sixth edition

Fundamentals of Early Childhood Education

GEORGE S. MORRISON

University of North Texas

PEARSON

Boston Columbus Indianapolis New York San Francisco Upper Saddle River
Amsterdam Cape Town Dubai London Madrid Milan Munich Paris Montreal Toronto
Delhi Mexico City Sao Paulo Sydney Hong Kong Seoul Singapore Taipei Tokyo

Vice President and Editor in Chief: Jeffery W. Johnston
Senior Acquisitions Editor: Julie Peters
Development Editor: Bryce Bell
Editorial Assistant: Tiffany Bitzel
Vice President, Director of Marketing: Quinn Perkson
Marketing Manager: Erica DeLuca
Senior Managing Editor: Pamela D. Bennett
Project Manager: Kerry J. Rubadue
Senior Operations Supervisor: Matthew Ottenweller
Operations Specialist: Laura Messerly
Senior Art Director: Diane Lorenzo
Text Designer: Candace Rowley

Cover Designer: Candace Rowley
Photo Coordinator: Sandy Schaefer
Permissions Administrator: Becky Savage
Cover Art: Getty Images
Media Producer: Autumn Benson
Media Project Manager: Rebecca Norsic
Full-Service Project Management: Thistle Hill Publishing Services, LLC
Composition: S4Carlisle Publishing Services
Printer/Binder: Courier/Kendallville
Cover Printer: Lehigh Phoenix Color/Hagerstown
Text Font: Garamond

Credits and acknowledgments borrowed from other sources and reproduced, with permission, in this textbook appear on appropriate page within text.

Photo Credits: Shutterstock, pp. 2, 3, 57, 69, 201 (top), 292 (bottom), 294 (bottom); David Mager/Pearson Learning Photo Studio, pp. 4, 14, 90, 132, 140, 142, 165 (bottom left), 227 (2nd from top), 234 (bottom), 250, 293 (top), 338; Michael Newman/PhotoEdit Inc., pp. 12, 146, 155; SuperStock, p. 30; Joe Atlas/Brand X Pictures, p. 31; Mac H. Brown/Merrill, p. 32; Robert Brenner/PhotoEdit Inc., p. 33; George Dodson/Lightworks Studio/PH College, pp. 34 (center), 94 (top), 183 (top), 296; Anthony Harris/Shutterstock, p. 34 (bottom); Corbis RF, p. 35; Frank Siteman, pp. 38, 165 (top left & right); Pearson Learning Photo Studio, pp. 42, 64, 242; Photos to Go, pp. 56, 264 (top), 352; iStockphoto.com, pp. 70 (all), 129, 183 (3rd from bottom), 186, 200 (top), 205, 226 (center & bottom), 234 (top), 292 (top), 293 (bottom), 339; Silver Burdett Ginn Needham, pp. 71, 309; BananaStock, pp. 74 (top & bottom right), 104, 183 (2nd from bottom); Annie Pickert/ABMerrill, pp. 74 (bottom left & center), 93 (center), 115, 145 (center), 147, 162, 204, 232, 313 (bottom left, 2nd from top, top right), 331; Krista Greco/Merrill, pp. 75, 80 (top & 2nd from bottom), 81, 93 (top), 163 (bottom), 188; Lori Whitley/Merrill, pp. 80 (2nd from bottom), 227 (top); Patrick White/Merrill, pp. 80 (bottom), 152, 270; Anthony Magnacca/Merrill, pp. 82, 91, 299, 324; Vanessa Davies © Dorling Kindersley, p. 93 (bottom); courtesy of Martha Magnia, p. 97 (both); T. Lindfors/Lindfors Photography, pp. 98, 229, 246, 317, 328 (left); Scott Cunningham/Merrill, p. 120; Pearson Scott Foresman, pp. 121, 239, 264 (bottom), 312; Modern Curriculum Press/Pearson Learning, p. 143; Laura Bolesta/Merrill, p. 145 (top & 2nd from bottom); Comstock Images/Jupiter Unlimited, pp. 145 (2nd from top), 170, 183 (2nd from top); Stockxpert/Jupiter Unlimited, pp. 145 (bottom), 165 (bottom right), 183 (bottom), 200 (bottom), 226 (top), 227 (2nd from bottom & bottom), 236, 297; Getty Images, Inc.–Photodisc, p. 163 (top); Comstock Royalty Free Division, p. 171; EyeWire Collection/Getty Images–Photodisc/Royalty Free, pp. 182, 280; Ruth Jenkinson © Dorling Kindersley, p. 183 (3rd from top); Photos.com/Jupiter Unlimited, p. 201 (bottom); Getty Images–Stockbyte, Royalty Free, p. 209; SW Productions/Getty Images–Photodisc/Royalty Free, pp. 223, 360; Tim Ridley © Dorling Kindersley, p. 227 (center); Robert Harbison, pp. 230, 313 (2nd from bottom); © Larry Williams/Corbis, p. 235; Karen Ahola/Silver Burdett Ginn, p. 237; BananaStock/Jupiter Unlimited, p. 265 (top); Katelyn Metzger/Merrill, pp. 265 (bottom), 274, 332, 336; Silver Burdett Ginn, p. 266; Bob Daemmrich/Bob Daemmrich Photography, Inc., pp. 267, 271 (top right), 315; courtesy of Gary W. Baird, p. 271 (left & bottom right); Ron Chapple/Photos to Go, p. 294 (top); Bill Aron/PhotoEdit Inc., p. 306; www.comstock.com, p. 325; Nancy Sheehan Photography, pp. 328 (right), 337; © Ellen B. Senisi, p. 344; Pearson, p. 345; PhotoDisc/Getty Images, p. 346; Anderson Ross/Getty Images, Inc.–Photodisc/Royalty Free, p. 350; Brand X Pictures/Jupiter Unlimited, p. 353; Geri Engberg/Geri Engberg Photography, p. 364.

Every effort has been made to provide accurate and current Internet information in this book. However, the Internet and information posted on it are constantly changing, so it is inevitable that some of the Internet addresses listed in this textbook will change.

Library of Congress Cataloging-in-Publication Data

Morrison, George S.
  Fundamentals of early childhood education/George S. Morrison.—6th ed.
    p. cm.
  Includes bibliographical references and index.
  ISBN-13: 978-0-13-703387-4 (pbk.)
  ISBN-10: 0-13-703387-7 (pbk.)
1. Early childhood education—United States. I. Title.
  LB1139.25.M67 2011
  372.210973—dc22

2009050234

10 9 8 7 6 5 4 3 2 1

www.pearsonhighered.com

ISBN 10:   0-13-703387-7
ISBN 13: 978-0-13-703387-4

FOR BETTY JANE—WHOSE LIFE IS FULL OF GRACE AND WHOSE HEART IS FULL OF LOVE.

ABOUT THE AUTHOR

GEORGE S. MORRISON is professor of early childhood education in the Department of Teacher Education and Administration, College of Education, at the University of North Texas. He teaches courses in early childhood education and teacher education to undergraduate and graduate students. Professor Morrison earned a Bachelor of Arts degree in history from Washington and Jefferson College; a Master's degree in elementary education from California State College of Pennsylvania, and an Ed.D. in elementary and early childhood education from the University of Pittsburgh. He is an experienced public school teacher and principal and has supervised student teachers. In addition to his affiliation with the University of North Texas, Dr. Morrison has been a professor at Edinboro University of Pennsylvania, the University of Tennessee at Martin, and Florida International University.

Professor Morrison's accomplishments include a Distinguished Academic Service Award from the Pennsylvania Department of Education and an Outstanding Service and Teaching Award from Florida International University. His books include *Early Childhood Education Today*, Eleventh Edition (also translated into Spanish and Mandarin Chinese); Fundamentals of Early Childhood Education, Sixth Edition (also translated into Mandarin Chinese); *Teaching in America*, Fifth Edition; *Education and Development of Infants, Toddlers, and Preschoolers; The World of Child Development; The Contemporary Curriculum;* and *Parent Involvement in the Home, School, and Community.*

Dr. Morrison is a popular author, speaker, and presenter. He serves on the editorial boards of *Annual Editions: Early Childhood* and the *International Journal of Early Childhood Education* and is the senior contributing editor for the *Public School Montessorian.* He also contributes his opinions and ideas to a wide range of publications. His speaking engagements and presentations focus on the future of early childhood education, the globalization of early childhood education, the changing roles of teachers, the influence of contemporary educational reforms on education, and the application of best practices to early childhood education. Dr. Morrison and his undergraduate and graduate students present regularly at the Annual Competition of the National Association for the Education of Young Children. Professor Morrison also lectures, conducts seminars, and gives keynote addresses on topics of early childhood education in Thailand, Taiwan, China. In 2009, Dr. Morrison gave the Keynote Address at the First Philippine Summit on Early Childhood Education.

PREFACE

When I ask my colleagues in early childhood education how I can help them be better professionals, their answers are always the same: They want an early childhood textbook that is user-friendly and applies theory to practice. *Fundamentals of Early Childhood Education,* Sixth Edition, is a textbook that is practical, is based on current research and thinking about how young children learn, and provides concrete, in the classroom examples for how best to teach children from birth to age eight.

Fundamentals captures the important changes occurring in early childhood education today and shows how they apply to teaching young children and to collaborating with parents and families. These changes include:

- New knowledge and ideas about how children grow and develop and the conditions that support optimal learning
- New views about how best to teach young children
- Changing roles and responsibilities of early childhood professionals
- Increasing demands from the public and politicians for accountability in ensuring that all children will learn to their fullest capacity
- The increasing integration of technology into instructional processes in early childhood classrooms
- The "greening" of early childhood programs and environments and the early childhood curriculum
- The rapid integration of the fields of early childhood education and early childhood special education

As you, other early childhood professionals, scientists, and the public respond to the changing field of early childhood education, more opportunities arise for new programs, curricula, and appropriate practices to meet the ever-changing needs of children and families. This textbook was designed to develop competent and confident early childhood education professionals, prepared to assume their professional roles in the ever-changing world of early childhood education.

WHAT'S NEW IN THIS EDITION?

Students and professors will benefit from new content and features in this sixth edition:

- Seventy percent of the research is new or updated.
- Chapter content is now aligned with the National Association for the Education of Young Children (NAEYC) Standards for Early Childhood Professional Development Programs.
- Many figures and tables have been revised and updated to reflect the latest research and the changes in the field of early childhood education.
- New *Accommodating Diverse Learners* topics in every chapter address the inclusion of all children, including ELLs, children with disabilities, and children with special needs. This feature recognizes the ongoing integration of the fields of early childhood education and early childhood special education.

- Updated *Diversity Tie-In* features.
- *Professionalism in Practice* features and *Program in Action* features have been combined to highlight what professionals and exemplary programs do in practice. *Professionalism in Practice* features have been updated, with five new *Professionalism in Practice* features added: *Native American Education: Then and Now,* in Chapter 3; *Using Blocks to Help Preschoolers Build Mathematical Skills,* in Chapter 8; *Teaching in Kindergarten Today: "What's for Dinner?"* in Chapter 9; *How to Teach Fluency in Mathematics in First Grade Without the Stress,* in Chapter 10; and *How to Implement a Successful Guided Reading Program,* in Chapter 10, and *Kids with Special Needs Need Extra Special Touch,* in Chapter 11.
- MyEducationLab is integrated throughout the text, extending and illustrating chapter content.
- In response to reviewers' comments, core content examples and illustrations have been increased and extended to make this sixth edition more practical and applied.
- Fifty percent of the book's content is new, to reflect the following:
  - Recent changes in the field of early childhood education influencing the care and education of young children
  - The politicization of the field, reflected in the use of early childhood education by politicians to implement national policies regarding the importance of a highly trained and educated workforce of the future
  - A growing emphasis on accommodating children with diverse needs, reflecting the increasingly diverse early childhood population and the growing number of children with disabilities

MYEDUCATIONLAB

The Power of Classroom Practice

> Teacher educators who are developing pedagogies for the analysis of teaching and learning contend that analyzing teaching artifacts has three advantages: It enables new teachers time for reflection while still using the real materials of practice; it provides new teachers with experience thinking about and approaching the complexity of the classroom; and in some cases, it can help new teachers and teacher educators develop a shared understanding and common language about teaching.[1]

As Linda Darling-Hammond and her colleagues point out, grounding teacher education in real classrooms—among real teachers and students and among actual examples of students' and teachers' work—is an important and perhaps even essential part of training teachers for the complexities of teaching in today's classrooms. For this reason, we have created a valuable, time-saving website—MyEducationLab—that provides the context of real classrooms and artifacts that research on teacher education tells us is so important. The authentic in-class video footage, interactive skill-building exercises, and other resources available on MyEducationLab offer unique teacher education tools.

MyEducationLab is easy to use and integrate into assignments and courses. Whenever the MyEducationLab logo appears in the text, follow the simple instructions to access the interactive assignments, activities, and learning units on MyEducationLab. For each topic covered in the course, you will find most or all of the following resources:

Connection to National Standards

Now it is easier than ever to see how coursework is connected to national standards. Each topic on MyEducationLab lists intended learning outcomes connected to the NAEYC *Standards for Early Childhood Professional Preparation.* And all of the

Assignments and Activities and all of the Building Teaching Skills and Dispositions in MyEducationLab are mapped to the appropriate national standards and learning outcomes as well.

Assignments and Activities

Designed to save instructors preparation time and enhance student understanding, these assignable exercises show concepts in action (through video, cases, and/or student and teacher artifacts). They help students synthesize and apply concepts and strategies they read about in the book.

Building Teaching Skills and Dispositions

These learning units help students practice and strengthen skills that are essential to quality teaching. Students are presented with the core skill or concept and then given an opportunity to practice their understanding of this concept multiple times by watching video footage (or interacting with other media) and then critically analyzing the strategy or skill presented.

IRIS Center Resources

The IRIS Center at Vanderbilt University (http://iris.peabody.vanderbilt.edu), funded by the U.S. Department of Education's Office of Special Education Programs (OSEP), develops training enhancement materials for pre-service and in-service teachers. The IRIS Center works with experts from across the country to create challenge-based interactive modules, case study units, and podcasts that provide research-validated information about working with students in inclusive settings. In your MyEducationLab course we have integrated this content where appropriate.

General Resources on Your MyEducationLab Course

The Resources section on MyEducationLab is designed to help students pass their licensure exams, put together effective portfolios and lesson plans, prepare for and navigate the first year of their teaching careers, and understand key educational standards, policies, and laws. This section includes:

- **Licensure Exams**—Contains guidelines for passing the Praxis exam. The Practice Test Exam includes practice multiple-choice questions, case study questions, and video case studies with sample questions.
- **Lesson Plan Builder**—Helps students create and share lesson plans.
- **Licensure and Standards**—Provides links to state licensure standards and national standards.
- **Beginning Your Career**—Offers tips, advice, and valuable information on:
  - **Resume Writing and Interviewing**—Expert advice on how to write impressive resumes and prepare for job interviews.
  - **Your First Year of Teaching**—Practical tips on setting up a classroom, managing student behavior, and planning for instruction and assessment.
  - **Law and Public Policies**—Specific directives and requirements educators need to understand under the No Child Left Behind Act and the Individuals with Disabilities Education Improvement Act of 2004.

Book-Specific Resources

Study Plan. A MyEducationLab Study Plan is a multiple-choice assessment tied to chapter objectives. A well designed Study Plan offers multiple opportunities to fully master required course content as identified by the objectives in each chapter:

- *Chapter Objectives* identify the learning outcomes for the chapter and give targets to shoot for as you read and study.
- *Multiple-Choice Assessments* assess mastery of the content. These assessments are mapped to chapter objectives, and students can take the multiple-choice quiz as many times as they want. Not only do these quizzes provide overall scores for each objective, but they also explain why responses to particular items are correct or incorrect.
- *Study Material: Review, Practice, and Enrichment* gives students a deeper understanding of what they do and do not know related to chapter content by including text excerpts.

Visit www.myeducationlab.com for a demonstration of this exciting new online teaching resource.

ACKNOWLEDGMENTS

In the course of my teaching, service, consulting, and writing, I meet and talk with many early childhood professionals who are deeply dedicated to doing their best for young children and their families. I am always touched, heartened, and encouraged by the openness, honesty, and unselfish sharing of ideas that characterize my professional colleagues. I thank all the individuals who contributed to the *Professionalism in Practice, Diversity Tie-In, and Technology Tie-In* features, as well as other program descriptions. They are all credited for sharing their personal accounts of their lives, their children's lives, and their programs.

I value, respect, and use the feedback and sound advice provided by the following reviewers: Annapurna Ganesh, Mesa Community College; Claire E. Hamilton, University of Massachusetts; Jeannie Ho, Montgomery College; Benita McCrann, Del Mar College; Elizabeth A. Persons, Pensacola Junior College; and Kenneth E. Smith, University of Nebraska at Omaha.

I am blessed to work with my colleagues at Pearson. My editor, Julie Peters, is always positive and upbeat, and she remains a constant source of bright and exciting ideas. Julie is continually opening new doors and possibilities. I can always count on her for wise counsel about how to make *Fundamentals* more engaging and relevant for students and professors. Development Editor Bryce Bell is a pleasure to work with. He is attentive to details, conscientious, and provides many insightful suggestions for making *Fundamentals* better. Because of Bryce's devotion to excellence, *Fundamentals* is a much better book. Tiffany Bitzel, Editorial Assistant, is an expediter *par excellence*. Tiffany is always pleasant and efficient and gets the job done. Project Managers Kerry Rubadue and Angela Williams Urquhart (Thistle Hill Publishing Services) are very attentive to detail and always make sure every part of the production process is done right. Many thanks, too, to Thistle Hill for a copyediting process that raised many questions that helped clarify issues of content and style.

Finally, I want to thank the "A-Team," Brittany Flournoy, Destine'e Davis, and Haley Garth. Thank you for your hard work! Brittany's positive energy keeps us all laughing and the pages turning! Haley is the spine of this book! Thanks Haley for staying late many days to make sure that all details were taken care of. Thank you Destine'e for being the glue that holds the book and team together. Destine'e is a great example of dedication, hard work, and positive attitude.

SUPPLEMENTS TO THE TEXT

All supplements are available online. To download and print supplement files, go to www.pearsonhighered.com and then click on "Educators."

Online Instructor's Manual This manual contains chapter overviews and activity ideas to enhance chapter concepts, as well as instructions for assignable MyEducationLab material.

Online Test Bank The Test Bank includes a variety of test items, including multiple choice, true/false, matching, and short answer items.

Pearson MyTest is a powerful assessment generation program that helps instructors easily create and print quizzes and exams. Questions and tests are authored online, allowing ultimate flexibility and the ability to efficiently create and print assessments anytime, anywhere! Instructors can access Pearson MyTest and their test bank files by going to www.pearsonmytest.com to log in, register, or request access. Features of Pearson MyTest include:

Premium assessment content

- Draw from a rich library of assessments that complement your Pearson textbook and your course's learning objectives.
- Edit questions or tests to fit your specific teaching needs.

Instructor-friendly resources

- Easily create and store your own questions, including images, diagrams, and charts using simple drag-and-drop and Word-like controls.
- Use additional information provided by Pearson, such as the question's difficulty level or learning objective, to help you quickly build your test.

Time-saving enhancements

- Add headers or footers and easily scramble questions and answer choices—all from one simple toolbar.
- Quickly create multiple versions of your test or answer key, and when ready, simply save to MS-Word or PDF format and print!
- Export your exams for import to Blackboard 6.0, CE (WebCT), or Vista (WebCT)!

Online PowerPoint Slides PowerPoint slides highlight key concepts and strategies in each chapter and enhance lectures and discussions.

BRIEF CONTENTS

CONTENTS

CHAPTER FOUR

Implementing Early Childhood Programs:
Applying Theories to Practice 90

CHAPTER FIVE

Standards and You:
Teaching Children to Learn 120

CHAPTER SIX

Observing and Assessing Young Children:
Guiding, Teaching, and Learning 142

CHAPTER SEVEN

Infants and Toddlers:
Critical Years for Learning 170

CHAPTER EIGHT

The Preschool Years:
Getting Ready for School and Life 204

CHAPTER NINE

CHAPTER TEN

CHAPTER ELEVEN

CHAPTER TWELVE

CHAPTER THIRTEEN

Parents, Families, and the Community:
Building Partnerships for Student Success 344

SPECIAL FEATURES

professionalism in practice

professionalism in practice

How Play Supports Literacy Development

Early childhood educators have long recognized the value of play for social, emotional, and physical development. Recently, however, play has attracted greater importance as a medium for literacy development. It is now recognized that literacy develops in meaningful, functional social settings rather than as a set of abstract skills taught in formal pencil-and-paper settings.

Literacy development involves a child's active engagement in cooperation and collaboration with peers; it builds on what the child already knows with the support and guidance of others. Play provides this setting. During observation of children at play, especially in free-choice, cooperative play periods, one can note the functional uses of literacy that children incorporate into their play themes. When the environment is appropriately prepared with literacy materials in play areas, children have been observed to engage in attempted and conceptual reading and writing in collaboration with other youngsters. In similar settings lacking literacy materials, the same literacy activities did not occur.

To demonstrate how play in an appropriate setting can nurture literacy development, consider the following classroom setting in which the teacher has designed a veterinarian's office to go

socially by collaborating and performing meaningful reading and writing activities with peers. The following anecdotes relate the type of behavior Ms. Meyers observed in the play area.

Jessica was waiting to see the doctor. She told her stuffed animal dog, Sam, not to worry, that the doctor would not hurt him. She asked Jenny, who was waiting with her stuffed animal cat, Muffin, what the kitten's problem was. The girls agonized over the ailments of their pets. After a while they stopped talking and Jessica picked up the book *Are You My Mother?* and pretended to read to her dog. Jessica showed Sam the pictures as she read.

Preston examined Christopher's teddy bear and wrote a report in the patient's folder. He read his scribble writing out loud and said, "This teddy bear's blood pressure is twenty-nine points. He should take sixty-two pills an hour until he is better and keep warm and go to bed." At the same time he read, he showed Christopher what he had written so he could understand what to do.

When selecting settings to promote literacy in play, choose those that are familiar to children and relate them to themes currently being studied. Suggestions for literacy materials and

diversity tie-in

diversity tie-in

Young English Language Learners

Linda M. Espinosa, Ph.D.
University of Missouri–Columbia
Columbia, Missouri

Increasingly, young children in the United States speak a language other than English in the home. The number of children enrolled in preschool and Head Start programs whose home language is not English (known as English language learners or ELLs) has been steadily increasing during the past two decades. During the 2006–2007 program year approximately 30 percent of children enrolled in Head Start did not speak English as their home language. Of these, the vast majority are from Spanish-speaking homes with 139 other language groups also reported.

Recent research has consistently shown that most young children are not only capable of learning two languages, but also enjoy cognitive, cultural, and economic advantages as a result of being bilingual. Bilingualism has been associated with a greater

immediate and extended families, and to thrive in a global, multilingual world.
• Becoming proficient in a language is a complex and demanding process that takes many years. As with any type of learning, children will vary enormously in the rate at which they learn a first and a second language.

TEACHING STRATEGIES THAT SUPPORT HOME LANGUAGE MAINTENANCE

Many specific teaching practices are available that support primary language development. Here are some things you can do:

• Provide instructional support including paraprofessionals (instructional assistants, parent volunteers, and older and more competent students) whenever possible.

technology tie-in

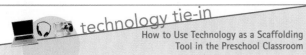

portraits of children

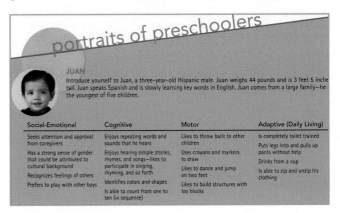

competency builder

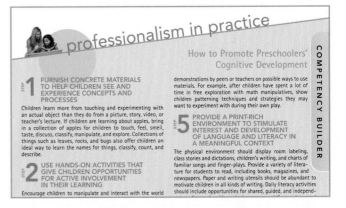

Fundamentals of Early Childhood Education

chapter one

YOU AND EARLY CHILDHOOD EDUCATION

Becoming a Professional

NAEYC Standards for Early Childhood Professional Preparation

Standard 1. Promoting Child Development and Learning

I use my understanding of young children's characteristics and needs, and of multiple interacting influences on children's development and learning, to create environments that are healthy, respectful, supportive, and challenging for each child.[1]

Standard 2. Building Family and Community Relationships

I know about, understand, and value the importance and complex characteristics of children's families and communities. I use this understanding to create respectful, reciprocal relationships that support and empower families, and to involve all families in their children's development and learning.[2]

Standard 3. Observing, Documenting, and Assessing to Support Young Children and Families

I know about and understand the goals, benefits, and uses of assessment. I know about and use systematic observations, documentation, and other effective assessment strategies in a responsible way, in partnership with families and other professionals, to positively influence the development of each child.[3]

Standard 4. Using Developmentally Effective Approaches to Connect with Children and Families

I understand and use positive relationships and supportive interactions as the foundation for my work with young children and families. I know, understand, and use a wide array of developmentally appropriate approaches, instructional strategies, and tools to connect with children and families and positively influence each child's development and learning.[4]

Standard 5. Using Content Knowledge to Build Meaningful Curriculum

I understand the importance of developmental domains and academic (or content) disciplines in an early childhood curriculum. I know the essential concepts, inquiry tools, and structure of content areas, including academic subjects, and can identify resources to deepen my understanding. I use my own knowledge and other resources to design, implement, and evaluate meaningful, challenging curricula that promote comprehensive developmental and learning outcomes for every young child.[5]

Standard 6. Becoming a Professional

I identify and conduct myself as a member of the early childhood profession. I know and use ethical guidelines and other professional standards related to early childhood practice. I am a continuous, collaborative learner who demonstrates knowledgeable, reflective, and critical perspectives on my work, making informed decisions that integrate knowledge from a variety of sources. I am an informed advocate for sound educational practices and policies.[6]

MARIA CARDENAS is excited about her new assignment as a pre-kindergarten teacher. After years of study and serving as an assistant teacher, Maria now has her own classroom of three- and four-year-olds. "I can't believe this day has finally come! I've worked so hard, and now my dream has come true! I can't wait to get started! I want my children to learn and be all they can be!"

Maria did not become a teacher overnight. She spent two years at a local community college and three at the university, learning the content, pedagogical, and professional knowledge and dispositions necessary to be a highly qualified early childhood teacher. There was never any doubt in her mind or mine that she would achieve her goals! I first met Maria as her faculty advisor when she entered a university teacher education program. From the beginning, Maria was enthusiastic about her career choice and determined that she would be a high-quality professional. In addition to all of her coursework, Maria volunteered in many community and school-based programs to get the experiences she needed to help her prepare for the day when she would have her "own" classroom. After five years of going to school part-time, Maria is ready to make a difference in the lives of "her" children. I hope you are as excited as Maria about your opportunity to teach young children.

Today, more than ever, the public and politicians all over the world are creating a lot of excitement by seeking ways to improve the quality of early childhood education and teaching.[7] As a result, you have a wonderful opportunity to work with young children and their families, develop new and better programs, and advocate for better practices and high-quality programs. Like Maria, you can be a leader in helping the early childhood profession make high-quality education a reality for all children.

WHO IS AN EARLY CHILDHOOD PROFESSIONAL?

Early childhood professionals promote child development and learning; build family and community relationships; observe, document, and assess to support young children and families; promote positive teaching and learning for young children; and identify with and conduct themselves as members of the early childhood profession.

Like Maria, you are preparing to be an early childhood professional, to teach children from birth to age eight. You are going to work with families and the community to bring high-quality education and services to all children. How would you explain the term **early childhood professional** to others? What does *professional* mean?

Professionals promote high standards for themselves, their colleagues, and their students. They are continually improving and expanding their skills and knowledge. They are multidimensional people who use their many talents to enrich the lives of children and families.

An early childhood professional is constantly changing in response to new jobs created by the expanding field of early childhood education. You can expect that you will participate in many professional development activities; will be constantly involved in new programs and practices; and will have opportunities to engage in new and different roles as a professional.

THE SIX STANDARDS OF PROFESSIONALISM

Being a professional goes beyond academic degrees and experiences. Professionalism in early childhood education is based on the six NAEYC Standards for professional development. All six of the standards are important for your professional development:

1. Promoting child development and learning
2. Building family and community relationships

FOCUS QUESTIONS

1. Who is an early childhood professional?

2. What are the six standards for an early childhood education (ECE) professional, according to the National Association for the Education of Young Children (NAEYC)?

3. How can you prepare for a career in early childhood education?

4. What roles are expected of early childhood professionals?

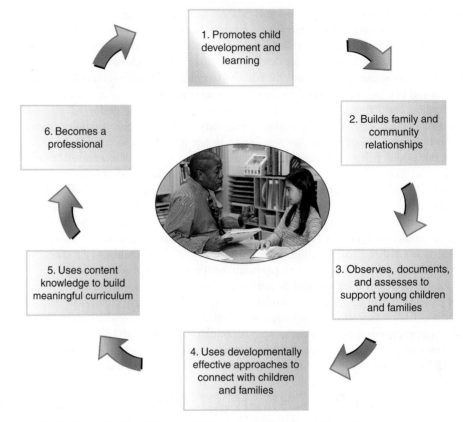

Figure 1.1 Six Standards of Early Childhood Professional Development

These six standards of your professional preparation provide guidelines for what you should know and be able to do in your lifelong career as an early childhood professional.

early childhood professional
An educator who successfully teaches all children, promotes high personal standards, and continually expands his or her skills and knowledge.

3. Observing, documenting, and assessing to support young children and families
4. Using developmentally effective approaches to connect with children
5. Using content knowledge to build meaningful curriculum
6. Becoming a professional (see Figure 1.1)

Each of these standards plays a powerful role in determining who and what a professional is and how professionals implement practice in early childhood classrooms. Let's review each of these standards and see how you can apply them to your professional practice.

Standard 1: Child Development and Learning

As an early childhood professional you will need to know how to promote child development and learning. Learning how to do this includes knowledge and understanding of young children's characteristics and needs and the multiple influences on children's development and learning. In addition, it includes knowing how to use developmental knowledge to create healthy, respectful, supportive, and challenging learning environments for young children.[8] This knowledge is drawn from a number of sources, including the Child Development Associate standards, the accreditation standards of the National Association for the Education of Young Children (NAEYC), the National Association of Early Childhood Specialists in State Departments of Education (NAECS/SDE), and state and national standards for teacher licensure and certification.

Child Development. Knowledge of child development is fundamental for all early childhood educators regardless of their roles or the ages of the children they teach. It enables you to confidently implement developmentally appropriate practices with all children. All early childhood professionals "use their understanding of young children's characteristics and needs, and of multiple interacting influences on children's development and learning, to create environments that are healthy, respectful, supportive, and challenging."[9]

Developmentally Appropriate Approaches. Knowledge of child development provides the foundation for conducting **developmentally appropriate practice (DAP)**. With your understanding of child development you will be able to select essential curricula and instructional approaches with confidence. All early childhood professionals use their understanding of child development as the foundation for their work with young children.

> **developmentally appropriate practice (DAP)** Teaching methods based on how children grow and develop and on individual and cultural differences.

Knowing Children. It is essential for you to have and demonstrate an understanding of child development. Child development knowledge enables you to understand how children grow and develop across all developmental levels—cognitive, linguistic, social, emotional, physical, language, and aesthetic domains as well as play, activity, learning processes, and motivation to learn.[10] Knowledge of individual children, combined with knowledge of child growth and development, enables you to provide care and education that is developmentally appropriate for each child. Developmentally appropriate practice (DAP) means basing your teaching on how children grow and develop, and DAP is the recommended teaching practice of the early childhood profession.

Core Considerations in Developmentally Appropriate Practice. Every day, early childhood practitioners make a great many decisions, both long-term and short-term. As they do so, they need to keep in mind the identified standards for children's learning and development and be intentional in helping children achieve these outcomes. The core of developmentally appropriate practice lies in this intentionality, the knowledge practitioners consider when they are making decisions, and that they always aim for goals that are both challenging and achievable for children.

Knowledge to Consider in Making Decisions. In all aspects of their work with young children, early childhood professionals consider three areas that are essential to the implementation of developmentally appropriate practice:

1. *What is known about child development and learning*—referring to knowledge of age-related characteristics that permits general predictions about what experiences are likely to best promote children's learning and development.

   Teachers who are knowledgeable about child development and learning are able to make broad predictions about what children of a particular age group typically will be like, what they typically will and won't be capable of, and what strategies and approaches will most likely promote their optimal learning and development. With this knowledge, teachers can make preliminary decisions with some confidence about environment, materials, interactions, and activities.

2. *What is known about each child as an individual*—referring to what practitioners learn about each child that has implications for how best to adapt for and be responsive to that individual variation.

   To be effective, teachers must get to know each child in the group well. They do this using a variety of methods—such as observation, interactions, examination of children's work, and talking with families. From this information, teachers make plans and adjustments to promote each child's individual development and learning as fully as possible. Developmental variation among children is the norm; but any one child's progress also will vary across domains and disciplines, contexts, and time. Children differ in many other respects, too—in their strengths, interests, preferences, personalities,

myeducationlab

Go to the Assignments and Activities section of Topic 8: DAP/ Teaching Strategies in the MyEducationLab for your course and complete the activity entitled *Designing Developmentally Appropriate Days.* Reflect on how individual and age-appropriate development and behavior influences your teaching of young children.

approaches to learning, knowledge and skills based on prior experiences, and more. Children may also have special learning needs; sometimes these have been diagnosed and sometimes they have not. Responding to each child individually is fundamental to developmentally appropriate practice.

3. *What is known about the social and cultural contexts in which children live*—referring to the values, expectations, and behaviors that practitioners must strive to understand in order to ensure that learning experiences are meaningful, relevant, and respectful for each child and family.

As we grow up in a family and in a broader social and cultural community, we all come to certain understandings about what our group considers appropriate—what it values, expects, and admires. We learn this through direct teaching from our parents and other important people in our lives, and by observing the behavior of those around us. Among these understandings we absorb "rules" about behaviors—such as how to show respect, how to interact with people we know well and those we have just met, how to regard time and personal space, how to dress, and countless other attitudes and actions. We typically absorb these rules very early and very deeply, so we live by them with little conscious thought. When young children are in a group setting outside the home, what makes sense to them and how they experience this world depend on the social and cultural contexts to which they are accustomed. Skilled teachers take such contextual factors into account, along with the children's age and their purely individual differences, in shaping all aspects of the learning environment.[11]

Ideas for how to conduct DAP are found throughout this book. These ideas and specific strategies for implementing DAP will serve as your road map of teaching. As you read about DAP suggestions, consider how you can begin to apply them in your professional practice.

> **developmentally and culturally responsive practice (DCRP)** Teaching methods that are sensitive and responsive to children's and families' developmental, cultural, and ethnic backgrounds and needs.

Appropriate Professional Practice. **Developmentally and culturally responsive practice (DCRP)** includes being sensitive to and responding to children's cultural and ethnic backgrounds and needs. The United States is a nation of diverse people, and this diversity will increase. Children in every early childhood program represent this diversity. When children enter schools and programs, they do not leave their uniqueness, gender, culture, socioeconomic status, and race at the classroom door. Children bring themselves and their backgrounds to early childhood programs. As part of your professional practice you will embrace, value, and incorporate multiculturalism into your teaching. Learning how to teach children of all cultures is an important part of your professional role. Figure 1.2 lists some popular and informative books that can help you achieve this goal. As you read these books, make a list of key ideas and how you can incorporate them into your teaching. In addition, the antibias curriculum information that follows offers guidelines that will help you teach children from diverse backgrounds.

> **multiculturalism** An approach to education based on the premise that all peoples in the United States should receive proportional attention in the curriculum.

Teaching Diverse Children. Think for a moment about all of the classrooms of children across the United States. What do you think their cultural, ethnic, and linguistic makeup is? More than likely, the demographics of these children are different from those of the children you went to school with in kindergarten or first grade. Consider these data about America's children:

- In 2008, 57 percent of U.S. children were white-alone, non-Hispanic; 21 percent were Hispanic; 14.5 percent were black-alone; 4 percent were Asian-alone; and 3.5 percent were all other races.[12]

- The percentage of children who are Hispanic has increased faster than that of any other racial or ethnic group.[13]

The increase in racial, ethnic, and cultural diversity in America is reflected in early childhood classrooms, which are also receiving increased numbers of children with disabilities and developmental delays. Consider the current student population at two elementary schools in different parts of the country. At Susan B. Anthony Elementary School

FIGURE 1.2

Books to Broaden Your Understanding of Multiculturalism in Schools and Other Programs

Delpit, L. (1996). *Other People's Children: Conflict in the Classroom.* New York: New Press.	In an interesting analysis of what is going on in American classrooms today, Lisa Delpit suggests that many of the academic problems attributed to children of color are actually the result of miscommunication as schools and "other people's children" struggle with the imbalance of power and the dynamics of inequality plaguing our system.
Derman-Sparks, L., & Ramsey, P. (2006). *What If All the Kids Are White? Anti-Bias Multicultural Education with Young Children and Families.* New York: Teachers College Press.	How do educators teach about racial and cultural diversity if all their students are white? The authors propose seven learning themes to help young white children resist messages of racism and build identity and skills for thriving in a multicultural country and world.
Espinosa, L. M. (2010). *Getting It Right for Young Children from Diverse Backgrounds: Applying Research to Improve Practice.* Upper Saddle River, NJ: Pearson.	This book reflects the current state of the field in terms of best practice and research. It provides a rich and comprehensive look at the needs of young children from diverse backgrounds. Espinosa also emphasizes the importance of collaboration among teachers and families to best serve students. Espinosa's book contains many concrete teaching strategies outlined and based on sound developmental theory.
Gonzalez-Mena, J. (2007). *Diversity in Early Care and Education: Honoring Differences*, 5th ed. McGraw-Hill Humanities/ Social Sciences/Languages.	This book explores the rich diversity encountered in programs and environments for children ages birth to eight, including those serving children with special needs. The emphasis is on the practical and immediate concerns of the early childhood professional and family service worker, though all information has strong theoretical support.
Marsh, M. M., & Turner-Vorbeck, T. (2007). *Other Kinds of Families: Embracing Diversity in Schools.* New York: Teachers College Press.	The authors contend that the vast diversity found in schools and society today suggests an urgent need to reconsider the ways in which families are currently represented and addressed in school curriculum and culture. They address such issues as multigenerational views of the schooling experiences of immigrant families, the educational needs of gay and lesbian families, the representation of adoption and adoptive families in children's literature, and the experiences of homeless students and their families with the educational system.

in Sacramento, California: 18 percent are Hispanic, 66 percent are Asian, 38 percent are African American, and 7 percent are white. Moreover, 95 percent of the children receive discounted/free lunches.[14] In San Angelo, Texas, at Alta Loma Elementary: 66 percent are Hispanic, 1 percent are Asian, 10 percent are African American, and 24 percent are white; 75 percent of the children receive discounted/free lunches.[15]

Meeting the Challenge. This diverse composition of early childhood classrooms challenges you to make your classroom responsive to the various needs of all your children, which is part of your professional responsibility. Developmentally appropriate practice also means that you will take into consideration the diverse nature of all children. In classrooms today, early childhood teachers work with children of varying cultural and socioeconomic backgrounds and needs.

Let's look at some of the things you can do to be a responsible professional who is culturally aware and who teaches with respect and equity:

Strategy 1: Be Concerned About Your Own Multicultural Development

- Honestly confront your attitudes and views as they relate to people of other cultures. You may be carrying baggage that you have to get rid of to authentically and honestly educate all of your children to their fullest capacity.
- Read widely about your cultural role as a professional.
- Learn about the habits, customs, beliefs, and religious practices of the cultures represented by your children.
- Ask some of your parents to tutor you in their language so you can learn basic phrases for greeting and questioning, the meaning of nonverbal gestures, and the way to appropriately and respectfully address parents and children.

Strategy 2: Make Every Child Welcome

- Make your classroom a place where diversity is encouraged and everyone is treated fairly. Create a classroom environment that is vibrant and alive with the cultures of your children. You can do this with pictures, artifacts, and objects loaned by parents.
- Support and use children's home language and culture. Create a safe environment in which children feel free to talk about and share their culture and language. Encourage children to discuss, draw, paint, and write about what their culture means to them.

Strategy 3: Make Every Parent Welcome

- Invite parents and families to share their languages and cultures in your classroom. Music, stories, and customs provide a rich background for learning about and respecting other cultures.
- Communicate with parents in their home languages.
- Work with parents to help them (and you) bridge the differences between the way schools operate and the norms of their homes and cultures.

Strategy 4: Collaborate with Your Colleagues

- Ask colleagues to share with you ideas about how to respond to questions, requests, and concerns of children and parents.
- Volunteer to form a faculty study group to read, discuss, and learn how to meet the cultural and linguistic needs of all children.

Strategy 5: Become Active in Your Community

- Learn as much as you can about your community and the cultural resources it can provide. Communities are very multicultural places!
- Collaborate with community and state organizations that work with culturally and linguistically diverse families and populations. Ask them for volunteers who can help you meet the diverse needs of your children. Children need to interact with and value role models from all cultures.
- Volunteer to act as a community outreach coordinator to provide families with services such as family literacy and school readiness information.

You can't be a complete early childhood professional without a cultural dimension. As you become more culturally aware, you will increase your capacity for caring and understanding—and you and your students will learn and grow together.

Reflect on your cultural awareness at http://www.prenhall.com/morrison.

Antibias Curriculum. Conducting a developmentally and culturally appropriate program also means that you will include in your curriculum activities and materials that help challenge and change all biases of any kind that seek to diminish and portray as inferior all children based on their gender, race, culture, disability, language, or socioeconomic status. You can accomplish this standard by implementing an **antibias curriculum**. The book *Anti-Bias Curriculum: Tools for Empowering Young Children*[16] is the profession's primary resource for understanding and implementing an antibias curriculum. If you have not read this book, you should put it at the top of your list of professional books to read. An antibias curriculum:

> embraces an educational philosophy as well as specific techniques and content. It is value based: Differences are good; oppressive ideas and behaviors are not. It sets up a creative tension between respecting differences and not accepting unfair beliefs and acts. It asks teachers and children to confront troublesome issues rather than covering them up. An anti-bias perspective is integral to all aspects of daily classroom life.[17]

Here are a few antibias strategies you should follow in your classroom:

- *Evaluate your classroom environment and instructional materials to determine if they are appropriate for an antibias curriculum.* Get rid of materials that are obstacles to your antibias goals, such as books that include children of only one race. In my visits to early childhood classrooms, I observe many that are "cluttered," meaning they contain too many materials that do not contribute much to a multicultural learning environment. Include photos and representations from all cultures in your classroom and community.

- *Develop a plan for redesigning your classroom.* For example, you may decide to add a literacy center that encourages children to "read" and "write" about cultural themes. Remember that children need the time, opportunity, and materials required to read and write about a wide range of antibias topics. In addition, since most classrooms don't have enough books on topics relating to gender, or with cultural and ethnic themes, make sure you provide them.

- *Evaluate your current curriculum and approaches to diversity.* This will help you understand how your curriculum is or is not supporting antibias approaches. Learning experiences should be relevant to your students, their community, and their families' cultures.

- *Observe children's play and social interactions to determine what you have to do to make sure that all children are accepted and valued.* For example, some children of different cultural backgrounds may not be included in particular play groups. This information allows you to develop plans for ensuring that children of all cultures and genders are included in play groups and activities.

- *Evaluate how you interact with children.* You can reflect on your teaching, videotape your teaching, and/or have a colleague observe your teaching. In this way you will gain invaluable insight into how you interact with all children and can make appropriate changes if necessary. For example, you may unknowingly give more attention to boys than to girls. Or you may be overlooking some important environmental accommodations that can support the learning of children with disabilities.

- *Include antibias activities in your daily and weekly classroom plans.* Intentional planning helps ensure that you are including a full range of antibias activities in your program. Intentional antibias planning also helps you integrate antibias activities into your curriculum for meeting national, state, and local learning standards.

- *Work with parents to incorporate your antibias curriculum.* Remember, parents are valuable resources in helping you achieve your standards.[18]

antibias curriculum An approach that seeks to provide children with an understanding of social and behavioral problems related to prejudice and seeks to provide them with the knowledge, attitude, and skills needed to combat prejudice.

Implementing an antibias curriculum will not be easy and it will require a lot of hard work and effort on your part. However, this is what teaching and being a professional is all about. You owe it to yourself, your children, and the profession to conduct programs that enable all children to live and learn in **bias-free** programs.

Creating Healthy, Respectful, Supportive, and Challenging Learning Environments. Research consistently shows that children cared for and taught in enriched environments are healthier, happier, and more achievement oriented.[19] To achieve this standard for all children, you must provide them with environments that are healthy, respectful, supportive, and challenging. **Healthy environments** provide for children's physical and psychological health, safety, and sense of security. **Respectful environments** show respect for each individual child, and for their culture, home language, individual abilities or disabilities, family context, and community. In **supportive environments** professionals believe each child can learn, and they help children understand and make meaning of their experiences. **Challenging environments** provide achievable and "stretching" experiences for all children.[20]

I discuss each of these four environmental essentials in detail, along with examples, in Chapters 7–10.

Standard 2: Building Family and Community Relationships

Families are an important part of children's lives. It makes sense to involve, work with, and advocate for parents and families. To do this, you need to know and understand the characteristics of children's families and the communities in which they live. Your collaboration with families will also involve supporting and empowering them. In addition, you will want and need to know how to involve families and communities in all aspects of children's development and learning.[21] It is very important to be respectful of children and their families to build strong relationships. Saying that you are respectful of children and families is one thing; putting it into practice means you will use your knowledge and skills of child development and family involvement to make respectfulness a reality. Here are some things you can do to demonstrate your respectfulness for children and families:

- When you plan cooking activities, talk with parents who have children with restricted diets to determine acceptable foods and recipes so all children can participate.
- Validate children's home languages by learning some words and teaching them to the other children. For example, when counting the days on the calendar, you can count in English, Spanish, Vietnamese, and so on.[22]

Learn and find out about families' child-rearing practices and how they handle routines relating to toileting, behavioral problems, and so on. Learning how to build family relationships is an important part of your professional development. Respectful and reciprocal relationships with parents and families empower them to be involved in their children's educations. Chapter 13, "Parents, Families, and the Community," will enable you to build family and community relationships in confident, respectful, and professional ways.

Standard 3: Observing, Documenting, and Assessing to Support Children and Families

One of your most important responsibilities as an early childhood professional will be to observe, document, and assess children's learning. As we discuss in Chapter 6, "Observing and Assessing Young Children," **assessment** is the process of collecting information about children's development, learning, behavior, academic progress, need for special services, and achievement to make decisions. The outcomes of your assessment will help guide you in making decisions about what and how to teach young children, and they will also provide you with abundant information to share with parents and families. You can consider

bias-free An environment, classroom setting, or program that is free of prejudicial behaviors.

healthy environment A learning environment that provides for children's physical and psychological health, safety, and sense of security.

respectful environment A learning environment that shows respect for each individual child and his or her culture, home language, individual abilities or disabilities, family context, and community.

supportive environment A learning environment where professionals believe each child can learn and where they help children understand and make meaning of their experiences.

challenging environment A learning environment that provides achievable and "stretching" experiences for all children.

assessment The process of collecting and recording information about children's development, learning, health, behavior, academic process, need for special services, and attainment in order to make a variety of educational decisions about children and programs.

assessment a three-way process: you the professional gathering data; using that data to make instructional decisions; and sharing assessment data with parents to get their comments, opinions, feedback, and advice about how best to teach their young children.

In your professional development, you can integrate methods for achieving your professional standards. Observation and documentation are just two forms of assessment that you will use in ongoing systematic ways. In fact, observation is one of your main means for gathering information about young children. You can sharpen your observation skills to help you also learn about child development.

Standard 4: Using Developmentally Effective Approaches to Connect with Children and Families

Selecting and using developmentally effective approaches is an essential part of your professional responsibility. In Standard 1, we discussed how to promote child development and learning. The use of developmentally appropriate practices and approaches supports Standard 4. Throughout this text, in each chapter, we will discuss how to use and apply developmentally appropriate practice. In fact, one of the hallmarks of this book is the integration of developmentally appropriate practices in all dimensions of providing high-quality learning environments for young children.

Using Developmentally Effective Approaches. Developmentally effective approaches and methods include: fostering oral language and communication; making the most of the environment and routines; capitalizing on incidental teaching, focusing on children's characteristics, needs, and interests; linking children's language and culture to the early childhood program; teaching through social interactions; creating support for play; addressing children's challenging behaviors; supporting learning through technology; and using integrative approaches to curriculum.[23]

In addition, as an early childhood professional, you will want to integrate your understanding of and relationships with children and families; your understanding of developmentally effective approaches to teaching and learning; and your knowledge of academic disciplines to design, implement, and evaluate experiences that promote positive developmentally appropriate learning for all children.[24] To be a professional in this area, you will want to demonstrate positive relationships with children and families. In the final analysis, all of education is about relationships: how you relate to your colleagues, how you relate to parents and other family members, and how you relate to children. In **responsive relationships** you are responsive to the needs and interests of children and their families. Throughout the book, I provide examples of suggestions for creating responsive relationships. Particularly, in Chapter 7, "Infants and Toddlers," I provide you with specific skills you can use to create responsive relationships with infants and toddlers.

responsive relationship The relationship that exists between yourself, children, and their families where you are responsive to their needs and interests.

Standard 5: Using Content Knowledge to Build Meaningful Curriculum

Content areas are important to children's learning. Content areas form the basis for children's learning to read, write, do mathematics and science, be creative, and be successful in school and in life. Consequently, early childhood professionals understand the importance of each content area in children's development and learning, demonstrate the essential knowledge and skills needed to provide appropriate environments that support learning in each content area, and demonstrate basic knowledge of the research base underlying each content area.[25]

Content Areas.   The content areas in early childhood are as follows:

- Language and literacy
- Reading

- The arts: music, creative movement, dance, drama, and art
- Mathematics
- Science
- Social studies (geography, history, economics, social relations/civics)
- Physical activity and physical education[26]

Much of the content knowledge in pre-K through third-grade programs is integrated in state and national standards, which we discuss in Chapter 5. However not all of the curriculum is specified by or through standards. What gets taught in early childhood programs is also based on children's interests and on the "teachable moment," when classroom, school, and communities lend themselves to teaching ideas, concepts, and skills. How you teach through and with standards is a result of your professional background and training. This is where Professional Standard 4—Using Developmentally Effective Approaches to Connect with Children and Families applies to your teaching. Throughout this book, you will learn what is included in each of the content areas and the competencies you can use to you teach each area.

content knowledge
Knowledge about the subjects (math, science, social studies, art, music, etc.) that teachers plan to teach.

pedagogical knowledge
Knowledge about how to apply instructional practices in order to develop meaningful learning experiences for children.

The knowledge that comes from content areas is known as **content knowledge**. Teachers must understand the content they teach (e.g., math, science, social studies). In addition to knowing content knowledge, teachers also must know *how* to teach students so they learn content knowledge. This is called *pedagogical content knowledge*. A third type of knowledge, general **pedagogical knowledge**, has to do with facilitating learning. This knowledge involves considering school, family, and community contexts, and children's prior experiences, to develop meaningful learning experiences. It also involves reflecting on teaching practice. Finally, high-quality teachers must know about and understand the students they teach. This is called *knowledge of learners and learning.*[27]

Early childhood educators are professionals who, in addition to teaching and caring for children, are ethical, engage in lifelong learning, collaborate with colleagues and families, are reflective practitioners, and advocate for children and families.

Building Meaningful Curriculum. In your work as an early childhood professional, you will participate in the designing, implementing, and evaluation of curriculum. You will participate with other professionals in this process. Today, *collaborative planning,* also known as *team planning,* is used by groups of teachers at the grade levels or across grade levels to plan curriculum daily, weekly, and monthly. One of the dimensions in today's planning for instruction is the incorporation of local and state standards. In Chapters 4, 7, 8, 9, and 10, I provide you with examples of standards for programs in grade levels and offer guidance for how you can incorporate state and local standards in your teaching in developmentally appropriate ways.

Standard 6: Becoming a Professional

Early childhood professionals conduct themselves as professionals and identify with their profession.[28] Your identification with and involvement in your profession enables you to say proudly that you are a teacher of young children. Being a professional means that you (1) know about and engage in ethical practice; (2) engage in continuous lifelong learning and professional development; (3) collaborate with colleagues, parents, families, and community partners; (4) engage in reflective practice; and (5) advocate on behalf of children, families, and the profession.[29] These competencies represent the heart and soul of professional practice. You should be committed to increasing your knowledge in these areas throughout your career.

Engaging in Ethical Practice. Ethical conduct—the exercise of responsible behavior with children, families, colleagues, and community members—enables you to confidently engage in exemplary professional practice. The profession of early childhood education has a set of ethical standards to guide your thinking and behavior. NAEYC has developed a Code of Ethical Conduct and Statement of Commitment (available online at http://www.naeyc.org/positionstatements/ethical_conduct), which states in part, as follows:

> As an individual who works with young children, I commit myself to furthering the values of early childhood education as they are reflected in the NAEYC Code of Ethical Conduct. To the best of my ability I will
>
> - Never harm children.
> - Ensure that programs for young children are based on current knowledge of child development and early childhood education.
> - Respect and support families in their task of nurturing children.
> - Respect colleagues in early childhood education and support them in maintaining the NAEYC Code of Ethical Conduct.
> - Serve as an advocate for children, their families, and their teachers in community and society.
> - Stay informed of and maintain high standards of professional conduct.
> - Engage in an ongoing process of self-reflection, realizing that personal characteristics, biases, and beliefs have an impact on children and families.
> - Be open to new ideas and be willing to learn from the suggestions of others.
> - Continue to learn, grow, and contribute as a professional.
> - Honor the ideals and principles of the NAEYC Code of Ethical Conduct.[30]

You can begin now to incorporate professional ethical practices into your interactions with children and colleagues. To stimulate your thinking, the Activities for Professional Development at the end of each chapter include an *ethical dilemma,* a set of circumstances defined as follows:

> An ethical dilemma is a situation an individual encounters in the workplace for which there is more than one possible solution, each carrying a strong moral justification. A dilemma requires a person to choose between two alternatives; each has some benefits but also some costs. Typically, one stakeholder's legitimate needs and interest will give way to those of another.[31]

As you reflect on and respond to each dilemma, use the NAEYC Code of Ethical Conduct as a valuable guide and resource.

> The goal of the NAEYC Code of Ethical Conduct is to inform, not prescribe, answers in tough decisions that teachers and other early childhood professionals must make as they work with children and families. The strategy inherent in the Code is to promote the application of core values, ideals, and principles to guide decision making.[32]

Continuous and Lifelong Professional Development Opportunities. A professional is never a "finished" product; you will always be involved in a process of studying, learning, changing, and becoming more professional. Teachers of the Year and others who share with you their philosophies and beliefs are always in the process of becoming more professional.

Becoming a professional means you will participate in training and education beyond the minimum needed for your current position. You will also want to consider your career objectives and the qualifications you might need for positions of increasing responsibility.

ethical conduct Responsible behavior toward students and parents that allows you to be considered a professional.

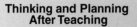

Thinking and Planning After Teaching

- Have I been self-reflective and thoughtful about my teaching?
- Did I assess the success of my students?
- How will I report students' achievements to parents?
- How will I provide feedback to my students?

Thinking and Planning Before Teaching

- What will I teach?
- How will I teach?
- What resources will I need?
- What background knowledge do my students have?

Thinking During Teaching

- Have I used students' prior knowledge to gain their interest and give them a focus?
- Am I presenting the lesson well?
- Am I constantly evaluating my students?
- Am I responding to the immediate needs of my students?
- Am I introducing new concepts and information?
- Am I motivating and challenging my students to pursue their own learning and investigation of the topic/subject/theme?

FIGURE 1.3 The Cycle of Reflective Practice: Thinking, Planning, and Deciding

Collaborating with Parents, Families, and Community Partners. Parents, families, and the community are essential partners in the process of schooling. Knowing how to effectively collaborate with these key partners will serve you well throughout your career. Chapter 13, "Parents, Families, and the Community," will help you learn more about this important topic.

Family education and support are important responsibilities of the early childhood professional. Children's learning begins and continues within the context of the family unit, whatever that unit may be. Learning how to comfortably and confidently work with parents and families is as essential as teaching children.

reflective practice The active process of thinking before teaching, during teaching, and after teaching in order to make decisions about how to plan, assess, and teach.

Reflective Practice. **Reflective practice** is a process that helps you think about how children learn and enables you to make decisions about how to best support their development and learning. Thinking about learning and understanding how children learn makes it easier for you to improve your teaching effectiveness, student learning, and professional satisfaction. Reflective practice involves deliberate and careful consideration about the children you teach, the theories on which you base your teaching, how you teach, what children learn, and how you will teach in the future. Although solitary reflection is useful, the power of reflective practice is more fully realized when you engage in such practice with your mentor teacher and colleagues. In a word, the reflective teacher is a thoughtful teacher. Reflective practice involves the three steps shown in Figure 1.3.

Advocacy.   **Advocacy** is the act of pleading the causes of children and families to the profession and the public and engaging in strategies designed to improve the circumstances of those children and families. Advocates move beyond their day-to-day professional responsibilities and work collaboratively to help others. Children and families today need adults who understand their needs and who will work to improve the health, education, and well-being of all young children. You and other early childhood professionals are in a unique position to know and understand children and their needs and to make a difference in their lives.

There is no shortage of issues to advocate for in the lives of children and families. Some of the issues that are in need of strong advocates involve quality programs, abuse and neglect prevention, poverty, good housing, and health. To change policies and procedures that negatively affect children, you must become actively engaged. The following are some of the ways in which you can practice advocacy for children and families:

- *Join an early childhood professional organization,* such as NAEYC, the Association for Childhood Education International (ACEI), and the Southern Early Childhood Association (SECA). These organizations have local affiliates at colleges and universities and in many cities and towns and are very active in advocating for young children. You can serve on a committee or be involved in some other way.
- *Become familiar with organizations that advocate for children and families.*
  - Children's Defense Fund
  - Stand for Children
  - Voices for America's Children[33]

Professional Dispositions

I'm sure that you have a favorite teacher. I know I have many favorite teachers who taught me or with whom I work. One reason why they are my favorite teachers is because they act as professionals. They demonstrate the dispositions of highly qualified professionals.

Professional dispositions are the values, commitments, and professional ethics that influence behaviors toward students, families, colleagues, and members of the community and affect student learning, motivation, and development as well as the educator's own professional growth. Dispositions are guided by beliefs and attitudes related to values such as caring, fairness, honesty, and responsibility. For example, they might include a belief that all students can learn, a vision of high and challenging standards, or a commitment to a safe and supportive learning environment.[34] We have already discussed other dispositions such as ethical conduct, collaborating with colleagues and families, and reflective practice. All programs that prepare professionals for the early childhood profession have a set of dispositions that are important for professional practice.

For the early childhood professional, *caring* is the most important of these dispositions. Professionals care about children; they accept and respect all children and their cultural and socioeconomic backgrounds. As a professional, you will work in classrooms, programs, and other settings where things do not always go smoothly—for example, children will not always learn ably and well, and they will not always be clean and free from illness and hunger. Children's and their parents' backgrounds and ways of life will not always be the same as yours. Caring means you will lose sleep trying to find a way to help a child learn to read and you will spend long hours planning and gathering materials. Caring also means you will not leave your intelligence, enthusiasm, and other talents at home but will bring them into the center, the classroom, administration offices, board of directors meetings, and wherever else you can make a difference in the lives of children and their families.

Go to the Teacher Talk section of Topic 12: Professionalism/Ethics in the MyEducationLab for your course and explore Robert Kelty's story about teachers becoming advocates for their children and promoting social and economic change for their students. Also watch Emily Jennette's story about instilling the power of hope in her children to achieve. She advocates for her children to create opportunities for them to succeed.

professional dispositions The values, commitments, and professional ethics that influence behavior toward students, families, colleagues, and members of the community and affect student learning, motivation, and development as well as the educator's own professional growth.

The theme of caring should run deep in your professional preparation and in your teaching. Listen to what Nel Noddings, a prominent teacher educator, has to say about caring:

> In an age when violence among school-children is at an unprecedented level, when children are bearing children with little knowledge of how to care for them, when the society and even the schools often concentrate on materialistic messages, it may be unnecessary to argue that we should care more genuinely for our children and teach them to care. However, many otherwise reasonable people seem to believe that our educational problems consist largely of low scores on achievement tests. My contention is, first, that we should want more from our educational efforts than adequate academic achievement and, second, that we will not achieve even that meager success unless our children believe that they themselves are cared for and learn to care for others.[35]

The Professionalism in Practice feature about caring and kindness illustrates this important point with many examples that you can use in your program or classroom.

PATHWAYS TO PROFESSIONAL DEVELOPMENT

The educational dimension of professionalism involves knowing about and demonstrating essential knowledge of the profession and professional practice. This knowledge includes the history and ethics of the profession, understanding how children develop and learn, and keeping up to date on public issues that influence early childhood and the profession.

Training and certification issues are a major challenge facing all areas of the early childhood profession and those who care for and teach young children. Training and certification requirements vary from state to state, and more states are tightening personnel standards for child care, preschool, kindergarten, and primary-grade professionals.

Many states have career ladders that specify the requirements for progressing from one level of professionalism to the next. Figure 1.4 outlines the early childhood practitioner's professional pathway for Oklahoma. What two things do you find most informative about this career pathway? How can you use the Oklahoma pathway to enhance your own professional development?

Associate Degree Programs

child care Comprehensive care and education of young children outside their homes.

Many community colleges provide associate degrees in *early childhood education,* the services provided by early childhood professionals. This degree qualifies recipients to be **child care** aides, primary child care providers, and assistant teachers. For example, Southwest Florida College with campuses at Fort Myers and Tampa, Florida, offers a two-year early childhood education program curriculum leading to an associate's degree in the field. Coursework emphasizes emergent literacy, the exceptional child, documenting observations and using the data to plan lessons to meet the needs of children, the creation of developmentally appropriate curricula, and assessment in classrooms. Students participating in the program are required to teach in an area school as the capstone course before graduating.

Baccalaureate Programs

pre-kindergarten A class or program preceding kindergarten for children usually from three to four years old.

Four-year colleges provide programs that result in early childhood teacher certification. The ages and grades to which the certification applies vary from state to state. Some states have separate certification for **pre-kindergarten** programs and nursery schools; in other states, these certifications are "add-ons" to elementary (K–6, 1–6, 1–4) certification. At the University of South Florida, the age three through grade three teacher certification program includes coursework and extensive field experiences in early childhood settings to enable students to integrate theory with teaching practice.

professionalism in practice

Caring and Kindness Are Keys to the Profession

Kindness is a simple eight-letter word that has the extraordinary power to make the world a better place. In our classroom we teach our students as we would want our own children to be taught. We practice what we teach by inspiring our students to share kindness with one another and to spread kindness wherever they go. To achieve that standard, we model kindness in these ways:

- Show enthusiasm for the subject matter and the children.
- Take time to know each child, both personally and academically (e.g., likes, dislikes, strengths, weaknesses, home environment).
- Be friendly and courteous, knowing that our attitudes can change children's attitudes.
- Be supportive and encouraging (e.g., saying "I am very proud of you," "Keep trying," "You're a great example for others").
- Avoid the use of criticism and ridicule.
- Don't choose favorites.
- Be sensitive to children's responses.
- Encourage mutual respect and trust.
- Create nurturing interactions with the children. (Our classroom motto, "Effort Creates Ability," makes students feel secure in trying new things.)

CLASSROOM PLEDGES

Each morning we begin the day by reciting our Kindness Promise:

Every day, in every way,
I will show kindness to others.

When an unkind act occurs in our classroom, we ask the students involved to repeat the Kindness Promise and make an apology to the parties involved.

We show acts of kindness in our classroom through these special activities:

- We pause each morning for a moment of silence. We think kind-and-happy thoughts for our students who are absent, as well as for friends, family, pets, and situations that could benefit from our actions.

- We make a "kindness critter," which is like a caterpillar. Each day our class thinks of one new way to show kindness. We write the idea on a new segment of the caterpillar. By the end of the school year, we have a very long critter with almost two hundred ways of showing kindness to others!
- We have regular class meetings to discuss situations in the classroom that relate to kindness (or its absence) and brainstorm solutions for those situations.

Kindness Outside the Classroom

There is no better way to promote and foster kindness and compassion in our world than by participating in community service projects. Here are ways we have taken caring and kindness outside our classroom:

- We raked leaves at the homes of veterans who live near our school on Veterans Day. We made patriotic wreaths for their doors and made no-bake cookies as a way of saying "thank you" to our veterans.
- We visited the pediatric floor of our local hospital. We used the bonus points from our Book Club to acquire age-appropriate books and prepared gift bags of hot chocolate, cups, and student-made bookmarks. Our theme was "Warm up with a good book—you'll feel so much better!" The books were given to each sick child as he or she was admitted to the hospital.
- We decorated lunch bags for our local Meals On Wheels program during our inside recess times. We were able to make 180 lunch bags per month for the elderly residents living near our school who depend on Meals On Wheels for a nutritious meal. Meals On Wheels provided the bags and it cost us nothing but our recess time to make many elderly and, often, lonely people happy!
- We collected cans of soup and donated them to our local food bank for our own "Souper Bowl." As a culminating activity, we had a "tailgate party," complete with hot dogs, popcorn, and root beer!

Contributed by Christa Pehrson and Vicki Sheffler, 2002 USA TODAY All-USA First Team Teachers, Amos K. Hutchinson Elementary School, Greensburg, Pennsylvania.

Master's Degree Programs

Depending on the state, individuals may gain initial early childhood certification at the master's level. Many colleges and universities offer master's programs for people who want to qualify as program directors or assistant directors or who want to pursue a career in teaching. Mary Ladd graduated with a bachelor's degree in business and worked for five years

Early Education Professional Development Career Pyramid

Advanced Level and Degrees - MS, MA, PhD, EdD, JD, MD, RN

Traditional:
- Early care and education Instructor at technology centers
- Teacher educator at a two year college or four year university
- Instructor/curriculum specialist
- Child development specialist
- Child guidance specialist
- Research/writer
- Early intervention
- Director/specialist in a child care resource and referral
- Family support and education

Related with further education/training/certifications:
- Social worker
- Teacher/administrator/special educator in a public or private elementary school – certification required
- Child advocate/lobbyist
- Librarian
- Pediatric therapist – occupational and physical
- Human resources personnel in industry
- Child life specialist in a hospital

- Speech and hearing pathologist – health department, public/private school, private practice, university teaching
- Early childhood consultant
- Entertainer/musician/song writer for children
- Career coach
- Agency administrator/director
- Author and illustrator of children's books
- Physician/Pediatrician
- Pedodontist (works only with children)
- Dietitian for children

- Counselor
- Child psychologist
- Psychiatrist
- Dietetic assistant
- Recreation supervisor
- Children's policy specialist
- Dental hygienist
- Scouting director
- Hospice care
- Domestic violence counselor
- Positions in elder care
- Child care center or playground/recreation center designer

- Probation officer
- County extension educator with 4-H
- Adoption specialist
- "Friend of the Court" counselor
- Psychometrist
- Attorney with primary focus on children/elderly
- Faith-based community coordinator and educator
- Family mediator
- Marriage and family therapy
- Infant/Child mental health specialist

Baccalaureate Level—Bachelors of Science (BS), Bachelors of Arts (BA) & Bachelors of Education (BEd)

Traditional:
- Early childhood teacher in public school, Head Start or child care settings–certification required
- Special education teacher
- Family child care home provider
- Nanny
- Administrator in a Head Start program
- Child care center director/owner/coordinator
- Child care center director in the armed services

Related with some positions requiring additional coursework at the baccalaureate level which will

be in a field other than early childhood:
- Child advocate/lobbyist
- Recreation director/worker/leader
- Web master
- Adult educator
- Journalist/author/publisher/illustrator of children's books
- Children's librarian
- Retail manager of children's toy or book stores
- Licensing worker

- Parent/family educator
- Family advocate
- Case manager in a state agency/recourse coordinator
- Parents as teachers coordinator
- Director of school-age (out of school time) program
- Mentor/coach

- Human resource personnel in industry
- Music teacher, musician/entertainer for children
- Recreation camp director
- Camp counselor/scouts camp ranger
- Domestic violence prevention and education
- Sex education and prevention
- Resource and referral trainer/data analyst
- Referral specialist/child care food program consultant

- Childbirth educator
- Gymnastic or dance teacher
- Pediatric nurse aide
- Child and parenting practitioner certification
- Producer of children's television shows and commercials
- Faith community coordinator and educator
- Substance abuse educator
- Foster care services

Associate Level—Associate of Arts (AA), Associate of Science (AS) & Associate of Applied Science (AAS)

Traditional:
- Child care center director
- School-age provider
- Early intervention/special needs program
- Para-professional assistant

- Parent educator

Related in addition to those listed at the core level:
- Family and human services worker
- LPN – specialized nurse training

- Entertainer for children at theme restaurants, parks or parties
- Social service aide
- Youth services
- Playground monitor

- Physical therapy assistant
- Nursing home aide/worker/technician
- Faith community coordinators for families and children

National Credential Level–Child Development Associate (CDA), Child Care Professional (CCP) & Oklahoma Certificate of Mastery (CoM)

Traditional:
- Head Start teacher (CDA required)

- Child care teacher – master teacher
- Family childhood care home provider

- Teacher assistant in public school classroom (additional college hours required)

- Child care center director
- Home visitor

- Nursing home aide/worker
- Nanny

Core Level—these positions require minimum education and training depending on the position

Traditional:
- Child care teaching assistant
- Family child care home provider
- Head Start teacher assistant
- Nanny
- Foster parent
- Church nursery attendant

Related some positions which involve working with children in settings other than a child care center, family child care home, Head Start or public school program may require specialized pre-service training:
- Children's storyteller, art instructor or puppeteer
- Recreation center assistant
- Salesperson in children's toys, clothing or bookstore
- School crossing guard

- Children's party caterer
- Restaurant helper for birthday parties
- Van or transportation driver
- Children's art museum guide
- Receptionist in pediatrician's office

- Camp counselor
- Special needs child care assistant
- Live-in caregiver
- Respite caregiver
- Cook's aide, camp cook, Head Start or child care center cook

FIGURE 1.4 Early Childhood Practitioner's Professional Pathway for Oklahoma

Source: Used with permission of Oklahoma Early Education Professional Development Council Career Advisement Committee, 2009.

in a high-tech company. However she kept feeling a call to teach and satisfy her desire to work with young children. Mary earned a master's degree and teacher certification and now teaches first grade in an urban setting, where she enjoys helping young children read.

The CDA Program

The **Child Development Associate (CDA)** National Credentialing Program is a competency-based assessment system that offers early childhood professionals the opportunity to develop and demonstrate competence in their work with children ages five and younger. Since its inception in 1975, the CDA program has provided a nationally recognized system that has stimulated early childhood training and education opportunities for teachers of young children in every state in the country and on military bases worldwide. The credential is recognized nationwide in state regulations for licensed centers as a qualification for teachers, directors, and/or family child care providers. The standards for performance that this program has established are used as a basis for professional development in the field.

The CDA program offers credentials to caregivers in four types of settings: (1) center-based programs for preschoolers, (2) center-based programs for infants/toddlers, (3) family child care homes, and (4) **home visitor programs**. Regardless of setting, all CDAs must demonstrate their ability to provide competent care and early educational practice in thirteen skill areas organized into six competency areas (which are outlined in Table 1.1). Evidence of ability is collected from a variety of sources including firsthand observational evidence of the CDA candidate's performance with children and families. This evidence is weighed against national standards. The CDA national office sets the standards for competent performance and monitors this assessment process so that it is uniform throughout the country.

> **Child Development Associate (CDA)** An individual who has successfully completed the CDA assessment process and has been awarded the CDA credential. CDAs are able to meet the specific needs of children and work with parents and other adults to nurture children's physical, social, emotional, and intellectual growth in a child development framework.

> **home visitor program** A program that involves visitation of children, parents, and other family members in their homes by trained personnel who provide information, training, and support.

Developing a Philosophy of Education

Professional practice entails teaching with and from a philosophy of education, which acts as a guidepost to help you base your teaching on what you believe about children.

A **philosophy of education** is a set of beliefs about how children develop and learn and what and how they should be taught. Your philosophy of education is based in part on your philosophy of life. What you believe about yourself, about others, and about life determines your philosophy of education. For example, we previously talked about optimism. If you are optimistic about life, chances are you will be optimistic for your children, and we know that when teachers have high expectations for their children, they achieve at higher levels. Core beliefs and values about education and teaching include what you believe about children, what you think are the purposes of education, how you view the teacher's role, and what you think you should know and be able to do.

> **philosophy of education** A set of beliefs about how children develop and learn and what and how they should be taught.

In summary, your philosophy of education guides and directs your daily teaching. The following guidelines will help you develop your philosophy of education.

Read. Read widely in textbooks, journals, and on the Web to get ideas for your philosophy. For example, these are some of the short philosophies of education for teachers of the year in Lee County, North Carolina:

> *Lisa Howard*, second-grade teacher: "It is my belief that the goal of education is to provide students with the tools necessary to achieve success. Through guidance and nurturing, teachers can empower students to become positive contributors to our society."

> *Candace Bloedorn*, third-grade teacher: "I believe that every child has the ability to learn. As an educator, I hope to create an environment where children are able to take risks, make mistakes, and learn from them. I hope to inspire and motivate our

TABLE 1.1 CDA Competency Goals and Functional Areas

CDA Competency Goals	Functional Areas
I. To establish and maintain a safe, healthy learning environment.	1. *Safe:* Candidate provides a safe environment to prevent and reduce injuries. 2. *Healthy:* Candidate promotes good health and nutrition and provides an environment that contributes to the prevention of illness. 3. *Learning Environment:* Candidate uses space, relationships, materials, and routines as resources for constructing an interesting, secure, and enjoyable environment that encourages play, exploration, and learning.
II. To advance physical and intellectual competence.	4. *Physical:* Candidate provides a variety of equipment, activities, and opportunities to promote the physical development of children. 5. *Cognitive:* Candidate provides activities and opportunities that encourage curiosity, exploration, and problem solving appropriate to the developmental levels and learning styles of children. 6. *Communication:* Candidate actively communicates with children and provides opportunities and support for children to understand, acquire, and use verbal and nonverbal means of communicating thoughts and feelings. 7. *Creative:* Candidate provides opportunities that stimulate children to play with sound, rhythm, language, materials, space, and ideas in individual ways and to express their creative abilities.
III. To support social and emotional development and to provide positive guidance.	8. *Self:* Candidate provides physical and emotional security for each child and helps each child to know, accept, and take pride in himself or herself and to develop a sense of independence. 9. *Social:* Candidate helps each child feel accepted in the group, helps children learn to communicate and get along with others, and encourages feelings of empathy and mutual respect among children and adults. 10. *Guidance:* Candidate provides a supportive environment in which children can begin to learn and practice appropriate and acceptable behaviors as individuals and as a group.
IV. To establish positive and productive relationships with families.	11. *Families:* Candidate maintains an open, friendly, and cooperative relationship with each child's family, encourages their involvement in the program, and suports the child's relationship with his or her family.
V. To ensure a well-run, purposeful program respective to participant needs.	12. *Program Management:* Candidate is a manager who uses all available resources to ensure an effective operation. Candidate is a competent organizer, planner, record keeper, communicator, and a cooperative co-worker.
VI. To maintain a commitment to professionalism.	13. *Professionalism:* Candidate makes decisions based on knowledge of early childhood theories and practices. Candidate promotes quality in child care services. Candidate takes advantage of opportunities to improve competence, both for personal and professional growth and for the benefit of children and families.

Source: The Council for Professional Recognition, *Overview of the National CDA,* October 2002, http://www.nova.edu/msi/onlinecda/national_cda.html. Reprinted with permission.

twenty-first century learners by incorporating technology and providing instruction that is meaningful and hands-on."

Donna Thomas, first-grade teacher: "Every child is unique and special. My role is to facilitate learning while guiding students toward self-discovery in an environment that is conducive to positive physical, social, cognitive, and emotional growth in an accepting, caring, supportive, and safe environment that encourages every child to reach his/her fullest potential."[36]

The Activities for Professional Development section at the end of the chapter will help you get started. In addition, Chapter 3, "History and Theories," provides helpful information for you to use in developing your philosophy.

Reflect. As you read through and study this book, make notes and reflect about your philosophy of education. The following prompts will help you get started:

- I believe the purposes of education are . . .
- I believe that children learn best when they are taught under certain conditions and in certain ways. Some of these are . . .
- The curriculum—all of the activities and experiences—of my classroom should include certain "basics" that contribute to children's social, emotional, intellectual, and physical development. These basics include . . .
- Children learn best in an environment that promotes learning. Features of a good learning environment are . . .
- All children have certain needs that must be met if they are to grow and learn at their best. Some of these basic needs are . . .
- I would meet these needs by . . .
- A teacher should have certain qualities and behave in certain ways. Qualities I think important for teaching are . . .

Discuss. Discuss with successful teachers and other educators their philosophies and practices. The personal accounts in the Professionalism in Practice boxes in each chapter of this text are evidence that a philosophy can help you be a successful, effective teacher. They also serve as an opportunity to "talk" with successful professionals and understand how they translate theory into practice.

Write. Once you have thought about your philosophy of education, write a draft and have other people read it. Writing and sharing will help you clarify your ideas and redefine your thoughts, because your philosophy should be understandable to others (although they do not necessarily have to agree with you).

Evaluate. Finally, evaluate your philosophy using this checklist:

- Does my philosophy accurately relate my beliefs about teaching? Have I been honest with myself?
- Is it understandable to me and others?
- Does it provide practical guidance for my teaching?
- Are my ideas consistent with one another?
- Does what I believe make good sense to me and others?

Now finalize your draft into a polished copy. A well-thought-out philosophy will be like a compass throughout your career. It may evolve but it will point you in the right direction and keep you focused on doing your best for children.

NEW ROLES FOR EARLY CHILDHOOD PROFESSIONALS

The role of the early childhood professional today is radically different from what it was even five years ago. Although the standards of professionalism and the characteristics of the high-quality professional remain the same, responsibilities, expectations, and roles have changed. Let's examine some of these new roles of the contemporary early childhood professional.

- *Teacher as instructional leader.* Teachers have always been responsible for classroom and program instruction, but this role is now reemphasized and given a much more prominent place in what early childhood teachers do, such as planning for what children will learn, guiding and teaching so that children learn, assessing what children learn, and arranging the classroom environment so that children learn. Today, the instructional emphasis is on children's learning and achievement.

- *Intentional teaching of national, state, district, and program goals and standards.* Intentional teaching occurs when instructors teach for a purpose, are clear about what they teach, and teach so that children learn specific knowledge and skills. In this context, teachers spend more time during the day actually teaching and make a conscious effort to be more involved in each child's learning process. Intentional teaching can and should occur in a child-centered approach for specified times and purposes throughout the school day.

- *Performance-based accountability for learning.* Teachers today are far more accountable for children's learning than at any time in American history. Previously, the emphasis was on the process of schooling. Teachers were able to explain their role as "I taught Mario how to. . . ." Today the emphasis is on "What did Mario learn?" and, "Did Mario learn what he needs to know and do to perform at or above grade level?"

- *Teaching of reading, math, science, and technology.* Although the teaching of reading has always been a responsibility of early childhood professionals, this role has been expanded. Today, every early childhood teacher is also a teacher of math, science, and technology.

- *Increased emphasis on linking assessment and instruction.* Today, all teachers use the results of assessment to plan for teaching and learning. Assessment and planning are an essential part of the teaching-learning process. Chapter 6, "Observing and Assessing Young Children," will help you learn how to use assessment in your teaching.

- *New meaning of child-centered education.* Early childhood professionals have always advocated child-centered education and approaches. However, today there is a rebirth of child-centered education processes. Essential to the child-centered approach are the ideas that each child can reach high levels of achievement, that each child is eager to learn, and that children are capable of learning more than many people previously thought they could learn. A new concept of child-centeredness embraces the whole child in all dimensions: social, emotional, physical, linguistic, and cognitive.

Cultural Diversity: Teaching in Early Childhood Today

Today, the United States is more diverse than ever before. The globalizing economy, world politics, and immigration make diversity in the United States a reality. Some states, such as California, Hawaii, New Mexico, and Texas, as well as the District of Columbia, are minority-majority states, or states in which minorities outnumber Caucasians by at least 50 percent.[37] Regardless of where you teach, you can be assured that students in your classroom will represent different ethnicities, religious beliefs, and cultures from yours. As an early childhood professional today, you should be prepared to accommodate the diverse backgrounds of your students and their families. The following are some things you can do to achieve your goal of being aware of your own cultural background.

- Examine your personal history, your relationships, and your personal beliefs about other cultures. Do you have any beliefs that may put you at odds with your students or their families? For example, do you find yourself saying, "Mexicans always . . ." or "All the white people I know . . ."? If you are honest with yourself, you may find biases or prejudices that will keep you from being an effective teacher of children from a different ethnic, religious, or cultural background from your own.

- Next, educate yourself on as many different cultures and religions as possible. Travel whenever possible, not to familiar haunts, but to places that are different for you. In addition, through the Internet you can take virtual trips or tours of different places.

- You should also read, read, and read some more. Magazines like *National Geographic* and *The Smithsonian* are available at most public libraries and provide information on diverse cultures that may exist right in your own neighborhood. Chicago, for example, is host to one of the largest traditional Hindu temples in the United States and one of the largest Indian outdoor markets. Calle Ocho ("Eighth Street") in Miami is well known for its Cuban festivals, and the city of Houston features a different country or culture every year in its International Festival.

- In addition, fiction is an excellent means of experiencing a culture. Books like *Three Cups of Tea* by Greg Mortenson, *The Joy Luck Club* by Amy Tan, and *Holy Cow* by Sarah Macdonald provide windows into different cultures. While fiction is not factual, it will challenge your perspective and make you aware of some of the forces at work in your students' lives.

- Once you have taken steps to explore diverse cultures for yourself, include the children in your classroom in your discoveries. Take these initial steps to represent and include other cultures in your classroom:
  - In your reading centers make a diverse array of materials available to your students that communicate other cultures. *Listen to the Wind* by Greg Mortenson and *For You Are a Kenyan Child* by Kelly Cunnane are examples of books that both inform and entertain.
  - In your dramatic play centers, go beyond the typical fireman, princess, and doctor costumes. Provide dashikis from Africa, grass skirts from Hawaii, kimonos from Japan, fur caps like those worn in Russia, and buckskins to represent early North America. Also go beyond clothing to represent diversity. Provide cultural tools used by our multicultural society such as play food and cooking items (plastic tortillas, wok, chopsticks, etc.) and items of daily life (keys, recycled MP3 players, phones, computer keyboards, etc.). Your children will begin to engage in play that represents what you are teaching them about cultural diversity and respect.

Modeling and Using Technology for Teaching and Learning

Technology is the application of tools and information to make products and solve problems. With this definition, technology goes far beyond computers and video games, but the most common use of the term refers to electronic and digital applications. In addition, technology also includes the applications involved in technology such as word processing, sending and receiving messages, publishing, and Web research. Today's teacher is a technological teacher. Today's students are technological students. One reality of society in education today is that technology permeates all facets of our life work, teaching, and learning. Effective early childhood teachers use technology of all kinds, such as computers, digital cameras, and cell phones, to involve all children in learning. In addition, high-quality

technology The application of tools and information to make products and solve problems. With this definition, technology goes far beyond computers and video games, but the most common use of the term refers to electronic and digital applications.

teachers use technology as a means of being positive role models for their students. Today's teachers use technology to:

- Create meaningful learning activities
- Teach children how to use technology and technological applications in their learning
- Assess children's achievement
- Model how they use technology in their teaching and professional development
- Connect children to learning experiences outside the classroom and around the world
- Teach children the technological skills they will need in the workforce of the future

You can learn more about technology and your role as a teacher by accessing the *ISTE National Educational Technology Standards (NETS-T) and Performance Indicator for Teachers* at the website of the International Society for Technology in Education, http://www.iste.org.[38]

The Future: You and The Early Childhood Profession

It is always risky to predict what the future holds for you and me as early childhood professionals. However, if the past is any indication of the future, I expect that we will practice our profession under the following conditions:

- *Rapid change.* The field of early childhood education will continue to undergo rapid and dramatic change. Old ways of doing things will be challenged by new ideas and methods. This means that you will have to adapt as the field changes. And you will have to transform your thinking continually as new ways make old habits obsolete.
- *Increased use of technology.* Technology will play an increasingly important and prominent role in how you teach, what you teach, and how children learn. You must constantly plan for how you will integrate technology into your teaching and children's learning.
- *Politicization of early childhood education.* Politics have always influenced education in one way or another. However, in the years to come, politics and politicians will play an even greater role in determining what and how children are taught. This means that advocacy will be a major dimension of your professional practice, allowing you to influence decisions on public policy at all levels.
- *Acceleration of early childhood teacher education and training.* As the field of early childhood changes, so do the knowledge and skills associated with it. This means that constant and continuous education will play a central role in your professional development. Many teachers will spend as much time educating themselves and being educated as they spend teaching their children.

Embrace these changes that the future holds. This is a wonderful and exciting time to be in the field of early childhood education. A bright future awaits you and your children.

The Professional Development Checklist

As the field of early childhood continues to change, the details of your role as an early childhood professional will continue to be refined. You will want to devote the time and energy necessary to keep yourself in the forefront of your field. Figure 1.5 contains a professional development checklist. Review this checklist throughout your teaching career to further refine your professional teaching role.

My purpose for writing this book is to support your professional development from the stage where you are—novice or midlevel to highly skilled expert. The professional development checklist in Figure 1.5 is a powerful tool you can begin to use now to achieve this goal. Each chapter emphasizes one or more professional outcomes from the checklist for you to consider and master. The Desired Professional Competencies come from a number of

PEARSON myeducationlab

Go to the Building Teaching Skills and Dispositions section of Topic 12: Professionalism/Ethics in the MyEducationLab for your course and complete the activity entitled *Becoming an Early Childhood Professional.*

PEARSON myeducationlab

Go to the Assignments and Activities section of Topic 12: Professionalism/Ethics in the MyEducationLab for your course and complete the activity entitled *Collaborating with Other Professionals.* As you watch this video, reflect on ways you can collaborate with other professionals to create an atmosphere of respect and cooperative learning for young children.

sources: the initial certification standards for early childhood certification of the National Council for Accreditation of Teacher Education and National Teachers of the Year, award-winning teachers, National Board Certified teachers, and professors of early childhood education.

ACTIVITIES FOR PROFESSIONAL DEVELOPMENT

ethical dilemma

"Should I Report Her To . . .?"

Elena is talking to Kim, her colleague at a preschool:

> Kim, you have been teaching here longer than I have, so maybe you can help me. I want to talk to you about the new preschool teacher they hired. I've talked with her a couple of times about how she implements the state pre-K standards, and she says she isn't too worried about them. I offered to help her with her lesson plans, but she told me she plans as she goes along. She said she knows what to do and developing a written plan gets in the way of her doing what comes naturally for her and the children. She also told me she thinks that the emphasis on early literacy is just a lot of hype—a passing fad. I'm concerned that her children won't be ready for kindergarten.

What should Elena do? Should she talk to her preschool supervisor and risk damaging her relationship with her fellow teacher and possibly hurt her career, or should she assume that another teacher's practices are not her business, even if they might be harmful to the children?

Application Activities

1. Recall the teachers who had a great influence on you. Which of their characteristics do you plan to incorporate into your philosophy of education?

2. Write your philosophy of education and share it with others. Ask them to critique it for comprehensiveness, clarity, and meaning. How do you feel about the changes they suggested?

3. Use a daily/monthly planner to develop a professional development plan for the next year. First list your career development goals and then on a monthly basis specify activities, events, and other ways that you will achieve these goals. For example, in addition to attending classes at a local community college, preschool teacher Rosa Vaquerio plans to read a book a month on a topic related to teaching.

4. Many local schools and school districts elect and honor their teachers of the year. Contact one of these teachers and have him or her share with you the core ideas and beliefs that enabled him or her to be selected as a teacher of the year. Ask the teacher to provide specific examples of how to apply ethical practice to teaching. How do you plan to integrate these qualities into your professional development plan?

5. You should constantly be on the alert for ways to grow professionally. Interview two pre-K to grade three teachers. Ask them to identify specific things they do to promote their own professional development.

6. Dispositions (for example, love of children, honesty, and respect for all children) are a good way to think about yourself, your beliefs, and your teaching role. Add to this list and then identify several dispositions that you plan to focus on during the coming year.

7. Developmentally appropriate practice will play an important role in your teaching. For example, knowledge of child development influences how teachers help children develop oral language skills. Research this topic by accessing the NAEYC website (http://www.naeyc.org/about/positions.asp) and reviewing the *Developmentally Appropriate Practice* position statement. Identity three other examples of how you would apply child development to your teaching to help children learn to communicate.

PEARSON
myeducationlab

To check your comprehension on the content covered in Chapter 1, go to the Book Specific Resources in the MyEducationLab for your course, select your text, and complete the Study Plan. Here you will be able to take a chapter quiz and receive feedback on your answers.

FIGURE 1.5

Seventeen Competencies for Becoming a Professional: A Professional Development Checklist

NAEYC Standard	Desired Professional Goals
Standard 1	**Promoting Child Development and Learning** I use my understanding of young children's characteristics and needs, and of multiple interacting influences on children's development and learning, to create environments that are healthy, respectful, supportive, and challenging for each child.
Standard 1	**Delivering Education and Child Care** I am familiar with a variety of models and approaches for delivering education and child care, and I use this knowledge to deliver education and child care in a safe, healthy learning environment.
Standard 1	**Guiding Behavior** I understand the principles and importance of behavior guidance. I guide children to be peaceful, cooperative, and in control of their behavior.
Standard 1	**Theories of Early Childhood Education** I understand the principles of each major theory of educating young children. The approach I use is consistent with my beliefs about how children learn.
Standard 2	**Building Family and Community Relationships** I know about, understand, and value the importance and complex characteristics of children's families and communities. I use this understanding to create respectful, reciprocal relationships that support and empower families, and to involve all families in their children's development and learning.
Standard 3	**Observing, Documenting, and Assessing to Support Young Children and Families** I know about and understand the goals, benefits, and uses of assessment. I know about and use systematic observations, documentation, and other effective assessment strategies in a responsible way, in partnership with families and other professionals, to positively influence the development of each child.
Standard 4	**Using Developmentally Effective Approaches to Connect with Children and Families** I use my knowledge of children and families, developmentally effective approaches, and academic disciplines to design, implement, and evaluate learning experiences for all children.
Standard 4	**Educating Diverse Students** I understand that all children are individuals with unique strengths and challenges. embrace these differences, work to fulfill special needs, and promote tolerance and inclusion in my classroom. I value and respect the dignity of all children.
Standard 4	**Developmentally Appropriate Practice** I understand children's developmental stages and growth from birth through age 8, and use this knowledge to implement developmentally appropriate practice. I do all I can to advance the physical, intellectual, social, and emotional development of the children in my care to their full potential.
Standard 4	**Technology** I am technologically literate and integrate technology into my classroom to help all children learn.
Standard 5	**Using Content Knowledge to Build Meaningful Curriculum** I understand the importance of developmental domains and academic (or content) disciplines in early childhood curriculum. I know the essential concepts, inquiry tools, and structure of content areas, including academic subjects, and can identify resources to deepen my understanding. I use my own knowledge and other resources to design, implement, and evaluate meaningful, challenging curricula that promote comprehensive developmental and learning outcomes for every young child.
Standard 6	**Becoming a Professional** I identify and conduct myself as a member of the early childhood profession. I know and use ethical guidelines and other professional standards related to early childhood practice. I am a continuous, collaborative learner who demonstrates knowledgeable, reflective, and critical perspectives on my work, making informed decisions that integrate knowledge from a variety of sources. I am an informed advocate for sound educational practices and policies.
Standard 6	**Ongoing Professional Development** I have a professional career plan for the next year. I engage in study and training programs to improve my knowledge and competence, belong to a professional organization, and have worked or am working on a degree or credential (CDA, AA, BS, or BA). I strive for positive, collaborative relationships with my colleagues and employer.

Level of Accomplishment? (Circle One)	If High, Provide Evidence of Accomplishment	If Needs Improvement, Specify Action Plan for Accomplishment	Target Date of Completion of Accomplishment	See the following for more information on how to meet the Desired Professional Outcomes
High Needs Improvement				Chapters 1, 4, 5, 6, 7, 8, 9, 10, 11, 12, and 13
High Needs Improvement				Chapters 3, 4, 7, 8, 9, 10, 11, and 12 and all chapters' Technology Tie-In features
High Needs Improvement				Chapter 12
High Needs Improvement				Chapters 3 and 4
High Needs Improvement				Chapters 2, 11, and 13 and all chapters' Diversity Tie-In features
High Needs Improvement				Chapters 1 and 6
High Needs Improvement				Chapters 1, 2, 3, 4, 5, 6, 7, 8, 9, 10, 11, 12, and 13
High Needs Improvement				Chapters 1, 2, 4, 6, 7, 8, 9, 10, 11, 12, and 13 and all chapters' Diversity Tie-In features
High Needs Improvement				Chapters 1, 2, 3, 4, 5, 6, 7, 8, 9, 10, 11, 12, and 13
High Needs Improvement				Chapters 7 and 9 and all chapters' Technology Tie-In features
High Needs Improvement				Chapters 1, 2, 3, 4, 6, 7, 8, 9, 10, and 11 and all chapters' Diversity Tie-In and Technology Tie-In features
High Needs Improvement				Chapters 1, 5, 6, and 13 and all chapters' Ethical Dilemma and Professionalism in Practice features
High Needs Improvement				Chapters 1 and 7 and all chapters' Activities for Professional Development and Ethical Dilemma features

(continued)

FIGURE 1.5   Continued

NAEYC Standard	Desired Professional Goals
Standard 6	**Philosophy of Teaching** I have thought about and written my philosophy of teaching and caring for young children. My actions are consistent with this philosophy.
Standard 6	**Keeping Current in an Age of Change** I am familiar with the profession's contemporary development, and I understand current issues in society and trends in the field. I am willing to change my ideas, thinking, and practices based on study, new information, and the advice of colleagues and professionals.
Standard 6	**Professional Dispositions** I work with students, families, and communities in ways that reflect the dispositions expected of professional educators as delineated in professional, state, and institutional standards. I recognize when my own dispositions may need to be adjusted and am able to develop plans to do so.
Standard 6	**Historical Knowledge** I am familiar with my profession's history, and I use my knowledge of the past to inform my practice.

Level of Accomplishment? (Circle One)	If High, Provide Evidence of Accomplishment	If Needs Improvement, Specify Action Plan for Accomplishment	Target Date of Completion of Accomplishment	See the following for more information on how to meet the Desired Professional Outcomes
High Needs Improvement				All chapters' Activities for Professional Development and Ethical Dilemma features
High Needs Improvement				Chapters 1, 2, 3, 4, 5, 6, 7, 8, 9, 10, 11, 12, and 13
High Needs Improvement				Chapters 1, 2, 5, 11, and 12 and all chapters' Professionalism in Practice, Activities for Professional Development, and Ethical Dilemma features
High Needs Improvement				Chapters 3 and 6

Note: These professional development outcomes are consistent with the core values of the NAEYC and the competencies of the CDA.[38]

Source: Adapted from Morrison, George S., *Early Childhood Education Today,* 11th ed., © 2009. Electronically reproduced by permission of Pearson Education, Inc., Upper Saddle River, New Jersey.

chapter two

EARLY CHILDHOOD EDUCATION TODAY

Understanding and Responding to Current Issues

NAEYC Standards for Early Childhood Professional Preparation

Standard 1. Promoting Child Development and Learning

I use my understanding of young children's characteristics and needs, and of multiple interacting influences on children's development and learning, to create environments that are healthy, respectful, supportive, and challenging for each child.[1]

Standard 6. Becoming a Professional

I identify and conduct myself as a member of the early childhood profession. I know and use ethical guidelines and other professional standards related to early childhood practice. I am a continuous, collaborative learner who demonstrates a knowledgeable, reflective, and critical perspective on my work, making informed decisions that integrate knowledge from a variety of sources. I am an informed advocate for sound educational practices and policies.[2]

ISSUES INFLUENCING THE PRACTICE OF EARLY CHILDHOOD EDUCATION

We hear a lot about change. Change is in the air! President Barack Obama ran for office on a platform of change. America wants change from its elected officials. America also wants change in its schools and in the way children are educated. This national demand for change is based on the many economic and social problems facing our nation. The call for educational change is a result of the many problems facing children and schools.

Child abuse, childhood diseases such as asthma and lead poisoning, poverty, low-quality care and education, and society's inability to meet the needs of all children are perennial sources of controversy and concern. New ideas and issues relating to the education and care of young children keep the field of early childhood education in a state of constant change. In fact, change is one constant in the field of early childhood education. As a result, you will be continuously challenged to determine what is best for young children and their families as you meet the demands of society today as an early childhood professional.

You are part of the solution to making it possible for all children to achieve their full potential. Politicians and the public look to you and your colleagues to help develop educational solutions to social and political problems.

Agencies serving children and families, such as the Parent Teacher Association (PTA), offer "a voice for children" by expressing their views. For example, Anna Marie Weselak, past president of the National PTA, says, "Every young mind needs a spark to light the way to a brighter future through learning. Teachers are that spark."[3] Anthony Mullen, the 2009 Connecticut Teacher of the Year, says ". . . the greatest institution for social change is the school and the greatest instrument of change is the teacher. No other democracy created by man to promote the welfare of all people has ever existed. Schools and teachers have always been *the* catalyst for human progress because knowledge and learning have created the world in which we live."[4]

So, in the spirit of making change in response to social and educational issues let's examine some topics in early childhood and consider how you can respond to them.

Changing Families

Families are in a continuous state of change as a result of social trends. Some of these include increased maternal employment, increased father absence, increased cultural diversity, and changing views about marriage. As a result, the definition of what a family is varies as society changes. Consider the following ways families are changing:

1. *Structure*. Many families now include arrangements other than the traditional nuclear family. Some of these contemporary families include single-parent families headed by a mother or a father; stepfamilies including individuals related by either marriage or adoption; heterosexual, gay, or lesbian partners living together as families; and extended families, which may include grandparents, uncles, aunts, other relatives, and individuals not related by kinship.[5] Grandparents as parents are growing in numbers and represent a fast-growing "new" family arrangement.[6] In Chapter 13, I discuss in more detail grandparents and their roles in children's lives.
2. *Roles*. As families change, so do the roles that parents and other family members perform. More parents work and have less time for their children and family affairs. Working parents must combine roles of both parent and employee. The numbers of hats parents wear increases as families change.

FOCUS QUESTIONS

1. What are some critical, contemporary issues that influence the practice of early childhood education?

2. What can I do to promote cultural diversity in my classroom?

3. How can I accommodate children with autism in my classroom?

4. How can I prevent violence, bullying, and abuse in my classroom?

5. How can I be politically aware and keep current in the rapidly changing field of early childhood education?

6. How are educators using green curricula in their classrooms?

7. What are some of the ways early childhood education is changing today?

3. *Responsibilities.* As a result, 15 million children are left unattended after school.[7] families change, many parents find it difficult to afford quality care for their children. Some parents find that buffering their young children from television and societal violence, child abusers, and crime is more than they can handle. Other parents are consumed by problems of their own and have little time or attention to give their children. Nonetheless, the responsibilities of parenthood remain and, increasingly, parents seek help from early childhood professionals to meet the demands and challenges of child rearing.

Families will continue to change. As they do, you must develop creative ways to provide services to children and families of all kinds.

Working Parents.   An increasing percentage of mothers with children are currently employed. In 51.4 percent of married-couple families in 2008, both the husband and the wife were employed.[8] Sixty-five percent of mothers with children under the age of six and 77 percent of mothers with their youngest child between the ages six to seventeen were in the workforce.[9] This creates a greater demand for early childhood programs. Unfortunately, much of child care in the United States is not high quality.[10] One of your professional responsibilities is to partner with parents to raise the quality of child care and to make it affordable and accessible.

Fathers.   Fathers are rediscovering the joys of parenting and interacting with young children. At the same time, early childhood educators have rediscovered fathers! Men are playing an active role in providing basic care, love, and nurturance to their children. Increasingly, men are more concerned about their roles as fathers and their participation in family events before, during, and after the birth of their children. Fathers want to be involved in the whole process of child rearing.

Because of the profession's increased understanding of the importance of fathers in children's development, there is now more research than ever before about fathers' roles in the lives of children. For example, research indicates that:

Research shows that involved fathers contribute to the quality of their children's lives more than uninvolved fathers. What can you do to encourage fathers to become a part of their children's lives at home? In your classroom?

- Children with involved, caring fathers have better educational outcomes.
- Fathers who are involved, nurturing, and playful with their infants have children with higher IQs, as well as better linguistic and cognitive capacities.
- Toddlers with involved fathers go on to start school with higher levels of academic readiness. They are more patient and can handle the stresses and frustrations associated with schooling more readily than children with less involved fathers.
- The influence of a father's involvement on academic achievement extends into adolescence and young adulthood. Children with involved, loving fathers are significantly more likely to do well in school, have healthy self-esteem, and exhibit empathy and pro-social behavior compared to children who have uninvolved fathers.[11]
- Highly involved biological fathers had children who were 43 percent less likely than other children to repeat a grade.[12]

As you can see, helping fathers be involved with their children benefits children, families, schools, and society.

Here are some things you can do to involve fathers in your program:

- *Offer activities that can reach out to fathers.* Encourage fathers to become involved by planning back-to-school events, planning a father volunteer day, and daddy-daughter dances and other events.
- *Schedule activities for after work hours on weekdays, or on weekends.* Plan according to when most working parents can attend. If additional father involvement is sought, care programs and activities should be scheduled accordingly.
- *Sponsor activities that teach fathers how to help their children learn.* Parenting programs that encourage fathers to be involved in their children's learning and in the emotional side of child rearing appeal to dads.
- *Tell dads how much you appreciate their involvement.* Fathers should be told "thank you" and given support throughout the year, not just on Father's Day. Dads contribute to the financial, emotional, and academic success of children, and deserve to be praised for their efforts.[13]

In Chapter 13, I provide additional ideas for how you can involve dads and working parents.

Single Parents. The number of one-parent families, both male and female, continues to increase. Certain demographic groups are disproportionately represented in single-parent families. These increases are due to several factors. First, pregnancy rates are higher among lower socioeconomic groups. Second, teenage pregnancy rates in poor Caucasian, Hispanic, and African American populations are sometimes higher because of lower education levels, economic constraints, and fewer life opportunities.[14] In 2007, 80 percent of single-parent families were headed by females and 20 percent were headed by males.[15]

The reality is that more women are having children without marrying. In fact, 38.5 percent of all births in 2007 were to unmarried women.[16] This phenomenon is likely to continue to grow. So working with single moms will be a major part of your teacher role.

Teenage Parents. Although teenage pregnancies had declined during the previous decade, they are now climbing once again, causing alarm among social agencies and early childhood educators. The largest increases were for non-Hispanic black teens.[17] Consider these additional facts:

- In 2006, 435,427 births occurred to mothers aged fifteen to nineteen years, a birthrate of 41.9 per 1,000 women in this age group. The teen birthrate rose between 2005 and 2006 for the first time since 1991.[18]
- As a group, Latino teenagers have the highest birthrate, with 83 births per 1,000.[19]
- Among the states, Mississippi has the highest birthrate of teens fifteen to nineteen years of age, with 68 births per 1,000. New Mexico reaches second with 64 per 1,000, and Texas is third with 63 per 1,000. The national teen birthrate average is 42 per 1,000.[20]

Concerned legislators, public policy developers, and national leaders view teenage pregnancy as a loss of potential for young mothers and their children. From an early childhood point of view, teenage pregnancies create greater demand for infant/toddler child care and for programs to help teenagers learn how to be good parents.

Teenage pregnancies continue to be a dilemma for a number of reasons. The financial costs of teenage childbearing are high, including costs to young mothers and their children. Teenage parents are less likely to complete their education and more likely to have limited career opportunities. How might early childhood programs help teenage parents meet their needs and the needs of their children?

Collaborating with Families

Early childhood professionals agree that a good way to meet the needs of children is through their families, whatever the family units may be. Review Figure 2.1, which shows processes for working with children and families. As families change, early childhood professionals have to develop new and different ways of meeting parents' and children's needs. Providing for children's needs through and within the family system makes sense for a number of reasons:

- The family system has the primary responsibility for meeting children's many needs. Parents are children's first teachers, and the experience and guidance they do or do not provide shapes their children for life. It is in the family that basic values, literacy skills, and approaches to learning are set and reinforced. This is why it is important to work with families and help them get a good start on parenting.
- Teachers frequently need to address family problems and issues simultaneously as they help children. For example, working with family services agencies to help parents access adequate, affordable health care means that the whole family, including children, will be healthier.

Early childhood education professionals provide:

- Basic health care and nutrition information designed to promote wellness and healthy living
- Parenting education to help parents learn basic child-rearing knowledge and skills
- Literacy programs to help children and families learn to read
- Readiness activities and programs designed to get children ready for school and ensure all children are ready to learn
- Family referrals to community agencies that can provide help. The Special Supplement Nutrition Program for Women, Infants, and Children (WIC) is a preventive health and nutrition program that promotes optimal growth and development

Family and child outcomes as a result of professional efforts include but are not limited to:

- Less family stress
- Healthier families and children
- More involvement of families in their children's education
- Increased school involvement and success
- Reduced child abuse and neglect
- Better quality of life for children and families

FIGURE 2.1 A Model for Meeting the Needs of Children and Families

- Early childhood professionals can work with children and their families and benefit both. Family literacy is a good example. Helping children, their parents, and other family members learn to read and write helps the whole family. Many early childhood programs have literacy programs for parents and children. For example, the Toyota Family Literacy Program (TFLP) partners with the National Center for Family Literacy and addresses the growing needs of Hispanic and other immigrant families by increasing English language and literacy skills for adults while also supporting parents' involvement in their children's education.[21]

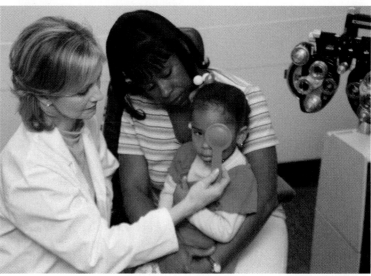

Families matter in the education and development of children. Working with parents becomes a win–win proposition for everyone. You are the key to making family-centered education work.

Wellness and Healthy Living

As you know, when you feel good, life goes much better. The same is true for children and their families. One major goal of all early childhood programs is to provide for the safety and well-being of children. A second goal is to help parents and other family members provide for the well-being of themselves and their children. Poor health and unhealthy living conditions are major contributors to poor school achievement and life outcomes.[22] A number of health issues facing children today put their chances for learning and success at risk.

When you think of children's illnesses, you probably think of measles, rubella, and mumps. Actually, asthma, lead poisoning, and obesity are the three leading childhood diseases.

Asthma. **Asthma**, a chronic inflammatory disorder of the airways, is the most common chronic childhood illness in the United States. An estimated 68 million children under the age of eighteen (almost 1.2 million children under the age of five) suffer from asthma; 4.1 million children have some kind of asthma attack each year.[23] Asthma is caused in part by poor air quality, dust, mold, animal fur and dander, allergens from cockroaches and rodent feces, and strong fumes. Many of these causes are found in poor and low-quality housing. You will want to reduce asthma-causing conditions in your early childhood programs and work with parents to reduce the causes of asthma in their homes. Some things you can do to reduce the causes of asthma are: (1) reduce or remove as many asthma and allergy triggers (such as smoke, mold, pet dander, cockroaches, and strong fumes or odors) as possible from homes and programs; (2) use air filters and air conditioners—and properly maintain them; (3) pay attention to the problem of dust mites, and (4) keep in mind that vacuum cleaners with poor filtration and design characteristics release and stir up dust and allergens.[24]

Lead Poisoning. Lead poisoning is also a serious childhood disease. The Centers for Disease Control and Prevention (CDC) estimate that approximately 250,000 U.S. children between birth and age five have dangerous blood lead levels.[25] These children are at risk for low IQs, short attention spans, reading and learning disabilities, hyperactivity, and behavioral problems. The major source of lead poisoning is from old lead-based paint that still exists in many homes and apartments; 83–86 percent of homes built before 1978 have

Children's development begins in the family system. The family system, with the help and support of early childhood programs, provides for children's basic needs. It is beneficial for the family to allow early childhood professionals to work with and through the family system to deliver their services.

asthma A chronic inflammatory disorder of the airways.

lead-based paint in them. Since then, lead has not been used in paint.[26] Other sources of lead are from car batteries and dust and dirt from lead-polluted soil. Lead enters the body through inhalation and ingestion. Young children are especially vulnerable since they put many things in their mouths, chew on windowsills, and crawl on floors. The Grace Hill Neighborhood Health Centers in St. Louis, Missouri, treat children for lead poisoning and send health coaches into the homes of children who have high levels of lead. These health workers cover peeling windowsills and provide vacuum cleaners with high-efficiency filters. For more information about the Grace Hill Neighborhood Health Centers, visit http://www.gracehill.org.

obesity A condition characterized by excessive accumulation and storage of fat in the body.

Obesity.   Today's generation of young children is often referred to as the "Supersize Generation" due to **obesity**. In fact, the Supersize Generation is getting younger! The 2008 statistical fact sheet of the American Heart Association reports that more than nine million children between the ages of six and nineteen are considered overweight; 11.5 percent of children between the ages of six months and twenty-three months are overweight; and nearly 14 percent of preschool children between the ages of two and five are overweight. Among preschool children, 11.5 percent of non-Hispanic whites are overweight; 13 percent of non-Hispanic blacks are overweight; and 19.2 percent of Mexican American children are overweight.[27] Obesity is such a national problem that it is now considered to be the number one health concern for children.[28] Additionally, the tipping point for early childhood obesity begins in infancy. More and more obesity prevention programs are geared toward infants and toddlers.[29]

In addition, new waves of research report the relationship of obesity to other diseases and health problems, especially later in life. Excess weight in childhood and adolescence predicts weight problems in adults. Overweight children, ages ten to fourteen, with at least one overweight or obese parent, were reported to have a 79 percent likelihood being of overweight into adulthood.[30] Obesity can also cause heart problems. A recent study revealed that children who are substantially overweight throughout much of their childhood and adolescence have a higher incidence of depression than those who aren't overweight. There were several significant findings related to this research involving one thousand children. First, a link was shown between obesity and psychiatric disorders. Second, researchers found that boys were at greater risk than girls for weight-related depression.[31]

The dramatic rise in obesity is due to a combination of factors, including less physical activity and more fat and calorie intake. More children spend more time in front of televisions and computer screens and fewer schools mandate physical education. Also, restaurant promotions to "supersize" meals encourage high-fat and high-calorie diets. Recent studies suggest that a ban on fast food advertisements on television, especially those targeting young children, could reduce the number of overweight children by as much as 18 percent. Although it is unlikely that such a ban would ever materialize, the study does demonstrate how advertising food and childhood obesity are linked.[32]

As the rate of obesity in American children continues to rise, it is especially important for you to keep yourself healthy and to model healthy habits for the children you teach to ensure that they have a good role model as encouragement to develop healthy nutritional habits.

What can you do to help children and parents win the obesity war?

- Provide parents with information about nutrition. What children eat—or don't eat—plays a major role in how they grow, develop, and learn. Diet also plays a powerful role in whether or not children engage in classroom activities with energy and enthusiasm. For example, send home copies of MyPyramid for Kids (see Figure 2.2). Also, you can log on to http://www.mypyramid.gov and individualize a food pyramid for each of your children. Be sure to note there are different pyramids depending on the child's age group. You can also send this information home to parents and share with them how to access and use the new MyPyramid.

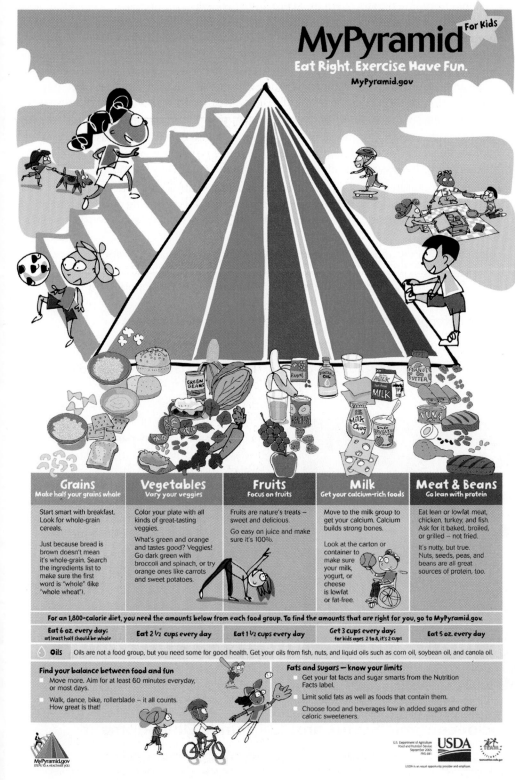

FIGURE 2.2 Good Nutrition for Young Children

Source: U.S. Department of Agriculture Food and Nutrition Service, retrieved January 26, 2009, from http://www.mypyramid.gov.

- Encourage your children to eat breakfast and encourage parents to serve breakfast. Also, investigate your school's lunch and breakfast programs. If your program does not serve breakfast to children, you can advocate for a breakfast program for children whose families' incomes make them eligible for federal- and state-supported nutrition programs. Research is very clear that serving breakfast to children who do not get it elsewhere significantly improves their cognitive abilities; this enables them to be more alert, pay better attention, and do better in terms of reading, math, and on standardized test scores.[33]

- Counsel parents to pull the plug on the television. TV watching at mealtime is associated with obesity because children are more likely to eat fast foods such as pizza and salty snack foods while they watch TV. Also, children who watch a lot of television tend to be less physically active, and inactivity tends to promote weight gain.

- Cook with children and talk about foods and their nutritional values. Cooking activities are also a good way to eat and talk about new foods. Cooking and other nutrition-related activities are ideal ways to integrate math, science, literacy, art, music, and other content areas.

- Integrate literacy and nutritional activities. Reading and discussing labels is a good way to encourage children to be aware of and think about nutritional information. For example, calories provide energy; too much fat and sugar are not good for us; and protein is important, especially in the morning.[34]

- Provide opportunities for physical exercise and physical activities every day.

For their part, schools are fighting the obesity war in the following ways:

- Banning the sale of sodas and candy bars in school vending machines during lunch hours[35]

- Teaching about and encouraging healthier lifestyles in and out of school

- Including salad bars as part of their cafeterias (for example, in Pittsburgh, Frazier School District Superintendent Dennis Spinella said, "Salad bars go hand in hand with allowing us to meet the goals of our wellness program and provide healthy eating choices and hopefully cut into the childhood obesity issue")[36]

- Banning cupcakes and other sweets at class birthday parties and being urged to consider healthier snack choices for homeroom celebrations[37]

- Restoring recess and physical education to the elementary school curriculum

- Working with parents to help them get their children to be more active and to eat healthier foods at home

Readiness is now viewed as promoting children's learning and development in all areas. Readiness includes general health such as being well rested, well fed, and properly immunized. More than 20 percent of toddlers (1 in 5) in the United States are not fully immunized.

Socioeconomic Status and Children's Development

Throughout the course of their in-school and out-of-school lives, children's successes and achievement are greatly influenced by their family's socioeconomic status (SES).[38] This chapter's Diversity Tie-In feature, "How You Can Advocate for Children and Families," discusses this topic further. SES consists of three broad but interrelated measures: parents' education levels, parents' employment status, and family income. These three measures, acting individually and as an integrated whole, influence: (1) how children are reared; (2) family–child interactions; (3) home environments and the extent to which they do or do

How You Can Advocate for Children and Families

As we have discussed, children from low socioeconomic backgrounds do not achieve as well as they could or should in school. This is an overgeneralization, of course; many do succeed, although many do not. You should use data about poverty and school achievement to advocate for policies that will help more poor children and their families find success in both school and life.

One thing is certain: We do not need to accept the status quo. We can work to ensure that all children start school on an equal footing. NAEYC Standard 6 is about becoming a professional and what this entails. How children are affected by their socioeconomic status is a critical area in which you can develop and use your advocacy skills.

Some things you can advocate for and support in order to help all children and families include the following:

- Support the development of and access to high-quality preschool and kindergarten programs for all children, to ensure that all children have equal opportunities to achieve. Also, advocate for preschool readiness programs to ensure that all children will enter preschool programs and kindergarten ready to learn.
- Advocate for family literacy programs and other programs that will enable families to help their children learn before they come to school. Insofar as possible, we want to eliminate achievement gaps before children come to school.
- Help create public awareness of the importance of early learning and how early learning, or the lack of it, shapes

children's futures. Part of your advocacy can include sharing data about socioeconomic status (SES) and school achievement. Also, you can share data that demonstrate the effectiveness of high-quality preschool programs. For example, the latest study by the High/Scope Educational Research Foundation shows that adults who had participated in a high-quality preschool program have higher earnings, are more likely to hold a job, and have committed fewer crimes. In addition, the study demonstrated a return to society of more than $17 for every tax dollar invested in the early care and education program.*

- Advocate for equitable funding for all preschool and elementary programs and schools. All children deserve and need high-quality learning environments and teachers.
- Create awareness of the importance that all children achieve state standards specified for their grade level. All children—not just some—must achieve the state standards. This means children from low-SES backgrounds will need more help and support from you, the schools, and the community.

....
*High/Scope Perry Preschool Study, "Lifetime Effects: The High/Scope Perry Preschool Study Through Age 40," 2005, available online at http://www.highscope .org/Content.asp?ContentId=219.

Source: V. E. Lee and D. T. Burkham, Inequality at the Starting Gate: Social Background Differences in Achievement as Children Begin School. Economic Policy Institute, www.epinet.org/content.cfm?id=616.

---

not support language development and learning; (4) kind and amount of discipline used; and (5) kind and extent of future plans involving children's education and employment.[39]

Poverty Defined.   **Poverty** has serious negative consequences for children and families. Around 12.8 million children live in poor families, meaning their parents' income is $20,000 or less. These parents are typically unable to provide their families with basic necessities like stable housing and reliable child care.[40] In addition, over one-third of all children in the United States live in low-income families, meaning that their parents earn no more than twice the federal poverty level, or $40,000 for a family of four. These families often face material hardships and financial pressures similar to those families who are officially counted as poor.

Poverty is a greater risk for children living in single-parent homes headed by females (approximately 43 percent) rather than males (approximately 21 percent).[41] Approximately 41 percent of African American children under the age of five live in poverty; this figure climbs to 58.5 percent in single-mother households. Poverty rates for Hispanic American children under the age of five are 31.3 percent overall and about 59.1 percent for those in single-mother homes.[42]

Effects of Poverty.   Living in poverty means children and their families don't have the income that allows them to purchase adequate health care, housing, food, clothing,

poverty The state of a person who lacks a usual or socially acceptable amount of money or material possessions.

and educational services. The federal government annually revises its poverty guidelines, which are the basis for distribution of federal aid to schools and student eligibility for academic services such as Head Start, **Title I** (a federal program that provides low-achieving students additional help in math and reading), and free and reduced-price school breakfasts and lunches. Living in a rural community and in a rural southern state increases the likelihood that families will live in poverty. Cities with the highest school-age poverty rate are in the South and East.[43] The following are some examples of the effects of poverty:

Title I A federal program designed to improve the basic skills (reading and mathematics) of low-ability children from low-income families.

- Poverty is detrimental to students' achievement and life prospects. For example, children and youth from low-income families are often older than others in their grade level, move more slowly through the educational system, are more likely to drop out, and are less likely to find work. Poor children are more likely to be retained in school, and students who have repeated one or more grades are more likely to become school dropouts. Poverty affects students' health prospects as well. For example, in 2008 the number of children under age eighteen without health insurance was 11 percent, or 8.1 million.[44]
- Children in poverty are more likely to have emotional and behavioral problems and are less likely than others to be "highly engaged" in school.[45]
- Children living in poverty have poorer health and shorter life spans. The longer children live in poverty, the less efficient their bodies become in handling environmental demands.[46]

So, improving the conditions that surround children of poverty is a major way teachers, politicians, and the public can collaborate to help children do better in all areas of life, including schooling.

PROVIDING FOR CULTURAL DIVERSITY

As a result of changing demographics, more students will require special education, bilingual education, and other special services. Issues of culture and diversity shape instruction and curriculum. These demographics also have tremendous implications for how you teach and how your children learn.

Diversity

The population of the United States is changing and will continue to change. For example, projections are that by 2050, minorities will constitute more than 47 percent of the American population.[47] The population of young children in the United States reflects the population at large and represents a number of different cultures and ethnicities. Thus, many cities and school districts have populations that express great ethnic diversity, including Asian Americans, Native Americans, African Americans, and Hispanic Americans. For example, the Charlotte-Mecklenburg School District in North Carolina has children from 141 countries, each with their own culture.[48] This constantly evolving population requires teachers to not only understand diversity, but embrace it in each classroom.

Multicultural Awareness

multicultural awareness Appreciation for and understanding of people's culture, socioeconomic status, and gender.

Multicultural awareness is the appreciation for and understanding of people's cultures, socioeconomic status, and gender. It includes understanding one's own culture. Cultural awareness programs and activities focus on other cultures while making children aware of the content, nature, and richness of their own. Learning about other cultures concurrently with their own culture enables children to integrate commonalities and appreciate differences without inferring inferiority or superiority of one or the other. Promoting multiculturalism in an early childhood program has implications far beyond your school, classroom, and program. Multiculturalism influences and affects work habits, interpersonal relations, and a child's general outlook on life. Early childhood professionals must take these cultural influences into consideration when designing curriculum and instructional processes for the impressionable children they will teach. One way to accomplish the primary goal of multicultural education—to positively change the lives of children and their families—is to infuse multiculturalism into early childhood activities and practices.

Being a culturally aware teacher means that you are sensitive to the socioeconomic backgrounds of children and families. For example, we know that low family socioeconomic status tends to dampen children's school achievement. The same is true with children's school achievement and maternal education. By learning about family background you can provide children from diverse backgrounds the extra help they may need to be successful in the school.

Multicultural Infusion

Multicultural infusion means that culturally aware and sensitive education permeates the curriculum to alter or affect the way young children and teachers think about diversity issues. In a larger perspective, infusion strategies are used to ensure that multiculturalism becomes a part of the entire center, school, and home. Infusion processes foster cultural awareness; use appropriate instructional materials, themes, and activities; teach to children's learning styles; and promote family and community involvement.

Fostering Cultural Awareness. As an early childhood professional, keep in mind that you are the key to a cultural classroom. The following guidelines will help you foster cultural awareness:

- *Recognize that all children are unique.* Children have special talents, abilities, and styles of learning and relating to others. Make your classroom a place in which children are comfortable being who they are. Always value uniqueness and diversity.
- *Get to know, appreciate, and respect the cultural backgrounds of your children.* Visit families and community neighborhoods to learn more about cultures and religion and the ways of life they engender.
- *Use authentic situations to provide for cultural learning and understanding.* For example, a field trip to a culturally diverse neighborhood of your city or town provides children an opportunity for understanding firsthand many of the details about how people live. Such an experience provides wonderful opportunities for involving children in writing, cooking, reading, and dramatic play activities. What about setting up a market in the classroom?
- *Use authentic assessment activities to asses fully children's learning and growth.* Portfolios are ideal for assessing children's learning in nonbiased and culturally sensitive ways.
- *Infuse culture into your lesson planning, teaching, and care giving and make it a foundation for learning.* Use all subject areas—math, science, language arts, literacy, music, art, and social studies—to relate culture to children's lives and cultural backgrounds. This approach makes students feel good about their backgrounds, cultures, families, and experiences.
- *Be a role model by accepting, appreciating, and respecting other languages and cultures.* In other words, infuse multiculturalism into your personal and professional lives.
- *Be knowledgeable about, proud of, and secure in your own culture.* Children will ask about you, and you should be prepared to share your cultural background with them.

Using Appropriate Instructional Materials. You need to carefully consider and select appropriate instructional materials to support the infusion of cultural education. The

myeducationlab

Go to the Assignments and Activities section of Topic 10: Cultural & Linguistic Diversity in the MyEducationLab for your course and complete the activity entitled *Understanding Culture.* You will have children from many diverse backgrounds in your classroom. This activity helps you understand how culture influences children's development and learning.

multicultural infusion A situation in which multicultural education permeates the curriculum to influence the way young children and teachers think about diversity issues.

following are some suggestions for achieving this goal.

- *Multicultural Literature.* Choose literature that embraces similarities and welcomes differences regarding how children and families live their *whole lives.*
- *Themes.* Early childhood professionals may select and teach thematic units that help strengthen children's understanding of themselves, their culture, and the cultures of others. Here are some appropriate theme topics, all of which are appropriate for meeting various state standards and the standards of the National Council for the Social Studies (NCSS):
- Getting to Know Myself, Getting to Know Others

- What Is Special About You and Me?
- Growing Up in the City
- Tell Me About Africa (or South America, China, etc.)
- *Personal Accomplishments.* Add to classroom activities, as appropriate, the accomplishments of people from different cultural groups, women of all cultures, and individuals with disabilities.

When you select materials for use in a cultural curriculum for early childhood programs, make sure of the following:

- Represent people of all cultures fairly and accurately.
- Include people of color, many cultural groups, and people with exceptionalities.
- Verify that historical information is accurate and nondiscriminatory.
- Do not use materials that include stereotypical roles and languages.
- Ensure gender equity—that is, boys and girls are represented equally and in nonstereotypic roles.

Promoting Family and Community Involvement. You will work with children and families of diverse cultural backgrounds. As such, you will need to learn about the cultural background of children and families so that you can respond appropriately to their needs.

It is important for you to understand that each family and child is unique. You should not assume values and beliefs just because a family speaks a particular language and is from a different country of origin. Take time to discover the particular values, beliefs, and practices of the families in the communities.

As a teacher of young children, you will teach children from different cultures whose first language is not English. Educating students with diverse backgrounds and special needs makes for a challenging and rewarding career and learning how to constantly improve your responses to students' special needs and improve learning environments and curricula will be one of your ongoing professional responsibilities. Society, families, and children change as diversity increases, and as more students with special needs come to school, you will have to change how and what you teach. It is your responsibility to teach these children and to help them learn.[49] The accompanying Professionalism in Practice Competency Builder provides six strategies for becoming a successful teacher of linguistically and culturally diverse children. Your students are waiting for you to make a difference in their lives!

As a result of new research, we are learning more about children than ever before. This new research accounts for the tremendous popularity of early childhood programs and curriculum. Practices in early childhood programs are now more research-based, especially those that support early literacy learning.

COMPETENCY BUILDER

How to Help English Language Learners Succeed

My attempts to learn Spanish have given me a lot of empathy for English language learners (ELLs). Perhaps you have had the same experience of frustration with comprehension, pronunciation, and understandable communication. English language learners face these same problems. Many come from low socioeconomic backgrounds. Others come to this country lacking many of the early literacy and learning opportunities we take for granted.

INCREASING NUMBERS

Many school districts across the country have seen their numbers of English language learners skyrocket. For example, in 2007, the Texas Education Agency reported there were 775,645 ELL students in early education through twelfth grade; 600,000 of those were in kindergarten through twelfth grade; 92 percent (711,388) were Spanish speakers. Prominent languages other than Spanish were Korean, Vietnamese, Urdu, and Arabic. Approximately 10 percent of ELLs are served by special education in schools.*

The chances are great that you will have English language learners in your classroom wherever you choose to teach. There are a number of approaches you can use to ensure that your children will learn English and will be academically successful.

TIPS FOR SUCCESS

Judith Lessow-Hurley, a bilingual expert, says, "It's important to create contexts in which kids exchange meaningful messages. Kids like to talk to other kids, and that's useful."[†] Lessow-Hurley also supports sheltered immersion. She says, "A lot of what we call 'sheltering' is simply good instruction—all kids benefit from experiential learning, demonstrations, visuals, and routines. A lot of sheltering is also common sense—stay away from idioms, speak slowly and clearly, [and] find ways to repeat yourself."[§]

Here are some other general tips Lessow-Hurley offers for assisting English language learners, along with some explicit classroom strategies:

STRATEGY 1
Develop Content Around a Theme
The repetition of vocabulary and concepts reinforces language and ideas and gives English language learners better access to content.

STRATEGY 2
Use Visual Aids and Hands-On Activities to Deliver Content
Information is better retained when a variety of senses are used.

- Rely on visual cues as frequently as possible.

- Have students create flash cards for key vocabulary words. Be sure to build in time for students to use them.
- Encourage students to use computer programs and books with CDs or DVDs.

STRATEGY 3
Use Routines to Reinforce Language
This practice increases the comfort level of second-language learners; they then know what to expect and associate the routine with the language. One helpful routine is daily reading. Use pictures, gestures, and a dramatic voice to help convey meaning.

STRATEGY 4
Engage English Language Learners with English Speakers
Cooperative learning groups, composed of children with mixed language abilities, give students a meaningful content for using English.

- Pair English language learners with native speakers to explain and illustrate a specific word or phrase frequently heard in the classroom.
- Ask the students to make a picture dictionary of the words and phrases they are learning, using pictures they have cut out of magazines.
- Have small groups make vocabulary posters of categories of common words, again using pictures cut from magazines.

STRATEGY 5
Allow Students to Use Nonverbal Responses
Permit students to demonstrate their knowledge and comprehension in alternative ways. For example, one teacher asks early primary students to hold up cardboard "lollipops" (green or red side forward) to indicate a yes or no answer to a question.

STRATEGY 6
Don't Correct All Nonstandard Responses
It's better to get students talking; they acquire accepted forms through regular use and practice. A teacher can always paraphrase a student's answer to model Standard English.[§]

*L. Ayala, Texas Education Agency, ELL Assessment Update, December 2008; retrieved April 7, 2009, from http://ritter.tea.state.tx.us/student .assessment/resources/conferences/tac/2008/ell_assessment_update.pdf.
[†]R. Allen, "Acquiring English: Schools Seek Ways to Strengthen Language Learning," Curriculum Update, Association for Supervision and Curriculum Development, Fall 2002, 6.
[†] Ibid.
[§]Ibid, 7.

ACCOMMODATING DIVERSITY: AUTISM SPECTRUM DISORDER

autism spectrum disorder A neurological developmental disorder characterized by a deficit in communication and social interactions as well as by the presence of restricted and repetitive behaviors. It is considered a "spectrum" of disorders because different people can have very different symptoms, ranging from mild to severe.

receptive language Language that a person "receives" or understands through spoken, written, or visual communication.

social story A personalized, detailed, and simple script that breaks down behavior and provides rules and directions.

Meet Sean: He has just turned four years old and was diagnosed with a mild **autism spectrum disorder**, a neurological developmental disorder characterized by a deficit in communication and social interactions as well as by the presence of restricted and repetitive behaviors. Sean is one of every 150 children in the United States who have autism. Sean is very attached to routine and while his **receptive language** skills appear to be typical—he can understand spoken, written, or visual communication—he has difficulty expressing himself. In addition, Sean's social interactions with peers are often contentious or stilted because he has difficulty deviating from his own plans or adapting to his peers'. How will you accommodate Sean in your classroom?

One way you can help Sean acclimate to your classroom rules and routines is for you to write a **social story** for him. A social story is a personalized, detailed, and simple script that breaks down behavior and provides rules and directions. Social stories can range from drawings featuring stick figures, to computer images, or even better, to digital photos featuring Sean. To write a social story you follow these steps:

1. Identify a behavior or activity you want Sean to comply with. You can use social stories to modify any kind of behavior, from toileting to peer interactions to transitions. However, each social story should focus on one thing at a time. For example, Sean is having difficulty transitioning from his mother's car to your classroom and the morning routine. Before writing the social story, observe Sean and talk with his parents to learn why the home-to-school transition is difficult for him. Is he concerned that his mother won't come back for him? Does Sean understand what will happen next? Are all transitions a source of worry for him? You will use this information to write Sean's social story.

2. Write on the first page: "This is Sean." Use a picture of Sean. You can draw it and label it or use an actual photo. The photo should depict a part of Sean's life that he will recognize. If he brings a Spiderman action figure to school every day, have Spiderman in the picture.

3. Write on the second page: "On Monday morning, Sean gets into Mommy's car to come to school." Include a photo of Sean getting into his mother's car.

This is Sean.

On Monday morning, Sean gets into Mommy's car to come to school.

4. Always use the child's own language. Sean calls his mother "Mommy," so you use the word "Mommy." Keep in mind that different cultures use different words for parents. For example, Ali, whose parents are from Pakistan, calls his father "Abba." Contact

Sean's parents and ask them questions about the words he uses. For Sean, using his language makes the story more real, more personal, and reinforces the importance of communication.

5. Provide routines. Children with autism like routines because they provide predictability. Sean's mother shares with you that if she takes a different route to school Sean has a meltdown. As a result, driving to school can be a daily trauma.

6. On the third page write: "Sometimes Mommy drives one way to school. If Mommy drives a new way to school, I will be safe. Mommy will keep Sean safe. If I feel worried, I can say, 'I am safe and I am still going to school' or 'It's okay if Mommy goes a different way. I am still going to school.'" Use a picture of Sean giving the "OK" or "thumbs-up" sign inside a car.

7. Write on the fourth page: "When Sean gets to school, he can say, "Bye Mommy! See you soon!" Use a picture of Sean with a big smile on his face waving good-bye. Social stories are a behavior model and a linguistic script, so whenever you use them be sure to model the behavior you wish to reinforce. If Sean is very attuned to time, instead of saying "See you soon," you can include the time his mother will return, saying "See you in

three hours at 12 o'clock!" Use a picture of his mother next to a picture of a clock showing the correct time on the same page.

8. Write on the fifth page: "Sean's job is to go to school. Sean can say, "Hi, (teacher's name)." Take a picture of yourself and insert it here.

9. If Sean's next step in the routine is to hang up his backpack, give him instructions for how to hang up his backpack. On the sixth page write: "Sean can hang his backpack on his hook. Now it is time to sit down." Use a picture of his hook with an arrow pointing to the next task of sitting down.

10. If Sean does not know how to greet his classmates, it is important to provide him with the steps and the words to do so. On the seventh page write: "When I sit down, I can say 'Hi, Johnny!'" Use a picture of his classmates waving or giving high fives.

11. Follow the same steps to make pages for Tuesday, Wednesday, Thursday, and Friday.

Social stories focus on the behavior you want Sean to use, not on negative behavior. Once you have written the social story, set aside time during the day to read it with Sean. Tell him that you made this very special book just for him. The first day, read it several times. You should read a social story as if it were a picture book with all the inflection and emotion you wish to model. Have Sean "practice" saying the words with you. Make a copy and send it home with Sean. Ask his parents to read it at home a few times but especially before bedtime and right before he leaves for school in the morning. On the drive to school, have Sean's mother let him hold the book and "read" it to himself. The first few days you use the new story, read it with him as he gets out of the car. Eventually Sean will not need this added support.

VIOLENCE, BULLYING, AND ABUSE

Violence

Violence seems to pervade American society. From television to video games to domestic violence, children are exposed to high doses of undesirable behavior. Children experience violence, both directly and indirectly, in these ways:

- Everyday in the United States, ten young children are murdered, sixteen killed in firearm accidents, and 8,042 are reported as physically abused.[50]
- Over three million children per year witness domestic violence in their homes.[51]
- Children in poverty are 22 times more likely to be physically abused and 60 more times likely to die from the abuse than those in the middle class.[52]
- By the time they reach middle school, children will have watched 100,000 acts of violence through television, including 8,000 depictions of murder.[53]
- Violence is not limited to movies, prime-time television, or the news. Saturday morning cartoons actually depict more acts of violence than prime-time television.[54]
- Television programs do not depict violence realistically. Instead, they depict violence as harmless or even comical. Only 16 percent of violent programs depict the long-term, realistic consequences of violent behavior.[55]
- On average, school-age children play video games fifty-three minutes per day; 49 percent of video games feature serious violence, and 40 percent show violence in a comic way.[56]

Research shows that violent behavior is learned and that it is learned early.[57] Your students' brains are remarkably **plastic**, or capable of being molded or adapting to conditions; the neurons are still arranging and rearranging connections. Brain plasticity usually works to children's advantage, because it enables them to learn and develop in spite of poor influences, allowing us to redirect neural pathways away from violence and toward amiable and peaceful conflict resolution. However, when children are routinely and repeatedly exposed to violence, their emotions, cognition, and behavior become centered on themes of aggression and violence.

plastic Capable of adapting to conditions, such as the neurons in a child's brain, which are constantly arranging and rearranging connections to form neural pathways.

Increasing acts of violence have led to proposals for how to provide violence-free homes and educational environments; how to teach children to get along nonviolently with others, such as by using puppets to discuss feelings with younger children or by role-playing and discussing appropriate ways to behave on the playground with older children; and how to reduce violence on television, in the movies, and in video games.[58] Reducing violence on television, for example, in turn leads to discussions and proposals for ways to limit children's television viewing. Such proposals include "pulling the plug" on television; using the V-chip, which enables parents to block out programs with violent content; boycotting companies whose advertisements support programs with violent content; and limiting violence shown during prime-time viewing hours for children. Here are some other steps you can take to prevent or reduce violence in children's lives:

- Show children photographs and have children identify various emotions; discuss appropriate responses to these emotions.
- Have children role-play how to respond appropriately to various emotions.
- Dr. Bruce D. Perry, internationally renowned specialist of brain development and childhood crisis, recommends that all classrooms foster six core elements to prevent violence: (1) attachment or a sense of friendship, (2) self-regulation or thinking before you act, (3) affiliation or the ability to join in, (4) awareness or thinking of others, (5) tolerance or accepting others, and (6) respect for yourself and others.[59]
- When guiding behavior, discuss with your students their behavior and the clear logical consequences of that behavior.
- When disagreements occur, have the children involved discuss with one another the feelings that caused their actions and think about how they could have done things differently.
- Discuss violence openly in your classroom. Be honest about the repercussions of violence. Focus on the pain and humiliation it causes. For example, if you are reading a book in class in which the characters engage in violence, discuss how the victim felt, what the character could have done differently, and what they themselves would have done in the same situation.
- Send home information about media violence and encourage parents to monitor and limit screen time.
- Encourage your school to offer parenting classes and parent–child relationship-building workshops. Such activities promote proactive and nonviolent problem solving, healthy and happy relationships, and community health.
- Read children books about handling emotions and discuss how the story characters handled their emotions. Some good books to read are:
  - *Handling Your Ups and Downs: A Children's Book About Emotions* by Joy Wilt Berry and Ernie Hergenroeder
  - *A to Z—Do You Ever Feel Like Me?* by Bonnie Hausman and Sandi Fellman
  - *The Oceans of Emotions* by Nicole K. Clark and John T. Clark

Bullying

bullying To treat abusively or affect by means of force or coercion.

Programs to prevent and curb **bullying** are another example of how educators are combating the effects of violence on children. Although in the past bullying has been dismissed as "normal" or "kids' play," this is no longer the case, because bullying is related to personal and school violence. Bullying includes teasing, slapping, hitting, pushing, unwanted touching, taking personal belongings, name-calling, and making sexual comments and insults about looks, behavior, or culture. Many schools are starting to fight back against bullies and bullying through bully prevention programs.

Here are some things you can do to help prevent bullying in your classroom:

- Talk to children individually and in groups when you see them engage in hurtful behavior. For instance: "Chad, how do you think Brad felt when you pushed him out of the way?"
- Be constantly alert to any signs of bullying behavior in your classroom and intervene immediately.

- Teach cooperative and helpful behavior, courtesy, and respect. Much of what children do, they model from others' behaviors. When you provide examples of courteous and respectful behavior in your classroom it sets a good example for children.
- Have children work together on a project. Then, have the students talk about how they got along and worked together.
- Make children and others in your classroom feel welcome and important.
- Talk to parents and help them understand your desire to stop bullying and have a bully-free classroom.
- Conduct a workshop for parents on anti-bullying behavior.
- Teach your students the "talk, walk, and squawk" method (or some other method your school uses) in response to bullying. Role-play and practice this technique in class:
  - *Talk:* Encourage your students to stand up for themselves verbally: "Leave me alone" or "You don't scare me" are some choices. Have children practice these responses in a calm and assertive voice.
  - *Walk:* Teach your students to walk away, but not to run away. If students run away, it is likely to increase the intensity of the bullying.
  - *Squawk:* The last step is to tell a teacher. Teachers can then take steps to halt the bullying behavior.[60]
- Keep parents informed of their child's interactions with violence in school. If a child is a bully or is being bullied, tell the parents so that you and they can collaborate to remediate the situation.
- Read books about bullying. You can read books about bullying to and with your children during story time, group reading lessons, guided reading, and shared reading. You can also send books home for parents to read with their children. Some books you might want to read are:
  - *Arthur's April Fool* by Marc Brown. Arthur worries about remembering his magic tricks for the April Fool's Day assembly, and the bully Binky threatens to pulverize him.
  - *Blubber* by Judy Blume. When overweight Linda gives an oral report on whales, the cruel and power-wielding class leader, Wendy, starts calling her "Blubber," and the name-calling escalates into more intense bullying and humiliation.
  - *The Rat and the Tiger* by Keiko Kasza. Even though one is just tiny and the other is a big tough guy, Rat and Tiger are best friends. They have lots of fun playing together, even though Tiger is a bit of a bully. One day Tiger takes the bullying too far, and Rat decides that he's not going to take it anymore. Rat stands up for himself and refuses to be Tiger's friend until Tiger learns to play fair and square.[61]
  - *Nobody Knew What to Do* by Becky R. McCain. When bullies pick on Ray, a boy at school, a classmate is afraid but decides that he must do something.
  - *Stop Picking on Me* by Pat Thomas. This picture book helps kids accept the normal fears and worries that accompany bullying, and suggests ways to resolve this upsetting experience.
  - *The Berenstain Bears and the Bully* by Stan Berenstain. When she takes a beating from the class bully, Sister Bear learns a valuable lesson in self-defense—and forgiveness.

Childhood Abuse and Neglect

Many of our views of childhood are highly romanticized. We tend to believe that parents always love their children and enjoy caring for them. We also envision family settings full of joy, happiness, and harmony. Unfortunately for children, their parents, and society, these assumptions are not always true. In fact, the extent of child abuse is far greater than we might imagine. In 2007, there were 3.2 million referrals to CPS agencies, involving the alleged maltreatment of about 5.8 million children.[62]

Child abuse is not new; abuse—in the form of abandonment, infanticide, and neglect—has been documented throughout history. The attitude that children are the property of the parents partly accounts for this record. Parents have believed, and some still do, that they own their children and can do with them as they please.

Valid statistics are difficult to come by because definitions of child abuse and neglect differ from state to state and reports are categorized differently. Because of the increasing concern over child abuse, social agencies, hospitals, child care centers, and schools are becoming more involved in identification, treatment, and prevention of this national problem.

Public Law 93-247, the Child Abuse Prevention and Treatment Act, defines *child abuse and neglect* as follows:

> Physical or mental injury, sexual abuse, negligent treatment or maltreatment of a child under the age of eighteen by a person who is responsible for the child's welfare under circumstances which indicate that the child's health or welfare is harmed or threatened thereby as determined in accordance with regulations prescribed by the secretary.[63]

In addition, all states have some kind of legal or statutory definition of child abuse and mistreatment, and many define penalties for child abuse.

Just as debilitating as physical abuse and neglect is *emotional abuse,* which occurs when parents, teachers, and others strip children of their self-esteem. Adults take away children's self-esteem by continually criticizing, belittling, screaming and nagging, creating fear, and intentionally and severely limiting opportunities. Because emotional abuse is difficult to define legally and difficult to document, the unfortunate consequence for emotionally abused children is that they are often left in a debilitating environment.

Table 2.1 will help you identify abuse and neglect, both of which adversely affect children's growth and development.

Remember that the presence of a single abuse symptom or sign does not necessarily indicate abuse. You should observe a child's behavior and appearance over a period of time and generally be willing to give parents the benefit of the doubt about a child's condition. Moreover, we also want to make sure we are practicing and upholding the best interest and welfare of each child.

TABLE 2.1 Signs of Child Abuse and Neglect

Physical Signs of Child Abuse	Sexual Signs of Child Abuse
Unexplained burns, cuts, bruises, or welts in the shape of an object	Inappropriate interest or knowledge of sexual acts
Bite marks	Nightmares and bed wetting
Antisocial behavior	Drastic changes in appetite
Problems in school	Overcompliance or excessive aggression
Fear of adults	Fear of a particular person or family member

Signs of Neglect	Emotional Signs of Child Abuse
Unsuitable clothing for weather	Apathy
Dirty or unbathed	Depression
Extreme hunger	Hostility or stress
Apparent lack of supervision	Lack of concentration
Failure to thrive	Eating disorders

Source: From Childhelp.org, *Signs of Child Abuse*, 2009, http://www.childhelp.org/signs-of-child-abuse. Used with permission.

Reporting Child Abuse. As a teacher you are a mandatory reporter of child abuse. Other mandatory reporters include physicians, nurses, social workers, counselors, and psychologists. Each state has its own procedure and set of policies for reporting child abuse. You need to be familiar with your state and district policies about how to identify child abuse and how to report it.

The following guidelines should govern your response to a child with suspected abuse or neglect:

- Remain calm. A child may retract information or stop talking if he or she senses a strong reaction.
- Believe the child. Children rarely make up stories about abuse.
- Listen without passing judgment. Most children know their abusers and often have conflicted feelings.
- Tell the child you are glad that he or she told someone.
- Assure the child that abuse is not his or her fault.
- Do what you can to make certain that the child is safe from further abuse.
- Do not investigate the case yourself. Report your suspicions to your principal or program administrator or to the child and family services agency.

How child abuse is reported varies from state to state. In Washington, D.C., for example, if child abuse or neglect is suspected, you are to call the reporting hotline immediately at 202-671-SAFE. To make a report, you would need to provide the following information:

- Name, age, sex, and address of the child who is the subject of the report; also names of any siblings and the parent, guardian, or caregiver
- Nature and extent of the abuse or neglect, as you know it (and any previous abuse or neglect)
- Any additional information that may help establish the cause and identity of persons responsible
- Your name, occupation, contact information, and a statement of any actions taken concerning the child

Seeking Help. What can be done about child abuse? There must be a conscious effort to educate, treat, and help abusers and potential abusers. The school is a good place to begin. Federal agencies are another source of help. For information, contact any of the following organizations:

- Child Welfare Information Gateway (formerly known as the National Clearinghouse on Child Abuse and Neglect Information), a service of the Administration for Children and Families, U.S. Department of Health and Human Services, which helps coordinate and develop programs and policies concerning child abuse and neglect; http://www.childwelfare.gov
- Childhelp USA, which handles crisis calls and provides information and referrals to every county in the United States; hotline 1-800-422-4453 or 4-A-CHILD
- National Committee to Prevent Child Abuse (NCPCA), a volunteer organization of concerned citizens that works with community, state, and national groups to expand and disseminate knowledge about child abuse prevention.

POLITICS AND EARLY CHILDHOOD EDUCATION

The more early childhood is in the news, the more it generates public interest and attention; this is part of the political context of early childhood education. Whatever else can be said about education, it is this: It is political. Politicians and politics exert a powerful influence in determining what is taught, how it is taught, to whom it is taught, and by whom it is taught. Early childhood education is no exception.

Federal and State Involvement in Early Childhood Programs

Federal and state funding of early childhood programs has greatly increased during the past decade.[64] This trend will continue for several reasons. First, politicians and the public recognize that the early years are the foundation for future learning. Second, spending money on children in the early years is more cost effective than trying to solve problems in the teenage years. For example, a study by the Federal Reserve Bank estimates that the returns on public investment in quality early childhood development programs for low-income children, in terms of reduced spending on public programs and increased tax payments, is 16 percent. Children with quality early childhood education do better in school, are less likely to become involved in the juvenile justice system, and are more likely to own homes and have jobs as adults.[65] Third, President Obama has endorsed a Zero-to-Five initiative that includes grants to states to improve pre-kindergarten programs.[66]

Expanded Federal Support for Early Childhood Education

At the same time states are exerting control over education, so is the federal government. One of the dramatic changes occurring in society is the expanded role of the federal government in the reform of public education. More federal dollars are allocated for specific early education initiatives than ever before.

No Child Left Behind Act A landmark act in education reform designed to improve student achievement and change the culture of America's schools.

The **No Child Left Behind Act** (Public Law 107-110) and other federal initiatives have focused national attention on developing educational and social programs to serve young children and families. Two areas in particular, reading and school readiness, are now major federal priorities in helping to ensure that all children succeed in school and life. The Early Reading First programs established by No Child Left Behind provide grants to school districts and preschool programs for the development of model programs to support school readiness of preschool programs and to promote children's understanding of letters, letter sounds, and the blending of sounds and words. You can learn more about how the government plays a major role in what young children learn in Chapter 5.

Public Schools and Early Education

Traditionally, the majority of preschool programs were operated by private agencies or agencies supported wholly or in part by federal funds to help the poor, the unemployed, working parents, and disadvantaged children. But times have changed and now many preschool programs are operated by the public schools. In 2007, approximately 1.7 million children were served by child care, and 59 percent of those children were enrolled in a center-based early childhood program.[67] As preschool programs admit more three- and four-year-olds nationwide, employment opportunities for teachers of young children will grow.

GREEN SCHOOLS—GREEN CURRICULUM

All across the United States, schools are going green. Green schools and curricula are a response to ecology issues around the world and represent ways to save energy, conserve resources, infuse curricula with environmental education, build school gardens, and offer more healthy school lunches. Green schools are those in which the building creates a healthy environment conducive to learning while saving energy, resources, and money.[68] At Evergreen Elementary in California, Maryland, two silo-like structures catch rainwater that is used to flush the toilets. Gardens of plants on the entrance canopy roof soak up additional rainwater and help eliminate runoff.[69]

Green Curriculum

Green schools are only one part of contemporary eco-friendly initiatives. Making the school curriculum greener is the other part. More schools and teachers are teaching children and their families about the environment and how to preserve it, as well as the benefits of green living. At Morikami Park elementary in Palm Beach, Florida, environmental issues are integrated into the schools' curriculum through the students' TV broadcasts on "Green News."[70] At the University City Children's Center in St. Louis, preschool children have a garden bed in which they raise vegetables that become part of their school lunches. "We eat what we grow," says the school director.[71] Child care programs are turning to eco-friendly diapers, organic baby foods, odor-free zero-VOC (volatile organic compounds) paints, and the use of nontoxic techniques to control pests.

Just as saving the environment permeates all of our daily lives, so too is the eco movement becoming an essential part of the schools and the curriculum. Throughout this text, but especially in Chapters 7, 8, 9, and 10, we will provide ideas and examples for how you can integrate green activities and projects into your teaching.

NEW DIRECTIONS IN EARLY CHILDHOOD EDUCATION

Changing needs of society and families and new research provide new directions in early childhood education. As a result, the field of early childhood education is constantly changing. These are some important changes occurring in early childhood education today that will influence how you and others practice the profession of early childhood education:

- *Full-day, full-year services.* Parents want full-day, full-year services for their children for several reasons. Such a schedule fits in with their work schedules and lifestyles. Working parents, in particular, find it difficult to patch together child care and other arrangements when their children are not in school. Parents also believe that full-day, full-year services support and enhance their children's learning. Parents want their children to do well academically. As a result, we will see more full-day, full-year early childhood programs of all kinds.
- *School readiness.* There is and will be an increase in programs designed to provide families, grandparents, and others with child development information, parenting skills, and learning activities that will help them get their children ready for school. Working with parents to help them get their children ready for learning and school is an important and growing part of early childhood services.

  For example, the Harlem Children's Zone (HCZ) Project is a unique, holistic approach to rebuilding a community so that its children can stay on track through college and go on to the job market. The goals is to create a "tipping point" in the neighborhood so that children are surrounded by an enriching environment of college-oriented peers and supportive adults, a counterweight to "the street" and the toxic popular culture. The HCZ pipeline begins with Baby College, a series of workshops for parents of children from birth to age three. For children to do well, their families have to do well. And for families to do well, their community must do well. That is why HCZ works to strengthen families as well as empowering them to have a positive impact on their children's development.[72]

- *Support for whole child education.* Early childhood professionals have always acknowledged that they must educate the whole child—physical, social, emotional, linguistic, and cognitive. The Association for Supervision and Curriculum Development (ASCD) is sponsoring the Whole Child Initiative.

  The Whole Child Initiative is straightforward. If students are to master world-class academics, they need to be physically and emotionally healthy. They need to be well fed and safe. They need to be intellectually challenged and have supportive adults who know them well and care about their success. And they need to be interested and engaged in what they are learning. It is common sense—a hungry student can't learn, a scared student can't think, and a student who is bored or intimidated by schoolwork will just slip through the cracks.[73]

  In addition, another facet of the whole child—spiritual development—has not received enough attention. A recent trend is a greater emphasis on supporting children's spiritual development through moral and character education.[74]

- *Early literacy learning.* Research supports the importance of early literacy development. There is a growing awareness of the critical role literacy plays in school and life success. Consequently, there are now more programs designed specifically to help young children get ready to read. This emphasis on early literacy will continue as the federal government funds programs such as Early Reading First (see Chapter 4). This emphasis on early literacy and learning to read is also evident in other chapters throughout this book.

- *Increased use of technology.* More early childhood programs are seeking ways to enhance their effectiveness by helping children gain the cognitive and literacy skills they need to be successful in school and life. Many are turning to technology as a means of achieving these goals.

- *The politicalization of early childhood education.* There has been a dramatic increase in state and federal involvement in the education of young children and this will continue. For example, the federal government is using Head Start as a means and model for reforming all of early childhood education. This federalization will likely continue and expand. Under the American Recovery and Reinvestment Act of 2009, Head Start and Early Head Start received an additional $2.1 billion in funding.[75]

Changes in society constantly cause changes in the field of early childhood education. One of your major challenges as an early childhood professional is to keep current in terms of new changes and directions in your field. In this way you will be able to judge what is best for young children and implement the best practices that will enable young children to succeed in school and life.

This is a great time for early childhood education and a wonderful time to be a teacher of young children. President Obama and Secretary of Education Arne Duncan are pressing for more legislation and increased awareness in early childhood education and programs. With these improvements in early childhood, education will continue to progress over the years to come. These changes and the issues that accompany them provide many opportunities for you to become more professional, and they enable all children to learn the knowledge and skills necessary for success in school and life.

ACTIVITIES FOR PROFESSIONAL DEVELOPMENT

ethical dilemma

iou smexy (handwritten)

"My Child's Not Fat!"

The faculty and administration at Belvedere Elementary set up a pilot program to develop a curriculum for helping overweight children learn good nutrition skills and lose weight. Amanda Jones was asked to select three children from her kindergarten class to participate. She selected three children based on a comparison of the height and weight of her students with a height and weight chart of the National Academy of Pediatrics. One of the children's parents contacted Amanda and is angry that she selected her child. The parent believes that her child is not obese and should not be in a program for "fat kids." She believes Amanda is discriminating against her child and is threatening to contact the school board and the media.

What should Amanda do? Should she give in to the parent and remove her child from the program and risk that the child, who Amanda believes is very overweight, will suffer health-wise and from bullying and taunting? Or, should she risk alienating the parent and insist that her child would benefit from the program?

Application Activities

1. Reading online news is one way to keep up to date in a changing society and in a changing early childhood educational environment. In my early childhood classes, I electronically post items that I call "Early Childhood in the News." My students respond by also posting articles they find interesting. Over a two-week period, share with your classmates some "Early Childhood in the News" items.

2. Think about problems that young children and their families face in education (e.g., children who have problems with reading or children with autism). What programs in your community are available to help intervene and assist families with these issues? How do these services influence early childhood education programs in your local community?

3. Over the next three or four months, keep an electronic journal about changes you notice in the field of early childhood. Include these topics:

   a. What changes intrigue you the most?

   b. Not all changes are for the better. Make a list of changes that you think have a negative effect on children (e.g., rising poverty).

   c. Document the things you are doing personally and professionally in response to changes in society and education.

4. Of all the issues we discussed in this chapter, which two do you think are the most detrimental to children's development and education? Why?

PEARSON myeducationlab

To check your comprehension on the content covered in Chapter 2, go to the Book Specific Resources in the MyEducationLab for your course, select your text, and complete the Study Plan. Here you will be able to take a chapter quiz and receive feedback on your answers.

chapter three

HISTORY AND THEORIES

Foundations for Teaching and Learning

· · · · · · · · ·

NAEYC Standards for Early Childhood Professional Preparation

Standard 4. Using Developmentally Effective Approaches to Connect with Children and Families

I understand and use positive relationships and supportive interactions as the foundation for my work with young children and families. I know, understand, and use a wide array of developmentally appropriate approaches, instructional strategies, and tools to connect with children and families and positively influence each child's development and learning.[1]

Standard 6. Becoming a Professional

I identify and conduct myself as a member of the early childhood profession. I know and use ethical guidelines and other professional standards related to early childhood practice. I am a continuous, collaborative learner who demonstrates knowledgeable, reflective, and critical perspectives on my work, making informed decisions that integrate knowledge from a variety of sources. I am an informed advocate for sound educational practices and policies.[2]

THE IMPORTANCE OF THE HISTORY OF EARLY CHILDHOOD EDUCATION

There is a history of just about everything: a history of teaching, a history of schools, and a history of early childhood education. While you don't need to know the history of comic books to read and enjoy one, if you are a comic book collector, knowing the history of comic books is essential! The same applies to you as an early childhood educator. You will be a much more informed and effective teacher if you know the history of your profession. Knowing the history of your profession is essential to being a professional.

When we know the beliefs, ideas, and accomplishments of people who have devoted their lives to young children, we realize that many of today's early childhood programs are built on enduring beliefs about how children learn, grow, and develop. There are at least three reasons why it is important to know about ideas and theories that have and are influencing the field of early childhood education.

Rebirth of Great Ideas

Great ideas and practices persist over time and tend to be reintroduced in educational thought and practices in ten- to twenty-year cycles. For example, many practices popular in the past—such as the teaching of reading through phonics, multi-age grades or groups, and teacher-initiated instruction—are now popular once again. I hope you will always be as amazed as I am about the way early childhood professionals recycle enduring ideas and practices and use them in their teaching.

Build the Dream—Again

Many ideas of famous educators are still dreams because of our inability to translate dreams into reality. For example, the idea of universal preschool in the United States has been around since 1830, when the Infant School Society of Boston submitted a petition to incorporate infant schools into the Boston Public Schools.[3] As we discuss in Chapter 8, we are *still* trying to implement universal preschool education. Horace Mann, a nineteenth century education reformer referred to as "the father of American public education," stressed the importance and necessity of educating all children.

This goal of educating all children remains elusive, but nonetheless the goal remains. As Secretary of Education Arne Duncan says:

> In today's era of global economics, rapid technological change, and extreme economic disparity, education is the most pressing issue facing America. Preparing young people for success in life is not just a moral obligation of society. It's an economic imperative. As President Obama has said many times, "The nations that out-teach us today will out-compete us tomorrow."[4]

The dream of educating all children to their full potential is a worthy one, and we can and should use it as a base to build meaningful teaching careers and lives for children and their families. We have an obligation to make the bright visions that others have had for children *our visions* as well. After all, if we don't have bright visions for children, who will?

Implement Current Practice

Beliefs of famous educators will help you better understand how to implement current teaching strategies, whatever they might be. For instance, Rousseau, Froebel, and Montessori all believed children should be taught with dignity and respect. Dignity and

FOCUS QUESTIONS

1. Why is it important to know the history of early childhood education?

2. Why is it important to know theories of learning?

3. Who were the famous individuals who have influenced early childhood education and what were their contributions?

4. What are basic beliefs essential for high-quality programs?

5. How have instructional practices to accommodate disabilities changed over time?

respect for all children are essential foundations of all good teaching and quality programs, and those traits apply today, just as they did hundreds of years ago. In addition, great educators always believed in educating the whole child, which is something that we always need to be reminded of. For example, the 2008 National Teacher of the Year Michael Giesen says:

> Students need to know that we value more than just being right all the time. We need to really honor their creativity, we need to honor their desire to learn useful skills that are going to be relevant in a 21st century world. These are skills such as innovation and creativity; people skills, like compassion and collaboration; and the ability not just to know the details but to really see how it fits into the big picture.
>
> This is our real challenge, to educate the entire child—not just the left side of their brain, but the entire child.[5]

THE IMPORTANCE OF THEORIES OF LEARNING

When you work with young children to help them discover and learn how plants grow, you talk about soil, sun, water, and the need for fertilizer. Perhaps you even use the word *photosynthesis* as part of your theory of plant growth. Describing the processes of mental and physical growth of children, however, is not as straightforward. How do children develop? How do children learn? I'm sure you have ideas and explanations based on your experiences to help answer these questions. We also have the theories of others to help us explain these questions.

A **theory** is a statement of principles and ideas that attempts to explain events and how things happen; in our case, it is learning more about children's early childhood. We will learn about theories that attempt to explain how children grow, develop, and learn.

Learning is the process of acquiring knowledge, behaviors, skills, and attitudes. As a result of experiences, children change in each of these areas. So, we can also consider learning to be changes that occur in behavior over a period of time. The children who enter your kindergarten class in September are not the same children who exit your kindergarten class in May. Learning is a complex process, and many educators have developed theories to explain how and why learning occurs in children. We use child development to examine changes in children's lives. **Child development** is the study of how children change over time from birth to age eight.

Theories about how children learn and develop are an important part of your professional practice for several reasons. Let's look at the role of educational theories.

theory A statement of principles and ideas that attempts to explain events and how things happen.

learning The acquisition of knowledge, behaviors, skills, and attitudes.

child development The study of how children change over time from birth to age eight.

Communicate

Theories enable you to explain to others, especially families, how the complex process of learning occurs and what you and they can expect of children. Communicating with clarity and understanding to parents and others about how children learn is one of the most important jobs for all early childhood professionals. To do this, you need to know the theories that explain how children develop and learn.

Evaluate Learning

Theories also enable you to evaluate children's learning. Theories describe behaviors and identify what children are able to do at certain ages. You can use this information to evaluate learning and plan for teaching. Evaluation of children's learning is another important job for all teachers. I discuss assessment of learning in Chapter 6.

Provide Guidance

Theories help us understand how, why, where, and when learning occurs. As a result, they can guide you in developing programs for children that support and enhance their learning. For example, as we will see shortly, what Piaget believed about how children learn directly influences classroom arrangement and what is taught and how it is taught. Developing programs and curriculum is an important part of your professional practice. Thus, the history of early childhood and theories about how children learn enable you to fulfill essential dimensions of your professional role. Table 3.1 summarizes the contributions of famous educators to the early childhood field. Those educators are profiled in the following section.

TABLE 3.1 Contributions of Famous Individuals to Early Childhood Education

Individual and Dates	Major Contributions	Influences on Modern Theorists
Martin Luther (1483–1546)	• Translated the Bible from Latin to vernacular language, allowing people to be educated in their own language. • Advocated establishing schools to teach children how to read.	• Universal education. • Public support of education. • Teaching of reading to all children.
John Comenius (1592–1670)	• Wrote *Orbis Pictus,* the first picture book for children. • Thought early experiences formed what a child would be like. • Said education should occur through the senses.	• Early learning helps determine school and life success. • Sensory experiences support and promote learning.
John Locke (1632–1704)	• Said children are born as blank tablets or *tabula rasa.* • Believed children's experiences determine who they are.	• Learning should begin early. • Children learn what they are taught—teachers literally make children. • It is possible to rear children to think and act as society wants them to.
Jean-Jacques Rousseau (1712–1778)	• Advocated natural approaches to child rearing. • Felt that children's natures unfold as a result of maturation according to an innate timetable.	• Natural approaches to education work best (e.g., family grouping, authentic testing, and environmental literacy).
Johann Pestalozzi (1746–1827)	• Advocated that education should follow the course of nature. • Believed all education is based on sensory impressions. • Promoted the idea that mother could best teach children.	• Family-centered approaches to early childhood education. • Home schooling. • Education through the senses.
Robert Owen (1771–1858)	• Held that environment determines children's beliefs, behaviors, and achievements. • Believed society can shape children's character. • Taught that education can help build a new society.	• Importance of infant programs. • Education can counteract children's poor environment. • Early childhood education can reform society.
Friedrich Froebel (1782–1852)	• Believed children develop through "unfolding." • Compared children to growing plants. • Founded the kindergarten "Garden of Children." • Developed "gifts" and "occupations" to help young children learn.	• Teacher's role is similar to a gardener. • Children should have specific materials to learn concepts and skills. • Learning occurs through play.

FAMOUS HISTORICAL FIGURES AND THEIR INFLUENCE ON EARLY CHILDHOOD EDUCATION

Throughout history many people have contributed to our understanding of what children are like and how to best teach them. The following accounts will help you understand the history of early childhood and theories about how to best teach children.

Martin Luther

Martin Luther (1483–1546) emphasized the necessity of establishing schools to teach children to read. Luther replaced the authority of the Catholic church with the authority of the Bible. Luther believed that individuals were free to work out their own salvation through the Scriptures. This meant that people had to learn to read the Bible in their native tongue.

Luther translated the Bible into German, marking the real beginning of teaching and learning in people's native language. In these ways, the Protestant Reformation encouraged and supported popular universal education and the importance of learning to read.

Today, literacy for all continues to be a national priority. As you can see by the accompanying Diversity Tie-In box, ensuring that all children can read and learn in their native language, as Luther suggested, are issues we still deal with today.

John Amos Comenius

John Amos Comenius (1592–1670) spent his life teaching school and writing textbooks. Two of his famous books are *The Great Didactic* and *Orbis Pictus* ("The World in Pictures"), considered the first picture book for children.

Comenius believed education should begin in the early years because "a young plant can be planted, transplanted, pruned, and bent this way or that. When it has become a tree these processes are impossible."[6] Today, new brain research reminds us again that learning should begin early and that many "windows of opportunity" for learning occur early in life.

Comenius also thought that sensory education forms the basis for all learning and that insofar as possible, everything should be taught through the senses. This approach to education was endorsed by Montessori and forms the basis for much of early childhood practice to this day.

John Locke

John Locke (1632–1704) is best known for his theory of the mind as a blank tablet, or *tabula rasa*. By this, Locke meant that environment and experience literally form the mind. According to Locke, development comes from the stimulation children receive from parents and caregivers and through experiences they have in their environment.

The implications of this belief are clearly reflected in modern educational practice. The notion of the importance of environmental influences is particularly evident in programs that encourage and promote early education as a means of helping children get a good foundation for learning early in life. These programs assume that differences in learning, achievement, and behavior are attributable to environmental factors such as home and family conditions, socioeconomic background, and early education and experiences. The current move toward universal schooling for three- and four-year-olds is based on the premise that getting children's education right from the beginning can help overcome negative effects of poverty and neglect and can help erase differences in children's achievement due to difference in socioeconomic levels.

Native American Education: Culture and Relationships

CULTURAL EDUCATION FOR NATIVE AMERICAN CHILDREN

Classroom approaches that are responsive to children's cultures promote academic achievement by providing cultural relevance—which honors and explores the unique culture that each family develops. Culture is viewed as a source of strength and expression of values and preferences and a rationale for accepting school. An understanding of the historical relationship between American Indian cultures and the American educational system is essential for contemporary educators of American Indian children. Tribal children need a learning environment that nurtures their natural curiosity and their path to knowing. A key issue for educators is to provide or facilitate classroom-based learning experiences that validate both cultures. For example, a teacher may successfully reframe the cultural norm of cooperation on tasks and practice before sharing with an elder a school norm of group time. This balanced preparation of tribal children fully enables them to participate in their place in tribal communities as well as in the larger world community.

The restructuring of classrooms to promote small-group cooperative learning activities, peer tutoring, and the recognition of group, rather than individual achievement, will allow the gradual development of individual competence as part of a group while emphasizing traditional values of sharing, helping others, and cooperation in group efforts. Young Native American students appreciate the presence of Native people in leadership roles because they are positive role models.

Attempts to maintain tribal culture and language face monumental challenges when more than one tribe lives on a reservation and their children attend the same early childhood program. Teaching Native culture and language in any early childhood setting requires a knowledgeable, skillful teacher. Educators and administrators must possess a level of cultural understanding, be reflective in their practice, and create an environment respectful of diversity. These attributes are important whether or not teachers are representative of the child's community. An educational leader in Native American communities needs to have a clear and focused personal vision of leading, teaching, and learning. The educator must place the family first, and develop a sense of family within the community.

Recognizing the strong interrelatedness between school and community and building these relationships into educational practice can yield powerful results in educational improvement, community vitality, and preservation of traditional cultural beliefs and practices.

Contributed by Lisa Blackmon-Hansard, child-care program specialist, Administration for Children and Families, Department of Health and Human Services, Dallas, Texas.

Jean-Jacques Rousseau

Jean-Jacques Rousseau (1712–1778) is best remembered for his book *Émile,* the opening lines of which set the tone for his education and political views: "God makes all things good; man meddles with them and they become evil."[7] Because of this belief, Rousseau advocated the "natural" education of young children, encouraging growth without undue interference or restrictions.

Rousseau also believed in the idea of **unfolding**, in which the nature of children—who and what they will be—unfolds as a result of development according to their innate timetables. Such an approach is at the heart of developmentally appropriate practice, in which childhood educators match their educational practices to children's developmental levels and abilities. Every day you will make decisions about how to make sure what you teach and how you teach it is appropriate for each child based on his or her developmental level.

unfolding Rousseau's belief that the nature of children—who and what they will be—unfolds as a result of development according to their innate timetables.

Johann Heinrich Pestalozzi

Johann Heinrich Pestalozzi (1746–1827) was influenced by both Comenius and Rousseau. Pestalozzi believed all education is based on sensory impressions and that through the proper sensory experiences, children can achieve their natural potential. To achieve this goal, Pestalozzi developed "object lessons," manipulatives that encouraged activities such as counting, measuring, feeling, and touching. Pestalozzi also wrote two books—*How Gertrude Teaches Her Children* and *Book for Mothers*—to help parents teach their young children in the home. Today, enter any major bookstore (either online or in the shopping mall) and you will see shelves jammed with books on how to parent, how to teach young children, how to guide children's behavior, and many similar topics. You will be able to help families by providing them with books and/or suggestions for books to read that will help them enhance their guidance skills.

Robert Owen

Robert Owen (1771–1858) believed children's environments contribute to their beliefs, behavior, and achievement just as we believe today. He maintained that individuals and society can use environments to shape children's character. Owen was also a *utopian,* believing that by controlling the circumstances and consequent outcomes of child rearing, it was possible to build a new and perhaps more perfect society. Such a view of child rearing makes environmental conditions the dominant force in directing and determining human behavior.

To implement his beliefs, Owen opened an infant school in 1816 in New Lanark, Scotland, designed to provide care for about a hundred children, ages eighteen months to ten years, while their parents worked in the cotton mills he owned. This emphasis on early education eventually led to the opening of the first infant school in London in 1818.

Several things about Owen's efforts and accomplishments are noteworthy. First, his infant school preceded Froebel's kindergarten by about a quarter century. Second, Owen's ideas and practices influenced educators concerning the importance of early education and the relationship between educational and societal improvements, an idea much in vogue in current educational practice. In addition, early childhood professionals also seek to use education as a means of reforming society and as a way of making a better world for everyone.

Friedrich Wilhelm Froebel

Friedrich Wilhelm Froebel (1782–1852) is known as the "father of the kindergarten." Froebel's concept of children and learning is based in part on the idea of unfolding, also held by Comenius and Pestalozzi. According to this view, the teacher's role is to observe children's natural unfolding and provide activities that enable them to learn what they are ready to learn when they are ready to learn it.

Froebel compared the child to a seed that is planted, germinates, brings forth a new shoot, and grows from a young, tender plant to a mature, fruit-producing one. He likened the role of teacher to a gardener. Think for a moment how we still use the teacher-as-gardener metaphor to explain our role as teachers of young children. For example, I view myself as a planter of seeds in my work with young children. Froebel wanted his *kindergarten,* or "garden of children," to be a place where children unfolded like flowers. Froebel believed development occurred primarily through self-activity and play. I will discuss play further in other chapters because the process of learning through play is as important today as it was in Froebel's time. The concepts of unfolding and learning through play are two of Froebel's greatest contributions to early childhood education.

To promote self-activity, Froebel developed a systematic, planned curriculum for the education of children based on "gifts," "occupations," songs, and educational games. Think of these as similar to the materials and toys we have today to promote children's learning. For example, we teach the alphabet and other concepts with songs, use blocks to teach size and shape, and use colored rods to teach concepts of length and seriation.

Gifts were objects for children to handle and use in accordance with teachers' instructions so they could learn shape, size, color, and concepts involved in counting, measuring, contrasting, and comparison. Figure 3.1 describes Froebel's gifts. Think of some specific examples of how they relate to educational toys and materials today.

Occupations were materials designed for developing various skills through activities such as sewing with a sewing board, drawing pictures by following the dots, modeling with clay, cutting, stringing beads, weaving, drawing, pasting, and folding paper. All of

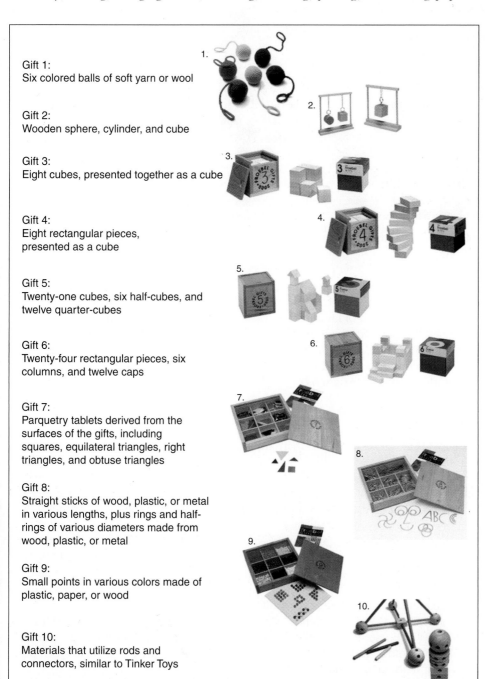

Gift 1:
Six colored balls of soft yarn or wool

Gift 2:
Wooden sphere, cylinder, and cube

Gift 3:
Eight cubes, presented together as a cube

Gift 4:
Eight rectangular pieces, presented as a cube

Gift 5:
Twenty-one cubes, six half-cubes, and twelve quarter-cubes

Gift 6:
Twenty-four rectangular pieces, six columns, and twelve caps

Gift 7:
Parquetry tablets derived from the surfaces of the gifts, including squares, equilateral triangles, right triangles, and obtuse triangles

Gift 8:
Straight sticks of wood, plastic, or metal in various lengths, plus rings and half-rings of various diameters made from wood, plastic, or metal

Gift 9:
Small points in various colors made of plastic, paper, or wood

Gift 10:
Materials that utilize rods and connectors, similar to Tinker Toys

FIGURE 3.1 Froebel's Gifts

Froebel's concept of learning through play remains one of the basic principles of early childhood practice.

Source: Used by permission of Scott Bultman, FroebelUSA.com.

these activities are part of early childhood programs today.

Froebel devoted his life to developing both a program for young children and a system of training for kindergarten teachers. Many of his ideas and activities form the basis for activities in preschools and kindergartens today.

Maria Montessori and the Montessori Theory

Maria Montessori (1870–1952) developed a system for educating young children that has greatly influenced early childhood education. The first woman in Italy to earn a medical degree, she became interested in educational solutions for problems such as deafness, paralysis, and mental retardation.

At that time she said, "I differed from my colleagues in that I instinctively felt that mental deficiency was more of an educational than medical problem."[8]

While preparing herself for educating children, Montessori was invited to organize schools for young children of families who occupied tenement houses in Rome. In the first school, named the *Casa dei Bambini,* or Children's House, she tested her ideas and gained insights into children and teaching that led to the perfection of her system. Chapter 4 provides a full description of the Montessori method, which is currently used in over four thousand early childhood programs.[9]

Froebel believed, as early childhood professionals believe today, that play is a process through which children learn. Learning flows from play. These children are engaged in play that supports their growth and development. Froebel urged early childhood educators to support the idea that play is the cornerstone of children's learning.

John Dewey and Progressive Education Theory

John Dewey (1859–1952) did more than any other person to redirect the course of education in the United States, and his influence is ongoing.

Dewey's theory of schooling, usually called *progressivism,* emphasizes children and their interests rather than subject matter. From this child-centered emphasis come the terms *child-centered curriculum* and *child-centered school,* two topics very much in the forefront of educational practice today. Dewey believed that education "is a process of living and not a preparation for future living" and that daily life should be a source of activities through which children learn about life and the skills necessary for living.[10] He also believed that "the child is more important than the subject" and that "schools should be based on democratic, not authoritarian principles."[11] For example, read the Professionalism in Practice feature, "How to Teach in a Child-Centered Program."

Classroom work in Dewey's school was a carefully designed extension of children's familiar life in the home. Rote exercises were minimized. Projects resembling those of a traditional household—crafts and cooking, for example—were used as ways to teach practical lessons of reading and arithmetic.[12]

Dewey's school was based on five basic principles, all of which are very contemporary and applicable to early childhood practice today:

- The child's early school experiences reflect the home life (cooking, sewing, construction); academic skills would be an outgrowth of these activities/occupations.[13]
- Children are part of a human community in school that focuses on cooperation.

PEARSON myeducationlab

Go to the Assignments and Activities section of Topic 1: History in the MyEducation-Lab for your course and complete the activity entitled *Montessori Classroom.* Observe the Montessori materials and how the classroom is organized. Compare this with what you have read about the Montessori program in this chapter.

How to Teach in a Child-Centered Program

The City & Country School, founded by Caroline Pratt in 1914, is located in the Greenwich Village district of New York City. It has a current enrollment of 250 students between the ages of two and thirteen and is an example of a progressive school that continues to educate children using the curriculum structure that was set forth over eighty years ago: "giving children experiences and materials that will fit their stage of development and have inherent in them unlimited opportunities for learning." Pratt, a teacher, sought to provide a school environment that suited the way children learn best—by doing.

BASIC VALUES OF A CHILD-CENTERED APPROACH

The essence of City & Country's philosophy is faith in children and their desire to learn. When we trust this truly child-centered ideal and set about developing materials, experiences, and environments that foster and guide it, we remain true to Caroline Pratt's work. Adults must constantly be open to learn from the children they teach and must be sensitive to their needs and experiences.

- What are the children interested in?
- What is going on in their environment that interests them and is relevant to their lives?

OPEN-ENDED MATERIALS AND METHODS

It is City & Country School's belief that an early childhood curriculum based on open-ended materials and methods fosters independence, motivation, and interest—all essential components of learning. The younger groups (ages two through seven) use basic, open-ended materials to reconstruct what they are learning about the world and to organize their information and thinking in meaningful ways. Materials such as blocks, clay, water, paint, and wood are chosen because of their simplicity, their flexibility, and the challenging possibilities that they offer. Children are encouraged to work out problems among themselves, with help from the teacher only when absolutely necessary.

Children move naturally into the more academic tasks as they need to find out more about what they're already doing. The three R's are viewed as useful tools to further a child's education, not as ends in themselves; but in no way did Pratt, nor do we, undervalue their importance. In fact, every possible method is used to empower all children with the crucial skill of reading. It can be a natural process for many, but others require extra directed instruction.

THE JOBS PROGRAM

The Lower School curriculum provides a firm foundation for the more formal academic skills that children must master in later years. The Jobs Program was developed to play this central role for students ages eight through thirteen. Each group of students has a specific job to perform that is related to the school's functioning as an integrated community. These jobs provide both a natural impetus for perfecting skills in reading, writing, spelling, and mathematics and a relevant framework for the exploration of social studies and the arts.

Beyond their work with blocks and jobs, children at City & Country are given opportunities to experience art, music, dramatics, foreign languages, science, computers, and woodworking, often integrated with their classroom work.

GUIDELINES FOR A CHILD-CENTERED PROGRAM

Even though children learn naturally, teachers should arrange and manage the classroom environment to stimulate that learning. The following guidelines promote active, independent learning:

GUIDELINE 1 Arrange the classroom to support child-centered learning.

GUIDELINE 2 Provide easily accessible materials and supplies.

GUIDELINE 3 Provide opportunities for children to move around and engage in active learning.

GUIDELINE 4 Provide materials and space for hands-on activities.

GUIDELINE 5 Arrange learning centers and desks so that children can work and play together.

GUIDELINE 6 Support cooperative learning.

GUIDELINE 7 Provide for individual differences and individualized instruction.

GUIDELINE 8 Incorporate project-based activities.

GUIDELINE 9 Provide ample time for children to engage in projects and other cooperative activities.

City & Country School remains committed to its founding principles and will continue to promote and exemplify child-centered education.

....

Contributed by Kate Turley, principal, City & Country School.

- Learning is focused on problems that children solve (e.g., numbers would be learned through understanding relationships rather than memorizing multiplication tables).
- Motivation is internal to the experiences and the child.
- The teacher's role is to know the children and to choose stimulating problems for them.

In a classroom based on Dewey's ideas, children are actively involved in activities, making and using things, solving problems, and learning through social interactions. Dewey felt that an ideal way for children to express their interests was through daily life-skills activities such as cooking and through occupations such as carpentry.

John Dewey represents a dividing line between the educational past and the educational present. This would be a good time for you to review and reflect on the "Time Line of the History of Early Childhood Education" in Appendix A.

John Dewey is important to the field of early childhood education in another way. His progressive education movement, based on children learning by doing, forms the foundation for, and is a transition to, constructivist education, which is the foundational theory for the practice of early childhood education. Dewey's ideas form a framework for contemporary constructivist ideas and practices.

Jean Piaget and Constructivist Learning Theory

Jean Piaget (1896–1980) was always interested in how humans learn and develop intellectually, beginning at birth and continuing across the life span. He devoted his life to conducting experiments, observing children (including his own), and developing and writing about his **cognitive theory** approach to learning. Piaget's theory is a constructivist theory.

cognitive theory Jean Piaget's proposition that children develop intelligence through direct experiences with the physical world. In this sense, learning is an internal (mental) process involving children's adapting new knowledge to what they already know.

Constructivism. **Constructivism** is a cognitive theory of development and learning based on the ideas of John Dewey and two other theorists you will learn about shortly, Jean Piaget and Lev Vygotsky. The *constructivist approach* supports the belief that children actively seek knowledge; it explains children's cognitive development, provides guidance for how and what to teach, and provides direction for how to arrange learning environments.

Constructivism is defined in terms of the individual's organizing, structuring, and re-structuring of experience—an ongoing lifelong process—in accordance with existing schemes of thought. In turn, these very schemes become modified and enriched in the course of interaction with the physical and social world.[14]

constructivism Theory that emphasizes the active role of children in developing their understanding and learning.

Constructivism and Cognitive Development. The **constructivist process** involves organization, structure, and restructure of children's experiences.[15] Constructivism rests on the notion that instead of absorbing or passively receiving knowledge, children should gain through experimental learning—personal involvement and self-initiated deep thinking where they can actively construct knowledge by integrating new information and experiences into what was taught. Pedagogy based on constructivist theory—such as class discussion, group presentation, and project work—is supportive in stimulating students' creativity and fostering their learning.[16]

constructivist process The continuous mental organizing, structuring, and restructuring of experiences, in relation to schemes of thought, or mental images, that result in cognitive growth.

Children, through activity and interaction with others, continuously organize, structure, and restructure experiences in relation to existing *schemes,* or mental images of thought. As a result, children build their own intelligence.

How Do Children Construct Knowledge? Even though children have parents, teachers, and others to provide for them and to take care of them and to create learning environments for them, nonetheless it is children who are constructing their cognitive and social development for themselves. Lev Vygotsky, a leading proponent and developer of constructivist ideas, says that learning nudges development, and this is true. But learning comes with the assistance of more competent others and the children themselves as they construct their world. How do children construct knowledge? Here are some processes they engage in, which make possible the "construction" of knowledge schemes and their understanding of the world:

- *Organization.* Children are self-organizing systems who gather information by experiencing the world around them through active involvement with people, places, and things. This self organization occurs through the cognitive processes of assimilation, accommodation, and equilibrium, which is discussed below.
- *Repetition.* Much of children's learning is characterized by repetition. When children continually bounce a ball, they are creating a relationship between the ball and themselves, their motor functions. So by bouncing the ball, they are developing and creating the muscle memory necessary to make ball bouncing possible. Children love to repeat poems and nursery rhymes over and over again. They sing a favorite song repeatedly. Such repetition is essential for the construction of knowledge and schemes.
- *Social interactions.* Lev Vygotsky repeatedly reminds us that cognitive development occurs in social contexts. Put another way, socialization is essential for construction of knowledge and learning. Children seek out others to establish relationships, to engage in experiences, and to test out their ideas. Socializing with others creates dynamic interactions in which children share their thoughts, ideas, and artifacts. Such interactions are the crucible for construction of knowledge. Reciprocally, socialization provides children access to others' ideas, thoughts, and points of view. This reciprocal socialization is an essential ingredient whereby children are able to construct knowledge.
- *Problem solving.* Children are great problem solvers. They are willing to repeat experiences and to keep working on a project in order to problem-solve. Environments, well designed activities, and materials (concrete objects, props, etc.) support children's experimenting and problem solving, which contribute to the construction of knowledge.[17]

Constructivism and Play. Play is one primary way in which children are actively involved in their environments and by which they think and learn. Play provides hands-on and "minds-on" opportunities so children can experience and learn through all kinds of materials—water, sand, clay, indoor and outdoor equipment, puzzles, blocks, real-life toys, housekeeping furniture, dolls, dress-up clothes, carpentry equipment, musical instruments, and so forth. The physical activity involved in play supports children's natural ways of learning by enabling them to touch, explore, feel, test, experiment, talk, and think. It is through these processes that children gain meaning of their world and learn how things work. As a result, children learn to make sense of the world.

The Constructivist Classroom. The constructivist classroom is child centered and learning centered. Here are some essential features of constructivism applied to teaching and learning:

- Children are physically and mentally active.
- Children are encouraged to initiate learning activities.
- Children carry on dialogues and conversations with peers, teachers, and other adults.
- Teachers create and support children's social interactions with peers, teachers, and other adults to provide a context for cognitive development and learning.
- Teachers provide rich social environments characterized by children's collaboration, projects, problem solving, and cooperative learning.
- Teachers arrange classroom desks, tables, and learning centers to support student collaboration and social interaction.
- Teachers create a classroom climate of mutual respect and cooperation.
- Teachers and children are partners in learning.
- Teachers provide guided assistance.

- Teachers can promote the construction of knowledge by observing individual children and asking questions or making suggestions that will further their thinking.[18]
- Teachers link children's prior knowledge and experiences with current classroom activities and experiences.

Piaget's Cognitive Development Theory.   Piaget's theory explains how individuals think, understand, and learn. Piaget believed that intelligence is the cognitive, or mental, process by which children acquire knowledge. *Intelligence* is "to know" and involves the use of *mental operations* developed as a result of acting mentally and physically in and on the environment. **Active involvement** is basic to Piaget's theory that children develop intelligence through direct hands-on experiences with the physical world. These hands-on experiences provide the foundations for a "minds-on" ability to think and learn.

Piaget also thought intelligence helped children adapt to their environments. For example, in the process of physical adaptation, children react and adjust to their environments. Piaget applied the concept of adaptation to the mental level, using it to explain how children change their thinking and grow cognitively as a result of encounters with parents, teachers, siblings, peers, and the environment.

Cognitive Development and Adaptation.   According to Piaget, the adaptive process at the intellectual level operates much the same as at the physical level. The newborn's intelligence is expressed through reflexive motor actions such as sucking, grasping, head turning, and swallowing. Early in life, reflexive actions enable children to adapt to the environment, and their intelligence develops from these adaptations.

Through interaction with the environment, children organize sensations and experiences and grow mentally. Obviously, therefore, the quality of the environment and the nature of children's experiences play a major role in the development of i--ntelligence. For example, Jason, with various and differing objects available to grasp and suck, and many opportunities for this behavior, will develop differentiated sucking organizations (and therefore an intelligence) quite different from those of Amber, who has nothing to suck but a pacifier. Consequently, one of your roles is to provide enriched environments for young children and to work with parents to provide rich home learning environments.

Learning as the Adaptation of Mental Constructs.   Piaget believed that adaptation is composed of two interrelated processes: assimilation and accommodation.

Assimilation.   **Assimilation** is the taking in of sensory data through experiences and impressions and incorporating the data into existing knowledge. Through assimilation, children use old methods or experiences to understand and make sense of new information and experiences. In other words, children use their experiences and what they have learned from them as a basis for learning more. This is why quality learning experiences are so important. All experiences are not equal. Out of all the possible learning experiences you could provide, make sure the ones you select have the highest potential to promote learning.

Accommodation.   **Accommodation** is the process of changing old methods and adjusting to new situations. Robbie has several cats at home. When he sees a dog for the first time, he may call it a kitty. He has assimilated *dog* into his organization of *kitty*. However, Robbie must change (accommodate) his model of what constitutes "kittyness" to exclude dogs. He does this by starting to construct or build a scheme for dogs and thus what "dogness" represents.[19]

The processes of assimilation and accommodation, functioning together, constitute *adaptation*.

Equilibrium.   If adaptation is the functioning together of assimilation and accommodation, then **equilibrium** is the balance between the two processes. According to Piaget's theory of intelligence, as assimilation and accommodation function with one another, there must be balance between the two in order to allow children to successfully understand new data.

Upon receiving new sensory and experiential data, children assimilate, or fit, these data into their already existing knowledge (scheme) of reality and the world. If the new data can be immediately assimilated, then equilibrium occurs. If unable to assimilate the data, children

active involvement The feature of Piaget's theory of cognitive development stating that children's active hands-on experiences with the physical world provide the foundations for a "minds-on" ability to think and learn.

Go to the Assignments and Activities section of Topic 2: Child Development/ Theories in the MyEducationLab for your course and complete the activity entitled *The Restaurant*. Note how the teacher facilitates, then slowly fades away to allow the girls more autonomy. Also notice how the girls change roles through their play and explore different ideas.

assimilation The taking in of sensory data through experiences and impressions and incorporating them into existing knowledge.

accommodation The process of changing old methods and adjusting to new situations.

equilibrium A state of balance between the cognitive processes of assimilation and accommodation, allowing children to successfully understand new data.

try to accommodate and change their way of thinking, acting, and perceiving to account for the new data and restore the equilibrium to the intellectual system. It may well be that Robbie can neither assimilate nor accommodate the new data; if so, he rejects the data entirely.

Rejection of new information is common if experiences and ideas children are trying to assimilate and accommodate are too different from their past experiences and their level of knowledge and understanding. This partially accounts for Piaget's insistence that new experiences must have some connection or relationship to previous experiences. Child care and classroom experiences should build on previous life and school experiences.

Schemes.   Piaget used the term **scheme** to refer to units of knowledge that children develop through adaptation. Piaget believed that in the process of developing new schemes, physical activity is very important. Physical activity leads to mental stimulus, which in turn leads to mental activity—our hands-on, minds-on concept. Thus, it is not possible to draw a clear line between physical activity and mental activity in infancy and early childhood. Teachers and parents should provide classrooms and homes that support active learning by enabling all children to explore and interact with people and objects in meaningful ways.

Piaget believed that the opportunity to be physically and mentally involved in learning is necessary to mental development in the early years. What are some examples of how children's active involvement contributes to their learning?

Stages of Intellectual Development.   Figure 3.2 summarizes Piaget's developmental stages and provides examples of stage-related characteristics. As you review these now, keep in mind that Piaget contended developmental stages are the same for all children and that all children progress through each stage in the same order. The ages identified with each stage are only approximate and are not fixed. The sequence of growth through the developmental stages does *not* vary; the ages at which progression occurs *do* vary.

scheme A unit of knowledge that a child develops through experience that defines how things should be.

Sensorimotor Stage.   The sensorimotor stage is the first of Piaget's stages of cognitive development. When children use their primarily reflexive actions to develop intellectually, they are in the **sensorimotor stage**. During this period from birth to about two years, children use their senses and motor reflexes to build knowledge of the world. They use their eyes to see, mouths to suck, and hands to grasp. These reflexive actions help children construct a mental scheme of what is suckable and what is not (what can fit into the mouth and what cannot) and what sensations (warm and cold) occur by sucking. Children also use the grasping reflex in much the same way to build schemes of what can and cannot be grasped. Through these innate sensory and reflexive actions, they continue to develop an increasingly complex, unique, and individualized hierarchy of schemes about their world. What children are to become physically and intellectually is related to these sensorimotor functions and interactions. This is why it is important for teachers and others to provide quality experiences and environments for young children.

The following are some characteristics of children in the sensorimotor stage.

sensorimotor stage The first of Piaget's stages of cognitive development, when children primarily use their senses and motor reflexes to develop intellectually.

- Children in this stage exhibit dependence on and use of innate reflexive actions, which are the basic building blocks of intelligence.
- They are beginning to develop *object permanency*—the understanding or awareness that objects exist even when they are not seen, heard, or touched.
- Children who are in the sensorimotor and preoperational stages are **egocentric**. They see themselves as the center of the world. They believe what they see, feel and think is true of everyone. Egocentric children are unable to see life and events from other

egocentric Centered on the self; an inability to see events from other people's perspectives.

Stage	Characteristics	Teacher's Role
Sensorimotor Birth to about 2 years	• Use innate sensorimotor systems of sucking, grasping, and gross-body activities to build schemes • Begin to develop object permanency • "Think" with their senses and their innate reflexive actions • "Solve" problems by playing with toys and using everyday "tools" such as a spoon to learn to feed themselves	• Provide interactive toys, such as rattles, mobiles, and pound-a-peg • Provide many and varied multisensory toys to promote investigation and sensory involvement; include household items such as pots, pans, and spoons • Provide environments in which infants and toddlers can crawl and explore, keeping infants out of their cribs as much as possible • Play hide-and-seek games that involve looking for hidden objects • Provide rich language environments to encourage interaction with people and objects
Preoperational 2 to 7 years	• Depend on concrete representations; "think" with concrete materials • Use the world of here and now as frame of reference • Enjoy accelerated language development; internalize events • Are egocentric in thought and action • Think everything has a reason or purpose • Are perceptually bound • Make judgments based primarily on how things look	• Provide toys and materials for pretend play • Provide building blocks of many kinds (review Froebel's gifts and occupations) • Provide materials for arts and crafts • Provide many and varied kinds of manipulative materials, such as puzzles, counters, and clay • Provide many concrete learning materials and activities • Provide many developmentally appropriate language opportunities involving speaking, listening, reading, and writing
Concrete Operations 7 to 12 years	• Are able to reverse thought processes • Are able to conserve • Depend on how things look for decision making • Are less egocentric • Structure time and space • Understand numbers • Begin to think logically; can apply logic to concrete situations	• Use props and visual aids, especially when dealing with sophisticated material • Give students a chance to manipulate and test objects • Make sure presentations and readings are brief and well organized • Use familiar examples to explain more complex ideas • Give opportunities to classify and group objects and ideas on increasingly complex levels • Present problems that require logical, analytical thinking • Provide opportunities for role playing, problem solving, and self-reflection.

FIGURE 3.2 Piaget's Stages of Cognitive Development

peoples' perspectives. Cognitively, they are unable to "put themselves in someone else's shoes."
- They are dependent on concrete representations (things) rather than symbols (words, pictures) for information.
- By the end of the second year, children in the sensorimotor stage are less reliant on sensorimotor reflexive actions, are beginning to use symbols for things that are not present.

Preoperational Stage. The second stage of cognitive development, the **preoperational stage**, begins at age two and ends at approximately seven years. Preoperational children are cognitively different from sensorimotor children in these ways:

- Rapidly accelerating language development
- Less dependence on sensorimotor actions
- Increased ability to internalize events and think by using symbols such as words to represent things

Preoperational children express their ideas mainly on how they see things. How things look to preoperational children is the foundation for several other stage-related characteristics. First, when children look at an object that has multiple characteristics, such as a long, round, yellow pencil, they will "see" whichever of those qualities first catches their eye. Preoperational children's knowledge is based mainly on what they are able to see, simply because they do not yet have operational intelligence or the ability to think using mental images.

Second, the inability to perform operations makes it impossible for preoperational children to *conserve,* or understand that the quantity of an object does not change simply because some transformation occurs in its physical appearance. For example, as shown in Figure 3.3, place two identical rows of pennies in front of preoperational children. Ask whether each row has the same number of pennies. The children should answer affirmatively. Next, space out the pennies in one of the rows, and ask whether the two rows still have the same number of pennies. They may insist that more pennies are in one row "because it's longer." Children base their judgment on what they can see—namely, the spatial extension of one row beyond the other row. This example also illustrates that preoperational children are not able to mentally reverse thoughts or actions, which in this case would require mentally putting the "longer" row back to its original length.

Furthermore, preoperational children believe and act as though everything happens for a specific reason or purpose. This explains their constant and recurring questions about why things happen and how things work.

Preoperational children believe everyone thinks as they think and acts as they do for the same reasons, and for this reason preoperational children have a hard time putting themselves in another's place. This egocentrism helps explain why it is difficult for them to be sympathetic and empathetic. The children tend to talk *at* each other rather than *with*

Preoperational children's inability to perform operations makes it impossible for them to determine that the quantity of a group of objects does not change because some changes occur in how the objects look. Try the penny experiment discussed in the text with several children and see how they are thinking and making sense of their world based on how things look to them.

preoperational stage The stage of cognitive development in which young children are not capable of mental representations.

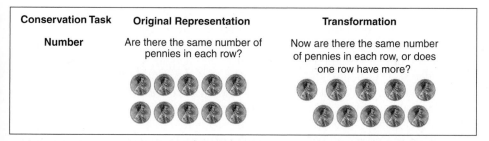

Conservation Task	Original Representation	Transformation
Number	Are there the same number of pennies in each row?	Now are there the same number of pennies in each row, or does one row have more?

FIGURE 3.3 Conservation of Number

each other. This dialogue between two children playing at a child care center illustrates one example of egocentrism:

Carmen: My mommy's going to take me shopping.
Mia: I'm going to dress this doll.
Carmen: If I'm good, I'm going to get an ice cream cone.
Mia: I'm going to put this dress on her.

The point is that egocentrism is a fact of cognitive development in the early childhood years. Developmentally appropriate practice means you will take this into account as you teach.

Another important characteristic of children in the preoperational stage is activity. As we previously discussed, activity is a critical developmental force in children's physical, social, emotional, linguistic, and cognitive development. Activity in the form of play provides children with opportunities to be active in early childhood classrooms.

During the preoperational stage, *make-believe play* (also called *dramatic play* or *pretend play*) is one of children's favorite types of play. They engage in it with seriousness and purposefulness. For young children, the world of make-believe play is their world.

Make-believe play helps children learn about their world, helps them deal with their feelings and emotions, enables them to try out roles (mommy, daddy, doctor, nurse, community helper, etc.), and helps them relate to others. Through make-believe play children also learn:

- About themselves, their families, and the world around them
- To talk to, get along with, and work with others—how others act, think, and feel
- To plan and decide what they want to do
- To be creative and solve problems
- To develop physical skills by using large and small muscles
- To stick with a task until it's finished

You can be supportive of children's make-believe play by providing:

- Time and opportunity for children to engage in make-believe play
- Props and materials (clothing and equipment) with which children can play
- A housekeeping area as a learning center where children can play
- A theater-drama area for puppets, costumes, and other props

concrete operations
Piaget's third stage of operational or logical thought, often referred to as the "hands-on" period of cognitive development because the ability to reason is based on tangible objects and real experiences.

operation A reversible mental action.

reversibility The notion that actions can be reversed. Awareness of reversibility develops during the concrete operations stage of development.

Concrete Operations Stage. Concrete operations is the third stage of operational or logical thought. Piaget defined an operation as an action that can be carried out in thought and in direct experiences and that is mentally and physically reversible. The concrete operations stage is often referred to as the "hands-on" period of cognitive development because children's ability to reason is based on tangible objects and real experiences.

Children in the concrete operations stage, from about age seven to about age twelve, begin to develop the understanding that change involving physical appearances does not necessarily change quality or quantity. They can reverse mental operations. For example, operational children know that the amount of water in a container does not change when it is poured into a different-shaped container. They can mentally reverse the operation by going back over and "undoing" the mental action just accomplished—a mental process that preoperational children cannot accomplish, known as reversibility. Awareness of reversibility allows the child to see physical transformations and then imagine reversing them so that the change is canceled out. Without being able to imagine, say, pouring liquid from a tall, narrow container back into a wider container, the preoperational child cannot "see" that the amount of liquid has not changed.

You can encourage the development of mental processes during this stage through the use of concrete or real objects when talking about and explaining concepts. For example, instead of just giving the children a basket of beads to play with, ask them to sort the beads into a red group, a blue group, a yellow group, and a green group.

The process of development from one cognitive stage to another is gradual and continual and occurs over a period of time as a result of maturation and experiences. No simple set of exercises will cause children to move up the developmental ladder. Rather, ongoing developmentally appropriate activities lead to conceptual understanding.

Other mental operations typical of this stage are:

- *One-to-one correspondence.* This is the basis for counting and matching objects. Concrete operational children have mastered the ability, for example, to give one cookie to each classmate and a pencil to each member of their work group.
- *Classification of objects, events, and time according to certain characteristics.* Classifying is a way of comparing.

  Classification refers to putting like things together and naming the group, such as big bears, little bears; shiny shells, dull shells; round buttons, square buttons; or smooth rocks, rough rocks. Classification schemes are important for young children to construct, as they are central to scientific thinking. Rocks, sea shells, birds, seeds, and just about everything in nature has a classification system.[20]

  For example, a child in the concrete operations stage can classify events as occurring before or after lunch.
- *Classification involving multiple properties.* Multiple classification occurs when a child can classify objects on the basis of more than one property, such as color and size, shape and size, or shape and color.
- *Class inclusive operations.* Class inclusion also involves classification. For example, if children in this stage are shown five apples, five oranges, and five lemons and asked whether there are more apples or more fruit, they are able to respond with "fruit."

classification The ability, developed during the concrete operations stage of cognitive development, to group things together according to their similar characteristics.

Lev Vygotsky and Sociocultural Theory

Lev Vygotsky (1896–1934), a contemporary of Piaget, increasingly inspires the practices of early childhood professionals. Vygotsky's theory of development is particularly useful in describing children's mental, language, and social development.

Social Interaction. Vygotsky believed that children's mental, language, and social development is supported and enhanced by others through social interaction. This view is opposite from the Piagetian perspective, in which children are much more solitary developers of their own intelligence and language. For Vygotsky, development is supported by social interaction: "Learning awakens a variety of developmental processes that are able to operate only when the child is interacting with people in his environment and in collaboration with his peers. Once these processes are internalized, they become part of the child's independent developmental achievement."[21] Vygotsky further believed that children seek out adults for social interaction beginning at birth; development occurs through these interactions.

Zone of Proximal Development. For early childhood professionals, one of Vygotsky's most important concepts is that of the **zone of proximal development (ZPD)**, which he defines as follows:

> The area of development into which a child can be led in the course of interaction with a more competent partner, either adult or peer. [It] is not some clear-cut space that exists independently of joint activity itself. Rather, it is the difference between what the child can accomplish independently and what he or she can achieve in conjunction with another, more competent person. The zone is thus created in the course of social interaction.[22]

zone of proximal development (ZPD) The range of tasks that children can perform with help from a more competent partner. Children can perform tasks below their ZPD on their own, but they are not yet able to learn tasks or concepts above their ZPD, even with help.

As Figure 3.4 illustrates, the ZPD represents the potential space between the child's level of independent performance and the child's level of maximally assisted performance.[23] Thus, the ZPD is the range of tasks a child can perform when helped by a more competent person—teacher, parent, teenager, another child, etc. Tasks below the ZPD are those that children can learn independently. Tasks, concepts, ideas, and information above the ZPD are those that children are not yet able to learn, even with help.

Experience and Development. Vygotsky believed that learning drives development. In this regard, the experiences children have influence their development. This is why it is important for you and others to provide high-quality learning experiences for all children.

Vygotsky also believed communication or dialogue between teacher and child is very important and literally becomes a means for helping children to *scaffold,* or develop new concepts and thus think their way to higher level concepts. **Scaffolding** is assistance in the ZPD that enables children to complete tasks they cannot complete independently. When adults "assist" toddlers in learning to walk, they are scaffolding from not being able to walk to being able to walk. Technology

The zone of proximal development is the mental and social state of concept development and learning in which children are about to "go beyond" and achieve at higher levels with the assistance of more competent "others." In this way, learning and development are very social processes.

scaffolding Assistance or support of some kind from a teacher, parent, caregiver, or peer to help children complete tasks they cannot complete independently.

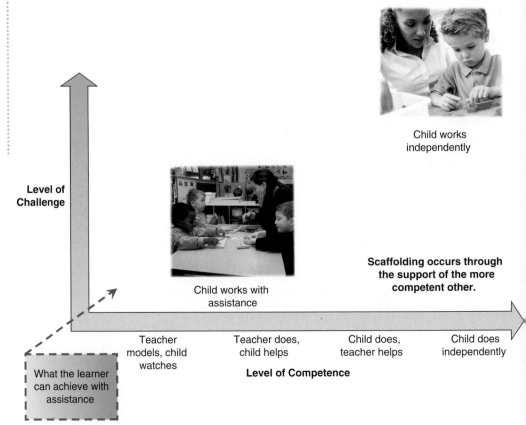

FIGURE 3.4 Teaching and Learning in the Zone of Proximal Development

How to Scaffold Children's Learning

Vygotsky believed that cognitive development occurs through children's interactions with more competent others—teachers, peers, parents—who act as guides, facilitators, and coaches to provide the support children need to grow intellectually. Much of that support is provided through conversation, examples, and encouragement. When children learn a new skill, they need that competent other to provide a scaffold, or framework, to help them—to show them the overall task, break it into doable parts, and support and reinforce their efforts.

THE SCAFFOLDING PROCESS

Here are the basic steps involved in effective scaffolding. Study them carefully and then look for them in the three examples that follow:

STEP 1
OBSERVE AND LISTEN
You can learn a great deal about what kind of assistance is needed.

STEP 2
APPROACH THE CHILD
Ask what he or she wants to do, and ask for permission to help.

STEP 3
TALK ABOUT THE TASK
Describe each step in detail—what is being used, what is being done, what is seen or touched. Ask the child questions about the activity.

STEP 4
REMAIN ENGAGED IN THE ACTIVITY
Adjust your support, allowing the child to take over and do the talking.

STEP 5
GRADUALLY WITHDRAW SUPPORT
See how the child is able to perform with less help.

STEP 6
OBSERVE THE CHILD PERFORMING INDEPENDENTLY
After you have withdrawn all support, check to be sure the child continues to perform the task successfully.

STEP 7
INTRODUCE A NEW TASK
Present the child with a slightly more challenging task, and repeat the entire sequence.

EXAMPLE—WORKING A PUZZLE

Celeste has chosen a puzzle to work and dumps the pieces out. She randomly picks up a piece and moves it around inside the frame. She tries another. Look at her face: Is she smiling or showing signs of stress? Is she talking to herself?

Perhaps Celeste needs a puzzle with fewer pieces. If so, you can offer her one. But from prior observation, you may know she just needs a little assistance. Try sitting with Celeste and suggesting that you will help. Start by turning all the pieces right side up. As you do this, talk about the pieces you see: This one is red with a little green, this one has a straight edge, this one is curved. Move your finger along the edge.

Ask Celeste whether she can find a straight edge on the side of the puzzle and then whether she can find a piece with a straight edge that matches the color. Ask what hints the pieces give her. Repeat with several other pieces. Then pause to give Celeste the opportunity to try one on her own. As she does, describe what she is doing and the position, shape, and color of the piece. Demonstrate turning a piece in different directions while saying, "I'll try turning it another way." (If you just say "Turn the piece," she will most likely turn it upside down.)

By listening to you verbalize and by repeating the verbalizing, Celeste is learning to self-talk—that is, to talk herself through a task. By practicing this private speech, children realize they can answer their own questions and regulate their own behavior. When the puzzle is complete, offer Celeste another of similar difficulty and encourage her to try it on her own while you stay nearby to offer assistance as needed, allowing her to take the lead.

Contributed by Catherine M. Kearn, EdD, early childhood professional and adjunct professor, Carroll College, Waukesha, Wisconsin. Also contributing were Elena Bodrova, senior researcher at Mid-Continent Research for Education and Learning, Denver, Colorado; and Deborah Leong, professor of psychology and director of the Center for Improving Early Learning, Metropolitan State College of Denver, Denver, Colorado.

provides another useful means for helping scaffold children's learning.[24] For example, Kid-Pix is a popular software program designed to reinforce basic skills such as language arts and math through technology. The accompanying Professionalism in Practice feature, "How to Scaffold Children's Learning," will help you learn how to put into practice the Vygotskian teaching skill of scaffolding.

Vygotsky believed that as a result of teacher–child collaboration, the child uses concepts learned in the collaborative process to solve problems when the teacher is not present. As Vygotsky said, the child "continues to act in collaboration even though the teacher is not standing near him. . . . This help—this aspect of collaboration—is invisibly present. It is continued in what looks from the outside like the child's independent solution of the problem."[25] According to Vygotsky, social interactions and collaboration are essential ingredients in the processes of learning and development.

Features of a Vygotskian Classroom. Many current practices such as cooperative learning, joint problem solving, coaching, collaboration, mentoring, and other forms of assisted learning are based on Vygotsky's theory of development and learning. Vygotsky believed that social and cultural features of the classroom play an important role in children's learning. The suggestions below will help you apply Vygotsky's theories and enable children to learn to their fullest. A Vygotskian classroom has the following features:

- Children are grouped by differing abilities.
- There is ample opportunity for make-believe play with peers and adults.
- Activities, materials, and learning centers support independent discovery.
- Teachers guide each child's learning in his or her zone of proximal development. Vygotsky believed that challenging tasks promote maximum cognitive growth.
- Diversity is valued, respected, and expected. Vygotsky believed children of different cultural backgrounds will develop somewhat different knowledge, skills, and ways of thinking.
- There is ample peer collaboration and cooperation on classroom projects.
- Children are encouraged to help each other.
- Children are provided with the opportunity, time, and materials necessary to explore, experiment, and learn.
- There is collaboration among adults, "expert" peers, and other more competent students (elementary, middle and high school students, and other adults).
- "Assisted discovery" is supported and encouraged as children help each other and as the teacher guides the children through scaffolding.
- Teachers guide learning with explanations, verbal prompts, demonstrations, and modeling of behavior.
- There is ample opportunity for child–children, teacher–child, and child–teacher conversations.

Abraham Maslow and Self-Actualization Theory

Abraham Maslow (1908–1970) developed a theory of motivation called **self-actualization** based on the satisfaction of human needs illustrated in Figure 3.5. Maslow identified self-actualization, or self-fulfillment, as the highest human need. However, Maslow maintains that people don't achieve self-actualization until the needs for life essentials, safety and security, belongingness and love, achievement and knowledge, and aesthetic are met. Helping children meet their basic needs is an important role for you, parents, and others.

Life Essentials. The most basic of human needs that must be met before self-actualization can be achieved are the life essentials. Life essentials are basic survival necessities such as food, water, and air. Everyone has these basic needs regardless of

self-actualization Abraham Maslow's theory of motivation based on the satisfaction of needs; Maslow maintained that children cannot achieve self-actualization until certain basic needs—including food, shelter, safety, and love—are met.

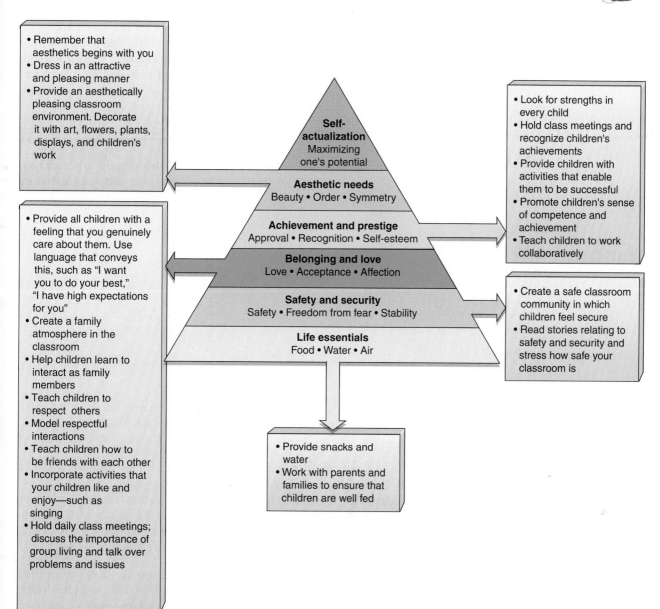

FIGURE 3.5 Maslow's Hierarchy of Human Needs

Source: From Maslow, Abraham H.; Frager, Robert D. (Editor); Fadiman, James (Editor), *Motivation and Personality,* 3rd ed., © 1987. Reproduced by permission of Pearson Education, Inc., Upper Saddle River, New Jersey.

sexual orientation, race, gender, socioeconomic status, or age. Satisfaction of basic needs is essential for children to function well and to achieve all they are capable of achieving.

Nutrition.   When children are hungry they perform poorly in school. Children who begin school without eating breakfast don't achieve as well as they should and experience difficulty concentrating on their school activities. Research shows far-ranging benefits of breakfast consumption affecting children's heath and learning through increased attendance, higher standardized test scores and grades, decreased classroom disruptions, and fewer trips to the nurse.[26] This explains why many early childhood programs provide children with breakfast, lunch, and snacks throughout the day.

Safety and Security. The next step to self-achievement is safety and security. Safety and security needs play an important role in children's lives. When children think that their teachers do not like them or are fearful of what their teachers say and how they treat them, they are deprived of a basic need. As a consequence, they do not do well in school and become fearful in their relationships with others. Some things you can do to provide for children's safety needs are:

- Develop routines and predictability to provide children with a sense of safety and security.
- Provide consistent behavioral rules and guidelines for how children are to act and behave. For example, classroom policies for Ms. Kelly Barker's kindergarten in Arlington, South Dakota, are:[27]

  1. Be Polite
  - Use an "inside" voice
  - Say please and thank you
  - Wait your turn/Share with others

  2. Be Respectful
  - Look at the person who is speaking
  - Raise your hand
  - Keep hands and feet to yourself

  3. Be Responsible
  - Remember planner/materials needed for class
  - Put your things away
  - Follow directions

- Provide a warm, loving, and comfortable classroom. Some teachers use plants to make the classroom attractive and have reading corners with pillows to provide comfort and security.

Belonging and Love. After safety and security, needs for belonging and love must be met. Children need to be loved and feel that they "belong" within their home and school in order to thrive and develop. All children have affectional needs that teachers can satisfy through smiles, hugs, eye contact, and nearness. For example, in my work with three- and four-year-old children, many want to sit close to me and want me to put my arms around them. They seek love and look to me and their teachers to satisfy this basic need.

Achievement and Prestige. Also before self-actualization can occur, children need to gain achievement and prestige. Recognition and approval are self-esteem needs that relate to success and accomplishment. Children who are independent and responsible, and who achieve well, have high self-esteem. Today, many educators are concerned about how to enhance children's self-esteem.

Friendship is a key to self-esteem. Teach children how to socialize and get along with others. Some children need help making friends. Teach cooperation and helpfulness. Instill new skills. Learning new skills forms the basis for achievement, and achievement is another cornerstone of high self-esteem. Have high and individually appropriate expectations for all of your children. Nothing diminishes self-esteem more than low or no expectations for a child. Provide many opportunities for children to be recognized for their achievement. Once children have their basic needs met, they can become self-actualized. They have a sense of satisfaction, are enthusiastic, and are eager to learn. They want to engage in activities that will lead to higher levels of learning.

Praise Children's Successes. Praising children's successes does wonders to boost children's abilities to do good work and keep on doing it. Give love and affection to every child every day. Feeling loved and wanted is a cornerstone of self-esteem. Pay attention to children. Show children that you are interested in them. Build a foundation on which children can succeed. This foundation is built on this four-step process:

1. Tell children what you want them to do.
2. Show/model for children what to do.
3. Have children practice and demonstrate.
4. Have children work independently.

Here are some examples to follow on praising your students:

- Give a particular student attention:

   "Jason, I really like the way you got right to work on your journaling, you must have some interesting things to share today."

- Help the student to understand the value of his or her accomplishments:

   "Your explanation of how you answered that word problem helped your classmates to see a new way that they might want to use to try to solve a similar problem."

- Credit the student's effort to succeed:

   "I see that you are working hard to improve your spelling, you spelled more words correctly this week than you did last week."

- Show students you focused on their work because you could see that they were enjoying their learning process:

   "I admire how you added some amazing details to your illustration. You looked like you were really enjoying what you were doing"[28]

Aesthetic Needs.   Finally, children need their aesthetic needs met before they can self-actualize. Children like and appreciate beauty. They like to be in classrooms and homes that are physically attractive and pleasant. As an early childhood professional, you can help satisfy aesthetic needs by being well dressed and providing a classroom that is pleasant to be in, one that includes plants and flowers, art, and music.

Erik Erikson and Psychosocial Theory

Erik H. Erikson (1902–1994) developed his theory of **psychosocial development**, based on the idea that cognitive and social development occur hand in hand and cannot be separated. According to Erikson, children's personalities and social skills grow and develop within the context of society and in response to society's demands, expectations, values, and social institutions such as families, schools, and child care programs. Adults, especially parents and teachers, are key parts of these environments and therefore play a powerful role in helping or hindering children in their personality and cognitive development. For example, school-age children must deal with demands to learn new skills or risk a sense of incompetence, or a crisis of "industry"—the ability to do, be involved, be competent, and achieve—versus "inferiority"—marked by failure and feelings of incompetence. Many of the cases of school violence in the news today are caused in part by children who feel inferior and unappreciated and who lack the social skills for getting along with their classmates. Figure 3.6 outlines the stages of psychosocial development according to Erikson.

psychosocial development Erik Erikson's theory that cognitive and social development occur simultaneously and cannot be separated.

Urie Bronfenbrenner and Ecological Theory

Urie Bronfenbrenner's (1917–2005) *ecological theory* looks at children's development within the context of the systems of relationships that form their environment. There are five interrelating environmental systems: the microsystem, the mesosystem, the exosystem,

Stage	Appropriate Age	Characteristics	Role of Early Childhood Educator
I. Basic trust versus mistrust: During this stage, children learn to trust or mistrust their environment and their caregivers. Trust develops when children's needs are met consistently, predictably, and lovingly. Children then view the world as safe and dependable.	Birth to 18 months	Infants learn to trust or mistrust that others will care for their basic needs, including nourishment, warmth, cleanliness, and physical contact.	• Meet children's needs with consistency and continuity. • Identify and take care of basic needs such as diapering and feeding. • Hold babies when feeding them—this promotes attachment and develops trust. • Socialize through smiling, talking, and singing. • Be attentive—respond to infants' cues and signals. • Comfort infants when in distress.
II. Autonomy versus shame and doubt: This is the stage when children want to do things for themselves. Given adequate opportunities, they learn independence and competence. Inadequate opportunities and professional overprotection result in self-doubt and poor achievement; children come to feel ashamed of their abilities.	18 months to 3 years	Toddlers learn to be self-sufficient or to doubt their abilities in activities such as toileting, feeding, walking, and talking.	• Encourage children to do what they are capable of doing. • Do not shame children for any behavior. • Provide for safe exploration of classrooms and outdoor areas.
III. Initiative versus guilt: During the preschool years children need opportunities to respond with initiative to activities and tasks, which gives them a sense of purposefulness and accomplishment. Children can feel guilty if they are discouraged or prohibited from initiating activities and are overly restricted in attempts to do things on their own.	3 to 5 years	Children are learning and want to undertake many adultlike activities, sometimes overstepping the limits set by parents, and may feel guilty.	• Observe children and follow *their* interests. • Encourage children to engage in many activities. • Provide environments in which children can explore. • Promote language development. • Allow each child the opportunity to succeed.
IV. Industry versus inferiority: In this period, children display an industrious attitude and want to be productive. They want to build things, discover, manipulate objects, and find out how things work. They also want recognition for their productivity, and adult response to their efforts and accomplishments helps develop a sense of self-worth. Feelings of inferiority result when children are criticized or belittled or have few opportunities for productivity.	5 to 8 years	Children actively and busily learn to be competent and productive or feel inferior and unable to do things well.	• Help children win recognition by making things. • Help ensure children are successful in literacy skills and learning to read. • Provide support for students who seem confused or discouraged. • Recognize children's achievement and success.

FIGURE 3.6 Erikson's Stages of Psychosocial Development

microsystem The various environmental settings in which children spend their time (e.g., children in child care spend about thirty-three hours a week in the microsystem of child care).

the macrosystem, and the chronosystem. Figure 3.7 shows a model of these environmental systems and the ways each influences development. Each system influences and is influenced by the other.

The **microsystem** encompasses the environments of parents, family, peers, child care, schools, neighborhood, religious groups, parks, and so forth. The child acts on and influences each of these and is influenced by them. For example, four-year-old April might

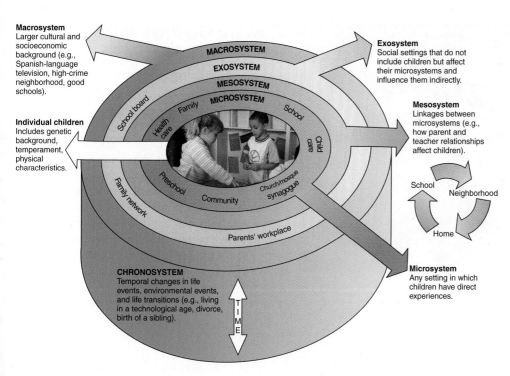

FIGURE 3.7 Ecological Influences on Development

have a physical disability that her child care program accommodates by making the class-room more accessible. Five-year-old Mack's aggressive behavior might prompt his teacher to initiate a program of bibliotherapy.

The **mesosystem** includes linkages or interactions between microsystems. Interactions and influences there relate to all of the environmental influences in the microsystem. For example, the family's support of or lack of attention to literacy may have a major influence on the child's performance in school. Likewise, school support for family literacy will influence the extent to which families value literacy.

The **exosystem** is the environmental system that encompasses those events with which children do not have direct interaction but which nonetheless influence them. For example, when school boards enact policies that end social promotion or when a parent's workplace mandates increased work time (e.g., a ten-hour workday), this action influences children's development with the parent and the school.

The **macrosystem** includes the culture, customs, and values of society in general. For example, contemporary societal violence and media violence influence children's development. Many children are becoming more violent, and many children are fearful of and threatened by violence.

The **chronosystem** includes environmental influences over time and the ways they impact development and behavior. For example, today's children are technologically adept and are comfortable using technology for education and entertainment. In addition, we have already referred to how the large-scale entry of mothers into the workforce has changed family life.

Clearly, there are many influences on children's development. Currently there is a lot of interest in how these influences shape children's lives and what parents and educators can do to enhance positive influences and minimize or eliminate negative environmental influences as well as negative social interactions.

mesosystem The links or interactions between microsystems that influence children's development.

exosystem The environments or settings in which children do not play an active role but which nonetheless influence their development.

macrosystem The broader culture in which children live (absence or presence of democracy, societal violence, religious freedom, etc.), which influences their development.

chronosystem The environmental influences and events that influence children over their lifetimes, such as living in a technological age.

According to Gardner's theory of multiple intelligences, children demonstrate many types of intelligences. How would you apply his theory in the early childhood environment?

multiple intelligences
Howard Gardner's concept that people can be "smart" in many different ways; those intelligences include verbal/linguistic, musical/rhythmic, mathematical/logical, visual/spatial, bodily/kinesthetic, interpersonal, intrapersonal, and naturalist.

Howard Gardner and Multiple Intelligence Theory

Howard Gardner (b. 1943) has played an important role in helping educators rethink the concept of intelligence. Rather than relying on a single definition of intelligence, Gardner's philosophy of **multiple intelligences** suggests that people can be "smart" in many different ways.

Gardner has identified nine intelligences: visual/spatial, verbal/linguistic, mathematical/logical, bodily/kinesthetic, musical/rhythmic, intrapersonal, interpersonal, naturalist, and existentialist. Gardner's view of intelligence and its multiple components has and will undoubtedly continue to influence educational thought and practice. Review Figure 3.8 to learn more about these nine intelligences and how to apply them to your teaching.

FROM LUTHER TO TODAY: BASIC BELIEFS ESSENTIAL FOR HIGH-QUALITY EARLY CHILDHOOD PROGRAMS

Throughout this chapter we have considered the basic beliefs that are essential for developing high-quality programs and for teaching young children. As you read the following beliefs, reflect on how you can embrace them and make them a part of your philosophy of education and how you can apply them to your teaching. Many people have influenced and changed the course of early childhood education. That process continues today. Part of your role as an early childhood professional is to stay up to date, be open to ideas and practices, and inspire children.

Basic Beliefs About Teaching Children

- Everyone needs to learn how to read and write.
- Children learn best when they use all their senses.
- All children are capable of being educated.
- All children should be educated to the fullest extent of their abilities.
- Education should begin early in life. Today especially there is an increased emphasis on beginning education at birth.
- Children should be appropriately taught what they are ready to learn when they are ready to learn it and should be prepared for the next stage of learning.
- Learning activities should be interesting and meaningful.
- Social interactions with teachers and peers are a necessary part of development and learning.
- All children have many ways of knowing, learning, and relating to the world.

Basic Beliefs About Teachers And Teaching

- Teachers should love and respect all children, have high expectations for them, and teach them to their highest capacities.
- Teachers should be dedicated to the teaching profession.

Intelligence/Child Characteristics	Teacher Support
Visual/Spatial Children who learn best visually and who organize things spatially. They like to see what you are talking about in order to understand. They enjoy charts, maps, tables, illustrations, art, puzzles, costumes—anything eye-catching.	• Allow student movement around the learning environment. • Provide a visually stimulating environment. • Work with manipulatives. • Utilize visual technologies such as KidPix and PowerPoint.
Verbal/Linguistic Children who demonstrate strength in language arts: speaking, writing, reading, and listening. These students have always been successful in traditional classrooms because their intelligence lends itself to traditional teaching.	• Introduce new vocabulary. • Encourage opportunities for speaking in front of class. • Incorporate drama into learning. • Provide opportunities for creative writing.
Mathematical/Logical Children who display an aptitude for numbers, reasoning, and problem solving. This is the other half of children who typically do well in traditional classrooms where teaching is logically sequenced and students are asked to conform.	• Present objectives at the beginning of an activity to provide structure. • Promote class experiments that test students' hypotheses. • Encourage classroom debate. • Incorporate puzzles into learning centers.
Bodily/Kinesthetic Children who experience learning best through activity: games, movement, hands-on tasks, building. These children were sometimes labeled "overly active" in traditional classrooms where they were told to sit and be still.	• Provide hands-on learning centers. • Offer experiences in movement to rhythm and music. • Engage students in hands-on science experiments. • Utilize manipulatives in math instruction. • Allow opportunities for building and taking apart.
Musical/Rhythmic Children who learn well through songs, patterns, rhythms, instruments, and musical expression. It is easy to overlook children with this intelligence in traditional education.	• Work with pattern blocks. • Have students move to rhythm. • Have students draw visual patterns. • Have students listen to music.
Intrapersonal Children who are especially in touch with their own feelings, values, and ideas. They may tend to be more reserved, but they are actually quite intuitive about what they learn and how it relates to themselves.	• Differentiate instruction. • Provide activities that offer learner choices. • Have students set goals for themselves in the classroom. • Include daily journal writing in classroom routine.
Interpersonal Children are noticeably people oriented and outgoing, and do their learning cooperatively in groups or with a partner. These children may be identified as "talkative" or "too concerned about being social" in a traditional setting.	• Allow interaction among students during learning tasks. • Include activities where students work in groups. • Form cooperative groups so each member has an assigned role. • Plan activities where students form teams.
Naturalist Children who love the outdoors, animals, and field trips. These students love to pick up subtle differences in meaning.	• Use graphic organizers. • Provide sorting and grouping tasks. • Build portfolios of student work.
Existential Children who learn in the context of where humankind stands in the "big picture" of existence. They ask, "Why are we here?" and "What is my role in my family, school, and community?" This intelligence is seen in the discipline of philosophy.	• Offer an overview before starting new instruction. • Discuss how topics are important to the classroom, school, and community. • Bring in resource people or offer additional perspectives on a topic. • Help students learn to summarize what they have learned.

FIGURE 3.8 Gardner's Nine Intelligences

Source: Reprinted with permission from Walter McKenzie, "Multiple Intelligences Overview," 1999; available online at http://surfaquarium.com/MI/overview.htm.

Go to the Assignments and Activities section of Topic 2: Child Development/Theories in the MyEducationLab for your course and complete the activity entitled *Applying Multiple Intelligences Theory.* Observe as a first-grade teacher develops a classroom activity on dragons to accommodate and provide for her children's multiple intelligences.

- Good teaching is based on a theory, a philosophy, goals, and objectives.
- Children's learning is enhanced through the use of concrete materials.
- Teaching should move from the concrete to the abstract.
- Observation is a key way to determine children's needs.
- Teaching should be a planned, systematic process.
- Teaching should be centered on children rather than adults or subjects.
- Teaching should be based on children's interests.
- Teachers should collaborate with children as a means of promoting development.
- Teachers should plan so they incorporate all types of intelligence in their planning and activities.

Basic Beliefs About Collaborating with Parents and Families

- The family is the most important institution in children's education and development. The family lays the foundation for all future education and learning.
- Parents are their children's primary educators; they are their children's first teachers. However, parents need help, education, and support to achieve this goal.
- Parents must guide and direct young children's learning.
- Parents should be involved in every educational program their children are involved in.
- Everyone should have knowledge of and training for child rearing.
- Parents and other family members are collaborators in children's learning.
- Parents must encourage and support their children's many interests and their unique ways of learning (see the Technology Tie-In feature).

What Are Your Beliefs?

Go to the Building Teaching Skills and Dispositions section of Topic 1: History in the MyEducationLab for your course and complete the activity entitled *Using History to Inform Current Practice.*

Throughout history all great educators have had a vision about what is best for young children and their families. Great educators are passionate about what they believe about children and how to best teach them what they need to know to be productive and involved citizens. The same is true today. Many educators, professional organizations, and politicians are passionately advocating for what they think are worthy goals and the best practices to achieve these goals. But how to do this is at the heart of many educational debates today. As a practicing professional you will be involved in these debates. You will be asked to identify ideas and theories that will help all children be successful in school and life. Knowing the history of your profession and the theories that guide approaches to education will help you in this critical part of your professional practice. See Table 3.2 for a summary of these theories.

epilepsy A neurological disorder in which electrical discharges in the brain cause a seizure.

Tourette's syndrome A genetic neuropsychiatric disorder characterized by multiple physical and/or vocal tics.

DISABILITIES THEN AND NOW

As an early childhood professional, it is important for you to know about and understand the nature of disabilities. It has not always been an American priority to accommodate differences. People with **epilepsy** (a neurological disorder in which electrical discharges in the brain cause a seizure) or **Tourette's syndrome** (a genetic neuropsychiatric disorder characterized by multiple physical and/or vocal tics) were once thought to be possessed by the devil. People with mental impairments were put in group homes, out of the public eye, and often abused. Deaf and mute children were often considered "idiots," and not worth teaching.

From Mozart to Montessori: Teaching the Fine Arts to Children

Since the beginning of the recorded history of early childhood education, music and the arts have had an important place in the education of young children. Educators have supported children's involvement in music and the arts in three ways: appreciation, performance, and creation. You and I may not agree on the kind of music and art we like, but one thing is certain: We all like music and the arts of some kind, and they all affect us in some way. The same is true for children. I have not met a child who does not like to sing, dance, paint, and create.

Aristotle believed that art and drama were good for people because through them they were able to work out their emotions vicariously and as a result be calmer and better persons. Maria Montessori believed that children should be involved in learning about art and artists. Art appreciation is part of the Montessori curriculum, and many Montessori classrooms have paintings by famous artists on display. We have read in this chapter about the high value Abraham Maslow places on creativity and the importance of creating aesthetically pleasing classrooms for young children. Some early childhood programs provide keyboard lessons and experiences for all children based on the link some research shows between learning music and high academic achievement. You can involve your children in music and the arts in many ways as appreciators, performers, and creators. All early childhood programs should involve all children in the arts. A 2006 research study done by Dr. Laurel Trainor, professor of psychology, neuroscience, and behavior at McMaster University in Hamilton, Ontario, stated:

> Young children who take music lessons show different brain development and improved memory over the course of a year, compared to children who do not receive musical training. Musically trained children performed better in a memory test that is correlated with general intelligence skills such as literacy, verbal memory, visuospatial processing, mathematics, and IQ.[29]

The journal *Nature Neuroscience* stated in an article released in April 2007:

> Playing a musical instrument significantly enhances the brainstem's sensitivity to speech sounds. This relates to encoding skills involved with music and languages. Experience with music at a young age can "fine-tune" the brain's auditory system.[30]

The following software suggestions are just one avenue you can use to encourage and support your children's fine arts skills:

Curious George Paint & Print Studio (ages 4–9), Sunburst Technology

Draw & Paint Plus (ages 4–9), Forest Technologies

JumpStart Music (ages 5–8), Knowledge Adventure

Kid Works Deluxe (ages 4–9), Knowledge Adventure

Reader Rabbit Toddler (ages 2–4), The Learning Company

Create and Draw in Elmo's World (ages 4–9), Sesame Street

TABLE 3.2 Learning Theories That Influence Early Childhood Education

Individual and Dates	Major Contributions	Influences on Modern Education
Maria Montessori (1870–1952)	• The Montessori method for educating young children. • Learning materials to meet the needs of young children. • Sensory-based materials that are self-correcting. • Prepared environments are essential for learning. • Respect for children is the foundation of teaching.	• Large number of public and private Montessori schools that emphasize her approach, methods, and materials. • Renewed emphasis on preparing environment to support and promote children's learning. • Teacher training programs to train Montessori teachers.
John Dewey (1859–1952)	• Progressive education movement. • Children's interests form the basis of the curriculum. • Educate children for today—not tomorrow.	• Child-centered education. • Curriculum based on children's interests. • Discovery learning.

(continued)

Individual and Dates	Major Contributions	Influences on Modern Education
Jean Piaget (1896–1980)	• Theory of cognitive development based on ages and stages. • Children are "little scientists" and literally develop their own intelligence. • Mental and physical activities are important for cognitive development. • Project approach to learning.	• Constructivist approaches to early childhood education. • Matching education to children's stages of cognitive development. • Active involvement of children in learning activities.
Lev Vygotsky (1896–1934)	• Sociocultural theory, which emphasizes importance of interpersonal relationships in social and cognitive development. • Concept of zone of proximal development—children can learn more with the help of a more competent person. • Communication between teachers and children can act as a means of scaffolding to higher levels of learning.	• Use of scaffolding techniques to help children learn. • Use of cooperative learning and other forms of social learning.
Abraham Maslow (1908–1970)	• Theory of self-actualization based on needs motivation. • Human development is a process of meeting basic needs throughout life. • Humanistic psychology.	• Importance of meeting basic needs before cognitive learning can occur. • Teachers develop programs to meet children's basic needs. • Growth of the self-esteem movement. • Emphasis on providing safety, security, love, and affection for all children.
Erik Erikson (1902–1994)	• Theory of psychosocial development—cognitive development occurs in conjunction with social development. • Life is a series of eight stages with each stage representing a critical period in social development. • How parents and teachers interact with and care for children helps determine their emotional and cognitive development.	• Play supports children's social and cognitive development. • The emotional plays as great a role as the cognitive in development. • All children need predictable, consistent love, care, and education.
Urie Bronfenbrenner (1917–2005)	• Ecological systems theory views the child as developing within a system of relationships. • Five interrelating systems—microsystem, mesosystem, exosystem, macrosystem, and chronosystem—have a powerful impact on development. • Each system influences and is influenced by the other. • Development is influenced by children and their environments.	• Teachers are more aware of how different environments shape children's lives in different ways. • Parents and educators strive to provide positive influences in each system and minimize or eliminate negative influences. • Teachers and parents recognize that children's development depends on children's natures and their environments.
Howard Gardner (b. 1943)	• Theory of multiple intelligences. • Intelligence consists of nine abilities. • Intelligence is not a single broad ability, but rather a set of abilities.	• Teachers develop programs and curricula to match children's particular intelligences. • Teachers individualize curricula and approaches to children's intelligences. • More awareness and attention to multiple ways in which children learn and think.

Because people with various disabilities were often hidden from the public eye or considered unable to contribute to society, our recent awareness and attention to children with diverse backgrounds and abilities may seem to exist in a contemporary vacuum. However, children and adults have always had learning differences, physical disabilities, and mental health deficits. Alexander the Great had epilepsy, Vincent Van Gogh had **bipolar disorder** (a mood disorder involving cycles of depression and mania that are severe and often lead to impaired functioning), Woodrow Wilson had **dyslexia** (a learning disability that is characterized by difficulties in reading, spelling, writing, speaking, or listening), Alexander Graham Bell had **mathematics disorder** (a learning disability characterized by decided lack of ability to calculate or comprehend mathematical problems), and Thomas Edison had **attention deficit hyperactivity disorder (ADHD)** (the inability to maintain attention and constrain impulsivity, accompanied by the presence of hyperactivity).

While individual differences have existed throughout human history, treating them, working with them, and attempting to improve the lives of those with differences is relatively new in the United States and other countries. It was not until 1790 in Paris that mental patients were no longer bound by iron shackles. Thereafter, professionals began to make more gains in attempts to accurately identify and address differences. *Rush's Medical Inquires and Observations,* published in 1805, is one of the first known attempts to explain mental disorders. Later, in 1845, Heinrich Hoffman wrote a book about his son who simply could not stop "fidgeting," or focus on tasks. In the 1890s Maria Montessori worked with children labeled by society as "uneducable" or "defective" and tailored her teaching methods to meet their needs, enabling them to excel in state board examinations. In the 1920s, researchers advanced the movement to accommodate children with disabilities by identifying specific interventions for reading disabilities. By the late 1970s, the U.S. federal government began to outline strategies for educational models, assistance, and teacher training to address the needs of students with learning differences.

Today, inclusionary classroom practices, medication, and various therapies attempt to address and accommodate the different needs of children. To accommodate differences in your classroom:

- Be well versed in differences you will see in your classroom such as ADD/ADHD, autism, and learning disabilities. Discover what treatments are available such as the DIR/Floortime model, assistive technologies (e.g., DynaMyte, alternative keyboards, and text-to-speech software), and listening therapy.

- Be available to parents to discuss their children's needs. Respond to their requests, questions, and concerns in a sensitive and timely manner in order to develop and maintain a close working relationship with them.

- Contact and collaborate with various professionals who specialize in working with and teaching children with disabilities. These professionals include occupational therapists, physical therapists, speech pathologists, counselors, and classroom tutors. As a member of a team, you can help your children more than if you worked alone.

bipolar disorder A mood disorder involving cycles of depression and mania that are severe and often lead to impaired functioning.

dyslexia A learning disability characterized by difficulties in reading, spelling, writing, speaking, or listening, despite at least average intelligence.

mathematics disorder A learning disability characterized by decided lack of ability to calculate or comprehend mathematical problems.

attention deficit hyperactivity disorder (ADHD) The inability to maintain attention and constrain impulsivity, accompanied by the presence of hyperactivity.

ACTIVITIES FOR PROFESSIONAL DEVELOPMENT

ethical dilemma

"Why Don't My Kids Get Their Fair Share?"

Latisha is a novice first grade teacher in the Rocky Springs School District. Her class of twenty-eight students includes fifteen Hispanic students, nine African American students, and four Vietnamese students. Latisha's room is sparsely furnished, many of the tables and chairs need repair, and the classroom library of thirty-seven books is old and worn. Last week at an orientation for pre-K–3 teachers held across town at the new Valley Ranch elementary school, Latisha learned that the students there are 90 percent white and class size averages nineteen. A tour of the classrooms revealed the latest in furniture, learning materials, and technology with well stocked classroom libraries. Latisha is concerned about the unequal distribution of resources in the school district, and she feels her children are not getting their fair share.

What should Latisha do? Should she just keep quiet and hope things get better, should she advocate for her children by getting a group of her colleagues together and sharing her concerns with them, or should she take some other course of action?

Application Activities

1. From John Dewey to the present, early childhood professionals have used children's interests as a basis for developing learning activities. In addition to being a good source of learning experiences, interests can also provide opportunities to develop skills and teach important information.

   a. Talk with some young children about what they like to do, their favorite activities, favorite television programs, and so on. Select several of these "interests" and plan three learning experiences you can use to teach skills related to literacy, math, and science.

   b. Do you think it is possible to base your entire curriculum and teaching activities on children's interests? Why or why not?

2. Throughout the history of education, great educators have been concerned with what they believed was best for children, how best to teach them, and what is worthwhile for children to know and be able to do.

   a. Based on the ideas and practices proposed by the educators discussed in this chapter, identify the teaching practices with which you most agree. State the learning outcomes you think are appropriate for all children.

   b. Review the curriculum goals and standards for the pre-K–3 grades in your local school district. Can you find examples to support that what educators identify as important knowledge and skills are substantiated by the beliefs of great educators?

3. Think for a minute what would happen if you gave six-month-old Emily some blocks. What would she try to do with them? More than likely she would put them in her mouth. She wants to eat the blocks. However, if you gave blocks to Emily's three-year-old sister Madeline, she would try to stack them. Both Emily and Madeline want to be actively involved with things and people as active learners. This active involvement comes naturally for them. Observe children in a number of early childhood settings and identify five ways they learn through active learning.

4. You have just been assigned to write a brief historical summary of the major ideas of the educational pioneers you read about in this chapter. You are limited to fifty words for each person and are to write as though you were the person. For example:

> Locke: "At birth the mind is a blank slate and experiences are important for making impressions on the mind. I believe learning occurs best through the senses. A proper education begins early in life and hands-on experiences are an important part of education."

chapter four

IMPLEMENTING EARLY CHILDHOOD PROGRAMS

Applying Theories to Practice

• • • • • • • • •

NAEYC Standards for Early Childhood Professional Preparation

Standard 1. Promoting Child Development and Learning

I use my understanding of young children's characteristics and needs, and of multiple interacting influences on children's development and learning, to create environments that are healthy, respectful, supportive, and challenging for each child.[1]

Standard 4. Using Developmentally Effective Approaches to Connect with Children and Families

I understand and use positive relationships and supportive interactions as the foundation for my work with young children and families. I know, understand, and use a wide array of developmentally appropriate approaches, instructional strategies, and tools to connect with children and families and positively influence each child's development and learning.[2]

When we talk about programs for children ages birth to eight, we mean the philosophy that guides our teaching and learning, the theories that underlie what we teach and how children learn, and the curricula that we select to guide the activities and experiences we provide for children. Early childhood programs are for all children, birth to age eight, and include all the services we provide for children in infant and toddler care, preschool programs, kindergarten, and grades one, two, and three. In other words, all programs for young children, regardless of what they are called, should be high quality and guided by basic philosophical beliefs.

Some teachers and administrators adopt a well recognized program such as Montessori as the basis for their school or classroom. Others use an *eclectic* approach in which they integrate the best from a number of programs into their own unique approach to educating young children. High-quality early childhood teachers think seriously about what they want their children to learn and be able to do and how best to achieve these goals. They make decisions based on their knowledge and understanding of various programs and how the basic features agree with their philosophies of teaching and learning. As we discuss in Chapter 5, current state and local standards specify what children in pre-kindergarten through third grade should know and do. Many programs incorporate these standards as the basis for developing their curriculum. Regardless of the approach you and your program select as your basis for teaching young children, the majority of early childhood professionals agree that the environment and teaching practices should be child centered, educate the whole child, and meet the needs of each child.

THE GROWING DEMAND FOR QUALITY EARLY CHILDHOOD PROGRAMS

Through 2008, the National Association for the Education of Young Children (NAEYC) accredited over 11,000 high-quality early childhood programs serving one million children.[3] These programs are only a fraction of the total number of early childhood programs in the United States. Think for a minute about what goes on in these and other programs from day to day. For some children, teachers and staff have developed well-thought-out and articulated programs that provide for their growth and development across all the developmental domains—cognitive, linguistic, emotional, social, and physical. This should be the goal of all programs that serve young children.

Early Childhood Programs

In the United States, early childhood programs come in many different varieties and are sponsored and supported by many different agencies. Unlike other countries with more centralized governments, the United States operates a more decentralized educational system, which accounts for the variety of programs for young children.

The federal government is a huge supporter of early childhood programs including Head Start and Early Head Start. The public schools are the largest provider of early childhood programs. These include preschool (for three- and four-year-old children), kindergarten, and grades one through three (which we discuss in Chapter 10). Public schools also provide before- and after-school care for children in the form of organized activities including help with schoolwork and enrichment activities such as music, art, and drama. Faith-based programs also provide many preschool and school options including mothers' day out (MDO) programs, preschools, kindergarten, and primary grade (one through three) programs.

FOCUS QUESTIONS

1. Why is there a growing demand for quality early childhood programs?

2. How does child care serve children and families?

3. What characteristics constitute quality education and care?

4. What are program models such as High/Scope, Montessori, and Reggio Emilia, and what are their basic features?

5. What early childhood programs does the federal government sponsor and fund?

6. Why is it important for you to know and understand early childhood programs?

FIGURE 4.1

The Ten Largest For-Profit Child Care Organizations in the United States

Organization	Headquarters	Centers	Capacity
Knowledge Learning Corporation	Portland, OR	1,746	231,673
Learning Care Group Inc.	Novi, MI	1,105	162,940
Bright Horizons Family Solutions	Watertown, MA	675	73,000
Nobel Learning Communities Inc.	West Chester, PA	178	28,000
Childcare Network	Columbus, GA	163	23,312
The Sunshine House	Greenwood, SC	157	20,867
Mini-Skool Early Learning Centers Inc.	Scottsdale, AZ	111	19,600
New Horizon Academy	Plymouth, MN	86	13,009
Children's Creative Learning Centers (CCLC Inc.)	Sunnyvale, CA	104	12,427
Minnieland Private Day School Inc.	Woodbridge, VA	101	12,025

Source: "The Exchange Top 50: North America's Largest For Profit Child Care Organizations," Trends in For Profit Care, Child Care Exchange, January/February 2009, 23; available online at http://www.childcareexchange.com/library/5018521.pdf.

Individuals and for-profit agencies are also large providers of child care, preschool, and other programs. The vast majority of the Montessori programs are provided by individual school owners, and the majority of infant/toddler child care is provided by individuals and for-profit programs. As you can see in Figure 4.1, Knowledge Learning Corporation is the largest corporate for-profit provider of infant/toddler, preschool, and kindergarten programs, along with nine other organizations all over the United States. In addition, many preschool programs adopt and use the Montessori, High/Scope, and Reggio Emilia models as a basis for their program approaches.

Regardless of the kind of programs they offer, parents, politicians, and the public want early childhood professionals to provide programs that:

- Ensure children's early school success, which enables them to succeed in school and life. The public believes that pre-kindergarten services are the smartest investments made.[4]
- Provide high-quality education for all children. The public is concerned by the growing achievement gap between African American and Hispanic American children and their white counterparts. Politicians and the public believe early childhood programs should help level the playing field of education for all children.[5]

Following are some of the goals these programs aim to meet:

- Include language and reading readiness activities in programs and curricula that enable children to learn and read well.[6]
- Help children develop the social and behavioral skills necessary for them to lead civilized and nonviolent lives. In response to daily headlines about shootings and

assaults by increasingly younger children, the public wants early childhood programs to assume an ever-growing responsibility for helping get children off to a nonviolent start in life. In addition, they want schools and other programs to keep their children safe.[7]

- Prepare children for the world shaped by global competition. Early childhood programs play a vital role in preparing the children of today for the world of tomorrow.[8] This is one reason why early childhood programs are placing more emphasis on science, math, technology, and learning a second language.

As you read about and reflect on the programs in this chapter, think about the ways each tries to best meet the needs of children and families and the goals above. Pause for a minute and review Table 4.1, which outlines the programs of early childhood education discussed in this chapter.

TABLE 4.1 Comparing Early Childhood Programs

Program	Main Features	Teacher's Role
Child Care 	• Comprehensive health, social, and education services are provided. • Program quality is determined by each program. • Each program has its own curriculum.	• Provides care and education for the whole child. • Provides a safe and secure environment. • Collaborates with and involves families.
High/Scope	• Theory is based on Piaget, constructivism, Dewey, and Vygotsky. • Plan-do-review is the teaching–learning cycle. • Emergent curriculum is not planned in advance. • Children help determine curriculum. • Key experiences guide the curriculum in promoting children's active learning.	• Plans activities based on children's interests. • Facilitates learning through encouragement.* • Engages in positive adult–child interaction strategies.*
Montessori	• Theoretical basis is the philosophy and beliefs of Maria Montessori. • A prepared environment supports, invites, and enables learning. • Children educate themselves—self-directed learning is a cornerstone. • Sensory materials invite and promote learning. • A set curriculum regarding what children should learn is offered. Montessorians try to stay as close to Montessori's ideas as possible. • Children are grouped in multiage environments. • Children learn by manipulating materials and working with others. • Learning takes place through the senses.	• Follows the child's interests and needs. • Prepares an environment that is educationally interesting and safe.* • Directs unobtrusively as children individually or in small groups engage in self-directed activity.* • Observes, analyzes, and provides materials and activities appropriate for the child's sensitive periods of learning.* • Maintains regular communications with the parent.

(continued)

TABLE 4.1 Comparing Early Childhood Programs *(Continued)*

Program	Main Features	Teacher's Role
Reggio Emilia 	• Theory is based on Piaget, constructivism, Vygotsky, and Dewey. • Emergent curriculum is not planned in advance. • Curriculum is based on children's interests and experiences. • Curriculum is project oriented. • The *Hundred Languages of Children* represents the symbolic representation of children's work and learning. • Learning is active. • A special teacher—the atelierista—is trained in the arts. • An art/design studio—the atelier—is used by children and teachers.	• Works collaboratively with other teachers. • Organizes environments rich in possibilities and provocations.* • Acts as recorder for the children, helping them trace and revisit their words and actions.*
Head Start 	• The program is federally sponsored and funded. • Programs must comply with federal performance standards and standards of learning. • The arts are integrated into all curriculum areas. • There is a comprehensive approach to educating the whole child. • Head Start offers comprehensive services, including health and nutrition. • The comprehensive program is designed to strengthen families. • Families and the community are involved in delivery of program services.	• Teaches to and provides for all children's developmental areas—social, emotional, physical, and cognitive. • Provides programs for children that support their socioeconomic, cultural, and individual needs in developmentally appropriate ways. • Involves families and the community in all parts.

*Information from C. P. Edwards, "Three Approaches from Europe: Waldorf, Montessori, and Reggio Emilia," *Early Childhood Research and Practice,* (4)1, Spring 2002, http://ecrp.uiuc.edu/v4n1/edwards.html.

CHILD CARE: SERVING CHILDREN AND FAMILIES

Child care is assuming an increasingly prominent role in the American education system. It is part of the seamless system of providing for the nation's children and youth that begins at birth and continues through high school and beyond. For this important reason, it is included in this chapter on early childhood programs.

Child care is a comprehensive service to children and families that supplements the care and education children receive from their families. Comprehensive child care includes high-quality care and education along with activities and experiences appropriate to support children's social, emotional, linguistic, physical, and academic development.

Child care is educational. It provides for children's cognitive development and helps engage them in the process of learning that begins at birth. Quality child care does not ignore the educational needs of young children but incorporates learning activities as part of the curriculum. Furthermore, child care staff work with parents to help them learn how to support children's learning in the home. A comprehensive view of child care considers the child to be a whole person; therefore, the major purpose of child care is to facilitate optimal development of the whole child and support efforts to achieve this goal.

The Importance of Child Care

Child care is popular and important for a number of reasons. First, recent demographic changes have created a high demand for care outside the home. There are more dual-income families and more working single parents than ever before. For example, over 58 percent of mothers with children under age three are employed, and it is not uncommon for mothers to return to work as early as six weeks after giving birth.[9]

Second, child care is viewed as a critical early intervention program for all children and families. High-quality early child care promotes pre-academic skills and school readiness, enhanced language performance, and increased positive developmental outcomes. Thus, child care plays a vital role in the health, welfare, and general social and academic well-being of all of the nation's children.

Third, for low-income families, quality child care is critical. High-quality child care provides safe places for children to be and grow. They provide good nutrition, environments for socialization, physical development, and learning.[10]

As demand for child care increases, you and your colleagues must participate in advocating for and creating high-quality child care programs that meet the needs of children and families.

Types of Child Care

Child care is offered in many places, by many persons and agencies that provide a variety of care and services. While the options for child care are almost endless, the following are some of the most popular.

Care by Family Members, Relatives, and Friends. Children are cared for by grandparents, aunts, uncles, other relatives, or friends, providing both continuity and stability of care. According to the Child Care Bureau, in 2007 the average monthly percentage of children served by relatives was 62 percent.[11]

Family Child Care. An individual caregiver provides care and education for a small group of children in his or her home. The Professionalism in Practice feature, "Magnia Child Care," will help you envision how good family child care is much more than babysitting. As you read, consider if you would want your child placed in a program like this.

Intergenerational Programs. In intergenerational programs, child care programs integrate children and the elderly in an early childhood and adult care facility. For example, the Mount Kisco Day Care Center in Mount Kisco, New York, and My Second Home/Family Services of Westchester, New York, are two nonprofit organizations whose shared vision has created a dynamic interactive community for young children and older adults under one roof. Mount Kisco Day Care Center provides early care and education for 139 infants, toddlers, preschool, and school-age children. My Second Home, an adult program, offers ninety-year-old adults a safe, supervised, home-like environment. The facility has been specially designed around the needs of older adults and children, providing optimal space for both structured programs and spontaneous interaction.[12]

Center-Based Care. Center-based child care is conducted in many types of facilities. Some of these facilities are constructed new, while others are refurbished homes and buildings. Others operate in churches and other such facilities. For example, KIDCO Child Care Centers in Miami, Florida, operate four centers, with enrollment of 443 children in renovated church and community buildings.

Employer-Sponsored Care. To meet the needs of working parents, some employers provide child care at the work site. Some employers may also provide for care in off-site facilities. For example, Bright Horizons Family Solutions is the world's leading provider of employer-sponsored child care and education. Through its full-service programs, children six weeks to six years experience a world rich with discovery, guided by skilled professionals who celebrate each child's individuality.[13]

I have been in the field of early care and education as a licensed family child care provider for sixteen years. My husband and I operate our program in our home. Magnia Child Care is accredited through the National Association for Family Child Care (NAFCC) and serves the needs of families with children from birth through age five. We are licensed for fourteen children and currently have eight enrolled. Because of the quality of our program, we are a training site for child development students from the local community college. As an Early Childhood Mentor Teacher—a program in California that pairs early childhood college students with experienced teachers in the field—I supervise these college students and offer firsthand experiences working with young children.

WHAT IS FAMILY CHILD CARE?

Family child care is the care of children in the provider's home. The provider must meet the necessary state and local licensing requirements, as well as health and safety standards. Family child care offers several benefits to parents that are not necessarily available in other early care settings:

- Smaller ratio of children to adults
- Mixed-age groups of children, allowing siblings to be together
- Consistent primary caregivers
- Flexibility to meet the needs of families
- The nurturing environment of a home

AN APPROPRIATE PROGRAM FOR ALL CHILDREN

At Magnia Child Care, we believe that our primary responsibilities include the following:

- Meeting the physical and emotional needs of children
- Maintaining a safe and healthy environment
- Supporting the parent–caregiver relationship
- Performing administrative tasks
- Continuing our professional growth and education

Because our program serves infants, toddlers, and preschool children, we offer a developmentally appropriate curriculum based on NAFCC guidelines. Along with planned activities for language and literacy, dramatic play, music and movement, and outdoor experiences, we also respect a child's ability to learn through self-discovery. Children in our program learn about science through their experiences with sand and water. They learn mathematics through the one-to-one ratio as they help pass out spoons or cups for lunchtime. They learn about their community as we take walks in the neighborhood and speak with the postal carrier, a repairman, or a police officer and visit a grocery store.

Children at Magnia Child Care have opportunities to explore the outdoors on our tricycle path, in our sandbox, on the climbing structures and swings, and in the places we've provided for them to discover nature. Indoor activities allow children to play in groups or to investigate on their own. Our schedule also provides a quiet time for rest and napping.

Proprietary Child Care. As mentioned earlier in this chapter, some child care centers are run by corporations, businesses, or individual proprietors for the purpose of making a profit. Refer again to Figure 4.1, which lists the ten largest for-profit child care providers in the United States. Despite the for-profit structure of these facilities, programs offered by proprietary child care centers often emphasize an educational component.

Before- and After-School Care. Public schools, center-based programs, community and faith-based agencies, and individuals all offer programs that extend the school day with tutoring, special activities, and a safe space. Some children are in school and child care up to ten hours a day.

However, regardless of the kinds of child care provided, the three key issues of *quality, affordability,* and *accessibility* are always part of child care delivery of services.

WHAT CONSTITUTES QUALITY EDUCATION AND CARE?

Although there is much debate about the quality of child care and what it involves, we can nonetheless identify the main characteristics of quality programs. The dimensions and indicators of quality child care include a healthy, respectful, supportive, challenging, and

RELATIONSHIPS WITH PARENTS

An important part of our work is the relationship we develop with parents. Together we form a partnership in caring for their children. We learn about the child from the parents, and in turn, the parents learn about their child's growth in our program. Over the years we have collected an assortment of articles on topics of interest to parents that relate to the typical skills of children, guidance suggestions, and dealing with difficult behaviors. Our Parent Files also include information on community resources that are available to children and their families. Coupled with our interactions with parents, this information serves to enhance the confidence of first-time parents as they inquire about their child's development.

AN EFFECTIVE FAMILY CHILD CARE PROVIDER

For an effective family child care provider, a strong background in child development is helpful. Understanding how children learn and how the environment affects their behavior, as well as learning about developmentally appropriate practices, influences the quality of child care. Taking part in professional organizations for early care and education is essential to our continued professional development.

A career in licensed family child care has many benefits. Being the director/owner of your own business is highly rewarding, as is incorporating your own program philosophy and developing your own policies, based on best practices. Your child care program can be flexible and accommodating to meet your needs and those of the families you serve.

Our greatest reward as licensed family child care providers is the pleasure we receive in working with young children and their families. It is gratifying to witness the growth and development of small infants into active, confident, ready-to-learn preschool children.

As with any profession, there are also challenges; unfortunately, some still assume that we are only babysitters. However, we continue to advocate and educate others about the valuable contribution that licensed family child care provides to children, to families, and to our communities.

....
Contributed by Martha Magnia, owner/director of Magnia Family Child Care and adjunct faculty at Fresno City College, where she teaches child development and family child care courses.

safe and pleasant environment, as outlined below. (Note that safe and pleasant are *necessary* environmental requirements.) Let's consider each of these child care environmental dimensions. Then we'll explore other factors that a quality early childhood program should consider.

A Healthy Environment

A healthy environment supports children's physical and mental health. A healthy environment is clean, well maintained, and has separate areas for toileting (and for changing diapers), eating, and sleeping. Caregivers teach infants and toddlers healthy habits, such as hand washing after toileting, before and after mealtime, and after other appropriate activities. A healthy environment also provides a relaxed and happy eating environment. Substantial research clearly indicates that a healthy diet and environment contribute to children's overall health and well-being.[14]

A healthy environment also supports children's mental health. Caregivers support children's mental health when they provide responsive and loving care and create environments that have a balance of small and large open areas. Small areas provide the opportunity for infants and toddlers to be alone or in small groups. The open areas

Family child care is the preferred method of child care for many parents. Parents like a program for their children that approximates a home-like setting. What are some characteristics of a home-like setting you can incorporate into your classroom?

encourage active involvement with larger numbers of children. In addition, child care staff collaborate with and involve parents to help them know about and understand the importance of children's mental health.

A Respectful Environment

A respectful environment is one in which caregivers deeply care about children and families (review again our discussion about caring as a professional disposition in Chapter 1). Caregivers create a respectful environment by listening, observing, and being aware of children's verbal and nonverbal communications. Caregivers interpret or "read" children's behavior by asking themselves: "What does the child's behavior say to me?" A respectful environment is also one in which children's unique individualities are honored and provided for. Each child's unique individuality is a product of such dimensions as temperament, gender, race, language, culture, and socioeconomic status, as well as other characteristics. As you honor each of these dimensions you create a respectful environment.

A Supportive Environment

A supportive environment means that you will spend time with children, pleasantly interact with them, and encourage and help them. Supportive environments encourage and promote children's routine social interactions. A supportive environment accommodates children's individual differences and provides for active play. It also offers a wide range of learning materials. This type of environment promotes children's mental health and encourages child-centered activities. In a supportive environment, you respond to children's physical, social, emotional, and cognitive needs.

A Challenging Environment

A challenging environment provides opportunities for infants and toddlers to be actively involved with other children, staff, and parents. These interactions are extremely important as children learn about their world and themselves. An environment that supports social interaction lays the foundation for children's school readiness and other life outcomes. A challenging environment provides materials and activities that are matched to the needs, interests and abilities of children and which provide for many hands-on activities that support seeing, touching, feeling, and moving. Supportive and challenging environments complement each other.

myeducationlab

Go to the Assignments and Activities section of Topic 5: Program Models in the MyEducationLab for your course and complete the activity entitled *Quality Child Care Settings*. Pay particular attention to what the narrator identifies as the factors that contribute to high-quality child care programs.

A Safe and Pleasant Environment

At all age levels, a safe and pleasant physical setting is important. Such an area should include a safe neighborhood free from traffic and environmental hazards, a fenced play area with well maintained equipment, child-sized equipment and facilities (such as toilets and sinks), and areas for displaying children's work, such as finger painting and clay models. The environment should also be attractive and pleasant. The rooms, home, or center should be clean, well lit, well ventilated, and cheerful. A pleasant and attractive environment supports Maslow's theory, which states that we must address and meet children's aesthetic needs.

Caregivers also provide a safe environment through responsive relationships and by developing close and nurturing bonds with the children they care for. Responsive and close relationships enable infants and toddlers to experience trust and to feel safe with you and in your program.

Other Considerations for a Quality Child Care Program

In addition to the environmental dimensions of quality care we just discussed, Table 4.2 identifies ten components of a high-quality child care program. Early childhood professionals also recognize these components as important. Other factors that contribute to a good early childhood education deserve our attention as well, and we explore these attributes next.

Caregiver-to-Child Ratio. The ratio of adults to children in child care programs should be sufficient to give children the individual care and attention they need. NAEYC guidelines for the ratio of caregivers to children are 1:3 or 1:4 for infants and toddlers and 1:8 to 1:10 for preschoolers, depending on group size.[15]

TABLE 4.2 The Ten Components of High-Quality Child Care

Component	Indicator
1. Licensed programs following appropriate health and safety practices	Licensing ensures that a child care setting meets basic health and safety requirements.
2. Staff well trained in early childhood development	The strongest indicators for long-term success tied to early education and care are related to the caregivers' education and level of participation in ongoing training in the field of early childhood development and care.
3. Age-appropriate environments	Learning is an interactive process that involves continuous opportunities for exploration and interactions.
4. Small groups with optimal ratios	Group size and ratios determine the amount of time and attention that each caregiver can devote to each child.
5. Primary caregiver and continuity of care	Positive relationships between caregivers and children are crucial to quality child care.
6. Active and responsive caregiving to support children's development	The active and responsive caregiver takes cues from each child to know when to guide, teach, and intervene.
7. Emerging language and emerging literacy	The path to literacy begins with interaction between caregivers and young children.
8. Curricula, observation, and individualized programming	Learning involves activities, materials, and opportunities for exploration and interaction.
9. Family involvement and cultural continuity	High-quality programs incorporate practices reflecting the values and beliefs of the families and the cultures of their communities.
10. Comprehensive support services with multidisciplinary teams	High-quality child care serves as a protective environment for the child and a source of support for the child's family.

Source: FSU Center for Prevention and Early Intervention Policy, "10 Components of Quality Child Care for Infants and Toddlers," April 8, 2003; available online at http://www.cpeip.fsu.edu/resourceFiles/resourceFile_1.pdf?CFID=57777&CFTOKEN=26715426. Reprinted by permission.

The American Public Health Association and the American Academy of Pediatrics recommends these ratios and standards:[16]

Age	Maximum Child-to-Staff Ratio	Maximum Group Size
Birth to 12 months	3:1	6
13 to 30 months	4:1	8
31 to 35 months	5:1	10
3-year-olds	7:1	14
4-year-olds	8:1	16
5-year-olds	8:1	16
6- to 8-year-olds	10:1	20

Research shows that when programs meet these recommended child-to-staff ratios and recommended levels of caregiver training and education, children have better outcomes.[17]

Developmentally Appropriate Programs. Programs should have written, developmentally based curricula for meeting children's needs. A program's curriculum should specify activities for children of all ages, which caregivers can use to stimulate infants, provide for the growing independence of toddlers, and address the readiness and literacy skills of four- and five-year-olds. All programs should include curricula and activities that meet the social, emotional, and cognitive needs of all children. Quality programs use developmentally appropriate practices to implement the curriculum and achieve their goals. You can develop a good understanding of developmentally appropriate practice by reading *Developmentally Appropriate Practice in Early Childhood Programs Serving Children from Birth Through Age 8.*[18]

Individual Needs. Good care and education provide for children's needs and interests at each developmental stage. For example, infants respond to good physical care and to continuity of care, love and affection, and **cognitive sensory stimulation**. Cognitive sensory stimulation is the process of providing appropriate sensory stimulation, which in turn supports cognitive development. Infants and toddlers learn through their senses. Indeed it is the way they learn. Providing children appropriate sensory stimulation through toys of different colors, shapes, and textures, such as foam balls and blocks, enables them to learn through their senses and develop cognitive schemes (see Chapter 3). Toddlers need safe surroundings and opportunities to explore. They need caregivers who support and encourage active involvement. However, within these broad categories of development, individual children have unique styles of interacting and learning that you must accommodate. Each child must feel valued and respected.

cognitive sensory stimulation The process of providing appropriate sensory stimulation, which in turn supports cognitive development.

Managing Behavior. Learning how to adapt your teaching to children's individual needs and learning styles and how to manage their behavior are two important teacher skills. Sometimes children's behavior can be difficult to manage. For example, a preschooler might demonstrate challenging behavior that makes it difficult for the teacher to help the child learn and be involved with others. A skillful teacher can redirect that behavior in order to help the child stay engaged and learn.

Accommodating Individual Needs. Providing for individual children's needs also means that you will accommodate their individual disabilities and developmental delays. For example, in your child care program, two-and-a-half-year-old Bobby has not learned to use the toilet. His parents have noticed that he shows interest in using the toilet, tells them after he urinates or defecates in his diaper, and does not say "no" as often as he did—all indications that Bobby is ready to start learning to use the toilet. Bobby, however, is not able to say when he needs to use the toilet. Here are some things you can do to accommodate Bobby, other children, and their parents:

- Discuss toilet-learning procedures with Bobby's parents. Discuss their wishes and views about toilet learning (Is Bobby using training pants or big boy underwear? What words do they use at home for urination and defecation?). Continuity is the key to success in toilet learning, so discuss with his parents what they are doing at home. Remember, different cultures have different approaches to toilet training. However, you cannot use harsh, punitive methods under any circumstances.

- Always keep the door open when you help children with toileting. Children are not yet concerned with privacy. In fact, some child care centers and schools mandate that doors remain open when adults are in the restroom with children.

- Start a schedule. To begin, take Bobby to the restroom every hour. Once you have an idea of his body rhythms, you can take him less or more often. Use the words that his family wants you to use (e.g., "pee," or "poop"), so that Bobby learns to tell you when he needs to use the toilet.

- Have Bobby help take off his own training pants or underwear and then sit on the toilet. Read him a short developmentally appropriate book about potty learning or sing several songs. If he has not done anything in the toilet by the end of the book or songs, then have him help put his clothes back on and try again in an hour.

- Encourage Bobby by saying, "You are so big. You are using the toilet (potty) just like Mommy and Daddy do."

- If Bobby has an accident, tell him the words he can use next time before he pees or poops. Be positive and encouraging at all times. Never scold Bobby for having an accident. Some children learn quickly and others slowly. Bobby's parents may want you to use a reward, such as a sticker, when he is successful.

If you take these steps to accommodate Bobby's individual needs, you will help him become more independent and developmentally on track.

The Effects of Care and Education on Children

Recent research reveals that high-quality early care and education have influences that last a lifetime. A valuable source of research about child care comes from the Study of Early Child Care and Youth Development (SECCYD) by the National Institute of Child Health and Human Development (NICHD).[19] The SECCYD is a comprehensive longitudinal study initiated by NICHD, designed to answer questions about the relationship between child care experiences and characteristics and children's developmental outcomes. Listed below are some of the study's findings on the use of child care and its effects on children and families. The study results make it clear that professionals must provide high-quality programs and must advocate for that high quality with the public and state legislators. Reflect on what surprises you most as you review the study results.

Child Care Arrangements

- During the first year of life the majority of children in nonparental care experienced more than two different child care arrangements.

- More than one-third experienced three or more arrangements.

Hours in Child Care

- At their first entry into nonmaternal care, children averaged 29 hours of care per week.

- By twelve months, children averaged 33.9 hours a week of care.

Type of Care

- Forty-four percent of children receive care in child care centers and 25 percent in child care homes; 12 percent are cared for by their father or their mother's partner; 10 percent are cared for at home by nannies or babysitters; and 9 percent are cared for by grandparents.

Child Care and Income

- Families with the lowest nonmaternal income were the most likely to place infants in care before the age of three months, probably because they were the most dependent on the mother's income.
- The higher their mothers' earnings, the more hours infants spent in nonmaternal care; however, the higher the *nonmaternal* earnings in the family, the *fewer* hours they spent in care.

Maternal Attitudes and Child Care

- Mothers who believed their children benefited from their employment tended to place their infants in care earlier, and for more hours, in nonauthoritarian, nonmaternal care.
- In contrast, mothers who believed maternal employment carried high risks for their children tended to put their infants in care for fewer hours and were especially likely to rely on the infant's father for child care.

Quality of Nonmaternal Care

- Observations at six months indicated that more-positive caregiving occurred when children were in smaller groups, child–adult ratios were lower, caregivers held less authoritarian beliefs about child rearing, and physical environments were safe, clean, and stimulating.

Social, Emotional, Cognitive, and Health-Related Child Outcomes

- Observed quality of caregivers' behavior—particularly the amount of language stimulation provided—was positively related to children's performance on measures of cognitive and linguistic abilities at ages fifteen, twenty-four, and thirty-six months.
- Quality of care was also related to measures of social and emotional development. At twenty-four months, children who had experienced higher quality care were reported by both their mothers and their caregivers to have fewer behavior problems and were rated higher on social competence by their mothers. At thirty-six months, higher quality care was associated with greater compliance and less negative behavior during mother–child interactions and fewer caregiver-reported behavior problems.
- Quality of care is associated with developmental outcomes throughout the preschool years.

It is clear that high-quality child care has beneficial outcomes for children and families. You will be involved in advising parents about child care. The research data above will help you be informed and knowledgeable.

Source: Reprinted by permission from Child Care and Child Development, *Results from the NICHD Study of Early Child Care and Youth Development* (New York: Guilford Press, 2005), 28–35.

PROGRAM MODELS

Models are guides that provide us with instructions, ideas, and examples. We use models to guide a lot of what we do in life. We model our lives after others we respect and admire. We adopt the fashions of models in advertisements—and, in early childhood education, we model our programs after highly respected models such as High/Scope, Montessori, and Reggio Emilia. While none of these individual models are intended for all children, they nonetheless are widely used in the United States and around the world. The High/Scope model, the first model we examine next, is widely used in Head Start, corporate-sponsored preschool programs, and public preschool programs.

High/Scope: A Constructivist Model

The **High/Scope educational model** uses curriculum that is geared to children's stages of development, promotes constructive processes of learning, and broadens the child's emerging intellectual and social skills.[20] The High/Scope model is based on Piaget's cognitive development theory (see Chapter 3). Three principles of the High/Scope model are:

- Active participation of children in choosing, organizing, and evaluating learning activities, which are undertaken with careful teacher observation and guidance in a learning environment that has a rich variety of materials located in various classroom learning centers
- Regular daily planning by the teaching staff in accord with a developmentally based curriculum model and careful child observations
- Developmentally sequenced goals and materials for children based on the High/Scope "key developmental indicators"[21]

Basic Principles and Goals of the High/Scope Model. The High/Scope program strives to develop in children a broad range of skills, including the problem-solving, interpersonal, and communication skills that are essential for successful living in a rapidly changing society. The curriculum encourages student initiative by providing children with materials, equipment, and time to pursue activities they choose. At the same time, it provides teachers with a framework for guiding children's independent activities toward sequenced learning goals. The teacher plays a key role in instructional activities by selecting appropriate, developmentally sequenced material and by encouraging children to adopt an active problem-solving approach to learning. This teacher–student interaction—teachers helping students achieve developmentally sequenced goals while also encouraging them to set many of their own goals—uniquely distinguishes the High/Scope curriculum from direct-instruction and teacher-centered curricula.[22]

Five Elements of the High/Scope Model. Professionals who use the High/Scope curriculum are fully committed to providing settings in which children actively learn and construct their own knowledge. Teachers create the context for learning by implementing and supporting five essential elements: active learning, classroom arrangement, the daily schedule, assessment, and the curriculum (content).

Active Learning. Teachers support children's active learning by providing a variety of materials, making plans and reviewing activities with children, interacting with and carefully observing individual children, and leading small- and large-group active learning activities.

Classroom Arrangement. The classroom contains five or more interest centers that encourage choice. The classroom organization of materials and equipment supports the daily routine. Children know where to find materials and what materials they can use. This encourages development of self-direction and independence.

The teacher selects the centers and activities to use in the classroom based on several considerations:

- Interests of the children (e.g., preschool children are interested in blocks, housekeeping, and art)
- Opportunities for facilitating active involvement in seriation (e.g., big, bigger, biggest), numbers (e.g., counting), time relations (e.g., before–after), classification

High/Scope educational model A constructivist educational model based on Piaget's cognitive development theory, providing realistic experiences geared to children's current stages of development.

Go to the Assignments and Activities section of Topic 5: Program Models in the MyEducationLab for your course and complete the activity entitled *The High/Scope Model*. Reflect on how you can guide children's learning through active play and key developmental indicators (key experiences).

(e.g., likenesses and differences), spatial relations (e.g., over–under), and language development

- Opportunities for reinforcing needed skills and concepts and functional (real-life) use of these skills and concepts

Classroom arrangement is an essential part of professional practice in order to appropriately implement a program's philosophy. This is true for High/Scope, as well as Montessori and every other program with which you may be involved.

Daily Schedule. The schedule considers developmental levels of children, incorporates a sixty- to seventy-minute plan-do-review process, provides for content areas, is as consistent throughout the day as possible, and contains a minimum number of transitions.

Assessment. Teachers keep notes about significant behaviors, changes, statements, and things that help them better understand a child's way of thinking and learning. Teachers use two mechanisms to help them collect data: the key developmental indicators note form and a portfolio. In addition, teachers use the Child Observation Record (COR) to identify and record children's progress in key behavioral and content areas.

Curriculum. The educational content of High/Scope preschool programs is built around fifty-eight "key developmental indicators" (KDIs) in five curriculum content areas. The curriculum content areas are as follows: (1) approaches to learning; (2) language, literacy, and communication; (3) social and emotional development; (4) physical development, health, and well-being; and (5) arts and sciences (math, science and technology, social studies, and arts).

The KDIs are early childhood milestones that guide teachers as they plan and assess learning experiences and interact with children to support learning.[23] For instance, the KDIs for language, literacy, and communication are: (1) talking with others about personally meaningful experiences; (2) describing objects, events, and relations; (3) having fun with language (e.g., listening to stories and poems, making up stories and rhymes); (4) writing in various ways (e.g., drawing, scribbling, letter-like forms, invented spelling, conventional forms); (5) reading in various ways (reading storybooks, signs and symbols, one's own writing); and (6) dictating stories.[24]

These developmental indicators are representative of the many that are available for teachers to choose from when identifying learning activities for children. In many ways, the KDIs are similar to standards that specify what children should know and do.

A Daily Routine That Supports Active Learning. The High/Scope curriculum's daily routine is made up of a plan-do-review sequence that gives children opportunities to express intentions about their activities while keeping the teacher intimately involved in the whole process. The following five processes support the daily routine and contribute to its successful functioning.

Children can learn mathematics skills through activities that involve the manipulation of concrete objects, like blocks. What other active learning experiences can you use to help children discover principles of mathematics?

Planning Time. Planning time gives children a structured, consistent chance to express their ideas to adults and to see themselves as individuals who can act on decisions.

The teacher talks with children about the plans they have made before the children carry them out. This helps children clarify their ideas and think about how to proceed. Talking with children about their plans provides an opportunity for the teacher to encourage and respond to each child's ideas, to suggest ways to strengthen the plans so they will be successful, and to understand and gauge each child's level of development and thinking style. Children and teachers benefit from these conversations and reflections. Children feel reinforced and ready to start their work, while teachers have ideas of what opportunities for extension might arise, what difficulties children might have, and where problem solving may be needed.

Key Developmental Indicators.   Teachers continually encourage and support children's interests and involvement in activities, which occur within an organized environment and a consistent routine. Teachers plan from key developmental indicators (KDIs) that may broaden and strengthen children's emerging abilities. Children generate many of these experiences on their own; others require teacher guidance. Many KDIs are natural extensions of children's projects and interests.

Work Time.   This part of the plan-do-review sequence is generally the longest time period in the daily routine. The teacher's role during work time is to observe children to see how they gather information, interact with peers, and solve problems. When appropriate, teachers enter into the children's activities to encourage, extend, and set up problem-solving situations.

Cleanup Time.   During cleanup time, children return materials and equipment to their labeled places and store their incomplete projects, restoring order to the classroom. All children's materials in the classroom are within reach and on open shelves. Clear labeling enables children to return all work materials to their appropriate places.

Recall Time.   Recall time, the final phase of the plan-do-review sequence, is the time when children represent their work time experience in a variety of developmentally appropriate ways. They might recall the names of the children they involved in their plan, draw a picture of the building they made, or describe the problems they encountered. Recall strategies also include drawing pictures, making models, physically demonstrating how a plan was carried out, or verbally recalling the events of work time. The teacher supports children's linking of the actual work to their original plan.

This review permits children to reflect on what they did and how it was done. It brings closure to children's planning and work time activities. Putting their ideas and experiences into words also facilitates children's language development. Most important, it enables children to represent their mental schemes to others.

Advantages of High/Scope.   Implementing the High/Scope approach has several advantages. First, it offers you a method for employing a constructivist-based program that has its roots in Piagetian cognitive theory. Second, it is widely popular and has been extensively researched and tested. Third, a rather extensive network of training and support is provided by the High/Scope Foundation. Fourth, High/Scope teachers emphasize the broad cognitive, social, and physical abilities that are important for all children, instead of focusing on a child's deficits. High/Scope teachers identify where a child is developmentally and then provide a rich range of experiences appropriate for that level. For example, they would encourage a four-year-old who is functioning at a two-year-old level to express his or her plans by pointing, gesturing, and saying single words, and they would immerse the child in a conversational environment that provided many natural opportunities for using and hearing language.[25] You can learn more about High/Scope through its website (http://www.highscope.org). Reviewing the website will help you decide if High/Scope is a program you would consider implementing in your classroom.

The Montessori Method

The **Montessori method** (see Chapter 3) is attractive to parents and teachers for a number of reasons. First, Montessori education has always been identified as a quality program for young children. Second, parents who observe a good Montessori program like what

Montessori method A system of early childhood education founded on the philosophy, procedures, and materials developed by Maria Montessori. Respect for the child is the cornerstone on which all other Montessori principles rest.

they see: orderliness, independent children, self-directed learning, a calm environment, and children at the center of the learning process. Third, some public schools include Montessori in their magnet programs, giving parents choices in the kind of program their children will have at their school.

During the past decade, the implementation of Montessori education has increased in both private and public school early childhood programs. Maria Montessori would probably smilingly approve of the contemporary use of her method once again to help change the nature and character of early childhood education.

Role of the Montessori Teacher. The Montessori teacher demonstrates certain behaviors to implement the principles of this child-centered approach. The teacher's six essential roles in a Montessori program are as follows: (1) respect children and their learning; (2) make children the center of learning; (3) encourage children's learning; (4) observe children; (5) prepare learning environments; and (6) introduce learning materials and demonstrate lessons. Review these six roles and consider how you can apply them to your practice regardless of what kind of program you implement. Which of these six do you think is the most essential? Why?

Maria Montessori contended, "It is necessary for the teacher to *guide* the child without letting him feel her presence too much, so that she may be always ready to supply the desired help, but may never be the obstacle between the child and his experience."[26] The teacher as a guide is a pillar of Montessori practice.

The Montessori Method in Action. In a prepared environment, certain materials and activities provide for three basic areas of child involvement: *practical life* for motor education, *sensory materials* for training the senses, and *academic materials* for teaching writing, reading, and mathematics. All of these activities are taught according to prescribed procedures.

Practical Life. The prepared environment emphasizes basic, practical, everyday motor activities, such as walking from place to place in an orderly manner, carrying objects such as trays and chairs, greeting a visitor, learning self-care skills, and doing other practical activities. For example, the "dressing frames" are designed to perfect the motor skills involved in buttoning, zipping, lacing, buckling, and tying. The philosophy for activities such as these is to make children independent of the adult and develop concentration. Water-based activities play a large role in Montessori methods, and children are taught to scrub, wash, and pour as a means of developing coordination. Practical life exercises also include polishing mirrors, shoes, and plant leaves; sweeping the floor; dusting furniture; and peeling vegetables.

Montessorians believe that as children become absorbed in an activity, they gradually lengthen their span of concentration. As they follow a regular sequence of actions, they learn to pay attention to details. Montessori educators also believe that concentration and involvement through the senses enable learning to take place. Teacher verbal instructions are minimal; the emphasis in the instruction process is on *showing how*—modeling and practice.

Practical life activities are taught through four different types of exercises. *Care of the person* involves activities such as using the dressing frames, polishing shoes, and washing hands. *Care of the environment* includes dusting, polishing a table, and raking leaves. *Social relations* include lessons in grace and courtesy. The fourth type of exercise involves *analysis and control of movement* and includes locomotor activities such as walking and balancing.

Sensory Materials. For many early childhood educators the core of the Montessori program is the specialized set of learning materials that help children learn and that support Montessori's ideas about how to best facilitate children's learning. Many of these materials are designed to train and use the senses to support learning. Figure 4.2 shows basic Montessori sensory materials. Montessori sensory materials are popular, attractive, and they support children's cognitive development. Authentic Montessori materials are very well made and durable.

As you review these materials, think about their purposes and how they act as facilitators of children's learning. Sensory materials include brightly colored rods and cubes and

Material	Illustration	Descriptions and Learning Purposes
Pink tower		Ten wooden cubes of the same shape and texture, all pink, the largest of which is ten centimeters. Each succeeding block is one centimeter smaller. Children build a tower beginning with the largest block. (Visual discrimination of dimension)
Brown stairs		Ten wooden blocks, all brown, differing in height and width. Children arrange the blocks next to each other from thickest to thinnest so the blocks resemble a staircase. (Visual discrimination of width and height)
Red rods		Ten rod-shaped pieces of wood, all red, of identical thickness but differing in length from ten centimeters to one meter. The child arranges the rods next to each other from largest to smallest. (Visual discrimination of length)
Cylinder blocks		Four individual wooden blocks that have holes of various sizes and matching cylinders; one block deals with height, one with diameter, and two with the relationship of both variables. Children remove the cylinders in random order, then match each cylinder to the correct hole. (Visual discrimination of size)
Smelling jars		Two identical sets of white opaque glass jars with removable tops through which the child cannot see but through which odors can pass. The teacher places various substances, such as herbs, in the jars, and the child matches the jars according to the smells. (Olfactory discrimination)
Baric tablets		Sets of rectangular pieces of wood that vary according to weight. There are three sets—light, medium, and heavy—that children match according to the weight of the tablets. (Discrimination of weight)
Color tablets		Two identical sets of small rectangular pieces of wood used for matching color or shading. (Discrimination of color and education of the chromatic sense)
Cloth swatches		Two identical swatches of cloth. Children identify them according to touch, first without a blindfold but later using a blindfold. (Sense of touch)
Tonal bells		Two sets of eight bells, alike in shape and size but different in color; one set is white, the other brown. The child matches the bells by tone. (Sound and pitch)
Sound boxes		Two identical sets of cylinders filled with various materials, such as salt and rice. Children match the cylinders according to the sounds the fillings make. (Auditory discrimination)
Temperature jugs or thermic bottles		Small metal jugs filled with water of varying temperatures. Children match jugs of the same temperature. (Thermic sense and ability to distinguish between temperatures)

FIGURE 4.2 Montessori Sensory Materials

sandpaper letters. One purpose of these sensory materials is to train children's senses to focus on some obvious, particular quality. For example, with red rods, it is the quality of length; with pink tower cubes, size; and with bells, musical pitch. Montessori felt that children need help discriminating among the many stimuli they receive. Accordingly, the sensory materials help children become more aware of the capacity of their bodies to receive, interpret, and make use of stimuli. In this sense, the Montessori sensory materials are labeled *didactic,* and are designed to instruct and help children learn.

Second, the sensory materials help sharpen children's powers of observation and visual discrimination. These skills serve as a basis for general beginning reading readiness. Readiness for learning is highly emphasized in early childhood programs.

Third, the sensory materials increase children's ability to think, a process that depends on the ability to distinguish, classify, and organize. Children constantly face decisions about sensory materials: which block comes next, which color matches the other, which shape goes where? These are not decisions the teacher makes, nor are they decisions children arrive at by guessing; rather, they are decisions made by the intellectual process of observation and selection based on knowledge gathered through the senses.

Finally, the sensory activities are not ends in themselves. Their purpose is to prepare children for the onset of the sensitive periods for writing and reading. In this sense, all activities are preliminary steps in the writing–reading process.

Materials for training and developing the senses have these characteristics:

- *Control of error.* Materials are designed so children, through observation, can see whether or not they have made a mistake while completing an activity. For example, if a child does not use the blocks of the pink tower in their proper order while building the tower, she does not achieve a tower effect.
- *Isolation of a single quality.* Materials are designed so that other variables are held constant except for the isolated quality or qualities. Therefore, all blocks of the pink tower are pink because size, not color, is the isolated quality.
- *Active involvement.* Materials encourage active involvement rather than the more passive process of looking. Montessori materials are "hands-on" in the truest sense of hands-on active learning.
- *Attractiveness.* Materials are attractive, with colors and proportions that appeal to children. In this sense, they help satisfy aesthetic needs for beauty and attractiveness.

Academic Materials for Writing, Reading, and Mathematics.   The third type of Montessori materials is academic, designed specifically to promote writing, reading, and mathematics. Exercises using these materials are presented in a sequence that supports writing as a basis for learning to read. Reading, therefore, emerges from writing. Both processes, however, are introduced so gradually that children are never aware they are learning to write and read until one day they realize they are writing and reading. Describing this phenomenon, Montessori said that children "burst spontaneously" into writing and reading. She anticipated contemporary practices such as the whole-language approach in integrating writing and reading and in maintaining that children learn to read through writing.

Montessori believed many children were ready for writing at four years of age. Consequently, children who enter a Montessori program at age three have done most of the sensory exercises by the time they are four. It is not uncommon to see four- and five-year-olds in a Montessori classroom writing and reading. In fact, children's success with early academic skills and abilities serves as a magnet to attract public and parental attention.

Additional Features.   Other features of the Montessori system are *mixed-age grouping* and *self-pacing.* A Montessori classroom always contains children of different ages, usually from two and a half to six years. This strategy is becoming more popular in many early childhood classrooms. Advantages of mixed-age groups are that children learn from one another and help each other, a wide range of materials is available for all ages of children, and older children become role models and collaborators for younger children. Contemporary instructional practices of student mentoring, scaffolding, and cooperative learning all have their roots in and are supported by multiage grouping.

In a Montessori classroom, children are free to learn at their own rates and levels of achievement. They decide which activities to participate in and work at their own pace. Through observation, the teacher determines when children have perfected one exercise and are ready to move to a higher level or different exercise. If a child is not able to correctly complete an activity, the teacher gives him or her additional help and instruction. Table 4.3 shows the instructional practices used in a Montessori program and how they apply to teacher roles and the curriculum. Review these practices now and think how they are similar to or different from instructional practices you have observed in other early childhood programs.

Montessori and Contemporary Practices. The Montessori approach has had a tremendous influence on approaches to early education. Many instructional practices used in contemporary early childhood programs have their basis in Montessori materials and practices. The Montessori method has many features to recommend it as a high-quality early childhood program and this accounts for its ongoing popularity.

Read now in the Technology Tie-In feature on page 112 how you can use technology to promote children's social development.

Reggio Emilia

Reggio Emilia, a city in northern Italy, is widely known for its approach to educating young children. Founded by Loris Malaguzzi (1920–1994), Reggio Emilia sponsors programs for children from three months to six years of age. Certain essential beliefs and practices underlie the **Reggio Emilia approach**. These basic features are what defines it, makes it

Reggio Emilia approach An early childhood educational program named for the town in Italy where it originated. The method emphasizes a child's relationships with family, peers, teachers, and the wider community; small-group interaction; schedules set by the child's personal rhythms; and visual arts programs coordinated by a specially trained atelierista.

TABLE 4.3 Montessori Instructional Practices

These instructional practices, combined with the roles of the Montessori teacher and the sensory materials, serve as the essential core of Montessori programs.

Integrated curriculum	Montessori provides an integrated curriculum in which children are actively involved in manipulating concrete materials across the curriculum—writing, reading, science, math, geography, and the arts. The Montessori curriculum is integrated by age and developmental level.
Active learning	In Montessori classrooms, children are actively involved in their own learning. Manipulative materials provide for active and concrete learning.
Individualized instruction	Curriculum and activities should be individualized for children. Individualization occurs through children's interactions with the materials as they proceed at their own rates of mastery.
Independence	The Montessori environment emphasizes respect for children and promotes success—both of which encourage children to be independent.
Appropriate assessment	Observation is the primary means of assessing children's progress, achievement, and behavior in a Montessori classroom. Well trained Montessori teachers are skilled observers of children and adept at translating their observation into appropriate ways for guiding, directing, facilitating, and channeling children's learning.
Developmentally appropriate practice	What is specified in developmentally appropriate practice is included in Montessori practice. It is more likely that quality Montessori practitioners understand, as Maria Montessori did, that children are much more capable than some early childhood practitioners think.

technology tie-in

Promote Children's Social Development with Technology

You can use computers and other technology to help children develop positive peer relationships, expanding their views of the world and themselves. These tools can also increase children's abilities of self-regulation and self-control, allowing them to function without constant supervision. Technology can aid in the development of positive self-esteem, the feelings children have about themselves. Here are some things you can do to accomplish these goals:

- Learning through technology is inherently a solitary activity, but you can find many ways to make it a cooperative and social learning experience. Have children work on projects together in pairs or small groups. Several children can work on the computer and other projects at the same time. For example, make sure that each computer has several chairs to encourage children to work together.
- Provide children opportunities to talk about their technology projects. Social development includes learning to talk confidently, explain, and share information with others.
- Encourage children to explore adult roles related to technology, such as newscaster, weather forecaster,

and photographer. Invite adults from the community to share with children how they use technology in their careers. Invite a television crew to show children how they broadcast from community locations.

- Read stories about technology and encourage children to talk about technology in their lives and the lives of their families.
- Use the Internet and e-mail to connect children to other children. Have them exchange ideas and work on short reports. Remember that social development can occur electronically!
- Use technology to encourage a socially isolated child to develop social skills: "Sophia, let's use the video camera to interview Mrs. Little, the cafeteria manager, on good nutrition ideas for use at home."
- Create a learning center devoted to technology. The writing and publishing of a classroom newspaper is a great way to promote social interactions. Make sure *all* children have a job, such as a reporter, writer, or photographer.

a constructivist program, and identifies it as a model that attracts worldwide attention. The Reggio approach has been adapted and implemented in a number of U.S. early childhood programs.

Beliefs About Children and How They Learn. As we have discussed, your beliefs about young children determine how you teach them, what kind of programs you provide for them, and your expectations for their learning and development. This is the case with Reggio. Their beliefs drive their program practices.

Relationships. Reggio education focuses on each child and is conducted in relation with the family, other children, the teachers, the school environment, the community, and the wider society. Each school is viewed as a system in which all of these interconnected relationships are essential for educating children. In other words, as Vygotsky believed, children learn through social interactions and, as Montessori maintained, the environment supports and is important for learning.

Teachers are always aware, however, that children learn a great deal in exchanges with their peers, especially when they interact in small groups. Such small groups of two, three, four, or five children provide possibilities for paying attention, hearing, and listening to each other, developing curiosity and interest, asking questions, and responding.

Time. Reggio Emilia teachers believe that time is not set by a clock and that learning continuity should not be interrupted by the calendar. Children's own sense of time and their personal rhythm are considered in planning and carrying out activities and projects. The full-day schedule provides sufficient time for being together among peers in an environment that is conducive to getting things done with satisfaction.

Teachers get to know the personal rhythms and learning styles of each child. This intensive getting to know children is possible in part because children stay with the same teachers and the same peer group for three-year cycles (infancy to three years and three years to six years).

Adults' Roles.   Adults play a powerful role in children's lives. Children's well-being is connected with the well-being of parents and teachers. The well-being of all is supported by recognizing and supporting basic rights. Children have a right to high-quality care and education that supports the development of their potentials. This right is honored by adults and communities who provide these educational necessities. Parents have a right to be involved in the life of the school. As one parent remarked, "I'm not a visitor at school; this is my school!" Teachers have the right to grow professionally through collaboration with other teachers and parents.

The Teacher.   Teachers observe and listen closely to children to know how to plan or proceed with their work. They ask questions and discover children's ideas, hypotheses, and theories. They collaboratively discuss what they have observed and recorded, and they make flexible plans and preparations. Teachers then enter into dialogues with the children and offer them opportunities for discovering, revisiting, and reflecting on experiences. In this sense, teachers support learning as an ongoing process. Teachers are partners and collaborators with children in a continual process of research and learning.

The Atelierista.   An **atelierista** is a teacher trained in the visual arts, who works closely with other teachers and children in every Reggio preprimary school and makes visits to the infant/toddler centers. The atelierista's specific training in the visual arts opens up another kind of dialogue, helping children use materials to create projects that reflect their involvement in and efforts to solve problems.

atelierista A Reggio Emilia teacher trained in visual arts who works with teachers and children.

Families.   Families are an essential component of Reggio, and they are included in the advisory committee that runs each school. Family participation is expected and supported and takes many forms: day-to-day interaction, work in the schools, discussion of educational and psychological issues, special events, excursions, and celebrations.

The Environment.   The infant/toddler centers and school programs are the most visible aspect of the work done by teachers and families in Reggio Emilia. They convey many messages, of which the most immediate is that they are environments where adults have thought about the quality and the instructive power of space.

The Physical Space.   In addition to welcoming whoever enters, the layout of physical space fosters encounters, communication, and relationships. The arrangement of structures, objects, and activities encourages children's choices, supports problem solving, and promotes discoveries in the process of learning.

Reggio centers and schools are beautiful. There is attention to detail everywhere: in the color of the walls, the shape of the furniture, the arrangement of objects on shelves and tables. Light from the windows and doors shines through transparent collages and weavings made by children. Healthy, green plants are everywhere.

The environment is highly personal and full of children's own work. Everywhere there are paintings, drawings, paper sculptures, wire constructions, transparent collages coloring the light, and mobiles moving gently overhead. Such things turn up even in unexpected spaces such as stairways and bathrooms.

The Atelier.   The **atelier** is a special workshop or studio, set aside and used by all the children and teachers in the school. It contains a great variety of tools and resource materials, along with records of past projects and experiences. In the view of Reggio educators, the children's use of many media is not art or a separate part of the curriculum but an inseparable, integral part of the whole cognitive/symbolic expression involved in the learning process.

atelier A special area or studio in a Reggio Emilia school for creating projects.

Go to the Assignments and Activities section of Topic 5: Program Models in the MyEducationLab for your course and complete the activity entitled *Comparing Program Models: Montessori and Reggio Emilia Approaches.* Reflect on the differences and similarities of the program models and how you can incorporate elements of both into your classroom.

Program Practices.   Cooperation is the powerful mode of working that makes possible the achievement of the goals Reggio educators set for themselves. Teachers work in pairs in each classroom. They see themselves as researchers gathering information about their work with children by means of continual documentation. The strong collegial relationships that are maintained with teachers and staff enable them to engage in collaborative discussion and interpretation of both teachers' and children's work.

Documentation.   Transcriptions of children's remarks and discussions, photographs of their activity, and representations of their thinking and learning using many media are carefully arranged by the atelierista and other teachers. These document children's work and the process of learning. This documentation has five functions:

1. To make parents aware of children's experiences and maintain their involvement
2. To allow teachers to understand children and to evaluate their own work, thus promoting professional growth
3. To facilitate communication and exchange of ideas among educators
4. To make children aware that their effort is valued
5. To create an archive that traces the history of the school and the pleasure of learning by children and their teachers

Curriculum and Practices.   The curriculum is not established in advance. In this sense, Reggio is a process approach, not a set curriculum to be implemented. Teachers express general goals and make hypotheses about what direction activities and projects might take. After observing children in action, teachers compare, discuss, and interpret together their observations and make choices that they share with the children about what to offer and how to sustain the children in their exploration and learning. In fact, the curriculum emerges in the process of each activity or project and is flexibly adjusted accordingly through this continuous dialogue among teachers and with children.

Projects provide the backbone of the children's and teachers' learning experiences. These projects are based on the conviction that learning by doing is of great importance and that to discuss in groups and to revisit ideas and experiences is the premier way of gaining understanding and learning.

Ideas for projects originate in the experiences of children and teachers as they construct knowledge together. Projects can last from a few days to several months. They may start from a chance event, an idea or a problem posed by one or more children, or an experience initiated directly by teachers.

Considerations.   As you consider the Reggio Emilia approach, keep in mind that its theoretical base rests within constructivism and shares ideas compatible with those of Piaget, Vygotsky, Dewey, and Gardner (refer to Chapter 3), and the process of learning by doing. In addition, like the Montessori approach, Reggio places a high value on respect for each child. In a Reggio program everyone has rights—children, teachers, and parents. Children with disabilities have special rights and are routinely included in programs for all children. The accompanying Professionalism in Practice feature, "A Reggio-Inspired Parent–Teacher Cooperative," shows how the Reggio approach inspires professionals to adapt it to their programs.

The Project Approach

Project Approach An educational approach that encourages in-depth investigation by an individual student or small group of students, or even by the whole class, of a topic the students want to learn more about.

The **Project Approach** is popular in early childhood education today, traces its roots back to John Dewey's project approach, and is based on constructivist ideas and practices. With the Project Approach, an investigation is undertaken by a small group of children within a class, sometimes by a whole class, and occasionally by an individual child. The key feature of a project is that it is a search for answers to questions about a topic worth learning more about, something the children are interested in.[27] The project approach can be

At Children First, a nonprofit NAEYC-accredited preschool, two teachers educate twelve children between the ages of thirty-three months and five years in one mixed-age group. The philosophy of the program is built on the belief that "children are strong, capable, infinitely valuable, and profoundly unique individuals."

The program focuses first on children as individuals, each with particular passions, strengths, challenges, and identities. Children have a great deal of choice about how they spend their time at school, and have continuous access to a rich variety of materials and art media that allow them to express their thinking and their feelings. Curriculum is built around the goals that teachers and parents set together for each child; and teachers focus their documentation efforts on tracing each child's developmental story in his or her portfolio.

At the same time, the program places tremendous value on individual children living together in a caring, lively community; that means friendship, inclusion, collaboration, conflict resolution, tradition, celebration, and diversity learning are all important parts of the curriculum.

Children First also works to strengthen children's connection and comfort with the natural world. The "outdoor classroom"—a playground with a garden, a creek, a mud river for digging, and a deck for sensory exploration and water play—is available throughout the morning, not just for a designated recess time. Children make regular visits to the nearby Eno River, their "wild home away from home." And teachers help children develop their capacities as natural scientists who are both curious about and respectful of plants and animals.

Children First works closely with parents to establish a strong parent–teacher cooperative: Parents serve on the board of directors and on various working committees; they participate in discussion groups with teachers; they are encouraged to volunteer in the classroom; and most importantly, they engage with teachers—through conversation, conferences, and the portfolios—to grow a shared appreciation and effective teaching plan for each child.

Children First takes a nontraditional approach to discipline. Teachers avoid punishment, direction, and praise, in favor of offering information, sharing feelings, and bringing children's attention to the effects of their choices on themselves and others. Teachers focus on helping children figure out what *to* do, rather than telling them what *not* to do. Children have a strong voice in constructing the rules, or "agreements," they live by as a community.

"Perhaps the most important thing Reggio has taught us to do here," says Donna King, teacher and administrator at Children First, "is to create a program, from day to day and year to year, that is built around and belongs to the people—children, parents, and teachers—who inhabit it." King advises educators interested in the Reggio approach to remember that the Reggio educators themselves urge us to look not at our practices and classrooms, but at the children and families in front of us, and to remember that all children are competent and have a right to be active in constructing a caring community. Also, educators must place absolute value on quality of life *now*—on beauty, joy, passion, nature, discovery, imagination, creativity—as opposed to focusing on "building the future" and "preparing for kindergarten," as so many American educators say.

Donna King is a teacher, administrator, and one of the founders of Children First. Information based on the Children First Parent Handbook. Children First is a nonprofit organization based in a private residence.

and is used in any kind of early childhood program regardless of its name. The project approach provides opportunities for children to be meaningfully and actively involved.

Learning Modalities

Regardless of the program (such as Montessori, constructivist, High/Scope, or Reggio Emilia) you use in your classroom, you should be aware that every child learns differently and thus experiences the world differently. Third grader Kate, for example, is a very physical child and comprehends material best when she can touch, feel, or move the information herself. Her classmate, Tenisha, a linguistic learner, learns best if she can write or read information. Eli, on the other hand, is very visual; he learns best if information is presented in pictures or diagrams. Unlike Eli, Juan learns best when material is presented to him in a musical manner. Combining visual, tactile, and auditory components is helpful for all of your students. When you teach in a multisensory way, you increase children's understanding, memory, and mastery of content, knowledge, and skills.

To accommodate diverse learners like Kate, Tenisha, Eli, and Juan in your classroom:

- Teach face-to-face with your students. Give directions and discuss subjects so all children can see and hear you. Children who are visual learners need to see your mouth moving and look at your facial expressions to completely hear your words. Ask children to "find my face" or to "give me your eyes and ears" when you give instructions so they understand you are telling them something important.

- Allow movement in your classroom. Children want and need to be active! Activity is the basis for active learning! Tactile, linguistic, and auditory learners like Kate, Tenisha, and Juan often tap their feet or pencils or scribble on paper while learning. Physical movement or scribbling helps them to internalize and concentrate. Movement is a self-help tool that helps students learn.

- Present information in a variety of ways.
  - When you discuss the day's schedule, in addition to talking about it have pictorial representations of the schedule for visual learners like Eli (snack time can be represented by a picture of crackers, math represented by a picture of an addition problem, etc.). Your visual schedule can be arranged vertically or horizontally to encourage the left-to-right, top-to-bottom reading process.
  - Attach pictures to the daily schedule with Velcro strips. Have tactile learners like Kate peel an activity off as it is finished. Kate can then put the picture of the activity in an "all-done" or "finished" box.
  - Accompany the schedule with a song such as, "our snack time is finished, our snack time is done," for auditory learners like Juan.

- Plan to include multisensory approaches in all your teaching. For example:
  - Discuss new words in a singsong fashion or set them to a popular children's tune such as "Baa Baa Black Sheep" for auditory learners like Juan.
  - Make learning letters and words a tactile experience. Children can mold words out of play dough, make letters 3-D by twisting them out of colorful pipe cleaners, trace words in shaving cream, or cut them out of sand paper. Also many letters—like "B," "D," "I," "V," and "L"—can be made with the hands and fingers. Encourage children to use their hands to help them remember which way letters orient and to demonstrate how they can be combined to form words. For example, to spell "bed," show students how to make their left hand in the shape of a "b," and their right hand into a letter "d." Use a written letter "e" to go in the middle.

- Form learning groups based on children's learning modalities.
  - Pair Eli, a visual learner, with Tenisha, a linguistic learner. Have them write and illustrate their own story. Eli can be the illustrator and Tenisha the writer. This allows them both to be co-authors!

The more senses you incorporate into your teaching, the more your students will learn and the more fun they will have.

FEDERAL PROGRAMS FOR YOUNG CHILDREN

The federal government exerts tremendous influence on early childhood education. Every dimension of almost every educational program—public, private, and faith based—is touched in some way by the federal government.

Head Start (children ages three to five) and Early Head Start (children from birth to age three) are comprehensive child development programs that serve children, families, and pregnant women. These programs provide comprehensive health, nutrition, educational, and social services in order to help children achieve their full potential and succeed in school and life. They are currently designed to serve poor children and families. In this regard, Head Start and Early Head Start are **entitlement programs**. This means that children and families who qualify, in this case by low income, are entitled to the services simply by meeting the qualifying criteria. However, only about one-third of eligible children and families receive these services because of the lack of funding to support full implementation.

entitlement programs Programs and services that children and families are entitled to because they meet the eligibility criteria.

Head Start Programs

Head Start, America's premier preschool program, was implemented during the summer of 1965. The first programs were designed for children entering first grade who had not attended kindergarten. The purpose of Head Start was literally to give children from low-income families a "head start" on their kindergarten experience and, ideally, on life itself. As public schools have provided more kindergarten and preschool programs, Head Start now serves younger children. It is administered by the Administration for Children and Families (ACF) in the Department of Health and Human Services. In 2007, Congress passed the Improving Head Start for School Readiness Act of 2007, which reauthorized Head Start through September 2012. In addition, the American Recovery and Reinvestment Act (ARRA) of 2009 earmarked $1.1 billion additional funding for the expansion of Head Start and $1.1 billion in funding for Early Head Start.

performance standards Specific examples of what students should know and do to demonstrate that they have mastered the knowledge and skills stated in content standards.

As of 2008, the National Head Start program has an annual budget of $6.9 billion and serves 908,412 low-income families. There are 1,604 Head Start programs nationwide, with a total of 18,275 centers and 49,400 classrooms. The average cost per child of the Head Start program is $7,326 annually. Head Start has a paid staff of 220,000 and 1,384,000 volunteers.[28]

Head Start Performance Standards. Both Head Start and Early Head Start must comply with federal **performance standards**, criteria designed to ensure that all children and families receive high-quality services.

The Head Start Program Performance Standards play a central role in defining quality services for low-income children and their families. These standards are the mandatory regulations that grantees and delegate agencies must implement to operate a Head Start and/or Early Head Start program. The standards define the objectives, features, and services of a quality Head Start program; they articulate the vision that services should be delivered to both young children and their families; and they require a group to monitor and enforce quality standards.[29]

Standards of Learning. Head Start programs implement *standards of learning* in early literacy, language, and numeracy skills. The nine indicators guide teacher planning and act as standards of learning for Head Start children. We discuss the standards in more detail in Chapter 5, and you can review them in Appendix B.

Head Start provides training for teachers to use the best methods of early reading and language skills instruction in order to implement these standards.[30]

Eligibility for Head Start Services. To be eligible for Head Start services, children must meet age and family income criteria. Head Start enrolls children ages three to five from low-income families. Income eligibility is determined by whether or not family incomes fall below the official poverty line, which is set annually by the U.S. Department

Federally funded programs such as Head Start are designed to provide for the full range of children's social, emotional, physical, and academic needs. Increasingly, however, federal- and state-supported early childhood programs are emphasizing literacy, math, and science skills. How can traditional play-based activities such as this one help children learn skills in these three areas?

TABLE 4.4 2009 Poverty Guidelines for the Forty-Eight Contiguous States and the District of Columbia

Size of Family Unit	Poverty Guidelines
1	$10,830
2	$14,570
3	$18,310
4	$22,050
5	$25,790
6	$29,530
7	$33,270
8	$37,010

Source: U.S. Department of Health and Human Services, "The 2009 HHS Poverty Guidelines," January 23, 2009; accessed June 15, 2009, at http://aspe.hhs.gov/POVERTY/09poverty.shtml.

of Health and Human Services. United States poverty guidelines for 2009 are shown in Table 4.4.

Ninety percent of Head Start enrollment has to meet the income eligibility criteria. The other 10 percent of enrollment can include children from families that exceed the low-income guidelines. In addition, 10 percent of a program's enrollment must include children with disabilities. Often, the actual enrollment in local programs for children with disabilities surpasses the 10 percent requirement. The accompanying Diversity Tie-In feature, "Inclusion and Collaboration," describes the operation of a fully inclusive Head Start Program.

Improving Head Start. The Improving Head Start for School Readiness Act of 2007 increased teacher qualifications by requiring that 50 percent of Head Start teachers nationwide have a minimum of a baccalaureate degree in early childhood education or a related field by 2013. It also requires Head Start programs to develop career ladders (see Chapter 1) and annual professional development plans for full-time staff. Also, it requires that all Head Start programs use research-based practices to support the growth of children's pre-literacy and vocabulary skills.

Head Start has always been and remains a program for children of poverty. Although it currently reaches a significant number of poor children, increasing federal support for Head Start will likely increase the number of poor children served. However, we must keep in mind that the federal government is using Head Start to reform all of early childhood education. Federal officials believe that the changes they make in the Head Start curriculum—what and how teachers teach and how Head Start operates—will serve as a model for other programs as well.

Early Head Start

Early Head Start (EHS), created in 1995, is designed to promote healthy prenatal outcomes for pregnant women; enhance the development of very young children (birth through age three); and promote healthy family functioning. Early Head Start enrolls pregnant women. When the child is born, the mother is provided family services. As with Head Start, EHS is a program for low-income families who meet federal poverty guidelines. Currently, 10 percent of the overall Head Start budget is used to serve low-income families with infants and toddlers through the Early Head Start program. EHS serves about 62,000 infants and toddlers with a budget of $687 million.[31] In addition, the American Recovery and Reinvestment Act

PEARSON
myeducationlab

Go to the Assignments and Activities section of Topic 3: Family/Community in the MyEducationLab for your course and complete the activity entitled *Family-Centered Practice in Head Start.* Note how families and teachers can work together to benefit students and also how educating the whole family is used to break the cycle of poverty.

Inclusion and Collaboration

The Head Start program of Upper Des Moines Opportunity Inc. operates twenty-five fully inclusive preschool classrooms. We have three classrooms specific to toddlers, ages eighteen to thirty-six months. We also have twenty-two classrooms set up for children ages three to five. Our programs are designated for all children, regardless of race or disability. We use the Creative Curriculum as a part of our ongoing instruction and observation of children in the classroom. We also use the Ages and Stages Questionnaire for developmental and social-emotional screening for children from birth to five years. In addition, we use positive behavior supports for guiding children's behavior.

Our Head Start programs take pride in the strength of our partnerships with local school districts and other local education agencies. Because of the strength of these relationships we are able to collaborate in program design and offer natural or least restrictive environments to all children.

In Early Head Start, our staff have been trained in case management of children with special needs. They have taken the lead position in coordination of services to our children and their families. These services can be provided in the home, in the classroom, or in a child care setting. Support service staff trained in specific areas of early childhood development facilitate our toddler rooms. We use the Child Study model to continually update staff on individual progress, concerns, and needs of our children. We employ many interpreters of different languages, as we serve a very diverse population.

Our Head Start classrooms for children ages three to five offer many opportunities for inclusion. In some centers we dually enroll children, allowing them the opportunity to spend half a day in Head Start and the other half in an early childhood special education (ECSE) classroom. We also have classrooms where Head Start teachers and ECSE teachers work side by side, allowing for full-day programming for all children in the least restrictive settings. We operate Head Start classrooms where the lead teacher has a degree in early childhood special education and associate(s) have backgrounds in early childhood, or the lead teacher has a background in early childhood and associate(s) are qualified to work with children having special needs. Support service staff facilitate all of our classrooms for three- to five-year-olds, and they, too, use the Child Study team approach to communicate the progress needs and concerns of all children.

Contributed by Mary Jo Madvig, private consultant and previous early childhood program director, Upper Des Moines Opportunity Inc., Des Moines, Iowa.

---

of 2009 allocated $1.1 billion for Early Head Start. EHS program services include: quality early education both in and out of the home; parenting education; comprehensive health and mental health services, including services to women before, during, and after pregnancy; nutrition education; and family support services.

Head Start's entry into the field of infant/toddler care and education has achieved several things. It has given Head Start an opportunity to work with a long-neglected age and socioeconomic population. As the public schools have enrolled preschoolers at an accelerated rate, the infant/toddler field gives Head Start a new group to serve. It has enabled Early Head Start to be a leader in the field of infant/toddler education. Without a doubt, EHS has been a pioneer and catalyst in providing high-quality programs for infants and toddlers.

EARLY CHILDHOOD PROGRAMS AND YOU

As an early childhood teacher it is important for you to know about various programs for young children. Knowing about programs will enable you to talk knowledgably with colleagues and parents and will enable you to critically compare and contrast features of one program with another. As you engage in this critical analysis you will be able to identify what you think are the strengths and weaknesses of each program and what features of each program you like the best. Knowing about early childhood programs enables you to always be clear about what you believe is best for children and families and to think, talk, and act as a confident professional.

myeducationlab

Go to the Building Teaching Skills and Dispositions section in Topic 5: Program Models in the MyEducation-Lab for your course and complete the activity entitled *Recognizing Character-istics of Early Childhood Program Models.*

The Politics of Early Childhood Education

As you learn more about early childhood education, you will learn that early childhood and its programs are very politicized. The politics of early childhood programs revolve around issues of which programs are most effective for which children, and which programs are capable of supporting children's learning so that they are ready for school and life. Today, the purposes of early childhood programs go far beyond merely educating young children. The purposes of early childhood programs also include developing curricula for closing the achievement gaps between African American and Hispanic American children and their white counterparts, getting children ready for school, and laying the foundation for a well prepared workforce. During 2008 and 2009 as the United States went through a very difficult recession, early childhood programs became more essential to the politicians and the public. Early childhood programs were then and are seen today as a way of enabling the United States to recover economically and to play a major role on the world's economic stage.

ACTIVITIES FOR PROFESSIONAL DEVELOPMENT

ethical dilemma

"Why Can't We Serve Them All?"

For the past five years Kim has worked as a lead teacher at a large Head Start center in a major city. She is a supporter of Head Start and believes in its mission of helping low-income children and families. Kim was ecstatic when she heard the news that Head Start would get additional funding under the American Recovery and Reinvestment Act of 2009. However, last week the regional Head Start office released data showing that 1,253 children who are eligible for Head Start in Kim's city will not be served. Kim believes that all children should have the benefits of Head Start, and she is sick and tired of people saying that children are the nation's greatest resource but not putting money where their mouths are! In frustration, Kim meets with Marty, the center director, to tell her that she has talked with a community activist who suggests that she call a meeting of parents with Head Start–eligible children to discuss how to demand additional funding under the federal government's economic stimulus plan. However, Marty becomes angry and defensive: "Look, Kim, I don't want you to rock the Head Start boat! We have to be satisfied with the additional funding we may receive. Head Start never has been and never will be fully funded in spite of all the new federal stimulus dollars."

What should Kim do? Does she ignore Marty and develop plans to organize the parents, perhaps risking her career and reputation, does she reluctantly agree with Marty and resign herself to the fact that there is nothing she can do about a large governmental agency like Head Start, or does she pursue some other course of action to help the children?

myeducationlab

To check your comprehension on the content covered in Chapter 4, go to the Book Specific Resources in the MyEducationLab for your course, select your text, and complete the Study Plan. Here you will be able to take a chapter quiz and receive feedback on your answers.

Application Activities

1. As an early childhood professional, you will need to make decisions about what to teach and how to teach it. Choose one of the programs you read about in this chapter and explain how you would implement it in your classroom. In your plans include a daily schedule and activities for children.

2. Make a chart with these headings:

   "Program Features I Like" and "Program Features I Dislike"

   Complete your chart for each of the programs we discussed in this chapter. Next, rank in order the programs according to your first choice, second, third, and so forth.

3. Review your philosophy of education again. Now write a paragraph about how your philosophy does or does not align with the theory and assumptions of each program we have discussed in this chapter.

4. Review the learning theories we discussed in Chapter 3. Explain, with specific examples, how these theories have influenced the programs discussed in this chapter.

5. The programs in this chapter reveal how fast the field of early childhood has changed and is changing. Which of these "changes" or new ideas surprised you?

chapter five

STANDARDS AND YOU

Teaching Children to Learn

· · · · · · · · ·

NAEYC Standards for Early Childhood Professional Preparation

Standard 4: Using Developmentally Effective Approaches to Connect with Children and Families

I understand and use positive relationships and supportive interactions as the foundations for my work with young children. I know, understand, and use a wide array of developmentally appropriate approaches, instructional strategies, and tools to connect with children and families and positively influence each child's development and learning.[1]

Standard 5: Using Content Knowledge to Build Meaningful Curriculum

I understand the importance of developmental domains and academic (or content) disciplines in early childhood curriculum. I know the essential concepts, inquiry tools, and structure of content areas, including academic subjects, and can identify resources to deepen their understanding. I use my own knowledge and other resources to design, implement, and evaluate meaningful, challenging curriculum that promotes comprehensive development and learning outcomes for every young child.[2]

When I visit early childhood classrooms and ask teachers "What are you teaching?" I get a lot of different responses. Some teachers reply that they are teaching about "animals" or "holidays." Others respond that they are teaching "themes," "social skills," and "beginning reading." But what are these teachers really teaching their children? And more importantly, what are the children learning?

"What should I teach?" is a question all teachers ask themselves. How do you answer this question? Perhaps you reply that you are going to teach your children reading, writing, and mathematics. But let's look at your answer for a minute. What reading skills will you emphasize? Are you going to teach phonics? Word meaning? Vocabulary development? In what order will you teach these skills? To what achievement level will you teach them? These questions are not easily answered and not all teachers answer them the same way. **Standards**, statements of what students should know and be able to do, help answer questions about what to teach children and what they should learn. National and state standards help us better answer the "What should students learn?" question. As a result, state and national standards have influenced every facet of early childhood education and will continue to do so in the decades to come.

WHAT ARE NATIONAL AND STATE STANDARDS FOR WHAT STUDENTS WILL LEARN AND DO?

Standards are statements that specify what students should know and be able to do. They also act as expectations for student learning. Often, standards are specified by content area and grade (e.g., first grade reading, second grade science); these are known as **content standards**. Today, from preschool to high school, professionals are emphasizing **standards-based education (SBE)**, which focuses on basing the **curriculum** (all of the experiences children have while in school), teaching, and testing on local, state, and national standards.

Performance standards (introduced in Chapter 4, in the discussion of Head Start) go into much greater depth than content standards. The performance standard incorporates the content standard, which tells teachers what students are expected to know (i.e., what concepts they are expected to master), and expands upon them by providing three additional items: suggested tasks, sample student work, and teacher commentary on that work. Performance standards provide clear expectations for assessment, instruction, and student work. They define the level of work that demonstrates achievement of the standards and identify the skills needed to use the knowledge and skills to problem-solve, reason, communicate, and make connections with other information. Performance standards also tell the teacher how to assess the extent to which the student knows the material or can manipulate and apply the information.[3] Here is a kindergarten reading content standard accompanied by performance standards:

Comprehension

Content Standard

The student gains meaning from orally presented text.

Performance Standard

The student will:

a. Listen to and read a variety of literary (e.g., short stories, poems) and informational texts and materials to gain knowledge and for pleasure.

FOCUS QUESTIONS

1. What are national and state standards for what students will learn and do?

2. Why are national, state, and local standards important?

3. How are standards changing teaching and learning?

4. What are issues associated with national, state, and local standards?

standards Statements of what pre-K–12 students should know and be able to do.

content standards Standards that are specified by content area and grade.

standards-based education (SBE) Curriculum, teaching, and testing based on local, state, and national standards.

curriculum The subject matter taught; all of the experiences children have while in school.

b. Make predictions from pictures and titles.

c. Ask and answer questions about essential narrative elements (e.g., beginning-middle-end, setting, characters, problems, events, resolution) of a read-aloud text.

d. Begin to distinguish fact from fiction in a read-aloud text.

e. Retell familiar events and stories to include beginning, middle, and end.

f. Use prior knowledge, graphic features (illustrations), and graphic organizers to understand text.

g. Connect life experiences to read-aloud text.

h. Retell important facts in the student's own words.[4]

As we discuss standards, keep in mind that constitutionally, education is a state responsibility. So this explains why states have taken the lead in developing standards for what students should know and do. However, the federal government also plays a powerful role in identifying standards for learning. And as you will discover, state governments are increasingly accepting the idea that there should be common national standards that apply to all fifty states.

Federal Initiatives and Standards

The current popularity of standards and the controversies surrounding them did not just suddenly happen overnight. In fact, the standards movement has been gaining momentum for the last several decades. Politicians view standards as a way to make sure that the nation's children learn and are prepared to do well in school and the workplace. Three federal initiatives have played a tremendous role in the creation of the SBE system we have today:

- *A Nation at Risk: The Imperative for Educational Reform, National Commission on Excellence in Education (1983).* The U.S. Department of Education created the National Commission on Excellence in Education to provide a report about the quality of education in America. The commission recommended, among other things, curriculum reform, higher expectations for the nation's students, and standards for learning.[5]

- *Goals 2000: Educate America Act (P.L. 103–227, 2000).* This act was designed to ensure that all students reached high levels of achievement. Goals 2000 established eight national education goals. Goal three specified that by the year 2000, "All students will leave grades 4, 8, and 12 having demonstrated competency over challenging subject matter including English, mathematics, science, foreign languages, civics and government, economics, the arts, history, and geography, and every school in America will ensure that all students learn to use their minds well, so they may be prepared for responsible citizenship, further learning, and productive employment in our nation's modern economy."[6]

- *No Child Left Behind Act (2001).* The No Child Left Behind Act (NCLB) is the main federal law affecting education from kindergarten through high school. NCLB is built on four principles: accountability for results, more choices for parents, greater local control and flexibility, and an emphasis on doing what works based on scientific research.[7] NCLB mandates numerous programs that have goals for improving education in elementary, middle, and high schools by setting high expectations for students, teachers, and administrators of each state with the result of greater educational achievement for all students.[8]

In addition, the federal government wants states and school districts to use standards to promote student achievement and learning. For example, Secretary of Education Arne Duncan is using $15 billion in federal funds to reward states, districts, and nonprofit organizations that have set high standards for the students they serve.[9] Duncan also wants to provide federal money to states and districts that have set rigorous standards linked to strong assessments and monitored by student-data systems.[10]

National Reports

A number of widely read and influential reports have also stimulated discussion and action regarding the importance of early learning: *Preventing Reading Difficulties in Young Children*,[11] *From Neurons to Neighborhoods: The Science of Early Childhood Development*,[12] and *Eager to Learn: Educating Our Preschoolers*.[13] These reports increased national interest in standards as a basis for making explicit and public what young children need to know and do to be successful in school and life.

NCLB Discussion

All states have responded to the No Child Left Behind Act of 2001 by writing learning standards for K–12. Many states have also written standards or guidelines for preschool education. Some states, such as Georgia, also have early learning guidelines (ELGs) for infants and toddlers. In addition, a federal early childhood initiative, "Good Start, Grow Smart," seeks to improve early learning for young children and encourages states to voluntarily develop early learning guidelines.[14] While the ELGs themselves are voluntary, they are a condition for receiving funding through the federal Child Care and Development Block Grant. This accounts for why most states have written preschool guidelines to guide the learning of three- and four-year-olds.

The No Child Left Behind Act of 2001 was intended to significantly reform K–12 education. Since its passage, it has radically and rapidly changed how America conducts its educational business. NCLB emphasizes state and district accountability, mandates state standards for what children should know and be able to do, puts in place a comprehensive program of testing in grades three to twelve, and encourages schools to use teaching methods that have demonstrated their ability to help children learn. The federal government's focus on using federal dollars on "programs that work" relies on **scientifically based** or **research-based programs**. This means that these programs are based on scientific research that demonstrates the programs can increase student achievement.

The NCLB Act targets six fundamental areas:

- Accountability
- Literacy
- Programs that work (based on scientific research)
- Professional development
- Educational technology
- Parental involvement

NCLB is a significant educational act that will continue to influence what and how you teach for many years to come. The act has influenced pre-kindergarten education because there is a major emphasis on getting children ready for school. Many federally funded programs now use guidelines and mandates in the No Child Left Behind Act to develop goals and objectives for their own programs. In other words, all facets of programs that serve young children have been and will continue to be influenced by NCLB. However, some educators oppose some of the provisions of NCLB, especially those that relate to testing. Critics of NCLB argue that the focus on assessment encourages teachers to teach a narrow range of skills. In addition, they argue that students are subjected to too much testing. Table 5.1 shows some pros and cons for NCLB.

scientifically based programs *or* **research-based programs** Programs based on scientific research that demonstrates they can increase student achievement.

TABLE 5.1 Pros and Cons of NCLB

The No Child Left Behind Act (NCLB) has caused a great deal of discussion and debate, which generally focuses around testing, academic standards, and accountability. The following are the major points in the NCLB pro-and-con debate.

Pros	Cons
• NCLB sets accountability standards which are measured annually by each state to guide educational growth and achievement. Results about how well students and schools perform are reported to parents.	• The federal government underfunds NCLB, but states have to comply with all provisions of NCLB in order to receive federal funding. • NCLB rewards schools that score well on standardized tests; therefore teachers are forced to teach a narrow set of test-taking skills and test a limited range of knowledge. • There is too much emphasis on testing. In efforts to ensure that children do well on tests, too much time is spent on testing, teaching to the test, and teaching children how to take tests—frequently referred to as *test besting*.
• NCLB emphasizes reading and math.	• Focus on reading and math "narrows" the curriculum. Other subjects such as the arts don't get the attention they deserve.
• NCLB links state academic content with student educational outcomes, and requires school improvement to be implemented using "scientifically based research."	• Emphasis on "scientifically based" curriculum takes away from teachers' creativity and using other curriculum materials.
• NCLB measures education status and growth by ethnicity, and helps close the achievement gap between white and minority students.	• Tests may contain cultural biases. Educational quality cannot necessarily be evaluated by objective testing.
• All children are held to high standards and achievement.	• Not all children, especially children with disabilities and ELLs, are able to meet the same standards.
• NCLB sets standards for teacher qualifications and certification. All teachers are to be highly qualified.	• Teacher qualification standards create problems for schools in obtaining qualified teachers. This is particularly true in urban school districts that already have teacher shortages.

What Is the Future of NCLB? It is likely that NCLB will be reauthorized by Congress in some form or another. Secretary of Education Arne Duncan supports the law's focus on accountability for student achievement. However, he wants to make the testing provision of the law less punitive and will push for a new version of the law.[15] What seems certain is that federal initiatives on standards and accountability will continue to have a powerful influence on early childhood programs.

Evaluation Research. According to the federal government, NCLB is making a difference in the lives of children. For example, the most recent national test scores show that:

- National average reading scores of fourth and eighth graders were higher in 2007 than in 1992, by 4 and 3 points, respectively.[16]
- From 1990 to 2007, the average National Assessment of Educational Progress (NAEP) mathematics scores increased 27 points for fourth graders and 19 points for eighth graders.[17]

The Early Reading First Program. The Early Reading First program was created to prepare young children to enter kindergarten with the necessary language, cognitive, and early reading skills to prevent reading difficulties and ensure school success in later grades.

Recent research on Early Reading First reveals that the program has had positive impact on the number of hours of professional development that teachers received as well as on the use of mentoring as a mode of training, the language environment of the classroom, children's book-reading practices, the variety and phonological-awareness activities, the materials and teaching practices to support print and letter knowledge and writing, and the extensiveness and recentness of child-assessment practices.[18]

Early Reading First had a positive impact on children's print and letter knowledge but not on phonological awareness or oral language.[19]

Becky Brinks, early childhood program director at Grand Rapids Community College, believes that:

> Through Early Reading First, preschool teachers receive professional development experiences and coaching in their own classrooms that enable them to immerse four-year-old children, who may be "at risk" of school failure, in research-based early literacy activities.[20]

The Reading First Program.   Reading First was enacted in 2002 as an initiative to teach reading to low-income children and is designed to promote instructional practices that are validated by scientific research. In 2008, $393 million was allocated for Reading First.[21] Reading First funding is used for:

- *Reading curricula and materials* that focus on the five essential components of reading instruction as defined in the Reading First legislation: (1) phonemic awareness, (2) phonics, (3) vocabulary, (4) fluency, and (5) comprehension
- *Professional development and coaching* for teachers on how to use scientifically based reading practices and how to work with struggling readers
- *Diagnosis and prevention* of early reading difficulties through student screening, interventions for struggling readers, and monitoring of student progress[22]

As with all things we do for and with children, we are interested in and concerned about its effectiveness in the lives of children. The *Reading First Impact Study Final Report* results indicate:[23]

- Reading First produced statistically significant positive impacts on multiple reading practices promoted by the program, such as the amount of instructional time spent on the five essential components of reading instruction and professional development in scientifically based reading instruction.[24]
- Reading First did not produce a statistically significant impact on student reading comprehension test scores in grades one, two, or three. However, there was a positive and statistically significant impact on first grade students' decoding skills in spring 2007.[25]

Congress did not reauthorize funding for Reading First beyond 2008. However, research-based reading instruction will continue in one form or another. Congress will likely authorize some kind of early reading program in the future.

Program Standards

Program standards are expectations that define the characteristics for quality in early childhood program settings, centers, and schools. For example, the National Association for the Education of Young Children (NAEYC) has developed standards for early childhood programs. The standards guide the NAEYC program accreditation process and help guide program administrators in maintaining quality. They also help parents and families make the right choice when they are looking for a child care center, preschool, or kindergarten. You can access the standards at http://www.naeyc.org/academy/primary/standardsintro.

program standards
Expectations that define the characteristics for quality in early childhood settings, centers, and schools.

NAEYC Early Learning Standards

Since standards are part of the early childhood landscape, it is reasonable to expect that professional organizations should become more involved in providing guidance and suggestions regarding the use and influence of standards. The NAEYC and the National Association of Early Childhood Specialists in State Departments of Education (NAECS/SDE) have issued a joint position statement designed to guide the development and implementation of standards for young children. As you review the following guidelines for developing standards, reflect about how they can help you as you engage in standards-based teaching.

A developmentally effective system of early learning standards must include four essential features:[26]

1. *Effective early learning standards emphasize significant, developmentally appropriate content and outcomes.*
   - Effective early learning standards give emphasis to all domains of early development and learning (including cognitive, language, physical, social, and emotional).
   - The content and desired outcomes of effective early learning standards are *meaningful and important* to children's current well-being and later learning.
   - Rather than relying on simplifications of standards for older children, the content and desired outcomes of effective early learning standards are based on research about the processes, sequences, and long-term consequences of early learning and development.
   - Effective early learning standards create appropriate expectations by linking content and desired outcomes to specific ages or developmental periods.
   - The content of effective early learning standards, and expectations for children's mastery of the standards, must accommodate variations—community, cultural, linguistic, and individual—that best support positive outcomes for all children. To do so, early learning standards must encompass the widest possible range of children's life situations and experiences, including disabilities.

2. *Effective early learning standards are developed and reviewed through informed, inclusive processes.*
   - The process of developing and reviewing early learning standards relies on relevant, valid sources of expertise.
   - The process of developing and reviewing early learning standards involves multiple stakeholders. Stakeholders may include community members, families, early childhood educators and special educators, and other professional groups. In all cases, those with specific expertise in early development and learning must be involved.
   - Once early learning standards have been developed, standards developers and relevant professional associations ensure that standards are shared with all stakeholders, creating multiple opportunities for discussion and exchange.
   - Early learning standards remain relevant and research based by using a systematic, interactive process for regular review and revision.

3. *Early learning standards gain their effectiveness through implementation and assessment practices that support all children's development in ethical, appropriate ways.*
   - Effective early learning standards require equally effective curriculum, classroom practices, and teaching strategies that connect with young children's interests and abilities, and that promote positive development and learning.
   - Tools to assess young children's progress must be clearly connected to important learning represented in the standards; must be technically, developmentally, and culturally valid; and must yield comprehensive, useful information.

- Information gained from assessments of young children's progress with respect to standards must be used to benefit children. Assessment and accountability systems should be used to improve practices and services and should not be used to rank, sort, or penalize young children.

4. *Effective early learning standards require a foundation of support for early childhood programs, professionals, and families.*
   - Research-based standards for early childhood program quality, and adequate resources for high-quality programs, build environments where standards can be implemented effectively.
   - Significant expansion of professional development is essential if all early childhood teachers and administrators are to gain the knowledge, skills, and dispositions needed to implement early learning standards.
   - Early learning standards have the most positive effects if families—key partners in young children's learning—are provided with respectful communication and support.

As the standards movement becomes more entrenched in early education, it is likely we will see more agencies issue position papers on the development and appropriate use of standards.

IMPORTANCE OF NATIONAL, STATE, AND LOCAL STANDARDS

By now, you have gained a pretty good idea that standards are playing an important role in the lives of children, teachers, families, and administrators. Let's examine some of the reasons for the prominent and important role standards have in education today.

Provide Clarity and Focus

Standards enable you to know what a district expects of its children and teachers. In this regard, they bring clarity and focus to the program curriculum and teaching. In order to know what skills need to be aligned with each other to produce the best learning experience for the child, standards have to identify the knowledge that needs to be taught. For example, reading standards for third grade have to show that students need to know how to recognize the distinguishing features of a paragraph (e.g., indentation of first word, topic sentence, supporting sentences, concluding sentences) or be able to use knowledge of prefixes (e.g., un-, re-, in-, dis-) to determine the meaning of words.

Integrate Concepts

By knowing what your district expects, you will be able to integrate concepts, ideas, and skills into your teaching. For example, if you are a preschool teacher, knowing about kindergarten standards enables you to provide your preschoolers with the language, literacy, and other skills they must have for a successful transition to kindergarten. It is important for you and other professionals to know what is expected of children at each grade level, pre-K–3, so that you can ensure your children are well prepared for learning in the next grade.

Identify What Children Should Know

Standards identify what every child in a particular state or district should know and be able to do. This is significant in that, with standards, the expectations are the same for all children, regardless of their socioeconomic backgrounds, their culture, their race or ethnicity, or where they go to school. In this sense, standards level the educational playing

Teaching, Standards, and You

There's a lot of discussion today about the education achievement gap. The achievement gap is the difference between what certain groups of children know and are able to do as opposed to what other groups of children know and are able to do. The achievement gap is wide between white children and black and Latino children. Consider this example:

> In 2007, the reading achievement gap between white and black fourth graders was smaller than in any previous assessment; however, the gap between white and Hispanic fourth graders was not measurably different in 2007 compared with 1992. In 2007, at the fourth grade level, African American children scored, on average, 27 points lower than white children (on a 0–500 scale), and Hispanics scored, on average, 26 points lower than their white peers.*

The standards are often cited as one way that teachers and schools can help all children learn what they need to know, and as a result close the achievement gap. Certainly standards do play a role in helping close achievement gaps; however, standards by themselves cannot close achievement gaps. A number of other things are required, including:

- Programs for young children at an early age that will help them gain the knowledge, skills, and behaviors necessary to succeed in school

- For every child, a high-quality teacher who is well prepared to teach all children regardless of diversity and socioeconomic background
- Programs designed to help parents gain knowledge and skills that will help them help their children get ready to learn before they come to school

In addition, here are some things you can do to make sure that you help all young children learn and close the achievement gap:

- Be familiar with your state and district standards. These standards are important because they outline what each and every child should know and be able to do, not just some children.
- Develop your lesson plans so that they incorporate state and district standards, and focus on the essential knowledge skills and behaviors that all children need to know.
- In your planning, focus on what your children will be tested on at the end of the year. You and other teachers should not "teach to the test"; however, you need to be aware of what your children will be tested on. In Chapter 6, I discuss the consequences of high-stakes testing.
- Differentiate your instruction so that you can provide for the diverse learning needs of your students. One approach

field and help ensure that all students will learn the same content and will achieve at a high level. Implementing standards is one way to help close the achievement gap. Read the accompanying Diversity Tie-In feature for steps on what you can do to help close the achievement gap.

Provide Accountability

Standards serve as one means by which states and local programs can be accountable for teaching and learning. Accountability implies that all students will achieve what the standards specify, leading to greater focus on student achievement. At the same time, advocates of greater accountability believe that more focus on student achievement for all students will narrow and hopefully eliminate the achievement gaps between races and socioeconomic classes.

All of the above reasons point to the fact that standards are an essential part of early childhood today. Hardly a teacher or classroom in the country is not impacted in some way by standards. The accompanying Professionalism in Practice feature by Gaye Gronlund, "The What and Why of Early Learning Standards," will help you make the best use of learning standards in your teaching.

does not fit all, and in today's educational environment increasing numbers of teachers differentiate their instruction to help ensure that all students can learn. Some ways to differentiate instruction are:

- Use reading buddies. Reading buddies don't have to be at the same reading level. What is important is that children are reading away from the teacher and are having opportunities to read.
- Group children for instructional purposes based on the skills they know and need to learn.
- Provide children with different levels of instructional materials. For example, see the discussion of leveled reading material in Chapter 9.
- Provide individual instruction to children who need help, such as struggling readers.
- Use peer teaching. Children learn from each other and they love to help others. Remember what Vygotsky said about "competent others" providing assistance in the zone of proximal development. (See Chapter 4.)
- Make the best use of your classroom time for instructional purposes. When children are meaningfully engaged in learning activities, there is a better chance for them to learn what they need to know and do. Remember that you have a limited amount of time with children, so strive to make the best use of it. At the same time, your teaching should be developmentally appropriate and children should be involved in activities they find interesting and worthwhile. Keep in mind also that children need opportunities to play and interact with each other.
- Integrate technology into your teaching and learning. Children enjoy technology, and technology adds interest

while at the same time it can help them learn what the standards specify.

- Work with families and parents to help them understand what you are teaching their children and why. Seek family members' cooperation so they can help support and encourage in the home what you are teaching in the classroom. Sending simple lessons home, such as a packet of learning activities that children and family members can do together, helps involve parents in the teaching–learning process and impresses on them and their children the importance of school achievement. One first grade teacher sends home each night a book bag containing books for children to read with their parents. Also included in the book bag is an evaluation sheet for the parents and students to fill out regarding the time they spent reading with their children and what they believe are areas in which they might need help.

Closing the achievement gap between cultures, races, and socioeconomic groups is always an ongoing process, but it is a process to which you have to dedicate yourself. After all, helping all children succeed is why we teach and is what we dedicate our lives to.

*National Center for Education Statistics, "Trends in the Achievement Gaps in Reading and Mathematics," Academic Outcomes: Indicator 16, November 2008; accessed February 13, 2009, from http://nces.ed.gov/programs/coe/2008/section2/indicator16.asp.

HOW ARE STANDARDS CHANGING TEACHING AND LEARNING?

As indicators of what children should know and be able to do, standards are changing the ways teachers teach, how and what students learn, and the ways schools operate. Let's review some of the ways standards are shaping teaching and learning.

Expectations of What Teachers Should Teach

When teachers ask the "What should I teach?" question, state and local standards help answer their question. However, good teachers teach more than the standards. They also teach an essential core of knowledge and skills that provides direction for the curriculum. Additionally, teachers teach individual children, plan for individual children's needs, and make decisions about what and how they should teach them. Therefore, standards serve as the baseline of expectations for teaching and learning. In this regard, standards give teachers a shared framework, based on developmentally appropriate practice, of what they should teach to children and how we know through their learning that they are growing socially, emotionally, physically, and academically.

myeducationlab

Go to the Assignments and Activities section of Topic 6: Curriculum Planning in the MyEducationLab for your course and complete the activity entitled *Designing Curriculum to Meet Standards*. Observe two teachers as they integrate and align standards with their curriculum and instructional activities.

Gaye Gronlund
Early childhood education consultant and author
Indianapolis, Indiana

As of 2009, early learning standards for preschool-age children had been developed by every state in the United States and many states are in the process of developing such standards for infants and toddlers. Early childhood educators in each state worked hard to define reasonable expectations for children from ages birth through five years that reflect the values and uniqueness of their state, as well as comply with accepted developmental understanding of how young children learn and develop. There are many similarities across these standards, as well as unique features. The National Institute for Early Education Research has a State Standards Database at its website (http://www.nieer.org) that enables comparison between the preschool standards for each state. In addition, most states have provided easy Internet access to the early learning standards they developed. Early educators should become familiar with the standards in their state and incorporate them in their curriculum planning and assessment practices.

MAKING THE BEST USE OF STANDARDS

There are benefits to early learning standards. There are also potential problems if they are used inappropriately. The benefits include:

- Reinforcement of the incredible potential for learning and growth in young children
- Help in establishing expectations for children at different ages and creating a commonality for communication among early educators
- Creation of a framework for accountability—a way for early educators to show parents, the community at large, and themselves just what children are learning

- Potential to be incorporated into curriculum that is developmentally appropriate for preschoolers—play and investigation, emergent curriculum and projects, small- and large-group times, and daily routines such as snack time, toileting and hand washing, outdoor times, and transitions
- The capability to be assessed in ways that are authentic, based on teacher observation and documentation of children's progress through photographs and work samples that can be used to show children's progress on the early learning standards

Caution should prevail when using early learning standards. Early educators committed to implementing them within a developmentally appropriate framework of curriculum and assessment must be careful to avoid the following:

- Teaching and curricular practices that overemphasize direct instruction and do not value child-initiated play and investigation with adult guidance and support
- Assessment practices that focus on testing or on-demand tasks that do not naturalistically reflect how the children demonstrate the early learning standards in everyday activities, play, investigation, and daily routines

Learning the standards for your state takes time. Figuring out ways to incorporate them into activities and daily routines, as well as assessing children's progress in authentic and naturalistic ways, may require training, dialogue among colleagues, and even some trial and error as you get started and see what works and doesn't work in your setting. Early learning standards have changed the climate of early childhood education. The accountability associated with them may be frightening or seem oppositional to traditional early childhood practices. This is not the case! They can be implemented within the context of best practices for young children. Time and effort on the part of teachers and administrators will be required to do so in ways that are just right for preschoolers.

Broad Statements About What Should Be Learned

benchmarks Statements that provide a description of student performance expected at specific grade levels, ages, or developmental levels. Benchmarks often are used in conjunction with standards.

Standards let the public, as well as parents or guardians, know what the state, district, or programs think their children should learn. Standards help early childhood teachers explain to parents what their children are learning and achieving through play. They make the job of explaining the how's and why's of what teachers do easier.

Benchmarks are more specific statements that clarify standards. They specify the level at which students will learn and identify mastery levels. As a result, teachers and parents can use the benchmarks to assess student progress. Think of benchmarks as smaller parts of the particular standards. For example, a reading standard stating that "students can comprehend what they read in a variety of literary and informational texts" may have a

STANDARDS IN A PRESCHOOL CURRICULUM

There are two ways to think about standards in a preschool curriculum: naturalistically and intentionally.

Naturalistic Approaches

Naturalistically, standards are imbedded in all that goes on in a preschool classroom. You can look back over the day with children and think about what you saw children do and heard them say. Then, you can identify which standards they were demonstrating as they played in the dramatic play area, or created at the art table, or built with the blocks.

This requires conscientious attention to what children are doing and familiarity with your state's early learning standards. The more you reflect and think about this and the more you dialogue with colleagues, the more you will see the children's progress!

Intentional Approaches

Thinking intentionally about standards is a proactive approach. You can plan for activities and materials that will directly address specific early learning standards. Again, you do not need to think in terms of direct instruction only. Your plans for children's play, projects, group times, and field trips can incorporate early learning standards. You can:

- Put together specific materials or activities that address that standard.
- Write the goals on a lesson or activity plan.
- Plan for how you will record what the children do in relation to that standard.

ASSESSING STANDARDS AUTHENTICALLY

As early educators work with children throughout each day, they are in a continual process of observing them and listening to them, as well as evaluating what they are seeing and hearing. Authentic assessment involves gathering information about a child as you work and play with him, watching him, listening to him, asking him open-ended questions to learn more about his thinking, and challenging him to try the next step. Then, you evaluate all of the information that you have learned about the child. This is where the standards come into play. They are the reference by which the child's accomplishments are measured. You ask yourself the following questions:

- Has the child accomplished a particular standard or not?
- If not, where is he on a spectrum of progress toward accomplishing the standard?
- If he has accomplished the standard, what is the next step in acquisition of skills and knowledge that he is ready for?
- What curricular plans will best meet this child where he is and help him to move on in his progress and accomplishments?

Authentic assessment through observation and reflection about each child's progress is time consuming. It is also the best and most appropriate way to get a true picture of how each child is developing in relation to the expectations in the standards. The time and effort put into documenting through observational notes, photographs, and work samples is worth it if the end result is a truer, more reliable evaluation of the child's capabilities.

CONCLUSION

Early learning standards have many benefits. They can be a wonderful guide to reasonable expectations and common goals for children in each state. They can be incorporated into developmentally appropriate preschool curriculum and authentic assessment practices. This takes commitment and hard work on the part of all involved to do what is right for young children!

Adapted with permission from Gaye Gronlund, *Make Early Learning Standards Come Alive: Connecting Your Practice and Curriculum to State Guidelines* (St. Paul, MN: Redleaf Press, 2006); special edition published unchanged in 2007 by Merrill/Prentice Hall as part of the Merrill Education/Redleaf Press College Textbook Series. © 2009 Gaye Gronlund.

benchmark stating that "students can determine the meaning of new words from their context." In another example, a standard may specify that children should get memory from print. Benchmarks for this standard would propose that infants can pay attention to books as they are read to them, that toddlers can "retell" a simple story, and that preschoolers can "read" picture books.

A Basis for Reform and Accountability

Standards help the public and politicians hold teachers and schools accountable for ensuring that children learn. As I pointed out in Chapter 2, using standards as a basis for accountability, teachers can no longer say, "I taught Maria reading." Now the question is: "Did Maria learn

What scientific foundational knowledge are children learning from this activity? Are they learning in a developmentally appropriate way? Identify two other activities that you could use to help kindergarten children learn scientific knowledge.

to read?" Even more important from an accountability point of view is the question: "Did Maria achieve the benchmark of being able to read at or above her grade level?"

Exert Federal and State Control of Education

Primarily, education is a state function. Historically, states have delegated the responsibility for education to local districts and programs. However, beginning in about 1995, states have increasingly taken more control for educating children, monitoring teaching, and holding schools accountable for student achievement. State standards are one example of this. Not everyone is happy about or satisfied with this state and federal control of education, for a number of reasons. First, they claim that federal control of education takes away from the ability of local programs to develop their own programs based on what they think are best for their children. Essentially this is a local control of schools idea and is embedded in the belief that local communities know what is best for their children. Second, some early childhood educators believe that federal control is leading to the implementations of programs that are developmentally inappropriate for young children, especially preschool and kindergarten children. However, standards are now a part of the political and educational landscape.

Meet the Educational Needs of Low-Achieving Students

Most standards are considered to be the minimum necessary for grade-level achievement. In this way, they help ensure that all children will be taught what they need to know to accomplish the skills appropriate for their grade level. There has always been a concern that low-socioeconomic-status children are not being taught or challenged to achieve. Teaching to the standards addresses this issue and helps to prevent failure and school dropout.

Make the Curriculum More Academic

In particular, standards have caused a greater emphasis on academics in pre-kindergarten and kindergarten. According to Pre-K Now, eighteen states currently meet eight or more of the ten-quality checklist criteria for its pre-kindergarten program, according to the National Institute for Early Education Research (NIEER).[27] Currently thirty-eight states and the District of Columbia have specified standards for pre-kindergarten.[28] While there are standards for music and the arts, standards for reading, writing, math, and science receive the majority of the teaching attention.

Align Teaching and the Curriculum

curriculum alignment
The process of matching curriculum to the standards and tests that measure student achievement.

In **curriculum alignment**, the official curriculum of the school district and that taught by individual teachers is matched to the content standards. **Alignment** is the process of making sure that the curriculum and what teachers teach are what the standards specify. Standards encourage curriculum alignment and, as a result, teachers select materials and learning experiences based on specific outcomes for children's learning. As federal pressure for

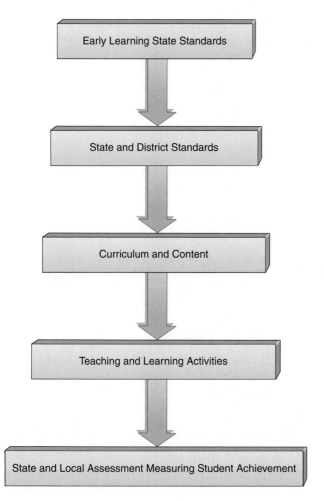

FIGURE 5.1 Alignment of Standards, Curriculum, Activities, and Assessment

accountability standards moves into the preschool arena, it is important for states to rapidly develop processes that align preschool standards with K–12 standards and evaluate how prepared children are to succeed in school. Figure 5.1 shows the way early learning standards, state and district standards, curriculum and content, teaching and learning activities, and assessment support learning objectives.

In Harold Yun's third grade class, he is teaching his students about plants. Read the example below to see how he uses alignment to help his children learn what the standards state.

Science—Third Grade

Life Science

Content Standard: 1.0 Cell Structure and Function

The student will investigate the structure and function of plant and animal cells.

Learning Expectations—Cell Structure

3.1.1 Recognize that living things are made up of smaller parts.

  • Use magnifiers to study the smaller parts of plants and identify their functions.

3.1.2 Recognize that smaller parts of living things contribute to the operation and well-being of entire organisms.
- Use magnifiers to observe and describe what occurs when a plant loses a specific part (e.g., leaves, roots).
- Recognize that smaller parts of organisms are essential to their well-being.

Third Grade Benchmarks

Investigate and describe how plants pass through distinct stages in their life cycle including growth, survival, and reproduction.

Instruction:	Read a book about the characteristics of plants.
Assessment of Learning:	Label parts of a plant on a drawing based on your observations.[29]

Integrating technology into the curriculum is another way to align standards, teaching, and learning. Technology is also a developmentally appropriate way to assess young children and measure their achievement. The accompanying Technology Tie-In feature helps you get a feeling for how one elementary school integrates technology across the curriculum to help children meet all state standards.

National Standards

National standards are, as the name implies, designed to be applicable to all children, regardless of individual state or local standards. Many professionals think some of the provisions of the No Child Left Behind Act, such as the emphasis on early literacy and reading, constitute national standards.

The Head Start performance standards are another example of national standards. In Chapter 4 we discussed these performance standards. The Head Start Program Performance Standards (http://www.acf.hhs.gov/programs/ohs/legislation/index.html) and Outcomes Framework (http://www.hsnrc.org/CDI/pdfs/UGCOF.pdf) guide programs in their operation. Major elements of the standards include early childhood development, health services, family and community partnerships, staffing, and program design and management. The Head Start Outcomes Framework acts as a national curriculum in that other preschool programs in addition to Head Start use them to guide what their children should know and do. The Outcomes Framework also helps ensure that all Head Start children, regardless of the state or program they are in, receive the same curriculum. Take a moment to review the Outcomes Framework shown in Appendix B.

Some professionals dislike the term "national" because it implies an erosion of state authority over public schools. On the other hand, proponents of the national standards argue that given the patchwork of state standards currently in place, it will be difficult if not impossible for the United States to compete on the global economic stage without national standards. Not everyone agrees that national standards from any source are good for the nation's children. Some argue that national standards, by their very nature, do not address the unique needs of children at the local level. They further argue that the needs of rural and urban children differ and that children's needs also differ by geographic region. However, others argue that national standards help ensure that all children in every state will learn a basic core of knowledge and skills. They further argue that this common curriculum does not preclude teachers in local districts and programs from teaching to the particular needs of their children.

The reality is that national standards are on the way in the form of common state standards. Governors and state commissioners of education across the country are committing to joining a state-led process to develop a common core of state standards in English language arts and mathematics for grades K–12. These standards will be research and evidence based, internationally benchmarked, aligned with college and work expectations, and will include rigorous content and skills.[30]

Technology Across the Curriculum

Preparing students to participate productively in a digital world is an important educational goal. Finding ways to achieve this goal is the challenge of all educators. Children, teachers, and schools all across the country are in different stages of using technology to facilitate and support teaching and learning. Many schools have progressed from simply teaching technology to integrating technology across the curriculum. As a result, teachers don't spend a lot of time teaching specific technology skills; rather, they integrate the technology skills into their curriculum.

Carolina Beach Elementary School and Anderson Elementary provide good examples of how teachers integrate technology in all curriculum areas. They use technology to teach skills and concepts related to the content areas (e.g., math, science, literacy), and knowledge and skills specified by North Carolina State Standards. Here are some examples of how technology is integrated into teaching lessons:

Reading: Kindergarten

- **Science**—Classify Animals—Students use interactive whiteboards to place animals into a Venn diagram.
- **Language Arts**—Students access Education City, a web-based program aligned with the North Carolina Standard Course of Study, to learn about sound and letter recognition.
- **Math**—Students use an interactive whiteboard to create patterns.

First Grade

- **Social Studies**—Students utilize Google Earth, an online resource, to virtually visit a location they've been learning about.
- **Science**—In KidPix, students create a Venn diagram to teach, compare, and contrast environments of animals. Label—Land, Water, and Both. Stamp animals in the correct area.
- **Language Arts**—Students use the word processing software Scholastic Keys MaxWrite to write their Core Words. Several software programs give students the individual help they need with blends, rhyming words, and beginning and ending sounds.
- **Math**—Students use a software program called Scholastic Keys MaxData to create spreadsheets with data obtained from tracking weather for a week.

Second Grade

- Use AlphaSmarts to create stories.
- **Science**—Students use a WebQuest on weather. Students create a picture with a sentence about each season during the year. At the end of the year they create a multimedia presentation in Scholastic Keys MaxShow.
- **Social Studies and Language Arts**—Students create a classroom book on community workers. Using a word-processing program, students write about their community workers and import a graphic on the subject for the book.
- Students search an Accelerated Reader database for books on their level.

Teachers at Carolina Beach and Anderson are enthusiastic about utilizing technology resources. For example, second grade teacher Cathy Byrd says, "Technology allows me to differentiate learning in my classroom in a way we couldn't have imagined even ten years ago. It also allows me to expand the walls of my classroom so the children can virtually travel around the community and world."

Your use of technology to help you be a high-quality teacher depends on a number of factors:

- Your belief in the power of technology to help children learn
- Your willingness to learn about and use technology in your teaching
- The technology resources available to you and your school
- The support of administrators for using technology in the classroom

Here are some things you can do to ensure that technology is an integrated part of your teaching:

- Collaborate with colleagues to develop ways to integrate technology in grade-level programs and across grades.
- Collaborate with and involve parents and the community. Many parents have technology skills and connections they can share with your students. Many community agencies, such as the police and health departments, use technology to solve problems. Community people make great classroom speakers and mentors.
- Create a classroom environment that encourages and enables students to help each other learn technology skills and applications. Children are very adept at helping their peers learn new skills.

WHAT ARE ISSUES ASSOCIATED WITH NATIONAL, STATE, AND LOCAL STANDARDS?

By now, through our discussion of standards, you are aware that a number of controversies and issues swirl around standards and their use. Let's examine some of these issues.

Standards and Achievement

Critics of standards-based education argue that standards focus too much on academic achievement and that other areas of the curriculum such as social and emotional development get left behind. High-quality teachers always teach to the whole child—the physical, social, emotional, linguistic, and cognitive. This is the foundation of early childhood education. For example, kindergarten teacher Karen Reid, 2009–2010 Teacher of the Year at Morris Grove Elementary, Chapel Hill–Carrboro City Schools in North Carolina, says:

> Assessment data is necessary to guide instruction, as well as to document progress, but educating the "whole child" often begins the process of helping the children realize their worth and their potential to make contributions as a well-rounded and productive citizen. Children need to know that we care about and value them.[31]

Standards and Play

Critics of standards assert that standards promote a traditional back-to-basics approach to early childhood education at the expense of play-based and child-centered teaching and learning. Whole-child education, child-centered education, and play-based education are three building blocks of early childhood education. Play and standards are not incompatible. I have provided you many examples of how teachers achieve standards through play (see for example the Professionalism in Practice feature, "How to Promote Preschoolers' Cognitive Development," in Chapter 8 on page 211).

Standards and the Curriculum

Many believe standards narrow the curriculum and force "teaching to the test." In some programs and classrooms, the standards may *become* the curriculum so that students pass state proficiency exams. While in a sense this issue may be true, it need not be so. There is no reason why standards should narrow the curriculum or what is taught. Effective teachers always have and always will teach a wide and rich range of knowledge and skills based on local community needs and the needs of young children. For example, here is how first grade teacher Jennifer Atkinson incorporates the community into her science teaching:

> Annually, the 1st grade at Metz Elementary School [Austin, Texas] hosts a visit from Fry's Farm to coincide with our science unit on animal groups. Each class gets uninterrupted time with several different furry, sweet mammals and fluffy comical ducks, chickens, and geese. The kids absolutely adore this special event and it adds to real life understanding of animal groups we are learning about in our science unit.[32]

Standards and Teacher Autonomy

Some argue that standards impose too much structure on early childhood teachers who have a tradition of having the freedom to develop their own curriculum and classroom activities. As I previously indicated, effective teachers always teach what they think is important in the best ways possible. I meet and interact with many teachers of the year. All of them emphasize that they teach children, not standards. LaWanda Rainey-Hall,

2009–2010 Teacher of the Year at Glenwood Elementary, Chapel Hill-Carrboro City Schools in North Carolina, says:

> I feel that my ability to differentiate instruction and challenge each student individually to produce his/her best work makes me an outstanding teacher. I'm constantly aware of the range of abilities that my learners have and as a result, I consistently assess and teach using a variety of teaching methods that embrace and incorporate different learning styles and varied learning experiences. Knowing my students' personalities and working with families helps me design a content-rich program that includes their diverse learning needs, but also can be fun for all of us.[33]

Standards and Testing

Critics of standards believe they lead to an overemphasis on assessment and testing. This may well be true, but proponents argue that testing is necessary to verify that children are learning. In reality, standards, instruction, and assessment, when well integrated, provide a process that helps ensure all children learn. See for example our discussion of data-driven instruction in Chapter 10.

Standards for All Students

Are state standards for all children? Not everyone agrees that they are. Many teachers of children with special needs believe that standards and tests designed for normally developing or native English-speaking children are inappropriate for children with disabilities or different linguistic backgrounds. However, they do apply to children with disabilities and special learning conditions. The U.S. Department of Education has been quite clear in this point. Under the No Child Left Behind Act (NCLB), states and local schools are held accountable for ensuring that all children—including children with disabilities—learn. Children with disabilities must be included in the assessment system required under NCLB, and schools must report their results through NCLB's adequate yearly progress (AYP) structure. The Individuals with Disabilities Education Act (IDEA) requires that the IEP team determine *how* the child with a disability is assessed, not *whether* the child is assessed (see Chapter 11 for information on IEPs). IDEA recognizes that children learn in different ways, with different methods of instruction and assessment. The IEP team is required to determine which accommodations are necessary, how to instruct the child, and how to assess the child.[34] The Accommodating Diverse Learners section below describes how standards apply to children with culturally diverse backgrounds.

Accommodating Diverse Learners

As an early childhood teacher you will have ELLs in your classroom and you will need to help them meet local and state standards. One way to make standards applicable to ELLs is to provide an environment that both stimulates and accommodates them. For all children, but especially English language learners (ELLs), the classroom should be a place your students feel welcome, comfortable, and safe. Here are some things you can do, for instance, to make your first grade classroom as inclusive as possible and conducive to both native speakers and English learners so that all children meet the standards:

- Label classroom objects in multiple languages. Use English and Spanish (or other languages) to label desks, art supplies, folders, and cubbies.
- Post class rules in English and in other languages. In addition, accompany the words with pictures to strengthen comprehension.
- Keep schedules and routines consistent until you are sure that all the ELL children understand the daily practices.

How to Plan Lessons That Meet Standards

When sitting down to create lesson plans, I always keep the following quotation in mind: "You cannot control the wind [i.e., state or district standards] but you can adjust your sails [i.e., personal lesson plans]." As you review the following steps, remember that lesson plans are to *guide* instruction; they are not a blueprint that must control your every word. You should always follow a wonderful teachable moment, even if it is not written into your lesson plan. You will never regret where it leads you and your students.

STEP 1 BECOME FAMILIAR WITH BOTH STATE AND DISTRICT STANDARDS

The objectives in my district's teacher's guide are clearly stated and are usually cross-referenced with the broader Florida Sunshine State Standards. Realize that standards encompass broad categories and often do not change significantly from one grade level to another. For example, "Reads for meaning" and "Uses context clues" apply to many grade levels; what changes is the level of presentation.

STEP 2 INCORPORATE IN YOUR PLANS WHAT WILL BE ASSESSED ON HIGH-STAKES TESTS

I work into my lesson plans for all subjects the Florida Comprehensive Assessment Test task cards (e.g., compare/contrast, vocabulary, author's purpose, main idea, details,

multiple representations of information, cause and effect) and the big five literacy components—phonological awareness, phonics, vocabulary, comprehension, and fluency.

STEP 3 PLAN A WEEK AHEAD

Planning ahead has several advantages:

- As you plan ahead, you think ahead. Just thinking about what you're going to teach enables you to see how standards and your instructional practices fit together.
- Planning ahead allows you to share ideas with your colleagues, get their advice, and make changes as appropriate.
- Planning ahead gives you time to gather all necessary materials and resources.

STEP 4 MEET WITH OTHER TEACHERS TO COORDINATE PLANS

As the chairperson for grade three, I hold a weekly planning meeting with the other third grade teachers. We explore the information required to be presented the following week and plan together. Because my district uses the same authored curriculum across the county, we all teach from a particular reading series. This is extremely helpful with our somewhat transient population in Miami and allows for continuity as students move.

- Have ELL children (and children with learning or language differences) sit in areas that provide adequate visual and tactile access to information, such as near you during circle time, close to the blackboard or overhead, and facing your direction while you are talking. Children who are learning a new language should not have to depend on purely auditory input to gain information.

- Color-code materials to reinforce word meaning, purpose, and categorization. For example, print all homework on blue paper, vocabulary on yellow paper, math on pink paper, handouts on white paper, and notes that go home on green paper. Pencils belong in a red container, while markers belong in an orange container, and so forth.

- Keep an open dialogue about different cultures, languages, and countries so that ELL students feel welcomed and included rather than unusual or excluded by engaging in active discussion, storytelling, and sharing.

- Encourage diversity and acceptance of individual differences.

- Allow ELL students time to use and develop their native languages. Bilingualism is an important and valuable skill!

You will want to set high standards for all your children and then help them meet them. For example South Bend, Indiana, 2009 Teacher of the Year Tania Harman teaches ELLs. Harman adjusts her teaching style to meet the needs of each student:

> Every student does not learn the same way, at the same pace, nor have the same schema to build on for meaningful lessons. My lessons reflect that knowledge. I present information to

STEP 5 CREATE AND SAVE A FRAMEWORK FOR YOUR LESSON PLANS

Because parts of lessons are repeated week after week, using a consistent framework saves valuable time. On a computer I can cut and paste from week to week, adding or removing entries quickly.

STEP 6 DIFFERENTIATE INSTRUCTION

Once the framework for lesson planning is understood you are ready to "adjust your sails"—that is, differentiate your instruction. As an inclusion teacher, one-third of my students have exceptional needs, so I differentiate my instruction. I must adjust my presentation rather than expecting my learners to modify themselves to my presentation. Because there are varied abilities and disabilities within any given classroom, instructional practices and approaches should always be adapted to the students served within the classroom. In other words, instruction should meet the learners wherever they are and appeal to them on a multisensory level.

For instance, I plan vocabulary practice daily within every lesson plan (e.g., math vocabulary, science vocabulary, story vocabulary). Because not all students are at the same level in vocabulary development, I do the following:

- Present vocabulary on an overhead.
- Use colored markers on the overhead to separate and isolate vocabulary words.
- Use hearing and seeing sticks (i.e., rulers with an ear or an eye and a vocabulary word stapled on them). Students raise the stick when they hear or see the vocabulary word.

- Use a highlighter stick (i.e., a yardstick with an index card stapled to the end of it). When the vocabulary words are projected on the wall, I can hold the index card over a word and actually lift the word off the wall by lifting the card.

OTHER PLANNING AND INSTRUCTIONAL GUIDELINES

I recommend overplanning. Activities that you think will take a certain amount of time will often take much less or much more. This is fine—you are working with children! Simply cut and paste a missed lesson into the next week's framework, or discontinue a lesson that is not working for you and move on to your next planned activity.

I also recommend moving your students often. Begin with a whole-group activity, and then transition to a partner activity. I place my students in groups of six rather than having them sit in rows. Within each grouping I place at least two children with special needs and have the group come up with a name and work as a small community. I also set up centers that allow for higher-order processing. Centers give me an opportunity to work with some students who may require more intensive instruction.

Lesson planning is a learned skill, and learned skills take time to master. Ask to see other teachers' lesson plans, ask them what works, and use any ideas that interest you.

....

Contributed by Lynn Carrier, third grade teacher, Gulfstream Elementary, Miami, Florida, and 2007 Miami–Dade County Teacher of the Year.

---

my students based on the effort to get to know them, and I differentiate instruction in order to teach to their differing strengths. Knowing my students is a powerful way to get to the heart of a lesson for each individual.[35]

The accompanying Professionalism in Practice feature by Lynn Carrier, "How to Plan Lessons That Meet Standards," provides an example of how you can develop lesson plans that meet students' needs and standards.

The Contributions of Standards

We can conclude our discussion of standards by asking ourselves: Why is this important to us?

The standards movement has done a number of things for the early childhood profession as well as teachers and young children. Standards have helped the profession sharpen its focus about what young children should know and be able to do. As a result, many early childhood professionals have come to the conclusion that young children are more capable than they realized or gave them credit for. As James J. Heckman, 2000 Nobel laureate in Economic Sciences, points out:

Learning starts in infancy, long before formal education begins, and continues throughout life. Early learning begets later learning and early success breeds later success, just as early failure breeds later failure. Success or failure at this stage lays the foundation for

success or failure in school, which in turn leads to success or failure in post-school learning. Recent studies of early childhood investments have shown remarkable success and indicate that the early years are important for early learning. Moreover, early childhood interventions of high quality have lasting effects on learning and motivation. As a society, we cannot afford to postpone investing in children until they become adults, nor can we wait until they reach school age—a time when it may be too late to intervene.[36]

As early childhood professionals have rediscovered the children they teach, they are in the process of rediscovering themselves. Teachers are engaged in more professional development than ever before and much of this professional development involves learning how to teach with standards. In this sense, standards have reenergized the teaching profession.

My hope for you is that you will embrace teaching with standards and that you will help all children learn to their highest levels.

Standards provide a number of challenges and opportunities for early childhood professionals. Determining developmentally effective ways to help children master the knowledge and skills in specified standards is one challenge, which can be met by involving children in active play with concrete materials that support their learning.

ACTIVITIES FOR PROFESSIONAL DEVELOPMENT

ethical dilemma

"Test or Leave?"

Michelle Hu teaches in a preschool for three- to four-year-olds that is funded with federal dollars. Her administrator has sent out a memo announcing they have developed a testing program designed to measure children's preschool achievement and the effectiveness of programs funded with federal dollars. All four-year-olds will be tested on their knowledge, skills, and readiness for kindergarten using the locally developed paper-and-pencil achievement test. Michelle believes such a test is developmentally inappropriate and it is unfair to "test" preschool children using the prescribed test.

What should Michelle do? Should she share her concerns with the school administrator and risk the administrator's disapproval, or should she administer a test she believes is developmentally inappropriate?

PEARSON
myeducationlab

To check your comprehension on the content covered in Chapter 5, go to the Book Specific Resources in the MyEducationLab for your course, select your text, and complete the Study Plan. Here you will be able to take a chapter quiz and receive feedback on your answers.

Application Activities

1. How can you answer the question: "Are standards meeting their intended purpose of helping ensure that each and every child will achieve and learn?" One way to answer this question is to create or join a blog. I find that many outstanding teachers have blogs that you can join and ask this and other questions.

2. Review your state standards for the grade you plan to teach. Did anything surprise you about what the standards specify children should know and learn? Create an online discussion with your classmates and ask for their opinions about standards.

3. Read again the Professionalism in Practice feature, "How to Plan Lessons That Meet Standards," on pages 138–139. Use the six steps to write a plan for the grade and subject of your choice.

4. Select the grade that you plan to teach (e.g., kindergarten) and compare the state standards for your grade with the standards from another state. One conclusion you may draw is that the content of standards across states is similar. What other conclusions can you draw? Which state do you think has the "better" standards? Why?

5. Interview one kindergarten and one third grade teacher. Ask them how state standards are affecting their teaching. Ask them to share with you their feelings—pros and cons—about standards.

chapter six

OBSERVING AND ASSESSING YOUNG CHILDREN

Guiding, Teaching, and Learning

NAEYC Standards for Early Childhood Professional Preparation

Standard 3: Observing, Documenting, and Assessing to Support Young Children and Families

I know about and understand the goals, benefits, and uses of assessment. I know about and use systematic observations, documentation, and other effective assessment strategies in a responsible way, in partnership with families and other professionals, to positively influence the development of every child.[1]

 Kindergarten Teacher Tyron Jones wants to make sure Amanda knows the initial beginning sounds he taught the class during the last two weeks. First grade teacher Mindy McArthur wants to see how many words on the class word wall César knows. Third grade team builder Shannon Keller wants to know if all the third graders are ready for the upcoming state exam. Decisions, decisions, decisions. All of these decisions relate to how to assess learning and teaching.

Teachers' minutes, hours, and days are filled with assessment decisions. Questions abound: "What is Jeremy ready for now?" "What can I tell Maria's parents about her language development?" "The activity I used in the large-group time yesterday didn't seem to work well. What could I have done differently?" Appropriate assessment can help you find the answers to these and many other questions relating to what to teach, how to teach, and what is best for children in their particular stages of development.

WHAT IS ASSESSMENT?

"Teaching without assessment is like driving a car without headlights."[2] Teaching in the dark does not benefit anyone, you or your children. In today's educational climate, assessment is an invaluable tool to guide your teaching and your students' learning.

Your children's lives, both in and out of school, are influenced by your assessment and the assessment of others. As an early childhood professional, assessment will influence your professional life and will be a vital part of your professional practice. Effective assessment is one of your most important responsibilities, and it can enhance your teaching and children's learning.

As defined in Chapter 1, according to the National Association for the Education of Young Children, *assessment* is the process of observing, recording, and otherwise documenting what children do and how they do it as a basis for a variety of educational decisions that affect the child:

> Assessment involves the multiple steps of collecting data on a child's development and learning, determining its significance in light of the program goals and objectives, incorporating the information into planning for individuals and programs, and communicating the findings to families and other involved people. Assessment of child progress is integral to curriculum and instruction. In early childhood programs, the various assessments of child progress procedures that are used serve several purposes:
> a. to plan instruction for individuals and groups
> b. to communicate with families
> c. to identify children who may be in need of specialized services or intervention
> d. to inform program development[3]

WHY IS IT IMPORTANT FOR YOU TO KNOW HOW TO ASSESS CHILDREN AND FAMILIES?

Assessment is important because it involves the majority of the decisions you will make about children when teaching and caring for them. The decisions facing our three teachers at the beginning of this chapter all involve how best to educate children. Like them, you will be called upon every day to make decisions before, during, and after your teaching. Whereas some of these decisions will seem small and inconsequential, others will involve high stakes, influencing the life course of children. All of your assessment decisions taken as a whole will direct and alter children's learning outcomes.

FOCUS QUESTIONS

1. What is assessment?

2. Why is it important for you to know how to assess children and families?

3. What are the purposes and uses of observation and assessment and what are some ways you can assess children's development, learning, and behavior?

4. What are the types of assessment teachers use?

5. What are the contexts that influence the use of assessments?

6. What are issues of assessment?

Figure 6.1 outlines for you some purposes of assessment and how assessment can enhance your teaching and student learning. All of these purposes are important; if you use assessment procedures appropriately, you will help all children learn well.

Principles of Assessment

As you think about the role assessment will play in your teaching, reflect on how the following general principles should guide both policies and practices for the assessment of young children:

- *Assessment should bring about benefits for children.* Gathering accurate information from young children is difficult and potentially stressful. Assessments must have a clear benefit—either in direct services to the child or in improved quality of educational programs.

- *Assessment should be tailored to a specific purpose and should be reliable, valid, and fair for that purpose.* Assessments designed for one purpose are not necessarily valid if used for other purposes. In the past, many of the abuses of testing with young children have occurred because of misuse.

- *Assessment policies should be designed recognizing that reliability and validity of assessments increase with children's age.* The younger the child, the more difficult it is to obtain reliable and valid assessment data. It is particularly difficult to assess children's cognitive abilities accurately before age six. Because of problems with reliability and validity, some types of assessment should be postponed until children are older, while other types of assessment can be pursued, but only with necessary safeguards.

- *Assessment should be age appropriate in both content and the method of data collection.* Assessments of young children should address the full range of early learning and development, including physical well-being and motor development; social and emotional development; approaches toward learning; language development; and cognition and general knowledge. Methods of assessment should recognize that children need familiar contexts to be able to demonstrate their abilities. Abstract paper-and-pencil tasks may make it especially difficult for young children to show what they know.

- *Assessment should be linguistically appropriate, recognizing that to some extent all assessments are measures of language.* Regardless of whether an assessment is intended to measure early reading skills, knowledge of color names, or learning potential, assessment results are easily confounded by language proficiency, especially for children who come from home backgrounds with limited exposure to English, for whom the assessment would essentially be an assessment of their English proficiency. Each child's first- and second-language development should be taken into account when determining appropriate assessment methods and in interpreting the meaning of assessment results.

- *Parents should be a valued source of assessment information, as well as an audience for assessment.* Because of the fallibility of direct measures of young children, assessments should include multiple sources of evidence, especially reports from parents and teachers. Assessment results should be shared with parents as part of an ongoing process that involves parents in their child's education.[4]

Reporting to and Communicating with Parents and Families

Part of your responsibility as a professional is to report to parents and, when appropriate, to other primary caregivers about the growth, development, and achievement of their children. Reporting to and communicating with families is one of your most important

FIGURE 6.1

Purposes of Assessment

Children

- Identify what children know.
- Identify children's special needs.
- Determine appropriate placement.
- Select appropriate curricula to meet children's individual needs.
- Refer children and, as appropriate, their families for additional services to programs and agencies.

Families

- Communicate with parents to provide information about their children's progress and learning.
- Relate school activities to home activities and experiences.

Early Childhood Programs

- Make policy decisions regarding what is and is not appropriate for children.
- Determine how well and to what extent programs and services children receive are beneficial and appropriate.

Early Childhood Teachers

- Identify children's skills, abilities, and needs.
- Make lesson and activity plans and set goals.
- Create new classroom arrangements.
- Select materials.
- Make decisions about how to implement learning activities.
- Report to parents and families about children's developmental status and achievement.
- Monitor and improve the teaching–learning process.
- Meet the individual needs of children.
- Group children for instruction.

The Public

- Inform the public regarding children's achievement.
- Provide information relating to students' school-wide achievements.
- Provide a basis for public policy (e.g., legislation, recommendations, and statements).

Report your assessment findings accurately and honestly to the parents of your students. How might such communication build trust?

jobs. The following guidelines will help you meet this important responsibility of reporting assessment information to parents:

- *Be honest and realistic with parents.* Too often, teachers do not want to hurt parents' feelings. They want to sugarcoat what they are reporting. However, parents and guardians need your honest assessments about what their children know, are able to do, and will be able to do. With this honest assessment you can solicit their help in helping their children.
- *Communicate with parents so they can understand.* What you communicate to parents must make sense to them. They must understand what you are saying. Reporting to parents often has to be a combination of written (in their language) and oral communication.
- *Provide parents with ideas and information that will help them help their children learn.* Remember that you and parents are partners in helping children be successful in school and life.

Systematic assessment of children represents a powerful way for you to learn about, guide, and direct children's learning and behavior. If you learn to use it well, you and your children will benefit.

USING OBSERVATON TO ASSESS

observation The intentional, systematic act of looking at the behavior of a child or children in a particular setting, program, or situation; sometimes referred to as *kid-watching*.

Professionals recognize that children are more than what is measured by any particular standardized test. Observation is an "authentic" means of learning about children—what they know and are able to do, especially as it occurs in more naturalistic settings such as classrooms, child care centers, playgrounds, and homes—and it is one of the most widely used methods of assessment. Observation is the intentional, systematic act of looking at the behavior of a child or children in a particular setting, program, or situation. Observation is sometimes referred to as "kid-watching" and is an excellent way to find out about children's behaviors and learning.

Purposes of Observation

Observation is designed to gather information on which to base decisions, make recommendations, develop curriculum, plan activities and learning strategies, and assess children's growth, development, and learning. For example, when professionals and parents sometimes look at children, they do not really "see" or concern themselves with what the children are doing or why. However, through a careful, planned, and systematic observation, you will be better able to "see" what your children are like and what they know and are able to do.

However, the significance and importance of critical behaviors go undetected if observation is done casually and is limited to "unsystematic looking." In order for you to make your observation meaningful, keep in mind that the purposes of observation are to:

- *Determine the cognitive, linguistic, social, emotional, and physical development of children.* Using a developmental checklist is one way professionals can systematically observe and chart the development of children. (Figure 6.6 later in this chapter shows a checklist for inclusive classrooms.)

Go to the Assignments and Activities section in Topic 4: Observation/Assessment in the MyEducationLab for your course and complete the activity entitled *Observing Children in Authentic Contexts.* This teacher is able to authentically assess the knowledge and skills acquired by the children during this self-selected play activity.

- *Identify children's interests and learning styles.* Today, teachers are very interested in developing learning activities, materials, and classroom centers based on children's interests, preferences, and learning styles.
- *Plan.* The professional practice of teaching requires planning on a daily, ongoing basis. Observation provides useful, authentic, and solid information that enables teachers to intentionally plan for activities rather than make decisions with little or no information.
- *Meet the needs of individual children.* Meeting the needs of individual children is an important part of teaching and learning. For example, a child may be advanced cognitively but overly aggressive and lacking the social skills necessary to play cooperatively and interact with others. Through observation, a teacher can gather information to develop a plan for helping the child learn how to play with others.
- *Determine progress.* Systematic observation, over time, provides a rich, valuable, and informative source of information about how individuals and groups of children are progressing in their learning and behavior.
- *Provide information to parents.* Professionals report to and conference with parents on an ongoing basis. Observational information adds to other information they have, such as test results and child work samples, and provides a fuller and more complete picture of individual children.
- *Provide self-insight.* Observational information can help professionals learn more about themselves and what to do to help children.

Systematic observation each day will enable you to meet children's learning needs and be a more effective teacher. In the Professionalism in Practice feature, "Making a Difference," second grade teacher Lu Ann Harger shares her perspective on assessment and evaluation.

Advantages of Gathering Data Through Observations

Intentional observation is a useful, informative, and powerful means for informing and guiding teaching and for helping ensure that all children learn. Knowing the advantages of gathering data through observation will enable the researcher to understand a child's development and learning style and assess them. Here are six advantages of gathering data through observation:

- *Enables professionals to collect information about children that they might not otherwise gather through other sources.* A great deal of the consequences, causes, and reactions to children's behavior can be assessed only through observation. Observation enables you to gather data that cannot be assessed by formal, standardized tests, questioning, and parent and child interviews.

Observing is an excellent way to find out about a child's behavior and how well he or she is learning. What do you think you can learn about children from watching them interact socially with each other to complete puzzles and other fine-motor activities?

- *Ideally suited to learning more about children in play settings.* Observation affords you the opportunity to note a child's social behavior in a play group and discern how cooperatively he or she interacts with peers. Observing a child at play gives professionals a wealth of information about developmental levels, social skills, and what the child is or is not learning in play settings.
- *Allows you to learn a lot about children's pro-social behavior and peer interactions.* It can help you plan for appropriate and inclusive activities to promote the social growth

Lu Ann Harger
Second grade teacher,
Hinkle Creek Elementary
Noblesville, Indiana

There are many ways to make a difference in a child's life. As a teacher, each year you are given the enormous honor of spending eight hours a day creating within a child a burning desire for learning. You have the opportunity to introduce your children to the wonders of numbers, letters, words, and the history of their nation. You have the ability to create the "what if" and the "tell me more" in minds each day. But where to start this daunting task is difficult to say.

BEGINNING OF THE SCHOOL YEAR

All things have a beginning, and nothing equals a sound beginning. Each year as the school year is ready to begin, I call all my students to introduce myself and our classroom, Camp Can Do, and put their minds at ease. Fear of the unknown is a great deterrent to success, and this phone call goes a long way in calming that fear. I ask them to bring a thinking cap along to help on tough assignments and, of course, I keep mine handy all year too!

As they begin the first week of school, activities are planned to get to know each other and to evaluate levels of learning. Students play the M&M game by choosing a handful and speaking about themselves according to the colors. Each child gets a chance to say the alphabet, show me crayons to match color words, read a set of selected grade-level word lists, and read a passage aloud to me. As a class, we sit in community circle and use cards to stimulate discussions. That way I can check for verbal expression, use of vocabulary words, life experiences, and comfort levels. Students also fill out a reading inventory on their likes and dislikes, play math games to show computation skills, and copy some basic words to evaluate their fine-motor skills.

FAMILY PARTICIPATION

Now that I am on the right track evaluating my students, I work on my other team members: my family members. At the beginning of each school year at Parent Night, parents and guardians are asked to provide information about their child. Sure, I have permanent records to look over but the primary caregivers are the experts. They share fears and acts of bravery, favorites, past school experiences, and special traits of their children. With their help I will gain a better understanding of their child, and they will understand how much I value their input. During the meeting I explain how our classroom, or Camp Can Do, is run and what we do each day. I also explain the importance of their role as communicator, coach, and study partner. In the end, I read *Leo the Late Bloomer* and reiterate that my plan this year is for everyone to make it, just like Leo. Now I have the complete package: family input, student files, and my classroom evaluations. This is a sound beginning. Using this information, I can set up learning profiles for all my students that will be used throughout the year.

ASSESSMENT AND CURRICULUM

As the year's curriculum begins to unfold, I gather new information. In math, I pretest before each chapter to see what students know and do not know. Then throughout the lessons I group students according to their needs. Students work in many different groups by the year's end as their mastery of math skills is checked. Students are able to work on weak areas like time and money, but expand areas in which they are strong, like addition computation. In spelling, lists are modified according to learning levels. Everyone gets an opportunity to try the bonus words and earn a chance for spelling prizes. In reading and language arts, students work in small and large groups. They begin to take home

of young children. Additionally, your observations can serve as the basis for developing multicultural activities to benefit all children.

- *Provides a basis for the assessment of what children are developmentally able to do.* Many learning skills are developed sequentially, such as the refinement of large-motor skills before fine-motor skills. Through observation, professionals can determine whether children's abilities are within a normal range of growth and development.

- *Useful to assess children's performance over time.* Documentation of daily, weekly, and monthly observations of children's behaviors and learning provides a database for the cumulative evaluation of each child's achievement and development.

- *Helps you provide concrete information for use in reporting to and conferencing with parents.* Increasingly, reports to parents about children involve professionals' observations and children's work samples so parents and educators can collaborate to determine how to help children develop cognitively, socially, emotionally, and physically.

simple readers or chapter books to become members of the Campfire Readers. Students work on partner reading books, enjoy the Scholastic Reader computer program books, and add up pages read, and use trade books for readers during the year as well. Weekly reading conferences are held between students and myself to check on comprehension.

The use of various assessment tools provides me with a wide range of knowledge about each student. Some assessments can be as easy to use as a book discussion to determine my students' comprehension or a game to show knowledge gained. Assessments can also take the form of a Venn diagram for comparison or a poster giving facts about the animal students researched. Ongoing assessments, such as writing portfolios, can provide a big picture of skill growth by storing information in a time line fashion. Other assessments may be standardized, such as a math or reading test. No matter what type of assessment I might use, I think it is critical that my students be aware beforehand how they will be assessed and afterward take part in a discussion of the assessment tool. When I give a test of any kind, my students have a chance to talk over the items they missed. When using a less formal assessment such as a rubric, I give these out in advance. This gives students an idea of my expectations and a way to determine what they would like to accomplish.

No matter how you choose to assess your students, the most important thing to remember is that the assessment is only as good as the teacher using it. To keep the information meaningful, I look at the assessments I use with each unit I teach. Is there an area that I forgot to include? Are my students missing a question on a test in large numbers? Did this assessment give me the information I needed to know about my students' learning? What do the students think of the assessment? Is the information easy for me to understand? Is it easy to share with my students and my parents? Good assessments gather meaningful information that enhances children's learning. If my assessments are doing that, great! If not, I need to make a change so they are.

MAKING LEARNING MEANINGFUL

All of this information would mean nothing to the students or me if they were not engaged in their learning. Seven years ago, two colleagues and I investigated the idea of integrated instruction. Taking all our textbooks, we rebuilt our second grade curriculum from the ground up using our social studies standards as the base. The result was a full year of learning that was connected and meaningful. Students could learn about community workers and be reading a story for language arts on the same topic that week. The math lesson would also use community helpers as a base for the skill taught that week. The effort to make this possible was enormous and continues today as the plan is refined each year, but the results are worth it. Learning has become an "I get it" experience for my students. They see that our story for the week is about money and so are the math lessons. They understand that we are working on the skill of compound words because they are in our story for the week. Suddenly learning has an order and pattern that make their gathering of knowledge so much more genuine and long term. This connection of learning also brings strengths and weaknesses together that help improve both. This is real, lifelong learning!

Creating an environment where learning occurs is a huge key to successful students. We use these lifelong guidelines: Be truthful. Be trustworthy. Do your personal best. Appreciate others. Be an active listener. By expecting everyone in our classroom, including myself, to follow these guidelines, we create a place that is consistent, caring, and safe. Students know what to expect from day to day. By taking the time to listen to a story from home, provide a worry box to stuff concerns in, use mistakes as learning opportunities, or help ease a fear, I am modeling these expectations. I am creating a place where my students feel comfortable, can take risks, and will grow as learners. From my most able student to my least, I hear them saying: I can do this, I will try.

Can this make a difference? We sure think so in Room 12, or Camp Can Do as we like to call it. Never underestimate the potential of a child. If they shoot for the moon and miss, they will still wind up in the stars.

....

Lu Ann Harger is part of the USA Today *ALL STAR Teacher Team.*

Steps for Conducting Observations

The four steps involved in the process of systematic, purposeful observation are listed in Figure 6.2. Review them now in preparation for our discussion of each of them.

Step 1: Plan for Observation. Planning is an important part of the observation process. Everything you do regarding observation should be planned in advance of the observation. A good guide to follow in planning for observation is to ask the questions *who, what, where, when,* and *how.*

Setting goals for observation is a crucial part of the planning process. Goals allow you to reflect on why you want to observe and thus direct your efforts to what you will observe. Stating a goal focuses your attention on the purpose of your observation. For example, suppose you want to determine the effectiveness of your efforts in providing an inclusive classroom or program, and in fully including an exceptional child into the classroom. In Figure 6.6, you will see how we incorporate assessment and goal planning for

FIGURE 6.2 Four Steps to Effective Observation

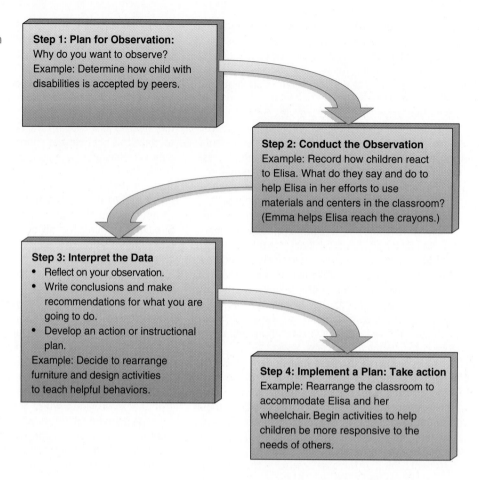

Step 1: Plan for Observation:
Why do you want to observe?
Example: Determine how child with disabilities is accepted by peers.

Step 2: Conduct the Observation
Example: Record how children react to Elisa. What do they say and do to help Elisa in her efforts to use materials and centers in the classroom? (Emma helps Elisa reach the crayons.)

Step 3: Interpret the Data
• Reflect on your observation.
• Write conclusions and make recommendations for what you are going to do.
• Develop an action or instructional plan.
Example: Decide to rearrange furniture and design activities to teach helpful behaviors.

Step 4: Implement a Plan: Take action
Example: Rearrange the classroom to accommodate Elisa and her wheelchair. Begin activities to help children be more responsive to the needs of others.

Elisa, a child with cerebral palsy (CP), and develop a plan for her successful assimilation in the inclusive classroom. As the teacher, your goals might read like this:

Goal 1: To determine what modifications might be necessary in the classroom to facilitate access to all parts of the classroom for Elisa in her wheelchair.

Goal 2: To assess the development of pro-social behavioral characteristics that other children display to Elisa while interacting in the classroom.

Goal setting sharpens your observation and makes it more effective.

Step 2: Conduct the Observation.   While conducting your observation, it is imperative that you be objective, specific, and as thorough as possible. For example, during your observation of Elisa and her peers, you notice that there is not enough room for Elisa to manipulate her wheelchair past the easel and shelf where the crayons are kept. None of her peers noticed that Elisa could not reach the crayons and so did not help her get them. Elisa had to ask one of the children to get the crayons for her. Now you have information that will enable you to take action.

Be sure to record your data as you observe. Here are four ways you can quickly and easily gather and manage observational data:

• Wear an apron (a carpenter's apron works very well) with pockets to carry pens, note cards, and Post-it notes.

• Use Post-it notes to record observations. These can be easily added to students' notebooks, folders, and so forth.

- Use the observation checklist for inclusive classrooms shown later in Figure 6.6, checklists you make yourself, and checklists found in other books.
- Use tape recorders, video cameras, and digital cameras to gather information. A problem with using a tape recorder is you have to transcribe your notes. Video cameras are probably best reserved for group observations. However, digital cameras are an excellent means of gathering and storing data.

Step 3: Interpret the Data. All observations can and should result in some kind of interpretation. **Interpretation** is a process that includes examining the gathered information, organizing and drawing conclusions from that information, and making decisions based on the conclusions. Interpretation serves several important functions. First, it puts your observations into perspective—that is, in relation to what you already know and do not know about events and the behaviors of your children. Second, interpretation helps you make sense of what you have observed and enables you to use your professional knowledge to interpret what you have seen. Third, interpretation has the potential to make you learn to anticipate representative behavior indicative of normal growth and development under given conditions, and to recognize what might not be representative of appropriate growth, development, and learning for each child. Fourth, interpretation forms the foundation for the implementation, necessary adaptations, or modifications in a program or curriculum. In your observation, you can note that Elisa's only exceptionality is that she has a physical disability. Her growth in other areas is normal, and she displays excellent social skills in that she is accepted by others, knows when to ask for help, and is able to ask for help. When Elisa asks for help, she receives it.

Step 4: Implement a Plan. The implementation phase means that you commit to do something with the results or the "findings" of your observation. For example, although Elisa's behavior in your observation was appropriate, many of the children can benefit from activities designed to help them recognize and respond to the needs of others. In addition, the physical environment of the classroom requires some modification in the rearrangement of movable furniture to make it more accessible for Elisa. Implementation means you report to and conference with parents or others as necessary and appropriate. Implementation is applying the results of your observations to real-life situations that can improve the child's circumstances and maintain consistent progress.

TYPES OF ASSESSMENT

Early childhood teachers use many kinds of assessments to help them learn about their children and plan for teaching. The following are examples of assessment that will be an important part of your professional toolbox as you enter the profession.

Authentic Assessment

Authentic assessment is the evaluation of children's actual learning and the instructional activities in which they are involved. Figure 6.3 outlines characteristics of authentic assessment. As you examine these characteristics, think about how you will apply them to your professional practice. Following the authentic assessment strategies shown in Figure 6.3 will help ensure that the information you gather will be useful and appropriate for all children.

Authentic assessment is also referred to as *performance-based assessment*. Authentic assessment requires children to demonstrate what they know and are able to do. Meaningless facts and isolated information are considered inauthentic.

Here are some characteristics of authentic assessment:

- *Assess children based on their actual work:* Use work samples, exhibitions, performances, learning logs, journals, projects, presentations, experiments, and teacher observations.

interpretation A three-step process that includes examining the information that has been gathered, organizing and drawing conclusions from that information, and making decisions about teaching based on the conclusions.

Go to the Assignments and Activities section in Topic 4: Observation/Assessment in the MyEducationLab for your course and complete the activity entitled *Opportunities for Authentic Assessment.* Watch for the different skills the children are learning and exhibiting on just one task. What are some of the skills the teacher is able to assess from her lesson?

authentic assessment Assessment conducted through activities that require children to demonstrate what they know and are able to do; also referred to as *performance-based assessment.*

Employs a number of different ways to determine children's achievement and what they know and are able to do

Takes into account children's cultural, language, and other specific needs

Is ongoing over the entire school year

Is curriculum-embedded; children are assessed on what they are actually learning and doing

Assesses children and their actual work with work samples, portfolios, performances, projects, journals, experiments, and teacher observations

Is a cooperative process—involves children, teachers, parents, and other professionals; goal is to make assessment child-centered

Assesses the whole child rather than a narrow set of skills

Is part of the learning process

FIGURE 6.3 Characteristics of Authentic Assessment

- *Assess children based on what they are actually doing in and through the curriculum.*
- *Assess what each individual child can do.* Evaluate what each child is learning, rather than comparing one child with another or one group of children with another.
- *Make assessment part of the learning process.* Encourage children to show what they know through presentations and participation.
- *Learn about the whole child.* Make the assessment process an opportunity to learn more than just a child's acquisition of a narrow set of skills.
- *Involve children and parents in a cooperative, collaborative assessment process.* The goal of authentic assessment is to be child-centered and to provide children with the resources they need to succeed.
- *Provide ongoing assessment over the entire year.* Assess children continually throughout the year, not just at the end of a grading period or at the end of the year.
- *Use many different assessment tools to evaluate your children.* Know ways to determine children's achievement and what they know and are able to do.

Traditional Assessment

traditional assessment
Assessment done with standardized tests or teacher-created tests, where students typically select an answer or recall facts, measuring how well children have learned specific information.

Another way to look at authentic assessment is to compare it with traditional assessment. **Traditional assessment** refers to the method of forced choice found in multiple-choice tests, fill-in-the-blanks, true-false, matching, and the like, where students typically select an answer or recall information to complete the assessment. These tests are usually standardized or teacher-created and administered locally or statewide.[5] In the traditional assessment model, the curriculum determines what is on the assessment. For an example,

FIGURE 6.4

Traditional Assessment Versus Authentic Assessment

Traditional	Authentic
Select a response	**Perform a task**
• Students are commonly given several choices (e.g., a, b, c, or d; true or false) and are asked to select the correct answer.	• Students are asked to demonstrate knowledge of a subject through application. For example, kindergarten students can show they know the vowels by singing, "A, E, I, O, U, and sometimes Y" and identifying the vowel in the word "cat."
Contrived	**Real-life**
• Tests often have several different editions, to show proficiency in a subject; this can increase the number of times a student demonstrates proficiency.	• Proficiency is assessed by application, by doing a task and showing mastery. For example, a first grade teacher can have an "assessment wall" filled with color-coded Post-its representing each pupil and whether he or she is making steady progress; as students show mastery in basic skills their individual Post-its move up the wall.
Recall/Recognition of knowledge	**Construction/Application of knowledge**
• Tests are designed to show how much knowledge students have acquired. However, they are less revealing about what students really know and can do.	• Instead of memorizing knowledge simply for the sake of passing a test (i.e., parts of the human body or farm animals), teachers construct unique tasks that allow the students to apply knowledge in real-life applications (e.g., singing a song that allows the children to become actively involved in learning the parts of the body).
Teacher-structured	**Student-structured**
• A student's attention is limited to and focused on what will be on the test.	• Assessments allow student choice in determining what to present as evidence of proficiency. There are usually multiple acceptable routes toward constructing a product or performance.
Indirect evidence	**Direct evidence**
• While evaluating a test, teachers can understand only that the student picked the correct answer. The teacher does not know what thinking led to the student picking the correct answer or if the student just got lucky.	• Assessments offer direct evidence of meaningful application and construction of knowledge. For example, reading about how to teach students how to read is not as fulfilling and meaningful as sitting down with a child and teaching him or her to read.

Source: Adapted from Jon Mueller, Professor of Psychology, North Central College, Naperville, IL, "Authentic Assessment Toolbox," 2008; retrieved March 30, 2009, from http://jonathan.mueller.faculty.noctrl.edu/toolbox/whatisit.htm.

each state has a list of basic and essential skills that each student should master at a certain grade level. A test is derived from these skills to assess how well the children have learned the information.

Figure 6.4 shows the difference between traditional and authentic assessment.

myeducationlab

Go to the Assignments and Activities section in Topic 4: Observation/Assessment in the MyEducationLab for your course and complete the activity entitled *Hearing and Vision Screening.* Observe how Head Start assesses the health of the whole child including vision and hearing. Assessing your children's physical health is important in creating a healthy and safe environment.

Formal Assessment

formal assessment
Assessment utilizing standardized tests that have set procedures and instruction for administration and have been normed, thus making it possible to compare a child's score with the scores of children who have already taken the same exam.

screening The process of identifying the particular physical, social, linguistic, and cognitive needs of children in order to provide appropriate programs and services.

screening procedures
Procedures that give a broad picture of what children know and are able to do, as well as their physical and emotional status.

Formal assessment involves the use of traditional tests that have set procedures and instructions for administration and have been *normed,* meaning that it is possible to compare a child's score with the scores of a group of children who have already taken the same exam. Table 6.1 lists other types of formal assessment measures commonly used in early childhood teaching. In the following pages we discuss screening procedures.

Screening.   In your work with children, have you ever wondered about the extent to which they are developing? **Screening** can help you, because it is the process of identifying the particular physical, social, linguistic, and cognitive needs of children in order to provide appropriate programs and services. Table 6.1 includes some common formal screening procedures used to assess children.

Screening procedures give you and others a broad picture of what children know and are able to do, as well as their physical and emotional status. As gross indicators of children's abilities, screening procedures provide much useful information for decisions about placement for initial instruction, referral to other agencies, and additional testing that may be necessary to pinpoint a learning or health problem. One out of every six children in the United States faces a developmental disability or disabling behavioral problem before age eighteen. Yet fewer than 50 percent of these children are identified before they start school.[6] Many school districts conduct a comprehensive screening assessment program in the spring for children who will enter kindergarten in the fall. Screening can include the following:

- Gathering information from parents about their children's health, learning patterns, learning achievements, personal habits, and special problems.
- Conducting a health screening, including a physical examination, health history, and a blood sample for analysis. (Recall from Chapter 2 that we identified lead poisoning as a major childhood disease.)
- Conducting vision, hearing, and speech screening.
- Collecting and analyzing data from former programs and teachers, such as preschools and child care programs.
- Using commercial screening instruments to help make decisions regarding children's placement in programs and need for special services.

TABLE 6.1 Formal Measures of Assessment Used in Early Childhood

Assessment Instrument	Age/Grade Level	Purpose
Ages and Stages Questionnaires®, Third Edition (ASQ-3)	Birth to 5 years	Provides developmental and social-emotional screening for children; looks at the child's developmental delays and educates parents about developmental milestones
BRIGANCE® screens and inventories	Pre-kindergarten to grade nine	Obtains a broad sampling of children's skills and behaviors to determine initial placement, plan appropriate instruction, and comply with mandated testing requirements
Developmental Indicators for the Assessment of Learning, Third Edition (DIAL-3)	Ages 3 to 6	Identifies children who may have special educational needs
Dynamic Indicators of Basic Early Literacy Skills (DIBELS)	Preschool and primary grades	Assesses three of the five Big Ideas of early literacy: phonological awareness, alphabetic principle, and fluency with connected text
Peabody Picture Vocabulary Test–Revised (PPVT-R)	Ages 2.5 to 40	Tests hearing vocabulary; is available in two forms

Schools and early childhood programs frequently conduct comprehensive screening programs for all children for one or two days. The data for each child are evaluated by a team of professionals who make instructional placement recommendations and, when appropriate, advise additional testing and make referrals to other agencies for assistance.

Screening measures are what you and other professionals use when you gather information and make decisions about such procedures as small-group placements, instructional levels, and so forth.

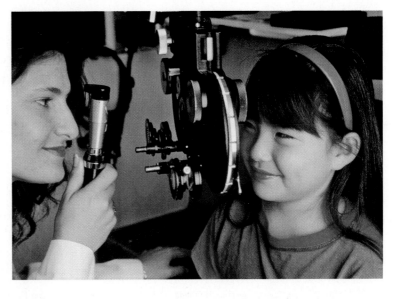

Informal Assessment

Informal assessment is a procedure for obtaining information that can be used to make judgments about children's learning, behavior, and development using means other than standardized instruments.[7] Informal assessments allow teachers to evaluate their children's progress and follow it throughout their learning experiences. Authentic assessment relies heavily on informal procedures.

Observations, checklists, and portfolios are just some of the methods of informal assessment available to you to help record and track your students' progress.

Observations. Early childhood professionals recognize that children are more than what is measured by any particular standardized test. As mentioned earlier in this chapter, *observation* is the intentional, systematic act of looking at the behavior of a child or children in a particular setting, program, or situation. It is an "authentic" means of learning about children—what they know and are able to do, especially as it occurs in more naturalistic settings such as classrooms, child care centers, playgrounds, and homes. It is one of the most widely used methods of assessment. As we have said, observation is sometimes referred to as "kid-watching" and is an excellent way to find out about children's behaviors and learning.

A sample observation form you can use is shown in Figure 6.5. This form can be a useful tool for gathering observational data and it will prove helpful when planning for teaching and finding your children's areas of improvement. In Figure 6.5, you will see how the teacher uses observations and a checklist to record the social pretend play skills of Eva, a student in her third grade theater class.

Checklists. Checklists are excellent and powerful tools for observing and gathering information about a wide range of student abilities in all settings. **Checklists** are a list of behaviors identifying children's skills and knowledge and can be used as a regular part of your teaching on a wide variety of topics and subjects. Some checklists can be developmental; others can help you assess behaviors, traits, skills, and abilities. In addition, the same checklists used over a period of time enable you to evaluate progress and achievement. Figure 6.6 is a checklist for assessing children in inclusive classrooms and can be used as a template or model to make other checklists. Review Figure 6.6 now and think about how you could modify it to assess children's technology use and skills. Some things for you to keep in mind when making and using checklists are:

- Each checklist should contain the qualities, skills, behaviors, and other information you want to observe. In other words, tailor each checklist to a specific situation.
- Make sure you are observing and recording accurately to prevent errors in assessment.

Many school districts conduct a comprehensive screening for children entering kindergarten, which may include vision, hearing, and speech tests.

informal assessment Assessment of students' learning, behavior, and development using means other than standardized tests.

checklist A list of behaviors or other traits, used in informal assessment to identify children's skills and knowledge.

FIGURE 6.5

A Checklist for Social Pretend Play

Date: May 1, 2011		Props			Roles			Themes			Social Skills		
Cast Members	Has a pretend scenario	Plays with realistic props	Uses props symbolically	Identifies role (Mommy, baby, etc.)	Plays more than one role	Plays with objects as actors	Incorporates multiple themes	Incorporates new themes from field trips, literature, etc.	Incorporates literacy in theme (reads books in center, writes, etc.)	Solves social problems that emerge in play	Plays with all children; does not exclude others	Resumes play after interruption	Incorporates teacher suggestions and support
Eva	X	X		X		X		X		X	X		X

Source: McAfee & Leong, *Assessing and Guiding Young Children's Development and Learning,* Figure 6.11, "Form for Recording Observations of a Group of Children's Social Pretend Play," p.119, © 2007. Reproduced by permission of Pearson Education, Inc.

portfolio A compilation of children's work samples, other artifacts, and teacher observations collected over time.

work sample An example of a child's work that demonstrates what the child knows and is able to do.

- File all checklists in students' folders to track their progress and for future reference and use.
- Use checklists as a basis for conferencing with children and parents.
- Use the information from checklists to plan for small-group and individual instruction.

Portfolios. Today many teachers use **portfolios**—a purposeful compilation of children's artifacts, as well as teacher observations collected over time—as a basis for assessing children's efforts, progress, and achievement. Before compiling students' portfolios, you will need to make decisions about the criteria you will use to decide what to put in the portfolios. Remember, a portfolio is not a dump truck. Only include samples of the child's work that you feel will be representative of the child's ability. Some questions to ask yourself when deciding what to include in student portfolios are:

- How will students participate in decisions about what to include?
- Do the materials show student progress over time?
- Do the materials demonstrate student learning of program and district standards and goals?
- Can you use the materials and products to adequately and easily communicate with parents about children's learning?
- Do the materials include examples to positively support students' efforts and progress?

Artifacts and Work Samples. As already stated, children's artifacts and teacher observations make up a portfolio. One type of artifact is a **work sample**, an example of a child's work that demonstrates what the child knows and is able to do. Work samples and other artifacts are pieces of evidence used to assess students' abilities and to document a child's accomplishments and achievements. These products can be electronic or nonelectronic and come in many different forms. The artifact in Figure 6.7 is an example of an electronic artifact that demonstrates a child's dreams to become a doctor and take care of her family.

Examples of electronic and nonelectronic artifacts are:

- Artwork, including scanned images
- Paper documents, such as written work samples
- Electronic documents

PEARSON myeducationlab

Go to the Assignments and Activities section in Topic 4: Observation/Assessment in the MyEducationLab for your course and complete the activity entitled *Portfolio Exhibitions.* Reflect on the importance of portfolios in children's learning and how you can celebrate and document leearning through portfolios.

FIGURE 6.6

Observation Checklist for Inclusive Classrooms

Teacher: *Graciela Gonzalez*　　　　　　　　　　　　　　　　Date: *December 8, 2010*

School: *Mission Hill*　　　　　　　　　　　　　　　　　　　Class: *Kindergarten*

Number of children in class: *16*

Number of children with disabilities in class: *1*

Types of disabilities: *Elisa has moderate cerebral palsy (CP) and must use a wheelchair.*

Physical Features of the Classroom

1. Are all areas of the classroom accessible to children with disabilities?
   No, Elisa cannot access the library/literacy center.
2. Are learning materials and equipment accessible for all children?
   There is not enough room for Elisa to manipulate her wheelchair past the easel and the shelf with art materials.
3. Are work and play areas separated to minimize distractions?
   Yes, but pathways are too narrow for Elisa's wheelchair.
4. Are special tables or chairs necessary to accommodate children's disabilities?
   Elisa has a large work board/table that attaches to her wheelchair.

Academic Features of the Classroom

1. What special accommodations are necessary to help children with disabilities achieve state and local standards?
   I have to check on this.
2. Are principles of developmentally appropriate practice applied to all children, including those with disabilities?
   Yes
3. Is there a wide range of classroom literature on all kinds of disabilities?
   I have a few books—but not enough.

Classroom Interaction

1. Are children with disabilities included in cooperative work projects?
   I will work on this next week.
2. Do nondisabled children interact positively with children with disabilities?
   Elisa is a very sociable child. Students interact well with her. Elisa could not reach the crayons by herself, so she asked Emma for help. She and Emma seem to get along well.

Play Routines

1. Are children with disabilities able to participate in all classroom and grade-level play activities?
   I need to talk to the P.E. teacher. I also need to observe Elisa during lunch and recess to see if she is involved in play and social activities during these times.

Conclusions

1. *I need to rearrange my classroom to make sure that Elisa has access to all learning centers and materials.*
2. *The children are not as helpful to Elisa as I want them to be.*
3. *The classroom library/literacy center needs books relating to children with disabilities.*
4. *There are a lot of questions I don't have the answers to at this time (e.g., meeting state standards).*
5. *I need to include more group work and cooperative activities in my planning.*

Recommendations

1. *I will ask a custodian to help me move a heavy bookshelf. I can move and rearrange the other things. I'll give the new arrangement a trial run and see how it works for all the children.*
2. *In our daily class meetings, I will talk about helpful behaviors and helping others.*
   a. *We can read books about helping.*
   b. *I plan to start a class buddy system; I can pair Elisa and Emma.*
3. *In my lesson plans, I need to include activities for learning helpful behaviors.*
4. *I will search for books about children with disabilities.*
   a. *I'll consult with the school librarian.*
   b. *I'll talk to my grade-level leader and ask for money for books.*
5. *I will talk with the director of special education about meeting state standards. Elisa is very smart, so I don't anticipate any problems.*
6. *I will develop a lesson involving group work and projects. I will include Elisa and observe the children's interactions.*
7. *I will observe Elisa at lunch and during recess.*

DeAr mOm And dAd,

Today I decided that I wanted to be a doctor, so I can fix you and dad when you get old and gray. LOL.

Love, Brittany

FIGURE 6.7 Electronic Artifact—Child's Letter to Parents

- Electronic images
- DVDs
- Documents such as word processors, spreadsheets, and databases
- Photographs of projects
- Voice recording of oral skills—reading, speaking, singing
- Video recordings of performances—sports, musical, theatrical
- Multimedia projects or Web pages exploring curriculum topics, current events, or social problems

Some teachers let children put their best work in their portfolios; others decide with children what will be included; still others decide for themselves what to include. Portfolios are very useful, especially during family–teacher conferences. Such a portfolio includes your notes about achievement, teacher- and child-made checklists, artwork samples, photographs, journals, and other documentation. The accompanying Technology Tie-In feature will give you an idea for using one type of technology, handheld computers, in the classroom.

Anecdotal Records. Another informal assessment tool is the **anecdotal record**, a brief written description of student behavior at one specific time (see Figure 6.8). These records are short and concise and tell the evaluator what needs to be known about the unique skills of a child or small group of children. They provide insight into a particular behavior and a basis for planning a specific teaching strategy. Some guidelines to remember about anecdotal records are to record only what is observed or heard, deal with the facts and include the setting, and what was said and done by the subjects being observed.

The accompanying Professionalism in Practice feature, "How to Evaluate Environments for Young Children," shows you how to use observation and records to create and maintain environments that are healthy, respectful, supportive, and challenging for all young children.

Running Records. **Running records** are a more detailed narrative of a child's behavior that focuses on a sequence of events that occur over a period of time. These records help to obtain a more detailed insight into behavior in general, rather than specific events like the anecdotal record. When using running records try to maintain objectivity and include as much detail as possible. Figure 6.9 gives an example of how a student

anecdotal record An informal assessment tool that gives a brief written description of a student's behavior during a single incident.

running record An informal assessment tool that provides a more detailed narrative of a child's behavior, focusing on a sequence of events that occur over a period of time.

Handheld Computers: Assessment Tools for a New Generation

A growing number of early childhood educators regard *formative assessment*—assessment conducted periodically during the school year—important in understanding students' learning needs and delivering instruction to meet these needs. Such assessment typically occurs three times each year to screen for students who are at risk and to monitor progress toward skill mastery. Many teachers find this scene familiar:

> Kindergarten teacher Carrie Huggins has papers spread all over her dining room table. She tabulates scores on a calculator, writes notes about achievement levels for each student in her classroom, and adds comments to report cards to help parents understand assessment results. Carrie shifts papers into different piles, trying to organize small groups of children needing intervention on the same skills. Then she will create activities and lesson plans for the next week. Carrie finds all of this tedious and labor intensive.

However, the above scene is being replaced by this one more and more:

> Rachel McBride uses a handheld computer to administer the assessment and record her students' responses. Later she connects her handheld device to a computer and uploads assessment results to a secure website where her students' data are recorded. Moments later, Rachel prints out a class summary, individual children summaries, small-group suggestions, and recommended instructional activities. The reports are easy to understand and include explanations of each skill assessed and the student's level. Rachel then makes phone calls to parents to request conferences, as the reports show critical need areas that need to be addressed. Rachel gathers the materials needed for the small-group activities she will teach the following week. The teacher drops an extra copy of the reports into the principal's and the reading coach's mail boxes.

Cindy Lewis, a pre-K bilingual teacher and the 2006 Texas Elementary Teacher of the Year, has experienced both scenarios. She says, "The difference between teaching without, and then with, a handheld device is astounding. Hours of work were replaced by a simple click of a button that gave me more accurate, efficiently organized data, and support for planning my instruction. I found that in the school as a whole, the faculty talked about data regularly and collaborated in developing the right strategies for our students. The obvious impact of using this technology in my classroom was that I could do what I was trained for and do it even better—*teach!*"

Currently in the United States, more than 100,000 teachers use handheld computers to assess more than two million students. Many are in grades pre-K–3, when formative assessment is usually observational—young children don't take bubble tests—and is often supported by federally mandated reading initiatives and funding. This number of teachers continues to grow as schools seek to impact all areas of teaching and learning through the more efficient collection and effective analysis of data. Benefits of using handheld computers for assessment include the following:

1. Teachers save time and can devote more instructional hours to the classroom.
2. Teachers can assess students more often for an understanding of what instruction they need.
3. All paperwork is eliminated.
4. Results are automatically delivered upon assessment completion.
5. The handheld promotes accurate administration and reliable results:
   - Prompts and instructions are displayed on the handheld, guiding the teacher and providing professional development in best practices.
   - Timing is integrated into the handheld—no need for a stopwatch.
   - Branching to the next assessment task is automated.
   - The handheld calculates all scores.
6. Immediate data aggregation and reporting support differentiated instruction:
   - Assessment information moves securely from the handheld to a secure website with a click of a button.
   - Reports allow educators to see student, class, school, and district progress toward key goals, growth over time, and all the key data needed to make critical instructional decisions.
   - Reports are individualized, allowing the teachers to select exactly which data they want to see.
   - Data are linked to instructional recommendations for individual students, groups, and classes.
   - Reports can be printed and shared, promoting conversations about data and learning among colleagues and with parents.

New educators have an advantage in using handheld devices because their generation has long been "plugged in." Veteran teachers might encounter a steeper learning curve, depending on their technology experience and willingness to try new approaches. But most educators quickly see that handheld technology makes assessment easier, more efficient, and more integral to their work in the classroom.

Contributed by Cindy Lewis, pre-K bilingual teacher and 2006 Texas Elementary Teacher of the Year.

FIGURE 6.8

Example of an Anecdotal Record

Child Name(s): *Melissa, Amanda, Kasie*
Age: *4*
Location: *Bayside Preschool*
Observer: *Delanna Sosap*
Type of Development Observed: *Social/Emotional*

Incident	Social/Emotional Notes or Comments
Amanda and Kasie were in the kitchen area pretending to fix a meal. Melissa came to the center and said she wanted to eat. The girls looked at her. Kasie said, "You can't play here, we're busy." Melissa stood watching the girls as they moved plastic fruit on the table. Melissa said, "I could be the third sister and do the dishes." Amanda thought for a minute, looked at Kasie, and replied, "Oh, all right, you can play."	*The girls play together frequently and tend to discourage others from entering their play. Melissa has learned how to enter a play group. She was careful not to upset the other girls. They relented when she offered to be helpful. Melissa is usually successful in being accepted into play activities.*

Source: Wortham, *Assessment in Early Childhood Education,* Figure 5-1, "Example of an Anecdotal Record," p. 120, © 2008. Reproduced by permission of Pearson Education, Inc.

FIGURE 6.9

Example of a Running Record

Child Name(s): *"Lisa"*
Age: *5*
Location: *Colonial Elementary, Kindergarten Room*
Time: *1:25 pm–2:08 pm*
Observer: *Destine'e Garth*
Type of Development Observed: *Social/Emotional Play*

(1:30 pm) Lisa went to the right corner of the room in the "Construction Zone," a play area filled with toys and manipulatives children use to build things (Legos, Jenga blocks, etc.), and sat down with "R" and asked her did she want to play with her. "R" turned her head to the right and said "No, I'm playing with "S."

(1:35 pm) Lisa sat there and stared at "R" for about 1 minute and got up and kicked the Lego blocks "R" and "S" were playing with. "R" began screaming to Ms. Myers saying, "Lisa kicked my blocks." She said this three times. Lisa stood in front of "R" and said "No, I didn't!" "R" screamed "Yes you did. S saw you too." Lisa began crying and ran into the "Reading Aquarium."

(1:42 pm) Ms. Myers went into the Reading Aquarium about 2 minutes later and asked Lisa was she ok. Lisa and Ms. Myers went to the conference table located at the front of the room by Ms. Myers' desk. They sat and started talking. "I did not do it Ms. Myers, I really am sorry." Ms. Myers sat with Lisa until she completely understood why it is important for her to accurately convey her feelings to her friends.

(1:52 pm) After speaking to Ms. Myers, Lisa wrote a "letter" to "R" and "S" apologizing for kicking the Lego blocks. "R" said that Lisa could play with them and that they were building a hotel just for kids.

(2:05 pm) Lisa smiled and joked with "R" and "S." In the middle of playing with the girls, Lisa got up and went up to Ms. Myers and gave her a hug and said, "Thank you." Ms. Myers replied, "You're very welcome, Lisa. I'm glad you worked everything out with your friends!"

observes a student during play time and the conflict that arises with her and two of her peers. Because the observer uses a running record to observe the student, the events are shown in chronological order and you can see how the problem begins and is solved with the help of the teacher.

Time Sampling. **Time sampling** records particular events or behaviors during specific, continuous time intervals (e.g., five minutes, one hour). When using the time sampling method, you take an interval such as five minutes and observe what behavior is occurring during that particular five minutes. Then you would repeat your observations over the course of a day or longer, during a series of five-minute periods chosen either systematically or at random. The purpose of this method is to help identify when a child demonstrates a specific behavior. It also helps answer the question, "Does this child do something all the time or just at certain times and events?" An important key to remember when using time sampling is to observe *only* during the specified time period. Figure 6.10 gives an example of how an observer uses the time sampling technique to show how a child has difficulty completing tasks.

Event Sampling. **Event sampling**, unlike time sampling, uses discontinuous intervals and focuses on a particular behavior during particular events. For example, Ms. Curry would look at Sebastian's behavior during lunchtime, on the playground, and during reading time. The behavior may occur infrequently or at random times, so event sampling is only used as a cause-and-effect type of observation. Once the behavior occurs, the observer looks at what happened to cause the behavior and what happened as a result of

time sampling An informal assessment tool that records particular events or behaviors during specific, continuous time intervals, such as three or four five-minute periods during the course of a morning.

event sampling An informal assessment tool that focuses on a particular behavior during a particular event.

FIGURE 6.10

Example of Time Sampling

Child Name(s): *Ashley*
Age: 5
Location: *Hilltop Kindergarten School*
Date and Time: *April 29, 2009; 2:00–2:30*
Observer: *Crystal Bueno*
Type of Development Observed: *Ashley has difficulty completing tasks*

Incident	Time	Notes or Comments
Art Center- leaves coloring activities on table without putting up supplies.	*2:00 pm*	*Some of Ashley's behaviors seem to be resulting from failure to follow procedures for use of materials.*
Library- leaves books out and does not return them to the shelf.	*2:12 pm*	*Behavior with the puzzles may come from frustration.*
Manipulative Center- gets frustrated with puzzle, throws pieces all over room, leaves the puzzle on table. Pulls out Jenga game, and starts piling the blocks up. When another child signals for Ashley to play Legos with her, she leaves the Jenga game out with the pieces all over the floor.	*2:14 pm* *2:30 pm*	*Ashley may need help in putting away with verbal rewards for finishing a task and putting materials away.* *Encourage Ashley to get help with materials that are too hard.*

Source: Wortham, *Assessment in Early Childhood Education*, Figure 5-4, "Examples of Time Sampling," p. 125, © 2008. Reproduced by permission of Pearson Education, Inc.

COMPETENCY BUILDER

How to Evaluate Environments for Young Children

One of your roles as an early childhood professional is to create and maintain environments that are healthy, respectful, supportive, and challenging for all young children. This exercise will help you achieve this goal, which is part of Standard 1 of NAEYC's *Standards for Professional Development*. In addition, you will learn to assess and evaluate environmental strengths and weaknesses, and to reflect and make decisions for improvement and changes. Before you begin, review and reflect on our discussion of healthy, respectful, supportive, and challenging environments on pages 99–101 in Chapter 4.

STEP 1 PLAN FOR THE OBSERVATION
Decide What, Where, and How You Will Observe

In our case, we will observe environmental features of classrooms and child care centers through photos.

Write Your Goals for Observation

Our goals for observing environments are:

- To assess features that contribute to environments being healthy, respectful, supportive, and challenging for each child
- To identify features that do not contribute to environments being healthy, respectful, supportive, and challenging
- To recommend changes leading to environments that are healthy, respectful, supportive, and challenging

Select Your Observation Tool

For our observation, a checklist will achieve our goals and provide the data necessary to make conclusions and recommendations. Review the information on checklists on pages 157–159. Then, using the following definitions and the questions in Step 2, develop a short checklist to use as we observe our three environments.

respectful and supportive: Respectful environments show respect for each individual child, and for each child's culture, home language, individual abilities or disabilities, family context, and community. In supportive environments, professionals believe each child can learn, and they help children understand and make meaning of their experiences.

challenging: Challenging environments provide achievable and "stretching" experiences for all children.

healthy: Healthy environments provide for children's physical and psychological health, safety, and sense of security.

STEP 2 CONDUCT THE OBSERVATION

1

---

rating scale An informal assessment tool, usually a numeric scale, that contains a list of descriptors for a set of behaviors.

interviewing An informal assessment tool by which observers and researchers obtain information about children by asking questions and engaging them in conversation.

the behavior occurring. In Figure 6.11, you can see how an observer uses the event sampling method to assess Rachel's frequent hitting behavior.

Rating Scales. **Rating scales** are usually numeric scales that contain a list of descriptors for a set of behaviors. If you have seen a rating scale before, you have noticed that they usually begin with the phrase, "On a scale of (a number) to (a number), you rate (the behavior) as . . ." Rating scales enable a teacher to record data when they are observed. When using rating scales, make sure that the key descriptors and the rating scales are appropriate for what is being observed.

Interviews. **Interviewing** is a common way that observers and researchers engage children in discussion through questions to obtain information. It allows children to explain behavior, work samples, or particular answers. Interviewing gives an eyewitness account to obtaining information and can describe more visible information, otherwise not

Observe the first photo. Using your checklist, answer these questions about a respectful and supportive environment:

- Is the teacher using positive interactions with the children?
- Does the teacher show interest in children's ideas and activities?
- Is the teacher supporting children's learning?
- What evidence is there that the teacher is supporting learning and wants the children to succeed?
- What background evidence can you identify in the classroom that would lead you to believe that this classroom environment is or is not respectful and supportive?

2

Observe the second photo and answer these questions about a challenging environment:

- What evidence is there that this environment contains materials that would provide challenging activities for the children?
- What evidence can you observe that the children are being challenged to succeed in their learning?

3

- What evidence can you observe that individual children are being challenged to learn?

Observe the third photo and answer these questions about a healthy environment:

- What are three characteristics of this environment that would make it safe, healthy, and supportive for these infants?
- What environmental features promote children's physical and psychological security?
- What evidence is there that this classroom is conducting healthy environmental practices?

STEP 3 INTERPRET THE DATA

Review your goals for observing:

- Look at the observation data as a whole. Place your observation in the context of all that you know about young children and about healthy, respectful, supportive, and challenging environments.
- Reflect on your observations and look for patterns.
- Make decisions about what actions you want to pursue based on your conclusions from the data.
- Your decision-making process can include consulting with other colleagues and professionals. Who could coach and mentor you in observing and developing environments that are healthy, respectful, supportive, and challenging?

STEP 4 IMPLEMENT A PLAN

Take action based on your interpretation of the data:

- What three things would you do to make the environment in the first photo more supportive and respectful?
- What three things would you do to make the environment in the second photo more challenging?
- What three things would you do to make the environment in the third photo healthier for children and adults?

---

shown through written records such as portfolios or checklists. When using interviewing, employ the hierarchy of questions in Bloom's Taxonomy of questioning to gain further insight into children's learning. (Refer to Figure 10.7, on page 290.)

WHAT ARE THE CONTEXTS OF ASSESSMENT?

We have taken a look at individual processes of assessment—observation, screening, and individual tests—to gather data about children to help ensure achievement and learning. Now let's put all of this in context. Notice the four steps in Figure 6.12 and how they are all linked to each other. The four steps, taken as a whole, make assessment a meaningful and child-appropriate process. Notice also that assessment is an ongoing process throughout the program year. Finally, notice how the purpose—the end product—of assessment is to promote, support, extend, and enrich children's learning so that children are successful in school.

FIGURE 6.11

Example of Event Sampling

Child Name(s): *Rachel*
Age: *4*
Location: *Betty's Child Care Center*
Date and Time: *December 8; 2:50-3:50*
Observer: *Haley Martin*
Type of Development Observed: *Social/Emotional; Rachel uses frequent hitting behavior*

Time	Antecedent Event	Behavior	Consequent Event
2:52	*Rachel and Rosinda are eating a snack. Rosinda takes part of Rachel's cracker.*	*Rachel hits Rosinda.*	*Rosinda calls to the teacher.*
3:47	*Sam is looking at a book in the Library Center. Rachel asks for the book. Sam refuses.*	*Rachel grabs the book and hits Sam.*	*Sam hits back and takes back the book. Rachel cries but soon gets another book and sits down.*

Source: Wortham, *Assessment in Early Childhood Education,* Figure 5-5, "Example of Event Sampling," p. 126, © 2008. Reproduced by permission of Pearson Education, Inc.

Appropriate Assessment

The NAEYC and NAECS/SDE also take the position that policy makers, the early childhood profession, and other stakeholders in young children's lives have a shared responsibility to make ethical, appropriate, valid, and reliable assessment a central part of all early childhood programs.

To assess young children's strengths, progress, and needs, teachers need to use assessment methods that are:

- Developmentally appropriate
- Culturally and linguistically responsive
- Tied to children's daily activities
- Supported by professional development
- Inclusive of families
- Connected to specific beneficial purposes

They also need to:

- Make sound decisions about teaching and learning.
- Identify significant concerns that may require focused intervention for individual children.
- Help programs improve their educational and developmental interventions.[8]

Indicators of Effective Assessment. The following are indicators of effective assessment that you can apply to your teaching.

Ethical principles guide assessment practices. Ethical principles underlie all assessment practices. Young children are not denied opportunities or services, and decisions are not made about children on the basis of a single assessment.

Assessment instruments are used for their intended purposes. Assessments are used in ways consistent with the purposes for which they were designed.

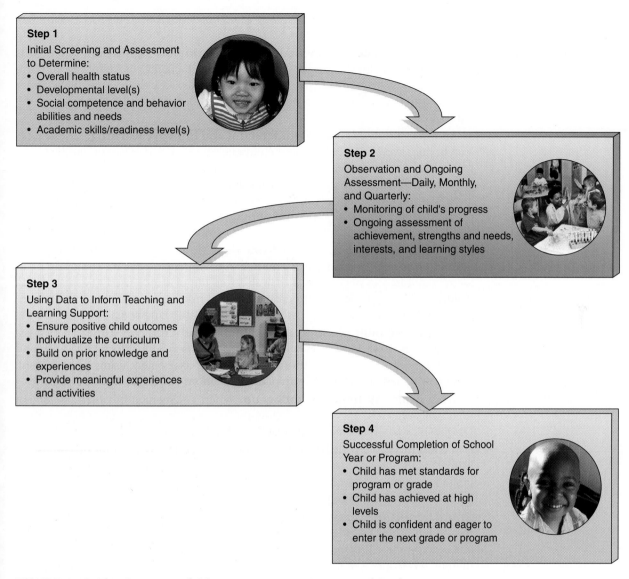

Step 1

Initial Screening and Assessment to Determine:
- Overall health status
- Developmental level(s)
- Social competence and behavior abilities and needs
- Academic skills/readiness level(s)

Step 2

Observation and Ongoing Assessment—Daily, Monthly, and Quarterly:
- Monitoring of child's progress
- Ongoing assessment of achievement, strengths and needs, interests, and learning styles

Step 3

Using Data to Inform Teaching and Learning Support:
- Ensure positive child outcomes
- Individualize the curriculum
- Build on prior knowledge and experiences
- Provide meaningful experiences and activities

Step 4

Successful Completion of School Year or Program:
- Child has met standards for program or grade
- Child has achieved at high levels
- Child is confident and eager to enter the next grade or program

FIGURE 6.12 The Contexts of Observation, Assessment, and Evaluation

If the assessments will be used for additional purposes, they are validated for those purposes.

Assessments are appropriate for ages and other characteristics of children being assessed. Assessments are designed for and validated for use with children whose ages, cultures, home languages, socioeconomic status, abilities and disabilities, and other characteristics are similar to those of the children with whom the assessments will be used.

Assessment instruments are in compliance with professional criteria for quality. Assessments are valid and reliable. Accepted professional standards of quality are the basis for selection, use, and interpretation of assessment instruments, including screening tools. NAEYC and NAECS/SDE support and adhere to the measurement standards set forth in 1999 by the American Educational Research Association, the American Psychological Association, and the National Council on

Measurement in Education. When individual norm-referenced tests are used, they meet these guidelines.

What is assessed is developmentally and educationally significant. The objects of assessment include a comprehensive, developmentally and educationally important set of goals, rather than a narrow set of skills. Assessments are aligned with early learning standards, with program goals, and with specific emphases in the curriculum.

Assessment evidence is used to understand and improve learning. Assessments lead to improved knowledge about children. This knowledge is translated into improved curriculum implementation and teaching practices. Assessment helps early childhood professionals understand the learning of a specific child or group of children; enhance overall knowledge of child development; improve educational programs for young children while supporting continuity across grades and settings; and access resources and supports for children with specific needs.

Assessment evidence is gathered from realistic settings and situations that reflect children's actual performance. To influence teaching strategies or to identify children in need of further evaluation, the evidence used to assess young children's characteristics and progress is derived from real-world classroom or family contexts that are consistent with children's culture, language, and experiences.

Assessments use multiple sources of evidence gathered over time. The assessment system emphasizes repeated, systematic observation, documentation, and other forms of criterion- or performance-oriented assessment using broad, varied, and complementary methods with accommodations for children with disabilities.

Screening is always linked to follow-up. When a screening or other assessment identifies concerns, appropriate follow-up, referral, or other intervention is used. Diagnosis or labeling is never the result of a brief screening or one-time assessment.

Use of individually administered, norm-referenced tests is limited. The use of formal standardized testing and norm-referenced assessments of young children is limited to situations in which such measures are appropriate and potentially beneficial, such as identifying potential disabilities.

Staff and families are knowledgeable about assessment. Staff are given resources that support their knowledge and skills about early childhood assessment and their ability to assess children in culturally and linguistically appropriate ways. Teacher training develops "assessment literacy," creating a community that sees assessment as a tool to improve outcomes for children. Families are part of this community, with regular communication, partnership, and involvement.

WHAT ARE THE ISSUES IN THE ASSESSMENT OF YOUNG CHILDREN?

myeducationlab
Go to the Building Teaching Skills and Dispositions section of Topic 4: Observation/Assessment in the MyEducationLab for your course and complete the activity entitled *Development of Infants and Toddlers.*

As with almost everything that has been and will be discussed in this book, issues surround essential questions about what is good practice, what is inappropriate practice, and what is best for children and families. Assessment is no different. Let's examine two important issues of assessment in early childhood.

Assessment and Accountability

There is a tremendous emphasis on the use of standardized tests to measure achievement for comparing children, programs, school districts, and countries. This emphasis will continue for a number of reasons. First, the public, including politicians and legislatures, sees

High-Stakes Tests Leave Minority Students Behind

Today, students from preschool to high school are subjected to an almost endless array of tests. These tests are designed to measure everything from achievement, abilities, interests, and reading level to friendship preferences. When these tests are used to make critical decisions about students that have serious school and life consequences, they are called *high-stakes tests*. For example, standardized achievement tests are used to make decisions about whether Maria or Mario should be promoted to the next grade or whether Jennifer or Johnny has to attend summer school. But grade promotion and summer school attendance are not the only high-stakes decisions about young children that are based on tests.

Take the case of Amir Diego Howard, a bright third grader at Sierra Vista Elementary School in Washo County, Nevada. Amir's teacher thought he was a perfect candidate for the school district's gifted and talented (GT) program, so she referred him. Amir did well in the first two steps of the district's three-step process for admission into GT. First, Amir had his teacher's recommendation. Second, he scored at the 96th percentile on a national standardized achievement test. The third step was the problem. Amir failed to score an IQ of 133 on the Kaufman Brief Intelligence Test. "Sometimes they gave me these huge words that you don't even know," said Amir about the IQ test. "Like 'autobiography.' I don't know what that means. I'm

only in the third grade." Unfortunately, across the country many language minority children like Amir fail to get into GT programs. Tests used to establish admission criteria discriminate against English language learners (ELLs) and minority students. As Joe Garret, Washo County GT curriculum coordinator, points out, "The kids that are English language learners, if they don't have the language and they don't have the background experiences, they are not going to do well on standardized tests we use to identify kids."

The good news is that increasing numbers of school districts are doing something about the inequities of high-stakes testing and how criteria for GT and other programs discriminate against English language learners. For example, districts are broadening and/or changing their criteria by:

- Placing more emphasis on nonverbal criteria such as learning styles and creative behavior
- Eliminating passing scores on high-stakes tests as a condition of program admission
- Placing more emphasis on teacher recommendation
- Changing admission criteria to ensure that more minority and ELL students are in GT programs
- Using language-free tests that don't discriminate against English language learners and minority children

assessment as a means of making schools and teachers accountable for teaching the nation's children. Second, assessment is seen as playing a critical role in the reform of education. As long as there is a public desire to improve teaching and achievement, we will continue to see an emphasis on assessment for accountability purposes.

High-Stakes Testing

High-stakes testing occurs when standardized or other kinds of tests are used to make important, and often life-influencing, decisions about children. Standardized tests have specific and standardized content, administration, and scoring procedures and norms for interpreting scores. High-stakes outcomes include decisions about whether to admit children into gifted or other special programs, whether to begin preschool or kindergarten, and whether to retain or promote children. Generally, the early childhood profession is opposed to high-stakes testing for young children because they are developing so rapidly in the early years. Also, high-stakes testing should be done by well trained personnel. However, as part of the accountability movement, many politicians and school administrators view high-stakes testing as a means of ensuring that children learn and that promotions are based on achievement. Many school critics maintain that in the pre-K and primary grades there is too much social promotion—that is, passing children from grade to grade merely to enable students to keep pace with their age peers. The Diversity Tie-In feature tackles the issue of bias against minorities in high-stakes testing.

high-stakes testing Using assessment tests to make important and often life-influencing decisions about children, such as whether to admit children into programs or promote them from one grade to the next.

ACTIVITIES FOR PROFESSIONAL DEVELOPMENT

ethical dilemma

"He's No Guinea Pig!"

Stacy Hibauch teaches in an inclusive kindergarten classroom. One of her children, Shaun, has Down syndrome. Shaun's mother is very protective of him and tends to be, in Stacy's opinion, overprotective. A professor from the local university contacted Stacy and asked her permission to send students to observe in her classroom. In his request he said, "I want my students to see how you accommodate a child with Down syndrome." Stacy thought it would be a good idea to tell Shaun's mom about the classroom observation. Her response caught Stacy off guard: "I don't want any college kids observing my Shaun! He's no guinea pig!" Stacy thinks the college students would benefit from observing in her classroom.

What should Stacy do? Let the college class observe, and not tell Shaun's mom? Or should she ask for a meeting with the school principal and Shaun's mom and try to work it out? Or should she just tell the college professor "No"?

Application Activities

1. Create an observation guide similar to Figure 6.5 or Figure 6.6. Observe in an early childhood classroom and determine how effective you are at observing some aspect of children's development and learning.

2. Observe a particular child during play or another activity. Before your observation, make sure you follow the steps presented in this chapter. Use the information you gathered to plan a learning activity for the child. As you plan, determine what information you need that you didn't gather through observation. When you observe again, what will you do differently?

3. Based on your knowledge and the information provided in this textbook, explain in fifty words or less why you think it is important for you to assess children. Provide three examples of how you will use observation to assess in your classroom.

4. Review the contents of several children's portfolios. How are they similar and different? What do the contents tell you about the children? What would you include that wasn't included? What would you delete?

5. Frequently articles in newspapers and magazines address assessment and testing. Over a two-week period, review these sources and determine what assessment and evaluation issues are "in the news." Put these materials in your portfolio or teaching file.

chapter seven

INFANTS AND TODDLERS

Critical Years for Learning

• • • • • • • • •

NAEYC Standards for Early Child Professional Preparation Programs

Standard 1. Promoting Child Development and Learning

I use my understanding of young children's characteristics and needs, and of multiple interacting influences on children's development and learning, to create environments that are healthy, respectful, supportive, and challenging for each child.[1]

Standard 4. Using Developmentally Effective Approaches to Connect with Children and Families

I understand and use positive relationships and supportive interactions as the foundation for my work with young children and families. I know, understand, and use a wide array of developmentally appropriate approaches, instructional strategies, and tools to connect with children and families and positively influence each child's development and learning.[2]

Standard 5. Using Content Knowledge to Build Meaningful Curriculum

I understand the importance of developmental domains and academic (or content) disciplines in early childhood curriculum. I know the essential concepts, inquiry tools, and structure of content areas, including academic subjects, and can identify resources to deepen my understanding. I use my own knowledge and other resources to design, implement, and evaluate meaningful, challenging curricula that promote comprehensive developmental and learning outcomes for every young child.[3]

 Interest in infant/toddler care and education is at an all-time high; it will continue at this level well into the future.[4] The growing demand for quality infant/toddler programs stems from the growing numbers of women with infants and toddlers in the workforce, as we discussed in Chapter 2. The popularity of early care and education is also attributable to a changing view of the very young and the discovery that infants are remarkably competent individuals.[5] We also know that the infant/toddler years are critical for growth and development. The experiences infants have—or don't have—influence everything from development to school readiness. Let's examine the ways that infants' and toddlers' early experiences shape their future development.

WHAT ARE INFANTS AND TODDLERS LIKE?

Think for a minute about your experiences with infants. What characteristics stand out most in your mind? I know that infants never cease to amaze me! Infants are capable of so many accomplishments. They are great imitators. Make a face at an infant and she will make a face back. Stick your tongue out at an infant and she will stick out her tongue at you. Talk to infants and they will "talk" back to you![6] One of the great delights and challenges of working with infants is that you will constantly discover the wonderful things they can do!

Have you ever tried to keep up with a toddler? Everyone who tries ends up exhausted at the end of the day! A typical response is "They are into everything!" And indeed they are! Toddlers are busy from morning until night getting up on and into things that parents and caregivers never expected! But, "getting into everything" is good for toddlers. Exploration helps toddlers learn about their world by using all of their senses. For parents and caregivers the challenge is to make sure toddlers can explore safely. Toddlers can even read your mind! Toddlers engage in "emotional eavesdropping" by listening and watching emotional reactions directed from one adult to another. They then use this emotional information to shape their own behavior.[7] Understanding other people's emotions is a critical school readiness skill. This is one reason infants and toddlers need emotionally stable teachers.

The infant and toddler years between birth and age three are full of developmental milestones and significant events. **Infancy**, life's first year, includes the first breath, first smile, first thoughts, first words, and first steps. Significant developments continue during **toddlerhood**, the period between one and three years. Two of the most outstanding developmental milestones of these years are walking and language acquisition. Mobility and language are the cornerstones of autonomy that enable toddlers to become independent. These unique developmental events are significant for children as well as those who care for and teach them. How you, other early childhood professionals, and primary caregivers respond to infants' first accomplishments and toddlers' quests for autonomy helps determine how they will develop and master life events.

As you work with infants, toddlers, and other children, constantly keep in mind that "normal" growth and development milestones are based on averages. Table 7.1, for instance, gives average heights and weights of infants and toddlers. Remember, though, that "average" is only the middle ground of development. Also consider the whole child and take into account cultural and family background, including nutritional and health history, to determine what is normal for individual children. Furthermore, when we provide children with good nutrition, health care, and a warm, loving emotional environment, development tends toward what is "normal" for each child.

FOCUS QUESTIONS

1. What are infants and toddlers like?

2. How does brain research influence your care and education of young children?

3. How can you support the psychosocial, emotional, motor, cognitive, and language development of infants and toddlers?

4. How can you provide developmentally appropriate and enriched environments to support infant and toddlers development?

5. How can you provide high-quality curricula for infants and toddlers?

6. What is infant/ toddlers mental health, and why is it important?

7. How can you accommodate for diversity in infant/toddler programs?

TABLE 7.1 Average Height and Weight of Infants and Toddlers

Age (months)	Males		Females	
	Height (inches)	Weight (pounds)	Height (inches)	Weight (pounds)
Birth	19.75	7.75	19.50	7.50
3	24.00	13.25	23.25	12.00
6	26.50	17.50	25.75	15.75
9	28.25	20.50	27.50	18.75
12	29.75	22.75	29.00	21.00
18	32.25	25.75	31.75	24.25
24	34.25	28.00	33.75	26.50
30	36.00	29.75	35.75	28.50
36	37.75	31.50	37.25	30.50

Source: Centers for Disease Control and Prevention, National Center for Health Statistics, "Clinical Growth Charts," 2001, http://www.cdc.gov/growthcharts.

infancy A child's first year of life.

toddlerhood The period of a child's life between one and three years of age.

Nature Versus Nurture

Does nature (genetics) or nurture (environment) play a larger role in development? This question is at the center of a never-ending debate. At this time there is no one right and true answer because the answer depends on many things. On the one hand, many traits are fully determined by heredity. For example, your eye color is a product of your heredity. Physical height is also largely influenced by heredity, as are temperament and shyness. Certainly height can be influenced by nutrition, growth hormones, and other environmental interventions, but by and large an individual's height is genetically determined.

On the other hand, nurturing and the environment in which children grow and develop also play an important role in development. For example, environmental factors that play a major role in early development include nutrition, quality of the environment, stimulation of the brain, affectionate and positive relationships, and opportunities to learn. Think for a moment about other kinds of environmental influences that affect development, such as family, neighborhood, school, and friends.

A decade or two ago, we believed that nature and nurture were competing entities and that one of these was dominant over the other. Today we understand that they are not competing entities; both are necessary for normal development, and it is the interaction between the two that makes children the individuals they are.

BRAIN DEVELOPMENT

Let's continue our look at young children with a discussion of the importance of the brain in ongoing growth and development. Brain and child development research has created a great deal of interest in the first three years of life. Research on the brain has enormous implications for early childhood education and for public policy. Brain research provides a strong basis for making decisions about what programs to provide for young children, as well as what environmental conditions promote optimal child development. Brain research also underscores the importance of early experiences and the benefits of early intervention services, thus pointing toward a positive economic return on investments in young children.

Public interest in the application of brain research to early childhood education has intensified. In many cases that research affirms what early childhood educators have

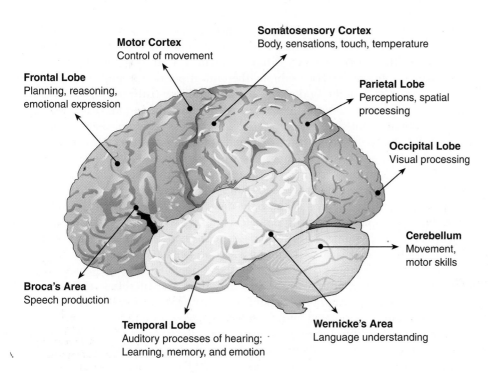

Frontal Lobe
Planning, reasoning,
emotional expression

Motor Cortex
Control of movement

Somatosensory Cortex
Body, sensations, touch, temperature

Parietal Lobe
Perceptions, spatial
processing

Occipital Lobe
Visual processing

Cerebellum
Movement,
motor skills

Broca's Area
Speech production

Temporal Lobe
Auditory processes of hearing;
Learning, memory, and emotion

Wernicke's Area
Language understanding

FIGURE 7.1 Brain Regions

always intuitively known: Good parental care, warm and loving attachments, and positive age-appropriate stimulation from birth onward make a tremendous difference in children's cognitive development for a lifetime. Let's review some interesting facts about infant and toddler brain development and consider the implications they have for your practice as a professional. Also review Figure 7.1, which shows the regions of the brain and their functional processes.

The brain is a fascinating and complex organ. Anatomically, the young brain is like the adult brain, except it is smaller. The average adult brain weighs approximately 3 pounds. At birth, the infant's brain weighs 14 ounces; at six months, 1.31 pounds; and at three years, 2.4 pounds. So you can see that during the first two years of life the brain undergoes tremendous physical growth. The brain finishes developing at about age ten, when it reaches its full adult size.

At birth, the brain has one hundred billion *neurons,* or nerve cells, which is the total amount it will ever have! It is important for parents and other caregivers to play with, respond to, interact with, and talk to young children because this is the way brain connections develop and learning takes place. Brain connections become permanent as they are used repeatedly. However, brain connections that are not used or used only a little may wither away. This withering away is known as **neural shearing** or **pruning**. This helps explain why children who are reared in language-rich environments do well in school, while children who are not reared in such environments may be at risk for academic failure.

Also, by the time of birth, these billions of neurons have formed over fifty trillion connections, or s*ynapses,* through a process called **synaptogenesis**, the proliferation of neural connections. This process will continue to occur until the age of ten. The experiences that children have help form these neural connections. Experiences count. If children don't have the experiences they need to form neural connections, they may be at risk for poor developmental and behavioral outcomes. In this regard, remember that while experiences count, not all experiences are equal! Children need high-quality experiences that contribute to their education and development.

neural shearing *or* pruning The process of brain connections withering away when they are not used.

synaptogenesis The formation of connections, or synapses, among neurons; this process of brain development begins before birth and continues until age ten.

critical periods Periods that represent a narrow window of time during which a specific part of the body is most vulnerable to the absence of stimulation or to environmental influences.

In addition, children need the right experiences at the right times. These "right times" are known as **critical periods**. Critical periods represent a narrow window of time during which a specific part of the body is most vulnerable to the absence of stimulation or to environmental influences.[8] For example, the critical period for language development is the first year of life. It is during this time that the auditory pathways for language learning are formed. Beginning at birth, an infant can distinguish the sounds of all the languages of the world. But at about six months, through the process of neural shearing or pruning, infants lose the ability to distinguish the sounds of languages they have not heard. By twelve months, their auditory maps are pretty well in place.[9] It is literally a case of "use it or lose it." An infant whose mother or other caregiver talks to her is more likely to have a larger vocabulary than an infant whose mother doesn't talk to her.

sensitive periods Periods of development during which it is easier to learn something than it is at other times.

Having the right experiences at the right time also relates to broad, developmental "windows of opportunity" or **sensitive periods** during which it is easier to learn something than it is at another time. Sensitive periods represent a less precise and often longer period of time when skills, such as acquiring a second language, are influenced. However, if the opportunity for learning does not arise, these potential new skills may not be lost forever. They may be harder to learn or they may not be learned fully.[10] During the last decade, scientists and educators have spent considerable time and energy exploring the links between brain development and classroom learning. Brain research provides many implications for how to develop enriched classrooms for children and for how to engage them in activities that will help them learn and develop to their optimal levels. Most importantly, brain research has made educators aware of the importance of providing young children stimulating activities early in life.

Applying Brain Research

Brain research also tells us a great deal regarding stimulation and the development of specific areas of the brain. For example, brain research suggests that listening to music and learning to play musical instruments at very early ages stimulate the brain areas associated with mathematics and spatial reasoning.[11] In addition, brain research suggests that gross-motor activities and physical education should be included in a child's daily schedule throughout the elementary years.[12] Regrettably, school systems often cut programs such as physical education and music in times of budget crisis, even though research shows that these programs are essential to a child's complete cognitive development. As you will see in our discussion of childhood obesity in Chapter 10, physical activities and exercise are essential for good physical health.

Brain-Based Guidelines for Teaching. As an early childhood professional, reflect on the following conclusions about the development of young children and consider the implications they have for your teaching:

1. Child development is shaped by a dynamic and continuous interaction between biology and experience. For example, the years from birth to age eight are extremely important environmentally, especially for nutrition, stimulation of the brain, affectionate relationships with parents and others, and opportunities to learn. Think a moment about how other kinds of environmental influences—such as family, school, and friends—affect development.

2. Culture influences every aspect of human development and is reflected in child-rearing beliefs and practices designed to promote healthy adaptations. For example, the kinds of foods parents feed their children, the ways they discipline, and their beliefs about the importance of education are based on cultural beliefs and customs.

3. The growth of self-regulation is a cornerstone of early childhood development that cuts across all domains of behavior. For example, children learn to regulate their

behaviors with the help of parents and teachers who provide help in controlling their behavior and who guide them in making good choices (see Chapters 4 and 12).

4. Children are active participants in their own development, reflecting the intrinsic human drive to explore and master one's environment. This drive to explore is especially evident in toddlers' constant exploring and "getting into things."

5. Child–adult relationships and the effects of these relationships on children are the building blocks of healthy development. For example, parents who read to children while on the rocking chair form positive relationships and happy memories of reading.[13]

6. The timing of early childhood experiences is important. However, children remain vulnerable to risks throughout the early years of life and into adulthood. For example, much of what represents a threat to healthy brain development involves what we call *toxic stress,* resulting from chronic negative experiences. Stressors include child abuse and neglect. We know that the presence of these stressors can change brain chemistry and affect behavior.[14] This is why professionals must help protect children from stress and harm.

PSYCHOSOCIAL AND EMOTIONAL DEVELOPMENT

We discussed Erik Erikson's theory of psychosocial development in Chapter 3. Review Figure 3.6 on page 80 before reading this section. The first of Erikson's psychosocial stages, basic trust versus basic mistrust, begins at birth and lasts about one and a half to two years. For Erikson, basic trust means that "one has learned to rely on the sameness and continuity of the outer providers, but also that one may trust oneself and the capacity of one's organs to cope with urges."[15] Whether children develop a pattern of trust or mistrust, says Erikson, depends on the "sensitive care of the baby's individual needs and a firm sense of personal trustworthiness within the trusted framework of their culture's life-style."[16]

Basic trust develops when children are reared, cared for, and educated in an environment of love, warmth, and support. An environment of trust reduces the opportunity for conflict among child, parent, and caregiver. In the accompanying Professionalism in Practice feature, "Power Tools for Teachers and Caregivers: The Three R's," Martha Pratt offers some ideas for how to use the three R's to improve your teaching to infants and toddlers.

Social Behaviors

Social relationships begin at birth and are evident in the daily interactions of infants, parents, and teachers. Infants are social beings who possess many behaviors that they use to initiate and facilitate social interactions. Everyone uses *social behaviors* to begin and maintain a relationship with others. Consequently, healthy social development is essential for young children. Regardless of their temperament, all infants are capable of and benefit from social interactions.

Crying is a primary social behavior in infancy. It attracts parents or caregivers and promotes a social interaction of some type and duration, depending on the skill and awareness of the caregiver. Crying also has a survival value; it alerts caregivers to the presence and needs of the infant. However, merely meeting the basic needs of infants in a matter-of-fact manner is not sufficient to form a firm base for social development. You must react to infants with enthusiasm, attentiveness, and concern for them as unique persons.

Imitation is another social behavior of infants. They have the ability to mimic the facial expressions and gestures of adults. When a mother sticks out her tongue at a baby, after a few repetitions, the baby will also stick out his tongue![17] This imitative behavior is satisfying to the infant, and the mother is pleased by this interactive game. Since the imitative behavior is pleasant for both persons, they continue to interact for the sake of interaction,

Power Tools for Teachers and Caregivers: The Three R's

Martha W. Pratt
Instructor, Early Childhood Education
College of Marin
Kentfield, California

Right now, every one of us is involved in a process of change. We can choose to ignore the process or we can choose to value the process. I call what follows the three R's for teachers. Making a commitment to use this process daily puts you on the path of assuming a personal responsibility to the children you care for and teach.

THE THREE R'S FOR TEACHERS
- Reflect
- Reevaluate
- Renew

REFLECT

Imagine yourself watching a video of what you are doing as you are doing it. What do you feel inside at the moment? Is there frustration or anger toward the baby or perhaps resentment toward a colleague?

- Kate has been an infant care specialist for about six months. She is rocking eight-month-old Tim. She usually has no trouble quieting Tim for his nap, but today it is just not working. Kate does some reflecting. She can't see anything amiss as she mentally watches herself. She checks her feelings and realizes that she is still holding on to the sharp words she and Liz exchanged earlier in the day.

REEVALUATE

As you watch the video, try objectively comparing what you see to what you know would be the "best possible" practice.

- As Nancy sets the lunches on the table in the toddler room she does a mental reevaluation of what she is doing. "Watching" herself she sees the mechanical, routine way she is doing the task. She is not proud of herself. She knows that if she had instead interacted with each individual child she could have made this experience rich with good feeling.

RENEW

Renew your commitment to improving your personal professional practice.

- Both Nancy and Kate are highly competent infant/toddler teachers and their use of the three R's helps them both catch themselves being less than competent from time to time. When this happens, they renew their commitment and improve their practice in the moment. How?
- Focus on the "you" of responding to infants and toddlers. Notice the inner thoughts you are having:
  - About yourself
  - About the baby you hold
  - About your beliefs concerning learning, teaching, and caregiving
  - About your *feelings* while you are *doing*
  - About what would make this moment better for this child

The change process continues. Your own willingness to *reflect, reevaluate,* and then *renew* your commitment to personal growth is what lets you take advantage of this ongoing process and become a better teacher and caregiver.

Remember, infants and toddlers learn how to see themselves by seeing their reflection through our eyes. We have a responsibility to make that a crystal clear reflection of them, not of our own preoccupations.

---

bonding A relationship between a parent and offspring that usually begins at the time of birth and that establishes the basis for an ongoing mutual attachment.

attachment An enduring emotional tie between a parent/caregiver and an infant that endures over time.

which in turn promotes more social interaction. Social relations develop from social interactions, but we must always remember that both occur in a social context, or culture.

Attachment and Relationships

Bonding and attachment play major roles in the development of social and emotional relationships. **Bonding** is a relationship that usually begins at the time of birth between a parent and child and establishes the basis for an ongoing mutual attachment.[18] It is a one-way process, which some maintain occurs in the first hours or days after birth. **Attachment,** on the other hand, is the enduring emotional tie between the infant and the parents and other primary caregivers; it is a two-way relationship and a strong affectional tie between a parent/caregiver and the child that endures over time.

Attachment behaviors serve the purpose of getting and maintaining proximity; they form the basis for the enduring relationship of attachment. Parent and teacher attachment behaviors include kissing, caressing, holding, touching, embracing, making eye contact, and looking at the face. Infant attachment behaviors include crying, sucking, eye contact, babbling, and general body movements. Later, when infants are developmentally able, attachment behaviors include following, clinging, and calling.

Adult speech has a special fascination for infants. Interestingly enough, given the choice of listening to music or listening to the human voice, infants prefer the human voice.[19] This preference plays a role in attachment by making the baby more responsive. Infants attend to language patterns they will later imitate in their process of language development; they move their bodies in rhythmic ways in response to the human voice. Babies' body movements and caregiver speech synchronize to each other: Adult speech triggers behavioral responses in the infant, which in turn stimulate responses in the adult, resulting in a "waltz" of attention and attachment.[20]

Multiple Attachments.   Increased use of child care programs inevitably raises questions about infant attachment. Parents are concerned that their children will not attach to them. Worse yet, they fear that their baby will develop an attachment with the caregiver rather than with them. However, children can and do attach to more than one person, and there can be more than one attachment at a time. Infants attach to parents as the primary teacher as well as to a caregiver, resulting in a hierarchy of attachments in which the latter attachments are not of equal value. Infants show a preference for the primary caregiver, usually the mother.

Parents should not only engage in attachment behaviors with their infants, but they should also select child care programs that employ caregivers who understand the importance of the caregiver's role and function in attachment. High-quality child care programs help mothers maintain their primary attachments to their infants in many ways. The staff keeps parents well informed about infants' accomplishments, but parents are allowed to "discover" and participate in infants' developmental milestones. A teacher, for example, might tell a mother that today her son showed signs of wanting to take his first step by himself. The teacher thereby allows the mother to be the first person to experience the joy of this accomplishment. The mother might then report to the center that her son took his first step at home the night before.

The Quality of Attachment.   The quality of infant–parent attachment varies according to the relationship that exists between them. A primary method of assessing the quality of parent–child attachment is the Strange Situation, an observational measure developed by Mary Ainsworth (1913–1999) to assess whether infants are securely attached to their caregivers. The testing episodes consist of observing and recording children's reactions to several events: a novel situation, separation from their mothers, reunion with their mothers, and reactions to a stranger. Based on their reactions and behaviors in these situations, children are described as being securely or insecurely attached, as detailed in Figure 7.2. The importance of knowing and recognizing different classifications of attachment is that you can inform parents and help them engage in specific behaviors that will promote the growth of secure attachments.

Temperament and Personality Development

Children are born with individual behavioral characteristics that, when considered as a collective whole, constitute **temperament**. This temperament—that is, what children are like—helps determine their personalities, which develop as a result of the interplay of their particular temperament characteristics and their environment.

temperament A child's general style of behavior.

FIGURE 7.2

Individual Differences in Attachment

Secure Attachment
Secure infants use parents as a secure base from which to explore their environments
and play with toys. When separated from a parent, they may or may not cry; but when
the parent returns, these infants actively seek the parent and engage in positive interaction.
About 65 percent of infants are securely attached.

Avoidant Attachment
Avoidant infants are unresponsive/avoidant to parents and are not distressed when
parents leave the room. Avoidant infants generally do not establish contact with a
returning parent and may even avoid the parent. About 20 percent of infants demonstrate
avoidant attachment.

Resistant Attachment
Resistant infants seek closeness to parents and may even cling to them, frequently
failing to explore. When a parent leaves, these infants are distressed and on the parentís
return may demonstrate clinginess, or they may show resistive behavior and anger,
including hitting and pushing. These infants are not easily comforted by a parent. About
10 to 15 percent of infants demonstrate resistant attachment.

Disorganized Attachment
Disorganized infants demonstrate disorganized and disoriented behavior. Children look
away from parents and approach them with little or no emotion. About 5 percent of
children demonstrate disorganized attachment.

Source: Based on Mary Ainsworth, *Patterns of Attachment: A Psychological Study of the Strange Situation*
(Hillsdale, NJ: Erlbaum, 1978).

The classic study to determine the relationship between temperament and personality development was conducted by Alexander Thomas, Stella Chess, and Herbert Birch.[21] They identified nine characteristics of temperament:

1. Level and extent of motor activity
2. Rhythm and regularity of functions such as eating, sleeping, regulation, and wakefulness
3. Degree of acceptance or rejection of a new person or experience
4. Adaptability to changes in the environment
5. Sensitivity to stimuli
6. Intensity or energy level of responses
7. General mood (e.g., pleasant or cranky, friendly or unfriendly)
8. Distractibility from an activity
9. Attention span and persistence in an activity

Thomas and his colleagues developed three classes or general types of children according to how these nine temperament characteristics clustered together: the *easy child,* the *slow-to-warm-up child,* and the *difficult child* (see Figure 7.3).

It is important to develop a match between children's temperament and the caregiver's child-rearing style. The parenting process extends beyond natural parents to include all those who care for and provide services to infants; therefore, it is reasonable to expect that all who are part of this parenting cluster will take infants' basic temperaments into account.

FIGURE 7.3

Children's Temperaments

Reflect on each of these three classifications based on temperament, and provide examples of how each temperament could affect the outcome of childrenís development.

Easy Children
- Few problems in care and training
- Positive mood
- Regular body functions
- Low or moderate intensity of reaction
- Adaptability and positive approach to new situations

Slow-to-Warm-Up Children
- Low activity level
- Slow to adapt
- Withdrawing from new stimuli
- Negative mood
- Low intensity of response

Difficult Children
- Irregular body functions
- Tense reactions
- Withdrawing from new stimuli
- Slow to adapt to change
- Negative mood

Source: Based on A. Thomas, S. Chess, and H. Birch, "The Origin of Personality," *Scientific American,* 223(2), August 1970, 102–109.

MOTOR DEVELOPMENT

Think for a minute of all the life events and activities that depend on motor skills. Motor skills play an important part in all of life! Even more so, motor development is essential for infants and toddlers because it contributes to their intellectual and skill development. Table 7.2 lists infant and toddler motor milestones.

Here are some general principles that govern motor development:

- Motor development is sequential.
- Maturation of the motor system proceeds from gross (large) to fine (small) behaviors. For example, as part of learning to reach, Maria sweeps toward an object with her whole arm. Over the course of a month, however, as a result of development and experiences, Maria's gross reaching gives way to a specific reaching, and she grasps particular objects.
- Motor development is from cephalo to caudal—from head to foot (tail). This process is known as *cephalocaudal development.* At birth, Maria's head is the most developed part of her body; she holds her head erect before she sits, and her being able to sit precedes her walking.
- Motor development also proceeds from the proximal (midline, or central part of the body) to the distal (extremities), known as *proximodistal development.* Maria is able to control her arm movements before she can control her finger movements.

Motor development also plays a major role in social and behavioral expectations. For example, toilet training is a milestone of the toddler period. Many parents want to

TABLE 7.2 Infant and Toddler Milestones

Children vary in the age at which they achieve major motor milestones.
The important thing to observe is that children achieve them.

Age	Milestone
Month 1	• Looks at faces • Lifts head when lying on stomach • Responds to sounds
Month 2	• Vocalizes, gurgles, and coos • Follows objects across field of vision • Holds head up for short periods
Month 3	• Watches faces intently • Raises head and chest when lying on stomach • Visually tracks moving objects • Begins to babble
Month 4	• Smiles and laughs • Can bear some weight on legs • Coos when spoken to
Month 5	• Can distinguish between bold colors • Plays with hands and feet • Can roll once
Month 6	• Turns toward sounds and voices • Imitates sounds • Rolls over in both directions • Reaches for objects
Month 7	• Sits without support • Enjoys playing games like pat-a-cake and peek-a-boo • Responds to name • Finds partially hidden objects
Month 8	• Says "mama" and "dada" to both parents • Grasps objects from hand to hand • Begins to crawl
Month 9	• Stands while holding onto something • Is beginning to understand object permanence
Month 10	• Waves good-bye • Crawls well, with belly off the ground
Month 11	• Says "mama" and "dada" to the correct parent • Stands alone for a few seconds
Month 12	• Imitates others' activities • Indicates wants with gestures • Speaks first word • Takes first steps
Month 13	• Uses two words skillfully • Walks with assistance

(continued)

TABLE 7.2 Infant and Toddler Milestones *(Continued)*

Children vary in the age at which they achieve major motor milestones.
The important thing to observe is that children achieve them.

Age	Milestone
Month 14	• Eats with fingers • Empties containers of contents • Walks without assistance
Month 15	• Plays with ball • Uses three words regularly
Month 16	• Turns pages of a book • Becomes attached to soft toy or other object
Month 17	• Can build a block tower using 3–4 blocks • Enjoys pretend games • Likes riding toys
Month 18	• Reads board books • Climbs; uses chairs and tables to reach toys
Month 24	• Names at least six body parts • Sorts by shape and color • Uses two- to four-word sentences • Kicks ball • Begins to run

accomplish toilet training as quickly and efficiently as possible, but frustrations arise when they start too early and expect too much of children. Toilet training is largely a matter of physical readiness, and most child-rearing experts recommend waiting until children are two years old before beginning the training process.

COGNITIVE DEVELOPMENT

Reflect on our discussion of cognitive development in Chapter 4, and think about how a child's first schemes are sensorimotor. Piaget said that infants construct (as opposed to absorb) schemes using reflexive sensorimotor actions.

Infants begin life with only reflexive motor actions that they use to satisfy biological needs. Consider sucking, for example, an innate sensorimotor scheme. Christina turns her head to the source of nourishment, closes her lips around the nipple, sucks, and swallows. As a result of experiences and maturation, Christina adapts or changes this basic sensorimotor scheme of sucking to include both anticipatory sucking movements and nonnutritive sucking, such as sucking a pacifier or blanket.

Children construct new schemes through the processes of assimilation and accommodation. Piaget believed that children are active constructors of intelligence through *assimilation* (taking in new experiences) and *accommodation* (changing existing schemes to fit new information), which results in *equilibrium* (see Chapter 3).

Stages of Sensorimotor Intelligence

Sensorimotor cognitive development consists of six stages (shown in Figure 7.4 Stages of Sensorimotor Cognitive Development and described in the following text). Let's follow Christina through her six stages of cognitive development.

Motor development plays a major role in cognitive and social development. For example, learning to walk enables young children to explore their environment, which in turn contributes to cognitive development. Can you think of other examples?

circular response Behavior that typically begins to develop in early infancy, in which an infant's own actions cause the infant to react or when another person prompts the infant to try to repeat the original action; similar to a stimulus–response relationship.

object permanence The concept that things out of sight continue to exist; this intellectual milestone typically begins to develop at four to eight months of age.

Stage 1: Birth to One Month. During this stage, Christina sucks and grasps everything. She is literally ruled by reflexive actions. Reflexive responses to objects are undifferentiated, and Christina responds the same way to everything. Sensorimotor schemes help Christina learn new ways of interacting with the world, which promotes her cognitive development.

Grasping is a primary infant sensorimotor scheme. At birth, Christina's grasping reflex consists of closing her fingers around an object placed in her hand. As Christina matures in response to experiences, her grasping scheme is combined with a delightful activity of grasping and releasing everything she can get her hands on!

Stage 2: One to Four Months. Sensorimotor behaviors not previously present in Christina's repertoire of behavior begin to appear: habitual thumb sucking (indicates hand–mouth coordination), tracking moving objects with the eyes, and moving the head toward sounds (indicates the beginning of the recognition of causality). Christina starts to direct her own behavior rather than being totally dependent on reflexive actions.

Primary circular reactions begin. A **circular response** occurs when Christina's actions cause her to react or when another person prompts her to try to repeat the original action. The circular reaction is similar to a stimulus–response, cause-and-effect relationship.

Stage 3: Four to Eight Months. Christina manipulates objects, demonstrating coordination between vision and tactile senses. She also reproduces events with the purpose of sustaining and repeating acts. The intellectual milestone of this stage is the beginning of **object permanence**, the concept that things that are out of sight continue to exist.

Secondary circular reactions begin during this stage. This process is characterized by Christina repeating an action with the purpose of getting the same response from an object or person. Christina will repeatedly shake a rattle to repeat the sound. Repetitiveness is characteristic of all circular reactions. "Secondary" here means that the reaction comes from a source other than the infant. Christina interacts with people and objects to make interesting sights, sounds, and events happen and last. Given an object, Christina will use all available schemes, such as mouthing, hitting, and banging; if one of these schemes produces an interesting result, she continues to use the scheme to elicit the same response. Imitation becomes increasingly intentional as a means of prolonging interest.

Stage 4: Eight to Twelve Months. During this stage, characterized by coordination of secondary schemes, Christina uses means to attain ends. She moves objects out of the way (means) to get another object (end). She begins to search for hidden objects, although not always in the places they were hidden, indicating a growing understanding of object permanence.

Stage 5: Twelve to Eighteen Months. This stage, the climax of the sensorimotor period, marks the beginning of truly intelligent behavior. Stage 5 is the stage of experimentation. Christina experiments with objects to solve problems, and her experimentation is characteristic of intelligence that involves tertiary circular reactions, in which she repeats actions and modifies behaviors over and over to see what will happen.

Christina and other toddlers are avid explorers, determined to touch, taste, and feel all they can. Novelty is interesting for its own sake, and Christina experiments in many

Stage 1: Reflexive action
Age: Birth to one month
Behavior:
- Innate reflexive actions—sucking, grasping, crying, rooting, swallowing
- Experiences enabling reflexes to become more efficient (e.g., amount of sucking required for nutrition)
- Little or no tolerance for frustration or delayed gratification
- Beginning to modify reflexes to accommodate the environment

Stage 2: Primary circular reactions
Age: One to four months
Behavior:
- Behaviors focused on own body
- Acquired adaptions
- Reflexive actions gradually being replaced by voluntary actions (e.g., repeatedly putting hand in mouth)
- Circular reactions resulting in modification of existing schemes

Stage 3: Secondary circular reactions
Age: Four to eight months
Behavior:
- Increased awareness of and response to people and objects in the environment
- Ability to initiate activities
- Fascination with effects of actions
- Beginning of object permanence

Stage 4: Coordination of secondary schemes
Age: Eight to twelve months
Behavior:
- Knowledge of cause-and-effect relationship
- Increased deliberation and purposefulness in responding to people and objects
- First clear signs of developing intelligence
- Continued development of object permanence
- Actively searching for hidden objects
- Comprehends meanings of simple words
- Combines new behavior to achieve goals
- Behaves in particular ways to achieve results; likes push-pull toys

Stage 5: Experimentation (tertiary circular reactions)
Age: Twelve to eighteen months
Behavior:
- Active experimentation through trial and error, leading to new outcomes
- Much time spent experimenting with objects to see what happens; insatiable curiosity
- Differentiates self from objects
- Realizes that "out of sight" is not "out of reach" or "out of existence"
- Initial understanding of space, time, and causality

Stage 6: Representational intelligence
Age: Eighteen to twenty-four months
Behavior:
- Development of cause-and-effect relationships
- Beginning of representational intelligence; child mentally representing objects
- Engages in symbolic, imitative behavior
- Beginning of sense of time
- Egocentric in thought and behavior

FIGURE 7.4 Stages of Sensorimotor Cognitive Development

different ways with a given object. For example, she will use any available item—a wood hammer, a block, a rhythm band instrument—to pound the pegs in a pound-a-peg toy.

Stage 6: Eighteen to Twenty-four Months. This is the stage of symbolic representation, which occurs when Christina can visualize events internally and maintain mental images of objects not present. Representational thought enables Christina to solve problems in a sensorimotor way through experimentation and trial and error and predict cause-and-effect relationships more accurately. She also develops the ability to remember, which allows her to try out actions she sees others do. During this stage, Christina can "think" using mental images and memories, which enable her to engage in pretend activities. Christina's representational thought does not necessarily match the real world and its representations, which accounts for her ability to have other objects stand for almost anything: a wooden block is a car; a rag doll is a baby. This type of play, known as *symbolic play,* becomes more elaborate and complex in the preoperational period.

LANGUAGE DEVELOPMENT

Language development begins at birth. The first cry, the first coo, the first "da-da" and "ma-ma," the first words are auditory proof that children are participating in the process of language development (see Figure 7.5). How does the infant go from the first cry to the first word a year later? How does the toddler develop from saying one word to several hundred words a year later? How does language development begin? What forces and processes prompt children to participate in this uniquely human endeavor? Let us examine some of the explanations.

Heredity and Language Development

Heredity plays a role in language development in a number of ways. First, humans have the respiratory system and vocal cords that make rapid and efficient vocal communication possible. Second, the human brain makes language possible. The left hemisphere is the center for speech and phonetic analysis and is the brain's main language center. However, it does not have the exclusive responsibility for language. The right hemisphere plays a role in our understanding of speech intonations, which enables us to distinguish between declarative, imperative, and interrogative sentences.[22] Without these processing systems, language as we know it would be impossible.

Theories of Language Development

Just as we have theories for how children develop mentally and socially, we also have theories that explain and help us understand children's language development. The following theories—while individually not necessarily fully explaining the process of children's language development—nonetheless, as a collective whole, do help us understand this important developmental process.

The Maturationist Theory. The **maturationist theory** of language development holds that language acquisition is innate in all children regardless of country or culture. This theory views speech production and related aspects of language acquisition as developing according to built-in biological schedules. They appear when the time is ripe and not until then, when a state of developmental "resonance" exists. Children become sensitive for language.

The idea of a sensitive period of language development makes a great deal of sense and held a particular fascination for Maria Montessori, who believed there are

maturationist theory A theory of language development stating that language acquisition is innate in all children regardless of culture, and that speech production and other aspects of language will develop as children mature, according to built-in biological schedules.

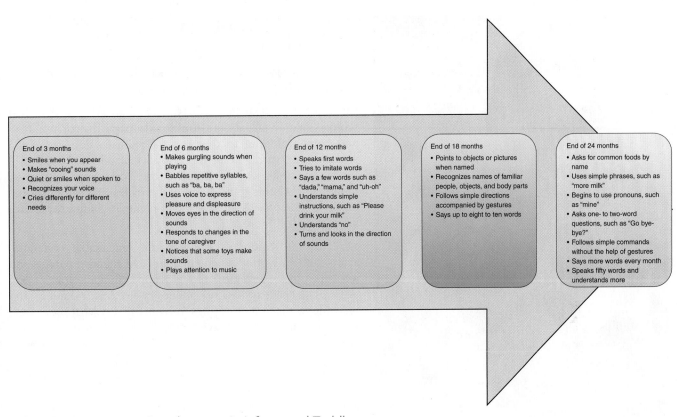

FIGURE 7.5 Language Development in Infants and Toddlers

two such sensitive periods. The first begins at birth and lasts until about three years. During this time, children unconsciously absorb language from the environment. The second period begins at three years and lasts until about eight years. During this time, children are active participants in their language development and learn how to use their power of communication. Refer again to Figure 7.5 for milestones of language development.

The Environmental Theory. In contrast to the maturationist theory, the **environmental theory** holds that while the ability to acquire language has a biological basis, the content of the language syntax, grammar, and vocabulary is acquired from the environment, which includes parents and other people as models for language. Development depends on talk between children and adults, as well as between children and children. Optimal language development ultimately depends on interactions with the best possible language models. The biological process may be the same for all children, but the content of their language will differ according to environmental factors. For example, ten-month babies learn words for new objects based on how interested they are in the object, whereas toddlers attach more importance to whether the parent or caregiver is interested in the object. This suggests that parents or caregivers should talk with babies about what the babies are interested in rather than what they are interested in.[23]

environmental theory
A theory of language development stating that while the ability to acquire language might have a biological basis, the content of language is acquired from the child's environment.

Language development begins at birth. Infants and toddlers need to be surrounded by a rich linguistic environment that enables them to develop the literacy skills necessary for successful learning.

holophrases One-word sentences that toddlers use to communicate.

symbolic representation The understanding, which develops at about age two, that something else can stand for a mental image; for example, a word can represent a real object or a concept.

The Sequence of Language Development

Children develop language in predictable sequences, and in an age–stage process, which is described next.

First Words. The first words of children are just that, first words. Children talk about people: dada, papa, mama, mommie, and baby (referring to themselves); animals: dog, cat, kitty; vehicles: car, truck, boat, train; toys: ball, block, book, doll; food: juice, milk, cookie, bread, drink; body parts: eye, nose, mouth, ear; clothing and household articles: hat, shoe, spoon, clock; greeting terms: hi, bye, night-night; and a few words for actions: up, no more, off.

Holophrasic Speech. Children are remarkable communicators without words. When children have attentive parents and teachers, they develop into skilled communicators, using gestures, facial expressions, sound intonations, pointing, and reaching to make their desires known and get what they want. Pointing at an object and saying, "uh-uh-uh" is the same as saying, "I want the rattle" or "Help me get the rattle." As a responsive caregiver you can respond by saying, "Do you want the rattle? I'll get it for you. Here it is!" One of the attributes of an attentive caregiver is the ability to read children's signs and signals, anticipating their desires even though no words are spoken.

The ability to communicate begins with "sign language" and sounds and progresses to the use of single words. Toddlers are skilled at using single words to name objects, to let others know what they want, and to express emotions. One word, in essence, does the work of a whole sentence. These single-word sentences are called **holophrases**.

The one-word sentences children use are primarily referential (used primarily to label objects, such as "doll"), or expressive (communicating personal desires or levels of social interaction, such as "bye-bye" and "kiss"). The extent to which children use these two functions of language depends in large measure on the teacher and parent. For example, children's early language use reflects their mother's verbal style. This makes sense and the lesson is this: How parents speak to their children influences how their children speak.

Symbolic Representation. Two significant developmental events occur at about the age of two. First is the development of **symbolic representation**. Representation occurs when something else stands for a mental image. For example, a word is used to represent something else not present. A toy may stand for a tricycle, a baby doll may represent a real person. Words become signifiers of things, such as ball, block, and blanket.

The use of mental symbols also enables the child to participate in two processes that are characteristic of the early years: symbolic play and the beginning of the use of words and sentences to express meanings and make references.

Vocabulary Development. The second significant achievement that occurs at about age two is the development of a fifty-word vocabulary and the use of two-word sentences. This vocabulary development and the ability to combine words mark the beginning of rapid language development. Vocabulary development plays a very powerful and significant role in school achievement and success. Research repeatedly demonstrates that children who come to school with a broad use and knowledge of words achieve better than their peers who do not have an expanded vocabulary. Adults are the major source of children's vocabularies.

Telegraphic Speech.   You have undoubtedly heard a toddler say something like "Go out" in response to a suggestion such as "Let's go outside." Perhaps you've said, "Is your juice all gone?" and the toddler responded, "All gone." These two-word sentences are called **telegraphic speech**. They are the same kind of sentences you would use if you wrote a text message. The sentences are primarily made up of nouns and verbs. Generally, they do not have prepositions, articles, conjunctions, and auxiliary verbs.

telegraphic speech
Two-word sentences, such as "Go out" or "All gone," used by toddlers.

Motherese or Parentese.   Many recent research studies have demonstrated that mothers and other caregivers talk to infants and toddlers differently than adults talk to each other. This distinctive way of adapting everyday speech to young children is called **motherese**[24] or **parentese**. Characteristics of motherese are:

motherese *or* **parentese** The distinctive way of adapting everyday speech to young children. *See also* parentese.

- The sentences are short, averaging just over four words per sentence with babies. As children become older, the length of sentences mothers use also becomes longer. Mothers' conversations with their children are short and sweet.
- The sentences are highly intelligible. When talking to their children, mothers tend not to slur or mumble their words. This may be because mothers speak slower to their children than they do to adults in normal conversation.
- The sentences are "unswervingly well formed"; that is, they are grammatical sentences.
- The sentences are mainly imperatives and questions, such as "Give Mommie the ball" or "Do you want more juice?" Since mothers can't exchange a great deal of information with their children, their utterances are such that they direct their children's actions.
- Mothers use sentences in which referents ("here," "that," "there") are used to stand for objects or people: "Here's your bottle." "That's your baby doll." "There's your doggie."
- Mothers expand or provide an adult version of their children's communication. When a child points at a baby doll on a chair, the mother may respond by saying, "Yes, the baby doll is on the chair."
- Mothers' sentences involve repetitions. "The ball, bring Mommie the ball. Yes, go get the ball. The ball, go get the ball."

In working with parents of infants, what would you do to encourage them to use motherese with their children?

Negatives.   If you took a vote on toddlers' favorite word, "no" would win hands down. When children begin to use negatives, they simply add "no" to the beginning of a word or sentence ("no milk"). As their "no" sentences become longer, they still put "no" first ("no put coat on"). Later, they place negatives appropriately between subject and verb ("I no want juice").

By the end of the preschool years, children have developed and mastered most language patterns. The basis for language development is the early years, and no amount of later remedial training can make up for development that should have occurred during this sensitive period for language learning.

Baby Signing.   Think of all the ways you use signs—gestures to communicate a need or emotion. You blow a kiss to convey affection and hold your thumb and little finger to the side of your head to signal talking on the telephone. I'm sure you can think of many other examples. Now apply this same principle to young children. Children have needs, wants, and emotional feelings long before they learn to talk. There is a growing movement of teaching children to use signs and gestures to communicate desires or signify objects and conditions. Beginning at about five months, babies can learn signals that stand for something else (e.g., a tap on the mouth for food, squeezing the hand for milk).

There is not universal agreement about whether to teach babies a common set of signs or to use ones that parents and children themselves make up. Linda Acredelo and Susan Goodwyn, popularizers of baby signing, identify these benefits: It reduces child and parent

A major part of your role as an early childhood professional is to provide a developmentally appropriate environment and activities for young children. This means that you must know infant/child development and individual children. You must also know how to apply that knowledge to a curriculum that will enable children to learn what they need to know for successful learning and living.

frustration, strengthens the parent–child bond, makes learning to talk easier, stimulates intellectual development, enhances self-esteem, and provides a window into the child's world.[25]

How to Promote Language Development in Infants and Toddlers

Providing a language-rich context supporting children's language and literacy is one of the most important things you can do as an early childhood professional. Following are some ways you can achieve this goal.

Treat Children as Partners in the Communication Process. Engage in conversations, smile, sing nursery rhymes, and make eye contact. Infant behaviors such as smiling, cooing, and vocalizing serve to initiate conversation.

Conduct Conversations. Talk to children clearly and distinctly. Conversations are the building blocks of language development.

Talk to Infants in a Soothing and Pleasant Voice. Mothers' language interactions with their toddlers are much the same as with infants. When conversing with toddlers who are just learning language, simplify your verbalization—but not by using "baby talk," such as "di-di" for diaper or "ba-ba" for bottle. Rather, speak in an easily understandable way. Instead of saying, "We are going to take a walk around the block so you must put your coat on," you would instead say, "Let's get coats on."

Use Children's Names. Use children's names while conversing with them. This personalizes the conversation and builds self-identity. The most important word to a child is his or her name. "My, Sarah! You look beautiful!" Infants who do not respond when their name is called may be more likely to be diagnosed with an autism spectrum disorder or another developmental problem at age two.[26]

Use a Variety of Means to Stimulate and Promote Language Development. Read stories, sing songs, and give children many opportunities to verbally interact with you and other children.

Converse and Share Information. Encourage children to talk and share information with you, other children, and adults.

Converse in Various Settings. Encourage children to learn to talk in various settings. Take them to different places—the library, the park, the supermarket, the post office—so they can use their language with a variety of people. This approach also gives children ideas and events for using language.

Have Children Use Language in Different Ways. Teach children how to use language to ask questions and to explain feelings and emotions. Tell children what they have done and describe things. "Mario! Great job! You got the book all by yourself!"

Teach the Language of Directions and Commands. Give children experiences in how language is used for giving and following directions. Help children understand that language can be used as a means to an end—a way of attaining a desired goal. "Bruce, let's ask Christina to help us put the blocks back in the basket."

Converse with Children About What They Are Doing and How They Are Doing It.   Help children learn language through feedback—asking and answering questions and commenting about activities—which shows children that you are paying attention to them and what they are doing. "Okay, let's read a story. Hillary, what book is your favorite?"

Use the Full Range of Adult Language.   Talk to children in the full range of adult language, including past and future tenses. Talk about what happened yesterday, before a diaper change, and what will happen next. "Okay, Cindy! We changed your diaper, now we are going to put on this pretty pink top."

Use New Words and Phrases.   Read stories and talk about new words. Children's vocabularies are a prediction of their learning to read.[27] Children with good vocabularies can engage others in conversations. So, you will want to develop children's vocabularies by reading to them and engaging them in conversations in which you use a rich vocabulary to identify people, places, and things.

DEVELOPMENTALLY APPROPRIATE INFANT AND TODDLER PROGRAMS

Most of the topics we discuss in this book have implications for infant/toddler education. First is the topic of developmental appropriateness. All early childhood professionals who provide care for infants and toddlers—indeed, for all children—must understand and recognize this important concept, which provides a solid foundation for any program. The NAEYC defines *developmentally appropriate* as having three dimensions:

- What is known about child development and learning—referring to knowledge of age-related human characteristics that permits general predictions within an age range about what activities, materials, interactions, or experiences will be safe, healthy, interesting, achievable, and also challenging for children
- What is known about the strengths, interests, and needs of each individual child in the group to be able to adapt for and be responsive to inevitable individual variation
- Knowledge of the social and cultural contexts in which children live to ensure that learning experiences are meaningful, relevant, and respectful for the participating children and their families[28]

Based on these dimensions, you must provide different programs of activities for infants and toddlers. To do so, you must get parents and your professional colleagues to recognize that infants, as a group, are different from toddlers and need programs, curricula, and environments specifically designed for them. For example, we know that sudden infant death syndrome (SIDS) occurs in very young babies—a developmental, researched fact. We also use the practice recommended by the American Academy of Pediatrics: that infants under the age of one year be put down for a nap or for the night on their *backs*.[29] As another example, we know that mobile infants and toddlers developmentally need lots of physical activity and opportunities to explore, so quality programs accommodate this need. Designing programs and practices specifically for different age groups is at the heart of developmentally appropriate practice. The early childhood education profession is leading the way in raising consciousness about the need to match what professionals do with children's development as individuals. We have a long way to go in this regard, but part of the resolution will come with ongoing training of professionals in child development and curriculum planning.

Finally, it is important to match teachers and child care providers with children of different ages. Not everyone is emotionally or professionally suited to provide care for infants

PEARSON
myeducationlab

Go to the Assignments and Activities section of Topic 2: Child Development/Theories in the MyEducationLab for your course and complete the activity entitled *Development of Infants and Toddlers*. Reflect on the mother's use of concrete materials to support and scaffold her child's development and how child caregivers help infants and toddlers through social interactions.

and toddlers. Both groups need adults who can respond to their particular needs and developmental characteristics. Infants need especially nurturing professionals; toddlers, however, need adults who are also nurturing and who can tolerate and allow for their emerging autonomy and independence.

Multiculturally Appropriate Practice

Children and families are not all the same. They do not all come from the same socio-economic and cultural backgrounds, and they do not all rear their children the same way. Consequently, it is important for teachers and caregivers to get to know children and families and to be culturally sensitive in their care and education practices. Even so, it may be that because of background and culture, families and professionals may not always agree on a particular policy or practice. For example, many infant/toddler programs teach self-help skills early and encourage children to become independent as soon as possible. These practices may conflict with some families' cultural beliefs and practices.

PREPARING ENRICHED ENVIRONMENTS TO SUPPORT INFANT AND TODDLER DEVELOPMENT

Research studies repeatedly show that children who are reared, cared for, and taught in environments that are enriched are healthier, happier, and more achievement oriented than children who are not raised in such environments.[30] Environments for infants and toddlers should be *inviting, comfortable, healthy, safe, supportive, challenging,* and *respectful.* You must plan in order to create environments with these features. Figure 7.6 shows an infant/toddler floor plan that you can refer to as you reflect on how you can create an enriched environment for infants and toddlers.

Also, as you plan, think about how you can make the environment as home-like as possible. Infants and toddlers like and need environments that are cozy, warm, and safe places to be. You can customize your children's home-like environment with curtains, family pictures on the walls, a couch, and so forth. Make sure that your home away from home includes objects from children's various cultures.

Following are some things you can do to provide an enriched environment for infants and toddlers.

Provide for Health and Safety

Safe environments are essential for infants, toddlers, teachers, and families. Some guidelines for providing safe environments for infants and toddlers include:

- Areas used for diapering and toileting are separate from areas used for cooking, eating, and children's activities.
- Mattresses used for infants are firm; avoid soft bedding, such as comforters, pillows, fluffy blankets, and stuffed toys.
- All infant and toddler toys are made of nontoxic, lead-free materials and are sanitized regularly.
- All required policies and plans of action for health emergencies requiring rapid response (such as choking or asthma attacks) are posted.
- Locations and telephone numbers of emergency response systems are posted and up-to-date.
- Family contact information and consent for emergency care are readily available.

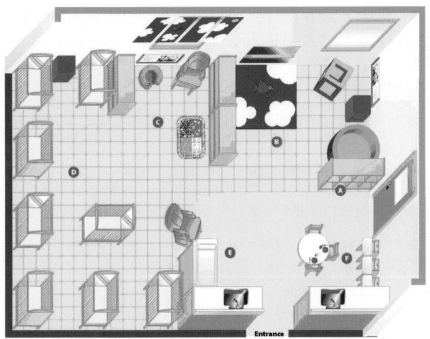

© 2007 Environments, Inc.

DIMENSIONS: 21' X 29' (609 square feet)
Each square on the floor represents 1 square foot.

- (A) Personal Storage
- (B) Mobile Infant Play
- (C) Non-Mobile Infant Play
- (D) Sleeping
- (E) Diapering
- (F) Eating

FIGURE 7.6 Infant/Toddler Floor Plan (0–18 months) for an Enriched Environment

Source: Environments, Inc., http://www.environments.com.

- Teachers, staff, volunteers, and children wash their hands with soap and running water after diapering and toilet use, before and after food-related preparation or activity, after hands have become contaminated with blood or other body fluids, after handling pets or other animals, before and after giving medications, before and after bandaging a wound, and after assisting a child with toileting.[31]

Provide for Basic Emotional Needs

Supportive environments enable infants to develop **basic trust** and toddlers to develop **autonomy** (see Chapter 3). Infant and toddler care should be loving and responsive to their needs. The trusting infant can depend on others to meet her needs. Toddlers want to do things for themselves and be independent.

- Meet infants' and toddlers' needs in warm, sensitive ways. Provide for their choices while taking into account their temperament, emotions, and individuality.
- Express love and be affectionate to your children. Tell them, "I love you!"
- Give infants and toddlers your undivided attention—respond to their actions.
- Treat each child as special and important.

basic trust An Erikson concept that involves trust, security, and basic optimism that an infant develops when nurtured and loved.

autonomy An Erikson concept that says as toddlers mature physically and mentally, they want to do things by themselves with no outside help.

Provide Space and Materials for Active Involvement

Young children need an environment that allows plenty of activity for them to grow both physically and intellectually. Here are some things you can do:

- Provide safe floor space indoors and grassy areas outdoors so children can explore and move freely.
- Provide low, open shelves that allow children to see and select their own materials.
- Have a cubby for each child's personal belongings. Personalize these with a picture of each child.
- Provide toys and objects that children can manipulate, feel, suck, and grasp.
- Provide objects and containers that children can use to put things in and dump out.
- Provide responsive toys that make sounds, pop up, and change color as children manipulate or act on them.
- Allow infants and toddlers to crawl, pull up, walk, move freely, and explore environments safely.
- Provide activities based on children's interests and abilities. This is a key to responsive and relational caregiving.
- Provide all kinds of books—stories, poems, and so on.
- Provide music as background and music to sing and dance to.

CURRICULA FOR INFANTS AND TODDLERS

Curricula for infants and toddlers consist of all the activities and experiences they are involved with while in your care. The curriculum provides for the whole child—the physical, emotional, social, linguistic, and cognitive aspects. Consequently, infant/toddler teachers plan for all activities and involvement: feeding, washing, diapering/toileting, playing, learning, having stimulating interactions, outings, being involved with others, and having conversations. You must plan the curriculum so it is developmentally appropriate.

All dimensions of the infant/toddler curricula are based on *responsive relationships*. This means that you are responsive to the *needs* and *interests* of each infant and toddler. For example:

> We should watch and observe our babies much more closely. What are they doing? How are they playing? What are they trying to achieve? Ask them who they are, what they need, how they can be helped. Then listen and watch for the answer and let that guide what we choose to do with our babies. In this way the baby will truly direct his or her care. The baby will lead. This is hard work for caregivers. To truly attend to and "be there" emotionally for babies is not a skill, but a way of being. Engaging in loving, responsive relationships with each individual baby while at the same time fully supporting the family/child relationship is a tall order. It requires that caregivers have a depth and breadth of knowledge about infant and toddler development; a high degree of self-awareness; a wellspring of emotional resources; and intense dedication to the well-being of other people's children.[32]

Provide Daily Routines

The infant/toddler curriculum is also built around routines of the daily organization and purposes of the programs. Routines include (1) arrivals and departures; (2) diapering and toileting; (3) feeding, mealtimes, and snacks; and (4) naps and sleep time.

Organizing the curriculum around routines and including routines in the curriculum provides children with consistency, security, a sense of safety, an increase of trust, and a general sense of well-being. Language development also provides you with an excellent opportunity to incorporate literacy into the curriculum.

Encourage Language Development

- Read, read, and read to infants and toddlers. Read aloud with enthusiasm, because this shows children how much you love to read.
- Read in all places and times—before naptime, when invited by children for special occasions, before and after outings, and so forth.
- Read from all kinds of books—stories, poems, and the alphabet.
- Provide books (washable, cloth, small board books, etc.) for children to "read," handle, manipulate, and mouth.
- Sing for and with children. Play a wide variety of music. Sing while changing diapers and doing other teacher–child activities.
- Read and sing nursery rhymes that provide children experiences with manipulating language.
- Talk, talk, talk.

As you promote and support children's language development you can also model and teach appropriate social interactions.

Promote Respectful Social Development and Interactions

- Use respectful language such "Please," "Thank you," and "Excuse me."
- Play games and engage in activities that include small groups of children.
- Play with toys that involve more than one child. For example, use a wagon and let one child pull another.

Encouraging children to help each other in activities such as block play allows them to learn and play cooperatively, which makes it easier for them to engage in challenging activities.

Provide Engaging and Challenging Activities

A challenging environment is one in which infants and toddlers can explore and interact with a wide variety of materials. It is important for you to provide all children with developmentally appropriate challenges. A challenging curriculum enables children to go from their present levels of development and learning to higher levels.

- Include a wide variety of multisensory, visual, auditory, and tactile materials and activities to support all areas of development—physical, social, emotional, and linguistic.
- Include materials for large and small muscles for reaching, grasping, kicking, pulling up, holding on, walking, and so forth.
- Provide materials for tactile and sensory stimulation.
- Hold, play with, and be responsive to infants and toddlers—you are the best toy a child has.
- Provide mirrors for infants and toddlers to look at themselves and others.
- Provide visually interesting things for children to look at, such as mobiles, family pictures, and murals.
- Take infants and toddlers on walks so they can observe nature and people.

Thinking about and planning for how you will relate and respond to infants and toddlers is based on the guidelines and the steps outlined in the Professionalism in Practice feature, "How to Plan a Curriculum for Infants and Toddlers: Day to Day the Relationship Way," a little later in this chapter.

INFANT/TODDLER MENTAL HEALTH

There is an ongoing emphasis on how to support the social and emotional competence of young children. Early childhood teachers recognize that robust social and emotional development plays an essential role in children's overall growth, development, and well-being. Figure 7.7 illustrates some of the causes of poor mental health in children, the associated outcomes, and some remedies available to early childhood professionals, community service

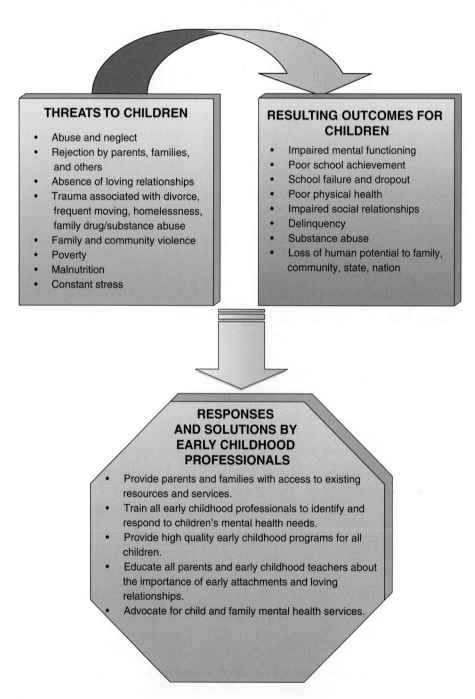

THREATS TO CHILDREN

- Abuse and neglect
- Rejection by parents, families, and others
- Absence of loving relationships
- Trauma associated with divorce, frequent moving, homelessness, family drug/substance abuse
- Family and community violence
- Poverty
- Malnutrition
- Constant stress

RESULTING OUTCOMES FOR CHILDREN

- Impaired mental functioning
- Poor school achievement
- School failure and dropout
- Poor physical health
- Impaired social relationships
- Delinquency
- Substance abuse
- Loss of human potential to family, community, state, nation

RESPONSES AND SOLUTIONS BY EARLY CHILDHOOD PROFESSIONALS

- Provide parents and families with access to existing resources and services.
- Train all early childhood professionals to identify and respond to children's mental health needs.
- Provide high quality early childhood programs for all children.
- Educate all parents and early childhood teachers about the importance of early attachments and loving relationships.
- Advocate for child and family mental health services.

FIGURE 7.7 Threats to Children's Mental Health, Resulting Outcomes, and Solutions

Infant Mental Health in a Cultural Context

The relational guidelines listed below identify cultural responsiveness as important for infant mental health.

Here are some things you can do to help ensure that your work with children and families is culturally appropriate and supports the positive development of infant mental health:

- Remember the important concept of individual differences. In any cultural group, there exist great differences between family practices, beliefs, and customs.
- Share stories about your own culture. Encourage others to share their culture and/or family's way of celebrating a particular holiday or milestone (e.g., birth of a child, wedding).
- Know and understand several basic phrases (e.g., hello, good-bye, thank you) in the language(s) represented by the families in your program.
- Explore your own cultural beliefs, practices, and assumptions.
- Provide training to staff in the role that culture plays in a child's development.

- Solicit songs and games from families from their home cultures—ask families and staff to provide bilingual labels for items found in the program.
- Ensure that all pertinent materials used by the program are available in the home languages of the families served.
- When food is served at a program-sponsored event, ensure that it is sensitive to the cultures of the families in the program.

As you reflect on these eight key cultural approaches to supporting infant mental health, consider what you will have to do to implement them into your program.

Source: Copyright © 2002 ZERO TO THREE. Adapted with permission of the copyright holder. Further reproduction requires express permission from ZERO TO THREE (http://www.zerotothree.org).

---

providers, mental health experts, and others. Providing for the whole child includes ensuring that children have high-quality social and emotional experiences and support. At the same time, with national interest in school readiness at an all-time high, early childhood teachers also recognize the major roles that emotional health and social competence play in children's cognitive development.

What Is Infant Mental Health?

Infant mental health is the "state of emotional and social competence of young children."[33] It occurs in the context of the interplay between nature and nurture. The nurture context consists of many "nested" and interrelated processes and factors, including parents' mental health, educational background, and socioeconomic status; parents' parenting knowledge and competence; home conditions; child care; school and community quality and resources; and the values and practices of family cultures.

Infant mental health then can be viewed as an interrelated set of relationships between children, parents, early childhood programs, and community agencies. The essential question for you and other early childhood professionals is how to best provide for infants' mental health. The Diversity Tie-In feature, "Infant Mental Health in a Cultural Context," provides you with ways to ensure that our work with infant and toddlers is culturally appropriate. Infant mental health is all about *relations*—relations among children, parents, child care programs, and other community agencies. Here are some relational guidelines you can follow:

- *Individualize attention.* Attention is given to the individual needs of infants and parents. Responsive caregiving of infants acknowledges and addresses their needs and behavioral temperament, and conveys the respect and security essential for early emotional development.
- *Emphasize strengths.* Early relationships emphasize the strengths and resources of infants and toddlers. Everyone has strengths, even the newborn. Helping parents understand their

infant mental health The overall health and well-being of infants and young children in the context of family, school, and community relationships.

How to Plan a Curriculum for Infants and Toddlers: Day to Day the Relationship Way

COMPETENCY BUILDER

Talitha (nine months old) leans against her teacher while laughing and giving her a quick hug while Marcus (thirteen months old) figures out how to make music with a small drum.

Kareem (eighteen months old) climbs into a teacher's lap with a book in his hand while Tanya (twenty-four months old) splashes water with her peers at a small water table.

All of these fortunate infants and toddlers have something in common. They attend programs in which teachers know how to plan a curriculum that is responsive and promotes relationships.

WHAT IS AN INFANT/TODDLER CURRICULUM?

A curriculum for infants and toddlers includes everything that they experience (from their perspective) from the moment they enter the program until they leave to go home. Every experience makes an impression on how children view themselves, others, and the world. Caring teachers plan a curriculum that is (1) relationship based and (2) responsive to infants' and toddlers' needs, interests, and developmental levels as well as their families' goals for their children.

WHY ARE RELATIONSHIPS IMPORTANT IN CURRICULUM?

A relationship is a bond of caring between two people that develops over time. In a relationship-based program, teachers support all the relationships that are key to children's development—parent–child, teacher–child, teacher–family, and child–child relationships. Children need these sustaining, caring relationships to give them a sense of self-worth, trust in the positive intentions of others, and motivation to explore and learn. They need protection, affection, and opportunities to learn to thrive.

HOW CAN YOU PLAN AND IMPLEMENT A RESPONSIVE CURRICULUM?

In a responsive curriculum, teachers interact with children and plan day to day the relationship way. Teachers make daily and weekly changes in the environment and in their interactions in response to each child's needs, interests, goals, and exploration of concepts. How do you do this? First, you *respect,* then you *reflect,* and then you *relate.*

STEP 1 — RESPECT

Respect that infants and toddlers are competent, motivated learners; recognize that play is the way young children learn; and honor individual differences. Recognize that infants and toddlers are active learners and thinkers who are using many different strategies to figure out how things work. In an emotionally supportive and interesting environment, they are motivated problem solvers, make good choices, and care about others. When infants and toddlers aren't sleeping or eating, they are usually playing with toys, people, and objects. As they make choices, infants and toddlers focus on *their* important goals for learning and nurturing—for example opening and closing a door on a toy, filling a hole on the playground, or playing with a friend. As they play, they explore concepts such as how objects fit into various spaces, cause and effect, object permanence, how to comfort another child, or what they can do with different sizes of paper (e.g., crumple, stack, make into a ball, etc.). Nurturing and responsive adults stay close by, support children's play, and meet their emotional needs by using all of the strategies described in the next sections. Respect that children are unique human beings with different styles (e.g., some eat fast and others slow), different interests, and one-of-a-kind personalities.

STEP 2 — REFLECT

Reflection is a process of wondering with families and other teachers about the child's unique interests, explorations, and culture. It is a process of observing children to know them well. You can use an observation and planning guide such as the one shown here to capture your observations.

As you reflect ask yourself the following questions: What is the child trying to do, and how is the child trying to do it? What is the child learning? (*Not:* What am I teaching?) What concepts (e.g., space, time, social interactions, expressing emotions, ways to open containers) is the child exploring? What is the child telling you he or she needs? (More positive attention, more affection, new strategies to use when another child takes a toy, more room to learn to walk?) What is new in the child's development? For example, is he or she learning to climb or jump, comfort peers, use two words together, or ask questions?

STEP 3 — RELATE

Relate to children by providing the basics—moment-to-moment responsive adult interactions.

- Comfort distressed children.
- Respond to children's cues and signals.
- Talk responsively with children, abundantly describe your own and the children's actions, and provide reasons and explanations.

- Sing, read, play with children, and respond to children's need for sleep, food, and comfort.
- Guide children to learn how to be prosocial by noticing when they are kind, modeling helpfulness, and demonstrating how to care for others.
- Be open and receptive to what each child is learning in the moment, and follow each child's lead.
- Encourage the children to experiment and problem-solve.

Individual Child Planning Guide

Child's Name: _Lamar_

Age: _2 years 5 months_

Plans for Week of: _July 6-10, 2010_

Person(s) Completing the Guide: _Kiki—toddler teacher_

Respect: Child's Emotions, Effort, Goals, Learning, and Relationships

Write an observation or use a photograph or other documentation here—date all notes:

7/6/09 - Lamar found the basket of balls in the active area. He pulled the basket into the center of the area, took out each ball one by one, and put them on the floor. As a ball would roll away, he would chase after it and bring it back. Mia joined him and he handed her two balls.

7/7 - Lamar's mother told us that Lamar loves balls of different sizes and textures and that he will throw a basketball into a short basketball net.

Reflect	Relate
What am I doing? Lamar is playing with balls of different sizes and shapes. *How am I feeling?* Lamar seems to be enjoying his uninterrupted time with the balls. *What am I learning?*	*What will you do to support my development and learning?* *Responsive Interactions and Building Relationships* As he plays with the balls a teacher could talk about what he is doing. Since Mia and Lamar enjoy being with each other we could have them sit together at lunch.
• *Emotional:* I am learning that the school environment is a safe place to play. • *Social with peers:* He is learning to give toys to other children. • *Cognitive:* He is learning about how toys fit into a space. He is learning how he can cause things to happen. He is learning about the properties of balls—that they roll. • *Language:* His experience with balls will help bring meaning to the word "balls." • *Motor:* He is using his large muscles as he runs after the ball and he is using the small muscles in his hands to remove the balls from the basket.	*Environment, Toys, Materials, and Experiences* We will bring in a sturdy box or basket so that Lamar can show the other children how to throw a ball into the basket. We will bring in other containers so he can continue to explore how things fit into the different sizes of containers.

Source: Wittmer & Petersen, *Infant and Toddler Development and Responsive Program Planning*, Box 12.4, "Individual Child Planning Guide: Version 1," p. 289, © 2010. Reproduced by permission of Pearson Education, Inc.

(continued)

(Continued)

- When a child becomes frustrated, scaffold the child's learning and motivation by helping just enough to support the child's learning how to do the task.
- Remember that sometimes you facilitate children's concentration and peer play by sitting near and observing with engaged interest.
- Relate during routines. Consider routines such as diapering/toilet learning, feeding/group eating, and nurturing to sleep as central parts of the curriculum for infants and toddlers. Use these times to support children's emotional development and other learning.
- Relate by using the observations and reflections to make changes—day to day and week to week in your interactions, the environment, opportunities, and routines.
- Plan new ways to support healthy relationships among teachers, children, peers, and families. For example, to help a child who has started to bite peers, plan for a teacher to stay near to help the child learn new behaviors to get needs met.
- Choose a few new songs to sing, books, toys, changes in the environment, and new opportunities (e.g., art and sensory materials, puzzles, manipulatives, large-motor equipment) based on the children's interests and learning. However, keep most of the environment and materials the same for the children's sense of security and stability.

In the following example, a teacher uses the *respect–reflect–relate model* to plan a responsive, relationship-based curriculum. She *respects* that each child is expressing a need or conveying an interest. She *reflects* by communicating with families, observing the child, and wondering about her observations. She *relates* by planning changes in the environment, opportunities for the child, and moment-to-moment responsive interactions to build healthy relationships.

Tommy (twelve months old) was dumping toys out of containers. His teacher observed the dumping and asked herself, What is he trying to do? How is he trying to do it? What is he learning? What does he need? She asked Tommy's mother how Tommy was playing with his toys at home. Tommy's teacher decided that he was interested in how a container can be full one minute and then empty the next. She provided more containers full of safe objects that Tommy could dump. Soon he also began to fill the containers as he explored different strategies for how objects fit into different spaces.

When teachers plan the curriculum in a responsive, relationship-based way, infants' and toddlers' motivation to learn and love gets stronger with each caring moment.

....

Contributed by Donna S. Wittmer and Sandra H. Petersen, authors of *Infant and Toddler Development and Responsive Program Planning: A Relationship-Based Approach* (Upper Saddle River, NJ: Merrill/Prentice Hall, 2006). Donna was a professor of early childhood education at the University of Colorado Denver for seventeen years. Sandy works for ZERO TO THREE.

infants' strengths, and the strengths that they bring to their caregiving, builds confidence within parents and supports their interactions with their infants.

- *Provide continuous and stable caregiving.* For the infant, continuous and stable caregiving builds confidence that their needs will be met. Especially in the earliest years, it is important for infants who are cared for out of the home to have a long-term relationship with a primary caregiver. For the parents, knowing that there are consistent people available to turn to—the child's caregiver, a home visitor, extended family, network of formal and informal support—is equally important.
- *Be accessible.* Relationships need to be accessible and responsive to when and how the infant and parent need attention and support. To achieve this for infants, adults need to understand the rhythm of the infants, being mindful of the cues infants send when seeking attention as well as those cues infants send when they are overstimulated. The parents and caregivers also need to be participants in supportive relationships. The extent to which the program staff and administration are available for parents helps to meet the individual needs of the adults, facilitating parents' responsive relationships with the infant.
- *Be culturally responsive.* You need to recognize the importance of understanding the values, beliefs, and practices of diverse cultures. Integrate diversity into your caregiving. In all interactions with children and their families, honor their home culture.[34] The accompanying Professionalism in Practice feature, "How to Plan a Curriculum for Infants and Toddlers: Day to Day the Relationship Way," demonstrates for you how to provide responsive and relational caregiving.

ACCOMMODATING DIVERSE LEARNERS

Infants' and toddlers' mental health and well-being is influenced by their parents. So, collaborating with parents and accommodating to their cultures and needs is an important professional role. As an early childhood professional, your students will come from home environments that are very diverse. For example, Hayden is a fifteen-month-old of West European ancestry and comes from a single-mother household. Eighteen-month-old Guadalupe is Mexican American and comes from the traditional two-parent household. Sixteen-month-old Lee is biracial with a Latino mother and a Chinese American father who works overseas six months of the year. James is a fifteen-month-old seventh-generation American, while at the other end of the spectrum eighteen-month-old Yahya's parents are refugees from Darfur. Families today represent a diverse group of parental parings, race, religion, socioeconomic statuses, and cultures. It is important to remember that culture influences parenting styles, beliefs about child rearing, education, and family responsibilities. As the teacher of all these children, you will want to make each and every parent and child feel welcome, safe, and valued. While at first you may find it overwhelming to effectively collaborate with so many diverse families, here are some tips:

- Care for and about all of your children, regardless of race, creed, or socioeconomic status. When you genuinely care for their children, parents are more likely to respond favorably to you. (See Chapter 1 for our discussion of the professional disposition of caring.)
- Talk with parents in order to learn about and incorporate aspects of children's lives at home into your classroom. Maintain continuity by using the same or similar books, providing opportunities to celebrate diverse holidays, and being respectful of religious and cultural traditions.
- Some parents may be dealing with feelings of separation anxiety or even guilt. You can help calm their fears by demonstrating that you know how to provide a high-quality education for their children. Provide classroom environments that are stimulating, safe, and inclusive.
- Keep a log in which you document children's developmental milestones. For example, on Tuesday, Lee was able to redress himself after toileting for the first time. Share this milestone with his parents. Take a digital photo of Lee dressed and proud of his success, write up his accomplishment on a piece of decorated paper, or provide a "certificate" of accomplishment. Parents will appreciate what their children have achieved—and will love that you appreciate it too!
- Maintain open communication with parents. Have a folder you send back and forth between home and school that contains behavior charts, art work, lists of daily schedules, and so forth.
- Help parents develop networks with other parents. A monthly coffee chat, a parents' night out, book clubs, joint resource libraries, or an Internet blog are excellent ways to encourage open discourse between parents. Such activities help break down cultural, economic, and language barriers and encourage development of family friendships.

PORTRAITS OF CHILDREN

I want you to understand what children are like. To help you achieve this goal, I have included two special features, Portraits of Infants and Portraits of Toddlers. The portraits, on pages 200–201, provide you with an "up-close" look at infants and toddlers. As you review each of these portraits, use them to consider how to apply what you have learned in this chapter. For example, for each child featured, what could you do to modify the environment to meet that child's particular needs?

Portraits of Infants

MARIA

Introduce yourself to Maria, a four-month-old Cuban female. Maria weighs 15 pounds and is 2 feet tall. She frequently expresses her mood through facial expressions and vocal sounds. Maria enjoys playing with her toys and has developed motor skills such as reaching, grasping, and kicking.

Social-Emotional	Cognitive	Motor	Adaptive (Daily Living)
Very vocal in expressing her needs and emotions	Attention is more efficient and focused	Holds up her head and chest	Is becoming more accepting of her primary caregiver
Indiscriminate when smiling at people around her	Recognition of people, places, and objects has improved	Reaches and grasps for toys	Has developed a cycle of bowel movements
Social smile and laughter have emerged	Babbles and coos a lot	Sits up with support	Is beginning to eat formula with rice—eats every four hours
Imitates father in face-to-face interaction	Attentive to surrounding environment—looks at everything	Rolls from her back to one side	Reaches and cries for caregiver when hungry

ETHAN

Introduce yourself to Ethan, a ten-month-old Caucasian male. Ethan weighs 21 pounds and is 2 feet 5 inches tall. He is inviting in nature and enjoys making eye contact with others. Ethan is very trusting but gets visibly nervous when his mother leaves the room. He is full of personality and is a very happy baby.

Social-Emotional	Cognitive	Motor	Adaptive (Daily Living)
Pouts when frustrated or angry	Is learning to talk—says "mama" and "dada"	Grabs caregivers' fingers and walks with their assistance	Is beginning to eat solid foods
Has special attachments to familiar caregivers	Knocks things down and points and laughs	Sits upright without assistance	Points to bottle and whines when hungry—grasps cup and tries to feed himself
Exhibits stranger anxiety—distressed when faced with a stranger	Plays peek-a-boo with his mom	Pulls to stand—walks while holding on to furniture	Prefers pacifier at bedtime rather than bottle
Sleeps with favorite blanket	Fits shapes into shape sorter	Manipulates small objects and toys in play	Is taking swimming lessons with his mom

Questions About Developmentally Appropriate Practice:

- What are some of the common traits between Maria and Ethan?
- What differences are there?
- What roles do Maria's and Ethan's caregivers play in their cognitive development?
- What roles do Maria's and Ethan's caregivers play in their social and emotional development?
- Why is it important for Maria's and Ethan's caregivers to talk to them on a frequent basis?
- Why is it so important for caregivers to verbally and physically interact with their infants at this age?
- What role might culture play in what Maria eats?
- Why is it important for you to be sensitive to cultural differences as you care for and teach young children?

Portraits of Toddlers

ABRIANNA

Introduce yourself to Abrianna, an eighteen-month-old Hispanic female. She weighs 24.5 pounds and is 2 feet, 5 inches tall. Abrianna is a very sociable girl and is talkative in Spanish. She loves to sing and is very independent; however, she looks for help from her caregiver when frustrated.

Social-Emotional	Cognitive	Motor	Adaptive (Daily Living)
Very sociable and talkative in Spanish	Loves to sing along with music	Walks up steps without help	Can feed self with spoon
Laughs when you call her name or make faces at her	Likes to pretend to be different animals; cats are her favorite	Can build a tower with four cubes	Looks for help from caregiver when frustrated
Makes eye contact and smiles	Uses twenty-five to fifty words	Scribbles with crayons; loves to "write"; enjoys playing with play dough	Likes to do things by herself—very independent
Is warm and affectionate	Points to named body parts	Throws and catches a ball with both hands	Can undress herself

ARIELA

Introduce yourself to Ariela, a twenty-four-month-old African American female. Ariela weighs 28 pounds and is 2 feet tall. She is a talkative child with an expansive vocabulary. Ariela is a highly creative child who enjoys drawing pictures as well as coloring in her coloring books.

Social-Emotional	Cognitive	Motor	Adaptive (Daily Living)
Self-conscious emotions such as pride, shame, embarrassment, and guilt are emerging	Knows the names of classmates; has vocabulary of more than 100 words	Mother began toilet training at twenty-one months—Ariela was responsive to the training and is now potty trained	Is beginning to use utensils when she eats
Shows signs of empathy—consoles her peers when they are upset	Knows names of colors and can count to ten	Is able to jump in place and walk on her tiptoes	Enjoys helping her mother with housekeeping activities
Does not share—very possessive	Interest in language has dramatically increased over the past two months	Walks up and down stairs without assistance	Gets upset when daily routine changes
Has favorite playmates	Can name familiar objects when caregiver points to them	Loves to draw—can draw both circular shapes and straight lines	Enjoys helping her mom choose her outfits for child care center

Questions About Developmentally Appropriate Practice:

- What role does Abrianna's and Ariela's cultural background play in their social-emotional development?
- In what ways are Abrianna and Ariela alike and different?
- Given their temperaments, what types of supervision would best fit Abrianna and Ariela?

ACTIVITIES FOR PROFESSIONAL DEVELOPMENT

ethical dilemma

"Should I Keep Quiet?"

Alexa is a toddler teacher at the Bent Tree Early Learning Center, a for-profit company. The state guidelines recommend a toddler ratio of 5:1. Generally, Alexa's room has ten children and two caregivers. However, the administration of Bent Tree overenrolls. The Bent Tree administrator justifies overenrollment in this way: "We can compensate for illnesses and other absences and always be fully enrolled. Full enrollment is important for our bottom line." As a result, on many days, Alexa has more children in her room than the recommended ratio. When the Bent Tree administration believes state licensing inspectors will visit the center, they shift children around from room to room so they are in compliance with the child–adult ratio. In addition, administrators often staff classrooms to comply with child–adult ratio guidelines.

What should Alexa do? Keep quiet and go along with the administration's juggling of child–adult ratios, or should Alexa talk to the administrators about her concern that they are unethically manipulating the system to be in state compliance?

Application Activities

PEARSON
myeducationlab

To check your comprehension on the content covered in Chapter 7, go to the Book Specific Resources in the MyEducationLab for your course, select your text, and complete the Study Plan. Here you will be able to take a chapter quiz and receive feedback on your answers.

1. You are invited to speak to a group of infant/toddler caregivers about relationship-based caregiving. Develop your presentation and list five specific suggestions you will make about key relationship-based practices for infants and toddlers. Share your presentation with others or online in an early childhood discussion group.

2. Observe children between the ages of birth and eighteen months. Identify the six stages of sensorimotor intelligence by describing the behaviors you observed. Cite specific examples of secondary and tertiary reactions. For each of the six stages, develop two activities that would be cognitively and developmentally appropriate for use with infants and toddlers.

3. Visit two programs that provide care for infants and toddlers. Observe the curriculum to determine whether it is relationship based. Before you observe, develop an observational checklist based on guidelines provided in Chapter 6. What suggestions do you have for making the program more developmentally appropriate?

4. Making the connection between how culture influences parenting and education is a difficult connection to make. Visit at least two centers that care for young children of different cultures to determine the role culture plays in how we care for and educate children. List the specific activities and materials that supported children's cultures.

THE PRESCHOOL YEARS

Getting Ready for School and Life

NAEYC Standards for Early Childhood Professional Preparation Programs

Standard 4: Using Developmentally Effective Approaches to Connect with Children and Families

I understand and use positive relationships and supportive interactions as the foundation for my work with young children and families. I know, understand, and use a wide array of developmentally appropriate approaches, instructional strategies, and tools to connect with children and families and positively influence each child's development and learning.[1]

Standard 5: Using Content Knowledge to Build Meaningful Curriculum

I understand the importance of developmental domains and academic (or content) disciplines in early childhood curriculum. I know the essential concepts, inquiry tools, and structure of content areas including academic subjects and can identify resources to deepen my understanding. I use my knowledge and other resources to design, implement, and evaluate meaningful, challenging curricula that promote comprehensive developmental and learning outcomes for every young child.[2]

The road to success in school and life begins long before kindergarten or first grade. It starts even earlier, in preschool. The preschool years are assuming a more important place in the process of schooling, and many view the preschool years as the cornerstone for learning.

WHAT IS PRESCHOOL?

Preschools are programs for children ages three to five to help ensure that they have the readiness behaviors and skills necessary for learning before they enter kindergarten. Today it is common for many children to be in a school of some kind as early as age two or three. In fact, 80 percent of all four-year-old children are in some kind of preschool.[3] Thirty-eight states currently invest in preschool education, in the form of public preschools or support for Head Start.[4] This widespread access to preschool is known as **universal preschool**, and more states are moving in this direction. In 2008, the fifty states spent $4.6 billion on preschool education.[5] There are approximately 552,000 preschool teachers in the United States who teach in many kinds of preschool programs.[6] What are these teachers like? Here are mini portraits of some preschool Teachers of the Year:

1. *Christine Lyall.* Christine Lyall works at the Culver City (California) Unified School District's Office of Child Development. Her teaching approach is sensitive to her children's various learning styles. For instance, she addresses logical-mathematical intelligence through hands-on materials and rhythmic patterning activities, which she creates herself.[7]

2. *Wendy Butler-Boyesen.* Science means success for Wendy Butler-Boyesen's students at EWEB Child Development center in Eugene, Oregon. She excites her young students by exploring different scientific themes each month, from hiking through local wetlands to studying the solar system.[8]

3. *Geralyn Dunckelman.* This Houma, Louisiana, teacher teaches Title I preschoolers often identified as at-risk, but refuses to use such labels, saying, "The only thing these children are at-risk of is making a difference in this world." Dunckelman embraces parents as the primary teachers of their children. When she became aware that one parent was illiterate while another spoke and read only Spanish, she recorded books in English for the family while recruiting a Spanish-speaking volunteer to create Spanish-language versions. These same parents eventually volunteered to read and teach Spanish to the class.[9]

4. *Lisa Frank.* Lisa Frank of McCloskey Elementary School in Philadelphia has students in her Bright Futures pre-K classroom try anything from yoga to sign language. She always makes it an enjoyable experience. For instance, once she transformed her classroom into a magical ocean environment, complete with blue cling wrap and sea-creature stickers on the window, an ocean-sound CD during naptime, and an edible ocean made of blueberry Jell-O and Swedish fish.[10]

5. *Karla Lyles.* Karla Lyles listens, observes, and engages her students in conversations. For example, when her students expressed interest in building houses, she took them on a construction-site field trip to explore the renovation of homes in their Chicago community. The class created a book filled with photos and captions from their excursion, and even enjoyed an on-site school visit by the backhoe driver they befriended on their trip.[11]

Benefits of Preschool

Figure 8.1 shows the educational and monetary benefits of investing in high-quality preschool programs. Often the public thinks that money invested in preschool programs does not have the impact that money invested in other programs has.

FOCUS QUESTIONS

1. What are preschools and why are they so popular?

2. What are preschoolers like and how can you support their physical, motor, social, emotional, cognitive, and language development?

3. What is school readiness?

4. What are preschool standards and how do they affect teaching and learning?

5. What does the preschool curriculum consist of?

6. What is the role of play in preschool programs?

7. How can you facilitate successful transitions to kindergarten?

universal preschool The idea that all children and families should have access to preschool, in the same way that kindergarten is available now.

FIGURE 8.1

What Research Says About Investing in Preschool

Program

Perry Preschool Project

- Children are educated through child-planned activities.
- Parents are involved through weekly home visits.
- Teachers are trained, supervised, and assessed.

Results and Benefits

- For every dollar spent, $7.16 was saved in tax dollars.
- At age forty, those who attended the preschool program had higher earnings, were more likely to hold a job, and had committed fewer crimes.
- The control group were 55 percent more likely to be arrested five or more times than the program group, at 36 percent.

Chicago Child–Parent Center Program

- Parents are required to participate in parent room or classroom activities at least twice a month.
- Parent education on nutrition, literacy, development, and so forth is provided in the parent room.
- Instructional approaches suit children's learning styles.

- For every dollar invested in the program, $7.10 was returned.
- Participants had a 51 percent reduction in child maltreatment.
- Participants had a 41 percent reduction in special education placement.

Abecedarian Project

- Primary medical care is provided on site.
- Each child has individualized educational activities.
- Activities promote cognitive, emotional, and social development, but focus on language.

- For every dollar invested, $4.00 was returned to taxpayers.
- 35 percent attended a four-year college, compared to 13 percent of the control group.
- 47 percent had skilled jobs, compared to 27 percent of the control group.
- Participants had significantly higher reading and math skills.

Sources: High/Scope Educational Research Foundation, "The Perry Preschool Study Through Age 40," http://www.highscope .org/Content.asp?ContentId=219; Chicago Public Schools, The Child–Parent Center and Expansion Program, http://www .waisman.wisc.edu/cls/Program.htm; The Carolina Abecedarian Project, http://www.fpg.unc.edu/~abc; and Pew Charitable Trusts, "The Trillion-Dollar Edge," http://www.pewtrusts.org/our_work_report_detail.aspx?id=29664.

Consider what the research outlined in Figure 8.1 reveals about spending taxpayer money in the early years. Today, more than ever, the federal and state governments are investing in preschool programs in order to build a stronger economy and country.

Why Are Preschools Growing in Popularity?

A number of reasons help explain the current popularity of preschool programs. With the falling economy and parents losing their jobs, finding affordable child care while trying to find a job has become a major burden on families. This in turn places a great demand on the early childhood profession to provide more programs and services, including programs for three- to five-year-olds. Many parents, however, are frustrated and dissatisfied with efforts to find quality programs for their children. They believe the federal and state governments, local communities, policy makers, and politicians should all work together to improve the quality of preschool education in the United States.[12]

Working Parents.   Working parents believe the public schools hold the solution to their child care needs so they advocate (rather strongly) for public schools to provide preschool programs. Some parents cannot afford quality child care; they believe preschools, furnished at the public's expense, are a reasonable, cost-efficient way to meet their child care needs. The alignment of the public schools with early childhood programs is becoming increasingly popular. Some think it makes sense to put the responsibility for educating and caring for all of the nation's children under the sponsorship of one agency—the public schools.

For their part, public school teachers and the unions that represent them are anxious to bring early childhood programs under the umbrella of the public schools. Public school teachers see their involvement as a step toward bringing higher quality programs to more children. The unions see preschool teachers as another source of growing membership.[13]

Highly Educated Workforce.   Second, a more highly educated workforce will increase economic growth.[14] Business leaders see early education as one way of developing highly skilled and more productive workers.[15] Many preschool programs include work-related skills and behavior in their curriculum. For example, approaches to learning or dispositions for learning are important preschool goals. Approaches to learning such as self-regulation and complying with rules and routines are essential workplace behaviors. We discuss approaches to learning again on pages 214–215. Likewise, being literate begins in the early years and literacy is an essential workforce skill. Research supports the importance of preschool early literacy learning as a basis for successful reading.[16] Learning to read is a high priority for our nation's schools. It makes sense to lay the foundation for reading as early as possible in the preschool years.

Equal Opportunity.   Third, many believe that early public schooling, especially for children from low-income families, is necessary if the United States is to promote equal opportunity for all. They argue that low-income children begin school already far behind their more fortunate middle-class counterparts and that the best way to keep them from falling hopelessly behind is for them to begin school earlier. Extensive research makes it apparent that investing in our children is important for all children—and not as expensive as some people believe.[17]

Cost Effective.   High-quality early education benefits children of all social and economic groups. It helps prepare young children to succeed in school and become better citizens; they earn more money; pay more taxes; and commit fewer crimes.[18] Advocacy exists for publicly supported and financed preschools as a means of helping ensure that all children and their families, regardless of socioeconomic background, receive the benefits of attending high-quality preschool programs.

The Perry Preschool Project—a longitudinal study that compared at-risk children who were from low socioeconomic backgrounds and at risk for school dropout but who received high-quality a preschool education against those who did not—attests to the benefits of high-quality preschool programs. The Perry Preschool Project found that those who received high-quality preschool educations were more likely to graduate from high school, earn more money, and own their own home, while they were less likely to have teenage pregnancies, engage in delinquency, be on public assistance, or be arrested for dealing drugs than children who did not attend high-quality preschool programs. The Perry Project shows us that in the long run and across multiple academic, social, and economic domains, it actually costs tax payers more *not* to provide high-quality education than it does to provide money for preschools.[19] The following is a comment typical of community leaders when discussing the value of preschools:

> You get what you pay for. Investing in high quality brings high return, not only in monetary, but also in human value. Socially and emotionally competent children who are well prepared to meet the challenges of school and life. Investing in bad or even mediocre programs yields at best, nothing, and at worst, children who enter kindergarten behind, many of whom never catch up. Further, as the Perry [Preschool] Project demonstrates, we get the biggest bang for our buck by investing in the neediest kids.[20]

PEARSON
myeducationlab

Go to the Building Teaching
Skills and Dispositions
section in Topic 2: Child
Development in the
MyEducationLab for your
course and complete the
activity entitled *Understanding How Young Children
Develop and Learn.*

What Are Preschools Like?

As preschool programs have grown in number and popularity, they have also undergone significant changes in purpose. In previous decades, the predominant purposes of preschools were to help socialize children, enhance their social-emotional development, and get them ready for kindergarten or first grade.[21] Today, there is a decided move away from socialization as the primary function for enrolling children in preschool. Preschools are now promoted as places to accomplish the following goals:

- Support and develop children's innate capacity for learning. The responsibility for "getting ready for school" has shifted from being primarily children's and families' responsibilities to being a cooperative venture among child, family, home, schools, and communities.[22]
- Provide children the academic, social, and behavioral skills necessary for entry into kindergarten. Today a major focus is on developing preschool children's literacy and math skills.[23]
- Use preschools to deliver a full range of health, social, economic, and academic services to young children and their families. Family welfare is also a justification for operating preschools.
- Solve or find solutions for pressing social problems. The early years are viewed as a time when interventions are most likely to have long-term positive influences. Preschool programs are seen as ways of lowering the number of dropouts, improving children's health, and preventing serious social problems such as substance abuse and violence.[24]

These goals of the "new" preschool illustrate some of the dramatic changes that are transforming how preschool programs operate and how preschool teachers teach. Given the changing nature of the preschool, it is little wonder that the preschool years are playing a larger role in early childhood education. They will continue to do so. In Charlottesville, Virginia, the preschool program is designed to provide a "stimulating environment and to provide and guide the educational experiences of each child."[25] To provide these educational experiences, a qualified lead teacher and teaching assistant work with up to sixteen children in one classroom. Charlottesville preschool programs focus on teaching students to make good decisions about their behaviors, to cooperate with other children and adults, to communicate with others about their experiences and feelings, to take initiative and solve problems, and to gain reading and math readiness skills and concepts.[26]

WHAT ARE PRESCHOOLERS LIKE?

Today's preschoolers are not like the children of previous decades. Many have already experienced one, two, or three years of child care. They have watched hundreds of hours of television. Many are technologically sophisticated and many use game-based computer entertainment. They have experienced the trauma of family divorce or the psychological effects of abuse. Many have experienced the glitz and glamour of boutique birthday parties or the poverty of being homeless. Both collectively and individually, the experiential backgrounds of preschoolers are quite different from those of previous generations. These factors raise a number of imperatives for you and preschool teachers:

- Observe and assess children so that you really understand what they know and are able to do.
- Conference and collaborate with families in order to discover their children's unique experiences, abilities, and needs.
- Develop programs to meet the needs of today's children, not yesterday's children. As children change, we must change our preschool programs to meet their needs and within the context of their experiences.

Physical and Motor Development

One noticeable difference between preschoolers and infants and toddlers is that preschoolers have lost most of their baby fat and taken on a leaner, elongated look. This process of "slimming down" and increasing motor coordination enables preschoolers to participate with more confidence in the locomotor activities so vitally necessary during this stage of growth and development. Both girls and boys continue to grow several inches per year throughout the preschool years. Table 8.1 shows the average height and weight for preschoolers. Compare these averages with the height and weight of preschoolers you know or work with.

Preschool children are learning to use and test their bodies. The preschool years are a time for learning what they can do individually and how they can do it. Locomotion plays a large role in motor and skill development and includes such activities as moving the body through space—walking, running, hopping, jumping, rolling, dancing, climbing, and leaping. Preschoolers use these activities to investigate and explore the relationships among themselves, space, and objects in space.

Preschoolers also like to participate in fine-motor activities such as drawing, coloring, painting, cutting, and pasting. Consequently, they need programs that provide action and play, supported by proper nutrition and healthy habits of plentiful rest and good hygiene. Good preschool programs provide for these unique physical needs of preschoolers and support their learning through active involvement.

Physical activities contribute to children's physical, social, emotional, linguistic, and cognitive development. It is essential that programs provide opportunities for children to engage in active play in both indoor and outdoor settings. What are some things that children can learn through participation in playground activities?

Social and Emotional Development

A major responsibility of preschool teachers is to promote and support children's social and emotional development. Positive social and emotional development enables children to learn better and to succeed in all of school and life activities.

During the preschool years (ages three to five), children are in Erikson's psychosocial development stage of initiative versus guilt (see Chapter 3). During this stage, children are fully involved in locomotive activities and the enjoyment of doing things. They want to plan and be involved in activities. They want to move and be active.

You can help support children's initiative in these ways:

- Give children freedom to explore in safe and secure indoor and outdoor environments.
- Provide projects and activities that enable children to discover and experiment. Preschool children like to work and play with their hands.

TABLE 8.1 Average Height and Weight of Preschoolers

	Males		Females	
Age	Height (inches)	Weight (pounds)	Height (inches)	Weight (pounds)
3 years	37.50	31.75	37.00	30.75
4 years	40.50	36.00	39.75	35.00
5 years	43.00	40.75	42.50	39.75

Source: Based on data from the National Center for Health Statistics in collaboration with the National Center for Chronic Disease Prevention and Health Promotion, 2000 (latest information), http://www.cdc.gov/growthcharts.

Go to the Assignments and Activities section of Topic 2: Child Development in the MyEducationLab for your course and complete the activity entitled *Art Development in Preschool.* Observe these children's artifacts. What conclusions can you make about each child's development?

self-regulation The ability of preschool children to control their emotions and behaviors, to delay gratification, and to build positive social relations with each other.

- Encourage and support children's attempts to plan, make things, and be involved. Preschool children like to build things and see the accomplishments of their efforts.

Self-Regulation. During the preschool years, children are learning **self-regulation**, the ability to control their emotions and behaviors, to delay gratification, and to build positive social relations with each other.

Teaching self-regulation (i.e., self-control or impulse control) is a major teacher task during the preschool years. The following guidelines will help you promote children's self-regulation:

- *Provide a variety of learning experiences.* Young children are very good at creating diversion when none is available. Often teachers think they cannot provide interesting learning experiences until the children are under control, when, in fact, the real problem is that the children are out of control because there is nothing interesting for them to do.
- *Arrange the environment to help children do their best.* Make sure block-building activities are accorded enough space and are protected from traffic. Avoid arrangements that invite children to run or get out of control, such as large open spaces.
- *Get to know each child.* Establish relationships with parents, and support children's strengths as well as their needs.
- *Set clear limits for appropriate and inappropriate behavior.* Enforce them with rational explanations in a climate of mutual respect and caring.
- *Develop a few simple group rules.* With preschool children, the simpler the rules, the better. I think it is best to begin the program year with a basic set of five (or less) rules such as:
  - Be nice to others.
  - Listen to the teacher.
  - Follow directions.
  - Hands are for helping.
  - Feet are for walking.

As you and the children discuss these rules and as the children get used to following them, you and they can modify, change, and add to the rules. Here are some other suggestions for helping preschoolers develop self-regulation:

- *Use children's home languages as often as possible.* Make every effort to show children you support their culture and respect their language.
- *Coach children to express their feelings verbally.* Help children use either their home language or English, and to solve social problems with others using words. For many children, this will mean not only providing the words and offering some possible solutions, but being there to assist when situations arise.
- *Model self-control by using self-talk.* "Oh, I can't get this lid off the paint. I am feeling frustrated [take a deep breath]. Now I'll try again."[27]

Cognitive Development

Children's preoperational characteristics have particular implications for you and other early childhood professionals. You can promote children's learning during the preoperational stage of cognitive development by following the steps presented in the accompanying Professionalism in Practice feature, "How to Promote Preschoolers' Cognitive Development." As you review these steps, start to plan for how you can apply them to your classroom.

Preschoolers are in the preoperational stage of intellectual development. As we discussed in Chapter 3, characteristics of the preoperational stage are (1) children grow in their

How to Promote Preschoolers' Cognitive Development

STEP 1
FURNISH CONCRETE MATERIALS TO HELP CHILDREN SEE AND EXPERIENCE CONCEPTS AND PROCESSES

Children learn more from touching and experimenting with an actual object than they do from a picture, story, video, or teacher's lecture. If children are learning about apples, bring in a collection of apples for children to touch, feel, smell, taste, discuss, classify, manipulate, and explore. Collections of things such as leaves, rocks, and bugs also offer children an ideal way to learn the names for things, classify, count, and describe.

STEP 2
USE HANDS-ON ACTIVITIES THAT GIVE CHILDREN OPPORTUNITIES FOR ACTIVE INVOLVEMENT IN THEIR LEARNING

Encourage children to manipulate and interact with the world around them. In this way, construct concepts about relationships, attributes, and processes. Through exploration, preoperational children begin to collect and organize data about the objects they manipulate. For example, when children engage in water play with funnels and cups, they learn about concepts such as measurement, volume, sink/float, bubbles, prisms, evaporation, and saturation.

STEP 3
GIVE CHILDREN MANY AND VARIED EXPERIENCES

Provide diverse activities and play environments that lend themselves to teaching different skills, concepts, and processes. Children should spend time daily in both indoor and outdoor activities. Give consideration to the types of activities that facilitate large- and fine-motor, social, emotional, and cognitive development. For example, outdoor play activities and games such as tag, hopscotch, and jump rope enhance large-motor development; fine-motor activities include using scissors, stringing beads, coloring, and using writing materials such as crayons, pencils, and markers.

STEP 4
SCAFFOLD APPROPRIATE TASKS AND BEHAVIORS

The preoperational child learns to a great extent through modeling. Children should see adults reading and writing daily. It is also helpful for children to view brief demonstrations by peers or teachers on possible ways to use materials. For example, after children have spent a lot of time in free exploration with math manipulatives, show children patterning techniques and strategies they may want to experiment with during their own play.

STEP 5
PROVIDE A PRINT-RICH ENVIRONMENT TO STIMULATE INTEREST AND DEVELOPMENT OF LANGUAGE AND LITERACY IN A MEANINGFUL CONTEXT

The physical environment should display room labeling, class stories and dictations, children's writing, and charts of familiar songs and finger-plays. Provide a variety of literature for students to read, including books, magazines, and newspapers. Paper and writing utensils should be abundant to motivate children in all kinds of writing. Daily literacy activities should include opportunities for shared, guided, and independent reading and writing; singing songs and finger-plays; and creative dramatics. Read to children every day.

STEP 6
ALLOW CHILDREN PERIODS OF UNINTERRUPTED TIME TO ENGAGE IN SELF-CHOSEN TASKS

Children benefit more from large blocks of time provided for in-depth exploration in meaningful play than they do from frequent, brief ones. It takes time for children to become deeply involved in play, especially imaginative and fantasy play. Morning and afternoon schedules should each contain at least two such blocks of time.

STEP 7
GUIDE CHILDREN IN PROBLEM-SOLVING SKILLS IN MATH AND SCIENCE

Apply and provide a variety of appropriate strategies to solve problems. Use graphic organizers in math. A graphic organizer such as a Venn diagram is a visual representation of material. The use of graphs is important. Children can graph many things—even their lunch requests! Many stories also offer a way to develop problem-solving skills. As you teach number concepts, use stories and visual representations. For example, there are five apples on the tree. Two apples fell on the ground. How many apples are on the tree? In science, ask questions such as "What do you think will happen if . . . ?"

diversity tie-in

Young English Language Learners

Linda M. Espinosa, Ph.D.
University of Missouri–Columbia
Columbia, Missouri

Increasingly, young children in the United States speak a language other than English in the home. The number of children enrolled in preschool and Head Start programs whose home language is not English (known as English language learners or ELLs) has been steadily increasing during the past two decades. During the 2006–2007 program year approximately 30 percent of children enrolled in Head Start did not speak English as their home language. Of these, the vast majority are from Spanish-speaking homes with 139 other language groups also reported.

Recent research has consistently shown that most young children are not only capable of learning two languages, but also enjoy cognitive, cultural, and economic advantages as a result of being bilingual. Bilingualism has been associated with a greater awareness of and sensitivity to linguistic structure, an awareness that is transferred and generalized to certain early literacy and nonverbal skills. There are several important implications of this research for early childhood professionals:

- Children who have the opportunity to speak two languages should be encouraged to maintain both, so they can enjoy the benefits that may accompany bilingual status.
- Maintaining the home language is essential not just to the child's future academic and cognitive development, but also to the child's ability to establish a strong cultural identity, to develop and sustain strong ties with their immediate and extended families, and to thrive in a global, multilingual world.
- Becoming proficient in a language is a complex and demanding process that takes many years. As with any type of learning, children will vary enormously in the rate at which they learn a first and a second language.

TEACHING STRATEGIES THAT SUPPORT HOME LANGUAGE MAINTENANCE

Many specific teaching practices are available that support primary language development. Here are some things you can do:

- Provide instructional support including paraprofessionals (instructional assistants, parent volunteers, and older and more competent students) whenever possible.
- Incorporate children's home language into the daily classroom activities through song, poetry, dances, rhymes, and counting.
- Create materials in the children's home language to represent familiar stories, songs, or poems that will improve early primary language literacy.
- Provide simple print material in the children's home language in learning centers, labeled objects, and writing utensils. This further supports early literacy abilities for non-English speakers. Each language can be printed on different colored paper to help children distinguish between them.

ability to use symbols, including language; (2) children are not capable of operational thinking (an *operation* is a reversible mental action), which explains why Piaget named this stage *preoperational;* (3) children center on one thought or idea, often to the exclusion of other thoughts; (4) children are unable to *conserve,* or understand that the quantity of something does not change simply because its appearance changes; and (5) children are egocentric.

Language Development

Children's language skills grow and develop rapidly during the preschool years. *Vocabulary,* the number of words children know, continues to grow. Sentence length also increases and children continue to master syntax and grammar.

During the preschool years, children's language development is diverse and comprehensive and constitutes a truly impressive range of learning. An even more impressive feature of this language acquisition is that children learn intuitively, without a great deal of instruction, the rules of language that apply to words and phrases they use. You can use many of the language practices recommended for infants and toddlers to support preschoolers'

- Encourage parents and other family members to continue to use the home language during family activities while also encouraging early literacy development in the primary language.
- Provide age-appropriate books and stories in the child's home language, loaning them to parents, with encouragement to engage in playful, interactive reading times. This will contribute to the child's motivation to read.
- Learn and use even just a few words of the students' home languages to communicate respect for the home language and culture. However, if you do attempt to speak the child's home language, it is important to pronounce the words correctly.
- Include family members and other community representatives in the classroom to provide language models in the home language. They can tell or read stories, help with translation if they are bilingual, and teach the rest of the class new words.

ENGLISH LANGUAGE FLUENCY

Many classroom instructional approaches are effective for English language learners. The following are specific suggestions to promote English acquisition for young children who are not native English speakers. These strategies are based on research and can also promote children's bilingual development if combined with home language support:

- Embed all instruction in context cues that connect words to objects, visuals, and body movements. This is what Tabors calls "doubling the message."* By connecting words with concrete objects and physical movements, you are increasing the probability that children will understand their meaning.
- Provide a consistent and predictable routine that frequently uses cooperative learning groups and small-group interactions. These regular opportunities for ELLs to converse informally with English speakers support second-language learning.
- Use small peer groups that give children opportunities to learn English in nonthreatening, secure environments. This can also promote friendships among children who speak different languages.
- Allow children to practice following and giving instructions for basic literacy tasks such as turning pages during reading, using pictures to tell a story, telling a story in sequence, and noting the names of main characters in a story.
- Allow for children's voluntary participation instead of strictly enforced turn-taking or teacher-led lessons.
- Help young English learners become a part of the social fabric of the classroom by systematically including a mix of first- and second-language children in organized small-group activities.
- Teach English-speaking children in the classroom to act as language resources for second-language learners, which could act as a catalyst to language development.
- Have students dictate stories about special personal events.
- Repeat words and directions frequently and explicitly throughout the day, calling attention to their sounds and meanings.
- Modify language use so that it is comprehensible for young second-language learners. Make it as simple, direct, and concrete as possible while systematically introducing new words that are unfamiliar.
- Speak at a standard speed with some pausing between phrases; use simple short sentences with clear referents; and use more gestures, movements, and facial expressions to help convey meaning.

*P. Tabors, One Child Two Languages: A Guide for Preschool Educators of Children Learning English as a Second Language (Baltimore: Brookes Publishing Company, 1997).

---

language development. The accompanying Diversity Tie-In feature provides you with specific examples of how you can support both home language and English language learning.

READY TO LEARN: READY FOR SCHOOL

School **readiness**—whether a child is "ready to learn" with the necessary knowledge, skills, and abilities—is a major topic of debate in discussions of preschool and kindergarten programs. The early childhood profession is reexamining readiness, its many interpretations, and the various ways the concept is applied to educational practices.

When asked "Does readiness matter?" the answer should be a big "Yes!" Research shows that students who enter kindergarten proficient across all readiness skills perform "significantly better" on standardized tests of English and math in third, fourth, and fifth grades than do children who have inadequate readiness skills or behaviors.[28]

Figure 8.2 shows important factors for kindergarten readiness. These are some of the things children should know and be able to do *before* coming to kindergarten. Thus they shape, influence, and inform the preschool curriculum and the activities of preschool

readiness Being ready to learn; possessing the knowledge, skills, and abilities necessary for learning and for success in school.

FIGURE 8.2 The Basic
Building Blocks of
Kindergarten Readiness

*Source: Kindergarten Observation
Form,* Applied Survey Research,
2009. Used with permission.

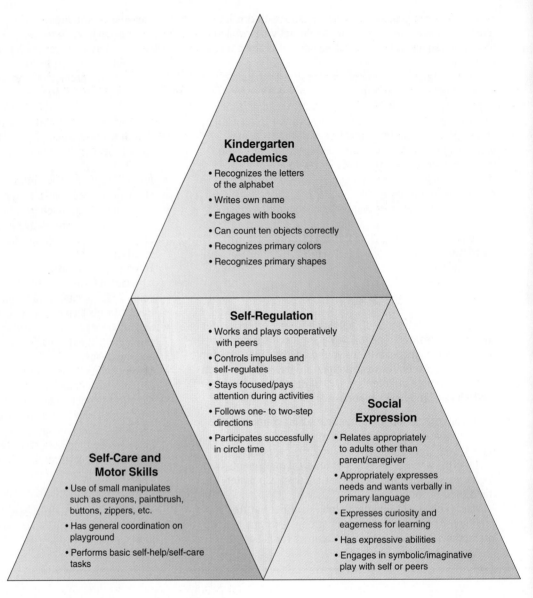

teachers. Review these now and think about their implications for what you will teach preschoolers to know and do.

Discussions about readiness have changed the public's attitude about what it means. Responsibility for children's early learning and development is no longer placed solely on children and their parents but rather is seen as a shared responsibility among children, parents, families, early childhood professionals, communities, states, and the nation.

School Readiness Skills and Dispositions

Readiness is not something that exists in the abstract. It consists of specific and well identified skills and dispositions. Some of these specific and well identified dispositions in "getting ready for school" are discussed next.

Approaches to Learning.

Four-year-old Luis is hard at work completing a puzzle. The puzzle, given to him by his teacher, is a little harder than the ones he has worked on before. He picks up a puzzle piece and looks at the puzzle, trying to decide where it might go. He tries it one way. It doesn't fit. He turns it around and tries again. Success! He has been working at the puzzle for a long time. His teacher comments, "Luis, you are working so hard to finish that puzzle."[29]

Luis has demonstrated that he has certain dispositions that will serve him well when he enters kindergarten. He is able to persist with a task, try something different when what he first tried did not work, and has the self-control necessary to pay attention. These dispositions are part of what we call **approaches to learning**. Approaches to learning are the inclinations, dispositions, and learning styles necessary to interact effectively with the learning environment. Approaches to learning include:[30]

1. *Curiosity/initiative.* The child is eager to learn and willing to try a variety of new and challenging activities.

2. *Persistence.* The child is able to persevere and complete a variety of tasks and activities, even if the first attempts are unsuccessful.

3. *Attention.* The child has the ability to concentrate when necessary and to pay attention during teacher-directed activities.

4. *Self-direction.* The child is able to set goals, make choices, and manage his or her time with increased independence.

5. *Problem solving.* The child is able to solve problems in a variety of ways, including finding more than one solution, investigation, and collaboration with peers.

6. *Creativity.* The child is able to address tasks with increased flexibility and originality.

Language.   Language is the most important readiness skill. Children need language skills for success in school and life. Important language skills include:

- *Receptive language,* such as listening to the teacher and following directions
- **Expressive language,** which includes the ability to talk fluently and articulately communicate needs and ideas with teacher and peers, to express oneself in the language of the school
- **Symbolic language,** or knowing the names of people, places, and things, knowing words for concepts, and knowing how to use adjectives and prepositions
- *Vocabulary development.* which should be three to four thousand words by the time preschoolers enter kindergarten[31]

Early Literacy Skills.   Reading and writing skills that are developed in the years from birth to age five have a clear and consistently strong relationship with later literacy skills. Six variables representing early literacy skills predict later measures of literacy development. These six variables are correlated with later literacy development:[32]

- **Alphabetic knowledge (AK):** Knowledge of the names and sounds associated with printed letters
- **Phonological awareness (PA):** The ability to detect, manipulate, or analyze the auditory aspects of spoken language (including the ability to distinguish or segment words, syllables, or phonemes), independent of meaning
- **Rapid automatic naming (RAN)** *of letters or digits*: The ability to rapidly name a sequence of random letters or digits
- *RAN of objects or colors*: The ability to rapidly name a sequence of repeating random sets of pictures of objects (e.g., "car," "tree," "house," "man") or colors
- *Writing or writing name*: The ability to write letters in isolation on request or to write one's own name
- **Phonological memory (PM):** The ability to remember spoken information for a short period of time

---

approaches to learning
Inclinations, dispositions, and learning styles necessary to interact effectively with the learning environment.

expressive language
A readiness skill that includes the ability to articulate fluently, to communicate needs and ideas with teacher and peers, and to express oneself.

symbolic language
A readiness skill that involves knowing the names of people, places, and things; understanding that words represent concepts.

alphabetic knowledge (AK)
Knowledge of the names and sounds associated with printed letters.

phonological awareness (PA)
The ability to detect, manipulate, or analyze the auditory aspects of spoken language (including the ability to distinguish or segment words, syllables, or phonemes), independent of meaning.

rapid automatic naming (RAN) The ability to rapidly name a random sequence, such as a random sequence of letters, digits, colors, or pictures of objects.

phonological memory (PM)
The ability to remember spoken information for a short period of time.

How to Use Technology as a Scaffolding Tool in the Preschool Classroom

Technology can be an exciting tool to help children acquire early literacy skills. Using cameras, printers, scanners, and software provides endless possibilities for personalizing literacy activities.

SELECT THE EQUIPMENT

You need several pieces of equipment to create literacy materials and activities.

Digital Camera

An inexpensive camera may work just as well as a special model designed for children. There are a number of features to consider:

- Resolution—the sharpness of the pictures expressed in pixels (the higher the resolution, the better the picture)
- Optical zoom—magnifies the images using a multifocal-length lens
- Image capacity—memory capability for images shot at high resolution
- Expansion slot for memory card
- LCD display for children to review pictures

Digital Video Camera

- Use to document events in the classroom.
- Use a tripod to ease use and avoid accidents.

Printer and Scanner

- A color printer is essential for book making and literacy material creation.
- Scanners can transfer children's writing samples and artwork into a digital format.

PDA (Personal Digital Assistant)

- These handheld devices usually include a date book, address book, task list, memo pad, clock, and calculator software. Some models have Internet access, color screens, and audio capabilities, enabling them to show multimedia content.
- This important documentation tool can record a child's progress.
- Children's work can be captured in photo form.
- Software application is key to use with children's portfolio items.

LEARN TO USE THE EQUIPMENT

Most equipment is fairly user-friendly, requiring very little, if any, instruction to operate.

- Become familiar with all options and test them.
- Make sure equipment is easy for children to use.

The manufacturer may have tutorials that are downloadable from its website. Online training sites may also offer tips and training on using technology.

CHOOSE THE SOFTWARE

Before you choose software, decide on the literacy activity:

- For creating simple books or class slide shows, use a photo-management type of program—such as *iPhoto*, *Kodak EasyShare*, or *Photo Kit Junior*.
- For interactive books, authoring software is best—such as *Classroom Suite*, *HyperStudio*, or even *Microsoft Word*.

Teaching English Language Learners. A reality of teaching in the preschool today is that some students will come to your classroom not speaking any English. Others will be in stages of English acquisition ranging from speaking very little English to speaking it very well. In 2007, 21 percent of children spoke a language other than English at home[33] and 5.3 percent had difficulty speaking English.[34] In all, over ten million children speak a language other than English in the home.[35] Other than English, in the United States, Spanish is the most often spoken home language. Other common home languages are Chinese and Vietnamese.[36] Furthermore, your chances of having to teach children English increases dramatically in high-minority population states such as Arizona, California, Florida, Illinois, New Jersey, New York, and Texas.[37]

As discussed in earlier chapters of this book, children whose home language is not English are called *English language learners* (ELLs). They are learning English as their second language. Preschool ELLs are like other preschoolers. Everything we have said about

CREATE LITERACY ACTIVITIES FOR THE CHILDREN

When they create their own electronic books, children learn many print concepts, including reading text left to right and top to bottom, separating words with a space, and learning that words have meaning.

Electronic Book Templates

- Each child can create a book about him- or herself or can base it on a field trip, class project, or favorite book.
- Children can add their own pictures, voices, and text.
- Page-turning buttons in the bottom corners of each page allow children to navigate forward and backward through the book.

Child-Created Books

Children in preschool classes can learn to use digital cameras, download pictures to the computer, and use software to create books.

- Explain how to plug the camera into the computer and download the pictures.
- Show children how to use the photo management application.
- Teach children how to enter text and sounds into the program.
- Encourage children to work in small groups to benefit from cooperative play.

DOCUMENT THE LEARNING

- **Daily documentation.** Take digital photos in the classroom on an ongoing basis. Pictures of children's construction, artwork, or play activities can be shared immediately with them. The teacher may also want to share the images with the class as a review of the week's activities and projects.
- **Wall displays.** Displaying digital pictures in a hallway or on a classroom wall gives children documentation of events and an opportunity to review and revisit. Children's language skills are sparked as they review the pictures. They may also dictate a narrative about the pictures and events.
- **Portfolios.** Have digital photos, scanned photos, writing samples, and artwork in children's individual electronic portfolio files. At the end of the year, copy the images to a CD or DVD for families, or create an electronic book or movie about each child. Families might also create their own books during a workshop at the end of the year. With simple instructions and a template, they can choose the images to place in children's books.

Technology is a scaffolding tool for literacy when educators and families know how to use equipment and apply it to young children's needs. Children gain print concepts and other early literacy skills, and the technology serves as a valuable documentation tool.

*L. Robinson, "Technology as a Scaffold for Emergent Literacy: Interactive Storybooks for Toddlers," Young Children, 58(6), November 2003, 42–48.

....

Contributed by Linda Robinson, assistant director, Center for Best Practices in Early Childhood, Western Illinois University, Macomb, Illinois.

children's cognitive, physical, linguistic, and social-emotional development applies to them. They are bright, active, and they want to learn!

The following guidelines will provide you with teaching strategies you can apply to your teaching of ELLs:

- *Keep ELLs active and involved.* Provide motor and kinesthetic activities such as playing games involving basic English words, acting out stories, and helping with classroom chores.
- *Create a buddy system.* Pair ELLs with other children who are native English speakers or who know English well.
- *Teach daily living and vocabulary words and phrases.* Teach vocabulary and phrases that enable ELLs to greet others and identify objects in the classroom and home. Teach words they need to get along in everyday life such as days of the week. Have children

make their own dictionaries of pictures labeled with words. They can have a picture dictionary for school and one for home. Help children learn oral language skills first. Then emphasize writing skills, followed by learning-to-read skills.

- *Incorporate children's culture into classroom activities.* Classroom activities and themes that focus on the children—such as "all about me"—enable you to support and celebrate children's unique cultural identities.
- *Integrate technology into children's English learning.* Use language-learning software to help your students learn English, such as the Zip Zoom English software by Scholastic that aids in developing critical language and reading skills for ELLs in grades K–3. The Technology Tie-In feature explores ways in which technology can assist in any child's literacy development.

Readiness and Culture

Every child is always ready for some kind of learning. Children always need experiences that will promote learning and get them ready for the next step. As early childhood educators, we should constantly ask such questions as: What does this child know? What can I do to help this child move to the next level of understanding?

> In the first five years of life, children learn to talk their people's language and play their people's daily life scripts—homemaking and going places, talking to friends and buying and selling, making and fixing, singing and dancing, and storytelling and celebrating rituals. Children's imitative and playful grounding in their culture is the foundation for identity development and for trust in the world as a predictable and a meaningful place.[38]

culture A group's way of life, including basic values, beliefs, religion, language, clothing, food, and various practices.

Many factors influence children's readiness for school. Reflect on the influence of parents, siblings, home, and schools on how children learn. Readiness is also a function of **culture**. Culture is a group's way of life, including basic values, beliefs, religion, language, clothing, food, and various practices. Teachers have to be sensitive to the fact that different cultures have different values regarding the purpose of school, the process of schooling, children's roles in the schooling process, and the family's and culture's roles in promoting readiness. You must learn about other cultures, talk with families, and try to find a match between the process and activities of schooling and families' cultures. Providing culturally sensitive, supportive, and responsive education is the responsibility of all early childhood professionals.

From teachers' standpoints, it is critical to identify those aspects of children's cultural backgrounds that have the greatest relevance for children's adjustment, motivation, and learning at school. Cultural dimensions that influence children's school readiness include (1) parents' attitudes and beliefs about early learning, (2) the nature and extent of parent–child interactions and other experiences that support the kinds of learning that schools tend to expect from children, and (3) social conventions that affect the ways in which knowledge and skills pertinent to early learning are communicated among and used by family members. The primary language used at home is also a profoundly important factor that affects children's adjustment to school.[39]

PRESCHOOL AND STATE STANDARDS

The purposes of preschool are changing dramatically. More and more, preschools are seen as places that get children ready for kindergarten. What was traditionally taught in kindergarten is now taught in the preschool. The preschool curriculum is now stressing academic skills related to reading, writing, and math as well as social skills. Increasingly, the responsibility for setting the preschool curriculum is being taken over by state departments of education through early learning guidelines or *standards,* statements of what preschoolers should know and be able to do. (Recall our discussion in Chapter 5.)

Currently, thirty-eight states have guidelines or standards for what preschool children should know and do before they enter kindergarten. These early learning standards include literacy, mathematics, science, social studies, fine arts, health and safety, personal and social development, physical development, and technology applications. Two important points are associated with state preschool standards. One is that preschool goals and learning standards are being set by state departments of education, and as a result, states are determining the preschool curriculum. Second, the preschool curriculum is becoming much more academic focused.

THE PRESCHOOL CURRICULUM

Although the curricula of individual preschools are varied and are influenced by state standards or guidelines, all programs should have certain essential curricular content areas. These include (1) social and emotional; (2) language and communication; (3) emergent literacy reading and writing; (4) mathematics; (5) science; (6) social studies; (7) fine arts; (8) physical development; and (9) technology. In other words the content areas for preschool are much like kindergarten and first grade.

It is more than likely that your state has preschool guidelines for what preschool children should know and do for each of these curriculum areas. Now would be a good time for you to review the preschool guidelines/standards for your state or another state. Pay particular attention to the math standards. Learning mathematics is a high priority in all of education from pre-K through grade twelve. More and more, the preschool years are viewed as the foundation for mathematics learning.

Daily Schedule

What should the preschool day schedule be like? Although a daily schedule depends on many things—your philosophy, the needs of children, families, beliefs, and state and local standards—the following descriptions illustrate what you can do on a typical preschool day. The preschool schedule described here is for a whole-day program; many other program arrangements are possible. Some preschools operate half-day, morning-only programs five days a week; others operate both a morning and an afternoon session; others operate only two or three days a week. However, an important preschool trend is toward public school full-day, full-year programs.

How you structure the day for your children will determine in part how and what they learn. You will want to develop your daily schedule with attention and care. Figure 8.3 is an example of a schedule for a full-day program.

Opening Activities. As children enter, the teacher greets each individually. Daily personal greetings make the children feel important, build a positive attitude toward school, and provide an opportunity to practice language skills. Daily greetings also give you a chance to check each child's health and emotional status.

Children usually do not arrive all at one time, so the first arrivals need something to do while others are arriving. Offering a free selection of activities or letting children self-select from a limited range of quiet activities (such as puzzles, pegboards, or markers to color with, journal "writing," etc.) are appropriate ways to involve children as they arrive.

Group Meeting/Planning. After all children arrive, you and they plan together and talk about the day ahead. This is also the time for announcements, sharing, and group songs, and for children to think about what they plan to learn during the day.

FIGURE 8.3 Sample of a Daily Schedule

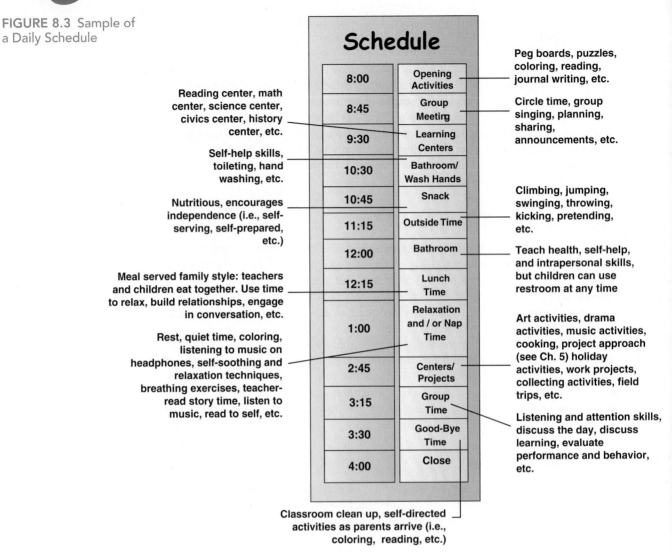

Schedule

8:00	Opening Activities
8:45	Group Meeting
9:30	Learning Centers
10:30	Bathroom/ Wash Hands
10:45	Snack
11:15	Outside Time
12:00	Bathroom
12:15	Lunch Time
1:00	Relaxation and / or Nap Time
2:45	Centers/ Projects
3:15	Group Time
3:30	Good-Bye Time
4:00	Close

Peg boards, puzzles, coloring, reading, journal writing, etc.

Reading center, math center, science center, civics center, history center, etc.

Circle time, group singing, planning, sharing, announcements, etc.

Self-help skills, toileting, hand washing, etc.

Nutritious, encourages independence (i.e., self-serving, self-prepared, etc.)

Climbing, jumping, swinging, throwing, kicking, pretending, etc.

Teach health, self-help, and intrapersonal skills, but children can use restroom at any time

Meal served family style: teachers and children eat together. Use time to relax, build relationships, engage in conversation, etc.

Rest, quiet time, coloring, listening to music on headphones, self-soothing and relaxation techniques, breathing exercises, teacher-read story time, listen to music, read to self, etc.

Art activities, drama activities, music activities, cooking, project approach (see Ch. 5) holiday activities, work projects, collecting activities, field trips, etc.

Listening and attention skills, discuss the day, discuss learning, evaluate performance and behavior, etc.

Classroom clean up, self-directed activities as parents arrive (i.e., coloring, reading, etc.)

Learning Centers.　After the group time, children are free to go to one of various learning centers, organized and designed to teach concepts. Table 8.2 lists types of learning centers and the concepts each is intended to teach. You should plan based on the state standards, and for the concepts and skills you want children to learn in each center. Also, every center should be a literacy center; that is, there should be materials for the development of writing and reading in every center.

Learning centers provide a number of useful functions. They enable you to meet the diverse learning needs and interests of your children and your community. In addition, learning centers:

- Encourage and promote collaboration, social interaction, and independent work
- Provide you with a classroom organization that enables you to work with individual children and small groups while other children are meaningfully and actively involved
- Provide for active and child-initiated learning

TABLE 8.2 Types of Classroom Learning Centers

Theme-Based Centers	Concepts
Use theme centers as an extension of classroom themes: • Space • Dinosaurs • The Ocean • All About Me • My Family Generally a classroom theme lasts for one to two weeks and occasionally longer. Children can use theme centers for varying amounts of time from fifteen to thirty minutes and during their free time.	• Use language skills, participate in sociodramatic play, and verbalize. • Identify role(s) as a family member. • Cooperate with others in joint activities. • Learn how to cooperate and practice good habits of daily living such as sharing, taking turns, and following rules.

Subject Centers	Concepts
• *Literacy/Language:* Be sure to change books frequently. Add ten new books every two to three weeks. The goal is to have preschoolers familiar with 100 books. Also include books from all genres: picture books, fiction, science, and so on.	• Verbalize; listen; understand directions; how to use books; colors, size, shapes, and names; print and book knowledge; vocabulary development; print awareness.
• *Writing:* Provide various and plentiful materials for writing: paper, blank books, folded paper, envelopes, markers, pencils, and so forth. Every center should have materials for writing.	• Learn alphabet, word knowledge, that words have meaning, that words make sentences, and so forth. • Learn that writing has many useful purposes, and that written words convey meaning.
• *Math:* Provide plastic number tiles, math cards, pegboards. There should be many concrete materials to promote hands-on experiences. The math center should also have picture books about math; read stories involving math.	• Understand meanings of whole numbers. • Recognize the number of objects in small groups without counting and by counting. • Understand that number words refer to quantity. • Use one-to-one correspondence to solve problems by matching sets and comparing number amounts and in counting objects to ten and beyond. • Understand that the last word stated in counting tells "how many." Count to determine number amounts and compare quantities (using language such as "more than" and "less than"). • Order sets by the number of objects in them. • Find shapes in the environment and describe them. • Build pictures and designs by combining two- and three-dimensional shapes. • Solve problems such as deciding which piece will fit into a space in a puzzle. • Discuss the relative positions of objects with vocabulary such as "above," "below," and "next to." • Identify objects as "the same" or "different," and "more" or "less," on the basis of attributes that can be measured. • Measure attributes such as length and weight. Make comparisons of objects based on length, weight, etc.

(continued)

TABLE 8.2 Types of Classroom Learning Centers *(Continued)*

Subject Centers	Concepts
• *Science:* Provide books on science; provide materials for observing, for discovering relationships, and for learning about nature, plants, animals, and the environment.	• Develop skills in observation, size, shape, color, whole/part, figure/ground, spatial relations, classifying, graphing, problem-solving skills. • Learn how to observe, make comparisons, classify, and problem-solve. • Investigate and explore.
• *Life Science:* Provide various plants and animals, terrariums, and habitats.	• Understand plant and animal care and habitats.
• *Art/Music/Creative Expression:* Provide materials for painting, coloring, drawing, cutting, pasting. Engage children in activities involving singing and movement. Provide puppets and puppet theater to encourage dramatic and creative expression.	• Listen to a wide range of musical styles. • Learn color relationships and combinations. • Engage in creative expression, aesthetic appreciation, satisfaction. • Create representations of homes and places in the community. • Participate in group singing, finger-plays, and rhythm.

Activity Centers	Concepts
• *Construction/Blocks:* Provide a variety of different kinds of blocks.	• Describe size, shape, length, seriation, spatial relationships. • Develop problem-solving skills.
• *Woodworking:* Make real tools and building materials available. Be sure to provide goggles and other precautions for children's safety.	• Learn to follow directions; learn how to use real tools; learn about planning and the construction process. • Discover whole/part relationships.
• *Dramatic Play:* Provide various materials and props for home activities, including a child-size stove, table, chairs, refrigerator, sink, etc. Provide clothing, hats, and shoes, as well as outfits and props from many occupations such as nurse/doctor, firefighter, construction worker.	• Learn language skills, sociodramatic play, functions, processes, social skills. • Engage in pretend and imaginary play. • Learn roles and responsibilities of community workers.
• *Water/Sand Play*	• Learn what floats; investigate capacity; compare volume. • Develop social skills and responsibility (i.e., cleanup).

Technology Centers	Concepts
• *Computer/Technology:* Provide computers, printer, scanner, fax machine, digital camera, video camera. A computer center can have one or more workstations or can have one or more laptops or handheld devices.	• Learn socialization, keyboarding, how technology can solve problems. • Learn basic technology skills. • Write (using e-mail, word processing). • Use technology to learn basic math and language skills. • Use technology to play games.

When developing learning centers, keep these guidelines in mind:

- Teach children how to use each center. Provide appropriate rules for use, care of materials, and so on. Such guidelines can be covered with the whole group as well as in small groups or with individuals.

- Develop centers around your state's/district's pre-K guidelines or standards, children's interests, and your learning goals for the children. For example, a state standard or learning expectation for preschool might specify that "children demonstrate emergent reading skills." To help meet this goal, you could develop a center that has a variety of age-appropriate printed materials such as books, magazines, catalogs, and so forth. You would also provide opportunities in the center for children to "read" and participate in literacy-related activities.

- Use children's interests to develop learning centers. For example, on a nature walk around the center, the children were very interested in dragonflies, grasshoppers, and crickets. You can develop a learning center in which children draw pictures of insects, record observations about insects, and sort pictures of insects by type.

- Develop ways for evaluating children's work processes and products while they are at the centers. Chapter 6 provides many ideas for how to observe and assess children's products and achievement.

Although we want children to be involved in child-initiated and active learning, sometimes it is necessary to directly teach children certain concepts or skills. What concepts or skills is this teacher directly teaching these children?

Bathroom/Hand Washing. Before any activity in which food is handled, prepared, or eaten, children should wash and dry their hands. Instructing children in proper hand-washing procedures can prevent the spread of illness and form lifelong habits. Hand washing has assumed a major role in the prevention of diseases such as the flu.

Snacks. After learning center activities, a snack is usually served. It should be nutritionally sound and something the children can serve (and often prepare) themselves. In Chapter 9 on pages 240–241, read how teacher Shannon Keller combines snack and rest times in the Professionalism in Practice feature, "Teaching in Kindergarten Today: 'What's for Dinner?'"

Outdoor Activity/Play/Walking. Outside play should be a time for learning new concepts and skills, not just a time to run around aimlessly. Children can practice climbing, jumping, swinging, throwing, and using body control. Teachers may incorporate walking trips and other events into outdoor play.

Bathroom/Toileting. Bathroom/toileting times offer opportunities to teach health, self-help, and intrapersonal skills. Children should also be allowed to use the bathroom whenever necessary.

Lunch. Lunch should be a relaxing time, and the meal should be served family style, with professionals and children eating together. Children should set their own tables and decorate them with place mats and flowers they can make in the art center or as a special project. Children should be involved in cleaning up after meals and snacks. On the other hand, in many programs, preschool children go to the school cafeteria for their lunch. Try to make this a relaxing experience also.

Relaxation. After lunch, children should have a chance to relax, perhaps to the accompaniment of teacher-read stories, CDs, or music. This is an ideal time to teach children breathing exercises and relaxation techniques.

Nap Time. Children who want or need to should have a chance to rest or sleep. Quiet activities should be available for those who do not need to or cannot sleep on a particular day. In any event, nap time should not be forced on any child.

Centers or Special Projects. Following nap time is a good time for center activities or special projects. Special projects can also be conducted in the morning, and some may be more appropriate then, such as cooking something for snack or lunch. Special projects might involve cooking, holiday activities, collecting things, work projects, art activities, and field trips.

Group Time. The day can end with a group meeting to review the day's activities. This meeting develops listening and attention skills, promotes oral communication, stresses that learning is important, and helps children evaluate their performance and behavior.

Good-Bye Time. This is a time for your children to participate in cleaning responsibilities. After the classroom is clean, your students can engage in self-directed activities until their parents arrive to pick them up. Such activities might include coloring or reading, playing in various centers, "reading" books and other materials, and other "free choice" activities.

PLAY IN PRESCHOOL PROGRAMS

Go to the Assignments and Activities section in Topic 6: Curriculum Planning in the MyEducationLab for your course and complete the activity entitled *Effective Teaching Strategies in Early Childhood Classrooms.* Note how the teacher is making an effort to involve each student. Many skills are being fostered and explored in this play, such as teamwork, creative thinking, experimenting, turn taking, communicating, and sharing.

Play has traditionally been at the heart of preschool programs. Children's play is and will continue to be important in preschool programs because it results in learning. Therefore, preschool programs should support learning through play.

The notion that children learn and develop through play began with Froebel. Since his time, most early childhood programs have incorporated play into their curricula. Montessori viewed children's active involvement with materials and the prepared environment as the primary means by which they absorb knowledge and learn. John Dewey believed that children learn through play and that children should have opportunities to engage in play associated with everyday activities (e.g., the house center, post office, grocery store, doctor's office). Piaget believed play promotes cognitive knowledge and is a means by which children construct knowledge of their world. He thought that through active involvement, children learn. Vygotsky viewed the social interactions that occur through play as essential to children's development. He believed that children, through social interactions with others, learn social skills such as cooperation and collaboration that promote and enhance their cognitive development.

These are some things children learn through play:

- Physical concepts associated with the five senses—touching, tasting, smelling, seeing, and hearing
- Logical-mathematical concepts associated with classification, seriation, numeration, space (over, under, etc.), and time (before, after, etc.)
- Sharing and taking turns
- Negotiating and compromising
- Leading and following
- Using fine and large muscles
- Conversation skills (e.g., taking turns and responding appropriately)
- Demonstrating accomplishments and abilities
- Relating own accomplishments to those of peers
- Making decisions

- Cooperating/collaborating with all others, including those who are different from the child culturally, racially, or in ability

Providing opportunities for children to choose among well-planned, varied learning activities enhances the probability that they will learn through play.

Accommodating Play

Preschool is the first opportunity Han Ling has had to go to school. Han Ling is **typically developing** (meaning that she reaches the majority of developmental milestones at the appropriate time and does not have deficits in social areas), enjoys coloring, story time and playing on the swing set outside. In preschool, Han Ling must learn the rules of a more structured environment, such as sitting for longer periods of time, and she must learn pre-math and language skills. With so much to teach her, it is easy to forget that Han Ling's first job as a preschool-aged child is play. Play is the true language of children. It is how they learn social norms, hone peer interactions, express their emotions, engage in their environment, and learn problem solving. However, play does not always erupt spontaneously, so here are some tips to encourage Han Ling in play:

- Provide different play opportunities by arranging your room in centers. Block centers with blocks of varying weights and sizes, dramatic play centers with dress-up clothes, home centers with pretend food and cooking appliances, and manipulative centers with toys like dolls, action figures, or cars are just a few examples of centers that elicit play.
- Change out your centers as you rotate your units. For example, if you are in a transportation unit, put toy boats, bicycles, cars, trucks, and trains in the manipulative center. Your students will begin to act out and internalize the information you've given them in their play.
- Start a rotation of three or four children grouped by their personalities, strengths, and weakness for each center. Don't put students in a center by themselves. Play is a wonderful opportunity to help Han Ling learn social skills and problem solving, which is much more difficult to do solo. It is natural and acceptable for centers and the children in them to occasionally blend into one another.
  - When children repeatedly combine, like the block center with the manipulative center or the home center and the dress up center, go ahead and combine them. This may make your groups larger but also more vibrant and conducive of greater social skill building.
  - Move children into different groups. You may not find the perfect group for every child right away.
- Play! Children don't always naturally know how to play, especially if they are unfamiliar with the toys, the other children, or if they are developmentally delayed. You notice that Han Ling seems unsure and doesn't participate very much. To start:
  - Choose similar or complementary toys. If Han Ling has a mommy doll, you pick up the daddy doll and the baby doll. Once you show interest, Han Ling will likely take the initiative and tell you what part to play or what to say. Let her lead you and don't ask too many direct questions.
  - If Han Ling does not take the initiative in play, you can ask for directions in a roundabout way, saying, "Hmm, I'm not sure which one to be, the dad or the baby . . ." She will likely take the lead and tell you what role to take.
  - To begin a play sequence, start with a scenario that Han Ling will be familiar with, like fixing breakfast or going to the grocery store. Once she is on familiar ground, Han Ling may become more directive and steer the pretending in other directions.

typically developing
Reaching the majority of developmental milestones at the appropriate time and not presenting deficits in social areas.

Using Blocks to Help Preschoolers Build Mathematical Skills

Froebel, the father of kindergarten, introduced blocks to the early childhood curriculum with his creation of gifts. Froebel created these gifts to facilitate children's creativity and provide opportunities for them to construct geometric forms. Enabling children to explore and experiment with blocks provides them with several opportunities to develop the foundation for mathematical concepts related to algebra, geometry, and measurement.

When reflecting on how to create opportunities for children to use blocks, consider the following ideas prior to using these materials.

1. Develop a Variety of Learning Opportunities for Children to Use Blocks

Offer young children different types of learning opportunities to use blocks that will foster their development of mathematical concepts.

- Give children time to explore freely with blocks during center time or other times in the day. Providing opportunities for free play allows children to develop various intuitive geometric concepts and problem-solving skills.

- Informally guide children during these experiences to help them connect prior learning experiences or deepen their understanding of a concept. Ask children questions to provoke mathematical conversations. For example, when a child sorts blocks into different groups, ask the child about these groupings with questions such as:
  - Why did you put these blocks together?
  - What other blocks could you put into this group?
- Use the blocks in the classroom to introduce or review mathematical concepts such as counting or identifying various shapes.

2. Provide Children with a Variety of Different Types of Blocks to Explore

Incorporate a variety of manipulatives—including different types of blocks—for young children to use in your preschool classroom. Providing these materials will allow children to explore mathematical concepts such as sorting, patterns, measurement, and geometry. The accompanying table lists some of the common types of blocks used in preschool classrooms and

Type of Block	Mathematical Concepts	Examples
Building/architect blocks 	Patterns, sorting, geometry, measurement, spatial relationships, counting	Children will build various structures with these materials. Consider playing an "I Spy" type of game where children find different shapes in their creations.
Pattern blocks 	Patterns, sorting, geometry, measurement, spatial relationships, counting	Children can practice creating patterns with these blocks or creating "new" shapes.
Snap cubes 	Patterns, sorting, measurement, counting	Children can use blocks to determine the length/width of various objects in the room.

Type of Block	Mathematical Concepts	Examples
Color tiles 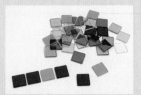	Patterns, sorting, measurement, counting	Children might use these blocks to measure objects in the classroom or to start thinking about how many color tiles might cover a certain object in the classroom (area).
Tangrams 	Patterns, sorting, geometry, measurement, spatial relationships, counting	Provide children with opportunities to create "new" shapes with tangrams. Children can trace the perimeter of these designs and have friends try to create their new shapes.
Three-dimensional geometric models 	Patterns, sorting, geometry, measurement, counting	These solids not only provide examples of various three-dimensional shapes, but also allow children different types of materials to sort.
Color cubes 	Patterns, sorting, measurement, counting	Children can use these cubes to start understanding the concept of capacity. For instance, have children explore how many cubes different objects in the classroom can hold.
Attribute blocks 	Patterns, sorting, geometry, measurement, counting	Children can practice sorting these blocks into various groups. Allow children to develop groups and labels instead of telling them to sort by color or by shape. Children will develop groupings that are more interesting with this flexibility.

(continued)

(Continued)

some of the possible mathematical concepts children might develop when using these materials.

3. Ask Children a Variety of Questions

It is important for you to ask students thought-provoking questions that will allow them to explore a variety of mathematical concepts. Asking children questions about their block structures not only provides them with the opportunity to engage in mathematical conversations about their work, but also gives you the occasion to explore children's mathematical knowledge. For example, if a preschooler made a pattern like this with pattern blocks, you might ask the following questions:

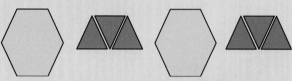

- Tell me about your creation. What did you make? (Give the child an opportunity to use her words to describe the blocks.)
- What type of pattern did you make?
- If I wanted to add to your pattern, what blocks would I have to use?
- Is there a block that looks the same as the three green triangles?

As you ask these questions, encourage children to use their own words to describe their work. Also, verify your understanding of the child's descriptions. For example:

Ms. Jones: What type of pattern did you make?
Alicia: We used one yellow block and then three green blocks.
Ms. Jones: So you used one yellow hexagon and three green triangles, and then another yellow hexagon and three green triangles?
Mason and Alicia: Yes.

Providing children with opportunities to explore and construct with blocks helps lay the foundation for future mathematical success. These experiences not only allow children to deepen their understanding of algebra, geometry, and measurement, but they also offer children opportunities to practice their problem-solving skills. In addition, children will engage in meaningful mathematical conversations with their peers and their teacher.

....

Contributed by Elisabeth Johnston, doctoral candidate at the University of North Texas. Her current research relates to young children's mathematical development. Elisabeth taught second grade at a gifted and talented magnet school for six years in Texas, where she was responsible for teaching math to a diverse range of second graders.

- Use play as an opportunity to observe your students. Through their play, they are communicating to you their strengths and weaknesses, their home lives, relationships, fears and insecurities, as well as greatest joys and interests. Use this information to become a better teacher for them.
- Remember that play is a way children "work things out," explore, and communicate. So if Han Ling uses language or acts out behavior that is overly aggressive or abusive, make a note of the situation, time, and date. Report it to the school counselor and your principal. Ask them whether you should notify the parents or Child Protective Services.

Play can be an adventure for both Han Ling and for you. If you accommodate play in your classroom, both you and your students will learn a lot and enjoy the school day.

Planning for Play

You are the key to promoting meaningful play, which promotes a basis for learning. How you prepare the environment for play and the attitudes you have toward it help determine the quality of the children's learning.

Plan to implement the curriculum through play. Integrate specific learning activities with play to achieve learning outcomes. Play activities should match children's developmental needs and be free of gender and cultural stereotypes. Teachers have to be clear about curriculum concepts and ideas they want children to learn through play.

- Provide time for learning through play. Include play in the schedule as a legitimate activity in its own right.
- Supervise play activities and participate in children's play, as we discussed above. In these roles, help, show, and guide. Model when appropriate and intervene only when necessary.

- Observe children's play. Teachers can learn how children play and the learning outcomes of play to use in planning classroom activities.
- Create environments that ensure children will learn through play. Create both indoor and outdoor environments that encourage play and support its role in learning.
- Organize the classroom or center environment so that cooperative learning is possible and active learning occurs.
- Provide materials and equipment that are appropriate to children's developmental levels and that support a nonsexist and multicultural curriculum.
- Question children about their play. Discuss what children did during play, and "debrief" children about what they have learned through play.
- Provide for safety in indoor and outdoor play.

Today, with all of the discussions about standards and academics, sometimes play gets pushed out of the curriculum. Through play, you can help children meet state standards and achieve high academic levels. When children play, they are involved in activities they are interested in. Through play, children learn by doing. Learning through interests and learning by doing are two hallmarks of developmentally appropriate practice.

As children play, teachers follow their lead and help them learn new concepts, knowledge, and skills. For example, a state standard asks students to be able to count and engage in one-to-one correspondence. During play in the housekeeping center, the children are setting the table for lunch. The teacher asks children to count out the number of forks they will need for each place setting (counting) and then asks them to put a fork at each place setting (one-to-one correspondence). The accompanying Professionalism in Practice feature, "Using Blocks to Help Build Mathematical Skills," demonstrates how block play helps children learn math standards.

Kinds of Play

Play occurs in many types and forms. Your understanding of each of these will enable you to implement a meaningful program of learning through play. We will now discuss the different types of play.

Social Play.   Children engage in many kinds of play. Mildred Parten, a children's play researcher, identified six stages and descriptions of children's social play:

- *Unoccupied play* is play in which the child does not play with anything or anyone; the child merely stands or sits, without doing anything observable.
- *Solitary play* is play where the child plays alone, seemingly unaware of other children.
- *Onlooker play* is play in which the child watches and observes the play of other children. The center of interest is others' play.
- *Parallel play* is play in which the child plays alongside but in ways similar to other children nearby, and with toys or other materials similar to those other children.
- In *associative play,* children interact with each other—perhaps by asking questions or sharing materials—but do not play together.
- In *cooperative play,* children actively play together, often as a result of organization by the teacher.[40]

Puppets and plays provide many opportunities for children to learn and interact with others through associative play. Indeed, the props that professionals provide for children to play with contribute to all of children's learning, but in particular their literacy development. What literacy skills are these children learning?

Observing children's social play is a good way to sharpen your observation skills and to learn more about children's play and the learning that occurs through play. Refer to and reflect on our discussion of observation in Chapter 3.

Social play supports many important functions. First, it provides the means for children to interact with others and learn many social skills. Children learn how to compromise ("OK, I'll be the baby first and you can be the mommy"), be flexible ("We'll do it your way first and then my way"), resolve conflicts, and continue the process of learning who they are. Second, social play provides a vehicle for practicing and developing literacy skills, as detailed in the accompanying Professionalism in Practice feature, "How Play Supports Literacy Development." Children have others with whom to practice language and from whom to learn. Third, play helps children learn impulse control; they realize they cannot always do whatever they want. And fourth, in giving a child other children with whom to interact, social play negates isolation and helps children learn how to have the social interactions so vital to successful living.

On the other hand, children cannot learn all they need to know through play. There is a place in the curriculum for teacher-initiated instruction. For example, after her assessment of children's number knowledge, a preschool teacher might decide that her children need more counting practice. She could then lead them in a lesson with counting bears in which the children count out five bears from the basket of bears on their table. Both child-initiated play and teacher-initiated instruction are used in programs we discussed in Chapter 4. In addition to social play, other types of play and their benefits and purposes are shown below. Carefully study these kinds of play and plan for how you will include them in your program.

Functional Play. Functional play occurs during the sensorimotor period and in response to muscular activities and the need to be active. Functional play is characterized by repetitions, manipulations, and self-imitation. Functional play allows children to practice and learn physical capabilities while exploring their immediate environments. Very young children are especially fond of repeating movements for the pleasure of it. They engage in sensory impressions for the joy of experiencing the functioning of their bodies. Repetition of language is also a part of functional play.

Symbolic Play. Piaget referred to symbolic play as "let's pretend" play. During this stage, children freely display their creative and physical abilities and social awareness in a number of ways—for example, by pretending to be something else, such as an animal. Symbolic play also occurs when children pretend that one object is another—that a building block is a car, for example—and may also entail pretending to be another person—a mommy, daddy, or firefighter.

This child is learning how to strengthen her gross-motor skills through functional play, by stacking blocks on top of each other. Children enjoy experiencing the functions and movements of their body through repetitions and manipulations.

Informal or Free Play. Informal play occurs when children play in an environment that contains materials and people with whom they can interact. Learning materials may be grouped in centers with similar equipment: a kitchen center, a dress-up center, a block center, a music and art center, a water or sand area, and a free-play center, usually with items such as tricycles, wagons, and wooden slides for promoting large-muscle development. The atmosphere of a free-play environment is informal, unstructured, and unpressured. Play and learning episodes are generally determined by the interests of the children. Outcomes of free play are socialization, emotional development, self-control, and concept development.

How Play Supports Literacy Development

Early childhood educators have long recognized the value of play for social, emotional, and physical development. Recently, however, play has attracted greater importance as a medium for literacy development. It is now recognized that literacy develops in meaningful, functional social settings rather than as a set of abstract skills taught in formal pencil-and-paper settings.

Literacy development involves a child's active engagement in cooperation and collaboration with peers; it builds on what the child already knows with the support and guidance of others. Play provides this setting. During observation of children at play, especially in free-choice, cooperative play periods, one can note the functional uses of literacy that children incorporate into their play themes. When the environment is appropriately prepared with literacy materials in play areas, children have been observed to engage in attempted and conceptual reading and writing in collaboration with other youngsters. In similar settings lacking literacy materials, the same literacy activities did not occur.

To demonstrate how play in an appropriate setting can nurture literacy development, consider the following classroom setting in which the teacher has designed a veterinarian's office to go along with a class study on animals focusing in particular on pets.

The dramatic play area is designed with a waiting room, including chairs; a table filled with magazines, books, and pamphlets about pet care; posters about pets; office hour notices; a "No Smoking" sign; and a sign advising visitors to "Check in with the nurse when arriving." On a nurse's desk are patient forms on clipboards, a telephone, an address and telephone book, appointment cards, and a calendar. The office contains patient folders, prescription pads, white coats, masks, gloves, a toy doctor's kit, and stuffed animals for patients.

Ms. Meyers, the teacher, guides students in using the various materials in the veterinarian's office during free-play time. For example, she reminds the children to read important information they find in the waiting area, to fill out forms about their pets' needs, to ask the nurse for appointment times, or to have the doctor write out appropriate treatments or prescriptions. In addition to giving directions, Ms. Meyers also models behaviors by participating in the play center with the children when first introducing materials.

This play setting provides a literacy-rich environment with books and writing materials; models reading and writing by the teacher that children can observe and emulate; provides the opportunity to practice literacy in a real-life situation that has meaning and function; and encourages children to interact socially by collaborating and performing meaningful reading and writing activities with peers. The following anecdotes relate the type of behavior Ms. Meyers observed in the play area.

Jessica was waiting to see the doctor. She told her stuffed animal dog, Sam, not to worry, that the doctor would not hurt him. She asked Jenny, who was waiting with her stuffed animal cat, Muffin, what the kitten's problem was. The girls agonized over the ailments of their pets. After a while they stopped talking and Jessica picked up the book *Are You My Mother?* and pretended to read to her dog. Jessica showed Sam the pictures as she read.

Preston examined Christopher's teddy bear and wrote a report in the patient's folder. He read his scribble writing out loud and said, "This teddy bear's blood pressure is twenty-nine points. He should take sixty-two pills an hour until he is better and keep warm and go to bed." At the same time he read, he showed Christopher what he had written so he could understand what to do.

When selecting settings to promote literacy in play, choose those that are familiar to children and relate them to themes currently being studied. Suggestions for literacy materials and settings to add to the dramatic play areas include the following:

- A fast-food restaurant, ice cream store, or bakery suggests menus, order pads, a cash register, specials for the day, recipes, and lists of flavors or products.
- A supermarket or local grocery store can include labeled shelves and sections, food containers, pricing labels, cash registers, telephones, shopping receipts, checkbooks, coupons, and promotional flyers.
- A post office to serve for mailing children's letters needs paper, envelopes, address books, pens, pencils, stamps, cash registers, and labeled mailboxes. A mail carrier hat and bag are important for children who deliver the mail and need to identify and read names and addresses.
- A gas station and car repair shop, designed in the block area, might have toy cars and trucks, receipts for sales, road maps for help with directions to different destinations, automotive tools and auto repair manuals for fixing cars and trucks, posters that advertise automobile equipment, and empty cans of different products typically found in service stations.

Source: L. M. Morrow, Literacy Development in the Early Years: Helping Children Read and Write, *6th ed. (Needham Heights, MA: Allyn & Bacon, 2008).*

Dramatic play promotes children's understanding of concepts and processes. These children are exploring their feelings and ideas as they pretend to shop for groceries.

Sociodramatic (Pretend) Play. Dramatic play allows children to participate vicariously in a wide range of activities associated with family living, society, and their own and others' cultural heritage. Dramatic play is generally of two kinds: *sociodramatic* and *fantasy*. Sociodramatic play usually involves everyday realistic activities and events, whereas fantasy play typically involves fairy tale and superhero play. In sociodramatic play, children have an opportunity to express themselves, assume different roles, and interact with their peers. Sociodramatic play acts as a nonsexist and multicultural arena in which all children are equal.

Outdoor Play. Children's play outside is just as important as inside play. Outdoor environments and activities promote large- and small-muscle development and body coordination as well as language development, social interaction, and creativity. The outdoor area is a learning environment and, as such, the playground should be designed according to learning objectives. Indoor learning can also occur outdoors. Easels, play dough, and dramatic play props can further enhance learning opportunities.

SUCCESSFUL TRANSITIONS TO KINDERGARTEN

transition A passage from one learning setting, grade, program, or experience to another.

A **transition** is a passage from one learning setting, grade, program, or experience to another. You can help ensure that the transitions preschool children make from home to preschool to kindergarten are happy and rewarding experiences.

You can help your children and families make transitions easily and confidently in these ways:

- Educate and prepare children ahead of time for any new situation. Children can practice routines they will encounter when they enter kindergarten. For example, children can practice some likely kindergarten routines such as putting away their things each day.

- Alert parents to new and different standards, dress, behavior, and parent–teacher interactions they will encounter in kindergarten. Inform parents that school attendance is important for children's achievement. Also, make them aware of your state's attendance requirements.

- Give children an opportunity to meet their new teachers. Invite a kindergarten teacher to your classroom to read to the children.

- Let parents know ahead of time what their children will need in the new program (e.g., lunch box, change of clothing, etc.).

- Provide parents of children with special needs and bilingual parents with additional help and support during the transition. Introduce them to new teachers and contact personnel.

- Offer parents and children an opportunity to visit programs. Children will better understand the physical, curricular, and affective climates of their new programs if they visit in advance.

- Cooperate with the staff of any program the children will attend to work out a transition plan.

- Exchange class visits between preschool and kindergarten programs. Class visits are excellent ways to have preschool children learn about the classrooms they will attend as kindergartners. Having kindergarten children visit the preschool and telling preschoolers about kindergarten provides for a sense of security and anticipation.

- Work with kindergarten teachers to make booklets about their program. These booklets can include photographs of children, letters from kindergarten children and preschoolers, and pictures of kindergarten activities. These books can be placed in the reading centers where preschool children can "read" about the programs they will attend.

- Hold a "kindergarten day" for preschoolers in which they attend kindergarten for a day. This program can include such things as riding the bus, having lunch, touring the school, and meeting teachers.

Remember that transitions can be traumatic experiences for children. When transitions are hurried, unplanned, and abrupt, they can cause social, emotional, and learning problems. Successful transitions can be good learning experiences for children.

PORTRAITS OF CHILDREN

Now that you have learned about transitions, this is a good time for you to think more about the children you will be helping to transition to kindergarten. Read, review, and reflect on the Professionalism in Practice feature "Portraits of Preschoolers" on pages 234–235. As you answer the questions about developmentally appropriate practice, think how you would meet the needs of each of these children in your classroom. Also, look ahead to the Portraits of Kindergartners in Chapter 9 and review what kindergarten children are like.

ACTIVITIES FOR PROFESSIONAL DEVELOPMENT

ethical dilemma

"There's Only One Way"

Tracy Hodgkin teaches a class of twenty-two three- and four-year-old children from diverse cultures in a school district with a history of low achievement test scores. The new superintendent has promised the board of education that he will turn the district around in three years. The superintendent has hired a new preschool coordinator because he believes that one of the best ways to close the district's achievement gap is to begin as early as possible. The new preschool coordinator has recommended the adoption of a skills-based curriculum that includes the use of direct instruction, other teacher-centered approaches, and a scripted curriculum. According to her, "There is only one way to teach children what they need to know, and that is to directly teach them. We can't fool around with all this play and child-centered stuff."

Direct instruction of basic skills and teacher-centered instructional practices are contrary to what Tracy learned in her teacher education classes at the university. In addition, these approaches do not fit with her view of child-centered and developmentally appropriate practice.

What should Tracy do? Should she inform the preschool coordinator that she will not use the materials when and if they are adopted, or should she convene a meeting of other teachers and ask their opinions about the materials, or should she keep her thoughts to herself and vow to use the new curriculum only when she has to? Or should she adopt another plan?

myeducationlab

To check your comprehension on the content covered in Chapter 8, go to the Book Specific Resources in the MyEducationLab for your course, select your text, and complete the Study Plan. Here you will be able to take a chapter quiz and receive feedback on your answers.

portraits of preschoolers

JUAN

Introduce yourself to Juan, a three-year-old Hispanic male. Juan weighs 44 pounds and is 3 feet 5 inches tall. Juan speaks Spanish and is slowly learning key words in English. Juan comes from a large family—he is the youngest of five children.

Social-Emotional	Cognitive	Motor	Adaptive (Daily Living)
Seeks attention and approval from caregivers	Enjoys repeating words and sounds that he hears	Likes to throw balls to other children	Is completely toilet trained
Has a strong sense of gender that could be attributed to cultural background	Enjoys hearing simple stories, rhymes, and songs—likes to participate in singing, rhyming, and so forth	Uses crayons and markers to draw	Puts legs into and pulls up pants without help
Recognizes feelings of others	Identifies colors and shapes	Likes to dance and jump on two feet	Drinks from a cup
Prefers to play with other boys	Is able to count from one to ten (in sequence)	Likes to build structures with toy blocks	Is able to zip and unzip his clothing

MACKENZIE

Introduce yourself to Mackenzie, a three-year-old Caucasian female. Mackenzie weighs 34 pounds, is 3 feet 2 inches tall, and is a quiet child who exhibits an "easy" temperament. Once she becomes familiar with new people or new surroundings, she is very talkative. She is an only child and receives a lot of attention from parents and extended family. Mackenzie loves to play "make-believe" and enjoys playing "dress-up."

Social-Emotional	Cognitive	Motor	Adaptive (Daily Living)
Is very outgoing and sociable	Is very curious and frequently asks "Why?"	Is able to use hand–eye coordination when stringing beads	Dresses herself for school without assistance
Enjoys meeting new people	Is able to categorize items by colors and shapes	Enjoys painting and coloring	Is able to use the restroom without assistance
Enjoys talking with her caregivers	Puts puzzles together	Balances on one foot	Is very self-confident and willing to try new things
Likes to play with selected friends	Has a very large vocabulary for a three-year-old	Is able to dress and undress herself when she is playing "dress-up"	Has no difficulty eating independently

Application Activities

1. Visit preschool programs in your area. Determine their philosophies and find out what goes on in a typical day.
   a. How do their philosophies compare to your philosophy?
   b. Make a list of activities and practices you thought were developmentally appropriate. Make another list of developmentally inappropriate practices you observed. How would you change the practices to make them appropriate?
2. Based on material presented in this chapter, develop a set of guidelines for ensuring that preschool programs are developmentally appropriate. Develop guidelines for the environment, curriculum, and teaching practices.

KYM

Introduce yourself to Kym, a four-year-old Asian female. Kym weighs 34 pounds and is 3 feet 3 inches tall. She is a very active and assertive preschooler. She enjoys coloring and playing in the home center at preschool. She is a natural leader and is very intelligent.

Social-Emotional	Cognitive	Motor	Adaptive (Daily Living)
Tends to be somewhat aggressive and bossy with other children	Is able to identify all the letters of the alphabet	Enjoys playing the piano	Washes her hands before eating and after using the restroom without prompting
Shows her frustration by raising her voice when she is upset	Is able to identify a variety of animals in picture books	Participates in a gymnastics class; is able to do a forward roll and other movements	Brushes her teeth after meals without prompting from her caregivers
Enjoys spending time with friends and also being by herself	Expresses herself clearly—communication is easy for her	Rides a bike with training wheels	Is beginning to tie her own shoes
Is very interested in learning new skills such as reading and writing	Likes to "read" books—has several favorites	Demonstrates good balance and body control	Dresses herself each morning before school

Questions about Developmentally Appropriate Practice:

- How do Juan, Mackenzie, and Kym differ in terms of their adaptive daily living skills?
- What might be some factors that have contributed to Mackenzie's language development?
- How might being from a large family affect Juan's social-emotional development?
- Since Mackenzie is an only child and Juan has two older brothers and two older sisters, how might these differing family dynamics play a role in their future development?
- Knowing Kym's tendency to be bossy with her peers, how could you help her develop a more prosocial approach with her classmates?
- What developmental skills do Juan, Mackenzie, and Kym need in preparation for attending kindergarten?

3. Observe children's play, and give examples of how children learn through play and what they learn. Record the children's names, setting, day, and time. Record some dialogue or the children's comments. Observe and record the materials used and your interpretations. Identify the type of play, based on Parten's stages of play.

4. Using the Internet, locate your state department of education's pre-kindergarten guidelines or standards. Compare these to another state's, such as the Illinois Early Learning Standards. Begin to decide how you can integrate your understanding of developmentally appropriate practice with what the state standards are requiring preschool children to know and be able to do.

chapter nine

KINDERGARTEN TODAY

Meeting Academic and Developmental Needs

NAEYC Standards for Early Childhood Professional Preparation

Standard 1. Promoting Child Development and Learning

I use my understanding of young children's characteristics and needs, and of multiple interacting influences on children's development and learning, to create environments that are healthy, respectful, supportive, and challenging for each child.[1]

Standard 4. Using Developmentally Effective Approaches to Connect with Children and Families

I understand and use positive relationships and supportive interactions as the foundation for my work with young children and families. I know, understand, and use a wide array of developmentally appropriate approaches, instructional strategies, and tools to connect with children and families and positively influence each child's development and learning.[2]

Standard 5. Using Content Knowledge to Build Meaningful Curriculum

I understand the importance of developmental domains and academic (or content) disciplines in early childhood curriculum. I know the essential concepts, inquiry tools, and structure of content areas, including academic subjects, and can identify resources to deepen their understanding. I use my own knowledge and other resources to design, implement, and evaluate meaningful, challenging curricula that promote comprehensive developmental and learning outcomes for every young child.[3]

As we begin our discussion of kindergarten children and programs, perhaps you are thinking back to your kindergarten or pre-first-grade school experiences. I am sure that you have many pleasant memories and they include your teachers and classmates, what you learned, and how you learned it. It is good that you have fond memories of your kindergarten and/or other preschool experiences. However, we can't use just memories to build our understanding of what today's high-quality kindergartens are or should be like. If you have not visited a kindergarten program lately, now would be a good time to do so. You will discover that kindergarten education is undergoing a dramatic change. Compare the following changes that are transforming the kindergarten you went to versus kindergarten today:

- *Emphasis on academics including math, literacy, and science.* Reasons for the emphasis on academics include:
  - Standards that specify what children should know and be able to do. (See Chapter 5.)
  - Political and public support for early education and skill learning because they reduce grade failure and school dropout.[4]
- *Enriched curriculum with emphasis on literacy designed to have children read by entry into first grade.* Reasons for emphasis on literacy in the kindergarten include:
  - Recognition that literacy and reading are pathways to success in school and life.
  - Kindergarten for all children, or **universal kindergarten**, is now becoming a permanent part of the American education system. Ninety-three percent of five-year-old children attend a kindergarten program.[5] Sixty percent attend a full-day kindergarten program.[6]
- *More funding provided by more states for districts to provide more kindergarten programs.*[7]
- *Longer school days and transition from half-day to full-day programs.* Reasons for longer school days and full-day programs include:
  - Changes in society
  - An increase in the number of working parents
  - Recognition that earlier is the best option
  - Research that shows a longer school day helps children academically[8]
- *Exploding kindergarten enrollment.*
- *More challenging kindergarten programs, with children being asked to do and learn at higher levels.*[9]
- *More testing.* Reasons for the increased testing include:
  - The accountability movement
  - Recognition that district testing that begins in third grade and earlier puts more emphasis on what kindergarten children should learn[10]

As a result of these and other changes we discuss in this chapter, the contemporary kindergarten is a place of high expectations and achievement for all children. Kindergarten education is literally changing before our eyes!

THE HISTORY OF KINDERGARTEN EDUCATION

Kindergarten has a long and interesting history that helps us better understand the kindergartens of today.

FOCUS QUESTIONS

1. What major changes has kindergarten education undergone from Froebel to the present?

2. What are kindergarten children like?

3. What children attend kindergarten?

4. What are environments for kindergarten children like?

5. What is included in the kindergarten curriculum?

6. How can you support children's approaches to learning?

Friedrich Froebel

Friedrich Froebel's educational concepts and kindergarten program were imported from Germany into the United States in the nineteenth century, virtually intact, by individuals who believed in his ideas and methods. His influence remained dominant for almost half a century. While Froebel's ideas still seem perfectly acceptable today, they were not acceptable to those in the mid-nineteenth century who subscribed to the notion of early education. Especially innovative and hard to accept was the idea that learning could be based on play and children's interests—in other words, that learning could be child centered. Most European and American schools were subject oriented and emphasized teaching basic skills. In addition, Froebel was the first to advocate a communal education for young children outside the home. Froebel's ideas for educating children as a group in a special place outside the home were revolutionary. Review and reflect on our discussion of Froebel in Chapter 3.

Margarethe Schurz

Margarethe Schurz established the first kindergarten in the United States. After attending lectures on Froebelian principles in Germany, she returned to the United States and, in 1856, opened her kindergarten at Watertown, Wisconsin. Schurz's program was conducted in German, as were many of the new kindergarten programs of the time, since Froebel's ideas of education were especially appealing to bilingual parents. Schurz influenced Elizabeth Peabody, who was not only fascinated but converted to Froebel's ideas.

Elizabeth Peabody

Elizabeth Peabody opened her kindergarten in Boston in 1860. She and her sister, Mary Mann, also published a *Kindergarten Guide*. Peabody almost immediately realized that she lacked the necessary theoretical grounding to adequately implement Froebel's ideas. She visited kindergartens in Germany, then returned to the United States to popularize Froebel's methods. Peabody is generally credited as kindergarten's main promoter in the United States.

Susan Blow

The first public kindergarten was founded in St. Louis, Missouri, in 1873 by Susan E. Blow, with the cooperation of the St. Louis superintendent of schools, William T. Harris. Elizabeth Peabody had corresponded for several years with Harris, and the combination of her prodding and Blow's enthusiasm and knowledge convinced Harris to open a public kindergarten on an experimental basis. Endorsement of the kindergarten program by a public school system did much to increase its popularity and spread the Froebelian influence within early childhood education. In addition, Harris, who later became the U.S. Commissioner of Education, encouraged support for Froebel's ideas and methods.

Patty Smith Hill

The kindergarten movement, at first ahead of its time, became rigid and teacher centered rather than child centered. By the turn of the twentieth century, many kindergarten leaders thought that programs and training should be open to experimentation and innovation rather than rigidly following Froebel's ideas. Patty Smith Hill thought that, while the kindergarten should remain faithful to Froebel's ideas, it should nevertheless be open to innovation. She believed that the kindergarten movement, to survive, had to move into the twentieth century, and was able to convince many of her colleagues. More than anyone else, Hill is responsible for kindergarten as it was known prior to its twenty-first century transformation.

Kindergarten Today

Kindergarten as it was known five years ago is not the same as kindergarten today. Kindergarten twenty years from now will be vastly different from today. Kindergarten is in a transitional stage from a program that focuses primarily on social and emotional development to one that emphasizes academics, especially early literacy, math and science, and activities that prepare children to think and problem-solve. These changes represent a transformation of great magnitude and will have a lasting impact on kindergarten curriculum and teaching into the future.

Regardless of the grade or age group they teach, all early childhood teachers have to make decisions regarding what curriculum and activities they will provide for their children. The accompanying Professionalism in Practice feature, "Teaching in Kindergarten Today: What's for Dinner?" will provide you with an inside look at kindergarten teacher Shannon Keller's classroom.

WHAT ARE KINDERGARTEN CHILDREN LIKE?

Kindergarten children are like other children in many ways. They have similar developmental, physical, and behavioral characteristics that characterize them as kindergartners—children ages five to six. Yet, at the same time, they have characteristics that make them unique individuals.

Physical Development

Kindergarten children are energetic. They have a lot of energy, and they want to use it in physical activities such as running, climbing, and jumping. Their desire to be involved in physical activity makes kindergarten an ideal time to involve children in projects of building—for example, making **learning centers** to resemble a store, post office, or veterinary office.

From ages five to seven, children's average weight and height approximate each other. For example, at six years, boys, on average, weigh 46 pounds and are 45 inches tall, while girls, on average, weigh about 44 pounds and are 45 inches tall. At age seven, boys weigh on average 50 pounds and are about 48 inches tall; girls weigh on average 50 pounds and are about 48 inches tall. Review Table 9.1, which shows average height and weight of kindergarten children.

Social and Emotional Development

Kindergarten children ages five to six are in Erikson's industry versus inferiority stage of social and emotional development. During this stage kindergarten children are continuing to learn to regulate their emotions and social interactions.

Some things you can do to promote kindergartners' positive social and emotional development are:

- Provide opportunities for children to be physically and mentally involved in activities involving problem solving and social activities with others.
- Teach and role-model how to make and keep friends.
- Model positive social and emotional responses. Read stories and discuss feelings such as anger, happiness, guilt, and pride.

learning centers Areas of the classroom specifically set up to promote student-centered, hands-on, active learning.

Today, kindergarten is a universal part of schooling, enrolling children from different cultures and socioeconomic backgrounds and, subsequently, different life experiences. How can professionals help ensure that kindergarten experiences meet the unique needs of each child?

Teaching in Kindergarten Today: "What's for Dinner?"

Ask any kindergarten teacher and she will tell you that if you can survive the first month of teaching then you can make it through anything! As a prerequisite for teaching in any kindergarten, you need to master the three R's of learning:

- **Relationships**—Establish a true connection with your students and their families.
- **Rules**—Establish and maintain classroom expectations in order for learning to happen.
- **Routines**—Establish day-to-day routines for the operation of the classroom and for the use and organization of centers and classroom materials.

A principal once shared with me that you must get to a student's heart (build a relationship) before you can ever get to the student's head (teaching). How true this is in kindergarten! You have to develop a relationship of trust with your students and offer them guidelines for learning (through the establishment of rules and routines), before successful learning can begin. This task can seem daunting on the first day of school—even through the first month—as twenty individuals with their own personalities, ideas, fears, and styles of learning look to you for leadership and guidance through this new world known as kindergarten.

A day in the life of a kindergarten teacher starts with the preparation of materials and supplies that you will use for the day. Kindergartners are dependent on their teacher, so you must organize and provide all materials and supplies needed for instruction—and you must make them easily accessible.

Each morning the bell rings and a whirlwind of learning begins as a sea of laughter and excitement rushes through the door in the form of kindergartners. I quickly engage my students in the learning process as they study math, reading, science, and social studies through center and calendar time. I use songs and movement activities as tools for helping my students learn a particular concept and to increase students' attention to a particular activity. Songs and movement are also valuable tools in classroom management.

I guide my children through a ten- to fifteen-minute mini-lesson on a particular skill or concept. One of my favorite ways to introduce a new kindergarten standard is through the 5E lesson model: I *engage* the students in the learning process and allow them opportunity to *explore* the key concepts of a lesson; students then collaboratively *explain* their discoveries and *elaborate* by extending what they've learned; and then I *evaluate* my students' understanding of the concept. For example, I might introduce my students to the Texas Kindergarten Math Standard, *"The student is expected to model and create addition and subtraction problems in real situations with concrete objects,"* by modeling on the document camera how there were 2 apples on the tree and 3 in the basket and how do we find out how many apples there are in all. I then work with them through a guided practice time where I monitor the students' understanding of creating addition and subtraction problems by having them work in pairs to solve addition and subtraction problems using red cubes and tree storyboards. After guided practice, the children independently practice what they learned in workstations or centers. Independent practice is a valuable time for both students and teachers. It allows students the opportunity to put into practice (independently) the new knowledge they learned and provides an opportunity for teachers to teach small groups of students who need additional instruction on a particular concept. It's a win–win situation for everyone as long as the foundation of the three R's mentioned above is firmly put into place the first month of school. Otherwise it could be an absolute disaster!

TABLE 9.1 Average Height and Weight of Kindergartners

Age	Males		Females	
	Height (inches)	Weight (pounds)	Height (inches)	Weight (pounds)
5 years	43.00	40.50	42.25	40.00
6 years	45.25	45.50	45.25	44.00
7 years	48.00	50.00	47.75	50.00
8 years	50.50	56.00	50.25	56.00

Note: Remember that averages are just that—averages. Children are different because of their individual differences. Ongoing growth and development tend to accentuate these differences.

Source: Centers for Disease Control and Prevention, National Center for Health Statistics, "Clinical Growth Charts," 2000 (latest information), http://www.cdc.gov/growthcharts.

I allot specific time for instruction in math, reading, science, and social studies throughout the school day as well as time for lunch, recess, P.E., music, art, and computers. You have to teach every subject area so you must learn to integrate the subject areas as much as possible, providing students with developmentally appropriate academic instruction in all subjects. I love combining the instruction of science and math because they have many similar standards and offer engaging lessons like the study of the seasons of the year. For example, I integrate science and math standards by reading the story of *Arnold's Apple Tree*, taking a fall walk and recording the seasonal changes the students observe on our daily calendar and in their science journals, and having students make an apple tree for their science journal using their handprints and paint.

Every day I provide some "down time" so my students can have the opportunity to take a fifteen- to twenty-minute mental break, whether through a rest time or a DEAR (Drop Everything and Read) time. In my classroom, this time is delightfully paired with a snack and classical or easy-listening music. My children and I relish the calmness that this fifteen minutes brings to our day!

Although the academic rigor of kindergarten has increased greatly over the years, children still need an opportunity for developmental creative play. My students choose and freely explore centers such as dramatic play, painting, puzzles, play dough, and blocks for the last twenty-five minutes of our day. It is truly amazing to observe students in free explore time. The social interaction and vocabulary development are so rich during this portion of our day!

As a kindergarten teacher, you must find the right balance in your teaching style to meet the demanding needs of a rigorous academic curriculum and provide a classroom where instruction meets the developmental needs of each learner. Here are four steps for successfully maintaining this balance:

STEP 1 Provide an environment where students can be risk-takers and discover learning in every corner— Students must feel comfortable to share their

thinking in the classroom. You create this environment through lots of praise and opportunities to discover and share learning through hands-on experiences and cooperative learning groups.

STEP 2 Celebrate daily the unique differences each child contributes to the learning environment— I choose a different student each week to be the "Star Student" of our classroom. This child brings in a special poster about himself or herself and various items that makes that child unique. The various items are used as tools for instruction. For example, a student's favorite shell collection might be placed in a baggie and used in an estimation lesson.

STEP 3 Nurture a love of learning in all children— Learning should be fun, exciting, and something that all children desire regardless of their learning abilities and learning styles. It is up to you to meet every student's learning needs no matter how much time and effort you must put forth for that to happen.

STEP 4 Magically facilitate learning to ensure that whatever concept you've taught "makes it to the dinner table" on a weekly basis—When my students' parents comment that their children shared what they learned that day at the dinner table, then I know that what I taught connected, mattered, and made a difference in the lives of my children. There is no greater compliment for a teacher than to have what you taught that day shared over dinner!

So from one teacher to another: "What's for dinner?"

Contributed by Shannon Keller, kindergarten teacher and team leader, Curtsinger Elementary, Frisco, Texas.

- Give children opportunities to be leaders in projects and activities.
- State your expectations for appropriate behavior and discuss them with your children.

Most kindergarten children, especially those who have been to preschool, are very confident, are eager to be involved, and want to and can accept a great deal of responsibility. They like going places and doing things, such as working on projects, experimenting, and working with others. Socially, kindergarten children are at the same time solitary and independent workers and growing in their ability and desire to work cooperatively with others. They want to be industrious and successful. Their combination of a "can do" attitude and their cooperation and responsibility make them a delight to teach and work with.

Cognitive and Language Development

Kindergarten children are in a period of rapid intellectual and language growth. They have a tremendous capacity to learn words and like the challenge of learning new words. This helps explain kindergarten children's love of big words and their ability to say and use

Children are born to learn. Learning is not something children "get ready for," but is a continuous process. What factors do you think are critical to support children's readiness to learn?

them. This is nowhere more apparent than in their fondness for dinosaurs and words such as *brontosaurus* or *triceratops*. Kindergarten children like and need to be involved in many language activities.

Additionally, kindergartners like to talk. Their desire to be verbal should be encouraged and supported by allowing many opportunities to engage in various language activities such as singing, telling stories, being involved in drama, and reciting poetry.

What children know when they enter kindergarten helps determine their success in school and what and how they are taught. Keep in mind that many kindergartners know more than people think, but many others know a great deal less. For example, many immigrant children in border states, such as Texas and California, are illiterate in their native language.

Accommodating Learning Disabilities

While it seems to many that every time you turn around, they've "come up with" a new disease or disorder, in actuality it is realistic and reasonable that as our scientific capabilities grow, so too do our abilities to help children who need help. One population that receives a lot of diagnostic and treatment attention is children with learning disabilities. In the United States, 15 percent of school-aged children have a learning disability of some kind.[11]

learning disability A disorder in one or more of the basic psychological processes involved in understanding or using spoken or written language, which may manifest itself in an imperfect ability to listen, think, speak, read, write, and spell or to do mathematical calculations.

The Individuals with Disabilities Education Act (IDEA) defines a **learning disability** as a "disorder in one or more of the basic psychological processes involved in understanding or in using spoken or written language, which may manifest itself in an imperfect ability to listen, think, speak, read, write, and spell or to do mathematical calculations."[12]

Despite what all we know about learning disabilities today, we still hear remarks such as, "He's just not trying hard enough . . ." "If she really wanted to, she would be good at reading . . ." "He's just not motivated . . ." "She's lazy . . ." or "He's just choosing not to do the work." Worst of all is the belief that the child with a learning disability is actually "just not smart."

Keep in mind that how children learn plays a major role in their school success. Some of your children will learn differently from how other children learn. These are learning differences. Learning differences are very real and can have serious consequences for young children, especially if you ignore them and do not accommodate for them. If learning disabilities are not caught early enough, they can seriously damage children's self-esteem, make goals seem unreachable, delay successes, impair social/peer relationships, and make the day-to-day experience of going to school painful. Here are some things to remember:

- Some common learning disabilities are:
  - *Expressive language disorder.* A problem expressing oneself using spoken language
  - *Mixed receptive-expressive language disorder.* A problem expressing oneself using spoken language combined with a problem understanding what people say
  - *Reading disorder.* A problem with reading comprehension, accuracy, and/or speed
  - *Mathematics disorder.* A difficulty in doing calculations as well as understanding word problems and mathematical concepts

- *Disorder of written expression.* A problem with both the physical reproduction of letters and words and the organization of thoughts and ideas in written compositions
- *Developmental coordination disorder.* The failure to develop normal motor coordination
- Know the signs. In kindergartners, some red flags of a learning disability are:
  - Difficulty in:
    - Following simple directions
    - Understanding questions
    - Manipulating small objects
    - Learning new words
    - Staying on task or changing activities
    - Understanding cause and effect, sequencing, and counting
  - Avoidance of drawing or tracing
  - Lack of interest in storytelling
  - Trouble with self-help activities
  - Easily frustrated

When you suspect a child has a learning disability, collaborate with other teachers and seek instructional accommodations.

WHO ATTENDS KINDERGARTEN?

Froebel's kindergarten was for children three to seven years of age. In the United States, kindergarten is for five- and six-year-old children before they enter first grade. Since the age at which children enter first grade varies, the ages at which they enter kindergarten also differ. Many parents and professionals support an older rather than a younger kindergarten entrance age because they think older children are more "ready" for kindergarten and will learn better. For example, Jack Haims, who turned six in late September, started kindergarten with many skills. He could read simple rhyming books, count to 100 and write his name. Jacks mother says, "He has a lot of self-confidence because he is older." Jack acquired his confidence and abilities thanks to an extra year of preschool.[13] Whereas in the past children had to be five years of age prior to December 31 for kindergarten admission in many districts, today the trend is toward an older admission age.[14]

Kindergarten Entrance Age

Undoubtedly, there will be ongoing debates and discussions about the appropriate age for kindergarten entrance. Current legislative policies and initiatives support delaying kindergarten entrance ages. For example, Maryland recently raised the age at which children can be admitted to kindergarten. Now children must be five by September 1 rather than the previous date of December 31. The state's superintendent of schools said the change was necessary because of the increased academic focus in today's kindergartens.[15]

Redshirting. You may have heard of the practice of redshirting college football players. This is the practice of holding a player out a year so he can grow and mature. The theory is that the extra year will result in better football players. The same practice applies to kindergarten children. The U.S. Department of Education estimates that about 9 percent of entering kindergarten children are *redshirted*—held out of school for a year.[16] Parents and administrators who practice redshirting think that the extra year will give children an opportunity to mature intellectually, socially, and physically. On the one hand, redshirting might have some benefit for children who are immature and whose birth dates fall close to the school entrance date cutoff. On the other hand, some affluent parents redshirt their children, their sons in particular, because they want them to be the oldest members of the kindergarten class. They reason that their children will be class leaders, will get more attention from the teachers, and will have another year under their belt, which will help them handle the increasing demands of the kindergarten curriculum.

Rather than the constant juggling of entrance ages, what is needed are early childhood programs designed to meet and serve the needs of all children, regardless of the ages at which they enter school. At the heart of this issue of age and time is whether maturation or school is the more potent factor in children's achievement. Research studies comparing age and school effects suggest educational intervention contributes more to children's cognitive competence than does maturation.[17]

These and other issues will continue to fuel the educational debates and will make learning about and teaching in kindergarten even more fascinating as the years go by.

Universal Kindergarten

Just as support is growing for universal preschools, it should come as no surprise that there is wide public support for compulsory and tax-supported universal public kindergarten. Forty-three states require school districts to offer at least a half-day kindergarten.[18] The national trend is for districts to offer full-day programs. Nine states require school districts to offer full-day kindergarten.[19] However, only fourteen states require mandatory kindergarten attendance of age-eligible children.[20] Nonetheless, because of the widespread availability of kindergarten, 98 percent of American children attend at least a half-day kindergarten before entering first grade.[21] As a result, public school kindergarten is now considered the first grade of school. It is important for you to know that kindergarten is considered a time for serious learning and accomplishment.

Today, full-day kindergarten offers several potential benefits. It provides continuity for children accustomed to full-day experiences outside of the home, provides continuity with schedules in first grade and beyond, reduces the number of disruptions and transitions children experience in a typical day, and allows teachers more time for both formal and informal instruction that provide meaningful learning opportunities. It also provides an important opportunity to align the policies and practices of the grades that follow kindergarten with those of the early learning programs that typically come before. Furthermore, results of empirical research on the effects of full- versus half-day kindergarten are encouraging. Studies not only show full-day programs have no detrimental effects on children who attend, but students show significantly stronger academic gains over the course of the kindergarten year than their counterparts in half-day programs.[22]

ENVIRONMENTS FOR KINDERGARTNERS

Both the physical environment and the social environment of the kindergarten classroom influence children's physical, cognitive, linguistic, and social-emotional development. In classrooms where the environment supports children's learning, research shows that the occurrence of problem behaviors is reduced and the rate of children's social cooperation with their peers increases.[23]

The Physical Environment

Environments that support kindergarten children's learning are essential if we want all kindergarten children to be successful.

Classroom Arrangement and Organization. The classroom is organized to promote interaction and learning. Desks, tables, and workstations are clustered together; work areas have a variety of learning materials to encourage group projects, experiments, and creative activities.

Also, a high-quality kindergarten classroom is one in which children feel at home. Children's work is prominently displayed and they feel a sense of ownership. Here are some things you can do to provide high-quality kindergarten environments:

- Provide many materials that support children learning to read and write. Learning to read and write is a high priority of kindergarten, so be sure to offer a wide variety of all kinds of books and writing materials.
- Organize the children into groups of different sizes and ability levels. This provides for social interaction and cooperative learning and encourages children to help others (scaffolding).
- Use a variety of different instructional approaches, such as:
  - Small group
  - Large group
  - Seat work
  - Center time
  - Free activity choice time
  - Individual teacher one-on-one work with children
  - Free play time
- Develop your classroom arrangement so that it supports district and state learning standards. For example, to meet reading content standards, make books easily accessible to students. Also, make sure the classroom has a comfortable area for group and individual reading times.
- Adapt your classroom arrangement so it meets the learning and social needs of your children. For example, set aside time for students to work in groups, assign group projects, and assign projects dealing with different cultures.
- Collaborate with your children to "personalize" your classroom. Make your classroom home-like and cozy. Use plants, rugs, beanbag chairs, pillows, and so on.
- Make supplies and learning materials accessible to children by storing them on open shelves with labels (using pictures and words).

The Social Environment

The social environment consists of the immediate physical surroundings, social relationships, and cultural settings in which children function and interact. To help create a supportive social environment, all children of all cultures, genders, socioeconomic levels, and backgrounds should be valued and respected. Teachers treat children courteously, talk with them about in- and out-of-school activities and events, and show a genuine concern for them as individuals with specific needs. Unfortunately, not all children get the respect they need and want at home or at school. Some children, especially children with behavior and attention problems, can be subjected to verbal abuse by teachers and children.[24] Also, for shy children, the social environment can provide them with the social interaction they need, but they may have a difficult time initiating the interaction, and teachers need to help them find playmates. On the other hand, under the direction of an unaware or uncaring teacher, classroom activities and social interactions may encourage isolation and separation.

In developing positive teacher–child relationships, which is a key element of the social environment, it is important to remember to:

- Engage in one-to-one interactions with children.
- Get on children's level for face-to-face interactions.
- Use a pleasant, calm voice and simple language.
- Provide warm, responsive physical contact.

- Follow children's lead and interest during play.
- Help children understand classroom expectations.
- Redirect children when they engage in challenging behavior.
- Listen to children and encourage them to listen to others.
- Acknowledge children for their accomplishments and effort.[25]

CURRICULUM IN THE KINDERGARTEN

All kindergarten classrooms should be child centered and support developmentally appropriate practice in planning and implementing curriculum. Developmentally appropriate practice involves teaching and learning that is in accordance with children's physical, cognitive, social, linguistic, individual, and cultural development. Professionals help children learn and develop in ways that are compatible with how old they are and who they are as individuals (e.g., their background of experiences and culture). Early childhood professionals who embody the qualities of good kindergarten teachers are those who teach in developmentally appropriate ways.

Developmentally appropriate practice in kindergarten includes the following:

- *Make learning meaningful to children and related to what they know.* Children find things meaningful when they are interesting and they can relate to them.
- *Individualize your curriculum as much as possible.* All children do not learn the same way, nor are they interested in learning the same things as everyone else all the time.
- *Make learning physically and mentally active.* Actively involve children in learning that includes building, making, experimenting, investigating, and working collaboratively with their peers.

- *Provide for hands-on activities with concrete objects and manipulatives.* Emphasize real-life activities as opposed to workbook and worksheet activities.

Kindergarten curriculum includes not only activities that support children emotionally and socially in learning to be more competent people, but also more academic experiences, such as those in literacy and reading, math, science, social studies, and the arts. All experiences, however, should first be approached by considering five- and six-year-olds' developmental capabilities and yearning to play as they learn.

Literacy and Reading in Kindergarten

Today, improving literacy is a major goal across all grade levels. All states and school districts have adopted an educational agenda with a strong literacy focus and have set the goal of having all children read on grade level by grade three.

The nation has set a goal of having all children read and write at or above grade level by grade three. What are some activities and practices you can implement to help ensure that all children achieve this national goal?

This all means that the reading goals for kindergarten learning are higher than they have ever been, and will continue to increase. Now would be a good time for you to review your kindergarten state standards for literacy and reading. Teaching and learning today functions in a standards-based environment.

Literacy and Reading. Early childhood professionals place a high priority on children's literacy and reading success. **Literacy** means the ability to read, write, speak, and listen. Professionals view literacy as a process that begins at birth (perhaps before) and continues to develop across the life span, through the school years.

The process of becoming literate is also viewed as a natural process; reading and writing are processes that children participate in naturally, long before they come to school. No doubt you have participated with or know of toddlers and preschoolers who are literate in many ways. They "read" all kinds of environmental print such as signs (McDonald's), labels (Cheerios), and menus and other symbols in their environments.

Language arts refers to the subjects, including reading, spelling, and composition, aimed at developing reading and writing skills in early childhood education. Figure 9.1 defines common terms used when discussing literacy. These are terms you will want to

literacy The ability to read, write, speak, and listen.

FIGURE 9.1

Reading/Literacy Instructional Terminology

Alphabet knowledge The knowledge that letters have names and shapes and that letters can represent sounds in language.
Example: Children recognize and name the letters of the alphabet.

Alphabetic principle Awareness that each speech sound or phoneme in a language has its own distinctive graphic representation and an understanding that letters go together in patterns to represent sounds.
Example: Letters and letter patterns represent sounds of the language. Introduce just letters that are used a lot such as M, A, T, S, P, and H. Teach consonants first for sound–letter relationships.

Comprehension In reading, the basic understanding of the words and the content or meaning contained within printed material.
Example: Keisha is able to retell the story. Mario is able to tell who the main character is.

Decoding Identifying words through context and phonics.
Example: James can figure out how to read a word he does not know by using his knowledge of letters and sounds. Also, he uses context clues (information from pictures and the sentence before and the sentence after a word) to "decode" it. He looked at the picture with a "pile" of wood to figure out *pile,* a word he did not know.

Phoneme The smallest unit of speech that makes a difference to meaning.
Example: The word *pig* has three phonemes, /p/ /i/ /g/.

Phonemic awareness The ability to notice, think about, and work with the individual sounds in spoken words.
Example: Alex can identify the words in a set that begin with the same sound: *boy, big, bike.*

Phonics The learning of alphabetic principles of language and knowledge of letter–sound relationships.
Example: Children learn to associate letters with phonemes (basic speech sounds) to help break the alphabetic code.

Phonological awareness The ability to manipulate language at the levels of syllables, rhymes, and individual speech sounds.
Example: Maria can identify words that rhyme from those that don't rhyme. Whitney can match words that sound alike. Caroline can segment words into sounds. Angie can blend sounds into words.

Print awareness The recognition of conventions and characteristics of a written language.
Example: Mario pretends to read a bedtime story to his teddy bear. Also, he recognizes the Pizza Hut sign on his way to school.

know and use. They are an important part of being able to "talk the talk" of your profession. You will use these terms in your work with parents, colleagues, and the community.

Developing Literacy and Reading in Young Children. Literacy and reading are certainly worthy national and educational goals, not only for young children but for everyone. However, how best to promote literacy has always been a controversial topic. What do children need to know to become good and skillful readers? Research identifies the following:[26]

- *Phonemic awareness.* The ability to focus on and use phonemes (the smallest units of spoken language) in spoken words. The English language has at least forty-one phonemes. Some words (e.g., *a* or *oh*) have only one phoneme. Most words, however, consist of a blend of phonemes (e.g., three phonemes in *chip: ch, i,* and *p*).
- *Phonics.* Learning letter–sound relationships and spelling patterns.
- *Fluency.* Reading with speed, accuracy, and proper expression.
- *Comprehension.* The ultimate goal of reading, integrating the skills involved with reading and understanding what is being read.
- *Vocabulary.* Knowing and understanding the words in written and spoken language.

Approaches to Literacy and Reading. As stated above, there are a variety of approaches to literacy and reading instruction. Basal approaches and materials used for literacy and reading development often emphasize one particular method. Your kindergarten may employ one (or more) of the following.

sight word approach Also called *whole-word* or *look-say,* an approach to reading that involves presenting children with whole words so they develop a "sight vocabulary" as opposed to "sounding out" words using phonics.

Sight Words. One of the most popular methods is the **sight word approach** (also called *whole-word* or *look-say*) in which children are presented whole words (*cat, bat, sat*) and develop a "sight vocabulary" that enables them to begin reading and writing. Many early childhood teachers label objects in their classrooms (door, bookcase, etc.) as a means of teaching a sight vocabulary. Word walls are popular in kindergarten and primary classrooms. A word wall is a bulletin board or classroom display area on the classroom wall on which high-frequency and new words are displayed. The words are arranged alphabetically.

phonics instruction A teaching method that emphasizes letter–sound correspondence so children can learn to combine sounds into words.

Phonics. A second popular approach is based on **phonics instruction**, which stresses teaching letter–sound correspondences. By learning these connections, children are able to combine sounds into words (C-A-T). The proponents of phonics instruction argue that letter–sound correspondences enable children to make automatic connections between words and sounds and, as a result, to sound out words and read them on their own. From the 1950s until the present time there has been much debate about whether phonics or the sight word approach to literacy development is best. Today, there is a decided reemphasis on the use of phonics instruction. One reason is that the research evidence suggests that phonics instruction enables children to become more proficient readers.[27]

language experience approach (LEA) A reading instruction method that links oral and written language.

Language Experience. Another method of literacy and reading development, the **language experience approach (LEA)**, follows the philosophy and suggestions inherent in progressive education philosophy. This approach to reading instruction is child centered, links oral and written language, and maintains that literacy education should be meaningful to children and should grow out of experiences that are interesting to them. LEA is based on the premise that what is thought can be said, what is said can be written, and what is written can be read. Children's experiences are a key element in such child-centered approaches. Many teachers transcribe children's dictated "experience" stories and use them as a basis for writing and for reading instruction. When children write stories, write in their journals, and write and illustrate cards and notes they are using their language experiences to learn to write and read.

Whole Language. Beginning about 1980, early childhood practitioners in the United States were influenced by literacy education approaches used in Australia and New Zealand.

These influences gradually developed into what is known as the **whole-language approach** to literacy development. Since "whole language" is a philosophy rather than a method, its definition often depends on who is using the term. This approach nonetheless advocates using all aspects of language—reading, writing, listening, and speaking—as the basis for developing literacy. Children learn about reading and writing by speaking and listening; they learn to read by writing, and they learn to write by reading.

The whole-language approach dominated early childhood practice from about 1990 through 1995. However, growing numbers of critics, including parents and the public, maintained that because it is a philosophy rather than a specific approach, it does not teach children skills necessary for good reading. In addition, some teachers have difficulty explaining the whole-language approach to parents, and some find it difficult to implement as well. There is argument that some children from diverse backgrounds or with disabilities sometimes lack the required background experiences to be successful using this approach to reading instruction. Further, some research has indicated that whole-language approaches do not result in the high levels of reading achievement claimed by its supporters.[28] As a result, proponents of phonics instruction are aggressively advocating a return to this approach to best meet the needs of children, parents, and society.

Shared Reading. Because children love books and reading, shared reading is a good way for you to capitalize on their interests and help them learn to read. **Shared reading** is a means of introducing young beginners to reading by using favorite books, rhymes, and poems. Teachers model reading for the students by reading aloud a book or other text and ultimately inviting students to join in.

Shared reading builds on children's natural desire to read and reread favorite books. The repeated reading of texts over several days, weeks, or months deepens children's understanding of them because each time the reading should be for a different purpose: to extend, refine, or deepen children's abilities to read and construct meaning.

The shared reading routine requires that you have on hand a big-book form of the book to be read, as well as multiple little-book copies for individual rereading later. You then follow these three steps:

1. *Introduce the book.* Gather the children where they can all see the big book.
   - Show and discuss the book cover: Read the title, author, illustrator, and other appropriate book features.
   - Discuss some of the pages in the book, but don't give away the entire story.
   - Invite children to predict what they think will happen in the book. If they have difficulty, model thinking aloud to show them how you would predict. Record their predictions on a chart for later reference.

2. *Read and respond to the book.* Read the book aloud to the children, holding it so they can see each page. As you read, run your hand or a pointer under each line of print to help children develop a sense of left-to-right orientation, speech-to-print match, and other concepts of print. If some children wish to join in, encourage them to do so.

   As you read, you may stop briefly to discuss the story or to respond to reactions, but you should progress through the entire book rather quickly to give children a complete sense of the story. At the conclusion of the reading, encourage children to respond, using questions such as these:
   - Were your predictions right?
   - What did you like in this story?
   - What was your favorite part?
   - What made you happy (or sad)?
   - Who was your favorite character? Why?

whole-language approach Philosophy of literacy development that advocates using all aspects of language—reading, writing, listening, and speaking— to help children become motivated to read and write.

shared reading A teaching method in which the teacher and children read together from a book that is visible to all.

Then return to the book, rereading the story and inviting children to read along. Many will feel comfortable doing this right away, but others may not join in until another day. After the second reading, many children will say, "Let's read it again"—especially for books, songs, or rhymes that are lots of fun. Under most circumstances, when children are excited and want to reread, you should reread.

After you have read the book again, have children respond, using activities such as these:

- Talk with a friend about a favorite part.
- Retell the story to a partner.
- Draw a picture about the story and write a word or a sentence about it.
- Draw and write about a favorite character.
- Write a list of favorite characters.

Help children become comfortable with making decisions by giving them only a couple of choices initially.

> Reading and written language acquisition is a continuum of development. Think of children as being on a continuous journey toward full literacy development! Regardless of what method you use to teach children how to read, the goal is that they should learn to read—and read on or above grade level—so they can do well in school and life.

3. *Extend the book.* You may want to wait until children have read a book several times before extending it, or you may wait unit they have read several books within a thematic unit and combine them for extension activities. Although each repeated reading may seem to be just for fun, each should have a particular focus. You might first invite children to recall what the title was and what the book was about, prompting and supporting them if necessary. Then tell the children why they are rereading the book, using statements such as the following:

- "As we reread this book, let's think about who the important characters are" (comprehension).
- "In our story today, notice how the author repeats lines over and over" (exploring language).
- "Today, as we reread one of our favorite stories, look for places to use phonic skills we have been learning" (decoding).[29]

Through shared reading, children learn to

- Track print from left to right and word by word
- Predict and infer
- Enjoy and participate in reading with a high level of support
- Build a sense of story
- Expand their vocabulary
- Find letters and sounds in context
- Attend to concepts of print (spacing, capitalization, punctuation)
- Sequence the events of a story
- Focus on story elements (characters, setting, beginning, middle, end)[30]

> **balanced approach** An approach to literacy in which there is a balance between whole-language methods and phonics instruction.

The Balanced Approach. As with most things, a **balanced approach** is the best, and many early childhood advocates are encouraging literacy approaches that provide a balance between whole-language methods and phonics instruction to meet the specific needs of individual children. One thing is clear: Systematic instruction that enables children to acquire the skills they need to learn to read is very much in evidence in today's early childhood classrooms. It is likely that the debate over "the best approach" will continue. At the same time, efforts will increase to integrate the best of all approaches into a unified whole to make all children confident readers.

Supporting Children's Learning to Read. A primary goal of kindergarten education is for children to learn how to read. Teachers must instruct, support, and guide children in helping them learn what is necessary for them to be successful in school and in life. Here are some of the things you can do to motivate children's learning to read:

- Include a variety of different types of books, such as picture books without words, fairy tales, nursery rhymes, picture storybooks, realistic literature, decodable and predictable books, information books, chapter books, biographies, big books, poetry, and joke and riddle books.
- Provide other types of print such as newspapers, magazines, and brochures.
- Introduce and discuss several books each week (may be theme related, same authors, illustrators, types of books, etc.).
- Have multiple copies of popular books.
- Provide a record-keeping system for keeping track of books read (may include a picture-coding system to rate or evaluate the book).
- Showcase many books by placing them so covers are visible, especially those that are new, shared in read-aloud sessions, or theme related.
- Organize books on shelves by category or type (may color-code).
- Provide comfortable, inviting places to read (pillows, rugs, a sofa, large cardboard boxes, etc.).
- Encourage children to read to "friends" (include stuffed animals and dolls for "pretend" reading).
- Have an Author's Table with a variety of writing supplies to encourage children to write about books.
- Have a Listening Table for recorded stories and tapes.[31]

The accompanying Professionalism in Practice feature, "How to Use the Project Approach," shows how effectively you can use projects to teach young children traditional academic subjects such as literacy through an active, hands-on approach.

Also, stop for a minute and reflect on what we said in Chapter 3 about Vygotsky's theory of scaffolding children's learning.

Math in Kindergarten

Like all other kindergarten subjects, the teaching of math in kindergarten today is not what it was in the past. A good place to begin to understand what mathematics is like in the kindergarten today is with your state standards. Now would be a good time for you to review them. Here are the kindergarten Mathematics Standards for one state:[32]

- Number, operation and quantitative reasoning.
  - The student uses numbers to name quantities.
  - The student describes order of events or objects.
  - The student models addition (joining) and subtraction (separating). The student is expected to model and create addition and subtraction problems in real situations with concrete objects.
- Patterns, relationships, and algebraic thinking.
  - The student identifies, extends, and creates patterns. The student is expected to identify, extend, and create patterns of sounds, physical movement, and concrete objects.
  - The student uses patterns to make predictions.
- Geometry and spatial reasoning.
  - The student uses attributes to determine how objects are alike and different.
  - The student recognizes attributes of two- and three-dimensional geometric figures.

COMPETENCY BUILDER

How to Use the Project Approach

Students in the K–1 classroom at University Primary School begin their day reading a daily sign-in question that is intended to provoke a thoughtful response:

Have you ever eaten the flowers of a plant?
Do you think a van is more like a car or like a bus?

Such questions are related to the topic under study and are used to engage children in discussing different views during their whole-group meeting later in the morning.

Opportunities for children to express themselves abound at University Primary School. In addition to an hour of systematic literacy instruction, authentic opportunities to read and write occur throughout the day in the course of the children's regular activities.

INTEGRATING LANGUAGE ARTS WITH THE PROJECT APPROACH

The Project Approach involves students in an in-depth investigation of worthy real-world topics.* Learning becomes meaningful for them as they pursue answers to their own questions. Students can carry out specific literacy-related activities in each phase of project investigation:

PHASE 1

EXPLORING PREVIOUS EXPERIENCES

- Brainstorm what is already known about a project topic.
- Write or dictate stories about memories and experiences.
- Label and categorize experiences.

PHASE 2

INVESTIGATING THE TOPIC

- Write questions, predictions, and hypotheses.
- Write questions to ask experts.
- Write questionnaires and surveys.
- Write thank-you letters to experts.
- Record findings.
- Record data.
- Make all types of lists (what materials need to be collected, what will be shared with others, who will do which tasks).
- Listen to stories and informational texts read aloud.
- Read secondary sources to help answer questions.
- Compare what was read with what the experts shared.

PHASE 3

SHARING THE PROJECT WITH PARENTS AND OTHERS

- Make charts, displays, and PowerPoint presentations.
- Write reports or plays that demonstrate new understanding.

- Write invitations to a culminating event.
- Share stories orally in readers' theater.

Throughout all phases of their project investigation, students have authentic contexts to read, spell, write words, and build their vocabulary. In addition, comparing what they knew with what they have learned from the primary and secondary sources, they develop their analytical thinking and comprehension skills. And they become more fluent readers and writers by using their skills to answer their own questions.

PROVIDING DIRECT INSTRUCTION IN READING AND WRITING

The five reading components articulated in the No Child Left Behind Act—phonemic awareness, phonics, fluency, vocabulary, and comprehension—are taught throughout the students' day within the context of project investigation and during small-group direct literacy instruction. Direct instruction includes a whole-group meeting during which the teacher reads books aloud (i.e., shared reading) for specific purposes. The teacher may choose to highlight the project topic or specific authors or illustrators or to focus on rhyming words or specific patterns of phonemes.

Following the shared reading time, students engage in writing activities related to the books they heard read aloud. These activities may include literature extensions that encourage students to write creatively. They may write a different ending to a story or write a related story from a different point of view. Students may also write their own stories, using the principles of writer's workshop, in which students learn to edit and extend their language skills. The teacher may also introduce extended minilessons on the tools of writing, such as alliteration, similes, metaphors, or syllabic rhythms.

After their noon recess, students choose books to read quietly while the teacher provides individual guided reading. Project-related books may be a popular choice. Students conclude their silent reading with approximately ten minutes to engage in buddy reading. During the buddy reading time, students talk about what they have just read with their buddy and read favorite excerpts of their books to their buddy. This collaboration reinforces comprehension skills and instills the love of literature that motivates all children to read.

At University Primary School, students are always improving and using their literacy skills to learn.

*L. G. Katz and S. C. Chard, *Engaging Children's Minds: The Project Approach*, 2nd ed. (Norwood, NJ: Ablex, 2000).

Contributed by Nancy B. Hertzog, associate professor, Department of Special Education, and director, University Primary School at the University of Illinois at Urbana-Champaign; and by Marjorie M. Klein, former head teacher in the K–1 classroom at University Primary School and now an educational consultant in St. Louis, Missouri.

- Measurement.
  - The student directly compares the attributes of length, area, weight/mass, capacity, and/or relative temperature. The student uses comparative language to solve problems and answer questions.
  - The student uses time to describe, compare, and order events and situations.
- Probability and statistics.
  - The student constructs and uses graphs of real objects or pictures to answer questions.
- Underlying processes and mathematical tools.
  - The student applies Kindergarten mathematics to solve problems connected to everyday experiences and activities in and outside of school.
  - The student communicates about Kindergarten mathematics using informal language.
  - The student uses logical reasoning and the student is expected to justify his or her thinking using objects, words, pictures, numbers, and technology.[33]

In addition, one of the leading kindergarten mathematics programs includes these math strands and topics:[34]

Number and Operations

- Zero to Five
- Six to Ten
- Comparing Numbers
- Money

Algebra

- Sorting and Classifying
- Patterns
- Fractions and Ordinals

Geometry

- Position and Location
- Geometry

Measurement

- Time
- Calendar

Data Analysis and Probability

- Graphing

Your teaching of mathematics in kindergarten should also be in alignment with the National Council of Teachers of Mathematics (NCTM) Curriculum Focal Points. Curriculum focal points are important mathematical topics for each grade level, pre-kindergarten through eighth grade. In addition, your integration of your curriculum with the curriculum focal points should promote these processes. Review now the NCTM kindergarten curriculum focal points in Figure 9.2.

Science in Kindergarten

Scaffolding with Science. We do not want to forget that in all of our teaching of young children, we should be alert as to how to practice the theories we discussed in Chapter 3. For example, science offers many wonderful opportunities to apply Vygotsky's ideas, especially scaffolding. In meeting the science content standard *science as inquiry*

FIGURE 9.2

Kindergarten Curriculum Focal Points

1. *Numbers and Operations:* Representing, comparing, and ordering whole numbers and joining and separating sets	Children use numbers, including written numerals, to represent quantities and to solve quantitative problems, such as counting objects in a set, creating a set with a given number of objects, comparing and ordering sets or numerals by using both cardinal and ordinal meanings, and modeling simple joining and separating situations with objects. They choose, combine, and apply effective strategies for answering quantitative questions, including quickly recognizing the number in a small set, counting and producing sets of given sizes, counting the number in combined sets, and counting backward.
	For example, they might sort solids that roll easily from those that do not. Or they might collect data and use counting to answer such questions as "What is our favorite snack?" They re-sort objects by using new attributes (e.g., after sorting solids according to which ones roll, they might re-sort the solids according to which ones stack easily).
2. *Geometry:* Describing shapes	Children interpret the physical world with geometric ideas (e.g., shape, orientation, and spatial relations) and describe it with corresponding vocabulary. They identify, name, and describe a variety of shapes, such as squares, triangles, circles, rectangles, (regular) hexagons, and (isosceles) trapezoids presented in a variety of ways (e.g., with different sizes or orientations), as well as such three-dimensional shapes as spheres, cubes, and cylinders. They use basic shapes and spatial reasoning to model objects in their environment and to construct more complex shapes.
	For example, children integrate their understandings of geometry, measurement, and number. For example, they understand, discuss, and create simple navigational directions (e.g., "Walk forward ten steps, turn right, and walk forward five steps").
3. *Measurement:* Ordering objects by measurable attributes	Children use measurable attributes, such as length or weight, to solve problems by comparing and ordering objects. They compare the lengths of two objects both directly (by comparing them with each other) and indirectly (by comparing both with a third object), and they order several objects according to length.
	For example, children identify, duplicate, and extend simple number patterns and sequential and growing patterns (e.g., patterns made with shapes) as preparation for creating rules that describe relationships.

Source: Reprinted with permission from "Curriculum Focal Points for Prekindergarten Through Grade 8 Mathematics: A Quest for Coherence," National Council of Teachers of Mathematics (NCTM), 2006, 11.

(see Chapter 10), a problem-solving chart like that shown in Figure 9.3 can help you not only teach science as inquiry but also help students learn the process of scientific inquiry in their study of plants and how they grow.

Social Studies in Kindergarten

In kindergarten, the social sciences most often included are history, geography, economics, and civics.[35] For each of these disciplines you will want to include knowledge, concepts, and themes. Your teaching of social studies should be content based and child centered, and you will want to make sure that you consult your state's content standards for social studies.

expanding horizons approach *or* expanding environments approach An approach to teaching social studies in which the student's world is the center of the initial units, with children at each grade level being exposed to a slowly widening environment.

Historically, social studies in kindergarten have focused on the **expanding horizons approach**, also called the **expanding environments approach**, for sequencing and selecting content. In this approach the children are at the center of expanding horizons; at each grade level they are immersed in a widening environment. In recent years, the expanding horizons approach has come under criticism. Critics of this approach maintain that it is simplistic, lacks rigorous social science content, and does not engage children in a serious exploration of social studies.

FIGURE 9.3

Sample Problem-Solving Chart

Identify Problem	Preview Solution	Assemble Resources
What kind of soil will a bean seed grow in: soil from outside our classroom, humus, sand, water, rocks, or clay?	We think that a bean seed will grow best in humus because it has nutrients in it.	We need soil from outside our classroom, humus, sand, water, rocks, clay, see-through cups, beans, and a well-lit place in our classroom.

Analyze Resources and Plans	Select Plan and Begin Doing It	Monitor the Process
We need to make sure each cup gets the same amount of light. We need to make sure we use the same amount of planting material.	Each group of four students needs to plan the experiment and do it.	What is happening to the seeds? • After 4 days? • After 8 days? Why is this happening?

Source: Launching Learners in Science, PreK–5 by Kerry C. Williams. Copyright 2007 by Sage Publications Inc. Books. Reproduced with permission of Sage Publications Inc. Books in the formats Textbook and Other Book via Copyright Clearance Center.

Although the expanding horizon approach is much maligned, nonetheless, the teaching of social studies generally begins with who the children are and where they are geographically. In addition, approaches to social studies in kindergarten also try to be child centered and developmentally appropriate.

Today's teaching of social studies is designed to provide children with content knowledge and skills from the four social sciences: history, geography, economics, and civics. So, in your teaching of social studies you will want to make sure that children are provided with authentic content and are engaged in activities that help them learn knowledge, apply knowledge, and engage in critical thinking.

Ideas for Teaching Social Studies. The following are some ideas that you can use to help you teach the social studies content standards of your state and school district:

• *Geography.* Gayle teaches her kindergarten class about different cultures by placing one end of a ribbon on a map on the United States and the other end on the country they are learning about. Gayle discusses with the students about the different modes of transportation that could be used to travel to the country. Pictures are placed on the map above that country pertaining to the culture there. Students are then instructed to draw a picture, write a story, or create a poem to put on the map as well.

• *Economics.* Ashley teaches her children about assembly lines through the use of creative arts. She draws pictures of stick figures with each line drawn using a different color crayon. After displaying the drawing up on the wall she then separates her class into small groups and gives each group member a different color crayon and one piece of paper per group. The piece of paper is passed down the line of students, and each student draws one line with their crayon matching Ashley's drawing. The class then discusses the importance of assembly lines, why each member must do his part, and the different products that are made by assembly lines.

• *Civics.* Eric has his kindergarten children make a U.S. flag collage using large paper, magazines, crayons, scissors, and glue. He then discusses with the class that the flag is a national symbol, explains what the stars and stripes stand for, and discusses the role national symbols play in society. Students then tell Eric where they've seen the American flag flown before, and he makes a list of these places on the chalkboard. After the discussion, students individually draw pictures of other flags they have seen.

- *History.* Sarah teaches her kindergarten children about ancient cultures through photographs and online reproductions of wall paintings from ancient civilizations that illustrate aspects of life as it was lived in ancient times. She then asks the students to give her ideas about which animals lived at that time, which animals the people hunted, and what games the people played. Sarah then has her students illustrate a picture of a day in their own lives using markers, crayons, or paint. The pictures include scenes such as coming to school, reading in class, recess, lunch, and playing with pets or siblings at home. After their drawings are complete, Sarah hangs the students' pictures next to the pictures of the ancient civilization. The class then holds a discussion about the similarities and differences in the ancient civilizations and their own.

Arts in Kindergarten

Teaching of the arts in kindergarten consists of knowledge, skills, and concepts from these four areas: music, art, dance, and theater. The standards were developed by the American Alliance for Theater and Education, Music Educators National Conference, the National Art Education Association, and the National Dance Association.

In your role as a kindergarten teacher, you will want to integrate the arts into everything that you do. Children love to participate in activities relating to the arts, so you should capitalize on their natural creative inclinations and provide them with these experiences. As with anything else, the integration of the arts depends on these factors: time, opportunity, and materials.

Time. By integrating the arts into your curriculum, you are solving the time issue by enabling children to participate in all of these activities while they are learning reading/literacy, math, science, and social studies. For example, here are some ideas for integrating the arts into each of these areas:

- *Reading/literacy.* Students can act out the stories of their favorite book; students can illustrate a story that they and/or the class have written.
- *Math.* Students can use art materials to make charts and graphs and design and make different kinds of shapes. Students can also develop rules to describe the relationships of one shape to another—for example, "You can put two identical triangles together to make a rectangle."
- *Science.* Children can use their artistic skills to draw and paint various examples of life cycles of organisms or write and produce a public service announcement on the importance of personal health in the kindergarten classroom.
- *Social studies.* Students can learn about and sing many of the songs popular in their state's history; students can learn the folk dances of various cultural groups in their state.

Opportunity. There are many opportunities during the school year for children to engage in projects that involve the arts. For example, puppetry can be integrated into all of the content areas, and stories provide many opportunities for children to engage in theater and dramatic play. For example, in preparation for, and while reading the story "The Three Billy Goats Gruff," children can make paper masks to depict the goats and could build a bridge out of blocks and/or other materials. Also, students could have a starring role playing the troll. Every thematic unit provides opportunities for all of the arts, and children should be encouraged to explore ways to express ideas from the thematic units in an artistic way.

Materials. Materials are just as important as time and opportunity. They include all of the materials related to the visual arts—paints, crayons, markers, brushes, and so on—as well as materials necessary for music and dance. For example, you could provide materials such as DVDs of folk dances, popular songs, and sing-along tunes. To encourage theater expression, children need props—clothes, hats, puppets, and plenty of materials such as cardboard boxes, glue, and tape for making their own stage settings and backgrounds. Keep in mind that the *process* of exploring the creative arts is more important than the finished *product*. Children are learning to enjoy learning when the process is respected by teachers.

LESSON PLANNING

In addition to knowing the curriculum, the "what" to teach, another dimension of being a high-quality kindergarten teacher is knowing *how* to teach. This involves planning for teaching. Recall in Chapter 1, we discussed the cycle of reflective practice: thinking, planning, and deciding. Reflective practice involves thinking before teaching, thinking during teaching, and thinking after teaching. Part of your role as a kindergarten teacher will be to write lesson plans, either individually or as a team member. Some school districts have prepared lesson plans that you will be required to use. Other districts may ask you to prepare lesson plans a week or two in advance. Whatever the case, a good lesson plan helps you be an effective teacher.

Many school districts use the 5E Model of Instruction for lesson plans. The five E's are:

- Engagement
- Exploration
- Explanation
- Expansion
- Evaluation

Read the accompanying Professionalism in Practice feature, "How to Integrate Science and Literacy in Kindergarten" and learn how teacher Lori Cadwallader integrates the 5-Es into her lesson planning.

Technology in the Kindergarten

Technology pervades everything that children do in and out of the classroom. Using technology in your classroom will help you teach and help children learn. Technological tools commonly found in many kindergarten classrooms include computers, computer programs, printers, DVDs, televisions, and digital cameras. Use technology to help you achieve learning standards and objectives and focus on the curriculum. State standards also include standards for the application of technology to everyday life activities and classroom learning activities. Your use of technology should also build on children's out-of-school experiences. In addition, provide technology experiences for all children while ensuring that those who lack technology competence receive appropriate assistance. Children who are more technologically experienced can partner with students who are less technologically savvy. Parents can also help children become more familiar with technology by extending in-school technology learning at home.

Incorporating technology into the early elementary classroom allows students to engage in all kinds of learning in multisensory ways. You will benefit from software that includes:

- Active learning with students making decisions
- Multisensory and multidimensional learning
- Age-appropriate expectations

myeducationlab

Go to the Building Teaching Skills and Dispositions section in Topic 7: Curriculum/Content Areas in the MyEducationLab for your course and complete the activity entitled *Developing Content Area Lesson Plans and Choosing Developmentally Appropriate Materials.*

COMPETENCY BUILDER

Lightning is flashing and thunder is rolling in my bilingual kindergarten classroom. The children are trying to say how the storm is scaring them. But they don't know how to describe what's going on. They can only say that there's a lot of rain and wind. They've never heard the words for thunder or lightning—in either Spanish or English! Since many of these children are performing at high levels in other areas, this underdevelopment of oral language in science is amazing. No wonder we see such high failure rates in state science test scores.

If our children are to develop a love of science and the ability to think and express themselves scientifically, they need to learn about scientific concepts, methods, and attitudes while they are young. This gives them a foundation for future work in the sciences, math, language, and the arts.

WHY IS TEACHING SCIENCE IN KINDERGARTEN IMPORTANT?

- Science is an ideal vehicle for developing children's questioning minds about the natural world.
- Implementing the National Science Education Standards can help our students take their place in a scientifically literate society.
- When children explore science they acquire oral and written language for scientific expression—and learn to read in new contexts.
- Science teaches children to appreciate the diversity of life and its interconnectedness.
- When children learn about nature they respect and care for our planet and its natural resources.
- Learning scientific methods teaches children to view themselves as scientists.
- Exciting lessons in science can foster a lifelong love for the subject.

Kindergartners Can Act Like Scientists

Teaching children what a scientist is and what scientists do is fundamental to science education. Scientists observe with their five senses (sight, touch, taste, smell, and hearing). They draw what they see, write about their observations, classify, ask questions, make predictions, create models, design experiments, count accurately, test their hypotheses, repeat their experiments, and keep on trying. Children learn this *scientific method* and practice it from pre-kindergarten to grade twelve.

ELEMENT 1 HOW TO INTEGRATE SCIENCE

PLAN AN ACTIVITY AND ADDRESS STANDARDS

Always plan activities that provide opportunities to engage, explore, explain, elaborate, and evaluate—the 5E model. Central to teaching science is developing scientific concepts and methodology rather than merely studying some favorite topic or, worse yet, displaying some dramatic effect, such as a foaming "volcano." State and district standards will have science learning objectives. Plan activities as you consider the standards.

Example: Use "Planting Pumpkin Seeds" (a small part of an ongoing unit) to teach the following objectives as stated in the *Texas Essential Knowledge & Skills* publication:

- Students will ask questions about organisms, objects, and events.
- Students will plan and conduct simple descriptive investigations and communicate their findings.
- Examples will follow.

ELEMENT 2 INCLUDE HANDS-ON EXPERIENCES

Because children come from diverse backgrounds, they may not all have experience with a particular topic. To "level the playing field," begin every science unit with an activity that engages the students with a shared, hands-on experience.

Example: Bring a real pumpkin to the classroom and let the children touch it. Ask them to describe it and encourage them to ask questions.

Teacher: "What do you notice about the pumpkin?"
Jonathan: "It's orange."
Sara: "It's like a ball."
Carolina: "It's has brown spots on it."
Anthony: "It has lines on it."

Edward: "It's big."
Teacher: "What do you wonder about the pumpkin?"
Kevin: "Is it real?"
Carolina: "Are there seeds inside?"
Daniela: "Will it get bigger?"
Pedro: "Is it heavy?"

ELEMENT 3 INCORPORATE WRITING AND DRAWING

- Model writing for the class by recording on a chart what children say about the pumpkin.
- Encourage interactive writing. With guidance from the teacher, children take turns with a marker on a large piece of paper writing their observations as a group and using invented spelling.
- Teach children to make direct observations by individually drawing only what they see—in their science journals or on recording sheets.
- Depending on the children's developmental levels, they will either write about their observations, or you will record their observations.

ELEMENT 4 INCORPORATE LITERATURE

- Incorporate both nonfiction and fiction materials for read-alouds, free reading, and research: *Apples and Pumpkins* (Anne Rockwell), *Calabazas/Pumpkins* (Melvin and Gilda Berger), *From Seed to Plant* (Allan Fowler), *From Seed to Pumpkin* (Wendy Pfeffer), *Pumpkin Circle* (George Levenson) (Spanish version: *El círculo de las calabazas*), *Pumpkin Jack* (Will Hubbell), *Perfect Pumpkins* (Jeff Bauer), *Pumpkin, Pumpkin* (Jeanne Titherington), *Too Many Pumpkins* (Linda White).
- Choose nonfiction books with photos (including children if possible): *Perfect Pumpkins* (Jeff Bauer), *Pumpkin Circle* (George Levenson) (Spanish version: *El círculo de las calabazas*).
- Use charts of songs and poems for shared reading to teach scientific vocabulary and concepts.
- Explain science textbook features such as table of contents, diagram labels, glossary, and index.

ELEMENT 5 ASK QUESTIONS TO PROMOTE STUDENT-DESIGNED EXPERIMENTS

- Start children wondering. Model asking testable questions for the children:
  "What would happen if we watered these seeds?"

  "What would happen if we didn't water some others?"
  "What would happen if these seeds got a lot of light?"
  "What would happen if these seeds got only a little light?"
- Ask: "Which of these would grow faster and how could we find out?"
- Now say:
  "Let's put three seeds in each cup with some soil."
  "We'll put one cup where it will get a *lot* of light and *water* the seeds."
  "We'll put one cup where it will get a *lot* of light and *not water* the seeds."
  "We'll put one cup where it will get a *little* bit of light and *water* the seeds."
  "We'll put one cup where it will get a *little* bit of light and *not water* the seeds."
- Prompt the class to make predictions and record their answers.

  Brandon: "I think the seeds will grow in three days."
  Samantha: "I think the seeds will grow in five days."
- The children will check the seeds every few days and record the results in their science journals.
- Use plastic connecting cubes or some other nonstandard unit of measure such as paper clips to determine which plants are growing faster.
- Discuss the results.

ADDITIONAL STRATEGIES

Go into depth with a few topics rather than scratching the surface of many. Place additional materials in the science center for the children to explore and extend their studies of seeds, plants, and life cycles. Some examples are a tray with paper, crayons, and rubbing plates of leaves; field identification guides of leaves, trees, and other plants; seeds for sorting and sorting sheets; rubber stamps of the life cycle of a plant for the children to use to sequence the life cycle of a plant; and plant puzzles.

....

Contributed by Lori D. Cadwallader, bilingual kindergarten teacher, Rivera Elementary School, Denton, Texas, and staff development trainer for "SALSA" (Science and Literacy Saturday Academy) and "The Nature of Science," Denton ISD, Denton, Texas.

As educators, we are constantly searching for innovative ways to meet the needs of each child and enrich our teaching program. I find the iPod to be tremendously useful, versatile, and easily assessable. In my classroom, I use iPods to increase fluency with English language learners, as a remediation resource with at-risk students, for ongoing longitudinal assessments, and for driving my instruction.

DEVELOPING FLUENCY

Fluency, the smoothness and ease of speaking, is a critical attribute in learning English. English language learners need to practice this, as much as possible, during the school day. To meet this need, I created an iPod Learning Center in the classroom where my students go to hear English, speak English, read English, and write English.

One of the California kindergarten standards is to be able to audibly recite poems, rhymes, and songs without missing a word. With this in mind, each month my students are responsible for learning a selection of songs, poems, rhymes, and chants. I record myself reciting poems, rhymes, songs, and chants, which the children listen to and learn on their iPods. By using iPods as one, the students have the time they need to hear and practice with correct English modeling. I have a chart that always accompanies the material. This enables the children to have a visual picture of what they are learning. My class of thirty-one five- to six-year-olds is very active and the iPod Learning Center provides my students the opportunity to explore learning materials in an easy and accessible way. The use of iPods by individuals and small groups seems to lower the children's anxiety level and enables them to be successful. I have also found that children engaged in iPod activities attend longer and are able to obtain the repetition needed to master the task. Since the implementation of this learning center, I have witnessed my students become quickly familiar with text, and have noted that both fluency and comprehension increase along with whole group participation.

REMEDIATION PLANS

The iPod has become an invaluable resource for devising individual remediation plans. Last year, I had a student whose fluency was top-notch. He could recite the poems of the month without missing a word, he was an attentive listener, and he worked well independently when given a series of tasks. The student's challenge was learning letters and letter sounds. His intervention plan needed to include a variety of learning modalities and incorporate his strengths. I decided to begin his intervention plan with an auditory strategy using an iPod. I downloaded ABC songs and chants that he listened to independently. A set of flash cards and charts accompanied the ABC songs, so he could see the letters as he listened. This strategy was not only successful, but also opened my eyes to other possibilities.

ASSESSMENTS AND DRIVING INSTRUCTION

In addition to using the iPod as a teaching tool, I also use it as a way to assess my students' progress and to drive my teaching instruction. One of the language arts kindergarten standards is to retell stories. I have the students who did not initially meet this particular kindergarten benchmark retell the story of "The Three Bears." I record the students by using the iPod. Later, as I listen to the students retell their version of the story, I can evaluate many things such as their use of pronouns and how they use present and past tense. With this information I am able to create appropriate lessons and offer my students opportunities to work on these concepts with each other.

THREE STEPS FOR USING IPODS IN THE CLASSROOM

1. Purchase an iPod and a microphone/speaker you can attach to the iPod.
2. Become familiar with the features and functions (downloading and recording).
3. Start small and have one focus. I began using the iPod with my English language learners to work on fluency. It grew to using it with at-risk students and then to conduct assessments.

You will find that iPods are a wonderful learning tool for you and your children. As you plan how you will use iPods in your classroom, think across the curriculum and discover how you can also use iPods to integrate all content areas in your teaching.

Contributed by Andrea J. Spillett-Maurer, kindergarten teacher, Arovista Elementary, Brea, California.

- Flexibility, ease of use, and open-ended operation
- Provision for children to explore without fear of making mistakes, that responds to their exploration in ways that encourage further investigation

Software that is open-ended allows children to explore, discover, and be creative. It also encourages hypothesizing, problem solving, collaboration, motivation, and a more positive attitude toward learning. In the accompanying Technology Tie-In feature, kindergarten teacher Andrea Spillett describes how she uses iPods, another technological application, in her classroom. After you read her story, think about how you can use this type of technology to enhance the kindergarten learning experience.

SUPPORTING CHILDREN'S APPROACHES TO LEARNING

Recall that in Chapter 8 we discussed children's approaches to learning as being an important dimension to learning. These approaches to learning are curiosity/initiative, persistence, attention, self-direction, problem-solving ability, and creativity. The experiences children have before they come to kindergarten often influence the success of their kindergarten years. Three areas are particularly important in influencing children's success in kindergarten: children's skills and prior school-related experiences, children's home lives, and preschool and kindergarten classroom characteristics. Research demonstrates the following in relation to these three areas:[36]

- Children who are socially adjusted do better in school. For example, kindergarten children whose parents initiate social opportunities for them are better adjusted socially and therefore can do better.
- Rejected children have difficulty with school tasks.
- Children with more preschool experiences have fewer adjustments to make in kindergarten.
- Children whose parents expect them to do well in kindergarten do better than children whose parents have low expectations for them. Children who have teachers with high expectations also do better in school.
- Books, videos, computer-based learning materials, and other materials designed for children in the home improve the chances that children will be successful in school.
- Developmentally appropriate classrooms and practices promote easier and smoother transitions for children from home to school, from grade to grade, and from program to program.

The nature, extent, creativity, and effectiveness of transitional experiences for children, parents, and staff will be limited only by the commitment of all involved. If we are interested in providing good preschools, kindergartens, and primary schools, then we will include transitional experiences in the curricula of all these programs.

How successful children are in kindergarten depends on how well all who have a stake in children's education cooperate. More and more we realize that when early childhood teachers work with parents, children's achievement increases. For example, you can involve your students' parents in a family literacy project that supports children's learning to read. One way to do this is to encourage children and their parents to "read together." The use of a reading log such as the one shown in Figure 9.4 motivates children to read at home and involves the whole family. You can also design your program to address specific cultural aspects of your students' families or your geographical region, as described in the accompanying Diversity Tie-In feature.

PORTRAITS OF CHILDREN

Now that we have discussed what kindergarten is like, let's return our attention to kindergarten children. The Professionalism in Practice feature, "Portraits of Kindergartners," on the following pages helps you get an up-close, real-life insight into what the children you will teach are like. As you study the portraits, respond to the accompanying questions as though each child were in your classroom.

FIGURE 9.4

Sample Reading Log

My Weekly Home Reading Journal

Name: Daniel Sheffield

Week of: December 12

Day	Book Read	Who I Read To
Monday:	*The Biggest, Best Snowman*	mother
Tuesday:	*A Bed for the Winter*	sister
Wednesday:	*The Penguin Who Wanted to Fly*	father
Thursday:	*Bad Kitty*	brother
Friday:	*Bear Snores On*	baby brother
Saturday:	*There Was an Old Lady Who Swallowed a Bell*	my dog "Butch"
Sunday:	*Who Will Help Santa This Year?*	mother

Parent's Signature: *Marie Sheffield*

Note: Reading logs encourage children and their parents to "read together."

ACTIVITIES FOR PROFESSIONAL DEVELOPMENT

ethical dilemma

"No More Social Promotion"

Maria's school district has implemented a new policy that all kindergarten students must pass a readiness test before they can be promoted to first grade. Two of Maria's children did not have a passing score on the test. She believes the school district's policy is unfair because it bases promotion on the results of one test score. In addition, she thinks the two children who did not pass the readiness test will do well in first grade.

What should Maria do? Should she keep quiet and say nothing, or should she talk with the school principal and present her case? Or should she organize the parents and ask them to help her change the school district's policy, or should she choose another ethically appropriate solution?

Application Activities

1. Do you think as a teacher you are oriented more toward a kindergarten program based on academics or social-emotional play? How would you explain your beliefs on this topic during an interview for a teaching job?

2. Do you support an earlier or a later entrance age to kindergarten? Why? If your local legislator wanted specific reasons, what would you say? Ask two other teachers their opinion on this topic and compare their viewpoints with yours.

3. Give examples from your observations of kindergarten programs to support one of these opinions:
   a. Society is expecting too much of kindergarten children.
   b. Many kindergartens are not teaching children enough.
   c. Current changes occurring in the kindergarten are necessary and appropriate.

4. How to conduct developmentally appropriate practices in the ever-changing kindergarten is a major issue. Search the Internet and make a list of your "Top Five Developmentally Appropriate Practices."

PEARSON myeducationlab

To check your comprehension on the content covered in Chapter 9, go to the Book Specific Resources in the MyEducationLab for your course, select your text, and complete the Study Plan. Here you will be able to take a chapter quiz and receive feedback on your answers.

The Kindergarten Achievement Gap Begins Before Kindergarten

In the opening pages of the new third edition of NAEYC's *Developmentally Appropriate Practice in Early Childhood Programs Serving Children from Birth Through Age 8,* the authors discuss the early childhood achievement gap as one of the critical issues faced by children and early childhood professionals. Here is what they say:

> All families, educators, and the larger society hope that all children will achieve in school and go on to lead satisfying and productive lives. But that optimistic future is not equally likely for all of the nation's schoolchildren. Most disturbing, low-income and African American and Hispanic students lag specifically behind their peers on standardized comparisons of academic achievement throughout the school years, and they experience more difficulties while in the school setting.*

The achievement gap between students of various races, cultures, and socioeconomic backgrounds is a serious issue, which all of us as early childhood educators must address. Many children come to school already behind their more advantaged counterparts because they are not prepared to meet the demands of contemporary schooling. For example, as the accompanying graph shows, children from low-income families are already well behind children in the highest socioeconomic groups.

The extent and seriousness of the achievement gap is further illustrated in the results of a survey of Michigan kindergarten teachers:

- Thirty-two percent of kindergarten teachers were not satisfied with the abilities of their kindergarten students when they started school, with an additional 50 percent being only somewhat satisfied.
- According to the teachers, only 65 percent of children entered kindergarten classrooms ready to learn the curriculum.

- Eighty-six percent of teachers report that students who are behind academically at kindergarten entrance impact a teacher's ability to effectively provide instruction to the rest of the class.[†]

Awareness of the extent of the problem is only one part of our efforts to reduce and eliminate achievement gaps. Taking effective action is the other part of the solution. Here are two things that we can do as early childhood professionals:

- Advocate that *all* children, particularly English language learners and children from low-income backgrounds, have the opportunity to participate in high-quality preschool programs. As we discussed in Chapters 2 and 8, there is growing consensus that providing universal preschool for all children will help them socially and academically as they continue through the elementary grades.
- Advocate for "ready schools and ready communities" so that the schools children attend and the communities they live in are united in their efforts to provide the health, nutrition, and educational experiences all children need in order to be successful in school and life.

In addition, there are many specific things that preschool and kindergarten teachers can do to help children catch up with their more advantaged peers. In Chapter 8 on pages 215 and 226–228 see our discussion of the specific literacy and mathematics skills children need to be successful. Intentional teaching of these skills will go a long way toward helping to eliminate the achievement gap.

*C. Copple and S. Bredekamp, eds., Developmentally Appropriate Practice in Early Childhood Programs: Serving Children from Birth Through Age 8, *3rd ed.,* (Washington, DC: NAEYC, 2009), 8.

[†] Information from http://www.ecic4kids.org/documents/kSurvey/keyFindingsNarrative.pdf.

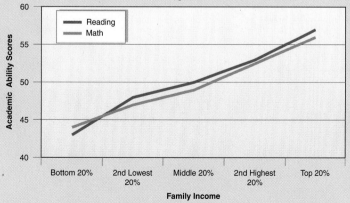

Children's Achievement by Socio-Economic Status

Source: U.S. Department of Education, National Center for Education Statistics, *Early Childhood Longitudinal Study, Kindergarten Class of 1998–99,* Fall 1998.

portraits of kindergartners

JORDAN

Introduce yourself to Jordan, a five-year-old African American male. He weighs 60 pounds and is 4 feet 7 inches tall. He is more physically mature than his peers and looks much older than most children his age. He loves school and gets along with his classmates. He is an active boy who loves to play sports and listen to music.

Social-Emotional	Cognitive	Motor	Adaptive (Daily Living)
Enjoys helping his peers with various tasks	Is able to sort and categorize objects by color and shape	Is well coordinated and a skilled athlete	Has memorized his phone number and knows how to dial 911
Participates in cooperative play and is very willing to share his toys with his peers	Follows simple, step-by-step directions without assistance	Has excellent hand–eye coordination	Expresses his needs, wants, and dislikes
Likes to please adults	Understands the concept of opposites	Has established hand preference	Tends to show off in front of strangers
Is an independent child who prefers to make decisions without assistance from his parents or teacher	Is eager to learn and able to read early beginner books	Is able to hop on one foot; has excellent balance	Has learned to tie his shoes without assistance

ISABELLA

Introduce yourself to Isabella, a five-year-old Hispanic female. She weighs 39 pounds and is 3 feet 11 inches tall. Isabella's family immigrated to the United States when she was an infant; therefore, her parents are learning the English language along with Isabella. She has been cared for by not only her parents but also her maternal grandmother, who has taught Isabella many traditional songs from their Hispanic culture.

Social-Emotional	Cognitive	Motor	Adaptive (Daily Living)
Given her bilingual status, she tends to talk to her classmates in Spanish, not realizing that they do not understand that language	Is able to recite the alphabet in both English and Spanish	Helps her grandmother make homemade tortillas	Has memorized her address and phone number
Seeks approval from the adults in her life (parents, grandmother, and teacher)	Is able to sing songs her grandmother taught her	Is learning to tie her shoes by herself	Is able to recognize her mother's car when she arrives to pick her up from school
Shows guilt over misbehavior	Recognizes many letters and words	Shows increased skill with simple tools and writing utensils	Enjoys playing noisy rhythm instruments
Is a vibrant child who is very talkative in school and at home	Is able to identify the parts of a story (beginning, middle, and end)	Enjoys skipping and hopping	Is able to bathe herself while her mother supervises her

Questions About Developmentally Appropriate Practice:

- How could Isabella's teacher incorporate Isabella's cultural heritage into the classroom so that the other classmates could learn about new cultures?
- Name several social tasks you think are important for Isabella and Jordan to master before reaching the first grade.
- How can a child's individuality become an asset in the classroom?
- Why do you think Jordan has mastered the skill of tying his shoes, whereas Isabella has not?
- How can you support Isabella's ongoing learning of her national language?

DANIEL

Introduce yourself to Daniel, a six-year-old Asian male. He weighs 54 pounds and is 4 feet tall. Daniel is a quiet child who has an "easy" temperament. He prefers to play in small groups and enjoys reading picture books by himself. Daniel is an attentive listener, but at times will remain focused on a task when being spoken to. He has tremendous concentration skills and tends to be a perfectionist when trying to write the letters in his name.

Social-Emotional	Cognitive	Motor	Adaptive (Daily Living)
Tends to keep to himself and exhibits shy behavior	Is reading above his grade level	Prefers less active activities such as reading, writing, and mathematics, rather than physical activities	Makes his bed every morning before going to school
Is more social in smaller groups	Loves to listen to stories being read to him	Has refined writing skills for his age; his printing is very legible	Is anxious to know how to do things so that he can do them by himself in the future
Tends to try to figure things out on his own rather than ask his teacher for help	Enjoys writing letters of the alphabet	Is able to stay in the lines while coloring	Is good about putting his dirty clothes into the dirty clothes hamper—does not like a "messy" environment

EMILY

Introduce yourself to Emily, a six-year-old Caucasian female. Emily weighs 39 pounds and is 3 feet 7 inches tall. She is an assertive kindergartner and loves to explore. She is involved in many extracurricular activities such as karate, choir, gymnastics, and Spanish lessons.

Social-Emotional	Cognitive	Motor	Adaptive (Daily Living)
Is adopted and very comfortable with the issue—her parents are open about her adoption	Enjoys being read to and reciting the story back to an adult	Enjoys dancing and perfecting her gymnastic routines	Expresses strong wants and dislikes
Enjoys playing with her neighborhood friends	Knows all the letters of the alphabet and can count to one hundred	Is very good at activities involving fine-motor skills	Is not a very neat child—she must be reminded to pick up after herself
Is very sensitive to criticism	Enjoys dramatic play	Is able to maintain balance while standing on one foot with eyes closed	Is becoming a finicky eater
Cries easily and is a somewhat impulsive child	Enjoys learning new Spanish words in her Spanish class	Is beginning to ride her bike without training wheels	Enjoys new responsibilities such as feeding the dog and cat

Questions About Developmentally Appropriate Practice:

- What could be some of the reasons why Daniel is a quiet child and Emily is an assertive child?
- Knowing that Emily is adopted, how could you as a teacher make sure she is socially and emotionally secure?
- How can children's individuality such as Emily's and Daniel's become assets in your classroom?
- Given that obesity is an epidemic in America, how could you encourage Daniel to do more physical activities rather than less active ones?

chapter ten

THE EARLY ELEMENTARY GRADES: 1–3

Preparation for Life

. . . .

NAEYC Standards for Early Childhood Professional Preparation Programs

Standard 1. Promoting Child Development and Learning

I use my understanding of young children's characteristics and needs, and of multiple interacting influences on children's development and learning, to create environments that are healthy, respectful, supportive, and challenging for all children.[1]

Standard 4. Using Developmentally Effective Approaches to Connect with Children and Families

I understand and use positive relationships and supportive interactions as the foundation for my work with young children and families. I know, understand, and use a wide array of developmentally appropriate approaches, instructional strategies, and tools to connect with children and families and positively influence each child's development and learning.[2]

Standard 5. Using Content Knowledge to Build Meaningful Curriculum

I understand the importance of developmental domains and academic (or content) disciplines in early childhood curriculum. I know the essential concepts, inquiry tools, and structure of content areas, including academic subjects, and can identify resources to deepen my understanding. I use my own knowledge and other resources to design, implement, and evaluate meaningful, challenging curricula that promote comprehensive developmental and learning outcomes for every young child.[3]

TEACHING IN GRADES ONE TO THREE

As we have discussed, reform is sweeping across the educational landscape, and nowhere is this more evident than in grades one to three, also known as the **primary grades**. Changes include how schools operate and are organized, how teachers teach, how children are evaluated, and how schools involve and relate to parents and the community. State governments are specifying curriculum and testing agendas. In an era in which the federal government is pouring huge amounts of money into school districts, under the American Recovery and Reinvestment Act of 2009, schools are being held to higher standards for learning and achievement. Reform and accountability are in; schooling as usual is out.

Contemporary Schooling and Contextual Factors

As we begin our discussion of living and learning in grades one to three, it will be helpful to look at the nature of these grades today. Here are some examples of what teaching and learning is like today as you prepare to teach children ages six to nine. First let's look at some mini portraits of teachers of the year in grades one, two, and three.

Nancy Berry, a first grade teacher at Liza Jackson Preparatory School, Fort Walton Beach, Florida, and an All-USA Today teacher, welcomes kids from diverse backgrounds and learning styles to "Berryland USA: A Place Where Children Love to Learn." Her classroom is alive with hermit crabs and oysters, uncaged caterpillars, chrysalises and butterflies. Berry accepts students unconditionally and treats them as if they are smart to make learning a self-fulfilling prophecy. She reassures kids that she made mistakes as a child, coaxing them to read, write, organize thoughts, and make decisions at a higher level. She uses singing, moving, reading, experiencing, applying, and writing to reach all types of learners. "I don't teach to a test," she says. "I teach to life."[4]

Elizabeth Parker, a second grade teacher at Fort Smith, Arkansas, and a Milken Family Foundation National Educator Award winner, is recognized by supervisors and colleagues as an outstanding literacy educator. According to her principal, "Beth is a teacher leader who constantly researches best teaching practices to better help her students achieve academic success in her classroom and to assist fellow teachers with curriculum and instructional questions." Parker's creative, well planned, motivating lessons and excellent classroom management skills have helped most of her students read above grade level. Parker's students have also experienced significant gains in math, with many scoring above the district average.[5,6]

Valorie Lewis of Stigler, Oklahoma, a third grade All-USA Today teacher, shares her story of overcoming poverty, teasing, and low expectations with her rural Oklahoma students to inspire them to believe in themselves because "there is no such thing as a child without the potential for success." Lewis holds a weekly "Community Circle" for her students to share thoughts and feelings and learn empathy. She fosters an environment where students respect and value others by having the children draw names each week and fill out "Positive Comment Cards" about that person each day to share with the class. Lewis uses multisensory lessons such as cooking to reach all students. She developed a daily review program to practice basic skills and Third Grade Brain Olympics, used in other classes and schools.[7]

Now, let's look at the school and social contexts of teaching in grades one, two, and three.

Diversity. Schools and classrooms are more diverse than ever before. This means you will be teaching children from different cultures and backgrounds, and you will

FOCUS QUESTIONS

1. What is teaching in grades one through three like?

2. What are children in grades one through three like?

3. What are environments like that support learning in the primary grades?

4. What is included in the curriculum of the primary grades?

primary grades Grades one to three.

have to take those differences into account in your planning and teaching. In addition to cultural and linguistic differences, diversity is also reflected in children's socioeconomic status and in their physical, cognitive, social, emotional, adaptive, and communication abilities. The percentage of racial/ethnic minority students enrolled in the nation's public schools increased to 43 percent in 2006.[8] This increase in minority enrollment largely reflects the growth in the percentage of students who were Hispanic. In 2006, Hispanic students represented 20 percent of public school enrollment. The distribution of minority students in public schools differs across regions of the country, with minority public school enrollment (55 percent) exceeding white enrollment (45 percent) in the West.[9] The number of school-age children who speak a language other than English at home is 10.8 million, or 20 percent of the population at this age range.[10] In 2007, some 6.7 million (about 9 percent) received speech education services.[11]

Take a look at our Diversity Tie-In feature, "The Rich Get Richer." It addresses issues and consequences of children from low socioeconomic homes, neighborhoods, and schools having fewer educational materials to learn from than children from higher socioeconomic backgrounds.

Achievement.   High-level achievement of all students is a national priority today as illustrated by the teacher vignettes at the beginning of this chapter. Schools and teachers place a premium on closing the achievement gap that exists between races and socioeconomic levels. High-quality teachers are dedicated to ensuring that each child learns.

Standards.   The curriculum of grades one through three is commonly aligned with local, state, and national standards. As a result, you will be teaching content designed to help students learn what state standards specify. In fact, many school districts provide their teachers with lesson plans that suggest activities and instructional strategies based on state standards. You won't always get to teach exactly what you want to teach, when you want to teach it, and how you want to teach it. However, good teachers always find ways to include in the curriculum what they believe is important and developmentally appropriate. As many teachers have learned and are learning, teaching with standards does not have to be dull and boring; you can make learning interesting and relevant to all your students' lives.

Testing.   Testing is a part of contemporary school culture. You will be involved in helping students learn appropriate grade-level content so they can pass local, state, and national tests. In addition, you will use test data as a basis for your planning and instruction. We discuss this more in the section on data driven instruction later in this chapter.

Changing Teacher Roles.   The role of the early childhood teacher is changing dramatically. This is particularly true for teachers in grades one to three. For example, it is likely that you will be a member of a grade-level team that meets regularly to plan, learn, debate, discuss, decide, and develop lessons and learning activities. You will collaborate with your colleagues on all types of projects. Today, schools place a premium on collaboration and being a team player.

Standards have transformed (some say reformed) teaching from an input model to an output model. As a result, teachers are no longer able to say, "I taught Mario the use of structural cues to decode words." Now the questions are, "Is Mario able to use and apply decoding skills?" and "Will Mario do well on decoding skills on the state test?" High-quality teachers have good ideas about what and how to teach, and they always will. However, the time and opportunity to act on those good ideas are reduced by increasing requirements to teach to the standards and teach so that students master the standards.

Curriculum Alignment.   Teaching issues are as old as teaching itself and involve frequently asked questions, such as "What should I teach?" and "How should I teach it?" As usual, the answer is, "It depends." It depends on what you and other teachers think is

The Rich Get Richer

INEQUALITY OF EDUCATIONAL RESOURCES

The title of this Diversity Tie-In may seem perplexing to you. After all, when we think about the rich getting richer, we think of money and other things associated with the rich and famous. However, the same applies to schools and schooling. Think for a moment about some of the things that contribute to rich learning experiences and environments, such as the children and the teacher. Although they are important, there are other dimensions to rich learning environments that contribute to student achievement. For example, in addition to high-quality teachers, children also need high-quality classroom environments with materials that support learning. To learn to read and write well, children need books and other materials that support their reading and writing processes. Unfortunately, these materials are not evenly distributed across all classrooms in the country. In fact, they are generally distributed by the socioeconomic status (SES) of the children who attend these classrooms.

INEQUALITIES OF LEARNING MATERIALS

Let's look at the inequality of distribution of classroom learning materials by SES status. We see that children from high-SES environments get more of the materials that support literacy than do their less-advantaged low-SES peers. So, in the very real world of learning to read, children who have adequate learning materials do indeed get richer in that they are able to learn to their fullest capacity. When researcher Nell Duke looked at classrooms of low-SES students, she found wide discrepancies between the classrooms of high-SES first graders and those of low-SES first graders. As the accompanying graph illustrates, children from high-SES schools had almost 50 percent more books and learning materials in their classroom libraries than did low-SES first graders. Additionally, Duke found that "it was not simply that the high-SES classroom libraries contained and displayed more materials; there were more opportunities for students to use them."

MAKING CLASSROOMS MORE EQUAL

So, what does this mean for you as a classroom teacher? Here are four things you can do:

1. Make sure that you're using all of your classroom materials to their fullest. Using materials and allowing children to have access to them is an essential first step in making sure that children are getting a foundation for reading and literacy.
2. Read, read, and read to your children. Reading to children is one of the best ways to improve vocabulary, word knowledge, and meaning, and to promote interest in and enthusiasm for reading.
3. Work with families and the community to get the materials that you need. You can be an advocate for getting your children the materials they need to learn how to read and write. Your advocacy will include conducting fund-raisers, seeking support from local businesses, and spreading the word that children need materials if they are to learn effectively and well.
4. Conduct family literacy programs for your parents. In these programs, you can help parents learn the importance of reading and literacy, and the vital role books and other reading materials play in children's lives.

Books and Materials in the First Grade Classroom Libraries of High- and Low-SES Children

Chart: Books and Magazines (y-axis, 0 to 800) vs Available Materials (x-axis). Low-SES districts approximately 400; High-SES districts approximately 680.

Legend: Low-SES districts; High-SES districts

Source: Nell K. Duke, "For the Rich It's Richer," American Educational Research Journal, 37(2), Summer 2000, 460.

important and what national, state, and local standards say is important. Therein lies the heart of the issue: how to develop meaningful curriculum that is aligned with standards. Learning how to develop strong lesson plans that also meet state standards is important for all teachers.

Increasing student achievement is at the center of the standards movement. Policy makers and educators view standards, tests, and teaching alignment as viable and practical ways

FIGURE 10.1 The Process of Data-Driven Instruction

to help ensure student achievement. Recall from Chapter 5 that *alignment* is the arrangement of standards, curriculum, and tests so that they complement one another. In other words, the curriculum is based on what the standards say students should know and be able to do; tests measure what the standards indicate. *Curriculum alignment* is the process of making sure that what is taught—the context of the curriculum—matches what the standards say students should know and be able to do.

data-driven instruction An approach to teaching in which analysis of assessment data drives the decisions about how to meet the instructional needs of each child.

Data-Driven Instruction. In **data-driven instruction**, teaching decisions are based on the analysis of assessment data to make decisions about how to best meet the instructional needs of each child. Figure 10.1 illustrates the process of data-driven instruction. Review Figure 10.1 and then read the following Professionalism in Practice feature, "How to Use Data-Driven Instruction." It will help you learn how to incorporate data-driven instruction into your planning and teaching.

Academics. The contemporary curriculum in grades one to three is heavy on reading, math, and science. There is also an emphasis on the arts, social studies, character education, and health and wellness through physical education. Many of these areas, however, are integrated with the basic curriculum. For example, to integrate academics with children's projects and activities, fifth grade teacher Patricia Doyle at Pine Grove Elementary in St. Petersburg, Florida, taught a Family Recipe classroom project. The project included third, fourth, and fifth grade students in an activity that also involved their extended family members. Doyle wanted the students to learn about their ancestors and their ethnicity by producing cookbooks made up of family favorite recipes. The project covered many skills in many subjects: social studies, writing, technology, reading, research, speaking and presentation, math, and science.[12]

Technology Use and Interaction. Children are different today from a decade ago because of new and different kinds of technology.[13] Today's generation is the "dot-com" or Net Generation. Children have grown up surrounded by technology and are familiar and comfortable with it. Children are much more comfortable writing their friends text messages than handwritten notes. Children's involvement with computer games enables them to think abstractly and to make rapid-fire decisions. The majority of children live in homes with access to the Internet. According to research, 63 percent of adult Americans now have broadband Internet connections at home, a 15 percent increase from a year earlier.[14] This connectivity enables children to have almost immediate access to vast

You don't have to go back to *Little House on the Prairie* to find a teaching style based on "getting through" the curriculum. Curriculum coverage is not the same as student learning. Accountability initiatives, including No Child Left Behind, have brought about a shift in focus from covering subject matter to meeting the needs of each student. There is only one way to determine whether or not the needs of each student are being met, and that is through an ongoing analysis of data collected by assessing children.

BACKGROUND

Lead Mine Elementary School reflects the changing demographics taking place in America today. More than 43 percent of our students are eligible for free or

reduced lunches, and for many students English is not their primary language. Yet despite these challenges, our test scores have shown steady growth over the years. Our teachers had to learn to teach smarter and to use technological resources as their ally.

WHAT IS DATA-DRIVEN INSTRUCTION?

Data-driven instruction is a system of teaching in which instructional decisions are based on an analysis of assessment data collected to determine how best to meet the needs of each individual student.

THE PROCESS OF IMPLEMENTING DATA-DRIVEN INSTRUCTION

STEP 1 START THE SCHOOL YEAR BY ANALYZING EXISTING DATA

Before your students arrive, examine their cumulative record files to get a general profile of each student. We conduct a formal initial assessment process for incoming kindergartners before creating our kindergarten class lists.

STEP 2 ALIGN ASSESSMENTS TO OBJECTIVES

Plan collaboratively with your grade-level colleagues to determine when and how you will teach district and state standards and how you will assess each standard. It is common and customary for grade-level teachers to meet regularly to make plans for how to teach standards and how to gather data based on student achievement.

STEP 3 BEGIN THE DATA COLLECTION PROCESS

There are a number of ways to collect classroom data. You may use formal assessments such as written assignments, quizzes, and tests. You may use informal assessments such as observation and discussions. You may also use technology to help you collect data. A variety of instructional learning systems on the market now allow you to track student progress with instructional software. For example, the Denton (Texas) Independent School District uses GradeSpeed to track student progress and use data to guide planning and instructional activities.

STEP 4 ANALYZE DATA

At the completion of the data collection process for a unit of study, meet with your grade-level colleagues and look at the data for trends. Did the majority of the students reach the standard? Do the data reveal student achievement needs you have to address? What standards did the students have trouble achieving? How will you reteach the knowledge and skills your students need more help with?

STEP 5 USE DATA ANALYSIS TO DECIDE THE NEXT COURSE OF STUDY

After examining the data, use it to guide your next steps in the instructional process. Which students are ready to move on? Which students need remediation? Which students need enrichment? In creating your plan to meet the needs of each student you may also involve resource teachers such as the academically gifted teacher, the ELL teacher, a special education teacher, the computer lab manager, or any other specialists in your school who can help you meet the specific needs of each child.

STEP 6 REPEAT THE PROCESS

Making data-based decisions to guide instruction is an ongoing process. Throughout the school year you are constantly assessing your students, analyzing their data, and readjusting the plans you have made to best meet their educational needs.

Contributed by Gary W. Baird, principal, Lead Mine Elementary School, Raleigh, North Carolina.

amounts of information that enrich their lives and learning. Also, consider how the use of cell phones and text messaging change the way children communicate. Here is what two third graders shared with each other about a school project through text messaging:

Student 1: do u want 2B partners 4 the project y/n?
Student 2: y. msg me L8tr on im wrking.

As a result of today's children being immersed in technology from the beginning of life, you need to find many opportunities for them to learn with technology. You can provide activities that enable children to access the Internet, use digital cameras to gather information and document learning, create and transport reports on the Internet, and engage in electronic creativity discussions and sharing of ideas.

Of course, not all students have the same access to technology. Making sure children have access to technology is an important factor when designing a classroom environment and planning curricula that promote learning and motivation. The accompanying Technology Tie-In feature "Blogging in Classroom" explains how blogging can be used to help children learn.

Health and Wellness.   Physical education at all levels, pre-K to twelve, is undergoing a renaissance. One reason for its rejuvenation, especially in the primary and elementary grades, is the concern about the national epidemic of childhood obesity and increases in childhood diabetes.[15] Physical education classes and programs are viewed as a way of providing children with the knowledge and activities they need to get in shape and stay that way for the rest of their lifetimes. The Institute of Medicine recommends that schools do all they can to "ensure that all children and youth participate in a minimum of thirty minutes of moderate to vigorous physical activity during the school day, including expanded opportunities for physical activity through classes, sports programs, clubs, lessons, after-school and community use of school facilities, and walking and biking to school programs."[16]

Ongoing Political Changes.   What politicians and lawmakers believe is best for children and how to teach them changes with each election. Changes in politics in turn change how we teach children and what we teach them. For the past decade, politicians have placed a major emphasis on standards and academic achievement. The No Child Left Behind Act of 2001 (NCLB) has focused teaching and learning on meeting state standards, especially in reading and math. What we expect of children, however, may not always be possible with the quality of the schools and materials we provide for them.

As a result of what we have discussed, you must look at teaching in grades one to three differently from how you would approach kindergarten education. You will want to consider new and appropriate approaches for teaching in these three important grades. We begin now our journey of rediscovering grades one to three with a look at what children (typically ages six, seven, eight, and nine) are like in these grades.

WHAT ARE CHILDREN IN GRADES ONE TO THREE LIKE?

All children share common developmental characteristics, yet each child is a unique individual. Although the common characteristics of children guide our general practice of teaching, we still must always account for the individual needs of children.

Physical Development

Two words describe the physical growth of primary age children: *slow* and *steady*. Children at this age experience continual growth, develop increasing control over their bodies, and explore the things they are able to do.

myeducationlab

Go to the Assignments and Activities section in Topic 5: Program Models of the MyEducationLab for your course and complete the activity entitled *Teaching in the Primary Grades*. You will observe how children in grades 1–3 are different from pre-K children. Note the distinguishing features and approaches of various types of educational settings serving children in the primary grades.

Blogging in the Classroom

I'm sure that in your life, you are involved in many kinds of technology. I'll bet some of you are bloggers! Just like you, children love technology and technology plays a great part in their world and in their lives. You can use technology to your advantage in your classroom by creating your own blog and getting your children blogging.

For those of you who don't blog, a *blog* is a Web publishing tool that allows you to self-publish commentary in a journal format, artwork, and links to other blogs or websites.

WHY BLOG?

Blogs:

- Motivate children and give them authentic reasons to write. We have talked about authentic assessment and authentic environments. Authentic also applies to children applying what they learn to real-life activities and events and using the real world as a source of ideas.
- Tie children to other children and people in the world, and let them know and understand that others are reading what they have written.
- Create a window into your classroom for parents, other children, and the world-wide community so they know what you are teaching and the children are learning. On the other hand, your blog opens a window to the world for you and your students.
- Third grade teacher Todd Wasil has three main goals for his classroom blog:
  - To keep students and parents updated on daily homework, weekly curriculum, and events
  - To allow students and parents to access information that will help them succeed in the third grade
  - To give students and parents a chance to express their ideas and comment on weekly posts

TIPS FOR GETTING STARTED

1. Make sure all students have an opportunity to blog because we want all children to be technologically literate.
2. Use a free source such as "Blogger," a blogging resource powered by Google. You can activate it with a Google account or with any other email address. Blogger is simple, easy to use, and accessible to most everyone (www.blogger.com).
3. Identify the goals you want to achieve through blogging.

Here is an excerpt from Kathy Cassidy's blog at the beginning of a new school year:

> Our first day of grade one. What an exciting day! In between sorting supplies and meeting new friends, we took some time to talk about what things we might learn this year and what goals we might make for the year. To help us think about what we might learn, we talked via Skype to some "experts" about what they learned in grade one. We talked to Cindi Crandall, a grade one teacher in California, and to Rodney Turner's grade four class in Glendale, Arizona.*

Ashley Hix, a first grade teacher at South Park Elementary in Moberly, Missouri, keeps a blog for her first grade class. Here is an excerpt of her blog from May, 2009:

> First graders are continuing to learn every day and I am amazed at their progress since the beginning of the year! This week we have had several end of the year assessments and I have seen remarkable growth! I am so proud of them . . . In science students are keeping track of the plants we are growing in our room by writing in a science journal. We planted green beans and peas. The class makes one journal entry a week by writing a sentence to describe what is happening. Students enjoy coming in each morning to see if anything has changed.[†]

*K. Cassidy, Mrs. Cassidy's Classroom Blog, *August 16, 2009; accessed September 29, 2009, from http://classblogmeister.com/blog.php?blogger_id=1337.*

[†]A. Hix, First Grade Newsletter, *May 10, 2009; accessed July 1, 2009, from http://moberly.k12.mo.us/blogs/ahix/2009/05/10/first-grade-newsletter-6.*

From ages six to nine, children's average weight and height approximate each other, as shown in Table 10.1 The weight of boys and girls tends to be the same until about age nine, when girls pull ahead of boys in both height and weight. Wide variations appear in both individual rates of growth and development and among the sizes of individual children. These differences in physical appearance result from genetic and cultural factors, nutritional intake and habits, health care, and experiential background. Refer now to the "Portraits of Children" at the end of this chapter to compare and contrast the development of primary grade children in all domains.

The primary years are also a time to use and test developing motor skills. Children's growing confidence and physical skills are reflected in games involving running, chasing,

TABLE 10.1 Average Height and Weight for Primary-Age Children

Conduct your own survey of the height and weight of primary-age children. Compare your findings with this table. What conclusions can you draw?

| | Males | | Females | |
Age	Height (inches)	Weight (pounds)	Height (inches)	Weight (pounds)
6 years	45.25	45.50	42.25	44.00
7 years	48.00	50.00	47.75	50.00
8 years	50.50	56.00	50.25	56.00
9 years	52.25	62.00	52.50	64.00

Source: Centers for Disease Control and Prevention, National Center for Health Statistics, "Clinical Growth Charts," 2000 (latest information), http://www.cdc.gov/growthcharts.

mastery-oriented attributions Personal characteristics that include trying hard, paying attention, determination, and stick-to-itiveness.

learned helplessness A condition that can develop when children lose confidence in their abilities and, in effect, learn to feel that they are helpless.

and kicking. A nearly universal characteristic of children in this period is their almost constant physical activity.

Differences between boys' and girls' motor skills during the primary years are minimal; their abilities are about equal. Therefore, you should not use gender as a basis for limiting boys' or girls' involvement in activities. Children in the primary grades are also more proficient at school tasks that require fine-motor skills, such as writing, making artwork, and using computers. In addition, primary-age children want to and are able to engage in real-life activities. They want the "real thing." In many ways this makes teaching them easier and more fun, since many activities have real-life applications.

Social Development

Children in grades one to three (ages six through nine) are in Erikson's industry versus inferiority stage of social-emotional development. This period is a time when children gain confidence and ego satisfaction from completing challenging tasks. Children want to act responsibly and are quite capable of achieving demanding tasks and accomplishments. Children take a lot of pride in doing well. All of this reflects the "industry" aspect of social-emotional development.

Children during this stage are at varying levels of academic achievement. Those who are high in academic self-esteem credit their success to such **mastery-oriented attributions** as trying hard (industriousness), paying attention, determination, and stick-to-itiveness. If children have difficulty completing a task, they believe that by trying harder they will succeed.

At the same time, children in this stage compare their abilities and accomplishments to their peers. When they perceive that they are not doing as well as they can or as well as their peers, they may lose confidence in their abilities and achievement. This is the "inferiority" side of this stage of social-emotional development. Some children attribute their failures to a lack of ability and develop **learned helplessness**, in which they learn

Today there is a greater emphasis on children's cognitive development and activities that promote reading, math, and science. What are some things you can do to help children be successful in these areas?

through failure to behave helplessly. This is where you the teacher can be helpful and supportive of children, providing them with tasks they can accomplish and encouraging them to do their best.

Here are some things you can do to accomplish this goal:

- Provide activities children can reasonably accomplish so they can experience the satisfaction that comes from a job well done.
- Apply Gardner's theory of multiple intelligences to your teaching (see Chapter 3). Let children excel at things they are good at. All children develop skills and abilities in particular areas. Build a classroom environment that enables children to be competent in their particular intelligence.
- Be supportive and encouraging of children's efforts. For example: "Good job, Carol! See what great work you can do when you really try!"

Emotional Development

Think for a moment about how important emotions are in your life and how emotions influence what and how you learn. When you are happy, life goes well! When you are sad, it is harder to get enthused about doing what you have to do. The children you teach are no different. Emotions are an important part of children's everyday lives. One of your responsibilities is to help them develop positive emotions and to express their emotions in healthy ways.

The following activities give you specific ideas for how to support the positive social-emotional development of children in the industry versus inferiority stage of development:

1. *Use literature to discuss emotions.* Children in grades one to three like to talk about their emotions and the emotions of characters in literature. They are able to make emotional inferences about characters' emotional states and discuss how they are or are not appropriate to the story. They can then relate these emotional states to their own lives and to events at home and in the classroom. Some good books to use to discuss emotional states include these:
   - *How Are You Peeling? Foods with Moods* by Saxton Freymann and Joost Elffers offers brief text and photographs of carvings made from vegetables that introduce the world of emotions by presenting leading questions such as "Are you feeling angry?"
   - *Today I Feel Silly. And Other Moods That Make My Day* by Jamie Lee Curtis follows a little girl with curly red hair through thirteen different moods including silly, grumpy, mean, excited, and confused.
   - *When Sophie Gets Angry . . . Really, Really Angry* by Molly Bang conveys young Sophie's anger when her mother allows her younger sister to play with her stuffed gorilla, the eventual calm she feels after running outside and crying, and the calm and relaxed return home.

2. *Encourage children to express their emotions.* Beginning and ending the day with a classroom meeting discussion is a good way to help children express their thoughts and feelings. This provides children a safe and secure outlet to say how they felt during their day.

3. *Write about feelings.* Give children opportunities to keep journals in which they write about home, life, and classroom events and how they feel about them. One teacher has her children keep several journals, one that they share only with her and another journal that they share with their classmates if they choose.

   Milissa Thornton has her third grade students keep electronic journals on the computer. Figure 10.2 is a journal entry written by Brianna about her dog Bella. Brianna writes about the first time she met and held Bella and the feelings she was having. In her journal entry, pay close attention to her detail and the way she expresses her emotions about her new puppy.

My Bella

My dogs name is Bella. She is brown and white. I got my dog when
she was only 1 week old. The first time I held my dog was when I just
got home from school. My mommy told me she had a surprise for
me. She said I had to go wash my hands. I was so happy and I ran as
fast as I could to the bathroom. I closed my eyes when I went to the
living room and my mommy said, open your eyes! There she was as
small as my hand. I picked her up and kissed her head and told my
mommy thank you.

That's the first day I met my Bella.

Brianna

FIGURE 10.2 A Nine-Year-Old's Electronic Journal Entry

4. *Provide for cultural differences.* Be aware of how various cultures express emotions. Some cultures are very emotive, whereas others are not. Work with parents to learn how their cultures express certain emotions such as joy and sadness and what are culturally acceptable and unacceptable ways to express emotions.

The Role of Play and Recess in Social and Emotional Development. Think for a minute how you feel when you have engaged in some kind of physical activity. Perhaps you feel good and in an upbeat mood. Physical activity has the same effects on children. It promotes their well-being, encourages a sense of contentment and happiness, and creates an atmosphere in which they are more inclined to engage in school and other activities.

Unfortunately, many of today's children do not have the opportunity to exercise as much as they need or sometimes want. Television viewing and passive activities such as computer games, which promote sedentary lifestyles, along with a general deemphasis of the value of physical activities all tend to undermine children's health.[17] In response to increased demands for academics, school districts have been decreasing the amount of time children have for physical activity and recess. On the other hand, the good news is that more schools that had deleted recess from the school day are now bringing it back. Currently 88 percent of elementary schools report offering recess once a day for their children. The average length of this recess time is 27.8 minutes per day. Also more schools are using more educational activities such as dance and even nontraditional ones such as kickboxing to make physical education classes more enjoyable.[18] Some states such as Texas have mandated 30 minutes of physical activity a day.[19] Many parents whose school districts are not offering opportunities for physical activity are upset that their children don't have an opportunity to participate in recess and other physical activities. Some are taking proactive steps to restore recess to the school day. For example, parents at Rivers Edge Elementary in Richmond, Virginia, have banded together to launch a "rescuing recess" campaign. They are involving children in letter-writing campaigns directed at school officials in which they explain the reasons for restoring recess.[20]

As an early childhood teacher, you will want to make sure that you provide time in your program for children to play indoors and outdoors, and to engage in group projects that enable children to be up out of their seats and active in the classroom.

Mental Health in Early Childhood. Just as we are concerned about the mental health of children from birth to age five, so, too, are we concerned about the mental health of children in the middle years. We are particularly concerned about **childhood depression**. As many as one in thirty-three children have depression.[21] Childhood depression manifests itself in the following ways:

- Persistent sadness; withdrawal from family, friends, and activities that they once enjoyed; increased irritability or agitation; changes in eating and sleeping habits (e.g., significant weight loss, insomnia, excessive sleep); frequent physical complaints, such as headaches and stomachaches; lack of enthusiasm or motivation; decreased energy level and chronic fatigue; play that involves excessive aggression toward self or others or that involves persistently sad themes; indecision, lack of concentration, or forgetfulness; feelings of worthlessness or excessive guilt; and recurring thoughts of death or suicide.[22]

Children's good mental health begins at home and continues in your classroom. Part of your role as an early childhood teacher is to work with parents to help them promote their children's mental health and to support children's good mental health in your classroom. In your work and collaboration with parents, here are some things you can advise parents to do:

- *Encourage children to play.* Play time is as important to a child's development as food. Play helps a child be creative, develop problem-solving skills and self-control, and learn how to get along with others.
- *Enroll children in an after-school activity, especially if they are otherwise home alone after school.* This is a great way for a child to stay productive, learn something new, gain self-esteem, and have something to look forward to during the week.
- *Provide a safe and secure home environment.* Fear can be very real for a child. Try to find out what could be frightening him or her. Be loving, patient, and reassuring, not critical.
- *Give appropriate guidance and discipline when necessary.* Be firm, but kind and realistic with your expectations. The goal is not to control the child, but to help him or her learn self-control.
- *Communicate.* Parents need to make time each day after work and school to listen to their children and talk with them about what is happening in their lives and to share emotions and feelings.[23]

In your teaching of young children, here are some things you can do:

- *Create a sense of belonging.* Feeling connected and welcomed is essential to children's positive adjustment, self-identification, and sense of trust in others and themselves.
- *Promote resilience.* Adversity is a natural part of life and being resilient is important to overcoming challenges and good mental health. Connectedness, competency, helping others, and successfully facing difficult situations can foster resilience.
- *Develop competencies.* Children need to know that they can overcome challenges and accomplish goals through their actions. Achieving academic success and developing individual talents and interests helps children feel competent and more able to deal with stress positively.
- *Ensure a positive, safe school environment.* Feeling safe is critical to students' learning and mental health. Promote positive behaviors such as respect, responsibility, and kindness. Prevent negative behaviors such as bullying and harassment.
- *Teach and reinforce positive behaviors and decision making.* Provide consistent expectations and support. Teaching children social skills, problem solving, and conflict resolution supports good mental health.

childhood depression A disorder affecting as many as one in thirty-three children that can negatively impact feelings, thoughts, and behavior and can manifest itself with physical symptoms of illness.

- *Encourage helping others.* Children need to know that they can make a difference. Pro-social behaviors build self-esteem, foster connectedness, reinforce personal responsibility, and present opportunities for positive recognition.
- *Encourage good physical health.* Good physical health supports good mental health.[24]

Cognitive Development

myeducationlab

Go to the Assignments and Activities section of Topic 12: Professionalism/Ethics in the MyEducationLab for your course and complete the activity entitled *Ethics and the Early Childhood Professional.* As you read, ponder what you would do in the same situation.

Concrete operational thought is the cognitive milestone that enables children in the primary elementary grades to think and act as they do. Logical operations, although more sophisticated than in preoperational children, still require concrete objects and referents in the here and now. Abstract reasoning comes later, in the formal operations stage during early adolescence.

Children in the *concrete operations stage*, from about age seven to about age twelve, begin to use mental images and symbols during the thinking process and can reverse operations. For example, operations include many mathematical activities involving addition and subtraction, greater than and less than, multiplication, division, and equalities. A child is able to reverse operations when she can understand that when, for example, she adds two to three to get five, she can reverse this operation by subtracting two from five to get three. This is why it is a good idea for you to use concrete materials (e.g., rods, beads, buttons, blocks) to help children physically see operations as an aid for mental representation.

Concrete operational children begin to develop the ability to understand that change involving physical appearances does not necessarily change quality or quantity. They also begin to reverse thought processes by going back over and "undoing" a mental action just accomplished. Other mental operations children are capable of during this stage include:

- *One-to-one correspondence.* One-to-one correspondence is the basis for counting and matching objects. The concrete operations child has mastered the ability, for example, to give one cookie to each of her classmates and a pencil to each member of her work group.
- *Classification of objects, events, and time according to certain characteristics.* For example, a child in the concrete operations stage can classify events as occurring before or after lunch.
- *Classification involving multiple properties.* Multiple classification occurs when a child can classify objects on the basis of more than one property such as color and size, shape and size, shape and color, and so forth.
- *Class inclusion operations.* Class inclusion also involves classification. For example, if you showed five apples, five oranges, and five lemons to a child in the concrete operations stage, and asked him if there were more apples or fruit, he would be able to respond "fruit."

The process of development from the preoperational stage to the concrete stage is gradual and continual and occurs over a period of time as a result of maturation and experiences. No simple sets of exercises will cause children to move up the developmental ladder. Rather, ongoing developmentally appropriate activities lead to conceptual understanding.

Moral Development

moral development The process of developing culturally acceptable attitudes and behaviors, based on what society endorses and supports as right and wrong.

Moral development is the process of developing culturally acceptable attitudes and behaviors toward others and the environment based on what society endorses and supports through rules, laws, and cultural norms as right and wrong. Although not everyone agrees about the particular dimensions of children's moral development, some frequently mentioned ones include empathy, honesty, fairness, respect, responsibility, and caring. Many school districts teach character traits through character education programs as a means of supporting children's moral development.

TABLE 10.2 Moral Development in the Primary Years

Theorist	Moral Stage and Characteristics	Implications for Teachers
Jean Piaget	1. *Relations of Constraint: Grades 1–2* Concepts of right and wrong are determined by judgments of adults. Therefore morality is based on what adults say is right and wrong. 2. *Relations of Cooperation: Grades 3–6* Children's exchange of viewpoints with others helps determine what is good/bad and right/wrong.	• Provide children with many opportunities to engage in decisions and make decisions about what is right and wrong. • Provide opportunities every day for children to make decisions and assume responsibilities. Responsibility comes from opportunities to be responsible.
Lawrence Kohlberg	1. *Preconventional Level: Ages 4–10* Morality is a matter of good or bad based on a system of punishment and reward as administered by adults in authority positions. • *Stage 1. Punishment and obedience:* Children operate within and respond to consequences of behavior. • *Stage 2. Instrumental–relativist orientation:* Children's actions are motivated by satisfaction of needs ("You scratch my back, I'll scratch yours").	• Provide many examples of moral behavior and decisions. Use children's literature to help you achieve this goal. • Use children's out-of-classroom experiences as a basis for discussion involving values and decision-making. • Provide children many opportunities to interact with children of different ages and cultures.

Character Education. Character education is closely aligned with pro-social and conflict resolution education and is now a high priority for all early childhood educators. Character education is rapidly becoming a part of many early childhood programs. Character education activities designed to teach specific character traits are now commonplace in the curriculum of the primary grades. The three R's have been expanded to six: reading, writing, arithmetic, respect, responsibility, and reasoning. Respect, responsibility, and reasoning are now part of the primary curriculum for a number of reasons. Although everyone believes children have to learn *how* to count, the public and educators also believe that schools have to teach children *what* counts.

Some common characteristics taught in the primary grades are:

• Responsibility, cooperation, respect for others, compassion, self-discipline, selflessness (friendship), tolerance, courage, friendship, optimism, honesty, perseverance, future-mindedness, and purposefulness.

Jean Piaget and Lawrence Kohlberg are the leading proponents of a developmental stage theory of children's moral development. Table 10.2 outlines their stages of moral development during ages six to ten. Implicit to children's moral development is the process of moving or developing from what is known as "other regulation" (by parents, teachers, etc.) to self-regulation (see Chapter 12). Review Table 10.2 now and consider how you can apply the implications to your teaching.

ENVIRONMENTS THAT SUPPORT LEARNING IN THE PRIMARY GRADES

As we have discussed, the environment plays a major role in children's learning and success and is also a major determinant of what and how well children learn. Figure 10.3 shows some of the critical features of an effective primary classroom designed to help children

learn in today's demanding educational environment. Classrooms not only support children's learning, but they also help ensure that all children learn to their full capacities. Part of your role is to use these features to help provide the best learning environment possible for all children. How might you do that in grades one to three?

The Physical Environment

The following conditions support learning in the primary classroom:

- Materials are in abundant supply for reading, writing, language development, and content area development (e.g., books about math, science, social studies, and the arts).
- Learning centers reflect content areas.
- Children are seated in chairs at tables or in clusters of desks for roughly three to six children.
- Literature of all genres supports content area learning centers, and materials provide for and emulate real work experiences (i.e., the waiting room, the restaurant).

Children not only have to learn *how* to count, but they need to know *what* counts. Helping children develop positive character traits is now a standard part of the curricula of many early childhood programs. What are some character traits that you believe should be taught to young children?

Thinking skills are taught and practiced.

Teachers believe that all children will learn.

Assessment is authentic and ongoing.

Literacy is emphasized across all contents.

All activities are multiculturally appropriate.

Teachers and administrators have high expectations for all children.

The majority of classroom time is spent on teaching, learning, and acquiring academic-related knowledge and skills.

The physical environment is prepared to enrich children's learning.

A high priority is placed on learning to read, to read on grade level, and to read with comprehension and fluency.

Families are in partnership with the school, children, and teachers.

A sense of community prevails. Children learn from each other, and teachers and children respect each other.

Math, science, social studies, and the arts as well as reading are important parts of the primary curriculum.

FIGURE 10.3 Features of Contemporary Classrooms: Grades 1–3

- Materials and instruction provide for interdisciplinary integrated approaches.
- Program, learning, and environment are coordinated so that materials support and align with outcomes and standards.
- Teacher instruction (teacher-directed instruction and intentional teaching) and active student involvement are balanced.
- Centers support literacy. All centers have materials that support reading and writing.
- Children's products are displayed and valued.
- Schedules are posted where children can read them.
- Technology supports and enriches basic skill and concept learning. Children use technology to make presentations, projects, and reports.

The Social Environment

The following conditions support an enriching emotional and social environment:

- Families, other adults, and the community are connected to classroom learning.
- Children are valued and respected. The classroom is a community of learners.
- Children live and learn in peace and harmony.
- High expectations for all are an essential part of the classroom culture.
- Assessment is continuous and appropriate and is designed to support teaching and learning.
- Thinking is considered a basic skill and is integrated through all areas of the curriculum.

Environments That Support Pro-Social and Conflict Resolution Education

All early childhood professionals, parents, and politicians believe that efforts to reduce incidents of violence and uncivil behavior begin in preschool, kindergarten, and grades one to three. Consequently, they place emphasis on teaching children the fundamentals of peaceful living, kindness, helpfulness, and cooperation. Follow these suggestions to foster the development of pro-social skills in your classroom:

- *Be a good role model for children.* Demonstrate in your life and relationships with children and other adults the behaviors of cooperation and kindness that you want to encourage in children. Civil behavior begins with courtesy and manners. You can model these and help children do the same.
- *Provide positive feedback and reinforcement when children perform pro-social behaviors.* When you reward children for appropriate behavior, they tend to repeat the behavior. ("I like how you helped Jake. I'll bet that made him feel better.")
- *Provide opportunities for children to help and show kindness to others.* For example, cooperative programs between your children and nursing and retirement homes and other community agencies are excellent opportunities to practice kind and helping behaviors.
- *Conduct conflict-free classroom routines and activities.* Provide opportunities for children to work together and practice skills for cooperative living. Design learning centers and activities for children to share and work cooperatively.
- *Provide practice in conflict resolution skills.* Classroom exercises here include taking turns, talking through problems, compromising, and working out problems.
- *Use examples from literature to make your point.* Read stories to children that exemplify pro-social behaviors and provide such literature for them to read.

- *Counsel and work with parents.* Encourage them to limit or eliminate altogether their children's watching violence on television, attending R-rated movies, playing video games with violent content, and buying CDs with objectionable lyrics.
- *Catch children "doing good."* Help children feel good about themselves, build strong self-images, and be competent individuals. Notice when children behave pro-socially and tell them that you are pleased with their actions. Children who are happy, confident, and competent feel good about themselves and are more likely to behave positively toward others.

CURRICULUM IN THE PRIMARY GRADES

The curriculum content of grades one, two, and three is pretty much determined by what state and local standards specify children should know and do in each content area. Take a few minutes now and review the curriculum standards for grades one, two, or three in your state.

The ways teachers help children achieve standards are many and varied. Teachers and children develop projects, write and put on plays, go on field trips, attend community events such as festivals and symphony orchestras, prepare for and hold arts and crafts exhibits, develop and update Web pages, and prepare for and take state exams. In other words, teaching in grades one, two, and three is fun, challenging, hard work, but worth the effort! A parent describes third grade teacher Robert Stephenson, the 2009 Michigan Teacher of the Year, this way:

> Mr. Stephenson creates an environment where the students thrive and enjoy education. He has the ability to make students feel great about themselves and their work. Mr. Stephenson makes learning fun by incorporating an extraordinary array of hands-on experiences. The kids love it, and more importantly—they learn![25]

Literacy and Reading in the Primary Grades

Just like preschool and kindergarten programs, today's primary grades emphasize literacy development, reading, and math. In fact, this emphasis is apparent in all the elementary grades, from pre-K to six. Parents and society want children who can speak, write, read well, and compute. As discussed in Chapter 9, more teachers use a balanced approach to reading. They integrate many different activities into a complete system of literacy development. For example, here are some things you can do as a teacher:

- Use the fundamentals of letter–sound correspondence, word study, and decoding, as well as many literacy activities, to involve children in reading, writing, speaking, and listening.
- Incorporate many reading approaches, such as shared reading (see Chapter 9), guided reading (discussed next), independent reading, and modeled reading (reading aloud).
- Use many forms of writing, such as shared writing, guided writing, and independent writing.
- Integrate literacy across the curriculum; for example, students write in journals or composition books about their experiences and investigations in math and science. Children write daily for different purposes. They write creative stories, answers to math word problems, personal narratives, journal entries, scientific observations, research reports, and responses to literature. They write fiction in different genres such as fables, poetry, and science fiction.
- Integrate literacy across cultures. That is, use technology to communicate with and about people in other cultures. (See this chapter's Technology Tie-In feature, "Blogging in the Classroom.")

- Use children's written documents as reading material, as well as literature books, vocabulary-controlled and sentence-controlled stories, and those containing predictable language patterns. Choose the best children's literature available to read to and with children.
- Organize literacy instruction around themes or units of study relevant to students.
- Have children create stories, write letters, keep personal journals, and share their written documents with others.

Connections with others, especially families, are important in making literacy meaningful for children.

Guided Reading. Guided reading is designed to help children develop and use strategies of independent reading and become good readers. Teachers provide support for small groups of readers as they learn to use various reading strategies (context clues, letter–sound relationships, word structure, and so forth).[26]

The accompanying Professionalism in Practice feature, "How to Implement a Successful Guided Reading Program," helps you learn how to implement guided reading with your children.

Math in the Primary Grades

Teachers are reemphasizing mathematics as an essential part of primary education. Just as reading is receiving a great deal of national attention, so too is mathematics. Some call this reemphasizing of mathematics the "new math." The term *new math* is not new, however. It has been around since the 1960s. What differentiates the "old" math from the "new"? Memorization and drill characterize the old or traditional math. The new math, sometimes referred to as the "new-new math," emphasizes hands-on activities, problem solving, group work and teamwork, application and use of mathematical ideas and principles to real-life events, daily use of mathematics, and an understanding of and use of math understandings and competencies. The new math seeks to have students be creative users of math in life and workplace settings but also includes the ability to recall addition sums and multiplication products quickly.

The ten standards of the National Council of Teachers of Mathematics (NCTM) identify these understandings and competencies as: number and operations, algebra, geometry, measurement, data analysis and probability, problem solving, reasoning and proof, communication, connection, and representation. The following sample standard from NCTM helps you understand the standard for algebra and its application to patterns, relations, and functions in the primary grades:

In prekindergarten through grade 2 all students should:
- Sort, classify, and order objects by size, number, and other properties;
- Recognize, describe, and extend patterns such as sequences of sounds and shapes or simple numeric patterns and translate from one representation to another;
- Analyze how both repeating and growing patterns are generated.[27]

Your teaching of math in the primary grades will also most likely be aligned with NCTM's Curriculum Focal Points, which outline important mathematical topics for each grade level. For example, the Curriculum Focal Points and children's connections to the focal points for grade two are shown in Figure 10.4.

Science in the Primary Grades

The National Science Content Standards set forth by the Center for Science, Mathematics, and Engineering help you teach science in the primary grades. Review these standards now in Figure 10.5.

myeducation**lab**

Go to the Assignments and Activities section in Topic 7: Curriculum/Content Areas of the MyEducationLab for your course and complete the activity entitled *Planning and Teaching the Inquiry Curriculum.* Observe how teachers promote and support hands-on learning and how young children assume the role of "scientists" as part of inquiry learning.

How to Implement a Successful Guided Reading Program

WHY IS GUIDED READING IMPORTANT?

Guided reading is beneficial for all students. For the more advanced readers, guided reading is a great way to introduce and practice skills that their peers may not be ready for. Guided reading offers struggling readers a safe setting for the extra support they need to master skills at a comfortable pace. Since I teach guided reading in small groups, I can reinforce skills as many times as needed for the students to achieve mastery. The children are not pressured from the feeling that they are the only ones "not getting it."

Guided reading is also very beneficial to me. Small-group instruction allows me to pinpoint the strengths and weaknesses of individual students. It is an easy way for me to differentiate instruction, which makes it much easier to teach all students on their current level. Guided reading is also a great time to level the students or group children with the same reading level, which is beneficial to me because it gives a great deal of information about which reading strategies the students are using, as well as showing the progress each student has made.

HOW TO IMPLEMENT GUIDED READING

ELEMENT 1

HOW OFTEN SHOULD I TEACH GUIDED READING?

You should teach guided reading every day. The guided reading sessions are short; fifteen minutes per group works well. Meeting with struggling readers daily is essential to their progress and success. Students reading on grade level should meet at least three times a week. Advanced readers need to meet at least once or twice a week as time permits. For example, here is the schedule I use:

Example Schedule:

	Monday	Tuesday	Wednesday	Thursday	Friday
9:00–9:15	Low Group	Low Group	Low Group	Low Group	Low Group
9:15–9:30	Mid Group 1	Mid Group 2	High Group	Mid Group 3	Mid Group 4
9:30–9:45	Mid Group 2	Mid Group 1	Mid Group 2	Mid Group 1	Mid Group 3

inquiry learning Involvement of children in activities and processes that lead to learning.

Today's science teaching is *inquiry based;* that is, it is all about helping children solve problems by asking questions. **Inquiry learning** is about involving children in activities and processes that lead to learning. The process of inquiry involves (1) posing questions, (2) observing, (3) reading and researching for a purpose, (4) proposing solutions and making predictions, and (5) gathering information and interpreting it.

What does an inquiry-based classroom look like? Figure 10.6 provides you with the essential features of an inquiry-based classroom. Such a classroom focuses on student-constructed learning, which is important for science concept development. Use the ideas in Figure 10.6 for implementing inquiry-based learning in your own classroom.

Social Studies in the Primary Grades

Social studies are the integrated study of the social sciences and humanities to promote civic competence. The primary purpose of social studies is to help children develop the ability to make informed and reasoned decisions for the public good as citizens of a culturally diverse, democratic society in an interdependent world.[28]

Teaching social studies is an important part of your responsibility as an early childhood teacher. While teachers devote a lot of instructional time to literacy/reading and math,

ELEMENT 2 — WHAT SHOULD I DO IN GUIDED READING?

Since time is limited, activities are short and simple; yet, they are quite effective due to the individualized instruction. Guided reading gives students time to practice the skill with the support of the teacher. Afterwards, students can apply the skills they learned as they play a learning game, use a book to go on a word hunt, or read leveled books. I am providing constant support, taking notes on student progress, and documenting the teaching strategies I used. These notes are very helpful because I can refer to them daily to plan future lessons or regroup the students based on their needs.

Here are some suggested materials for guided reading:

- Dry erase boards/markers
- Magnetic letters
- Index cards
- Teacher-made skill practice games (*Concentration, I Spy*, etc.)
- Pencils/sticky notes
- Leveled books

ELEMENT 3 — HOW DO I GROUP STUDENTS FOR GUIDED READING?

When you set up guided reading groups, give much thought and serious consideration to how to group the students based on ongoing assessment of their reading skills. Regroup students who have similar needs. As students master the skills practiced, they should then be regrouped. Students generally do not know what group they are in because the groups change constantly. It is easiest to call individual students to the reading table for instruction rather than naming each group, due to the constant regrouping that should be happening and to protect the self-esteem of each student.

ELEMENT 4 — WHAT ARE BOOK BAG BOOKS AND BROWSING BOXES?

Book bag books are leveled books that students read during Self-Selected Reading (SSR), throughout the day, and at home. The students choose these books based on individual interests from browsing boxes that are set up within reach of the students. Browsing boxes are set up according to levels to ensure that students are reading books that are just right for them. You can also keep books used in guided reading in the book bag and let students take home for practice.

ELEMENT 5 — HOW CAN I MANAGE GUIDED READING AND LEARNING CENTERS SIMULTANEOUSLY?

You can teach guided reading effectively while the other students are in literacy centers. You must use good classroom management skills. I explicitly teach center expectations, activities, and routines and have children practice them for several weeks before I begin guided reading. I monitor, praise good choices, and give consequences when needed for reinforcement. When I implement guided reading, children know well the center expectations and procedures. However, I consistently reinforce procedures, rules, and expectations before, during, and after guided reading.

Guided reading is a great way to help each student learn the skills he or she needs to be a successful reader and to achieve in all the subject areas. Good luck!

....

Contributed by Candice M. Bookman, first grade teacher, Lawrence Elementary School, Mesquite Independent School District, Mesquite, Texas.

---

you need not neglect social studies. Keep in mind that you can integrate social studies content with reading and math, so that children are reading and engaged in math processes "across the social studies curriculum." Be sure you are familiar with your state standards for the grade level you are teaching in order to incorporate them into your planning and teaching. Following are some ideas for incorporating social studies into your curriculum.

Culture. The best place to begin teaching about culture is with you and your students. At the beginning of the school year, third grade teacher Alessia Rossi shares information about her Italian background with her students by showing where her ancestors came from. She uses social studies tools such as maps and globes to help her students put Italy in the world geographic context. She invites members of the local Italian Sons and Daughters of America (ISDA) to share Italian culture and heritage. She introduces Italian words and ties these to the reading lessons. She has books about the Italian culture in the reading center and DVDs with Italian songs and dances. In the process of Rossi's sharing, her students feel comfortable and start to share their cultures and backgrounds. At the end of the school year, the class hosts a Cultural Heritage Festival.

Time, Continuity, and Change. Just as culture is all around us, so we are surrounded by time, continuity, and change. Second grade teacher Kelie Shipley involves her students

FIGURE 10.4

NCTM Curriculum Focal Points for Grade 2

The set of three NCTM curriculum focal points and related connections for mathematics in grade two follow. These topics are the recommended content emphases for this grade level. It is essential that these focal points be addressed in contexts that promote problem solving, reasoning, communication, making connections, and designing and analyzing representations.

Grade 2 Curriculum Focal Points	Connections to the Focal Points
Number and Operations: Developing an understanding of the base-ten numeration system and place-value concepts Children develop an understanding of the base-ten numeration system and place-value concepts (at least to 1,000). Their understanding of base-ten numeration includes ideas of counting in units and multiples of hundreds, tens, and ones, as well as a grasp of number relationships, which they demonstrate in a variety of ways, including comparing and ordering numbers. They understand multi-digit numbers in terms of place value, recognizing that place-value notation is shorthand for the sums of multiples of powers of 10 (e.g., 853 as 8 hundreds + 5 tens + 3 ones).	Children use place value and properties of operations to create equivalent representations of given numbers (such as 35 represented by 35 ones, 3 tens and 5 ones, or 2 tens and 15 ones) and to write, compare, and order multi-digit numbers. They use these ideas to compose and decompose multi-digit numbers. Children add and subtract to solve a variety of problems, including applications involving measurement, geometry, and data, as well as non-routine problems. In preparation for grade three, they solve problems involving multiplicative situations, developing initial understandings of multiplication as repeated addition.
Number and Operations and Algebra: Developing quick recall of addition facts and related subtraction facts and fluency with multi-digit addition and subtraction Children use their understanding of addition to develop quick recall of basic addition facts and related subtraction facts. They solve arithmetic problems by applying their understanding of models of addition and subtraction (such as combining or separating sets or using number lines), relationships and properties of number (such as place value), and properties of addition (commutativity and associativity). Children develop, discuss, and use efficient, accurate, and generalizable methods to add and subtract multi-digit whole numbers. They select and apply appropriate methods to estimate sums and differences or calculate them mentally, depending on the context and numbers involved. They develop fluency with efficient procedures, including standard algorithms, for adding and subtracting whole numbers, understand why the procedures work (on the basis of place value and properties of operations), and use them to solve problems.	Children use number patterns to extend their knowledge of properties of numbers and operations. For example, when skip-counting, they build foundations for understanding multiples and factors.
Measurement: Developing an understanding of linear measurement and facility in measuring lengths Children develop an understanding of the meaning and processes of measurement, including such underlying concepts as partitioning (the mental activity of slicing the length of an object into equal-sized units) and transitivity (e.g., if object A is longer than object B and object B is longer than object C, then object A is longer than object C). They understand linear measure as an iteration of units and use rulers and other measurement tools with that understanding. They understand the need for equal-length units, the use of standard units of measure (centimeter and inch), and the inverse relationship between the size of a unit and the number of units used in a particular measurement (i.e., children recognize that the smaller the unit, the more iterations they need to cover a given length).	Children estimate, measure, and compute lengths as they solve problems involving data, space, and movement through space. By composing and decomposing two-dimensional shapes (intentionally substituting arrangements of smaller shapes for larger shapes or substituting larger shapes for many smaller shapes), they use geometric knowledge and spatial reasoning to develop foundations for understanding area, fractions, and proportions.

Source: Reprinted with permission from *Curriculum Focal Points for Prekindergarten Through Grade 8 Mathematics: A Quest for Coherence*, copyright 2006 by the National Council of Teachers of Mathematics. The complete document may be viewed at National Council of Teachers of Mathematics (NCTM), "Curriculum Focal Points for Grade 2," 2009; accessed June 4, 2009, at http://www.nctm.org/standards/focalpoints.aspx?id=326.

FIGURE 10.5.

Science Content Standards for Grades K–4

Science As Inquiry	Physical Science	Life Science	Earth and Space Science
• Abilities necessary to do scientific inquiry • Understandings about scientific inquiry	• Properties of objects and materials • Position and motion of objects • Light, heat, electricity, and magnetism	• Characteristics of organisms • Life cycles of organisms • Organisms and environments	• Properties of earth materials • Objects in the sky • Changes in earth and sky

Science and Technology	Science in Personal and Social Perspectives	History and Nature of Science	
• Abilities of technological design • Understandings about science and technology • Abilities to distinguish between natural objects and objects made by humans	• Personal health • Characteristics and changes in populations • Types of resources • Changes in environments • Science and technology in local changes	• Science as a human endeavor	

Source: Reprinted with permission from *National Science Education Standards*, 1996, and *Inquiry and the National Science Education Standards*, 2000, by the National Academy of Sciences, Courtesy of the National Academies Press, Washington, DC.

FIGURE 10.6.

Essential Features of an Inquiry-Based Classroom and Their Variations

Essential Feature	Variations			
1. Learner engages in scientifically oriented questions.	Learner poses a question.	Learner selects among questions, poses new questions.	Learner sharpens or clarifies question provided by teacher, materials, or other source.	Learner engages in question provided by teacher, materials, or other source.
2. Learner gives priority to evidence in responding to questions.	Learner determines what constitutes evidence and collects it.	Learner directed to collect certain data.	Learner given data and asked to analyze.	Learner given data and told how to analyze.
3. Learner formulates explanations from evidence.	Learner formulates explanation after summarizing evidence.	Learner guided in process of formulating explanations from evidence.	Learner given possible ways to use evidence to formulate explanation.	Learner provided with evidence and how to use evidence to formulate explanation.
4. Learner connects explanations to scientific knowledge.	Learner independently examines other resources and forms the links to explanations.	Learner directed toward areas and sources of scientific knowledge.	Learner given possible connections.	
5. Learner communicates and justifies explanations.	Learner forms reasonable and logical argument to communicate explanations.	Learner coached in development of communication.	Learner provided broad guidelines to use to sharpen communication.	Learner given steps and procedures for communication.

Source: National Research Council. 2002. *Inquiry and the National Science Education Standards: A Guide for Teaching and Learning.* Washington, DC: National Academies Press. Reprinted with permission from the National Academies Press, Copyright 2002, National Academy of Sciences.

in a community history project in which her students research not only the history of their town, but also how the town is changing and why. In the course of their research the children discovered that on one of the dedication plaques, the name of the person for whom their school is named was misspelled. They wrote letters to school and city officials, resulting in a new plaque. At the new dedication, relatives of the school's namesake came and talked about what school was like when they were in the second grade.

People, Places, and Environment.　Your local museums, art institutes, and historical centers are wonderful resources for involving your students in learning about people, places, and the environment. For example, the Allen Memorial Art Museum in Oberlin, Ohio, collaborates with the Asian Art/Educational Outreach Funding Initiative of the Freeman Foundation and has developed Asian art educational programming for children and teachers. One of the lessons involves children ages five through eight in *gyotaku*, a Japanese art of fish painting, and *haiku*, a form of Japanese poetry. (You can learn more about this program and reflect on how you could involve your students in similar activities and learning experiences at http://www.oberlin.edu/amam/asia/about.html.)

Individual Development and Identity.　First grade teacher Ashley Gotkins incorporates the North Carolina Grade 1 Social Studies Standards into her teaching. They focus on neighborhoods and communities around the world. Gotkins, whose grandmother was one-sixteenth Cherokee, uses her cultural heritage to teach about Native Americans and the Cherokee tribes. She builds her Native American lessons around these North Carolina Standards:[29]

- Describe the roles of individuals in the family.
- Identify various groups to which individuals and families belong.
- Compare and contrast similarities and differences among individuals and families.
- Explore the benefits of diversity in the United States.

Individuals, Groups, and Institutions.　On the first day of school, first grade teacher Tanika Ramsey holds a "morning meeting" in which all of the children introduce themselves. Then she talks about families and what a family is. The children brainstorm about what things they can do to live peacefully in their classroom family. In the following days, Ramsey expands the discussion to include what children can do to live harmoniously in the school. The children discuss school rules, interview administrators, staff, and other teachers and develop a "blueprint for school living." They share their "blueprint" with other first grade classes.

Power, Authority, and Governance.　Classroom living requires a lot of compromises and getting along with others. First grade teacher Jacki Aochi believes she should share her "power" with children and can accomplish this goal by teaching her children how to resolve conflicts. She uses the Betsy Evans "Conflict Resolution with Young Children" program (http://www.kidsandconflict.com/contact.htm). In addition, Aochi conducts a morning meeting that consists of three parts. Each part takes about five minutes:

- *Announcements.* Both she and the students make announcements related to classroom and school events and activities as well as life events such as birthdays, sporting events, and family activities.
- *Concerns.* The children discuss events inside and outside of the classroom and suggest resolutions for how they and others can turn the concern into a positive situation.
- *Being a good citizen.* Children have an opportunity to state what they are going to do during the day or week to be good citizens in the classroom, school, home, and community.

Production, Distribution, and Consumption.   Matt Blair teaches his third graders about the production, distribution, and consumption of consumer products by creating, selling, and distributing handmade cards. The children design and illustrate get-well, birthday, and thank-you cards and provide original verses and sentiments. They also package, sell, and distribute their cards. As part of the project, children visit design studios and printers and consult with marketing executives of local businesses. All proceeds from the sales of the cards go to a community charity selected by the children.

Science, Technology, and Society.   Second grade teacher Beverly Haung integrates her teaching of science, technology, and society with the teaching of the scientific method. She involves the children in a project in which they survey their homes and community to determine the ways in which computers influence how people live and work. The children post their own research questions, develop their surveys—both online and hard-copy versions—analyze their data, draw conclusions, write their results in their science journals, and publish the results in their school newspaper.

Global Connections.   Melissa Gloria's students are third graders whose first language is primarily English, but they are learning Spanish as a second language. They are studying world cultures and use ePals Global Community (http://www.epals.com) to exchange letters, postcards, photographs, and journal entries via e-mail with their electronic pals in Colombia. They collaborate by exchanging information about culture and history.

Civic Ideals and Practices.   First grade teacher Gretchen Reich uses the local community to teach civic pride. Her students engage in a project of learning about community agencies and how they help others. The students select agencies they would like to know more about, such as the Salvation Army, and invite agency members to their classroom to talk about what they do. As a result of their community civic involvement, the children decided to collect pennies to support the Salvation Army Red Kettle drive. In six weeks, the children raised $50. Also, once a month, the children bake cookies and take them to homes for senior citizens.

Arts in the Primary Grades

In the primary grades, the creative arts most often include music, theater, dance, and art. For each of these disciplines you will want to include knowledge, concepts, and themes. Your teaching of the arts should be content based and child centered, and you will want to make sure that you consult your state's content standards for the arts.

Ideas for Teaching Creative Arts.   Today's teaching of the arts is designed to provide children with content knowledge and skills from the four disciplines listed in the preceding paragraph. So, in your teaching of the arts you will want to make sure that children are provided with authentic content and are engaged in activities that help them learn and apply knowledge of the arts. The following is an idea that you can use to help you teach your students about music and dance:

- *Dancing to Music.* Katie Dwyer encourages her students to appreciate and examine different styles of music as well as create dance presentations that are specifically related to the music. She plays music and asks her students to listen to it carefully, thinking about what it is about and how it makes them feel. She plays the music again and asks her students to move to the music. If the music is fast, she encourages them to move fast. At the same time, she asks her students to show her how the music makes them feel—happy, sad, and so forth.[30]

Teaching Thinking

As we previously discussed, reasoning has been added as one of the six R's of early childhood programs. Educators believe that if students can think, they can meaningfully engage in subject matter curriculum and the rigors and demands of the workplace and life. As a result, many teachers are including the teaching of thinking in their daily lesson plans.

Figure 10.7 shows examples of questions you can use to promote thinking. They are based on Benjamin Bloom's hierarchy of questioning levels. A major teaching objective is

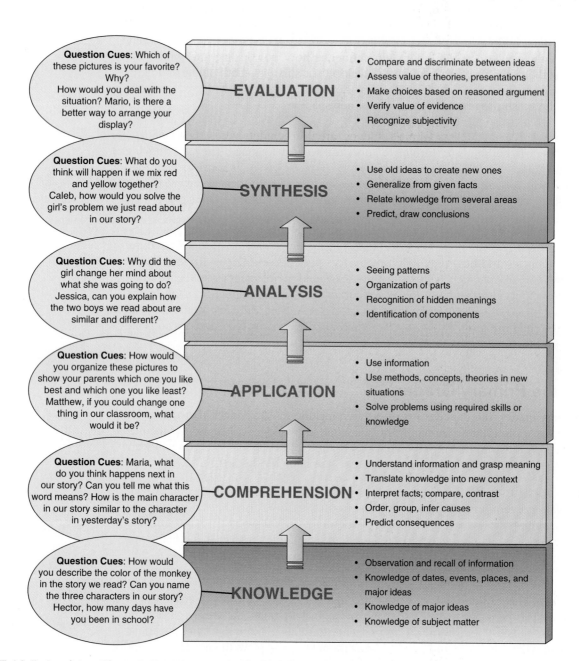

FIGURE 10.7 Applying Bloom's Taxonomy to Early Childhood Classrooms

Source: Based on "Learning Skills: Bloom's Taxonomy," University of Victoria, Counselling Services, http://www.coun.uvic.ca/learn/program/hndouts/bloom.html. From B. S. Bloom, ed., *Taxonomy of Educational Objectives: The Classification of Education Goals, Handbook I. Cognitive Domain* (New York and Toronto: Longmans, Green, 1956).

to ask students questions that move them up the hierarchy into higher level thinking. Your questions not only challenge children to think, but they also promote linguistic, social, and behavioral skills. For example, recall of knowledge is the lowest level of thinking and evaluation is the highest; therefore, instead of asking children merely to recall information, teachers should encourage them to think critically about information, solve problems, and reflect. To promote thinking in your classroom follow these guidelines:

- Give children the freedom and security to be creative thinkers.
- Encourage children to search for other answers and alternative solutions rather than settling for one "right" answer. Ask open-ended questions ("Why do you think that?") rather than questions that require a yes or no response.
- Create classroom cultures in which children have the time, opportunity, and materials with which to be creative.
- Integrate thinking into the total curriculum so that children learn to think during the entire school day.

PORTRAITS OF CHILDREN

We have discussed a lot of information about the curriculum and environments of the primary grades, but what about the children? Classrooms and programs are for the children, and we must always remember that children are the reason we teach. On the following pages are three Professionalism in Practice features offering some portraits of children ages seven, eight, and nine for you to review. As you read these, think about how you would teach each one in your classroom.

ACTIVITIES FOR PROFESSIONAL DEVELOPMENT

ethical dilemma

Program Incentives

Amy and Allison teach first grade in a middle- to low-income school district where a lot of children have difficulty learning to read. Allison believes that the parents should do more to support their children's learning to read. She has joined the sales force of a national company that markets a beginning reading program targeted at struggling readers. Allison has asked Amy for names, addresses, and phone numbers of families of children in her class who are experiencing reading difficulty. Allison feels she can help the children and at the same time make some extra money to supplement her teaching salary.

What should Amy do? Should she give Allison the list of names? Or should she refuse Allison's request and risk alienating her as a coworker? Or should Amy pursue another plan of action?

RAUL

Meet Raul, a seven-year-old Hispanic male. Raul weighs 47 pounds and is 3 feet 11 inches tall. He is a talkative first grader and loves learning anything that involves animals. Raul has a hard time paying attention in class and is easily distracted.

Social-Emotional	Cognitive	Motor	Adaptive (Daily Living)
Comes from a single-parent family and does not have a male role model	Easily memorizes odd facts about animals	Likes to climb and run during recess	Helps his mother with household chores
Spends a lot of time with his grandmother because his mother works full-time	Is beginning to learn to add and subtract small numbers	Likes to play competitive sports and games	Makes his own breakfast in the morning
Shows off in new situations	Is confident with individual sounds	Is action oriented, rather than verbal	Is becoming more independent
Tries very hard to fit in with other boys	Likes to read by himself	Is somewhat aggressive and tends to get into fights	Folds and puts away his own clothes

LYNNE

Meet Lynne, a seven-year-old African American female. Lynne weighs 45 pounds and is 3 feet 9 inches tall. She is a very boisterous child who is outgoing and loves to talk with her friends in class. Lynne is highly intelligent and loves to read. Her parents are both upwardly mobile lawyers.

Social-Emotional	Cognitive	Motor	Adaptive (Daily Living)
Likes to tell riddles and jokes	Is able to count to 200 without difficulty	Enjoys participating in her cheerleading class and has great coordination	Is able to fix a snack by herself
Tends to get in "trouble" at school for talking too much in class	Enjoys learning about space and the solar system	Likes to create dance routines with her friends	Likes to do her own hair each morning
Shows a growing concern about popularity among her peers	Has concrete math concepts	Is able to ride a bicycle without training wheels	Knows how to cross a street safely
Is often "performing" songs for her parents	Is able to recognize denominations of currency	Likes to draw the planets of the solar system	Puts herself to bed

Questions About Developmentally Appropriate Practice:

- What are the major differences between Raul and Lynne? How might their unique characteristics and home backgrounds affect their approaches to learning?
- As a teacher, how could you help Raul and Lynne grow socially and emotionally? Do you think having role models is important for Raul and Lynne? What can you do to provide Raul with positive adult male influences?
- As Raul's teacher, what would you do to help him pay attention?

TOMAS

Meet Tomas, an eight-year-old Hispanic male. He weighs 68 pounds and is 4 feet 3 inches tall. Tomas is an active child who is impulsive and very social. He can become aggressive while playing and his teachers frequently have to remind him to "settle down" while on the playground. Tomas has difficulty with reading and is showing a growing dislike for math.

Social-Emotional	Cognitive	Motor	Adaptive (Daily Living)
Is very loud and tends to yell out answers in class before raising his hand	Is a creative thinker who enjoys making up fictional stories	Has difficulty writing in paragraph form the fictional stories he likes to make up	Is able to make his own breakfast in the morning
Has difficulty controlling his emotions when he is upset	Prefers being read aloud to rather than reading quietly to himself	Is able to dribble and shoot a basketball and understands the basic rules of sports and games	Feeds his dog each morning and night
Is easily embarrassed	Resists adult guidance at times		Is beginning to understand his role in household duties
Often intimidates his peers with his aggressive behavior and impulsive social skills	Is able to multiply double-digit numbers with little difficulty	Writes and draws with increasing skill	Is able to manage his small weekly allowance
		Is learning to write in cursive	

MAKAYLA

Meet Makayla, an eight-year-old African American female. Makayla weighs 58 pounds and is 4 feet 4 inches tall. Makayla is very outspoken and likes to be the center of attention. Makayla enjoys extra attention from her teacher.

Social-Emotional	Cognitive	Motor	Adaptive (Daily Living)
Lives full-time with her grandmother	Is gradually learning concepts related to addition and subtraction	Is somewhat aggressive when playing with other children	Makes her bed every morning
Is extremely social and talkative—is a very happy child	Learns best in a tactile environment	Likes to play jump rope with other children on the playground	Has a strong, loving relationship with her grandmother—makes friends easily
Is beginning to become concerned about her height and weight	Is proud when she completes tasks	Has a lot of energy and stamina	Is very independent—likes to do things for herself
Is influenced by others, especially older females	Enjoys science but not math or reading	Likes to braid classmates' hair	Gets her own snacks without assistance from her grandmother

Questions About Developmentally Appropriate Practice:

- As a teacher, identify three activities that you could use to teach to Makayla's and Tomas's strengths.
- What gender differences between Tomas and Makayla influence their classroom behavior?
- What are some things you might do to help Makayla's grandmother become more involved?
- How could you use math to help Tomas with his reading?

DUY

Meet Duy, a nine-year-old Asian male. Duy weighs 70 pounds and is 4 feet 7 inches tall. Duy is a very intelligent third grader who excels when he is challenged. He prefers individual activities to those that involve a group. He is somewhat reserved and shy. He enjoys the company of adults rather than children his own age.

Social-Emotional	Cognitive	Motor	Adaptive (Daily Living)
Is an introverted child and keeps to himself	Reads two grades above the third grade level	Is nonaggressive in physical play	Dresses and grooms himself before school
Is very sensitive	Enjoys reading chapter books	Writes very legibly in cursive	Is very attached to his parents—prefers to stay "close" to them
Tends to be critical of himself	Uses reference books and the Internet to write research papers	Has very good manual dexterity	Shows a strong desire to complete his tasks
Is shy around children his age but is very interactive with adults	Excels in all subjects except physical education	Enjoys art activities and likes to paint and draw	Helps his mother with chores around the house such as sweeping and putting away dishes

MADISON

Meet Madison, a nine-year-old Caucasian female who is in the third grade. Madison weighs 69 pounds and is 4 feet 5 inches tall. Madison attends a private school and is in accelerated reading and math classes. She is a sensitive child with a studious nature. Madison spends most of her time reading or talking with her best friend. She is very outgoing, mannerly, and makes friends easily.

Social-Emotional	Cognitive	Motor	Adaptive (Daily Living)
Can have her feelings hurt rather easily but bounces back—has a positive attitude	Loves to read—has read all the books on the "Fun to Read" list	Has excellent balance and is able to twist on her tiptoes without falling—enjoys her ballet classes	Very fashion conscious and likes to be well dressed
Has a large circle of friends in and outside of school	Can write lengthy paragraphs with little assistance and minimal spelling errors—enjoys using the computer to write stories	Is involved in many out-of-school activities—has won a blue ribbon for her equestrian skills	Has her own cell phone and enjoys talking to her friends—also adept at text messaging
Very independent and self-assured	Has developed personal standards of right and wrong	Draws with great detail—thinks she may be an artist when she grows up	Is very curious—wants to know about everything
Actively seeks praise and affirmation of her good accomplishments	Is above average in math skills	Likes to dance and is able to stand on one leg for long periods of time without falling	Is becoming "boy" conscious and can be "silly" in relationships with them

Questions About Developmentally Appropriate Practice:

- How could you as a teacher help Duy be more socially interactive?
- Would it be helpful to pair Duy and Madison with children who are not so academically advanced? How would you involve them in mentoring their classmates?
- What can you do to further enhance Madison's development and education?
- What are some possible reasons for Madison's "advanced" education and development?

Application Activities

1. One of the curriculum goals of many states is that all children should be able to read on grade level by grade three.

    a. Why do you think this is such an important goal?

    b. Why do you think this goal is set for grade three rather than another grade level such as grades one or two?

    c. What are three things you can do to help all children achieve the goal of reading on or above grade level by grade three?

2. Early childhood teachers are able to articulate their reasons for wanting to teach a particular grade. Many of my early childhood students say they want to teach only in kindergarten. Others are not sure. One student, Chris, wants to teach fourth or fifth grade. He says he prefers working with children who are more mature.

    a. Write a 200-word paragraph about why you do or do not want to teach in grades one, two, or three.

3. What do you think are the most important subjects of the primary grades? Why? How would you agree or disagree with those who think any subjects other than reading, writing, and arithmetic are a waste of time?

4. We have discussed the importance of using technology to support teaching and learning. Search for teacher blogs and identify five features that you would use in your blogging with children and families.

chapter eleven

EDUCATING CHILDREN WITH DIVERSE BACKGROUNDS AND SPECIAL NEEDS

Ensuring Each Child Learns

• • • • • • • • •

NAEYC Standards for Early Childhood Professional Preparation Programs

Standard 1: Promoting Child Development and Learning

I use my understanding of young children's characteristics and needs, and of multiple interacting influences on children's development and learning, to create environments that are healthy, respectful, supportive, and challenging for all children.[1]

Standard 2: Building Family and Community Relationships

I know about, understand, and value the importance and complex characteristics of children's families and communities. I use this understanding to create respectful, reciprocal relationships that support and empower families, and to involve all families in their children's development and learning.[2]

Standard 4: Using Developmentally Effective Approaches to Connect with Children and Families

I understand and use positive relationships and supportive interactions as the foundation for my work with young children and families. I know, understand, and use a wide array of developmentally appropriate approaches, instructional strategies, and tools to connect with children and families and positively influence each child's developmental learning.[3]

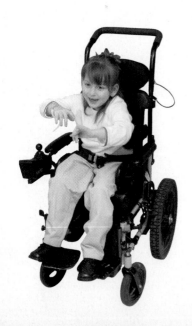

Gayle Solis Zavala, the 2009 National Special Education Teacher of the Year, is constantly finding ways to improve her students' receptive and expressive language through multisensory activities. To appeal to both children with physical and cognitive disabilities and their nondisabled peers, she draws on board games, gardens, Polaroid cameras, and puppetry. Her students have performed in a local arts festival, which helps them embrace different cultures and languages. Zavala has also developed school-wide projects to teach her students entrepreneurship, respect, and other important life skills; these projects have included a pickle sale and an indoor plant care service.[4]

Children with diverse backgrounds and special needs are in every program, school, and classroom in the United States. You will teach students with a variety of special needs. They might come from low-income families and various racial and ethnic groups; they might speak very little or no English; they may have exceptional abilities or disabilities. Like Gayle Solis Zavala, you will be challenged to provide for all students an education that is appropriate to their physical, intellectual, linguistic, social, and emotional abilities and to help them achieve their best.

Children with special needs and their families should receive education and services that will help them succeed in school and life. You are a key player in the process of ensuring that they receive such services. The federal government has passed many laws protecting and promoting the rights and needs of children with disabilities. One of the most important federal laws is the Individuals with Disabilities Education Act (IDEA), which was originally enacted in 1975 and was reauthorized by Congress in 2004.

As with many special areas, the field of children with special needs has a unique vocabulary and terminology. The terms defined in Figure 11.1 will help you gain a deeper meaning of and appreciation for your teaching of children and as you collaborate with their families.

THE INDIVIDUALS WITH DISABILITIES EDUCATION ACT (IDEA)

The purpose of IDEA is to ensure that all children with disabilities have available to them a free appropriate public education that emphasizes special education—now often called *exceptional student education*—and related services designed to meet their unique needs; to ensure that the rights of children with disabilities and their parents or guardians are protected; to assist states and localities to provide for the education of all children with disabilities; and to assess and ensure the effectiveness of efforts to educate children with disabilities.[5]

IDEA defines **children with disabilities** as those children with mental retardation, hearing impairments (including deafness), speech or language impairments, visual impairments (including blindness), serious emotional disturbance, orthopedic impairments, autism, developmental delays, traumatic brain injury, other health impairments, or specific learning disabilities; and who, by reason thereof, need special education and related services.[6] Figure 11.2 shows how many children between the ages of six and eleven were served by IDEA in 2007.

About 10 to 12 percent of the nation's children have disabilities.[7] What this means for you is that in your classroom of twenty to twenty-five students you will have at least two to three children with some kind of disability.

FOCUS QUESTIONS

1. What is the Individuals with Disabilities Education Act (IDEA) and why is it important?

2. Who are children with disabilities and how do you teach them?

3. Who are English language learners and how do you teach them?

4. What is multicultural education and how can you infuse multicultural content into your programs and activities?

FIGURE 11.1

Terminology Related to Children with Special Needs

Adaptive education: Modifying programs, environments, curricula, and activities to provide learning experiences that help all students achieve desired education goals.

Children with disabilities: Children who need special education and related services; replaces former terms such as *handicapped.* To avoid labeling children, do not use the reversal of these words (e.g., *disabled children*).

Co-teaching: The process by which a regular classroom professional and a special educator or a person trained in exceptional student education team-teach a group of regular and mainstreamed children in the same classroom.

Disability: A physical or mental impairment that substantially limits one or more major life activities.

Early intervention: Providing services to children and families as early in the child's life as possible to prevent or help with a special need or needs.

English language learners (ELLs): Students with a primary language other than English.

Exceptional student education: The education of children with special needs; is now often used in place of the term *special education.*

Full inclusion: The mainstreaming or inclusion of all children with disabilities into natural environments such as playgrounds, child care centers, preschool, kindergarten, and primary grade classrooms.

Individualized education program (IEP): A written plan for a child with a disability, stating what will be done, how it will be done, and when it will be done.

Individualized family service plan (IFSP): A written plan for providing early intervention services for an infant or toddler and the child's family that is based on the child's strengths and needs. The plan lists outcomes and describes the services and coordination that will get to those outcomes. Family members decide what is written on the plan; they can veto any input from professionals; and the plan can be amended at any time by the family.

Integration: The education of children with disabilities along with typically developing children. This education can occur in mainstream, reverse mainstream, and full-inclusion programs.

Least restrictive environment (LRE): The notion that children with disabilities should be educated with children who have no disabilities, to the greatest extent appropriate. Special classes, separate schooling, or other removal of children with disabilities from the regular educational environment should occur only when the nature or severity of the disability is such that education in regular classes with the use of supplementary aids and services cannot be achieved satisfactorily.

Limited English proficiency (LEP): A term to describe children who have limited English skills.

Mainstreaming: The social and educational integration of children with special needs into the general instructional process, usually in a regular classroom program.

Merged classroom: A classroom that includes—merges—children with special needs and children without special needs and teaches them together in one classroom.

Natural environment: Any environment where it is natural for a child to be—such as home, child care center, preschool, kindergarten, and primary grades.

Response to Intervention (RTI): An approach that seeks to prevent academic failure through early intervention, frequent progress measurement, and increasingly intensive research-based instructional interventions for children who continue to have difficulty.

Reverse mainstreaming: The process by which typically developing children are placed in programs for children with disabilities. In reverse mainstreaming, children with disabilities are in the majority.

Typically developing children: Children who are developing according to and within the boundaries of normal growth and development.

Universal design (UD): The use of teaching strategies and instructional support (technology, etc.) designed to make the curriculum and instructional strategies accessible to each student.

FIGURE 11.2

Number of Children Served by IDEA, 2007

- All disabilities: 2,733,616
- Specific learning disabilities: 851,421
- Speech and language impairments: 989,357
- Mental retardation: 156,659
- Emotional disturbance: 123,156
- Multiple disabilities: 49,494
- Hearing impairments: 32,226
- Orthopedic impairments: 28,255
- Other health impairments: 250,798
- Visual impairments: 12,128
- Autism: 142,984
- Deaf-blindness: 548
- Traumatic brain injury: 7,961
- Development delay: 88,629

Note: Data include children ages six through eleven.

Source: IDEA Data, "Children and Students Served Under IDEA, Part B, in the US and Outlying Areas by Age Group, Year, and Disability Category: Fall 2007, Age Group 6–11"; accessed May 6, 2009, from http://www.ideadata.org/TABLES31ST/AR_1-11.htm.

children with disabilities As defined by IDEA, children who need special education and related services because of mental retardation, hearing impairments, speech or language impairments, serious emotional disturbances, orthopedic impairments, autism, traumatic brain injury, other health impairments, or specific learning disabilities.

zero reject principle A rule under IDEA that prohibits schools from excluding any student with a disability.

IDEA Parts B and C

IDEA applies to infants and toddlers (ages 0 to 3) and students (age 3 through 21). Infants and toddlers have needs unlike those of older children. Therefore, IDEA consists of two parts, each of which is age-specific—Part B and Part C. Part B benefits students who are ages 3 through 21. Part C gives states discretion whether to serve infants and toddlers, and Part C benefits any child under age 3 who needs early intervention services because of developmental delays. Part C also gives each state the option of serving at-risk toddlers. These are children who would be at risk of experiencing a substantial developmental delay if they did not receive early intervention services.

IDEA's Six Principles

IDEA establishes six basic principles to follow as you provide educational and other services to children with special needs:

1. *Zero reject.* IDEA calls for educating all children and rejecting none from receiving an appropriate education. Whereas before IDEA many children were excluded from certain educational programs or were even denied an education, this is not the case today. The **zero reject principle** prohibits schools from excluding any student with a disability.

All early childhood programs should address the individual needs of children with disabilities. How can you use the IEPs to ensure that those needs are being met?

2. *Nondiscriminatory evaluation.* The tests and procedures used to decide whether a child has a disability cannot be culturally or racially discriminatory. Further, if it is determined that a child has a disability, nondiscriminatory evaluation is used to determine the kind of special education and services the student should receive.

3. *Appropriate education.* Instruction and related services need to be individually designed to provide educational benefits in making progress toward meeting the unique needs of each student. Basically, IDEA provides for a **free appropriate public education (FAPE)** for all students between the ages of three and twenty-one. *Appropriate* means that children must receive an education suited to their age, maturity level, condition of disability, past achievements, and parental expectations.

4. *Least restrictive placement/environment.* All students with disabilities have the right to learn in the **least restrictive environment (LRE)**—an environment consistent with their academic, social, and physical needs. Such a setting may or may not be the general classroom, but 96 percent of children with disabilities spend at least part of their school day in general classrooms.[8]

5. *Procedural due process.* IDEA provides schools and parents with ways of resolving their differences by mediation and/or hearings before impartial hearing officers or judges.

6. *Parent and student participation.* IDEA specifies a process of shared decision-making whereby educators, parents, and students collaborate in deciding a student's educational plan.[9]

Figure 11.3 lists the disabilities covered under IDEA. You can be reasonably assured that you will have children with some of these disabilities in your classroom. Make yourself familiar with each of these and consider how you might meet the needs of children with these disabilities.

Federal Funds for IDEA: Guaranteeing a Free and Appropriate Education

As previously mentioned, IDEA mandates a free appropriate public education (FAPE) for all persons between the ages of three and twenty-one. To back this up, IDEA provides federal money to state and local educational agencies.

State and local agencies, however, must agree to comply with the federal law or else they will not receive federal money. One of the facts of public education is that there is a lot of federal money for special services to children, such as the school lunch program, ELL programs, and special/exceptional student education. Some of the exceptional education and related services specified by IDEA are listed in Figure 11.4. When providing services for children with disabilities, it is important for them to receive specific services that will help them learn. This is why IDEA identifies some, but not all, of the services that will help achieve this goal.

Creating an Individualized Education Program

Exceptional student education laws mandate the creation of an **individualized education program (IEP)**, which requires a plan for the individualization of each student's instruction. The IEP is one of the most important documents in the education of children with disabilities. It literally constitutes a contract between the school system, the children, and parents. Writing an IEP and the document itself are the most important parts of compliance with IDEA. When the IEP is prepared as intended by law:

- The student's needs have been carefully assessed.
- A team of professionals and the parents have worked together to design an education plan to best meet the student's needs.
- Goals and objectives are clearly stated so that progress in reaching them can be evaluated.[10]

free appropriate public education (FAPE) The requirement under IDEA that children must receive a free education suited to their age, maturity level, condition of disability, achievements, and parental expectations.

least restrictive environment (LRE) As part of IDEA, the notion that a child with a disability should have the opportunity to be educated with children who are not disabled, to the greatest extent possible.

individualized education program (IEP) As required by IDEA, a written instruction plan for a child with a disability, assessing the child's needs and setting clear goals and objectives so that progress can be evaluated.

FIGURE 11.3

Disabilities Covered Under IDEA

As an early childhood educator, you will have children with special needs in your classroom. The following disabilities qualify children for special education services under IDEA:

1. *Autism:* A developmental disability significantly affecting verbal and nonverbal communication and social interaction, generally evident before age three, that adversely affects educational performance.

2. *Deaf-blindness:* Simultaneous hearing and visual impairment, the combination of which causes such severe communication and other developmental and educational problems that a child cannot be accommodated in special education programs solely for children with deafness or children with blindness.

3. *Deafness:* A hearing impairment so severe that a child is impaired in processing linguistic information through hearing, with or without amplification, which adversely affects educational performance.

4. *Developmental delay:* A delay in one or more of the following: (a) physical development; (b) cognitive development; (c) communication; (d) social or emotional development; or (e) adaptive (behavioral) development.

5. *Emotional disturbance:* A condition exhibiting one or more of the following characteristics over a long period of time and to a marked degree, which adversely affects educational performance: (a) an inability to learn that cannot be explained by intellectual, sensory, or health factors; (b) an inability to build or maintain satisfactory interpersonal relationships with peers and teachers; (c) inappropriate types of behavior or feelings under normal circumstances; (d) a general pervasive mood of unhappiness or depression; or (e) a tendency to develop physical symptoms or fears associated with personal or school problems. The term includes children who have schizophrenia. The term does not include children who are socially maladjusted, unless it is determined that they have an emotional disturbance.

6. *Hearing impairment:* A hearing impairment, whether permanent or fluctuating, which adversely affects a child's educational performance but which is not included under the definition of "deafness."

7. *Mental retardation:* Significantly subaverage general intellectual functioning existing concurrently with deficits in adaptive behavior and manifested during the developmental period, which adversely affects a child's educational performance.

8. *Multiple disabilities:* Simultaneous impairments (such as mental retardation/blindness or mental retardation/orthopedic impairment), the combination of which causes such severe educational problems that the child cannot be accommodated in a special education program solely for one of the impairments.

9. *Orthopedic impairment:* A severe orthopedic impairment that adversely affects a child's educational performance. The term includes impairments caused by a congenital anomaly (e.g., clubfoot, absence of a limb).

10. *Other health impairment:* Having limited strength, vitality, or alertness due to chronic or acute health problems such as a heart condition, attention deficit disorder, rheumatic fever, nephritis, asthma, sickle cell anemia, hemophilia, epilepsy, lead poisoning, leukemia, or diabetes, which adversely affects a child's educational performance. According to the Office of Special Education and Rehabilitative Services' clarification statement of September 16, 1991, eligible children with AIDS may also be classified under this category.

11. *Specific learning disability:* A disorder in one or more of the basic psychological processes involved in understanding or in using language, spoken or written, which may manifest itself in an imperfect ability to listen, think, speak, read, write, spell, or do mathematical calculations. The term includes such conditions as perceptual disabilities, brain injury, minimum brain dysfunction, dyslexia, and developmental aphasia. The term does not include children who have learning problems that are primarily the result of visual, hearing, or motor disabilities, of mental retardation, of emotional disturbance, or of environmental, cultural, or economic disadvantage.

12. *Speech or language impairment:* A communication disorder, such as stuttering, impaired articulation, a language impairment, or a voice impairment, which adversely affects a child's educational performance.

13. *Traumatic brain injury:* An injury to the brain caused by an external physical force, resulting in total or partial functional disability or psychosocial impairment, or both, which adversely affects educational performance. The term does not include brain injuries that are congenital or degenerative, or brain injuries induced by birth trauma.

14. *Visual impairment, including blindness:* A visual impairment that, even with correction, adversely affects a child's educational performance. The term includes both children with partial sight and those with blindness.

Source: Adapted with permission of the National Dissemination Center for Children with Disabilities (NICHCY), "Categories of Disability Under IDEA Law," http:// www.nichcy.org/Disabilities/Categories/Pages/Default.aspx.

FIGURE 11.4

Services Provided by IDEA

The related services apply to Part B and students ages three through twenty-one unless I note that they belong to Part C only and thus only to children ages birth through two.

- *Assistive technology and services:* Acquiring and using devices and services to restore lost capacities or improve impaired capacities (Part C, but also a "special consideration" for Part B students' IEPs)
- *Audiology:* Determining the range, nature, and degree of hearing loss and operating programs for treatment and prevention of hearing loss
- *Counseling services:* Counseling by social workers, psychologists, guidance counselors, or other qualified professionals
- *Early identification:* Identifying a disability as early as possible in a child's life
- *Interpreting services:* Various means for communicating with children who have hearing impairments or who are deaf-blind
- *Family training, counseling, and home visits:* Assisting families to enhance their child's development (Part C only)
- *Health services:* Enabling a child to benefit from other early intervention services (Part C only)
- *Medical services:* Determining a child's medically related disability that results in the child's need for special education and related services
- *Occupational therapy:* Improving, developing, or restoring functions impaired or lost through illness, injury, or deprivation
- *Orientation and mobility services:* Assisting a visually impaired or blind student to get around within various environments
- *Parent counseling and training:* Providing parents with information about child development
- *Physical therapy:* Services by a physical therapist
- *Psychological services:* Administering and interpreting psychological and educational tests and other assessment procedures and managing a program of psychological services, including psychological counseling for children and parents
- *Recreation and therapeutic recreation:* Assessing leisure function, recreation programs in schools and community agencies, and leisure education
- *Rehabilitative counseling services:* Planning for career development, employment, preparation, achieving independence, and integration in the workplace and community
- *School health services:* Attending to educationally related health needs through services provided by a school nurse or other qualified professional
- *Service coordination services:* Assistance and services by a service coordinator to a child and family (Part C only)
- *Social work services in schools:* Preparing a social or developmental history on a child, counseling groups and individuals, and mobilizing school and community resources
- *Speech pathology and speech-language pathology:* Diagnosing specific speech or language impairments and giving guidance regarding those impairments
- *Transportation and related costs:* Providing travel to and from services and schools, travel in and around school buildings, and specialized equipment (e.g., special or adapted buses, lifts, and ramps)
- *Vision services:* Assessing vision in an infant/toddler (Part C only)

Source: Turnbull, A., Turnbull, R., & Wehmeyer, M. L. (2010). *Exceptional Lives: Special Education in Today's Schools,* Sixth Edition. Upper Saddle River, NJ: Pearson Education. Copyright © 2010 by Pearson Education, Inc.

An IEP requires creating learning objectives and basing students' learning plans on their specific needs, disabilities, and preferences, as well as on those of their parents. A collaborative team of regular and special educators creates these objectives. The IEP must specify what will be done for the child, how and when it will be done, and by whom, and this information must be in writing. In developing the IEP, a person trained in diagnosing disabling conditions, such as a school psychologist, must be part of the IEP team, which includes the parent and, when appropriate, the child. An IEP team member may fill more than one of the team positions if properly qualified and designated. For example, the school system representative may also be the person who can interpret the child's evaluation results. As mandated by federal law, certain individuals must be involved in writing a child's Individualized Education Program:

- The parents of the child with a disability
- At least one regular education teacher of the child (if the child is or may be participating in a regular classroom environment)
- At least one special education teacher or at least one special education provider
- A representative of the public agency who is (1) qualified to provide/supervise the provision of special education, (2) knowledgeable about the general curriculum, and (3) knowledgeable about the availability of resources of the public agency
- Transition Services participants, individuals who can help the child and parents transition between home, school, clinics, and programs which provide special services such as speech, hearing, physical, and behavior therapy
- A qualified individual who can interpret implication of the evaluation results
- Other individuals with knowledge or special expertise regarding the child, such as an occupational therapist (OT), speech therapist, tutor, etc.
- When appropriate, the child with a disability[11]

Purposes of the IEP

The IEP has several purposes, including these:

- Protecting children and parents by ensuring that planning of special education services takes place
- Guaranteeing that children will have plans tailored to their individual strengths, needs, and learning styles
- Helping professionals and other instructional and administrative personnel focus their teaching and resources on children's specific needs, and promoting the best use of everyone's time, efforts, and talents
- Ensuring that children with disabilities will receive a range of services from other service-providing agencies by not only including an educational component, but also specifying how the child's total needs will be met
- Helping clarify and refine decisions as to what is best for children, where they should be placed, and how they should be taught and helped
- Ensuring that reviews are conducted at least annually, encouraging professionals to consider how and what children have learned, determining whether what was prescribed is effective, and prescribing new or modified strategies

An example of a completed IEP for a preschooler is shown in Appendix C.

The Individualized Family Service Plan

Infants, toddlers, and their families also have the right to an **individualized family service plan (IFSP)**, which specifies what services they will receive. The IFSP is designed

individualized family service plan (IFSP) As required by IDEA, a plan created for infants and toddlers with disabilities and their families, specifying what services they will receive to help them reach their specific goals.

to help families reach the goals they have for themselves and their children. The IFSP provides for:

- Multidisciplinary assessment developed by a multidisciplinary team and the parents. Planned services must meet developmental needs and can include special education, speech and language pathology and audiology, occupational therapy, physical therapy, psychological services, parent and family training and counseling services, transition services, medical diagnostic services, and health services.
- A statement of the child's present levels of development; a statement of the family's strengths and needs with regard to enhancing the child's development; a statement of major expected outcomes for the child and family; the criteria, procedures, and timeliness for determining progress; the specific early intervention services necessary to meet the unique needs of the child and family; the projected dates for initiation of services; the name of the case manager; and transition procedures from the early intervention program into a preschool program.

Helping parents of children with disabilities is an important role of all early childhood professionals. Administrators can help teachers and parents by:

- Establishing parent resource centers to help parents and teachers develop good working relationships
- Providing basic training to help parents understand special education and the role of the family in cooperative planning as well as offering workshops on topics requested by parents
- Making available up-to-date information and resources for parents and teachers
- Encouraging creation of early childhood and preschool screening programs and other community services that can be centered in the schools

In addition, here are some things you can do as a teacher:

- Make it clear to parents that you accept them as advocates who have an intense desire to make life better for their children.
- Provide parents with information about support groups, special services in the school and the community, and family-to-family groups.
- Offer parents referrals to helpful community groups such as Parents Helping Parents.
- Encourage parents to organize support systems, pairing families who can share experiences with each other during school activities.
- Involve parents in specific projects centered on hobbies or special skills that parents can share with students in one or several classes.
- Discuss a child's special talents with parents and use that positive approach as a bridge to discuss other issues.[12]

Go to the Assignments and Activities section of Topic 11: Special Needs/Inclusion in the MyEducationLab for your course and complete the activity entitled *Understanding Inclusion*. As you watch, consider what an inclusion classroom might have to offer children with disabilities. What kind of message might seclusion practices send to both children with and without disabilities?

Chapter 13 provides you with a comprehensive program for involving and collaborating with parents and families.

A Continuum of Inclusive Services

A continuum of services means that a full range of services is available for children from the most restrictive to the least restrictive placements. This continuum implies a graduated range of services, with one level of services leading directly to the next. For example, a continuum of services for students with disabilities would define institutional placement as the most restrictive and a general education classroom as the least restrictive. There is considerable debate over whether providing such a continuum is an appropriate policy. Advocates of inclusion say that the approach works against developing truly inclusive

Level	Educational Delivery System	Professional Responsibility

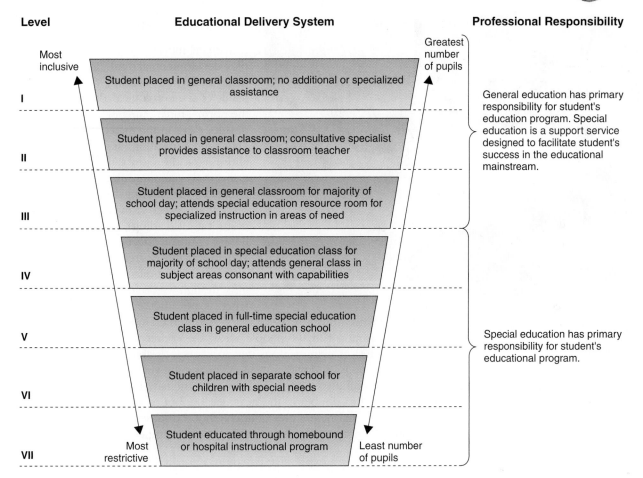

FIGURE 11.5 Educational Service Options for Students with Disabilities

Source: From HARDMAN. *Human Exceptionality, 8e.* © 2006 Wadsworth, a part of Cengage Learning, Inc. Reproduced by permission. www.cengage.com/permissions.

programs in regular education classrooms. Figure 11.5 shows educational options for students with disabilities that range from the most integrated, in which the regular classroom teacher meets most of a child's needs with help and support, to the least integrated, a residential setting providing a therapeutic environment.

Inclusive classrooms offer many benefits for children. They demonstrate increased acceptance and appreciation of diversity, develop better communication and social skills, show greater development in moral and ethical principles, create warm and caring friendships, and demonstrate increased self-esteem.

CHILDREN WITH DISABILITIES

These are exciting times for children with disabilities, their families, and their teachers because today's educational practices make a real difference in the lives of children with disabilities. As a result, life for children with disabilities is remarkably different from what it was only a few years ago. Furthermore, we know tomorrow holds the promise of even more opportunities for accomplishment and fewer barriers. So, in this context of optimism, let's take a closer look at children with disabilities and discuss how you can teach them.

Inclusive classrooms educate students with disabilities in the least restrictive educational environment. What would you say to a parent of a child without a disability who questions the idea of an inclusive classroom?

Children with Autism

Autism, as introduced in Chapter 2, is a complex developmental disability that typically appears during the first three years of life. It is the result of a neurological disorder that affects the normal functioning of the brain, impacting development in the areas of social interaction and communication skills.[13] Children with autism typically show difficulties in verbal and nonverbal communication, social interactions, joint attention (sharing one's experience of observing an object or event by following gaze, gesturing, or leading), and leisure or play activities. Autism affects each child differently and to varying degrees.[14] Autism is currently diagnosed four times more often in boys than girls, though we do not know why.[15] Its prevalence is not affected by race, region, or socioeconomic status. Since autism was first diagnosed in the United States, the occurrence has climbed to an alarming 1 in 150 people across the country.[16]

Autism is the fastest growing serious developmental disability in the United States.[17] More children will be diagnosed with autism in the coming years than children with AIDS, diabetes, and cancer combined. Spectrum delays cost the nation more than $35 billion per year, a figure expected to double in the next decade, but receive less than 5 percent of the research funding of many less prevalent childhood diseases.[18]

Children with autism typically demonstrate the following characteristics:

- Deficits in receptive and expressive communication skills
- Repetitive or "stereotyped" behaviors[19]
- Difficulty initiating and sustaining symbolic play and social interactions[20]
- Limited interests
- Trouble keeping up with conversations[21]

The cause of autism remains unknown. Dr. Christopher Wash, chief of genetics at Children's Hospital Boston, remarks that "Almost every kid with autism has their own particular cause of it."[22] However, evidence points to genetic factors playing a prominent role. Twin and family studies have suggested an underlying genetic vulnerability to autism.[23] Currently genetics can account for about 15 percent of autism cases. Other research suggests that in infancy and toddlerhood brain synapses are pruned in such a way as to "turn on or off" the autism gene, indicating that autism is a synaptic disorder.[24] Still other researchers have found that there may be environmental triggers for autism spectrum disorders.[25] Research into the causes of developmental disorders is ongoing. Regardless of the cause, autism is a prevalent presence in American society and will continue to be.

Autism can be diagnosed as early as 18 months of age, and the earlier children with autism receive intense and consistent intervention, the more likely they are to have positive experiences in school, social, familial, and later, occupational realms.[26] There are many effective interventions for autism. One effective intervention you can apply to children with developmental delays in your classroom is **applied behavior analysis (ABA)**. Applied behavior analysis is the theory that behavior rewarded is more likely to be repeated than behavior ignored. To reinforce behavior, ABA therapists initiate a sequence of stimuli, responses, and rewards. For example, an ABA therapist who is working on joint attention with Hayden, a child with **pervasive developmental disorders (PDD)**, will ask

applied behavior analysis (ABA) The theory that behavior rewarded is more likely to be repeated than behavior ignored.

Hayden to "show me" the red block (stimulus). If Hayden points to the red block (response), the ABA therapist gives him an M&M (reward) or another appropriate reward such as a sticker. If Hayden does not respond or points to a different colored block, the therapist ignores the behavior and repeats the stimulus.

Another effective intervention for children on the PDD spectrum is **play therapy**. Play therapy uses developmentally appropriate practices and models to incorporate social experiences and enjoyable interactions to enhance a child's pretend skills, joint attention, communication skills, and appropriate behavior. Play therapy can take place individually between one child and a therapist, in groups with other children, or can involve the parents in the intervention. Unlike ABA, play therapy is generally child-led.[27] For example, a play therapist working with Kate, who has autism, would use different toys to engage her. Over time, the play therapist would challenge Kate's manner and content of play by initiating different play scenarios and by reflecting Kate's emotions and activities in order to elicit and reward language development, play skills, and relationship development.

Music, art, and occupational therapies are also highly effective interventions for children with autism.[28] Music therapists or art therapists use their respective expressive mediums (musical instruments, singing, painting, clay, etc.) to provide children who have spectrum delays with different means of experiencing relationships, self-expression, and expanding various other skills. These therapies are unique in that they give children with spectrum delays an opportunity to develop skills that have social utility. As a result, children gain in peer interaction, self-esteem, and improve their everyday functioning. Physical and occupational therapists use a more body-centered approach to reach children with developmental delays. By swinging, receiving deep compressions to their body, climbing, and jumping, children's bodies are challenged and made more comfortable, thereby eliciting more language, social reciprocity, and joint attention. These types of therapies can also be done individually, in groups, or with parents to maximize the effects of therapy. For example, an occupational therapist would put Benjamin in a hammock swing and push him in it to stimulate his vestibular needs while engaging him in developmentally appropriate conversation.

Other methods of effective intervention include a highly supportive teaching environment; predictability and routine; family involvement; and working with young children in small teacher-to-child ratios, often one-to-one in the early stages. Recall the example in Chapter 2, describing how teachers can accommodate a child with autism disorder through the creation of a *social story*.

Children with Attention Deficit Hyperactivity Disorder (ADHD)

As you learned in Chapter 3, students with *attention deficit hyperactivity disorder (ADHD)* generally display cognitive delays and have difficulties in three specific areas: attention, impulse control, and hyperactivity. ADHD is usually diagnosed in childhood. Though commonly considered a childhood condition, at least two out of three children with ADHD maintain symptoms such as inattention, impulsivity, and hyperactivity into adulthood.[29] To be classified as having ADHD, a student must display for a minimum of six months before age seven at least six of the characteristics outlined here in at least two different settings:[30]

Inattention

- Often fails to give close attention to details or makes careless mistakes in schoolwork, work, or other activities
- Has difficulty sustaining attention in tasks or play activities
- Does not seem to listen when spoken to directly
- Does not follow through on instructions and fails to finish schoolwork or chores
- Has difficulty organizing tasks and activities

pervasive developmental disorders (PDDs) A category of neurological disorders characterized by severe and pervasive impairment in several areas of development.

play therapy A method that incorporates social experiences and enjoyable interactions into a therapeutic approach to working with children with developmental delays in order to enhance communication skills and other appropriate behavior.

- Avoids, dislikes, or is reluctant to engage in tasks that require sustained mental effort
- Frequently loses things necessary for tasks or activities
- Is often easily distracted by extraneous stimuli[31]

Impulsivity

- Blurts out answers before questions have been completed
- Has difficulty waiting turn
- Interrupts or intrudes on others[32]

Hyperactivity

- Fidgets with hands or feet or squirms in seat
- Frequently leaves seat in classroom or in other situations in which remaining seated is expected
- Often runs about or climbs excessively in situations in which it is inappropriate
- Has difficulty playing or engaging in leisure activities quietly
- Is often "on the go" or acts as if "driven by a motor"
- Talks excessively[33]

There are three types of ADHD: *predominantly inattentive*, in which the child is easily distracted, forgetful, disorganized, and has dificulty beginning or finishing tasks; *predominantly hyperactive-impulsive*, in which the child's difficulties are related to impulsivity, over-activity, rapid movement, and disorganized behavior; and *combined*, a combination of inattentive and hyperactive-impulsive types.[34] Frequently, the term *attention deficit disorder (ADD)* is used to refer to ADHD, but ADD is a form of a learning disorder, whereas ADHD is a behavioral component of that disorder.

ADHD is diagnosed about three times more often in boys than in girls, though they are no more likely to have it, and affects 4 to 12 percent of all students.[35] Boys are more likely to have the hyperactive component, and thus are identified with ADHD more often and more quickly, whereas girls tend to show the symptoms of ADHD in different ways.[36] However, both boys and girls can have any combination of symptoms. Some speculate that the typical hyperactive symptoms of boys disrupt the classroom more, and as a result, teachers are more likely to recommend testing and diagnosis. Hallmark symptoms for boys tend to be impulsivity and inability to sit still or concentrate.[37]

Researchers speculate that because girls are socialized to please parents and teachers, they are more likely to compensate for their ADHD in behavior-appropriate ways.[38] Symptoms for ADHD in girls are nonstop, uncontrollable talking; friendship difficulties; inordinate messiness; and difficulty paying attention, which may sometimes be interpreted as simply "not getting it." Some researchers have found that when these symptoms are identified, teachers tend to see them as evidence of a lack of the girl's academic abilities or intelligence rather than a symptom of a learning and behavior disorder.[39]

Some estimate that as many as 50 to 75 percent of girls who have ADHD are not diagnosed.[40] As a result, girls may not get the help they need. In addition, girls are often diagnosed five years later than boys, at around age twelve in comparison to boys at age seven.[41]

When ADHD and ADD are left untreated, children are more likely than their counterparts who have gotten help for their ADHD/ADD or those who don't have ADHD/ADD to experience lower educational achievement and are less likely to graduate from high school or college.[42] They are also more inclined to have low self-esteem, antisocial thoughts, a pessimistic outlook on their future, and problems with their romantic relationships and jobs.[43] With the right combination of medication and intervention, children with ADHD and ADD have a better chance at a successful academic, personal, and career life.

Interventions for ADHD include various medications such as Adderall, Concerta, Focalin, and Ritalin; and behavior therapy.[44] Each medication affects children differently, and children may need to try different types and at different dosages before a right fit is found. Teachers work with school psychologists and other professionals to help correctly identify children with ADHD. Remember, the primary purpose of identification is to provide appropriate services, instruction, and programs.

Instructional Processes for Teaching Children with Disabilities

Sound teaching strategies work well for all students, including those with disabilities. You must plan how to create inclusive teaching environments for each child. Here are some ideas to help you teach children with disabilities and create inclusive settings that enhance the education of all students.

- Accentuate the positive. One of the most effective strategies is to emphasize what children can do rather than what they cannot do. Children with disabilities have talents and abilities similar to other children, and by exercising your professional knowledge and skills you can help all children reach their full academic potential.

Children learn best when they are involved in hands-on activities. Students can be involved in learning to tell time by making a clock face out of a paper plate.

- Use appropriate assessment, including work samples, cumulative records, and appropriate assessment instruments. Discussions with parents and other professionals who have worked with individual children are sources of valuable information and contribute to making accurate and appropriate plans for children.
- Use concrete examples and materials. Special education students often need a hands-on approach to learning. Manipulatives (counting bears, blocks, counting straws, pictures with moveable pieces, etc.) help special education students by providing concrete and hands-on representations of abstract math concepts. Learning how to tell time and counting money are two concepts in particular that students struggle with but that can be made easier to learn with manipulatives. For example, a paper plate can be made into the face of a clock and fake money can be used to learn the value of each coin.
- Develop and use multisensory approaches to learning. For example, when conducting a lesson on counting, have the children learn simple dance movements for each number and speak them aloud.
- Model what children are to do rather than just telling them what to do. Have a child who has mastered a certain task or behavior model it for others. Ask each child to perform a designated skill or task with supervision. Give corrective feedback.
- Let children practice or perform a certain behavior, involving them in their own assessment of that behavior.
- Make the learning environment a pleasant, rewarding place to be. For example, make the physical setting of the classroom accessible to all students; create clear classroom rules accompanied by pictures; be cautious of too many visual or audio distractions; vary instructional materials and teaching styles; and be sure to reward students for participation, good behavior, and so on.
- Create a dependable classroom schedule. Young children develop a sense of security when daily plans follow a consistent pattern. Allowing for flexibility also is important, however.
- Use **differentiated instruction (DI)**. Differentiated instruction involves providing students with different avenues to acquiring content; to processing, constructing, or making sense of ideas; and to developing teaching products so that all students within a classroom can learn effectively, regardless of differences in ability.[45] You can use different assignments or activities to differentiate instruction. For example, when teaching how to measure, some students are taught basic measuring skills including using a ruler

myeducationlab

Go to the Assignments and Activities section of Topic 11: Special Needs/Inclusion in the MyEducationLab for your course and complete the activity entitled *Modifying and Adapting the Curriculum.* Watch how Mrs. Tucker and her colleagues adapt assessments and teaching to the individual child.

differentiated instruction (DI) Instruction that involves planning and teaching in response to the diverse needs of students, so that all students within a classroom can learn effectively, regardless of differences in ability.

myeducationlab

Go to the Assignments and Activities section of Topic 11: Special Needs/Inclusion in the MyEducationLab for your course and complete the activity entitled *Differentiating Instruction to Meet the Needs of Children.* Read how teachers work together to meet the individual needs of the students in their classrooms.

to measure length. Other students might also measure perimeter. Also, read again the Professionalism in Practice feature, "How to Implement a Guided Reading Program," on pages 284–285 in Chapter 10 for another example of how to differentiate instruction.

- Use multiple means of assessment. For example, don't just use formal assessment tools and screening instruments (i.e., state-mandated standardized testing). Also, use other forms of assessments such as observations, portfolio and work samples, and running records to piece together a more accurate picture of children's abilities, accomplishments, and needs (see Chapter 6 for more about how to assess).

- Identify appropriate tasks children can accomplish on their own to create in them an opportunity to become more independent of you and others.

- Embed instruction. **Embedded instruction** is used to promote child engagement, learning, and independence in everyday activities by identifying times and activities when instructional procedures designed to achieve particular goals are implemented in the context of naturally occurring activities, routines, and transitions in the classroom.[46] For example, many teachers embed instruction in naturally occuring transition activities such as lining up. Kindergarten teacher Jen Sherman might ask her children to line up for lunch alphabetically according to their first names, or she might have them line up according to height—shortest to tallest. When identifying classroom helpers, Sherman might say, "This child's name begins with the same sound as 'candy.'" Kindergarten teacher Lauren Gonzalez embeds mathematics standards in her daily calendar activity.

embedded instruction An approach to teaching that embeds lessons into naturally occurring classroom activities.

The accompanying Technology Tie-In feature provides tips for ensuring that all your students achieve and are successful. Good teaching is good teaching regardless of where you teach. However, you will want and need to make modifications in your program and curriculum to meet the unique needs of children with disabilities. Also, Figure 11.6 outlines a model for how you can teach effectively in your inclusive classroom. As the figure indicates, you will need special kinds of knowledge and skills about students, the curriculum, and working with others. Which knowledge and skills do you possess? Which will you have to make a special effort to acquire?

universal design The process of adapting teaching strategies and technology to make the learning environment, the curriculum, and the instruction methods accessible to each young child, regardless of physical limitations or learning disabilities.

Universal Design. **Universal design** in education describes the adaptation of teaching strategies and technology to make the learning environment, the curriculum, and the instruction processes accessible to each young child—much in the same way that universal design in architecture incorporates curb cuts, automatic doors, ramps, and other accommodations for people with disabilities. Universal design is about ensuring that learning is accessible to all students, and that success and achievement are feasible for students regardless of their differences. Universal design was established in order to integrate a greater number of students with disabilities into general education classroom settings.

Universal design is based on two best practices: (1) instruction is developmentally appropriate, and (2) teaching is based on a constructivist approach to learning. Developmentally appropriate practices and constructivist learning are based on the belief that children need multiple means of engagement and multiple means of expression, as well as practical experiences that support what they have learned.

For example, when teachers teach oral language and conversation skills, they use different modes of presenting the material and provide positive reinforcement. Teachers might record children's thoughts and ideas via written language, audio, or video in order to provide alternate ways for children to interact with the material. If the teacher is focusing on written language writing, she would embed writing into a variety of activities across the curriculum accept all students' attempts, and remain sensitive to the physical demands of writing that may be difficult for some students. She would also provide computers and other electronic devices to promote alternate routes to written expressive language.

When it comes to universal design, flexibility is the key. For example, in a lesson on whole numbers and comparing number values according to Indiana's Grade 1 Mathematics

Using Assistive Technology (AT) to Help Children with Disabilities Learn to Read

IDEA defines assistive technology (AT) as "any item, piece of equipment, or product system, whether acquired commercially off the shelf, modified, or customized, that is used to increase, maintain, or improve functional capabilities of individuals with disabilities."

Assistive technology covers a wide range of products and applications, from battery-operated toys to computer-assisted instruction. Assistive technology should be included as an important tool in your work with children with special needs.

One of your students with special needs may have trouble holding a pencil. Putting a pencil grip on her pencil makes it easier for her to hold it. The pencil grip is an example of low-tech assistive technology.

Dictionary skills are an important part of language and literacy. If a student has trouble holding and handling a dictionary, an assistive technology solution would be to use an electronic dictionary on the Internet, which also has voice pronunciation.

As this textbook has stressed, literacy development and learning to read are given a high priority in all early childhood grades, from pre-K to grade three. Children with special needs can learn to read with the help of assistive technology. Here are some software programs that can help you achieve this goal.

PHONEMIC AWARENESS/EMERGENT LITERACY SKILLS

Earobics-Cognitive Concepts

Sesame Street Elmo's Reading: Preschool & Kindergarten, The Learning Company

First Phonics, SUNBURST

Daisy Quest, McGraw-Hill Children's Publishing/Teachers Paradise

PHONOLOGICAL DECODING

Curious George Learns Phonics, Houghton Mifflin Interactive

Let's Go Read: 1 & 2, Riverdeep & Edmark

Jumpstart Phonics, Knowledge Adventure

Sound It Out Land: A Musical Adventure in Phonics and Reading, Learning Upgrade LLC

READING COMPREHENSION

Reader Rabbit Learn to Read with Phonics, The Learning Company

Reading Blaster, Knowledge Adventure

Arthur's Reading Games, The Learning Company

Reading Readiness 1, School Zone

TALKING STORYBOOKS

Discis Books, Harmony Interactive

Disney's Animated Storybooks, Disney Interactive

Interactive Storybooks, Encore Software

Source: "Assistive Technology Device," U.S. Department of Education, Building the Legacy: IDEA 2004, Title I/A/602/1, 2004; accessed May 5, 2009, from http://idea.ed.gov/explore/view/p/%2Croot%2Cstatute%2CI%2CA%2C602%2C1%2C.

academic standards, the teacher would present numbers and value comparison using multiple media, such as oral directions, charts or diagrams, storybooks, blocks, or even cooking activities.[47] The idea is to reach each child at the level he or she understands best. The teacher may introduce the concept of value comparison through graphs and group discussion one day, and then use a cooking experiment to demonstrate the concept practically ("Which is more: two cups of flour, or three cups of water?"), while encouraging groups of students to write their own stories featuring number value concepts the next day.

Response to Intervention/Response to Instruction (RTI). Response to Intervention/Response to Instruction is a multi-tier instructional approach to the early identification and support of students with learning and behavior needs. It is the opposite of the "wait to fail" approach. RTI seeks to prevent academic failure through early intervention, frequent assessment, and increasingly intense instructional processes for children who continue to have difficulty. The RTI process begins with high-quality instruction and universal, ongoing assessment of all children in the general education classroom.

Response to Intervention/Response to Instruction (RTI) A multi-tier approach to the early identification and support of students with learning and behavior needs; it evaluates assessment data and employs differentiated instruction, so that students who are struggling can receive more intense intervention.

KNOWLEDGE OF STUDENTS AND THEIR NEEDS

- Learn characteristics of each student with special needs.
- Learn legislation regarding students with special needs.
- Develop a willingness to teach students with special needs.
- Foster social acceptance of all students with special needs.
- Use assistive and educational technologies.

CLASSROOM LEADERSHIP AND CLASSROOM MANAGEMENT SKILLS

- Plan and manage the learning environment to accommodate students with special needs (see for discussion of universal design).
- Provide inclusion in varied student groupings and use peer tutoring.
- Manage the behavior of all students.
- Motivate each student.

KNOWLEDGE AND SKILLS IN CURRICULUM AND INSTRUCTION

- Develop and modify instruction for students with special needs.
- Use a variety of instructional styles and media and increase the range of learning behaviors.
- Provide instruction for students of all ability levels.
- Modify assessment techniques for students with special needs.
- Individualize instruction and integrate the curriculum.

PROFESSIONAL COLLABORATION SKILLS

- Work closely with special educators and other specialists such as physical therapists, speech therapists, occupational therapists, and behavior intervention specialists.
- Work with and involve parents.
- Participate in planning and implementing IEPs.

FIGURE 11.6 Effective Teaching in Inclusive Classrooms

Tiered classroom instruction (see Figure 11.7) is high quality and relies on scientifically based programs. Under No Child Left Behind, teachers must use curriculum and instructional methods that are based on research to ensure children's academic success (see Chapter 5). Throughout the instruction, students are assessed for their learning and level of achievement. The data from these assessments are then used when determining which students need closer monitoring or intervention. Decisions regarding students' instructional needs are based on multiple assessment data taken over time. Students who are struggling receive services provided by a variety of personnel, including general education teachers, special educators, and specialists. Educational decisions about the intensity and duration of interventions for struggling students are based on individual students' responses to instruction.

RTI works by efficiently differentiating instruction for all students at their developmental level. Students who are responsive to the initial high-quality instruction continue to be taught in the manner that is effective for them, while students who have difficulty for a variety of reasons are engaged in increasingly smaller groups with increasingly need-oriented instruction until they succeed. RTI is successful because it incorporates increasing

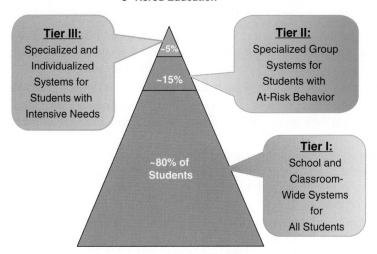

FIGURE 11.7 3-Tiered Education

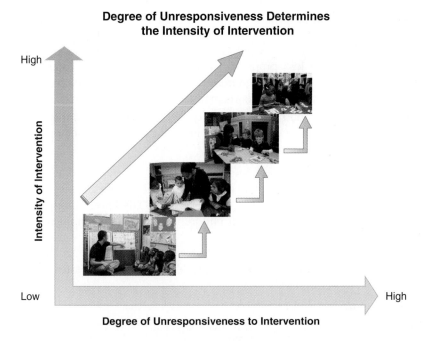

FIGURE 11.8 Degree of Unresponsiveness Determines the Intensity of Intervention

intensities of instruction based on research-based interventions that match the individual needs of the students, as shown in Figures 11.7 and 11.8.

TEACHING ENGLISH LANGUAGE LEARNERS (ELLs)

The United States is experiencing a rapid increase in immigration, and by 2015 the Census Bureau estimates that immigrant children will account for 30 percent of the school-age population.[48] If you are working in Arizona, California, Nevada, Texas, New York, or

New Jersey—the states that currently have the greatest immigrant representation—you will teach students from immigrant families.[49] Some of the difficulties immigrant families face are:

- Nine out of ten children of immigrants are citizens, but 81 percent of children of immigrants under age six have a noncitizen parent while 29 percent have an undocumented parent, which contributes to family instability and fear.[50]
- One in every five children in immigrant families have difficulty speaking English.[51]
- Twenty-seven percent of immigrant children live in linguistically isolated homes. This means that in their homes, they are the only ones under the age of fourteen who know English.[52]
- Depending on their immigration status, children of immigrants are largely uninsured (between 25 and 59 percent). This contributes to the health disparities between immigrant and native-born children—7 percent of immigrant children are reported to be in poor or fair health compared to only 3 percent of native-born children.[53]
- Fifty-six percent of young children of immigrants live in impoverished or low-income families.[54] Though the majority of immigrant parents work one or more full-time jobs, these jobs often don't provide adequate income for their family.[55] However, even in legal families, fear or lack of knowledge keeps many immigrants from accessing federally provided help.[56]
- Twenty-six percent of immigrant children's parents do not have a high school diploma or equivalent. Thirteen percent of immigrant children's parents do not have the equivalent of a ninth grade education.[57] This means that immigrant children will not get as much help with school or homework activities as native-born children; and children of immigrants may be less prepared than their counterparts to start kindergarten. Three- and four-year-old children in immigrant families are less likely to participate in nursery school or preschool programs than their peers.[58]
- Spanish is second only to English as the most spoken language in the United States.[59] Spanish speakers often face discrimination in public and private sectors for not knowing English.

Supporting English Language Learners.   José is a bright and energetic second grader. He excels in math, enjoys playing soccer, and collects baseball cards. He struggles with English as his second language. He and his family immigrated only six months ago. José is one of 15.7 million children of immigrant families in the United States.[60]

As José's teacher, you will want to provide him with the knowledge and experiences necessary so he can be successful in school and life in the United States. Here are some steps you can take to help Elián:

- Play to José's strengths and interests.
  - José is good at math, so appeal to his analytical nature by providing reading material that is factual and observable. Magazines for children—like *Kids Discover*, *Muse*, and *Yes Mag*—are rich in graphs, tables, and photos and provide information José will find interesting.
  - José is interested in soccer, so provide stories and books about soccer to enrich his English-speaking and reading skills.
  - Help José organize soccer games during recess. Encourage him to take a leadership role, like team captain, and to teach others how to play. A leadership role and helping others will increase his acceptance into the classroom and will allow José to make friendships more easily.
- Make sure José understands you. After giving directions to the entire class, ask José quietly if he understands the directions and if he needs you to repeat anything more slowly or in more detail.

Go to the Assignments and Activities section of Topic 10: Cultural & Linguistic Diversity in the MyEducationLab for your course and complete the activity entitled *Strategies for Teaching Diverse Learners.* Pay particular attention to how flexible the teachers are in their teaching strategies.

- Make sure your body language conveys to José that you accept him as a person and learner. When José feels accepted and welcomed by you, he is more likely to come to you for help rather than not seeking help at all.

- Initiate a buddy system. Assign a classmate to José to run interference in language and cultural differences. This buddy will be a mentor to José when he needs it. A buddy system increases familiarity and encourages José's acceptance into your classroom.

- Accommodate cultural differences.
  - Be knowledgeable of José's culture. Do a little research. Familiarize yourself with cultural norms so that you can appropriately respond to José. For example, certain symbols in certain cultures may mean different things. While you may use it to signal acceptance or a job well done, José may take it as an insult.

- Incorporate Spanish (or another language) into your classroom. Doing so helps lay the foundation for language learning. For example, when introducing new vocabulary words, ask José for a translation in Spanish. The role of translator will give José a position of worth and knowledge in the classroom and will enhance his self-esteem.

- Encourage José to speak English when appropriate, but allow him to communicate with others freely in either Spanish or English.

- Have a "Spanish Hour" once a week in which José reads a book in Spanish to the class. The class can translate the story into English. This process encourages cultural discussions, acceptance, sharing, and language skills.

MULTICULTURAL EDUCATION

bilingual education
Education in two languages (for example, the student's native language and English).

The population of the United States is changing and will continue to change. For example, projections are that by 2050, over one-fifth of the population will be Hispanic.[61]

The population of young children in the United States reflects the population at large and represents a number of different cultures and ethnicities. Thus, many cities and school districts have populations that express great ethnic diversity, including Asian Americans, Native Americans, African Americans, and Hispanic Americans. For example, the Dade County, Florida, school district has children from 172 countries, each with its own culture.[62] Table 11.1 shows the proportion of minority students in the nation's ten largest school districts. As a result of changing demographics, more students will require special education, **bilingual education** (being taught in both their native language and in English), and other special services. Issues of culture and diversity will shape instruction and curriculum. These demographics also have tremendous implications for how you teach and how your children learn.

Multicultural Awareness

As we discussed in Chapter 2, *multicultural awareness* is the appreciation for and understanding of people's cultures, socioeconomic status, and gender and includes understanding one's own culture. Multicultural awareness programs and activities focus on other cultures while making children aware of the content, nature, and richness of their own. The terms and concepts related to multicultural education are shown in Figure 11.9.

Early childhood educators must consider the diverse needs of students—including gender, ethnicity, race, and socioeconomic factors—when planning learning opportunities for their classes.

TABLE 11.1 Proportion of Minority Students in the Ten Largest Public School Districts in the United States

Name of Reporting School District (in order of size of student enrollment)	State	Percentage of Minority Students
New York City Public	NY	85.8
Los Angeles Unified	CA	91.2
City of Chicago	IL	91.7
Dade County	FL	90.2
Clark County	NV	60.5
Broward County	FL	66.6
Houston Independent	TX	91.5
Hillsborough County	FL	53.5
Philadelphia City	PA	86.7
Hawaii Department of Education	HI	80.1

Source: U.S. Department of Education, National Center for Education Statistics, "Characteristics of the 100 Largest Public Elementary and Secondary School Districts in the United States: 2005–06," http://nces.ed.gov/pubs2008/100_largest_0506/tables/table_a09.asp#f3.

FIGURE 11.9

Terminology Related to Multicultural Education

The following terms will assist you as you provide bias-free and multiculturally appropriate education for your children and their families.

bias-free: Curriculum, programs, materials, language, attitudes, actions, and activities that are free from biased perceptions.

bilingual education: Education in two languages. Generally, two languages are used for the purpose of academic instruction.

cultural diversity: The diversity between and within ethnic groups. The extent of group identification by members of ethnic groups varies greatly and is influenced by many factors such as skin color, social class, and professional experience.

cultural pluralism: The belief that cultural diversity is of positive value.

culturally fair education: Education that respects and accounts for the cultural backgrounds of all learners.

diversity: The relationships among background, socioeconomic status, gender, language, and culture of students, parents, and communities.

dual language: Two-way or developmental programs that allow students to develop proficiency in two languages by receiving instruction in English and another language in a classroom that is usually comprised of half native English speakers and half speakers of another language.

dual language learners: Children who acquire two or more languages simultaneously, as well as learn a second language while continuing to develop their first language. The term "dual language learners" encompasses other terms frequently used, such as Limited English Proficient (LEP), bilingual, English language learners (ELL), English learners, and children who speak a language other than English (LOTE).

English as a second language (ESL): Instruction in which students with limited English proficiency attend a special English class.

infusion: The process of having multiculturalism become an explicit part of the curriculum throughout all the content areas.

multicultural awareness: Ability to perceive and acknowledge cultural differences among people without making value judgments about these differences.

multiculturalism: An approach to education based on the premise that all peoples in the United States should receive proportional attention in the curriculum.

Knowing the terminology of the profession is important. Review these terms, become familiar with them, and use them appropriately. Learning about other cultures concurrently with their own culture enables children to integrate commonalities and appreciate differences without inferring the inferiority or superiority of one or the other.

Promoting multiculturalism in an early childhood program has implications far beyond your school, classroom, and program. Multiculturalism influences and affects work habits, interpersonal relations, and a child's general outlook on life. You must take these multicultural influences into consideration when designing curriculum and instructional processes for the children you will teach.

Being a multiculturally aware teacher means you are sensitive to the socioeconomic backgrounds of children and families. For example, we know that children that come from families with low socioeconomic status will learn less.[63] The same is true with children's school achievement and maternal education, as the accompanying Diversity Tie-In feature illustrates. By learning about family background you can provide children from diverse backgrounds the extra help they may need to be successful in school.

Use Appropriate Instructional Materials. Carefully consider and select appropriate instructional materials to support the infusion of multicultural education. The following are some suggestions for achieving this goal.

Multicultural Literature. Choose literature that stresses similarities and differences regarding how children and families live their *whole lives*. Here are some examples of good books you can use with your children:

- *Princesas: Olvidadas o desconocidas* (*Princesses: Forgotten or Unknown*) by Philippe Lechermeier and Rebecca Dautremer: A story of unique princesses that all have their own positive and negative attributes.
- *El mejor mariachi del mundo* (*The Best Mariachi in the World*) by J. D. Smith: A tale about finding one's own talent.
- *Teo en la nieve* (*Teo in the Snow*) by Violeta Denou: A story about Teo and his friends who go on a winter excursion in the mountains and do not always make safe choices in the pursuit of having fun.
- *León y Beto* (*Leon and Bob*) by Simon James: A story about a boy whose father is away in the army and his imaginary friend who is his confidant and playmate.
- *¡Ay, No!* (*Oh, No!*) by Rotraut Susanne Berner: A story about a hen who complains about everything, her friend who has a solution to every complaint, and their discovery that things are not always black and white.

Themes. Early childhood teachers often select and teach with thematic units that help strengthen children's understanding of themselves, their culture, and the cultures of others. Some appropriate theme topics are:

- Getting to Know Myself, Getting to Know Others
- What Is Special About You and Me?
- Growing Up in the City

All classrooms must be places where people of both genders and all cultures, races, socioeconomic backgrounds, and religions are welcomed and accepted. If students learn to embrace diversity within the classroom, they will also embrace diversity outside of it.

myeducationlab

Go to the Assignments and Activities section of Topic 10: Cultural & Linguistic Diversity in the MyEducationLab for your course and complete the activity entitled *Incorporating Children's Culture within Teaching Practices*. Note how teachers are providing for diversity in their classrooms by respecting children's culture. What are possible consequences of teaching without concern for an individual's culture?

Race, Socioeconomic Status, and Student Achievement

Socioeconomic status (SES), the social and economic back- grounds of children, is a reflection of family income, maternal education level, and family occupation. You may be surprised by the inclusion of maternal education level in this list, but in fact it is a powerful predictor of how well students do in school. As a mother's education increases, so does student achievement. This helps explain why, from a social and educational policy perspec- tive, a U.S. priority is to prevent teenage mothers, indeed all girls, from dropping out of school.

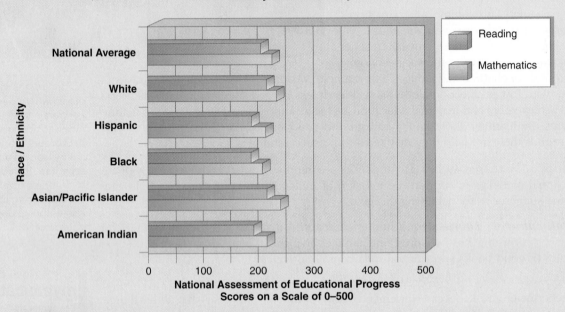

Reading and Mathematics Achievement Scores by Race/Ethnicity

National Center for Education Statistics, National Assessment of Educational Progress (NAEP), NAEP Data Explorer, "Reading Grade 4" and "Mathematics Grade 4," 2007, accessed May 10, 2009, from http://nces.ed.gov/ nationsreportcard/naepdata/dataset.aspx.

- Growing Up in the Country
- Tell Me About Africa (South America, China, etc.)

All of these themes are appropriate for meeting various state standards and standards of the National Council for the Social Studies (NCSS).

Personal Accomplishments. Add to classroom activities, as appropriate, the accomplishments of people from different cultural groups, women of all cultures, and individuals with disabilities.

When selecting materials for use in a multicultural curriculum for early childhood pro- grams, make sure:

- People of all cultures are represented fairly and accurately.
- To represent people of color, many cultural groups, and people with exceptionalities.

Sadly, as the accompanying graph "Reading and Mathematics Achievement Scores by Race/Ethnicity" shows, there is a correlation between school achievement and students' race/ethnicity. Minority students tend to have lower reading and mathematics achievement scores than do their nonminority peers. Whether this is due to testing bias, cultural bias, or other sociocultural factors, we do not know, but the fact remains that we must do serious educational work to increase minority children's achievement scores.

Family income also correlates with how well students do in school, whether or not they drop out, the kind and type of schools they attend, and the quality of their teachers. Students' socioeconomic status is used to determine eligibility for many state and federal programs such as Head Start and Title I programs. One Head Start eligibility criterion, for example, is that the child's family meets federal poverty income criteria for enrollment, and many schools provide free or reduced school lunches based on family income. As the graph "Reading and Mathematics Scores by Percent of Students Eligible for National School Lunch Program" shows, as with race, there is also a correlation between children's family income and their achievement scores.

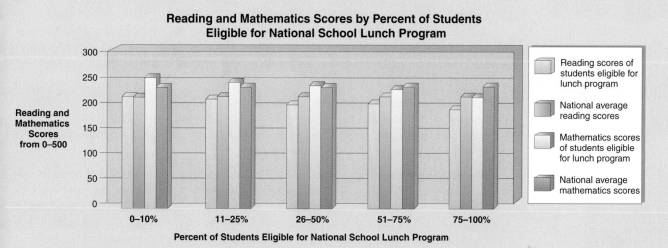

National Center for Education Statistics, National Assessment of Educational Progress (NAEP), NAEP Data Explorer, "Reading Grade 4" and "Mathematics Grade 4," 2007, accessed May 10, 2009, from http://nces.ed.gov/nationsreportcard/naepdata/dataset.aspx.

- Historical information is accurate and nondiscriminatory.
- Materials do not include stereotypical roles and language.
- There is gender equity—that is, boys and girls are represented equally and in nonstereotypic roles.

Teach to Children's Learning Styles and Intelligences.   Every child has a unique learning style. Although every person's learning style is different, we can cluster learning styles for instructional purposes.

Different Children, Different Learning Styles.   It makes sense to consider students' various learning styles and account for these differences when organizing the environment and developing activities: "Learning style is the way that students of every age are affected by their (1) immediate environment, (2) own emotionality, (3) sociological

learning style The way a child learns—specifically, how the child's environment, emotions, sociological needs, physical characteristics, and psychological inclinations come into play as he or she works to master new or difficult information or skills.

needs, (4) physical characteristics, and (5) psychological inclinations when concentrating and trying to master and remember new or difficult information or skills."[64]

Learning styles consist of the following elements:

- Environmental—sound, light, temperature, and design
- Emotional—motivation, persistence, responsibility, and the need for either structure or choice
- Sociological—learning alone, with others, or in a variety of ways (perhaps including media)
- Physical—perceptual strengths, intake, day or night energy levels, and mobility
- Psychological—global/analytic, hemispheric preference, and impulsive/reflective

Teaching to children's learning styles is a good way to infuse multiculturalism into your program.[65] Also, review now our discussion of Gardner's multiple intelligence theory in Chapter 3.

The accompanying Professionalism in Practice feature describes how a 2009 National Teacher of the Year, Gayle Solis Zavala, brings her classroom of children with disabilities and general education children together and enriches the education and development of both.

Promote Family and Community Involvement. You will work with children and families of diverse cultural backgrounds. As such you will need to learn about the cultural background of children and families so that you can respond appropriately to their needs. For example, let's take a brief look at the Hispanic and Asian cultures and their implications for parent and family involvement.

The Hispanic Culture. Throughout Hispanic culture is a widespread belief in the absolute authority of the school and teachers. In many Latin American countries it is considered rude for a parent to intrude into the life of the school. Parents believe that it is the school's job to educate and the parent's job to nurture, and that the two jobs do not mix. A child who is well educated is one who has learned moral and ethical behavior.

Hispanics, as a whole, have strong family ties, believe in family loyalty, and have a collective orientation that supports community life. They have personalized styles of interaction, a relaxed sense of time, and a need for an informal atmosphere for communication. Given these preferences, a culture clash may result when Hispanic students and parents are confronted with the typical task-oriented style of most American teachers.

Whereas an understanding of the general cultural characteristics of Hispanics is helpful, it is important not to overgeneralize. Each family and child is unique, and care should be taken not to assume values and beliefs just because a family speaks Spanish and is from Latin America. It is important that you spend the time to discover the particular values, beliefs, and practices of the families in the community.

The Asian Culture. In addition to having Hispanic children in your classroom or program, chances are you will also have children from one of the many Asian American family subgroups. Asian Americans now represent one of the fastest growing minority populations in the United States.

It is always risky to generalize about peoples and their cultures. When we do make generalizations about ethnic groups that compromise the domain of Asian Americans, we run the risk of assuming that the generalization applies to all groups. It may not. In addition, we always have to consider individual children and families, regardless of their cultural background. With this in mind, some broad generalizations about Asian Americans and values that influence the rearing and education of children include the following: a group orientation as opposed to an individual orientation, the importance of family and family responsibilities, emphasis on self-control and personal discipline, educational achievement, respect for authority, and reverence for the elderly.[66]

Kids with Special Needs Need Extra Special Touch

Gayle Solis Zavala
2009 CEC Teacher of the Year

STEP 1 PROVIDE A WARM WELCOME

I want to emphasize the importance of the "warm welcome" each day. A handshake or friendly pat on the back is a personal gesture that lets the students know they are important and you are glad to see them.

STEP 2 SUPPORT INDEPENDENCE

Call this first day of school—Independence Day. Students with disabilities just as students without disabilities find themselves facing this day with many of the same feelings and anxieties. Students with disabilities however, especially students with English as a second language, may oftentimes have little or no way to communicate their needs or feelings. They may walk or dash away or squat down refusing to move in fear of what is waiting ahead. In the cafeteria it's like entering another world altogether, where once again they will be asked to wait in a line, but this time there are choices to make, a cashier to greet, a table that stretches for miles to sit at, and food wrapped in plastic bags and cartons to figure out how to open.

The waiting in line part is something even as adults we will have to learn to do the rest of our lives and hopefully without bothering the person in front of us. The choices for breakfast, and later for lunch, are eventually communicated by the students in a way that begins to give them independence and a communicative voice (i.e., pointing, verbalizing part or all of a word, sign language, or picture communication board). The same will be expected of the students as they encounter the cashier or other friendly staff. Cafeteria staff give students PIN numbers to use whenever they get breakfast or lunch. Students carry their numbers with them to key in on what looks like a debit card machine. The seasoned teacher will consult with the cafeteria staff ahead of time to gain support and their patience in the importance of allowing the students to use this functional and practical opportunity to learn numbers and add another important independent skill. For those students in which cognitive and/or physical limitation is a challenge, a communication board or simple one-message voice output device could be used to convey any needed communicative message.

STEP 3 SCAFFOLD

Scaffolding as a teaching strategy is needed when orienting and teaching students with disabilities during the early childhood years. As students are learning to sign, verbalize, and select what they want to say on their picture boards, the teacher or staff may need to model or provide assistance to help a student learn a more independent response. Continuing on with the cafeteria scenario, the adult's first reaction may be to open up a student's juice carton or wipe a soiled mouth or clothing. But, if the students are to learn to take care of themselves, they need to repeatedly practice these self-help skills. The reward is evident as the students finally open their own cartons and wave their hands in the air with delight and look to their teacher for praise.

STEP 4 PRAISE

You will find that praise is one of the biggest teaching tools in managing behavior:

"I like the way Jesus is staying in line. Great job, Jesus!"
"I like the way Ashley is keeping her hands to herself (gesturing with folded arms or hands in pocket)."
"Look how nice Antwan said 'Thank you' to Ms. Vargas. Nice words, Antwan."

STEP 5 DEVELOP A SOCIAL CONTRACT

The students are always watching to see what gets teachers' and staff's attentions. It is always more beneficial to voice positive praise, especially with the most challenging students.

Once the first day of school gets going, establishing a written social contract (pictures can be added to cue understanding) between the students and the teaching staff is essential. Even if students are nonverbal or have limited communication skills, teachers can model appropriate choices on positive social interaction, use picture prompts, or capture the targeted behavior when it happens to add to the social contract. Allowing students to participate in creating the social contract is another example of giving them independence and self advocacy. Some of the social contract behaviors could be:

- Listen quietly to one another.
- Use nice words with each other.
- Establish eye contact.
- Enjoy humor (have fun), but not hurtful (don't make fun of one another).

A social contract is also an important opportunity to emphasize to paraprofessionals, volunteers, or other classroom personnel how the climate of the classroom should be. Everyone signs the contract and we review it at least once a day to maintain its importance.

Establishing independence, opportunities to communicate, and a safe, nurturing climate is a recipe for success with all children.

PEARSON
myeducationlab

Go to the Building Teaching Skills and Dispositions section in Topic 11: Special Needs/Inclusion of the MyEducationLab for your course and complete the activity entitled *Making Accommodations to Support Inclusive Practices.*

THE CHALLENGE FOR TEACHERS

Educating students with diverse backgrounds and special needs makes for a challenging and rewarding career. As society, families, and children change, as diversity increases, and as more students with special needs come to school, you will have to change how and what you teach. How to constantly improve your responses to students' special needs and improve learning environments and curricula will be one of your ongoing professional responsibilities. Your students with special needs are waiting for you to make a difference in their lives!

ACTIVITIES FOR PROFESSIONAL DEVELOPMENT

ethical dilemma

"We Shouldn't Cater to Them!"

Beth has just been hired to teach first grade in River Bend School District, which has had an influx of minority students during the past few years. The minority students are almost the majority. Not everyone thinks that the rapid increase in the minority student population is beneficial to the school district or town. Some of Beth's colleagues think that the school district is bending over (too far) backward to meet minority students' needs. At Beth's first meeting with Harry Fortune, her new mentor teacher, he remarked, "Respecting minorities and catering to them are two different things. I'm going to stress with my parents that this is America and American culture comes first, and that includes speaking English!"

What should Beth do? Should she agree with her mentor teacher, adopt a policy of English first, or should she seek out the director of multiculturalism for her school district and discuss Harry's comments with her, or should she pursue another course of action?

PEARSON
myeducationlab

To check your comprehension on the content covered in Chapter 11, go to the Book Specific Resources in the MyEducationLab for your course, select your text, and complete the Study Plan. Here you will be able to take a chapter quiz and receive feedback on your answers.

Application Activities

1. Visit a classroom or program where children with special needs are included, and observe the children during play activities. You can develop an observational checklist based on guidelines provided in Chapter 6. Follow a particular child and note the materials available, the physical arrangement of the environment, and the number of other children involved. Try to determine whether the child is really engaged in the play activity. Hypothesize about why the child is or is not engaged. Discuss your observations with your colleagues.

2. As we have discussed in the chapter, the number of children diagnosed with autism is growing rapidly. There is a lot of public interest in autism, its causes, treatments, and especially how to educate children with autism.

   a. Search the Internet for the latest developments regarding autism diagnosis. What are the latest developments in terms of diagnosing children with autism?

   b. Many parents believe that thimerosal, the preservative used in children's immunizations, is a leading cause of autism. Again, search the Internet for research that substantiates or refutes this claim.

3. In your textbook we talked about applied behavior analysis (ABA) as one means of educating children with autism. Go to YouTube.com and observe teachers implementing ABA approaches in their classrooms. What are two conclusions you can draw from watching these YouTube videos?

4. How does a teacher modify the classroom environment, classroom routines, learning activities, student groupings, teaching strategies, instructional materials, assessments, and homework assignments to meet all students' special needs? What human and material resources

for successful inclusion are available to teachers and to students with special needs? How do students show social acceptance of their classmates with special needs? Go online and search for tips on how to include children with disabilities in the regular classroom. Make a "Top Ten" list of things to do.

5. Effective educational programs provide children with opportunities to develop an understanding of other persons and cultures. List ways for how you would accomplish the following objectives in your classroom:

   a. Provide children with firsthand, positive experiences with different cultural groups.
   b. Help children reflect on and think about their own cultural group identity.
   c. Help children learn how to obtain accurate information about other cultural groups.

6. Select ten children's books that have multicultural content. Decide how you would use these materials to promote awareness and acceptance of diversity. Read these books to children and get their reactions.

chapter twelve

GUIDING CHILDREN'S BEHAVIOR

Helping Children Act Their Best

• • • • • • • •

NAEYC Standards for Early Childhood Professional Preparation Programs

Standard 1: Promoting Child Development and Learning

I use my understanding of young children's characteristics and needs, and of multiple interacting influences on children's development and learning, to create environments that are healthy, respectful, supportive, and challenging for each child.[1]

Standard 4. Using Developmentally Effective Approaches to Connect with Children and Families

I understand and use positive relationships and supportive interactions as the foundation for my work with young children and families. I know, understand, and use a wide array of developmentally appropriate approaches, instructional strategies, and tools to connect with children and families and positively influence each child's development and learning.[2]

WHY GUIDE CHILDREN'S BEHAVIOR?

Think for a moment of the early childhood classes you have observed. In some of the classes children were actively involved in meaningful activities based on state and district standards. In other classrooms, the children and teachers seemed disorganized with little real learning occurring. What makes the difference? Three things: a community of learners, a well organized classroom, and a well-thought-out and implemented plan for guiding children's behavior and learning.

As an early childhood professional, you will assume major responsibility for guiding children's behavior in up-close and personal ways. You will spend many hours with young children as a parent/family surrogate. As a result, you need to know how to best guide children's behavior and help them become responsible. There are a number of reasons for knowing how to best guide children's behavior:

- Helping children learn to guide and be responsible for their own behavior is as important as helping them learn to read and write. Think for a moment about how many times you have said or have heard others say, "If only the children would behave, I could teach them something!" Appropriate behavior and learning go together. One of your primary roles as an early childhood teacher is to help children learn the behaviors and skills that will help them act responsibly.

- Helping children learn to act responsibly and guiding their behavior will lay the foundation for lifelong responsible and productive living. As early childhood educators, we believe that the early years are the formative years. Consequently, what we teach children about responsible living, how we guide them, and the skills we help them learn will last a lifetime.

- The roots of delinquent and deviant behavior are in the early years. From research we know which behaviors lead to future problems. For example, research shows that children who rebound between home and school with an aggressive attitude toward their peers and teachers and a tendency to cause disruption are more likely to suffer a range of negative outcomes as adults. They are at greater risk of failing school, becoming addicted to drugs, engaging in antisocial behavior, and succumbing to depression or anxiety.[3]

- The public is increasingly concerned about the erosion of civility, and what it perceives as a general breakdown of personal responsibility for bad behavior. One reason the public funds the public educational system at all levels is to help keep society strong and healthy. Parents and the public look to early childhood professionals for assistance in helping children learn to live cooperatively and civilly in a democratic society. Getting along with others and guiding one's behavior is a culturally and socially meaningful accomplishment.

What Is Guiding Behavior?

Guiding children's behavior is a process of helping build positive behaviors. Discipline is not about compliance and control but involves **behavior guidance**, a process by which all children learn to control and direct their behavior and become independent and self-reliant. In this view, behavior guidance is a process of helping children develop skills useful over a lifetime.

As you work with young children, one of your goals will be to help them become independent and have the ability to regulate or govern their own behavior. Recall from Chapter 8 that *self-regulation* is the child's ability to plan, guide, and monitor his or her own behavior according to changing life circumstances.

FOCUS QUESTIONS

1. What is guiding behavior and why is it important?

2. What does it mean to guide behavior in a community of learners?

3. What is the social constructivist approach to guiding behavior?

4. What are twelve steps you can use to guide children's behavior?

GUIDING BEHAVIOR IN A COMMUNITY OF LEARNERS

behavior guidance A process by which teachers help all children learn to control and direct their behavior and become independent and self-reliant.

As we will emphasize in this and have emphasized in other chapters, cognitive and social development and behavioral characteristics are interconnected. More early childhood teachers recognize that it does not make sense to teach children reading, writing, and arithmetic and not also teach them skills necessary for responsibly guiding their own behavior.

The Community of Learners

Classrooms are and should be a community of learners in which children of all ages take shared responsibly for the physical, the social, and the learning environments. You, the teacher, must help children develop the behaviors for living and learning in the community.

A learning community is child centered. All that we do in classrooms should focus on children's growth and development as persons and as learners. The practices we use and teach for guiding children's behavior should be for their benefit. As a result of our guiding children's behavior—and helping them guide their own behavior—children should be successful, confident, responsible, and contributors to the learning community.

Democratic Living

In our efforts to help prepare all children to live effectively and productively in a democracy, we place increasing emphasis on providing experiences that will enable them to productively live and learn in democratic school and classroom communities. The idea of teaching democratic living through classrooms that are miniature democracies is not new. John Dewey was an advocate of this approach and championed democratic classrooms as a way of promoting democratic living. However, running a democratic classroom is easier said than done. It requires a confident professional who believes it is worth the effort.

Key Foundational Practices. Learning communities are grounded in key foundational practices. These include:

Go to the Assignments and Activities section in Topic 9: Guiding Children of the MyEducationLab for your course and complete the activity entitled *Strategies to Guide Behavior.* Note how the teacher facilitates the children's conflict resolution without actually solving the problem for them.

- *Cooperative living and learning.* You can promote cooperative living in which children help each other direct their behavior. Recall from Chapter 3 our discussion of Vygotsky's theory of social relations. Children are born seeking social interactions, and social relations are necessary for children's learning and development. Peers help each other learn.

  Children's natural social groups and play groups are ideal and natural settings in which to help children assist each other in learning new behaviors and being responsible for their own behavior. The classroom as a whole is an important social group. Classroom meetings in which teachers and children talk can serve many useful functions. They can talk about expected behaviors from day to day ("When we are done playing with toys, what do we do with them?"), review with children what they did in a particular center or situation, and help them anticipate what they will do in future situations ("Tomorrow morning when we visit the Senior Citizen Center . . ."). In all these situations, children are cooperatively engaged in thinking about, talking about, and learning how to engage in appropriate behavior.

  In addition, you can initiate, support, and foster a cooperative, collaborative learning community in the classroom in which children are involved in developing and setting guidelines and devising classroom norms and, by extension, individual norms of behavior. Teachers "assist" children but do not do things for them, and they ask questions that make children think about their behavior—how it influences the class, themselves, and others. This process of cooperative living occurs daily. Discussions grow out of existing problems, and guidance is provided based on the needs of children and the classroom.

- *Respect for children.* Throughout this text I have repeatedly emphasized the necessity for honoring and respecting children as human beings. When children are respected and honored then they are much more likely to engage in behavior that is respectful and honorable.
- *Time and opportunity to talk about behavior and develop strategies for guiding their behavior.* A good way to provide children time and opportunity to talk about behavior and classroom problems is through a class meeting. (An excellent resource for learning about and how to conduct class meetings is the NAEYC resource book, *Class Meetings: Young Children Solving Problems Together* by Emily Vance and Patricia Jimenez Weaver.) Democratic learning environments require that students develop responsibility for their own and others' behaviors and learning, that classrooms operate as communities, and that all children are respected and respectful of others.
- *Character education as a means of promoting responsible behavior.* Providing character education will continue to be an important means of promoting fundamental behaviors that early childhood professionals and society believe are essential for living in a democratic society.
- *Civility.* Civil behavior and ways to promote it are of growing interest at all levels of society. The specific teaching of **civil behavior**—how to treat others well and in turn be treated well—is seen as essential for living well in contemporary society. At a minimum, civil behavior includes manners, respect, and the ability to get along with people of all races, cultures, and socioeconomic backgrounds.

civil behavior In interactions with others, treating them well and in turn being treated well.

WHAT IS THE SOCIAL CONSTRUCTIVIST APPROACH TO GUIDING BEHAVIOR?

In Chapter 3 we discussed theories of learning and development and how you can use them in your teaching. Reacquaint yourself now with the theories of Piaget, Vygotsky, Maslow, and Erikson so their ideas will be fresh in your mind as we apply them to guiding children's behavior.

The Social Constructivist Approach: Piaget and Vygotsky

Piaget's and Vygotsky's theories support a social constructivist approach to learning and behavior. Teachers who embrace a **social constructivist approach** believe that children construct or build a set of behaviors as a result of learning from experience and from making decisions that lead to responsible actions. Your primary role in the constructivist approach is to guide and help children as they construct or build their behavior and use it in socially appropriate and productive ways. This process begins in homes and classrooms.

In Chapter 3 we also discussed Vygotsky's theories of *scaffolding* and the *zone of proximal development (ZPD)*. We now apply these two theories to our approach for guiding children's behavior, and add two additional essentials to Vygotskyian constructivist theory: **adult–child discourse** and child **self-discourse** (or **private speech**). Foundational to Vygotskyian and constructivist theory are the central beliefs that the development of a child's knowledge and behaviors occurs in the context of social relations with adults and peers. This means that learning and development are socially mediated as children interact with more competent peers and adults. As children gain the ability to master language and appropriate social relations, they are able to intentionally regulate their behavior.

social constructivist approach A theory that says children construct or build their behavior as a result of learning from experience and from making decisions that lead to responsible behavior.

adult–child discourse A conversation between an adult/parent and a child.

self-discourse *or private speech* An internal conversation between a person and himself or herself.

Guiding Behavior in the Zone of Proximal Development

The ZPD is the cognitive and developmental space that is created when the child is in social interaction with a more competent person (MCP) or a more knowledgeable other (MKO). As Vygotsky explains, the ZPD is the "actual development level as determined by independent problem solving and the level of potential development as determined through problem solving under adult guidance or in collaboration with more capable peers."[4] Problem solving is what guiding behavior is all about. Teachers take children from the behavioral and social skills they have in their ZPD and guide them to increasingly higher levels of responsible behavior and social interactions. Also, although we often think of guiding behavior as a one-on-one activity, this is not the case. Your role in guiding behavior includes large and small groups, as well as individual children. Figure 12.1 illustrates the ZPD and provides ideas for how to guide children's behavior within it. The ZPD is constantly moving and changing, depending on children's behavioral accomplishments and the assistance and scaffolding provided by others.

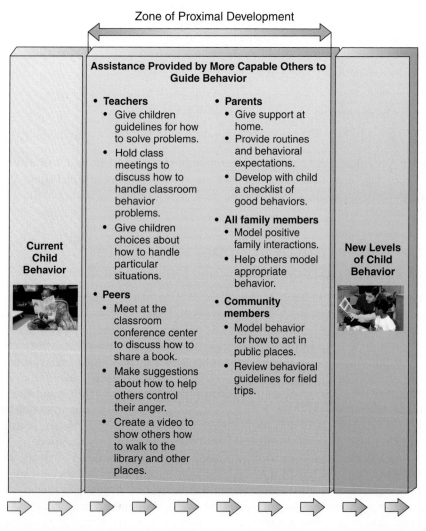

FIGURE 12.1 The Zone of Proximal Development Applied to Guiding Behavior

Guiding Behavior with Scaffolding

Scaffolding is one of the ways teachers can guide children in the ZPD. Recall that scaffolding is the use of informal methods such as conversations, questions, modeling, guiding, and supporting to help children learn concepts, knowledge, and skills that they might not learn by themselves. When more competent others provide "help," children are able to accomplish what they would not have been able to do on their own. In the ZPD, children are capable of far more competent behavior and achievements as they receive guidance and support from teachers and parents.

Adult–Child Discourse

The scaffolding script that follows is illustrative of adult–child discourse. Discourse also involves talking about how children might solve problems, guide their own behavior, interact and cooperate with others, understand norms of social conduct, and learn values related to school and family living. Teachers must initiate and guide these discourses and help children learn new skills that will assist them in developing self-regulation. Here is an example of a "learning conversation" that invites student participation. This discourse centers on how student authors should act while they are sharing their stories:

Ms. Anthony: Maybe we should now think about how to behave as the author during author's chair. What do authors do? Who can remember? Stephanie, would you like to start?

Stephanie: The author sits in the author's chair and speaks loud and clear.

Joyce: The author should not be shy and should be brave and confident.

Ms. Anthony continues to invite students to participate by providing ideas and suggestions, using this type of scaffolding. The children create a list of responsibilities to guide their behaviors while sharing stories.[5]

Private Speech and Self-Guided Behavior

Jennifer, a four-year-old preschooler, is busily engrossed in putting a puzzle together. As she searches for a puzzle piece, she asks herself out loud, "Which piece comes next?" I'm sure you have heard children talk to themselves. More than likely, you have talked to yourself while working on a task! Such conversations are commonplace in the lives of young children and adults.

Private speech plays an important role in problem solving and self-regulation of behavior. Children learn to transfer problem-solving knowledge and responsibility from adults to themselves:

> Self-regulation is focused on the ability of a child to regulate him or herself through private speech by comprehending what is asked in a given task or situation. The student must also be able to monitor his or her behaviors to see if there is coordination with the given task at hand and be able to maintain or avert what he is doing based on his own judgments.
>
> Self-regulation is important in school and teachers are the first to acknowledge this. A self-regulated student can stay in his designated area and focus on the task given to him by the teachers, capable of paying attention when the teacher is discussing or reading aloud without losing the attention focused on the teacher, especially to the learning process the student experiences. The child will soon learn to talk and may use "self-talk" to help regulate his or her behavior.[6]

TWELVE STEPS FOR GUIDING BEHAVIOR

As with many things in life, you accomplish goals by having a well-thought-out, conceptual plan for what you want to achieve. Guiding children's behavior is no different. It involves many dimensions and there is a lot to think about. The following twelve steps for guiding behavior are designed to give you practical, achievable, and successful ideas that you can relate to and use in your daily practice. As you read and reflect on each of the twelve steps, consider how you can apply them to your teaching and how you can begin to personalize them to your professional practice so they become your own and are strategies that you use automatically in helping children be their best.

Step 1: Use Constructivist Guidance Guidelines

Based on the constructivist theory, here are some strategies you can use to guide children's behavior:

- Guide problem solving:
  - "Tanya, what are some things you can do to help you remember to put the books away?"
  - "Eugene, you and Maria want to use the easel at the same time. What are some ideas for how you can both use it?"
- Ask questions that help children arrive at their own solutions:
  - "Tommy, you can't use both toys at the same time. Which one do you want to use first?"
  - "Rene, here is an idea that might help you get to the block corner. Ask Amelia, 'Would you please move over a little so I can get to the blocks?'"
- Model appropriate skills:
  - Practice social skills and manners. For example, say "Please" and "Thank you."
  - Listen attentively to children and encourage listening. For example, say "Harry has something he wants to tell us. Let's listen to what he has to say."

These are some of the major concepts associated with constructivist ideas and practices. Using these strategies effectively requires much determination and practice. They are worth the effort, and you will be rewarded with their beneficial results as you learn to guide children's behavior.

Step 2: Clarify What You Believe About Guiding Behavior

A good way to clarify your beliefs is to develop a philosophy about what you believe concerning children, guidance, and child rearing. Review the information on how to develop your philosophy of education in Chapter 1 to help you do this. Knowing what you want for your children at home and school helps you decide what to do and how to do it. Knowing what you believe also makes it easier for you to share with parents, help them guide behavior, and counsel them about discipline. Take a few minutes now and write a paragraph titled "My Basic Beliefs About Guiding Children's Behavior." This will help you get started on clarifying your beliefs.

Step 3: Know and Use Developmentally Appropriate Practice

Knowing child development is the cornerstone of developmentally appropriate practice. Children cannot behave well when adults expect too much or too little of them based on their development or when parents expect them to behave in ways inappropriate for them as individuals. Thus, a key for guiding children's behavior is to *really know what they are like*. This is the real meaning of developmentally appropriate practice. You will want to study children's development and observe children's behavior to learn what is appropriate for all children and individual children based on their age, needs, gender, and culture. The portraits of children in Chapters 7, 8, 9, and 10 will help you learn and apply developmentally appropriate practice.

Step 4: Meet Children's Needs

A major reason for knowing children and child development is so that you will be able to meet their needs. Abraham Maslow felt that human growth and development were oriented toward *self-actualization*, the striving to realize one's potential. Review Maslow's hierarchy in Chapter 3 and consider how children's physical needs, safety and security needs, belonging and affection needs, and self-esteem needs culminate in self-actualization. An example of each of these needs will illustrate how to apply them to guiding children's behavior.

Physical Needs.   Children's abilities to guide their own behaviors depend in part on how well their physical needs are met. Children do their best in school, for example, when they are well nourished. Families and schools should provide for children's nutritional needs by giving them breakfast. Recent brain research, discussed in Chapter 2, also informs us that the brain needs protein and water to function well. You should encourage children to drink water throughout the day and also provide frequent nutritional snacks.

Safety and Security.   Learning communities help children feel safe and secure. Just as you can't teach when you are fearful for your safety, children can't learn in fear. Children should feel comfortable and secure in your classroom. Consider also the dangers many children face in their neighborhoods, such as crime, drugs, and violence, and the dangers they face at home, such as abuse and neglect. Part of guiding children's behavior includes providing safe and secure communities, neighborhoods, homes, schools, and classrooms. For many children your classroom may be their only haven of safety and security. In addition, you may need to assume a major role of advocacy for safe communities.

Belonging and Affection.   You need love and affection and children do too. Love and affection needs are satisfied when parents hold, hug, and kiss their children and tell them, "I love you." Teachers meet children's affectional needs when they smile, speak pleasantly, are kind and gentle, treat children with courtesy and respect, and genuinely value each child. Today, many children are starving for affection and recognition. For these children you may be their sole or main source of emotional needs.

Self-Esteem.   Children who view themselves as worthy, responsible, and competent feel good about themselves and learn better. Children's views of themselves come from parents and early childhood professionals. Experiencing success gives children feelings of high self-esteem. It is the responsibility of parents and teachers to give all children opportunities for success. Success and achievement are the foundations for self-esteem.

Self-Actualization.   Self-actualization is a process of becoming all you can be, and we want this goal for each child. Children want to do things for themselves and be independent. Teachers and parents can help children become independent by helping them learn to dress themselves, go to the restroom by themselves, and take care of their classrooms. They can also help children set achievement and behavior goals ("Tell me

Helping children become more independent by warmly supporting their effort is one of the most effective forms of guidance. Identify some ways you and other teachers can support your students' efforts to do things for themselves.

what you are going to build with your blocks") and encourage them to evaluate their behavior ("Let's talk about what you did in the literacy center").

Step 5: Help Children Build New Behaviors

Helping children build new behaviors means that you help them learn that they are primarily responsible for their own behavior and that the pleasures and rewards for appropriate behavior are internal, coming from within themselves as opposed to always coming from outside (i.e., from the approval and praise of others). This concept is known as **locus of control**, the source or place of control. The preferred and recommended locus of control for young children is internal.

The process of developing an internal locus of control begins at birth, continues through the early childhood years, and is a never-ending process throughout life. When their locus of control is external, children are controlled by others; they are always told what to do and how to behave. We want children, however, to control their own behavior. In addition, we want children to take responsibility for their behavior. What we want to avoid is having children blame their behavior on others ("Chandra took my pencil") or on circumstances ("I didn't have time"). Legitimate excuses are appropriate, but always blaming others or external events is not. Learning to do it right and trying again after a failure are other important positive behaviors.

Affirming and acknowledging children's appropriate behaviors is a good way to build new behaviors—everyone likes to be praised and affirmed for a job well done, good efforts, and their best work. Helping children learn new behaviors and change or modify old behaviors is also an important part of guidance. Ways of affirming and acknowledging behavior verbally, socially, and nonverbally are:

Verbal

- "I like the way you . . .", "Great," "Cool," "Wow," "Way to go," "Super," "Terrific," "Excellent," "Fantastic," "Awesome," "You're working hard," "Good job," "Tremendous," "Beautiful"

Social (as a result of good behavior in classrooms, small groups, etc.)
- Parties, group approval, class privileges, or individual privileges; time to do a favorite activity (e.g., read books, play games)

Nonverbal
    Facial: Smiling, winking, or raising of eyebrows
    Gestures: Clapping of hands, waving, forming an okay sign (thumb + index finger), victory sign, nodding head, or shrugging shoulders
    Proximity: Standing near someone, shaking hands, getting down on child's level, hugging, rubbing on child's back, or holding child's arm up

Responsible choices and support are key ways to help children develop responsible behavior that internalizes their locus of control.

Step 6: Empower Children

Helping children build new behaviors creates a sense of responsibility and self-confidence. As children are given responsibility, they develop greater self-direction, which means that you guide them at the next level in their zone of proximal development. Some teachers and parents hesitate to let children assume responsibilities, but without responsibilities

---

Guiding children's behavior consists of essential guidelines, including helping children build new, appropriate behaviors and helping them to be responsible for their behaviors. Why is it important for children to learn to guide their own behavior rather than having teachers and parents always telling them what to do?

locus of control The source of control over an individual's behavior; the locus may be external (controlled by others) or internal (within oneself). The goal of behavioral guidance is to help children learn that their locus of control is internal, that they are responsible for their own behavior.

children are bored and frustrated and become discipline problems—the very opposite of what is intended. Guidance is not a matter of adults getting children to please them by making remarks such as "Show me how perfect you can be," "Don't embarrass me by your behavior in front of others," "I want to see nice groups," or "I'm waiting for quiet." Learning communities are child centered, not teacher centered.

To reiterate, guiding behavior is not about compliance and control. Rather, it is important to instill in children a sense of independence and responsibility for their own behavior. For example, you might say, "You have really worked a long time cutting out the flower you drew. You kept working on it until you were finished. Would you like some tape to hang it up with?"

You can do a number of things to help children develop new behaviors that result in empowerment:

- *Give children responsibilities.* All children, from an early age, should have responsibilities—that is, tasks that are their job to do and for which they are responsible. Being responsible for completing tasks and doing such things as putting away toys and learning materials promotes a positive sense of self-worth and conveys to children that in a community people have responsibilities for making the community work well.

- *Give children choices.* Life is full of choices—some require thought and decisions; others are automatic, based on previous behavior. But every time you make a decision, you are being responsible and exercising your right to decide. Children like to have choices, and choices help them become independent, confident, and self-disciplined. Making choices is key for children developing responsible behavior and inner control. Learning to make choices early in life lays the foundation for decision-making later. Guidelines for giving children choices are as follows:

  - Give children choices when there are valid choices to make. When it comes time to clean up the classroom, do not let children choose whether they want to participate, but let them pick between collecting the scissors or the crayons.

  - Help children make choices. Rather than say, "What would you like to do today?" say, "Sarah, you have a choice between working in the woodworking center or the computer center. Which would you like to do?"

- *Support children.* As an early childhood professional, you must support children in their efforts to be successful. Arrange the environment and make opportunities available for children to be able to do things. Successful accomplishments are a major ingredient of positive behavior.

The accompanying Technology Tie-In feature will give you another perspective on how you can use technology to help support children in their efforts to guide their own behavior.

Step 7: Establish Appropriate Expectations

Expectations set the boundaries for desired behavior. They are the guideposts children use in learning to direct their own behavior. Like everyone, children need guideposts along life's way.

Set high and appropriate expectations for children. When children know what to expect, they can better achieve those expectations. Up to a point, the more we expect of children, the more and better they achieve.

The following are some things you can do to promote appropriate expectations.

Set Limits.　Setting limits is closely associated with establishing expectations and relates to defining unacceptable behavior. Setting clear limits is important for three reasons:

1. Setting limits helps you clarify in your own mind what you believe is acceptable, based on your knowledge of child development, children, their families, and their culture.

2. Limits help children act with confidence because they know which behaviors are acceptable.

3. Limits provide children with security. Children want and need limits.

technology tie-in

Helping Kids Help Themselves—Electronically

Every classroom has children with emotional and behavioral disabilities. Computer programs, called electronic performance support tools, can help children take responsibility for their own learning and behavior by providing easy-to-use templates to personalize and use independently in school and home settings.

The *KidTools* (http://kidtools.missouri.edu/) programs assist children with problem solving and using self-management skills. The early childhood version, *eKidTools*, provides tools for children to identify behaviors, develop strategies to change or control these behaviors, prepare self-talk cues, and create self-monitoring cards. The software consists of fifteen tool templates that are kid-friendly with colorful graphics, text-with-audio directions, and simple formats.

The *KidSkills* programs provide organizational and learning strategy tools for children to support independence and success. The early childhood version, *eKidSkills*, provides tools for children to get organized, learn new information, complete homework, and do projects.

In both programs, graphic characters serve as "guides" to the different tools and provide audio directions in children's voices. The text and audio utilize the natural language of children. The audio directions supplement the simplified text instructions and can be turned off or on as desired.

Children and teachers who use the software in their classrooms enthusiastically support the programs. Children say *eKidSkills* is "cool" and it "helps you be better because you pay attention to how you act." Teachers report that children are intrigued by the software and became independent with it. Many describe behavior change attributed in part to the approaches that help children think before they act.

Gail Fitzgerald, co-developer of the programs, believes the use of electronic computer tools provides a nonintrusive method of supporting children with behavioral disabilities by providing easy-to-use tools that are functional and motivating. Gail says, "Often teachers attempt to control children's behavior without really involving them in that decision-making process or giving them the resources to be successful. The focus in this software is to help children make the shift from external to internal management."

Source: G. Fitzgerald and K. Koury, The KidTools Support System (KTSS) (Columbia: The University of Missouri–Columbia). Funded in part by the United States Department of Education Project H327A000005. (© 2007 The Curators of the University of Missouri, a public corporation. All rights reserved. Used with permission.)

PEARSON myeducationlab

Go to the Assignments and Activities section in Topic 9: Guiding Children of the MyEducationLab for your course and complete the activity entitled *Promoting Socially Appropriate Behavior in Kindergarten*. Pay particular attention to how the teachers use modeling to encourage cooperation and mutual respect in their classrooms.

As children grow and mature, the limits change and are adjusted to developmental levels, programmatic considerations, and life situations. Knowing what they can and cannot do enables children to guide their own behavior.

Develop Classroom Rules. Plan classroom rules from the first day of class. As the year goes on, you can involve children in establishing classroom rules, but in the beginning, children want and need to know what they can and cannot do. For example, rules might relate to changing groups and bathroom routines. Whatever rules you establish, they should be fair, reasonable, and appropriate to the children's age and maturity. Keep rules to a minimum; the fewer the better. See Figure 12.2 to see a sample of classroom rules for pre-kindergarten through third grade.

Step 8: Arrange and Modify the Classroom Environment

The classroom environment plays a key role in children's ability to guide their behavior. Arrange the environment so that it supports the purposes of the program and makes appropriate behavior possible. Appropriate room arrangements signal to children that they are expected to guide and be responsible for their own behavior and enable teachers to observe and provide for children's interests. Also, it is easier to live and work in an attractive and aesthetically pleasing classroom or center. We all want a nice environment—children should have one, too. The guidelines shown in Figure 12.3 can help you think about and arrange your classroom to support children as they guide their own behavior.

FIGURE 12.2

Examples of Classroom Rules, Pre-K–3

Pre-kindergarten	• Helping Hands • Listening Ears • Looking Eyes • Quiet Voices • Walking Feet
Kindergarten	• Be kind to everybody. • Raise your hand when you want to speak. • Use inside voices. • Walk inside the room. • Listen to the teachers. • Follow the school rules.
First grade	• Respect other people. • Keep your hands and feet to yourself. • Raise your hand for permission to speak in class. • Walk quietly in the hallways. • Move about quietly in the classroom.
Second grade	• Be a good listener. • Be a good friend. • Be polite. • Be a hard worker. • Be the best you can be.
Third grade	• Listen to and follow directions. • Raise your hand. • Work quietly. • Keep hands and feet to yourself. • Walk silently in the halls. • Be kind to others.

Note: Based on Carrollton Elementary School, Carrollton, Texas (pre-kindergarten); Chapin Elementary School, Chapin, South Carolina (kindergarten); Garrison-Pilcher Elementary School, Thomasville, Georgia (first grade); Elwood Public School, Elwood, Nebraska (second grade); and H. L. Horn Elementary, Vinton, Virginia (third grade).

Apart from the physical environment, other characteristics of classrooms that support children as they learn how to guide their own behavior include:

- An atmosphere of respect and caring
- Consistent behavior from teachers and staff, who model appropriate behavior and expect it of children
- Established and maintained routines
- A belief shared by all staff that children can and will learn, and also a belief that they are good teachers
- A partnership between teachers and children
- A classroom community and a culture of caring
- Open communication between:
  - Children–children
  - Teacher–children
  - Children–teacher

Make the classroom a rewarding place to be. It should be comfortable, safe, and attractive.

Locate materials so that children can easily retrieve them. When children have to ask for materials, this promotes dependency and can lead to behavior problems.

Create center areas that are well-defined and accessible to children and have appropriate and abundant materials. Provide children with guidelines for how to use centers and materials, and make center boundaries low enough so that you and others can see over them for proper supervision and observation.

Establish a system so that materials are easily stored, and so that children can easily put them away. A rule of thumb is that there should be a place for everything and everything should be in its place.

Have an open area in which you and your children can meet as a whole group. This area is essential for story time, general class meetings, and so on. Starting and ending the day with a class meeting provides an opportunity for children to discuss their behaviors and suggest ways they and others can do a better job.

Provide for all kinds of activities, both quiet and loud. Try to locate quiet areas together (reading area and puzzle area) and loud centers together (woodworking and blocks).

Provide opportunities for children to display their work.

FIGURE 12.3 How to Arrange the Classroom to Support Positive Behavior

- Teacher–parents
- Parents–teacher
- Clear expectations and high expectations
- Sufficient materials to support learning activities

This chapter's Diversity Tie-In feature details how a child's environment influences how he or she behaves.

Step 9: Model Appropriate Behavior

Telling is not teaching. Actions speak louder than words. Children see and remember how other people act. Modeling plays a major role in helping children guide their behavior.

Teachers and parents lay the first—and most important—foundation for children's appropriate habits and behaviors. You must be the best role model you can for children and help parents be good role models too. Whether they want to or not, or like it or not, teachers have to accept responsibility for helping raise responsible children who will become responsible adults.

Another good way both you and parents can become good role models for children is through books that encourage pro-social behaviors. The picture books listed in Figure 12.4 provide you many opportunities to model appropriate behavior through good books.

You can use the following techniques to help children learn through modeling:

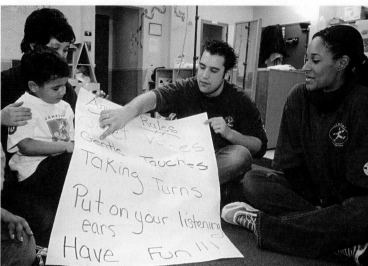

- *Show.* For example, show children where the block corner is, how and where the blocks are stored.
- *Demonstrate.* Perform a task while students watch. For example, demonstrate the proper way to put the blocks away and how to store them. Extensions of the demonstration method are to have children practice the demonstration while you supervise, or to ask a child to demonstrate to other children.
- *Supervise.* Supervision is a process of reviewing, reminding, maintaining standards, and following up. If children are not performing the desired behavior, you will need to review the behavior. You must be consistent in your expectations of desired behavior. Children will soon learn they do not have to put away their blocks if you allow them not to do it even once.

The classroom environment is one of the most important factors that enable children to develop and use appropriate behavior. The classroom should belong to children, and their ownership and pride in it makes it more likely they will act responsibly.

FIGURE 12.4

Children's Books That Encourage Pro-Social Behaviors in Young Children

Mad Isn't Bad: A Child's Book About Anger by Michaelene Mundy. Illustrated by R. W. Alley. Saint Meinrad, IN: One Caring Place/Abbey Press, 1999 (Ages 4–8).

This book shows children they have choices—just as caring adults have choices about what to teach children about anger. Through understanding what anger feels like and what triggers it, children and teachers learn and teach healthy ways to control it.

Big Pink Pig by Trevor Ricketts and Christopher O'Hare. New York: Random House, 2001 (Ages 4–8).

A big pink pig decides he needs to lose some weight, but after trying weight-lifting, aerobics, and jogging he comes to the realization that there is nothing wrong with a pig being big.

Happy to Be Me!: A Kid Book About Self-Esteem by Christine Adams and Robert J. Butch. Saint Meinrad, IN: Abbey Press, 2001 (Ages 4–8).

This colorful book leads the young reader through a process of self-discovery: exploring uniqueness, building a healthy-self-image, and preparing for challenging situations. Every child in the world is special, gifted, and wonderful. And each one deserves to feel "happy to be me"!

The Man Who Walked Between the Towers by Mordicai Gerstein. Brookfield, CT: Roaring Brook, 2003 (Ages 6–7).

Based on the true story of Philippe Petit who walked a tightrope strung between the two towers of the World Trade Center. Students learn courage and persistence, and consider a new perspective on these historic buildings.

It's Hard to Be Five: Learning How to Work My Control Panel by Jamie Lee Curtis. Illustrated by Laura Cornell. New York: HarperCollins, 2004 (Ages 4–8).

This book is about a five-year-old's challenges of learning self-control. He faces challenges of controlling his temper when dealing with a younger sibling, avoiding dirt, and starting school. However, he sees many advantages of being five, such as walking by himself and many fun activities at school that his younger brother cannot yet experience.

Fathers, Socioeconomic Status, and Children's Behavior

The majority of our discussion in this chapter has focused on what you can do in your classroom to guide children's behavior. However, the behaviors children bring to classrooms and programs are the result of many different experiences and environments. For example, look at the figure below, which shows a few of the home/family environmental factors that influence children's behavior. For example, families' home environments, children's experiences in previous classrooms, and children's temperaments all help determine how children behave.

Family socioeconomic status (SES) and parental background in particular exert powerful influences on children's behavior, their approaches to solving problems, and their particular life views regarding learning and social relationships. While a lot of attention is focused on mother–child interaction in the guiding of behavior, we must also consider how fathers influence their children's behavior.

Let's focus on fathers' SES and see how it influences their approach to guiding their children's behavior. Low-SES fathers report that they use more frequent verbal and corporal punishment when disciplining their children than do fathers from higher socioeconomic backgrounds.* Research is clear that verbal and physical punishments are good predictors of behavior problems. Across all SES levels, punitive parenting practices are associated with higher levels of disruptive behavior. So, punitive parenting practices exacerbate the behaviors parents are trying to eliminate or discourage. When fathers use punitive guidance practices with their children who are already disruptive, they may be providing a double whammy of negative behavior.

So, what can you do to help all low-SES parents—but particularly fathers—who need your help in learning how to positively guide children's behavior? Parents' sources of parenting information come mainly through discussions with other parents, and reading books on parenting.[†] You can use parent meetings and parent libraries to provide parents with resources they want and need in order to help them learn and use appropriate ways to deal with their children's misbehavior and help them develop new behaviors.

*A.D. Burbach, R.A. Fox, and B.C. Nicholson, "Challenging Behaviors in Young Children: The Father's Role," *Journal of Genetic Psychology,* 165(2), June 2004, 169–183.

[†]Christine Ateah, "Disciplinary Practices with Children: Parental Sources of Information, Attitudes, and Educational Needs," *Issues in Comprehensive Pediatric Nursing,* 26(1), April–June 2003, 89–101.

Child Environment

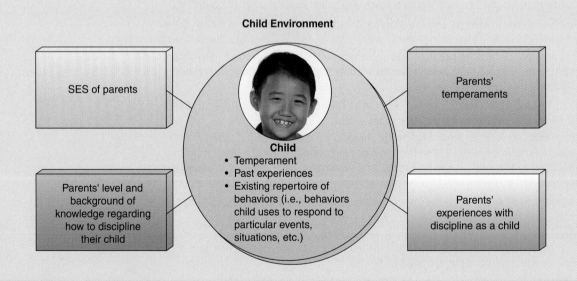

Step 10: Avoid Problems

It's easy to encourage children's misbehavior. Often teachers expect perfection and adult behavior from children. If you focus on building responsible behavior, there will be less need to solve behavior problems. The Professionalism in Practice feature on the following page profiles the successes of a school employing the positive discipline philosophy.

Ignoring inappropriate behavior is probably one of the most overlooked strategies for guiding children's behavior. Some early childhood professionals feel guilty when they use this strategy. They believe that ignoring undesirable behaviors is not good teaching. Ignoring some inappropriate behavior can be an effective strategy, but it must be combined with positive reinforcement of desirable behavior. Thus, you ignore inappropriate behavior and at the same time reinforce appropriate behavior. A combination of positive reinforcement and ignoring can lead to desired behavior.

When children do something good or are on task, tell them. Catch children being good; that is, look for good behavior. This helps improve not only individual behavior, but group behavior as well.

Step 11: Develop a Partnership with Parents, Families, and Others

Involving parents and families is a wonderful way to gain invaluable insights about children's behaviors. Some things you can do to collaborate with parents on guiding children's behaviors are these:

- Share your philosophy of guiding behavior with parents. Your classroom web site is a good place to do this.
- Share classroom rules and expectations with parents.
- Hold meetings for and with parents and share with them the information in this chapter and how to apply it to their learning about how to guide children's behavior in the home.
- Always be available in person, on the phone, or via e-mail to discuss with parents questions or concerns they might have about their children's behavior.

Chapter 13 provides many helpful ideas to use in your collaboration with parents.

Social relationships play a powerful role in children's and teachers' everyday behavior. Teachers must promote positive child–child and teacher–child relationships. What are some things you can do to promote positive social relationships in your classroom or program?

Step 12: Use and Teach Conflict Management

Quite often, conflicts result from children's interactions with others. Increasingly, teachers advocate teaching children ways to manage and resolve their own conflicts.

Positive Guidance: Responsible, Motivated, Self-Directed Learners

The Grapevine (Texas) Elementary School staff had a vision. The vision emphasized the desire to encourage all learners to be responsible, intrinsically motivated, and self-directed in an environment of mutual respect. As we looked for a discipline management system that fit this philosophy, we recognized that we needed one that emphasized personal responsibility for behavior and cooperation instead of competition and that focused on developing a community of supportive members. We also discovered that we held several beliefs in common that should be the foundation of our discipline management plan:

1. All human beings have three basic needs—to feel connected (the ability to love and be loved), to feel capable (a sense of "I can" accomplish things), and to feel contributive (I count in the communities to which I belong).
2. Problem solving and solutions encourage responsible behavior. Punishment, by contrast, encourages rebellion and resentment.
3. Children can be creative decision makers and responsible citizens when given opportunities to direct the processes that affect the day-to-day environment in which they live.
4. Every inappropriate action does not necessitate a consequence, but rather can be used as a cornerstone of a problem-solving experience, ultimately leading to a true behavior change.

Our desire was, and is, to address the needs of the whole child as we educate our children to be responsible citizens.

ADOPTING THE PLAN

After much research, we decided to implement *Positive Discipline*, a discipline management system based on the concept of responsibilities rather than rules. Teachers established the following Grapevine Star Responsibilities:

I will be responsible for myself and my learning.
I will respect others and their property.
I will listen and follow directions promptly.
I will complete my class work and homework in a quality manner.

Furthermore, we decided that rewards—whether in the way of stickers, pencils, or award ceremonies—were not, on the whole, consistent with encouraging intrinsic motivation and the belief that all children should continuously monitor their own learning and behavior. Rather, the term *reward* should be replaced with *celebration*, and these celebrations should be based on what children find personally significant.

Teachers also discussed the understanding that they would become facilitators of decision-making sessions instead of "general in command"; and they would encourage self-evaluation by students leading to solutions.

ENGAGING STUDENTS

Throughout the course of the year, students set goals each six-week period (usually one academic goal and one behavioral goal) and confer with their teachers at the end of the six weeks to determine the extent of their achievement toward that goal. At the end of the year, students participate in a celebration of achievement. Each student choses the goal that holds the most personal significance and receives a certificate that details the goal. The principal reads each chosen goal in the grade-level celebrations as the student walks across the stage and shakes hands with the principal. Teachers, parents, and students all enjoy this ceremony, which emphasizes the worth of each individual and affirms that learning was, and is, the ultimate goal of education and school (as opposed to a grade or series of marks on a report card).

Irene Boynton, a first grade teacher, notes that Positive Discipline allows children to experience the rewards of feeling confident and healthy about making respectful, responsible choices because it is the "right" thing to do, not because they will receive something for their choice.

THE BENEFITS

Teachers at Grapevine Elementary, when asked to comment on Positive Discipline, say such things as "Is there any other way to teach?" and "We would never go back to playing referee again!" Students no longer ask "What am I going to get?" in response to a request to go the extra mile for another student or while working on a project. They are developing respect for themselves and for the rights and needs of others. The skills learned through Positive Discipline extend into academic areas, where we find that students are becoming more thoughtful, introspective, self-motivated, and effective problem solvers. We believe that we are fostering a safe, respectful community where children and adults thrive together in an atmosphere of mutual respect.

You can visit Grapevine Elementary on the Web at http://www.gcisd-k12.org/ges/site/default.asp.

Source: Contributed by Alicia King (original author: Nancy Robinson). For more information on implementing additional components of Positive Discipline—such as class meetings, "I" messages, and role-playing—refer to *Positive Discipline in the Classroom* (Three Rivers Press, 2000) by Jane Nelsen, Lynn Lott, and Stephen Glenn.

Teaching conflict resolution strategies is important in the learning community for several reasons. First, it makes sense to give children the skills they need to handle and resolve their own conflicts. Second, teaching conflict resolution skills to children enables them to use these same skills as adults. Third, the peaceful resolution of interpersonal conflicts contributes, in the long run, to peaceful homes and communities. Children who are involved in efforts to resolve interpersonal behavior problems peacefully and intuitively learn that peace begins with them. Strategies used to teach and model conflict resolution include:

- *Model resolutions.* You can model resolutions for children: "Sasha, please don't knock over Brittany's building because she worked hard to build it"; "Lauren, what is another way (instead of hitting) you can tell Porcha that she is sitting in your chair?"

- *Do something else.* Teach children to get involved in another activity. Children can learn that they do not always have to play with a toy someone else has. They can get involved in another activity with a different toy. They can do something else now and play with the toy later. Chances are, however, that by getting involved in another activity they will forget about the toy for which they were ready to fight.

- *Talk it over.* Children can learn that talking about a problem often leads to a resolution and reveals that there are always two sides to an argument. Talking also helps children think about other ways to solve problems. Children should be involved in the solution of their interpersonal problems and classroom and activity problems.

- *Taking turns.* Taking turns is a good way for children to learn that they cannot always be first, have their own way, or do a prized activity. Taking turns brings equality and fairness to interpersonal relations.

- *Share.* Sharing is a good behavior to promote in any setting. Children have to be taught how to share and how to behave when others do not share. Children can be helped to select another toy rather than hitting or grabbing.

- *Teach children to say "I'm sorry."* Saying "I'm sorry" is one way to heal and resolve conflicts. It can be a step toward good behavior. Children need to be reared in an environment in which they see and experience others apologizing for their inappropriate actions toward others.

The Professionalism in Practice feature on pages 342–343 gives you guidelines for ensuring success for children who are hard to manage.

Applying the Twelve Steps

The twelve steps for guiding children's behavior we have discussed here will help you build learning communities in which you and your children can live happily and productively. These twelve steps lay the foundation for building learning communities and provide you with guidelines that will ensure you and the children are successful.

The first eight years of children's lives provide us many opportunities for helping children develop the skills and behaviors that will enable them to live healthy and productive lives. Enabling children to guide their own behavior and to live cooperatively and peacefully with other children will help them be better persons and good citizens. Guiding children's behavior is fundamental to making sure that all children have the opportunity to succeed in school and life.

I wish you much success as you joyfully and confidently empower children to guide their behavior.

myeducationlab

Go to the Assignments and Activities section in Topic 9: Guiding Children of the MyEducationLab for your course and complete the activity entitled *Peaceful Conflict Resolution.* Notice how the teacher is a facilitator, not a problem-solver. The teacher remains open and listens closely to each child. Pay particular attention to how the teacher reflects the girls' feelings.

How to Guide Hard-to-Manage Children to Help Ensure Their Success

Tyrone entered the kindergarten classroom on the first day of the school year, trailing several feet behind his mom, who appeared to be unaware of his presence. She called out a greeting to another mom, and the two of them had an extended discussion about events in the neighborhood. Tyrone glanced around the room and headed purposefully toward the housekeeping center, where he grabbed a baby doll, threw it out of the doll bed, and then ran to the block box and grabbed a large block in each hand. At this point I deflected his trail of destruction and redirected his progress: "Good morning, welcome to my class. My name is Ms. Cheryl. What's your name?" The whirlwind stopped briefly to mumble a response that I could not understand and glared at me in open hostility. "Let's go talk to Mom," I suggested, touching his shoulder and directing him toward his mom.

BACKGROUND

My school is in an area that includes mostly low-socioeconomic households; ours is a Title I school, with 95 percent of our students on free or reduced-fee lunches. In any given year, one-half to two-thirds of our students entering kindergarten have had no preschool experience. Nevertheless, as an early childhood educator, it is my job to help these students develop behaviors that will ensure their success in education. That does not mean that I need only to teach them to write their names, recognize all their letters and numbers, sit quietly in their chairs, and raise their hands before they speak. These tasks are not ends in themselves but are important steps in encouraging children to love learning and to gain the self-regulation that supports it.

UNDERSTANDING BEHAVIOR

In our opening scenario, what important facts should we as educators recognize as signals that Tyrone has some behaviors that require adjustment to ensure his success in school? He seems unaware of the expected protocol for entering a classroom—that is, looking for an adult in charge to give him directions. His mother's apparent lack of interest in her child's behavior could be an indicator that Tyrone does not expect the adults around him to be involved with his activities. He may have been in an atmosphere that requires very little from him when it comes to following rules and, as indicated by his hostility, may see adult intervention as only restrictive rather than supportive and nurturing. Tyrone may even have an undiagnosed speech problem that prohibits adults and other children from understanding his needs. If adults in his world have failed to observe and interact with him, he is also probably lacking in basic language skills and vocabulary, which would limit his understanding. He appears to deal with his world in a very physical manner.

BEHAVIORS NECESSARY FOR SUCCESS IN SCHOOL

The following behaviors are necessary for children to succeed in school:

Behavior #1: *Recognition of authority*—Tyrone was not even aware that an adult was in charge of the classroom.

Behavior #2: *Trust in adults*—The process of building trust is lengthy, but Tyrone needs to learn to see adults as nurturing and supportive.

Behavior #3: *Use of verbal skills rather than physical reactions*—If Tyrone is lacking in language, I can help provide language experiences, defining words, explaining everything in detail, showing and describing pictures, reading books aloud, helping with activities, and talk, talk, talking.

PEARSON
myeducationlab

Go to the Building Teaching Skills and Dispositions section in Topic 9: Guiding Children of the MyEducationLab for your course and complete the activity entitled *Guiding Children to Help Ensure Their Success.*

ACTIVITIES FOR PROFESSIONAL DEVELOPMENT

ethical dilemma

"Just Give Him a Good Whack"

Eduardo, age six, has just been assigned to Rachel's class. Eduardo acts out, hits other children, and screams when he doesn't get his own way. In a team meeting, Rachel asks for ideas on how to help guide Eduardo's behavior. One of Rachel's colleagues suggests that when he hits another child, she should "just give him a good whack on the bottom, and he'll soon get the message not to hit others."

How should Rachel handle disagreeing with a colleague over the best course of action to follow when dealing with a child's behavior problems? Should she suggest immediately that giving children "a good whack" is developmentally and culturally inappropriate, or should she talk after the meeting and share her views that she doesn't think physical punishment is a way to guide children's behavior, or should she report her colleague to the central administration, or pursue another course of action?

Behaviors #1 and #2 are especially complex; they stem from children's environments and experiences. However, I am committed to being one of the reasons a child succeeds and will dedicate great amounts of time and energy to changing behaviors that interfere with student learning. I follow certain steps to guide destructive behaviors into more successful ones.

STEP 1 PLAN

Before that first day of school, I plan—what activities I will offer my students, what part of the day I will use for centers, how I can show my students the best ways to use materials, where I want them to keep their belongings, how I can explain my expectations about dealing with conflict, how I will deal with behavior that is inappropriate, and what I am going to say about procedures for our classroom.

STEP 2 BE EXPLICIT

Many of my students are not accustomed to having an adult schedule their time for six hours, and many behavior problems stem from this new pressure to conform to an unfamiliar structure. Therefore, I want to be sure that all of my students fully understand what I expect. For example, I state exactly how I want them to move about the classroom, the cafeteria, the playground, and the school hallways. If they do not follow my instructions, I require them to practice. Many behaviors that inhibit success in school occur because students are not made aware of appropriate and inappropriate school procedures.

STEP 3 MODEL BEHAVIOR

I model or have my students role-play expected behavior in interpersonal actions. Students who take other students' belongings, hit other students, or push and shove other students are taught to handle these issues through conflict-resolution methods. However, it takes numerous rounds of modeling and role playing to make an impact on behavior that has been ingrained for five years at home and is still the norm when students return home.

STEP 4 ROLE-PLAY

I spend some time each day having students role-play scenarios with incorrect behavior. We brainstorm about what the correct behavior would be. Hitting, pushing, name calling, and destroying property are all common problems among my students. I ask my students how they feel if someone calls them a name (or exhibits any of the other negative behaviors).

STEP 5 DEVELOP CLASSROOM RULES

I have five classroom rules:

1. We listen to each other.
2. We use our hands for helping, not hurting.
3. We use caring language.
4. We care about each other's feelings.
5. We are responsible for what we say and do.

STEP 6 REINFORCE

Helping hard-to-manage children learn to guide their own behavior takes consistent reteaching and reinforcement. I correct every misbehavior I see, either using the "I don't like it when you . . ." statement or stating which rule has been broken. I use a very calm voice when I talk to my students and do not allow them to "tell" on each other. When a student comes to me with a tale of misbehavior, I ask, "Did you tell [*specific name*] how you feel?" Usually by the end of the first nine-week grading period, my students are using the behaviors and statements we have learned, and the tone of my classroom changes from a volatile one to a caring one. Spending some time at the beginning of the year changing behaviors and stating expectations gives my students the guidance they need to begin and to continue successful student careers.

....

Contributed by Cheryl Doyle, National Board Certified preschool teacher, Caribbean Elementary, Miami, Florida.

Application Activities

1. On the Internet, identify physical features of the classroom setting and atmosphere that influence classroom behavior. How will you use this information in your classroom?

2. In this chapter you learned twelve steps for guiding children's behavior. Although they are all important, rank-order the twelve in importance to you. Your first choice will be 1, your second, 2, and so on.

3. List five behaviors you think are desirable in toddlers, five in preschoolers, and five in kindergartners. For each behavior, give two examples of how you would encourage and promote development of that behavior in your program or classroom.

4. Research Internet sources devoted to discipline and guiding behavior. Determine what are various meanings of "discipline." Identify specific examples for how to discipline in various situations. Do you agree with the methods recommended? What implications does your research have for your role as a teacher of young children?

PEARSON
myeducationlab

To check your comprehension on the content covered in Chapter 12, go to the Book Specific Resources in the MyEducationLab for your course, select your text, and complete the Study Plan. Here you will be able to take a chapter quiz and receive feedback on your answers.

PARENTS, FAMILIES, AND THE COMMUNITY

Building Partnerships for Student Success

NAEYC Standards for Early Childhood Professional Preparation Programs

Standard 2: Building Family and Community Relationships

I know about, understand, and value the importance and complex characteristics of children's families and communities. I use this understanding to create respectful, reciprocal relationships that support and empower families, and to involve all families in their children's development and learning.[1]

Standard 3: Observing, Documenting, and Assessing to Support Young Children and Families

I know about and understand the goals, benefits, and uses of assessment. I know about and use systematic observations, documentation, and other effective assessment strategies in a responsible way, in partnership with families and other professionals, to positively influence the development of every child.[2]

One thing we can say with certainty about today's educational landscape is that parents, families, and communities are as much a part of the educational process as are the students, teachers, and staff. Efforts to involve families and communities in the process of educating the nation's children are at an all-time high. One primary reason for these renewed efforts is the overwhelming evidence that the effect of involving parents, families, and communities in the schools increases student achievement and promotes positive educational outcomes. Many research studies confirm the benefits of parent/community support.[3]

A positive and convincing relationship exists between family involvement and benefits for students, including improved academic achievement. This relationship holds across families of all economic, racial/ethnic, and educational backgrounds, as well as students of all ages. Students with involved parents, no matter their background, are more likely to earn higher grades and test scores, adapt well to school, attend regularly, have better social skills and behavior, and graduate and go on to higher education. Family involvement also has a protective effect; the more families can support their children's progress, the better their children do in school and the longer they stay in school.[4]

The public believes that nothing has a greater effect on students' level of achievement than parents. In fact, the public thinks that parents matter more than teachers![5] This makes parental involvement in children's education even more important.

NEW VIEWS OF PARENT/FAMILY AND COMMUNITY INVOLVEMENT

The current accountability and reform movements we discussed in Chapter 2 have convinced families that they should no longer be kept out of their children's schools. Families believe their children have a right to effective, high-quality teaching and care by high-quality teachers.[6] Parents have become more militant in their demands for high-quality education. Schools and other agencies have responded by seeking ways to involve families in this quest for quality. Educators and families realize that mutual cooperation is in everyone's best interest.[7]

Schools and other agencies are expected to involve and collaborate with parents and families in significant ways. In addition to using traditional methods of involving parents in fund-raising and children's activities, schools now involve parents in decisions about hiring new teachers, school safety measures, and appropriate curriculum to help ensure that all children learn.

Parents, families, and the community are now viewed as the "owners" of schools. As one parent said to me, "I don't consider myself a visitor at school. I'm an owner!"

Today, a major emphasis is on increasing student achievement. One of the best ways to do this is through involving parents in at-home learning activities with their children. Parent involvement is, now more than ever, a two-way street—from school to home and from home to school. The same reciprocal process applies to school–community collaboration.

For example, Karen Marler, principal of Lacoochee (Florida) Elementary, helps parents take ownership of their children's education in order to increase student achievement.

Teodora Romero wanted to help her children succeed in school, but she didn't know how. A Mexican immigrant who speaks almost exclusively Spanish, Romero felt overwhelmed by the assignments her third-grade son Luis and kindergarten daughter Berniece brought home from Lacoochee Elementary School. Worse, she lacked the comfort level with English to approach their teachers or others who work at the school. "I was intimidated," Romero said quietly, with the help of a bilingual friend.[8]

FOCUS QUESTIONS

1. What are new views of family and community involvement?

2. How do changes in families change the ways that you involve parents and families?

3. What are the six types of parent/family involvement?

4. What are some activities you can use to involve families and the community?

5. How will you confront the challenge of making the lives of children, their families, and their community better through parent/family/ community involvement?

So, Principal Marler decided to do something about it. She developed Parent University. Parent University offers classes to help parents help their children and themselves. Classes include: Help Children Read; Volunteering at School; and Parent Involvement.

Teacher Paula McCullough at Lakehoma (Oklahoma) Elementary also helps parents take ownership of their children's education in order to increase student achievement. Her Professionalism in Practice feature "Home and School: An Unbeatable Team!" will show you how helping parents can help your students.

Parent and family involvement means that while teachers work with parents to help children learn, they also have to teach parents how to work with their children. Review again our discussion of building family and community relationships in Chapter 1.

Also, as a result of more parents having to work to make ends meet, they look to schools for help raising their children. Working parents are demanding safe and high-quality child care as they turn their young children over to others for care and education. Parents and other family members need more help with rearing children. As a result, opportunities have blossomed for child-serving agencies, such as child care centers and preschools, to assist and support parents in their child-rearing efforts. Over the next decade additional programs will provide more parents with child development and child-rearing information and training.

CHANGING PARENTS AND FAMILIES: CHANGING INVOLVEMENT

Grandparents acting as parents for their grandchildren are a growing reality in the United States today. What are some things you can do to ensure that grandparents will have the educational assistance and support they need so that their grandchildren will be successful in school?

As we discussed in Chapter 2, the family of today is not the family of yesterday, nor will the family of today be the family of tomorrow. Today's parents are single, married, heterosexual, gay, lesbian, cousins, aunts, uncles, grandparents, brothers, and sisters. These changes in who and what parents are and what a family is have tremendous implications for parenting, child rearing, and education.

Grandparents as Parents

Since the early 1990s, more grandparents are raising their grandchildren than ever before in American history. One in ten grandparents are caregivers of the nation's youth, and most of the grandparents that act as parents are grandmothers.[9] Nearly 6.1 million children, or 8 percent of all children under age eighteen, are living in homes maintained by grandparents.[10] Many of the children in homes headed by grandparents are "skipped-generation" children—neither parent is living with them, perhaps because of drug abuse, divorce, mental or physical illness, abandonment, teenage pregnancy, child abuse and neglect, incarceration, military deployment, or even the death of the parents.[11] Grandparent-parents in these skipped-generation households must provide for their grandchildren's basic needs and care, as well as make sure that they do well in school. Grandparents who are raising a new generation of children, often unexpectedly, need your support. Keep in mind that they are rearing their grandchildren in a world very different from the one in which they reared their own children. You can help grandparents with this responsibility in a number of ways, including linking them with support groups such as Raising Our Children's Children (ROCC) and the Grandparent Information Center of the American Association of Retired Persons (AARP).

professionalism in practice

Home and School: An Unbeatable Team!

Paula McCullough
USA Today All-USA Teacher Team

STEP 1 · FORM PARTNERSHIPS WITH PARENTS

My philosophy of teaching is very simple: It is to teach the whole individual child, not a subject. Each child is unique, with different strengths and weaknesses, different likes and dislikes. To achieve my goal, I must form a partnership with the home. By working together, we can build a team whose mutual goal is the educational success of the child.

STEP 2 · COMMUNICATE WITH FAMILIES

A strong relationship needs to exist between the school and home in order for the child to get the best education possible. This "unbeatable team" is established through communication. Communication needs to be varied, timely, and honest. Proper communication is the tool that allows me to motivate parents to find the necessary time to work with and support their children's educations. I use weekly newsletters, phone calls, notes home, weekly homework bags, parent conferences/meetings, and parent volunteers.

STEP 3 · SEND NEWSLETTERS

I send out a weekly newsletter to inform my parents of "current events" in our classroom. Included in the newsletters are weekly progress reports, a list of spelling words, current areas of study, and special events/dates. I also include helpful tips on learning, such as how to help their child study spelling words, how to encourage reading for enjoyment and comprehension, or what games to play at home to practice reading/math skills.

STEP 4 · ENCOURAGE FEEDBACK

To encourage a two-way communication between home and school, I include a place for comments in the newsletters. Individual notes are sent home and phone calls made when needed. Sometimes it is necessary to keep parents informed on a daily basis about their child's progress, behavior, and/or work habits. I send home a daily note that is signed by the parent and returned to school. I have found it helpful to write these notes on a carbonless-copy message book so that I always have a copy (for those times when the student conveniently does not make it home with the note). Using different forms of communication keeps parents well informed of their child's progress, classroom policies/procedures, curriculum goals, and ideas on how best to help their child succeed at school.

STEP 5 · PROVIDE HOMEWORK BAGS

Homework bags are sent home each week. Each bag contains a worksheet to practice the skills (math/reading) taught in class, a practice reader, a reading activity, and a parent response form. The homework bags become increasingly more difficult as the student advances in abilities. A variety of reading activities are included to keep students excited about learning. The reading activities are determined by the lesson and the practice reader enclosed in the homework bag. They include games (board games, teacher-made folder games, card games, etc.), art projects (with the materials included), writing projects (a suitcase with a variety of writing materials), and simple cooking recipes.

These homework bags encourage parent–child interaction as they work together on the same skills that are covered at school. The parents have firsthand experience in watching the academic growth of their child and discovering their child's weaknesses and strengths. The child gets to practice needed skills in a safe, warm environment with the added bonus of parental approval.

STEP 6 · TEACH PARENTS

At the first of the year, I hold a meeting for my parents. I explain classroom procedures and how first graders learn to read and solve math problems. The parents are supplied with handouts on activities they can do at home to improve math and reading skills. I do not assume the parents are knowledgeable about how to help their child at home. I conduct a minilesson on the parents' role in teaching children to read. I model for them how they should guide their children when reading together by asking predicting questions, discussing cause/effect, using context clues, and so forth. At the end of the meeting, parents are given the opportunity to ask questions concerning their children's education. This gives me the opportunity to clarify any concepts or activities I had not clearly explained. Usually the questions asked need to be heard by the entire group. Parents realize that everyone has some of the same concerns: getting a reluctant child to read, homework hassles, improving weak math/reading skills, and challenging high achievers. Parents see that they are not alone in their child's educational journey.

STEP 7 · RECRUIT PARENTS

Every year, I recruit parent volunteers to become involved in my class. These "helping hands" are used to encourage my students to develop skills and/or interests. Parents listen to my students read, play games with them, help individual students learn math facts or spelling words, make learning centers, and aid students in creating art projects. The use of parent volunteers helps to strengthen the relationship between school and home. It also makes parents more aware of the importance their role plays in the education of children.

By using a variety of activities, I get parents involved in their children's educations. If both members of the team—parents and teacher—meet their educational responsibilities, an unbeatable team is formed with the same goal in mind—*children excited about learning.*

....

Paula McCullough is a transitional first grade teacher at Lakehoma Elementary, Mustang, Oklahoma.

Given the changes in families today, you can do a number of things to ensure that all parents and families are meaningfully involved. The following are some ideas for working with today's changing families:

- *Provide support services.* Support can extend from being a "listening ear" to organizing support groups and seminars on single parenting. You can help families link up with other agencies and groups, such as Big Brothers and Big Sisters or Families Without Partners. Through newsletters and fliers, you can offer families specific advice on how to help children become independent and how to meet the demands of living in single-parent families, stepfamilies, grandparent families, and other family configurations.

- *Provide child care.* As more families need child care, be an advocate for establishing care where none exists, extending existing services, and helping arrange cooperative babysitting services. Providing child care for parent–teacher conferences and other school–parent/family activities is one way to meet parents' needs and make parent involvement programs successful.

- *Avoid criticism.* Be careful not to criticize parents for the jobs they are doing. They may not have extra time to spend with their children or know how to appropriately guide their behavior. Regardless of their circumstances, families need help, not criticism.

- *Adjust programs.* Adjust classroom and center activities to account for how particular children cope with their home situations. Children's needs for different kinds of activities depend on their experiences at home. For example, opportunities abound for role playing, and such activities help bring into the open situations that children need to talk about. Create opportunities to discuss families and the roles they play. Make it a point in the classroom to model, encourage, and teach effective interpersonal skills.

- *Be sensitive.* There are specific ways to sensitively approach today's changing family patterns. For example, avoid having children make presents for both parents when it is inappropriate to do so, and do not award prizes for bringing both parents to meetings. Be sensitive to the demands of school in relation to children's home lives.

- *Seek training.* Request in-service training to help you work with families. In-service programs can provide information about referral agencies, guidance techniques, ways to help families deal with their problems, and child abuse identification and prevention. Be alert to the signs of all kinds of child abuse, including mental, physical, and sexual abuse.

- *Increase parent contacts.* Encourage greater and different kinds of parent involvement through visiting homes; talking to families about children's needs; providing information and opportunities to parents, grandparents, and other family members; gathering information from families (such as through interest inventories); and keeping in touch with parents. Make parent contacts positive.

TYPES OF PARENT/FAMILY INVOLVEMENT

parent/family involvement
A process of helping parents and family members use their abilities to benefit themselves, their children, and the early childhood program.

Parent/family involvement is a process of helping parents and family members use their abilities to benefit themselves, their children, and the early childhood program. Families, children, and the program are all part of the process; consequently, all three parties should benefit from a well planned program of involvement. Nonetheless, the focus in interactions between parent/family and the child is the family—and you must work with and through families if you want to be successful.

As you think about your role in parent and family involvement, read about the six types of parent involvement in the accompanying Professionalism in Practice feature. These six types of parent/family involvement constitute a comprehensive approach to your work with parents. A worthy professional goal would be for you to try to have some of your parents involved in all six of these types of parental involvement through the program year.

Education as a Family Affair

Education starts in the home, and what happens there profoundly affects development and learning. The greater the family's involvement in children's learning, the more likely it is that they will receive a high-quality education. Helping parents learn about child development, providing them with activities they can use to teach their children in the home, and supporting parents in their role as their children's first teachers are powerful ways to help parents and children be successful.

Family-Centered Teaching

Family-centered teaching and learning focus on meeting the needs of children through the family unit. Family-centered teaching and learning make sense for a number of reasons. First, the family unit has the major responsibility for meeting children's needs. Children's development begins in the family system. The family is a powerful determiner of developmental processes, for better and for worse. What you want to do is maximize the best and diminish the worst. Helping parents and other family members meet their children's needs in appropriate ways means that everyone benefits. Enabling individuals in the family unit to become better parents and family members helps children and consequently promotes their success in school and life.

Second, family issues and problems must be addressed first to help children effectively. For instance, helping parents gain access to adequate and affordable health care increases the chances that the whole family, including children, will be healthy.

Third, you can do many things concurrently with children and their families that benefit both. Literacy is a good example. Adopting a family approach to literacy means that helping parents learn to read so they can read aloud to their children helps ensure children's literacy development as well. Figure 13.1 helps you understand more about the outcomes of family-centered teaching.

Two-Generation and Intergenerational Family Programs

Two-generation programs involve parents and their children and are designed to help both generations and strengthen the family unit. Use the following guidelines to effectively involve all parents and families, including grandparents:

- *Support parents in their roles as first teachers of their children.* Support can include information, materials, and help with parenting questions.
- *Learn how families rear children and manage their families.* Political, social, cultural, and moral values of families all have implications for parent participation and ways to teach children.
- *Educate parents to be mentors, classroom aides, tutors, and homework helpers.* Also, communicate guidelines for helping students study for tests.
- *Support fathers in their roles as parents.* By supporting and encouraging fathers, you support the whole family.
- *Ask parents what goals they have for their children.* Use these goals to help you in your planning. Encourage parents to have realistically high expectations for their children.
- *Work with and through families.* Ask parents to help you in working with and involving other parents. Parents respond positively to other parents, so it makes sense to have parents helping families.
- *Get to know your children's parents and families in order to build relationships with them.* This allows for better communication. Home visits are a good way to do this.
- *Learn how to best communicate with parents based on their cultural communication preferences.* Take into account cultural features that can inhibit collaboration.

As you think about your role in involving parents and families, it would be helpful to review the six types of involvement shown in the accompanying figure. Let's take a closer look at what you can do with each type, along with examples from actual practice.

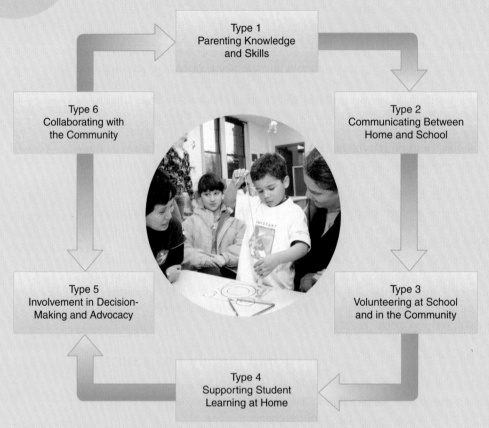

Source: Epstein, J. L. et al. (2009). *School, family, and community partnerships: Your handbook for action, 3rd ed.* Thousand Oaks, CA: Corwin Press..

1. **Parenting**—Assist families with parenting and child-rearing skills, understanding child and adolescent development, and setting home conditions that support children as students at each age and grade level. Assist schools in understanding families.

*Carstens Elementary School
Detroit, Michigan*

Carstens Elementary School's Parent Involvement Planning Team established a Parent University, where the parents of at-risk children could brush up on or acquire the skills they need to be effective partners in their children's education. The Parent University offered sixteen weeks of classes on *relevant parenting topics. The program also familiarized parents with local school policies and procedures, giving them an opportunity to be more actively involved in school governance through the PTA and School Improvement Team.*

The Parent University was specifically targeted to parents whose children had been identified as "at-risk" because of previous expulsions, chronic absences, or academic deficiencies. The administration at Carstens devised the program after surveying three hundred parents about what they wanted at the school. The planning team developed the curriculum.

In the weekly three-hour sessions, parents learned about parenting skills, family communications, peer mediation, family budgeting, parent involvement, activity planning, healthy practices, school governance, and advocacy. The school provided a structured curriculum for these sessions. While the parents were in class, their children enjoyed recreational activities in another part of the school.

2. **Communicating**—Communicate with families about school programs and student progress through effective school-to-home and home-to-school communications.

Wing Luke Elementary School
Seattle, Washington

While good communication is an issue in many schools, it presents an even greater challenge at Wing Luke Elementary because the students speak more than fifteen different native languages. With mathematics as the common denominator, school staff undertook four Family Cultural Math Nights. These get-togethers gave families the opportunity to learn about the school's math curriculum from teachers and speak to other parents who share their native tongue.

Math teachers, working with the staff of Wing Luke's ELL department, designed the program for these math nights. School newsletters and specific invitations went home with students, inviting parents in many languages.

School staff members grouped parents by language. "We met with families with the topic of math in mind, but the goal for the evenings was that parents would talk among themselves with their own ethnic/language group about math and any needs they perceived in the area of math instruction," said the principal, Ellen Punyon. The school brought translators so that the different groups could communicate.

3. **Volunteering**—Improve recruitment, training, tasks, and schedules to involve families as volunteers and audiences at school or in other locations to support students and school programs.

Scott Elementary School and Ellsworth Elementary School
Naperville, Illinois

With students from many different cultures, ethnic groups, and backgrounds, two Naperville elementary schools used their growing diversity as the basis for successful school-wide events for parents, students, teachers, and administrators.

The Ellsworth celebration was an evening of games, performances, art exhibits, craft demonstrations, food, and, most importantly, sharing cultures and customs. Among the countries represented were Greece, Japan, Mexico, Morocco, Sweden, Cuba, and India. As students entered the gymnasium, they received a color map of the world to guide them as they visited the various exhibits and presentations, many of them made by parents and students.

"Around the World at Scott School" was the second successful multicultural fair at Scott Elementary. The school community transformed a dozen classrooms into an international festival. "When you entered the room, it would appear as if you had entered another country," said one

organizer. Parent volunteers created the displays and programs that typified the countries where they were born. Visitors could say "hello" in a different language, see what the various countries looked like, and participate in activities that acquainted them further with the countries.

In the gym, students and others performed music and dances from the various countries. Each student received a "passport" when he or she arrived at the fair; students could have them stamped as they visited different countries around the school. About 150 parents and 300 hundred students attended the Scott Fair.

4. **Learning at home**—Involve families with their children in learning activities at home, including homework and other curriculum-related activities and decisions.

Hill Field Elementary School
Clearfield, Utah

Even with 95 percent of its students living in military families and half of its students moving in and out each year, Hill Field Elementary was able to attract someone for its literacy night that everyone recognized—Dr. Seuss! The school's principal dressed up as the popular children's author, accompanied by the some of his friends—the Cat in the Hat, the Grinch, and Thing One and Thing Two—for a celebration of literacy and Dr. Seuss's birthday.

And what a celebration it was, with more than three hundred people attending. "It was a hugely successful event and exceeded my expectations," said one teacher, who is a member of the literacy council. The event ended with everyone eating cake and punch and singing "Happy Birthday" to Dr. S. All of the children took home goodie bags of books and other things to read.

Because its student body is in constant flux, the Hill Field staff decided to involve parents in as many activities as possible to add some stability to the children's education. By holding a literacy night, Hill Field hoped to educate parents about the components of literacy: independent reading, reading aloud, fluency, and comprehension. Testing in the school indicated that students needed to improve in all of these skill areas.

Students arrived in their pajamas with their families. They visited stations where they read books, made crafts related to fairy tales and Dr. Seuss stories, and attended readers' theaters, where older students dramatically read stories out loud. Literacy night exposed students to the fun of reading. Parents learned how to help their children at home and how to access materials to learn even more.

5. **Decision making**—Include families as participants in school decisions, governance, and advocacy through PTA/PTO, school councils, committees, and other parent organizations.

Parents Plus
Milwaukee, Wisconsin

With an armload of free tickets to a popular ice-skating show, Parents Plus helped a small Milwaukee elementary

(continued)

(continued)

school launch its Action Team for Partnerships (ATP). Parents who completed a survey on school needs and volunteer potential received a free ticket and transportation for every family member to the touring ice show. In return, the school got almost a 100 percent response to its surveys, giving it a strong foundation for its parent involvement program. The tickets were donated to a Parents Plus staff member for use at the school.

Parents Plus is Wisconsin's Parent Information and Resource Center (PIRC), funded through a grant from the U.S. Department of Education. Its mission is to support positive parenting skills and increase parent involvement in schools to improve student achievement. The Parents Plus representatives and school administrators wrote the survey questions so that they allowed parents to say how they felt about the school, what their needs were, and how willing they were to volunteer their time and talents for both the ATP and other school needs. Working on a team with school and community members empowers parents and "having a voice will make advocating an easier thing for parents to do," a Parents Plus representative said.

6. **Collaborating with the community**—Coordinate resources and services for families, students, and the school with businesses, agencies, and other groups, and provide services to the community.

Frederick Law Olmsted School #64/56
Buffalo, New York

Parents often spend a great deal of time, energy, and money trying to find constructive after-school activities for their children. At Frederick Law Olmstead School, however, that is no longer necessary. The after-school enrichment program provides an hour of creative activities and experiences every day, while furthering the school's goals and preparing students for required tests.

During two six-week sessions, about one hundred Olmstead students participated in crafts, yoga, and cooking, as well as many other fun and educational activities. Parents and community partners of the two-site elementary-middle school contributed heavily to the successful program:

- The Explore and More Children's Museum conducted hands-on, culture-themed crafts activities.
- The Himalaya Institute provided a yoga instructor.
- The Darlene Ceglia Dance Project taught hip hop dancing, while the Buffalo Inner-City Ballet prepared beginning dancers well enough to perform in *The Nutcracker* at Shea's Performing Arts Center, downtown Buffalo's largest theater.
- Two professional chefs taught fifth and sixth graders how to read recipes and safely prepare a variety of dishes.
- More than twenty parents volunteered their time and talents.

Source: Epstein, J. L., et al. (2009). *School, family, and community partnerships: Your handbook for action, 3rd ed.* (Thousand Oaks, CA: Corwin Press, 2009) or online at http://www.partnershipschools.org.

TEACHERS, PRE-K–3, PROVIDE

- Family education
  - Literacy and math help
  - Nutrition education activities
  - Homework help
  - Technology education
- Basic counseling
  - Parenting help and skills
  - Assistance with problems of daily living
- Referrals to community agencies
  - Help with food, clothing, shelter

OUTCOMES/BENEFITS

- Increase knowledge, skills, and understanding of education process
- Help families and children address and solve problems
- Provide greater range of resources and more experts than school alone can provide
- Relieve families and children/youth of stress to make learning more possible
- Increase student achievement
- Promote school retention and prevent dropout

FIGURE 13.1 Family-Centered Teaching

The Federal Government and Parent Involvement

Given the key role that parents play in student education, it should come as no surprise that federal and state governments are taking a leading role in ensuring that parents are involved in schools. The No Child Left Behind Act of 2001 (NCLB) changed the way schools interact with parents. Prior to NCLB, parental involvement was largely determined by school district policies and administrator and teacher discretion. This is no longer the case: NCLB mandates a wide range of required procedures and activities relating to parental involvement.

The extent and range of parental involvement under NCLB is specific and comprehensive, at both the district and schoolhouse level. NCLB requires that each school must:

- Convene an annual meeting at a convenient time, to which all parents of participating children are invited and encouraged to attend; inform parents of their school's participation; and explain the requirements and the right of the parents to be involved.

- Involve parents in an organized, ongoing, and timely way in the planning, review, and improvement of programs, including the planning, review, and improvement of the school parental involvement policy and the joint development of the school-wide program plan.

- Provide parents with timely information about programs, a description and explanation of the curriculum, and the forms of academic assessment used to measure student progress and the proficiency levels students are expected to meet.

- Provide opportunities, if requested by parents, for regular meetings to formulate suggestions and to participate, as appropriate, in decisions relating to the education of their children and respond to any such suggestions as soon as practicably possible.[12]

NCLB also requires that the district, parents, schools, and students enter into a compact of shared responsibility for ensuring high student achievement. The school compact describes the school's responsibility to provide high-quality curriculum and instruction in a supportive and effective learning environment.[13]

ACTIVITIES FOR INVOLVEMENT

Unlimited possibilities exist for family involvement, but a coordinated effort is required to build an effective, meaningful program that can bring about a change in education and benefit all concerned: families, children, professionals, and communities. Following are some activities you can implement to ensure successful and significant parent and family involvement. The activities are organized according to the six types of parent/family involvement previously outlined.

Type 1—Parenting Knowledge and Skills

- *Participation in workshops.* These workshops introduce families to the school's policies, procedures, and programs. Most families want to know what is going on in the school and would do a better job of helping their children at home if they knew school policies and classroom procedures.

Families continue to change and, as they do, you must adapt and adopt new ways of involving family members and providing for their needs. For example, due in part to the 2008–2009 recession, growing numbers of fathers have responsibility for rearing their children. What can you do to ensure the involvement of single fathers in your programs?

Go to the Assignments and Activities section in Topic 3: Family/Community of the MyEducationLab for your course and complete the activity entitled *Involving Families: Super Smile Day.* Observe how members of the community work together with families and children to the benefit of all.

Go to the Assignments and Activities section in Topic 3: Family/Community of the MyEducationLab for your course and complete the activity entitled *Daily Conversations with Families.* Discuss with classmates what you noticed about the teacher/parent relationships.

- *Attending adult education classes.* These classes provide members of the community with opportunities to learn about a range of subjects.
- *Attending training programs.* These programs give parents, family members, and others skills as classroom aides, club and activity sponsors, curriculum planners, and policy decision makers. When parents, family members, and community persons are viewed as experts, empowerment results.
- *Participation in classroom and center activities.* While not all families can be directly involved in classroom activities, encourage those who can. Those who are involved must have guidance, direction, and training. Involving parents and others as paid aides is also an excellent way to provide employment and training. Many programs, such as Head Start, actively support such a policy.
- *Resource libraries and materials centers.* Families benefit from books and other articles relating to parenting. Some programs furnish resource areas with comfortable chairs to encourage families to use these materials.

Type 2—Communicating Between Home and School

- *Support services such as car pools and babysitting.* This makes attendance and involvement possible.
- *Performances and plays.* These, especially ones in which children have a part, tend to bring families to school; however, the purpose of children's performances should not be solely to get families involved.
- *Telephone hotlines.* When staffed by families, hotlines can help allay fears and provide information relating to child abuse, communicable diseases, and special events. Schools can organize telephone networks to help children and parents with homework.
- *Newsletters.* When planned with parents' help, newsletters are an excellent way to keep families informed about program events, activities, and curriculum information. Newsletters written in parents' native language help keep all families informed.
- *Home learning materials and activities.* Putting out a monthly calendar of activities is a good way to keep families involved in their children's learning.
- *Involvement of families in writing individualized education programs (IEPs) for children with special needs.* Such involvement in writing an IEP is not only a legal requirement but also an excellent learning experience.

Type 3—Encouraging Volunteering at School and in the Community

- *Child care.* Families may not be able to attend programs and become involved if they do not have child care for their children. Child care makes their participation possible and more enjoyable.
- *Service exchanges.* When operated by early childhood programs and other agencies, exchanges help families in their needs for services. For example, one parent provided child care in her home in exchange for having her washing machine repaired. The possibilities for such exchanges are endless. In tough economic times in particular, foster and exchange programs have become more popular.
- *Welcoming committees.* A good way to involve families in any program is to have other families contact them when their children first join a program.

Type 4—Supporting Student Learning at Home

- *Provide books and other materials for parents and children to use at home.* Provide material for parents to read to their children. For example, in the Professionalism in Practice feature "Home and School: An Unbeatable Team!" at the beginning of this chapter, you learned how teacher Paula McCullough uses book bags to encourage parental awareness of student learning.

Homework assignments for all children are a growing reality in many of today's primary classrooms. Over the past decade homework has increased by 50 percent. First grade teacher Karen Alverez at Aldama Elementary School in Los Angeles assigns her students forty-five minutes of homework every day, Monday through Thursday. Like Karen, teachers are assigning homework in response to higher standards and state tests that begin as early as kindergarten. Many teachers believe homework is one way of helping children learn the knowledge and skills mandated by school districts. Parents not only support homework, but they also expect their children to have homework.

Homework can be a challenge for parents and children. One of the issues parents and children have with homework is how to get the help they need with completing homework assignments. Keep in mind that quite often when you assign homework to children you are also assigning it to parents who are responsible for seeing that their children complete it! Over half of all parents are involved in their children's homework in one way or another.

The Internet is one source of help. B. J. Pinchbeck was nine years old when he founded B. J. Pinchbeck's Homework Helper (http://www.bjpinchbeck.com), which lists more than seven hundred links to educational sites and is affiliated with the Discovery Channel. Other sources for homework help are:

- Education Planet: http://www.educationplanet.com
- Ask Kids: http://www.askkids.com
- Fact Monster Homework Center: http://www.factmonster.com
- Yahooligans: http://kids.yahoo.com/learn
- KidsClick!: http://www.kidsclick.org

Pick a grade from kindergarten through third and develop a homework assignment for your class. Use these Internet sites to complete it. Develop a set of guidelines for how children can use the Internet to help them with their homework.

- *Develop a "home learning kit" around a content area such as math or science.* This can consist of activities and materials (books, activity packets, etc.). Send these kits home with children.
- *Give suggestions to parents.* Provide parents with tips for how to help their children with homework. (The accompanying Technology Tie-In feature, "Homework Helpers," presents some ideas for parents that one teacher is using in her classroom.)
- *Develop a website for parents.* A website informs them about the activities of your classroom. Give suggestions for how parents can extend and enrich classroom projects and activities at home.

Type 5—Involvement in Decision Making and Advocacy

- *Fairs and bazaars.* Schools should involve families in fund-raising.
- *Hiring and policy making.* Parents and community members can and should serve on committees that set policy and hire staff.
- *Curriculum development and review.* Parents' involvement in curriculum planning helps them learn about and understand what constitutes a quality program and what is involved in a developmentally appropriate curriculum. When families know about the curriculum, they are more supportive of it.

Type 6—Collaborating with the Community

- *Family nights, cultural dinners, carnivals, and potluck dinners.* Such events bring families and the community to the school in nonthreatening, social ways.
- *Parent support groups.* Parents need support in their roles. Support groups can provide parenting information, community agency information, and speakers.

Conducting Home Visits

Two home visits per year are required in the Head Start program, and home visits are becoming more commonplace in many school districts.[14] Teachers who do home visiting are trained prior to going on the visits. Although not every state or district pays extra for home

PEARSON
myeducationlab

Go to the Assignments and Activities section in Topic 3: Family/Community of the MyEducationLab for your course and complete the activity entitled *Home Visits to Connect with Families.* After reading the case study, consider how you would like to conduct home visits. What are some of the concerns you have?

visits, more schools are building home visits into the school calendar, with a certain number of days being set aside for home visiting. Some districts and programs provide released time for visitation by hiring substitute teachers to enable classroom teachers to make home visits.

A home visiting program demonstrates that teachers, principal, and school staff are willing to "go more than halfway" to involve all parents in their children's education. Home visits help teachers demonstrate their interest in students' families and understand their students better by seeing them in their home environment. For example, Susan Drinker, who teaches at Main Street School in Exeter, New Hampshire, makes sure parents partner in their children's education. She makes home visits at the beginning of each school year, promoting literacy by taking each family a book and a related stuffed toy.[15]

The importance of home visits is reflected in the fact that the American Recovery and Reinvestment Act of 2009 authorizes school districts to use funds to support home visits.

These visits should not replace parent–teacher conferences or be used to discuss children's progress. When done early before any school problems can arise, they avoid putting parents on the defensive and signal that teachers are eager to work with all parents. Teachers who have made home visits say they build stronger relationships with parents and their children, and improve attendance and achievement. Although many "home" visits do occur in the home, they do not always have to. Sometimes parents are more comfortable meeting teachers away from the home in places such as community centers, churches, or the local YMCA or YWCA. These visits are still considered "home" visits.

Here are some guidelines for how you can be successful in your program of home visitation:

- Schedule the visits:
  - Some schools have scheduled home visits in the afternoon right after school. Others have found that early evening is more convenient for parents. Some schedule visits right before a new school year begins. A mix of times may be needed to reach all families.
  - Work with community groups (e.g., Boys and Girls Clubs, housing complexes, 4-H, YMCAs, and community centers) to schedule visits in neutral but convenient spaces.
- Make parents feel comfortable:
  - Send a letter home to parents explaining the desire to have teachers make informal visits to all students' homes. Include a form that parents can mail back to accept or decline the visit.
  - State clearly that the intent of your thirty-minute visit is to introduce yourself to family members and not to discuss the child's progress.
  - Suggest that families think about special things their children would want to share with you, the teacher.
- Reduce parents' worries. One school included a note to parents that said "No preparation is required. In fact, our homes need to be vacuumed and all of us are on diets!" This touch of humor and casualness helps set a friendly and informal tone.
- Make a phone call to parents who have not responded to explain the plan for home visits and reassure parents that it is to get acquainted and not to evaluate students.
- Enlist community groups, religious organizations, and businesses to help publicize the home visits.[16]

Conducting Parent–Teacher Conferences

Significant parent involvement occurs through well planned and well conducted conferences between parents and early childhood teachers, informally referred to as parent–teacher conferences. Such conferences are often the first contact many families have with school.

Conferences are critical both from a public relations point of view and as a vehicle for helping families and professionals accomplish their goals. The following guidelines will help you as an early childhood professional prepare for and conduct successful conferences:

- *Plan ahead.* Be sure of the reason for the conference. What are your objectives? What do you want to accomplish? List the points you want to cover and think about what you are going to say.
- *Get to know the families.* This is not wasted time; the more effectively you establish rapport with families, the more you will accomplish in the long run.
- *Avoid an authoritative atmosphere.* Do not sit behind your desk while families sit in children's chairs. Treat families and others like the adults they are.
- *Communicate at parents' levels.* Do not condescend or patronize. Instead, use familiar words, phrases, and explanations families understand. Do not use jargon or complicated explanations, and speak in your natural style.
- *Accentuate the positive.* Make every effort to show and tell families that children are doing well. When you deal with problems, put them in the proper perspective: what a child is able to do, what the goals and purposes of the learning program are, what specific skill or concept you are trying to get the child to learn, and what problems the child is having in achieving the goal or purpose. Most importantly, explain what you plan to do to help the child achieve and what specific role families can have in meeting the achievement goals.
- *Give families a chance to talk.* You will not learn much about families and children if you do all the talking, nor are you likely to achieve your goals. Some teachers are accustomed to dominating a conversation, and many families will not be as verbal as you, so you will have to encourage some families to talk.
- *Learn to listen.* An active listener holds eye contact, uses body language such as head nodding and hand gestures, does not interrupt, avoids arguing, paraphrases as a way of clarifying ideas, and keeps the conversation on track.
- *Follow up.* Ask families to schedule a definite time for the next conference as you are concluding the current one. Having another conference is the best method of solidifying gains and extending support, but other acceptable means of follow-up are telephone calls, written reports, notes sent with children, and brief visits to the home. Although these types of contacts may appear casual, they should be planned for and conducted as seriously as any regular family–teacher conference.
- *Develop an action plan.* Never leave families with a sense of frustration, not knowing what you are doing or what they are to do. Every communication with families should end on a positive note, so that everyone knows what can be done and how to do it.

PEARSON
myeducationlab

Go to the Assignments and Activities section in Topic 3: Family/Community of the MyEducationLab for your course and complete the activity entitled *Parent-Teacher Conference.* Observe how a teacher has a conference with a parent to learn more about the student and help her succeed in the classroom.

Making Contact by Telephone

Making a telephone call is an efficient way to contact families when it is impossible to arrange a face-to-face conference. Here are some tips you can use for your telephone contacts with parents:

- Since you cannot see someone on a telephone, it takes a little longer to build rapport and trust. The time you spend overcoming families' initial fears and apprehensions will pay dividends later.
- Constantly clarify what you are talking about and what you and the families have agreed to do, using such phrases as "What I heard you say then . . ." and "So far, we have agreed that . . ."
- Do not act hurried. There is a limit to the amount of time you can spend on the phone, but you may be one of the few people who care about the parent and the child. Your telephone contact may be the major part of the family's support system.

Involving Parents Electronically

The Internet provides another way for you to reach out to parents and keep them informed and involved. For example, teachers use the Internet to post calendars, newsletters, discussion topics, assignments, assessment tools, spelling lists, and tips. Here are some ways you can electronically connect with families:

- *E-mail.* E-mail is fast, convenient, and is increasingly a preferred mode of communication for many. E-mail can be used not only to increase communication between families and teachers, but also to increase communication between faculty and outside personnel involved in working with individual students.

- *Teacher website.* Most school districts have a website that provides general information about the district and individual schools. Many teachers have their own classroom website as well. Web pages are excellent ways to give parents and community members general information and let them virtually experience school and classroom events and accomplishments. For example, through the Internet, you can access many teachers' websites. Now would be a good time for you to do this.

- *Twitter.* Twitter, a social-networking website delivering short (140 characters or less), text-based posts, is useful on many levels. Teachers can use Twitter to send out homework so that parents are automatically updated. Parents can follow teachers and see what their children are up to from any computer (from work, home, coffee shops) at any time of the day. Twitter can also bring students into contact with their community on a local and global level. Students in two Maine elementary schools have been exchanging messages through Twitter. Teachers say the exercise was initiated to help students develop their writing skills by composing messages that must be 140 characters or less.[17]

- *Video chat.* Teachers can use free video chat providers such as Skype or Gmail to hold convenient conferences with parents. If a parent is away on a business trip or can't get away from the office, with the click of a button the parent can take part in a conference with teachers and other parents on their lunch break. In Olathe, Kansas, teachers are using Skype to allow both students and their families to attend parent–teacher conferences.[18]

- *Teacher–parent blog.* Teachers can use a blog to connect with students and their families. Blogs can feature lesson summaries, concept introduction and exploration, and classroom notes, reminders, and news. Parents can leave comments, be more informed, and communicate with other parents in the class. "I can whip out something in maybe five minutes and immediately post it," says Melanie Sullivan, a third grade teacher in Needham, Massachusetts. Sullivan started her first classroom blog last school year with her first grade class. "Parents just want to know what's going on. The more they know, the more they understand where you're coming from and what you're trying to accomplish in your room." Parents concur. One Needham parent said the blog gave her something to talk about with her first grade son: "Instead of saying 'what did you learn today' I say, 'you know, I heard that your first grade class got some chicks,' and he would get so excited about the subject matter, he would start blabbering on."[19]

Before you set up your class Web page or begin communicating with parents via e-mail or Twitter, here are some things to consider:

- Check with your school or program technology coordinator for guidelines and policies for Web page development and communicating electronically with parents.
- Remember that not all parents are connected to the Internet. There is still a "digital divide" in the United States; low-income parents and minorities are less likely to have Internet access. Consider how to provide families without Internet access the same information you provide to families who have Internet service.

Here are some guidelines to follow when you communicate with parents on the Internet:

- Observe all the rules of politeness and courtesy that you would in a face-to-face conversation.
- Observe all the rules of courteous Internet conversations. For example, don't use all capital letters (this is similar to SHOUTING).
- Remember that just like handwritten notes, electronic mail can be saved. In addition, electronic notes are much more easily transferred.
- Be straightforward and concise in your electronic conversations.
- Establish ground rules ahead of time about what you will and will not discuss electronically.

Involving Single-Parent Families

Many of the children you teach will be from single-parent families. Depending on where you teach, as many as 50 percent of your children could be from single-parent families. In fact, recent data reveal that 40 percent of all new births are to single mothers.[20] Here are some things you can do to ensure that single-parent families are involved:

- Many adults in one-parent families are employed during school hours and may not be available for conferences or other activities during that time. You must be willing to accommodate family schedules by arranging conferences at other times, perhaps early morning, noon, late afternoon, or early evening. Some employers, sensitive to these needs, give release time to participate in school functions, but others do not. In addition, professionals and principals need to think seriously about going to families, rather than having families always come to them.
- Remember that single parents have a limited amount of time to spend on involvement with their children's school and with their children at home. Therefore, when you talk with single-parent families, make sure that (1) the meeting starts on time, (2) you have a list of items to discuss, (3) you have sample materials available to illustrate all points, (4) you make specific suggestions relative to one-parent environments, and (5) the meeting ends on time. Because one-parent families are more likely to need child care assistance to attend meetings, child care should be planned for every parent meeting or activity.
- Suggest some ways that single parents can make their time with their children meaningful. If a child has trouble following directions, show families how to use home situations to help in this area. For example, children can learn to follow directions while helping with errands, meal preparation, or housework.
- Get to know families' lifestyles and living conditions. For instance, you can recommend that every child have a quiet place to study, but this may be an impossible demand for some households. You need to visit some of the homes in your community before you set meeting times, decide what family involvement activities to implement, and determine what you will ask of families during the year. Keep in mind the condition of the home environment when you request that children bring certain items to school or carry out certain tasks at home. And when asking for parents' help, be sensitive to their talents and time constraints.
- Help develop support groups for one-parent families within your school, such as discussion groups and classes on parenting for singles. And be sure to include the needs and abilities of one-parent families in your family involvement activities and programs. After all, single-parent families may represent the majority of families in your program.
- Avoid making the assumption that students live with both biological parents.
- Avoid the traditional "Dear Parents" greeting in letters and other messages; instead use "Dear Parent," "Dear Family," "Friends," or some other form of greeting.

PEARSON
myeducationlab

Go to the Building Teaching Skills and Dispositions section in Topic 10: Cultural & Linguistic Diversity of the MyEducationLab for your course and complete the activity entitled *Creating Culturally Diverse Environments to Facilitate Children's Development.*

linguistically diverse parents Parents whose English proficiency is minimal and who lack a comprehensive knowledge of the norms and social systems in the United States.

Your role as an early childhood professional includes learning how to effectively involve linguistically diverse parents and families of many different cultures. How will you prepare yourself for this important role?

Involving Linguistically Diverse Parents and Families

Forty-three percent of public school populations are considered to be members of a racial or ethnic minority group.[21] The fact that the minority is now almost the majority is due largely to the growth in the proportion of students who are Hispanic. Hispanic students represent 20 percent of public school enrollment.[22]

Linguistically diverse parents are individuals whose English proficiency is minimal and who lack a comprehensive knowledge of the norms and social systems in the United States. Linguistically diverse families often face language and cultural barriers that greatly hamper their ability to become actively involved, although many have a great desire and willingness to participate in their children's education.

Because the culture of linguistically diverse families often differs from the majority in a community, those who seek truly collaborative community, home, and school involvement must take into account the cultural features that can inhibit collaboration. Traditional styles of child rearing and family organization, attitudes toward schooling, organizations around which families center their lives, life goals and values, political influences, and methods of communication within the cultural group all have implications for parent participation.

Linguistically diverse families often lack information about the U.S. educational system, including basic school philosophy, practice, and structure, which can result in misconceptions, fear, and a general reluctance to respond to invitations for involvement. Furthermore, this educational system may be quite different from schools with which these families are familiar. The accompanying Diversity Tie-In feature, "Getting Hispanic Parents Involved in Schools," offers suggestions for involving minority parents.

Accommodating Diverse Learners: Homeless Children

Meet Liliana, an eight-year-old second grader in Texas. She loves to play the violin, enjoys learning new math concepts, plays four-square at recess, and has two younger brothers. Until recently, Liliana only had eight-year-old worries. But then both her parents lost their jobs. Unable to find work and make mortgage payments, Liliana and her family were forced to move into a two-bedroom apartment with relatives; now she worries about the bugs that crawl over her as she sleeps on her cousin's floor.

Unfortunately, Liliana's story is very common. America is currently seeing a surge of homeless children. The National Center on Family Homelessness estimates that 1.5 million children are homeless. Arkansas, Georgia, and Texas have the highest levels of child homelessness.[23] Regardless of state residence, one in every fifty children were homeless in 2009.[24] In some cities, the rates are even worse; in Minneapolis, one in ten children were homeless.[25] The majority of children who are homeless are between the ages of birth and thirteen, the very group of children you will be teaching.[26]

Homelessness has long-lasting and devastating effects on children. They have at least twice as much traumatic stress, overall health problems, and emotional disturbances as children who are not homeless.[27] Many do not know where they will be sleeping at night, what they will get to eat the next day, or even if they will get to eat at all. Liliana, like so many of her homeless peers, suffers from nightmares, is teased by her classmates, and has trouble staying awake during the day. Homelessness affects Liliana's emotional and physical well-being as well as her ability to learn.

The American Recovery and Reinvestment Act of 2009 allocated $70 million to aid homeless children. But with over fifteen thousand school districts nationwide, there is still not enough money to go around.[28] Many school districts are aggressively combating homelessness. Here are some things that they have done:

- Nationwide, the McKinney-Vento Homeless Assistance Act requires school districts to establish "liaisons" between children who are homeless and their schools. In Richmond, California, liaisons established a community organization named Families in Transition (FIT), which uses these liaisons to identify and aid children who are homeless. FIT not only builds community ties, but also monitors homeless children's school attendance and grades.[29]

- In Albuquerque, New Mexico, the school districts utilize liaisons to gain grant funding and to implement summer school programs, career programs, biweekly free tutoring, support groups, and free food programs for children who are homeless.[30]

- In Minneapolis, Minnesota, the school districts help to ensure that homeless students stay enrolled in one school continuously by providing free transportation, whether by taxi, bus, or school bus, regardless of the pick-up or drop-off site. Minneapolis Public Schools (MPS) districts train their staff to recognize the signs of children who are between homes so that they can get them help. MPS also provides brand-new backpacks and school supplies for homeless children and allocates a certain amount of funding to keep homeless children involved in extracurricular activities like sports, dance, music, and art.[31]

Regardless of where you teach and your district's policies, there are things you can do in your classroom and your community to aid children like Liliana. Here are some tips:

- Challenge your own conception of homelessness. Regardless of your beliefs about adults who are homeless and accompanying stereotypes, children in general and your students in particular are not responsible for their families' poverty or home situation. Treat students and their families who are having economic difficulties respectfully and professionally, with empathy and an open mind.

- Know the signs of homelessness such as hesitancy about what home address to use, inability or difficulty in contacting parents, wearing the same clothes to school on consecutive days, or wearing inappropriate clothing for the weather. Other indicators are poor hygiene, fatigue (may fall asleep in class), and malnutrition/chronic hunger. Pay close attention to social factors such as difficulty or avoidance in making friends, seeming "old" beyond their years, fear of abandonment, difficulty trusting people, and anxiety late in the school day.[32]

- To help Liliana in your classroom:
  - Be patient and sensitive. Due to her economic situation, Liliana is facing a lot of difficulties that may interfere with her schoolwork. If she falls asleep or is disruptive, remain calm and empathetic. Offer her a chance to take a nap during recess or free time.
  - Build Liliana's self-esteem by providing her an outlet to pursue the activities she enjoys and is good at. She enjoys the violin, so praise her often and appeal to the school's music teacher to provide free lessons.
  - Make sure that you are approachable and available to listen to Liliana. Be reassuring, encouraging, empathetic, and respectful. If you feel that Liliana needs more emotional support than you know how to give, help her connect with a school

Getting Hispanic Parents Involved in Schools

Because parents play such a powerful role in their children's educational development, early childhood programs must make every effort to involve the parents and families of *all* children. Unfortunately, many minority parents are not included at all, or not to the extent they should be. The urgency of involving minority parents becomes more evident when we look at the population growth of minorities. Strong growth in Hispanic enrollment is expected to continue for decades, according to a recently released U.S. Census Bureau population projection. The Census Bureau projects that the Hispanic school-age population, aged five to seventeen, will increase by 166 percent by 2050 (to 28 million from 11 million in 2006), while the non-Hispanic school-age population will grow by just 4 percent (to 45 million from 43 million) over this same period. In 2050, there will be more school-age Hispanic children than school-age non-Hispanic white children.[*]

Due in part to the immigration backlash of the 1990s and early 2000s, based on the assumption that Latinos were taking jobs of U.S. citizens, wanting free handouts, not contributing to the U.S. economy, and are not assimilating to mainstream society, many immigrant families are resentful of these sentiments and believe that educational, community, and human service programs harbor some degree of prejudices that create a deep sense of *desconfianza* or mistrust. As a result, Latino parents inherently distrust the intentions of program developers, as they perceive that their role is not particularly valued or respected. Programs need to be deeply concerned with developing trust with these families by focusing on building interpersonal relationships. These interpersonal relationships need to be based on respect, dignity, and kindness.[†]

The St. Joseph School District in St. Joseph, Missouri, in attempts to generate and sustain respectful, dignified, and kind relationships between schools and linguistically diverse families, established the English for Speakers of Other Languages (ESOL) Program. The district's ESOL philosophy—integration, not assimilation—is visible in its ESOL office, appropriately called "The Welcome Center." The Welcome Center serves as an enrollment center for language minority families. The Welcome Center also serves as a resource center and gathering place for students' families.[†]

Furthermore, family outreach is the focus of bimonthly meetings that are held at the ESOL office. Family Fun Nights are regular events at the center schools, and all materials are offered in several languages. English classes are offered to students' parents and other members of the family through the district's adult English as a Second Language (ESL) program. St. Joseph's Parents-as-Teachers program employs one bilingual parent educator and aggressively recruits non-English-speaking families. The ESOL staff is on hand to help parents negotiate parent–teacher conferences, and can provide a translated report card upon request. The motto of the program is that when students feel good and when their families feel good, both are more likely to be involved in education. Many families helped by the Welcome Center have reported that the ESOL program was a great help in navigating their first months in St. Joseph and that the staff guided the

counselor. Ask the school counselor for tips on how to be emotionally supportive of Liliana and her family.

- Watch for academic difficulties. If Liliana starts to fall behind, give her special attention and help. An older student can act as both a tutor and as a big brother/big sister to Liliana, providing her with both the extra academic support and the emotional support she needs.
- Be open, frank, and respectful with Liliana's parents. Provide them with information on free after-school activities that can both enrich Liliana's experience and act as child care so that they can work.
- Collaborate with parents. Discuss with parents their wishes and how best to get them the help they need.[33]
- Be an advocate. Work with local groups to obtain funds and resources to help homeless children and their families.

Encouraging Community Involvement

A comprehensive program of parent and family involvement is not complete without community involvement. More early childhood teachers realize that neither they alone nor the limited resources of their programs are sufficient to meet the needs of many children and family through the enrollment process and continues to help them understand the public school system.[§]

Across the country, educators will place more emphasis on how to make Hispanic and other minority parents feel welcome and involved in their children's schools. Programs that have successfully involved Hispanic parents recommend the following strategies:

- **Personal touch**—Use face-to-face communication in the Hispanic parents' primary language when first making contact. It may take several personal meetings before parents gain sufficient trust to actively participate.
  - Make home visits if possible, taking Spanish-speaking parents with you to interpret for you. Remember, parents trust parents!
  - Have parents invite other parents to school, where you can talk personally to a small group.
  - Always greet parents whenever they come to school for any reason.
- **Nonjudgmental communication**—Avoid making Hispanic parents feel that they are to blame for or are doing something wrong. Support parents for their strengths rather than judging them for perceived failings.
  - Be an active listener—pay close attention to what parents are saying and how they are saying it.
  - Be willing to compromise.
- **Bilingual support**—Communicate with Hispanic parents in both Spanish and English.
  - Send all notes and flyers home in Spanish.
  - Spanish-speaking parents can help you compose notes and announcements.

- Designate a Hispanic parent as the contact for your classroom to keep other parents informed about upcoming meetings.
- Establish a Spanish book corner where students and parents can check out bilingual or Spanish books to read together.
- **Staff development focused on Hispanic culture**—All staff must understand the key features of Hispanic culture—Latino history, traditions, values, and customs—and their impact on students' behavior and learning styles. For example, Hispanic children like peer-oriented learning, so mixed-age grouping and cooperative learning strategies work well. You should learn as much as possible about the children and their culture.
- **Community outreach.** Many Hispanic families can benefit from family literacy programs, vocational training, ESL programs, improved medical and dental services, and other community-based social services.[**]

[*]R. Fry and F. Gonzales, Pew Hispanic Center, "One in Five and Growing Fast: A Profile of Hispanic Public School Students," August 26, 2008; retrieved June 5, 2009, from http://pewhispanic.org/reports/report.php?ReportID=92.

[†]P. Springer, C. S. Hollist, and K. Buchfink, "Engaging Latinos in Culturally Specific Educational Programming: A Multidisciplinary Approach," *Family and Consumer Sciences Research Journal*, 37(3), July 2009, 310–328.

[‡]M. Hines-Dochterman, "Educating Every Child for Success," *PTA Magazine: Our Children 2008*, January 2008; accessed May 10, 2009, from *http://www.pta.org/2092.htm*.

[§]Ibid.

[**]L. Espinosa, "Hispanic Parent Involvement in Early Childhood Programs," *ERIC Digest*, ED382412, May 1995, *http://www.ericdigests.org/1996-1/hispanic.htm*.

families in the twenty-first century. Consequently, early education professionals are seeking ways to link families to community services and resources.

The task facing early childhood professionals is this: Seeking merely to involve parents in school activities is no longer a sufficient program of parent involvement. Today, we can make the lives of families and their children better by making families the focus of our involvement activities. In our effort to do this, community resources provide valuable tools, and businesses can partner with schools to enhance both educational opportunities and the lives of families.

Community Resources. The community offers a vital and rich array of resources for helping you teach better and for helping you meet the needs of parents and their children. Schools and teachers cannot address the many issues facing children and youth without the partnership and collaboration of powerful sectors of society, including community agencies, businesses, and industry.

Following are suggested actions you can take to learn to use your community in your teaching:

- *Know your students and their needs.* Through observations, conferences with parents, and discussions with students, you can identify barriers to children's learning and discover what kind of help to seek.

- *Know your community.* Walk or drive around the community. Ask a parent to give you a tour to help familiarize you with agencies and individuals. Read the local newspaper, and attend community events and activities.

- *Ask for help and support from parents and the community.* Keep in mind that many business and community leaders will not be involved unless you personally ask them. The only encouragement many individuals and local businesses need is your invitation.

- *Develop a directory of community agencies.* Consult the business pages of local phone books, contact local chambers of commerce, and ask parents what agencies are helpful to them.

- *Compile a list of people who are willing to come to your classroom to speak to or work with your students.* You can start by asking parents to volunteer and to give suggestions and recommendations of others.

Only by helping families meet their needs and those of their children will you create opportunities for these children to reach their full potential. For this reason alone, family involvement programs and activities must be an essential part of every early childhood program.

School–Business Partnerships.   School–business partnerships are excellent means of strengthening programs and helping children and families. For their part, businesses are eager to develop the business–school connection in an effort to help schools better educate children.

Schools and businesses all over the country have partnered to help both the schools and local businesses build involvement and community. For example in Durham, North Carolina, the school district sponsors an annual information session with the Durham Regional Association of Realtors. At this annual event, area real estate professionals learn all about Durham Public Schools so they can better respond to requests from home buyers (parents) who are moving to Durham.[34]

In the town of Keizer, Oregon, the weekly newspaper *Keizertimes* offers a free quarter-page of space for Keizer Elementary School and Gubser Elementary School to promote events and general communications. This space in the weekly paper helps foster a cooperative relationship between the schools and the Keizer community. The *Keizertimes* also provides another quarter-page in its "Keizer Connections" section, in which student reporters write articles that are published monthly. The publisher of the paper sends e-mails to students to remind them of their deadline dates and makes school visits to third grade reporters to talk with them about what makes a good reporter.[35]

Community businesses and civic organizations offer many opportunities for collaborative partnerships that can lead to the achievement of common goals for making education better. Begin now to plan for ways that you will reach out to and involve the community in your classroom.

Partnerships between schools and local businesses range from the simple and informal to highly structured and professional. Partnerships are often managed by teachers. A partnership can be between a local business or community organization and the entire school, a single class, or even just a few students. Community partners range from large corporations to smaller local businesses such as an independently owned pharmacy, the local branch of the YMCA, or a neighborhood grocery store. For example, some partnerships help schools promote a green agenda. Corinne Dowst, head of fund-raising for the

Parent Teacher Association at Henniker (New Hampshire) Community School, says she was looking for new fund-raising ideas when she saw an ad for Greenraising, a company that sells eco-friendly products. The school organized a spring sale around Earth Day, and circulated copies of the Greenraising catalog, which features such products as recycled gift-wrap paper and reusable water bottles. The result was the school's most successful fund-raiser in nearly three years, grossing about $2,500. Greenraising has helped about five hundred schools and nonprofits raise money.[36]

THE CHALLENGE

The challenge for you and all early childhood professionals is quite clear: how to make families the focus of your involvement activities so that their lives and their children's lives are made better. Anything less will not help families and children access and benefit from the opportunities of the twenty-first century.

However, this is not your only challenge. There are many challenges to working with children and their families. In every chapter I have outlined challenges you will face in your role as teachers: from academics to disabilities, from standards and testing to education models and actual application, the challenges are varied and many. However, as numerous and diverse as the challenges are, working with children and families and improving their lives is the real reward of teaching.

ACTIVITIES FOR PROFESSIONAL DEVELOPMENT

ethical dilemma

"I Really Don't Want to Get Involved"

Tyler Cove Elementary School has enrolled a number of new families who were displaced by a recent hurricane. Six-year-old Tamika, her mother, and three siblings arrived in town with only the clothes on their backs. Tamika has not had a change of clothing in several days. Although Carrie has no hurricane-displaced children in her third grade class, she is very much concerned about their well-being. She mentions to Tamika's teacher that several community agencies are involved in hurricane relief and could provide Tamika and her family with clothing and other resources. Tamika's teacher is unresponsive: "I know, Carrie, but I don't have the time to mess around with this stuff. I've got all I can do to keep up with the things I have to do in the classroom. I don't want to make a lot of extra work for myself. Besides, I really don't want to get involved with these families; they just don't fit in to our community."

What should Carrie do to help Tamika and her family? Should she report Tamika's teacher to the principal? Or should she offer to buy Tamika and her family clothing? Or should she call her friend at the Salvation Army for help? Or should she develop another strategy?

Application Activities

1. Develop a plan for parent/family involvement in a grade in which you plan to teach.
   a. Write objectives for the program.
   b. Use the six types of parent/family involvement to develop specific activities for involving families and for providing services to them.
   c. Explain how you would involve fathers, language-minority families, and families of children with disabilities.

2. Visit social services agencies in your area, and list the services they offer.

   a. Describe how you can work with these agencies to meet the needs of children and families.

   b. Invite agency directors to meet with your class to discuss how you and they can work cooperatively to help families and children.

   c. As families change, so, too, do the services they need. Conduct a family survey of several families to determine what services they believe are most needed. Tell how you could help provide those services.

3. Parents of children with disabilities may need help with accessing community resources for their children with disabilities.

   a. Use the Internet and other resources to identify resources in your community you think could help children and families. How would you share this information with parents? How could you help parents access these services?

   b. Develop one specific example for how you will electronically involve a family of a child with a disability.

4. Review teacher websites for grades one, two, and three.

   a. Do the websites specifically "reach out" to parents and families and provide them with useful information?

   b. What improvements would you make to each of the websites?

APPENDIX A

Time Line of the History of Early Childhood Education

1524 Martin Luther argued for public support of education for all children in his *Letter to the Mayors and Aldermen of All the Cities of Germany in Behalf of Christian Schools.*

1628 John Amos Comenius's *The Great Didactic* proclaimed the value of education for all children according to the laws of nature.

1762 Jean-Jacques Rousseau wrote *Émile,* explaining that education should take into account the child's natural growth and interests.

1801 Johann Pestalozzi wrote *How Gertrude Teaches Her Children,* emphasizing home education and learning by discovery.

1816 Robert Owen set up a nursery school in Great Britain at the New Lanark Cotton Mills, believing that early education could counteract bad influences of the home.

1836 William McGuffey began publishing the *Eclectic Reader* for elementary school children; his writing had a strong impact on moral and literary attitudes in the nineteenth century.

1837 Friedrich Froebel, known as the "father of the kindergarten," established the first kindergarten in Blankenburg, Germany.

1856 Mrs. Margaretha Schurz established the first kindergarten in the United States in Watertown, Wisconsin; the school was founded for children of German immigrants, and the program was conducted in German.

1860 Elizabeth Peabody opened a private kindergarten in Boston, Massachusetts, for English-speaking children.

1871 The first public kindergarten in North America was started in Ontario, Canada.

1873 Susan Blow opened the first public kindergarten in the United States in St. Louis, Missouri, as a cooperative effort with the superintendent of schools, William Harris.

1876 A model kindergarten was shown at the Philadelphia Centennial Exposition.

1892 The International Kindergarten Union (IKU) was founded.

1896 John Dewey started the Laboratory School at the University of Chicago, basing his program on child-centered learning with an emphasis on life experiences.

1907 Maria Montessori started her first preschool in Rome, called Children's House; her now-famous teaching method was based on the theory that children learn best by themselves in a properly prepared environment.

1911 Margaret and Rachel McMillan founded an open-air nursery school in Great Britain in which the class met outdoors; emphasis was on healthy living.

1915 Eva McLin started the first U.S. Montessori nursery school in New York City.

1918 The first public nursery schools were started in Great Britain.

1919 Harriet Johnson started the Nursery School of the Bureau of Educational Experiments, later to become the Bank Street College of Education.

1922 Abigail Eliot, influenced by the open-air school in Great Britain and basing her program on personal hygiene and proper behavior, started the Ruggles Street Nursery School in Boston.

1924 *Childhood Education,* the first professional journal in early childhood education, was published by the IKU.

1926 The National Committee on Nursery Schools was initiated by Patty Smith Hill at Columbia Teachers College; now called the National Association for the Education of Young Children (NAEYC), it provides guidance and consultant services for educators.

1926 The National Association of Nursery Education (NANE) was founded.

1930 The IKU changed its name to the Association for Childhood Education.

1943 Kaiser Child Care Centers opened in Portland, Oregon, to provide twenty-four-hour child care for children of mothers working in war-related industries.

1946 Dr. Benjamin Spock wrote the *Common Sense Book of Baby and Child Care.*

1950	Erik Erikson published his writings on the "eight ages or stages" of personality growth and development and identified "tasks" for each stage of development; the information, known as "Personality in the Making," formed the basis for the 1950 White House Conference on Children and Youth.
1952	Jean Piaget's *The Origins of Intelligence in Children* was published in English translation.
1960	Katherine Whiteside Taylor founded the American Council of Parent Cooperatives for those interested in exchanging ideas in preschool education; it later became the Parent Cooperative Preschools International.
1965	The Head Start program began with federal money allocated for preschool education; the early programs were known as child development centers.
1971	The Stride Rite Corporation in Boston was the first to start a corporate-supported child care program.
1972	The National Home Start Program was initiated for the purpose of involving parents in their children's education.
1975	Public Law 94-142, the Education for All Handicapped Children Act, was passed, mandating a free appropriate public education for all children with disabilities and extending many rights to parents of such children.
1984	The High/Scope Educational Foundation released a study that documented the value of high-quality preschool programs for poor children. This study would be cited repeatedly in coming years by those favoring expansion of Head Start and other early years programs.
1986	Public Law 99-457, the Education of the Handicapped Act Amendments, established a national policy on early intervention that recognizes its benefits, provides assistance to states for building systems of service delivery, and recognizes the unique roles of families in the development of their children with disabilities.
1988	Even Start was established by the U.S. Department of Education as a parent education/literacy program.
1995	Head Start Reauthorization established a new program, Early Head Start, for low-income pregnant women and families with infants and toddlers.
2001	The No Child Left Behind Act (NCLB) was passed, providing funding for early literacy and learning to read.
2003	Beginning of the Literacy Decade: All early childhood professionals are called to action by the United Nations to fight against illiteracy worldwide.
2007	Montessorians around the world celebrate one hundred years of Montessori education.
2009	The world marks the two hundredth anniversary of Louis Braille, inventor of the Braille system of writing used by the blind and visually impaired worldwide. Braille represents one of the world's great assistive technologies.
2009	The American Recovery and Reinvestment Act of 2009 provides $2.1 billion for Head Start and Early Head Start.

APPENDIX B

Head Start Child Outcomes Framework

Domain	Domain Element	Indicators
LANGUAGE DEVELOPMENT	Listening & Understanding	• Demonstrates increasing ability to attend to and understand conversations, stories, songs, and poems. • Shows progress in understanding and following simple and multiple-step directions. ☆ **Understands an increasingly complex and varied vocabulary.** ☆ **For non–English-speaking children, progresses in listening to and understanding English.**
	Speaking & Communicating	☆ **Develops increasing abilities to understand and use language to communicate information, experiences, ideas, feelings, opinions, needs, questions, and for other varied purposes.** • Progresses in abilities to initiate and respond appropriately in conversation and discussions with peers and adults. ☆ **Uses an increasingly complex and varied spoken vocabulary.** • Progresses in clarity of pronunciation and towards speaking in sentences of increasing length and grammatical complexity. ☆ **For non–English-speaking children, progresses in speaking English.**
LITERACY	☆ Phonological Awareness	• Shows increasing ability to discriminate and identify sounds in spoken language. • Shows growing awareness of beginning and ending sounds of words. • Progresses in recognizing matching sounds and rhymes in familiar words, games, songs, stories, and poems. • Shows growing ability to hear and discriminate separate syllables in words. ☆ **Associates sounds with written words,** such as awareness that different words begin with the same sound.
	☆ Book Knowledge & Appreciation	• Shows growing interest and involvement in listening to and discussing a variety of fiction and nonfiction books and poetry. • Shows growing interest in reading-related activities, such as asking to have a favorite book read; choosing to look at books; drawing pictures based on stories; asking to take books home; going to the library; and engaging in pretend-reading with other children. • Demonstrates progress in abilities to retell and dictate stories from books and experiences; to act out stories in dramatic play; and to predict what will happen next in a story. • Progresses in learning how to handle and care for books; knowing to view one page at a time in sequence from front to back; and understanding that a book has a title, author, and illustrator.
	☆ Print Awareness & Concepts	• Shows increasing awareness of print in classroom, home, and community settings. • Develops growing understanding of the different functions of forms of print such as signs, letters, newspapers, lists, messages, and menus. • Demonstrates increasing awareness of concepts of print, such as that reading in English moves from top to bottom and from left to right, that speech can be written down, and that print conveys a message. • Shows progress in recognizing the association between spoken and written words by following print as it is read aloud. ☆ **Recognizes a word as a unit of print,** or awareness that letters are grouped to form words, and that words are separated by spaces.

369

Domain	Domain Element	Indicators
LITERACY (cont.)	Early Writing	• Develops understanding that writing is a way of communicating for a variety of purposes. • Begins to represent stories and experiences through pictures, dictation, and in play. • Experiments with a growing variety of writing tools and materials, such as pencils, crayons, and computers. • Progresses from using scribbles, shapes, or pictures to represent ideas, to using letter-like symbols, to copying or writing familiar words such as their own name.
	Alphabet Knowledge	• Shows progress in associating the names of letters with their shapes and sounds. • Increases in ability to notice the beginning letters in familiar words. ☆ Identifies at least ten letters of the alphabet, especially those in their own name. ☆ Knows that letters of the alphabet are a special category of visual graphics that can be individually named.
MATHEMATICS	☆ Number & Operations	• Demonstrates increasing interest and awareness of numbers and counting as a means for solving problems and determining quantity. • Begins to associate number concepts, vocabulary, quantities, and written numerals in meaningful ways. • Develops increasing ability to count in sequence to 10 and beyond. • Begins to make use of one-to-one correspondence in counting objects and matching groups of objects. • Begins to use language to compare numbers of objects with terms such as more, less, greater than, fewer, equal to. • Develops increased abilities to combine, separate, and name "how many" concrete objects.
	Geometry & Spatial Sense	• Begins to recognize, describe, compare, and name common shapes, their parts, and attributes. • Progresses in ability to put together and take apart shapes. • Begins to be able to determine whether or not two shapes are the same size and shape. • Shows growth in matching, sorting, putting in a series, and regrouping objects according to one or two attributes such as color, shape, or size. • Builds an increasing understanding of directionality, order, and positions of objects, and words such as *up, down, over, under, top, bottom, inside, outside, in front,* and *behind.*
	Patterns & Measurement	• Enhances abilities to recognize, duplicate, and extend simple patterns using a variety of materials. • Shows increasing abilities to match, sort, put in a series, and regroup objects according to one or two attributes such as shape or size. • Begins to make comparisons between several objects based on a single attribute. • Shows progress in using standard and nonstandard measures for length and area of objects.
SCIENCE	Scientific Skills & Methods	• Begins to use senses and a variety of tools and simple measuring devices to gather information, investigate materials, and observe processes and relationships. • Develops increased ability to observe and discuss common properties, differences, and comparisons among objects and materials. • Begins to participate in simple investigations to test observations, discuss and draw conclusions, and form generalizations. • Develops growing abilities to collect, describe, and record information through a variety of means including discussion, drawings, maps, and charts. • Begins to describe and discuss predictions, explanations, and generalizations based on past experiences.

Domain	Domain Element	Indicators
SCIENCE (cont.)	Scientific Knowledge	• Expands knowledge of and abilities to observe, describe, and discuss the natural world, materials, living things, and natural processes. • Expands knowledge of and respect for their body and the environment. • Develops growing awareness of ideas and language related to attributes of time and temperature. • Shows increased awareness and beginning understanding of changes in materials and cause–effect relationships.
CREATIVE ARTS	Music	• Participates with increasing interest and enjoyment in a variety of music activities, including listening, singing, games, and performances. • Experiments with a variety of musical instruments.
	Art	• Gains ability in using different art media and materials in a variety of ways for creative expression and representation. • Progresses in abilities to create drawings, paintings, models, and other art creations that are more detailed, creative, or realistic. • Develops growing abilities to plan, work independently, and demonstrate care and persistence in a variety of art projects. • Begins to understand and share opinions about artistic products and experiences.
	Movement	• Expresses through movement and dancing what is felt and heard in various musical tempos and styles. • Shows growth in moving in time to different patterns of beat and rhythm in music.
	Dramatic Play	• Participates in a variety of dramatic play activities that become more extended and complex, such as in using finger-plays. • Shows growing creativity and imagination in using materials and in assuming different roles in dramatic play situations.
SOCIAL & EMOTIONAL DEVELOPMENT	Self-Concept	• Begins to develop and express awareness of self in terms of specific abilities, characteristics, and preferences. • Develops growing capacity for independence in a range of activities, routines, and tasks. • Demonstrates growing confidence in a range of abilities and expresses pride in accomplishments.
	Self-Control	• Shows progress in expressing feelings, needs, and opinions in difficult situations and conflicts without harming themselves, others, or property. • Develops growing understanding of how their actions affect others and begins to accept the consequences of their actions. • Demonstrates increasing capacity to follow rules and routines and use materials purposefully, safely, and respectfully.
	Cooperation	• Increases abilities to sustain interactions with peers by helping, sharing, and discussion. • Shows increasing abilities to use compromise and discussion in working, playing, and resolving conflicts with peers. • Develops increasing abilities to give and take in interactions; to take turns in games or using materials; and to interact without being overly submissive or directive.
	Social Relationships	• Demonstrates increasing comfort in talking with and accepting guidance and directions from a range of familiar adults. • Shows progress in developing friendships with peers. • Progresses in responding sympathetically to peers who are in need, upset, hurt, or angry; and in expressing empathy or caring for others.

Domain	Domain Element	Indicators
SOCIAL & EMOTIONAL DEVELOPMENT (cont.)	Knowledge of Families & Communities	• Develops ability to identify personal characteristics including gender and family composition. • Progresses in understanding similarities and respecting differences among people, such as gender, race, special needs, culture, language, and family structures. • Develops growing awareness of jobs and what is required to perform them. • Begins to express and understand concepts and language of geography in the contexts of their classroom, home, and community.
APPROACHES TO LEARNING	Initiative & Curiosity	• Chooses to participate in an increasing variety of tasks and activities. • Develops increased ability to make independent choices. • Approaches tasks and activities with increased flexibility, imagination, and inventiveness. • Grows in eagerness to learn about and discuss a growing range of topics, ideas, and tasks.
	Engagement & Persistence	• Grows in abilities to persist in and complete a variety of tasks, activities, projects, and experiences. • Demonstrates increasing ability to set goals and develop and follow through on plans. • Shows growing capacity to maintain concentration over time on a task, question, set of directions, or interactions, despite distractions and interruptions.
	Reasoning & Problem Solving	• Develops increasing ability to find more than one solution to a question, task, or problem. • Grows in recognizing and solving problems through active exploration, including trial and error, and through interactions and discussions with peers and adults. • Develops increasing abilities to classify, compare, and contrast objects, events, and experiences.
PHYSICAL HEALTH & DEVELOPMENT	Fine Motor Skills	• Develops growing strength, dexterity, and control needed to use tools such as scissors, paper-punch, stapler, and hammer. • Grows in hand-eye coordination, in building with blocks, putting together puzzles, reproducing shapes and patterns, stringing beads, and using scissors. • Progresses in abilities to use writing, drawing, and art tools including pencils, markers, chalk, paint brushes, and various types of technology.
	Gross Motor Skills	• Shows increasing levels of proficiency, control, and balance in walking, climbing, running, jumping, hopping, skipping, marching, and galloping. • Demonstrates increasing abilities to coordinate movements in throwing, catching, kicking, bouncing balls, and using the slide and swing.
	Health Status & Practices	• Progresses in physical growth, strength, stamina, and flexibility. • Participates actively in games, outdoor play, and other forms of exercise that enhance physical fitness. • Shows growing independence in hygiene, nutrition, and personal care when eating, dressing, washing hands, brushing teeth, and toileting. • Builds awareness and ability to follow basic health and safety rules such as fire safety, traffic and pedestrian safety, and responding appropriately to potentially harmful objects, substances, and activities.

☆ Indicates the four specific Domain Elements and nine Indicators that are legislatively mandated.

Source: "Head Start Child Outcomes Framework," Head Start Resource Center, http://www.hsnrc.org/CDI/pdfs/UGCOF.pdf.

APPENDIX C

An Example of a Preschool IEP

Individualized Education Program (IEP)

Jeremy Carlson   September 26, 2010

Student Name   Date of Meeting to Develop or Review IEP

Note: For each student with a disability, beginning at age 14 (or younger, if appropriate) a statement of the student's transition service needs must be included under the applicable parts of the IEP. The statement must focus on the courses the student needs to take to reach his or her post-school goals.

[a general statement of the transition needs of the student; must be updated annually]

Present Levels of Educational Performance

[includes a description of how the disability affects involvement and progress or (for preschool children) how the disability affects participation]

- When asked to write his name, Jeremy can print the letter "J" but does not print the remaining letters.
- Given a free-play setting, Jeremy has difficulty selecting play items, changing activities, and remaining engaged in activities.
- When given the opportunity, Jeremy can greet familiar adults and peers and make unprompted eye contact with them, but he does not do so consistently.

Measurable Annual Goals [Including Benchmarks or Short-Term Objectives]

[clearly stated goals that lay out the plan for meeting the child's needs for improvement as well as all other educational needs]

- By the end of the school year, Jeremy will demonstrate comprehension of a spoken story's main idea by selecting representative pictures from arrays of three, with 90 percent accuracy.
- By the end of the school year, Jeremy will utter two- and three-word phrases as the result of natural environmental cues without prompting in eight out of every ten opportunities presented to him.
- By the end of the school year, Jeremy will greet three specific peers (Manny, Sarah, and Roland) at least once a day with unprompted eye contact and unprompted one- and two-word greetings such as "Hi, Manny," "Hey, Sarah," and "Roland!"

Jeremy's Benchmarks

- At the end of the first month of instruction, Jeremy will point as prompted with 100 percent accuracy to one pictorial representation (selected from an array consisting only of that picture) of a spoken story's main character or event.
- At the end of the third month of instruction, Jeremy will point as prompted with 60 percent accuracy to the correct pictorial representation (selected from an array consisting of two pictures) of a spoken story's main character or event.
- At the end of the fifth month of instruction, Jeremy will point as prompted with 90 percent accuracy to the correct pictorial representation (selected from an array consisting of two pictures) of a spoken story's main character or event.
- At the end of the seventh month of instruction, Jeremy will point as prompted with 70 percent accuracy to the correct pictorial representation (selected from an array consisting of three pictures) of a spoken story's main character or event.
- At the end of the ninth month of instruction, Jeremy will point, without prompting and with 90 percent accuracy, to the correct pictorial representation (selected from an array consisting of three pictures) of a spoken story's main character or event.

When Services, Modifications, and Accommodations Will Begin and Their Anticipated Frequency, Duration, and Location

- Services will begin as soon as parental agreement is obtained and will continue throughout the school year. Special education and related services will be delivered daily in the preschool.
- Upon receipt of parental agreement, speech/language therapy will occur in the preschool therapy room for thirty minutes each day for the first three months the IEP is in effect, and will be offered for thirty minutes, three times per week thereafter.
- The early childhood special education teacher and the Montessori teacher will develop a schedule of periodic visits (i.e., biweekly, then weekly) for Jeremy (with and without his parents) to the Montessori classroom during the last month of this year's preschool program.

[listing of all services, aids, and special modifications needed along with specific details]

- The lead special education teacher and paraprofessionals, as necessary, will develop and use pictorial "social stories" to describe and exemplify acceptable and successful ways of greeting peers. Three peers (one with and two without disabilities) will serve as peer supports for this instruction. Other personnel at the preschool will cooperate with modeling and prompting as necessary.[*]
- The lead special education teacher and paraprofessionals, as necessary, will use "comic strip conversations" to establish nonverbal, unobtrusive ways to provide Jeremy with feedback and cues as he interacts with his peers.[†]
- The speech-language therapist and the lead special education teacher will collaborate, plan, and deliver spoken-language training in comprehension and production on the basis of the training model developed by Ivar Lovaas.[‡]

Explanation of Extent, if Any, to Which Child Will Not Participate in Regular Education Classroom

[description of child's lack of interaction with other children in regular class setting]

- Jeremy is in an integrated preschool and participates fully with nondisabled children.

ADMINISTRATION OF STATE AND DISTRICT-WIDE ASSESSMENTS OF STUDENT ACHIEVEMENT

Any Individual Modifications in Administration Needed for Child to Participate in State or District-Wide Assessment(s)

[a listing of any special requirements needed for child to participate in assessments]

- Jeremy will not take these tests as a preschool child. Typically, children are first assessed in the intermediate elementary grades.

If IEP Team Determines That Child Will Not Participate in a Particular State or District-Wide Assessment

- Why isn't the assessment appropriate for the child?
- Describe alternative assessment.

How Child's Progress Toward Annual Goals Will Be Measured

[clear statement of measurement procedures]

- In light of the intent to place Jeremy in a general kindergarten program next year, progress monitoring is essential. Jeremy's IEP team will review each goal's status on a monthly basis. His lead teacher will prepare a brief report of this review for Jeremy's parents. The teacher will offer to call meetings for clarification purposes as necessary.
- Jeremy's progress toward annual goals will be assessed monthly through a review of his relevant performance data by the IEP team. His parents will receive monthly written reports of these reviews.

How Child's Parents Will Be Regularly Informed of Child's Progress Toward Annual Goals and Extent to Which Child's Progress Is Sufficient to Meet Goals by End of Year

[description of plan for working with parents and informing them of child's progress]

- Developing and maintaining clear communication between Jeremy's parents and all the professionals involved with him will be important. Formal progress reports will be provided to Jeremy's parents each month. It would be a good idea, however, to establish weekly "check-ins," either by phone or by e-mail.

[Beginning at age 16 or younger if determined appropriate by IEP team]
Statement of Needed Transition Services (Including, If Appropriate, Statement of Interagency Responsibilities or Any Needed Linkages)

[takes into account special considerations involved with older children, including student preferences and interests]

- Jeremy is too young for postsecondary transition services to be considered. However, he will make a critical transition next year to a Montessori kindergarten. Although it is not required, it would be wise for the IEP team to begin concerted planning for this transition early in the fourth quarter of the school year.

- As suggested in the preceding section, the team should arrange for Jeremy, with and without his parents, to make periodic visits to the Montessori classroom during the last month of this year's preschool program.

- Although moving from an integrated preschool to kindergarten is not part of the explicit intent of the transition statement in the IEP, the IEP team should nonetheless acknowledge the importance of Jeremy's transition to the Montessori kindergarten program by providing a plan for coordinating this transition.

[In a state that transfers rights to the student at the age of majority, the following information must be included beginning at least one year before the student reaches the age of majority]

- The student has been informed of the rights under Part 8 of IDEA, if any, that will transfer to the student on reaching the age of majority.

[guarantees that student is fully informed of rights regarding services available under IDEA]

*C. Gray, Writing Social Stories with Carol Gray (Arlington, TX: Future Horizons, 2000).

†M. F. Rogers and B. S. Myles, "Using Social Stories and Comic Strip Conversations to Interpret Social Situations for an Adolescent with Asperger's Syndrome," *Intervention in School and Clinic*, 36(5), May 2001, 310–313.

‡J. J. McEachin, T. Smith, and O. Lovaas, "Long-Term Outcome for Children with Autism Who Received Early Behavioral Treatment," *American Journal on Mental Retardation*, 97(4), January 1993, 359–372.

Sources: IEP outline from G. S. Morrison, *Teaching in America*, 4th ed. (Boston: Allyn & Bacon, 2006). Copyright © 2006 by Pearson Education; reprinted by permission of the publisher. Adapted from U.S. Department of Education, Office of Special Education and Rehabilitative Services, *A Guide to the Individualized Education Program*, July 2000, available at http://www.ed.gov/parents/needs/speced/iepguide/iepguide.pdf. Examples from E. Knowlton, *Developing Effective Individualized Education Programs: A Case Based Tutorial*, 2nd ed., © 2007; electronically reproduced by permission of Pearson Education Inc., Upper Saddle River, New Jersey.

ENDNOTES

Preface

1. L. Darling-Hammond and J. Bransford, eds., *Preparing Teachers for a Changing World* (San Francisco: Wiley, 2005).

Chapter 1

1. National Association for the Education of Young Children, *NAEYC Initial Licensure Standards*, "Initial Licensure Programs" (Washington, DC: NAEYC, 2008), 11. (Includes all numbered entries)
2. Ibid.
3. Ibid.
4. Ibid.
5. Ibid.
6. Ibid.
7. Department of Education, Republic of the Philippines, "DepEd Training to Improve Teachers' Competence Continues," August 15, 2008; accessed August 10, 2009, at http://www.deped.gov.ph/cpanel/uploads/issuanceImg/aug16-trng.pdf.
8. W. Barnett, K. Robin, J. Hudstedt, and K. Schulman, *The State of Preschool 2008: State Preschool Yearbook* (Rutgers, NJ: National Institute for Early Childhood Education Research, 2008); accessed August 10, 2009, at http://www.nieer.org/yearbook/pdf/yearbook.pdf, 12.
9. National Association for the Education of Young Children, *NAEYC Standards for Early Childhood Professional Preparation* (Washington, DC: NAEYC, 2008), 12.
10. National Association for the Education of Young Children, *NAEYC Initial Licensure Standards*, "Initial Licensure Programs" (Washington, DC: NAEYC, 2008), 12.
11. National Association for the Education of Young Children, *NAEYC Position Statement on Developmentally Appropriate Practice, 2008 Revision* (Washington, DC: NAEYC, 2008).
12. Children's Defense Fund, "Children in the United States", November 2008 http://www.childrensdefense.org/child-research-data-publications/data/state-data-repository/cits/children-in-the-states-2008-all.pdf.
13. U.S. Census Bureau, *U.S. Hispanic Population Surpasses 45 Million Now 15 Percent of Total (2008),* accessed September 14, 2009, at http://www.census.gov/Press-Release/www/releases/archives/population/011910.html.
14. SchoolDigger.com, "Anthony (Susan B.) Elementary (Sacramento, CA)," accessed August 13, 2009, at http://www.schooldigger.com/go/CA/schools/3384005282/school.aspx.
15. SchoolDigger.com, "Alta Loma Elementary (San Angelo, TX)," accessed August 13, 2009, at http://www.schooldigger.com/go/TX/schools/3870004296/school/aspx.
16. L. Derman-Sparks and the A.B.C Task Force, *Anti-Bias Curriculum: Tools for Empowering Young Children* (Washington, DC: NAEYC, 1989).
17. Ibid.
18. Ibid.
19. National Association for the Education of Young Children, *NAEYC Initial Licensure Standards*, "Initial Licensure Programs" (Washington, DC: NAEYC, 2008), 19.

20. Ibid.
21. Ibid.
22. S. Sandall, M. L. Hemmeter, B. J. Smith, and M. E. McLean, *DEC Recommended Practices* (Longmont, CO: Sopris West, 2005), 113–118.
23. National Association for the Education of Young Children, *NAEYC Standards for Professional Preparation, 2008,* accessed April 30, 2009, at http://www.naeyc.org/.
24. National Association for the Education of Young Children, *NAEYC Initial Licensure Standards*, "Initial Licensure Programs" (Washington, DC: NAEYC, 2008), 15.
25. National Association for the Education of Young Children, *NAEYC Standards for Early Childhood Professional Preparation* (Washington, DC: NAEYC, 2008), 20.
26. Ibid., 20–23.
27. National Council for Accreditation of Teacher Education, *NCATE Unit Standards* (Washington DC: NCATE, 2007).
28. Ibid., 24.
29. Ibid., 24–25.
30. S. Feeney and K. Kipnis, *Code of Ethical Conduct and Statement of Commitment* (Washington, DC: NAEYC, 2005). Used with permission.
31. S. Feeney and N. K. Freeman, *Ethics and the Early Childhood Educator: Using the NAEYC Code* (Washington, DC: NAEYC, 2005).
32. Ibid.
33. Used with the permission of Mary Nelle Brunson, Assistant Chair, Department of Elementary Education, Stephen F. Austin State University, Nacogdoches, Texas.
34. National Council for Accreditation of Teacher Education, *NCATE Unit Standards: Glossary* (Washington, DC: NCATE, 2006), 53.
35. N. Noddings, "Teaching Themes of Care," *Phi Delta Kappan,* 76(9), 1995, 675.
36. Word Press.com, Teacher of the Year bios, May 1, 2009, accessed September 14, 2009, at http://ezureick.wordpress.com/2009/05/01/teacher-of-the-year-bios/.
37. US Census Bureau, *Orange, Fla., Joins the Growing List of 'Majority-Minority' Counties,* accessed September 1, 2009, at http://www.census.gov/Press-Release/www/releases/archives/population/013734.html.
38. International Society for Technology in Education, *The ISTE National Educational Technology Standards (NETS-T) and Performance Indicators for Teachers,* 2008, http://www.iste.org.
39. National Association for the Education of Young Children, *NAEYC Standards for Professional Preparation, 2008,* accessed April 30, 2009, at http://www.naeyc.org/.

Chapter 2

1. National Association for the Education of Young Children, Draft Core *NAEYC Standards for Early Childhood Professional Preparation,* August 7, 2008, 1–3; accessed August 14, 2009, at http://208.118.177.216/about/positions/pdf/draftprepstds0808.pdf.
2. Ibid.

3. J. Clifford, "If You Can Read This, Take Time to Say Thanks to a Teacher," *San Diego Union Tribune,* May 6, 2006, http://www.signonsandiego.com/uniontrib/20060506/news_1c06clifford.html.

4. A. J. Mullen, 2009 Connecticut Teacher of the Year acceptance speech, December 3, 2008, http://www.sde.ct.gov/sde/cwp/view.asp?a=2678&Q=322238&pp=12&n=1.

5. K. Freeman, "The Different Types of Families," *Associated Content,* October 28, 2008; retrieved January 15, 2009, from http://www.associatedcontent.com/article/1130783/the_different_types_of_families.html?cat=9.

6. K. R. Tremblay, C. E. Barber, and L. Kubin, "Family: Grandparents as Parents," Colorado State University Extension, January 2006; retrieved January 15, 2009, from http://www.docstoc.com/docs/9577339/Grandparent-Rights-Colorado.

7. Afterschool Alliance, "America After 3 PM," October 2009, www.afterschoolalliance.org/AA3PM.cfm.

8. U.S. Bureau of Labor Statistics, *Employment Characteristics of Families Summary,* September 14, 2009, http://www.bls.gov/news.release/famee.nr0.htm.

9. National Association of Child Care Resource and Referral Agencies, "High Quality Child Care Matters," 2009, http://www.naccrra.org/policy/background_issues/high-quality-child-care-matters; and U.S. Bureau of Labor Statistics, *Employment Characteristics of Families Summary,* September 14, 2009, http://www.bls.gov/news.release/famee.nr0.htm.

10. National Association of Child Care Resource and Referral Agencies, "High Quality Child Care Matters," 2009, http://www.naccrra.org/policy/background_issues/high-quality-child-care-matters.

11. U.S. Department of Health and Human Services, "Promoting Responsible Fatherhood," 2006; retrieved January 22, 2009, from http://fatherhood.hhs.gov.

12. Child Welfare Information Gateway, "The Importance of Fathers in the Healthy Development of Children," 2006, http://www.childwelfare.gov/pubs/usermanuals/fatherhood/chaptertwo.cfm.

13. R. McClure, "Involve Dad in Early Childcare Programs"; retrieved January 15, 2009, from http://childcare.about.com/od/volunteerism/a/dadcare.htm.

14. Department Of Health and Human Services: Centers For Disease Control And Prevention, "NCHS Data On Teenage Pregnancy," October, 2008, accessed September 2009, at http://www.cdc.gov/nchs/data/infosheets/infosheet_teen_preg.htm.

15. Bureau of Labor Statistics, "Table 4: Families with Own Children: Employment Status of Parents by Age of Youngest Child and Family Type, 2004–05 Annual Averages," April 27, 2006; accessed August 15, 2009, at http://www.bls.gov/news.release/history/famee_04272006.txt.

16. W. Dunham, "US Teen Births Tilt Up, Unmarried Rate Hits Record," Reuters North American News Service, December 5, 2007; retrieved January 16, 2009, from http://www.reuters.com/article/domesticNews/idUSN0561785120071205.

17. Ibid.

18. B. E. Hamilton, J. A. Martin, and S. J. Ventura, "Births: Preliminary Data for 2006," *National Vital Statistics Reports,* 56(7), 2007, http://www.cdc.gov/nchs/data/nvsr/nvsr56/nvsr56_07.pdf; and "Teen Pregnancy and Birth Rates: Birth Rates in Teen Girls Ages 15–19, 2006," Centers for Disease Control and Prevention, 2008, http://www.cdc.gov/Features/dsTeenPregnancy/#source.

19. Centers for Disease Control and Prevention, "CDC 2007 National Youth Risk Behavior Survey Telebriefing," June 4, 2008; accessed August 15, 2009, at http://www.cdc.gov/media/transcripts/2008/t080604.htm.

20. M. Stobbe, "Mississippi Has Highest Teen Birth Rate, CDC Says," January 7, 2009, http://www.physorg.com/news150541455.html.

21. National Center for Family Literacy, "Toyota: Committed to Moving Families Forward," accessed June 10, 2009, from http://www.famlit.org/toyota.

22. Centers for Disease Control and Prevention, "Healthy Youth! Student Health and Academic Achievement," March 2, 2009, http://www.cdc.gov/HealthyYouth/health_and_academics/index.htm.

23. American Lung Association, Childhood Asthma Overview, April 2008, http://www.lungusa.org/site/pp.asp?c=dvLUK9O0E&b=22782.

24. Centers for Disease Control and Prevention, "Asthma: Basic Information," updated May 5, 2009, http://www.cdc.gov/asthma/faqs.htm; and Centers for Disease Control and Prevention, *You Can Control Your Asthma,* September 2006, http://www.cdc.gov/asthma/pdfs/asthma_brochure.pdf.

25. Centers for Disease Control and Prevention, National Center for Environmental Health, "Childhood Lead Poisoning," 2009, http://www.cdc.gov/lead/.

26. Omaha Healthy Kids Alliance, 2007, "Lead Facts: About Lead," retrieved January 13, 2009, at http://www.omahahealthykids.org/leadfacts.html.

27. American Heart Association, "Overweight and Obesity—Statistics," 2008 update, http://www.americanheart.org/downloadable/heart/1197994908531FS16OVR08.pdf.

28. University of Michigan Health System, "Obesity Is Number One Heath Concern for Kids in 2008," *Science Daily,* July 20, 2008; retrieved January 16, 2009, from http://www.sciencedaily.com/releases/2008/07/080714170957.htm.

29. Children's Hospital of the King's Daughters, "Two Years Old: A Childhood Obesity Tipping Point? Research Suggests That Childhood Obesity Begins in Infancy," *Science Daily,* August 5, 2008; retrieved January 16, 2009, from http://www.sciencedaily.com/releases/2008/08/080804100803.htm.

30. The Obesity Society, "Childhood Overweight," 2001, http://www.obesity.org/information/childhood_overweight.asp.

31. National Institute on Media and the Family, "Fact Sheet: Media Use and Obesity Among Children," June 2009, http://www.mediafamily.org/facts/facts_tvandobchild.shtml.

32. Leigh University, "Ban on Fast Food TV Advertising Would Reverse Childhood Obesity Trends, Study Shows," *Science Daily,* November 29, 2008; retrieved January 16, 2009, from http://www.sciencedaily.com/releases/2008/11/081119120149.htm.

33. L. Brown, W. Beardslee, and D. Prothrow-Smith, *Impact of School Breakfast on Children's Health and Learning: An Analysis of the Scientific Research,* November 17, 2008, http://www.sodexofoundation.org/hunger_us/Images/Impact %20of %20School%20Breakfast%20Study_tcm150-212606.pdf.

34. J. Clarke, "The Importance of Healthy Eating for Young Children," *Early Years Update,* June 2007, http://www.teachingexpertise.com/articles/the-importance-of-healthy-eating-for-young-children-2254.

35. Robert Wood Johnson Foundation, "Arkansas Schools, Parents Adjusting Well to State Efforts to Curb Obesity," June 17, 2008, http://www.rwjf.org/newsroom/product.jsp?id=31911.

36. J. Oliver, "Fighting Obesity in the Frazier School District," *Pittsburgh Tribune Review,* July 8, 2007, http://www.pittsburghlive.com/x/tribunereview/news/fayette/s_515979.html.

37. K. Zelman, "School Nutrition: Making the Grade?" MedicineNet.com, September 15, 2006, http://www.medicinenet.com/script/main/art.asp?articlekey=64158&pf=3&page=1.

38. National Governors Association, "State Strategies to Reduce Child and Family Poverty," June 5, 2008, http://www.nga.org/Files/pdf/0806POVERTYBRIEF.PDF.

39. Ibid.

40. A. Douglas-Hall, M. Chau, and H. Koball, "Basic Facts About Low-Income Children: Birth to Age 18," National Center for Children in Poverty, September 2006, http://www.nccp.org/publications/pub_678.html.

41. U.S. Census Bureau, "People in Families by Family Structure, Age, and Sex, Iterated by Income-to-Poverty Ratio and Race: 2007," *Current Population Survey,* August 2008, http://pubdb3.census.gov/macro/032008/pov/new02_100_01.htm.

42. Ibid.

43. U.S. Census Bureau, "Region, Division and Type of Residence—Poverty Status for People in Families with Related Children Under 18 by Family Structure: 2007," *Current Population Survey,* August 2008, http://pubdb3.census.gov/macro/032008/pov/new43_100_01.htm.

44. "Census: Fewer Americans Lack Health Insurance," CNNhealth.com, August, 26, 2008, http://www.cnn.com/2008/HEALTH/08/26/census.uninsured/index.html.

45. National Governors Association, "State Strategies to Reduce Child and Family Poverty," June 5, 2008, http://www.nga.org/Files/pdf/0806POVERTYBRIEF.PDF.

46. "How the Physiological Effects of Poverty on Young Children Takes Its Toll on Health," *Medical News Today,* November 8, 2007, http://www.medicalnewstoday.com/articles/88146.php.

47. B. Hayes, "Increasing the Representation of Underrepresented Minority Groups in U.S. Colleges and Schools of Pharmacy," *American Journal of Pharmaceutical Education,* 72(1), February 15, 2008, 14.

48. Charlotte-Mecklenburg Schools, *ESL Program,* January 2008; retrieved February 11, 2009, from http://www.cms.k12.nc.us/mediaroom/aboutus/documents/english%20as%20a%20second%20Language%20(ESL).pdf.

49. National Association for the Education of Young Children, "Linguistic and Cultural Diversity—Building on America's Strengths," *Young Children,* 1996; retrieved February 6, 2009, at http://oldweb.naeyc.org/ece/1996/03.asp.

50. Centers for Disease Control and Prevention, "Violence Prevention," January 27, 2009; accessed June 11, 2009, from http://www.cdc.gov/ViolencePrevention/.

51. Ibid.

52. Ibid.

53. *NewScientist,* "Editorial: In Denial About On-Screen Violence," April 21, 2007; accessed June 11, 2009, from http://www.newscientist.com/article/mg19426003.600-editorial-in-denial-about-onscreen-violence.html.

54. National Youth Violence Prevention Resource Center, "Media Violence Facts and Statistics: Prevalence of Media Violence," February 26, 2008; accessed June 11, 2009, from http://www.safeyouth.org/scripts/faq/mediaviolstats.asp.

55. Ibid.

56. Ibid.

57. National Institute on Media and the Family, "Children and Media Violence," November 2006; accessed June 11, 2009, from http://www.mediafamily.org/facts/facts_vlent.shtml.

58. Eyes on Bullying, Education Development Center Inc., "Child Care," 2008; retrieved February 10, 2009, at http://www.eyesonbullying.org/childcare.html.

59. B. D. Perry, "Keep the Cool in School: Promoting Non-Violent Behavior in Children," *Early Childhood Today;* accessed August 16, 2009, from http://teacher.scholastic.com/professional/bruceperry/cool.htm.

60. WebMD, Health and Parenting, "Bullying—What Children Should Do If They Are Bullied," January 31, 2007; accessed June 11, 2009, from http://www.webmd.com/parenting/tc/bullying-what-children-should-do-if-they-are-bullied.

61. K. Kasza, *The Rat and the Tiger,* Penguin Group, 2007, available online at http://us.penguingroup.com/nf/Book/BookDisplay/0,9780142409008,00.html?The_Rat_and_the_Tiger_Keiko_Kasza#.

62. U.S. Department of Health and Human Services, Administration on Children, Youth, and Families. *Child Maltreatment 2007* (Washington, D.C.: U.S. Government Printing Office, 2009).

63. *U.S. Statutes at Large,* 88(1976): 5.

64. S. Urahn and S. Watson, "A Movement Transformed," *The American Prospect,* November 19, 2007; retrieved February 10, 2009, from http://www.prospect.org/cs/articles?article=a_movement_transformed.

65. J. D. Black, "The Business of Child Care," *Great Falls Tribune,* February 1, 2009; retrieved February 10, 2009, from http://pqasb.pqarchiver.com/greatfallstribune/access/1688989991.html?FMT=ABS&date=Feb+01,+2009.

66. M. McNeil, "Campaign K–12 is now… Politics K–12," *Education Week,* November 6, 2008; retrieved February 11, 2009, from http://blogs.edweek.org/edweek/campaign-k-12/prekindergarten/.

67. U.S. Department of Health and Human Services, Administration for Children and Families: Child Care Bureau, "FFY 2007 CCDF Data Tables (Preliminary Estimates)," table 1, October 2008; accessed June 10, 2009, from http://www.acf.hhs.gov/programs/ccb/data/ccdf_data/07acf800_preliminary/table1.htm.

68. Green Building Council, "Green Building Research" (2008), accessed September 14, 2009, at http://www.usgbc.org/DisplayPage.aspx?CMSPageID=1718; and The Baltimore Sun, "Schools Going Green Big-Time," September 7, 2009; retrieved September 14, 2009, from http://www.baltimoresun.com/features/green/bal-md.gr.greenschool07sep07,0,5804340.story.

69. Green Schools Recognition Program, "Congratulations Green Schools!," May 21, 2009; retrieved September 14, 2009, from http://www.ourgreenschools.com/congratulations-green-schools/.

70. St. Louis Post-Dispatch, "Growing Minds Love Growing Gardens," September 9, 2009; retrieved September 14, 2009, from STLToday.com.

71. U.S. Department of Health and Human Services, Administration for Children and Families: Child Care Bureau, "FFY 2007 CCDF Data Tables (Preliminary Estimates)," table 3, October 2008; accessed June 10, 2009, from http://www.acf.hhs.gov/programs/ccb/data/ccdf_data/07acf800_preliminary/table3.htm.

72. The Harlem Children's Zone Project, "100 Blocks, One Bright Future," 2007; accessed June 10, 2009, from http://www.hcz.org/programs/the-hcz-project.

73. Association for Supervision and Curriculum Development, "About the Whole Child," http://www.wholechildeducation.org/about/.

74. Association for Supervision and Curriculum Development, "Whole Child Resolution Tool Kit: Frequently Asked Questions," 2009, http://www.wholechildeducation.org/blackboard/faqs/#faq1.

75. U.S. Department of Health and Human Services, "Head Start, Early Head Start Programs to Receive Over $2 Billion in Recovery Act Funding," April 2, 2009; accessed June 10, 2009, from http://www.hhs.gov/news/press/2009pres/04/20090402a.html.

Chapter 3

1. National Association for the Education of Young Children, *NAEYC Standards for Early Childhood Professional Preparation: Initial Licensure Programs,* NAEYC Initial Licensure Standards (Washington, DC: NAEYC, August 2008), 2.

2. Ibid.

3. B. Beatty, "Past, Present, and Future," *The American Prospect,* online edition, November 1, 2004; accessed September 4, 2007, at http://www.prospect.org/cs/articles?article=past_present_and_future.

4. A. Duncan, *Testimony of Education Secretary-Designate Arne Duncan Before the Committee on Health, Education, Labor, and Pensions,* United States Senate, January 13, 2009, http://help.senate.gov/Hearings/2009_01_13/Duncan.pdf.

5. "Teacher of the Year: Congrats and Good Speech," ShopFloor.org, May 1, 2008, http://www.shopfloor.org/2008/05/01/teacher-of-the-year-congrats-and-good-speech.

6. J. A. Comenius, *The Great Didactic of John Amos Comenius,* ed. and trans. M. W. Keating (New York: Russell & Russell, 1967), 58.

7. J.-J. Rousseau, *Emile, or Education,* trans. B. Foxley (New York: Dutton, Everyman's Library, 1933), 5.

8. M. Montessori, *The Discovery of the Child,* trans. M. J. Costelloe (Notre Dame, IN: Fides, 1967), 22.

9. North American Montessori Teachers' Association, *Frequently Asked Questions About Montessori Education,* 2009; accessed June 11, 2009, at http://www.montessori-namta.org/Namta/geninfo/faqmontessori.html.

10. R. D. Archambault, ed., *John Dewey on Education: Selected Writings* (New York: Random House, 1964), 430.

11. L. Benson, I. Harkavy, and J. Puckett, *Dewey's Dream: Universities and Democracies in an Age of Education Reform* (Philadelphia: Temple University Press, 2007).

12. W. Harms and I. DePencier, *Experiencing Education: 100 Years of Learning at the University of Chicago Laboratory Schools* (Orlando Park, IL: Alpha Beta Press, 1996), available online at http://www.ucls.uchicago.edu/about/history/education.shtml.

13. J. Wolfe, *Learning from the Past: Historical Voices in Early Childhood Education* (Mayerthorpe, Alberta, Canada: Piney Branch Press, 2002).

14. D. M. Brodzinsky, I. E. Sigel, and R. M. Golinkoff, "New Dimensions in Piagetian Theory and Research: An Integrative Perspective," in I. E. Sigel, D. M. Brodzinsky, and R. M. Golinkoff, eds., *New Directions in Piagetian Theory and Practice* (Hillsdale, NJ: Erlbaum, 1981), 5.

15. Ibid.

16. Y. Jumani, "Does Experiential Learning Facilitate Learners to Construct Their Own Knowledge," Bizcovering: Education and Training, August 5, 2008, http://bizcovering.com/education-and-training/does-experiential-learning-facilitate-learners-to-construct-their-own-knowledge.

17. H. K. Cook, "How Do Children Construct Knowledge?" Online Montessori Learning Environment, Success with Languages, November 26, 2008, http://childhoodspeech.com/2008/11/how-to-construct-knowledg.

18. Ibid.

19. P. G. Richmond, *An Introduction to Piaget* (New York: Basic Books, 1970), 68.

20. G. A. Davis, and J. D. Keller, *Exploring Science and Mathematics in a Child's World* (Columbus, OH: Pearson, 2009), 12.

21. L. S. Vygotsky, *Mind in Society* (Cambridge, MA: Harvard University Press, 1978), 244.

22. Ibid.

23. J. R. H. Tudge, "Processes and Consequences of Peer Collaboration: A Vygotskian Analysis," *Child Development,* 63(6), 1992, 1365.

24. Ibid.

25. E. Bodrova and D. J. Leong, "Scaffolding Emergent Writing in the Zone of Proximal Development," *Literacy Teaching and Learning,* 3(2) 1998, 1–18; available online at http://www.mcrel.org/our_work/scaffolding.pdf.

26. WAECE-AMEI (World Association of Early Childhood Educators) Newsletter, "Study on the Relationship Between Nutrition and Learning," Bulletin No. 398, February 6, 2009.

27. K. Barker, "Classroom Policies for Our Kindergarten Classroom," retrieved April 13, 2009, at http://lk094.k12.sd.us/Classroom%20Rules.htm.

28. J. Atkinson, "Effective Praise," Inside Jennifer's 1st Grade Classroom, August 13, 2008, http://blogs.scholastic.com/1_2/2008/08/effective-prais.html.

29. T. Fujioka, B. Ross, R. Kakigi, C. Pantev, and L. J. Trainor, "One Year of Musical Training Affects Development of Auditory Cortical Evoked Fields in Young Children," *Brain,* 129(10), 2593–2608.

30. P. C. M. Wong, E. Skoe, N. M. Russo, T. Dees, and N. Kraus, "Musical Experience Shapes Human Brainstem Encoding of Linguistic Pitch Patterns," *Nature Neuroscience,* 10, April 2007, 420–422; retrieved from *Nature Neuroscience* database at http://www.nature.com/neuro/journal/v10/n4/abs/nn1872.html#abs.

Chapter 4

1. National Association for the Education of Young Children, *NAEYC Standards for Early Childhood Professional Preparation: Initial Licensure Programs,* NAEYC Initial Licensure Standards (Washington, DC: NAEYC, August 2008), 2.

2. Ibid.

3. National Association for the Education of Young Children, "NAEYC Accreditation: Stats and Facts"; accessed March 13, 2009, at http://www.rightchoiceforkids.org/docs/NAEYC_stats_and_facts.pdf.

4. Pre-K Now, "Leadership Matters: Governors Pre-K Proposals Fiscal Year 2009," April 2008, accessed September 14, 2009, at http://www.preknow.org/media/lm_fy09_natl_release.pdf.

5. K. McCartney, "Finally Getting Smart About Investing in Learning," *Boston Globe,* March 13, 2009; accessed April 22, 2009, at http://nieer.org/news/?NewsID=2132.

6. Harvard Programs in Professional Education, "Pre-K to 3: Promoting Early Success," November 2008; retrieved September 14, 2009, at http://www.fcd-us.org/usr_doc/HarvardPK-3Institute.pdf.

7. Kern County Superintendent of Schools, "Keeping Schools Safe—The Goal," 2009; accessed April 22, 2009, at http://kcsos.kern.org/news/stories/storyReader$2135.

8. W. S. Barnett and D. J. Yarosz, "Who Goes to Preschool and Why Does it Matter?" National Institute for Early Education Research, *Preschool Policy Brief,* issue 15, November 2007; accessed April 1, 2009, at http://nieer.org/resources/policybriefs/15.pdf.

9. Bureau of Labor Statistics, *Current Population Survey,* "Table 6. Employment Status of Mothers with Own Children Under 3 Years Old by Single Year of Age of Youngest Child and Marital Status, 2006–07 Annual Averages," 2008; accessed March 13, 2009, at http://data.bls.gov/cgi-bin/print.pl/news.release/famee.t06.htm.

10. Enterprise Partners, "The Importance of Early Care and Education," 2006; retrieved April 22, 2009, at http://www.practitionerresources.org/cache/documents/639/63935.doc.

11. Child Care Bureau, United States Department of Health and Human Services, Administration for Children and Families, "Table 5. Preliminary Estimates of Children in Settings Legally Operating Without Regulation, Average Monthly Percent Served by Relatives vs. Non-Relatives (FFY 2007)," October 2008; accessed June 15, 2009, at http://www.acf.hhs.gov/programs/ccb/data/ccdf_data/07acf800_preliminary/table5.htm.

12. Generations United, "The 2008 Intergenerational Shared Site Best Practice Awards," 2008; accessed April 22, 2008, at http://www.gu.org/documents/A0/Shared_Site_Best_Practices_Final.pdf.

13. Bright Horizons Family Solutions, "Employer-Sponsored Child Care," 2009; accessed June 17, 2009, from http://www.brighthorizons.com/employer/care.aspx.

14. M. Story, K. Kaphingst, R. Robinson-O'Brien, and K. Glanz, "Creating Healthy Food and Eating Environments: Policy and Environmental Approaches," *Annual Review of Public Health,* 29, April 2008, 253–272 (first published November 21, 2007); accessed April 1, 2009, at http://publhealth.annualreviews.org.

15. Debra J. Ackerman and W. Steven Barnett, *Does Preschool Education Policy Impact Infant/Toddler Care?,* March 2009, accessed September 14, 2009, at http://nieer.org/resources/policybriefs/21.pdf.

16. National Resource Center for Health and Safety in Child Care, *Caring for Our Children,* 2nd ed. (Elk Grove Village, IL: American Academy of Pediatrics/American Public Health Association/NRC, 2005).

17. NICHD Early Child Care Research Network, "Child Outcomes When Child Care Center Classes Meet Recommended Standards for Quality," *American Journal of Public Health,* 88(7), 1998, 1072–1077.

18. S. Bredekamp, and C. Copple, *Developmentally Appropriate Practice in Early Childhood Programs Serving Children from Birth Through Age 8,* 3rd ed. (Washington, DC: NAEYC, 2009).

19. National Institute of Child Health and Human Development, "NICHD Study of Early Child Care and Youth Development (SECCYD)," http://www.nichd.nih.gov/research/supported/seccyd.cfm. See also *Results from the NICHD Study of Early Child Care and Youth Development* (New York: Guilford Press, 2005), 28–35.

20. High/Scope Education Research Foundation, *The High/Scope K–3 Curriculum: An Introduction* (Ypsilanti, MI: High/Scope, 1989), 1.

21. Ibid.

22. Ibid.

23. High/Scope Educational Research Foundation, "KDIs (Key Experiences)";accessed April 2, 2009, at http://www.highscope.org/Content.asp?ContentId=275.

24. Ibid.

25. High/Scope Educational Research Foundation, "Preschool: Adults and Children—Partners in Learning"; accessed December 10, 2007, at http://www.highscope.org/Content.asp?ContentId=63.

26. M. Montessori, *Dr. Montessori's Own Handbook* (New York: Schocken Books, 1965), 131.

27. H. Helm and L. Katz, *Young Investigators: The Project Approach in the Early Years* (New York: Teachers College Press, 2001).

28. U.S. Department of Health and Human Services, Administration for Children and Families, Early Childhood Learning and Knowledge Center, "Head Start Program Fact Sheet: Fiscal Year 2008";accessed April 1, 2009, at http://eclkc.ohs.acf.hhs.gov/hslc/About%20Head%20Start/dHeadStartProgr.htm.

29. U.S. Department of Health and Human Services, Administration for Children and Families, *FY 2009 Office of Head Start Monitoring Protocol: Program Design and Management,* February 27, 2009; accessed June 17, 2009, at http://eclkc.ohs.acf.hhs.gov/hslc/Program%20Design%20and%20Management/Head%20Start%20Requirements/FY%202008%20OHS%20Monitoring%20Protocol/2009PDF/OHS%20Monitoring%20Protocol%20PDM.pdf.

30. Ibid.

31. U.S. Department of Health and Human Services Administration for Children and Families, "Head Start Programs Fact Sheet", Fiscal Year 2008, accessed September 14, 2009, at http://www.acf.hhs.gov/programs/ohs/about/fy2008.html.

Chapter 5

1. National Association for the Education of Young Children, Draft Core *NAEYC Standards for Early Childhood Professional Preparation,* August 7, 2008, 1–3.

2. Ibid.

3. Georgia Department of Education, "Georgia Standards—Curriculum Frequently Asked Questions"; accessed February 27, 2009, at http://www.gatechlit.org/faqs.aspx#q4.

4. Georgia Department of Education, "Performance Standards, English Language Arts and Reading: Kindergarten," June 12, 2008; accessed April 17, 2009, at https://www.georgiastandards.org/standards/Georgia%20Performance%20Standards/Kindergarten-GPS.pdf.

5. A. G. de Leon, "After 20 Years of Educational Reform, Progress, but Plenty of Unfinished Business," Carnegie Corporation of New York, *Carnegie Results,* (1)3, Fall 2003; accessed August 21, 2006, at http://www.carnegie.org/results/03/index.html.

6. K. Paris, "Summary of Goals 2000: Educate America Act," North Central Regional Educational Laboratory, 1994; accessed February 23, 2009, at http://www.ncrel.org/sdrs/areas/issues/envrnmnt/stw/sw0goals.htm.

7. U.S. Department of Education, "Four Pillars of NCLB," 2004; accessed February 23, 2009, at http://www.ed.gov/nclb/overview/intro/4pillars.html.

8. Ibid.

9. A. Klein, "To Duncan, Incentives a Priority," *Education Week,* January 30, 2009; accessed February 6, 2009, at http://www.edweek.org/login.html?source=http://www.edweek.org/ew/articles/2009/02/04/20duncan.h28.html&destination=http://www.edweek.org/ew/articles/2009/02/04/20duncan.h28.html&levelId=2100.

10. Ibid.

11. C. Snow, M. S. Burns, and P. Griffin, eds., *Preventing Reading Difficulties in Young Children* (Washington, DC: National Academy Press, 1998).

12. J. P. Shonkoff and D. Phillips, eds., *From Neurons to Neighborhoods: The Science of Early Childhood Development* (Washington, DC: National Academy Press, 2000).

13. B. T. Bowman, S. Donovan, and M. S. Burns, eds., *Eager to Learn: Educating Our Preschoolers* (Washington, DC: National Academy Press, 2000).

14. U.S. Department of Health and Human Services, Administration for Children and Families, "Good Start, Grow Smart"; accessed February 20, 2009, at http://www.acf.hhs.gov/programs/ccb/initiatives/gsgs/gsgs_guide/guide.htm.

15. E. Ramirez and K. Clark, "What Arne Duncan Thinks of No Child Left Behind," *Education Week,* February 5, 2009; accessed February 27, 2009, at http://www.usnews.com/articles/education/2009/02/05/what-arne-duncan-thinks-of-no-child-left-behind.html.

16. National Center for Educational Statistics, *The Condition of Education 2008,* Section 2—Learner Outcomes, "Indicator 12: Reading Performance of Students in Grades 4, 8, and 12," June 2008; available online at http://nces.ed.gov/pubs2008/2008031_2.pdf.

17. National Center for Educational Statistics, *The Condition of Education 2008,* Section 2—Learner Outcomes, "Indicator 13: Mathematics Performance of Students in Grades 4 and 8," June 2008; available online at http://nces.ed.gov/pubs2008/2008031_2.pdf.

18. U.S. Department of Education, Institute of Education Sciences, National Center for Education Evaluation and Regional Assistance, "National Evaluation of Early Reading First," May 2007; accessed February 23, 2009, at http://ies.ed.gov/ncee/pubs/20074007/index.asp.

19. Ibid.

20. Grand Rapids Community College, "Summer of Success for our Education Department," October 2008; accessed February 13, 2009, at http://www.grcc.edu/files/sdever/Teacher_Ed_Fall_08.pdf.

21. U.S. Department of Education, "Reading First—Funding Status," September 2008; available online at http://www.ed.gov/programs/readingfirst/funding.html.

22. National Center for Education Evaluation and Regional Assistance, Institute of Education Sciences, *Reading First Impact Study: Final Report,* Executive Summary, November 2008; accessed February 18, 2009, http://ies.ed.gov/ncee/pdf/20094039.pdf.

23. National Center for Education Evaluation and Regional Assistance, Institute of Education Sciences, *Reading First Impact Study Final Report,* November 2008; accessed February 13, 2009, at http://nces.ed.gov/pubsearch/pubsinfo.asp?pubid=NCEE20094038.

24. National Center for Education Evaluation and Regional Assistance, Institute of Education Sciences, *Reading First Impact Study Final Report,* Executive Summary, November 2008; accessed February 18, 2009, http://ies.ed.gov/ncee/pdf/20094039.pdf.

25. Ibid.

26. National Association for the Education of Young Children, "Early Learning Standards: Creating the Conditions for Success," November 19, 2002; available online at http://208.118.177.216/about/positions/pdf/executive_summary.pdf.

27. Pre-K Now, "Fact Sheets: Pre-K Across the Country," 2008; accessed April 22, 2009, at http://www.preknow.org/policy/factsheets/snapshot.cfm?print=1.

28. National Institute for Early Education Research, *The State of Preschool 2008: State Preschool Yearbook;* available online at http://nieer.org/yearbook/pdf/yearbook.pdf.

29. Tennessee Department of Education, "Science—Third Grade," Life Science Standards; accessed April 25, 2009 from http://www.state.tn.us/education/ci/sci/grade_3.shtml.

30. National Governors Association, "News Release: Forty-Nine States and Territories Join Common Core Standards Initiative," June 1, 2009; accessed June 9, 2009 from http://www.nga.org/portal/site/nga/menuitem.6c9a8a9ebc6ae07eee28aca9501010a0/?vgnextoid=263a584a61c91210VgnVCM1000005e00100aRCRD&vgnextchannel=759b8f2005361010VgnVCM1000001a01010aRCRD.

31. Chapel Hill–Carrboro City Schools, "2009–2010 Teachers of the Year (Karen Reid)"; accessed June 9, 2009, from http://www2.chccs.k12.nc.us/education/components/scrapbook/default.php?sectiondetailid=72588&PHPSESSID=bac1144723306d8fe6c57718e656fb9f.

32. J. Atkinson, "Fry's Farm Visits Metz," Inside Jennifer's 1st Grade Classroom, April 5, 2009; accessed June 9, 2009 from http://blogs.scholastic.com/1_2.

33. Chapel Hill–Carrboro City Schools, "2009–2010 Teachers of the Year (LaWanda Rainey-Hall)"; accessed June 9, 2009 from http://www2.chccs.k12.nc.us/education/components/scrapbook/default.php?sectiondetailid=72588&PHPSESSID=bac1144723306d8fe6c57718e656fb9f.

34. R. Pierangelo and G. Giuliani, *Learning Disabilities: A Practical Approach to Foundations, Assessment, Diagnosis, and Teaching* (Columbus, OH: Pearson Education, 2006), 361.

35. Indiana District of Education, "South Bend Educator Named 2009 Teacher of the Year," September 22, 2008; accessed June 9, 2009, from http://www.doe.in.gov/news/2008/09-September/TOY.html.

36. J. J. Heckman, "Invest in the Very Young," *Encyclopedia on Early Childhood Development,* September 1, 2004; accessed February 16, 2009, at http://www.child-encyclopedia.com/pages/PDF/HeckmanANGxp.pdf.

Chapter 6

1. National Association for the Education of Young Children, Draft Core *NAEYC Standards for Early Childhood Professional Preparation,* August 7, 2008, 1–3.

2. Literacy Links, "Spotlight on Using Assessment to Guide Instruction," 2006; accessed September 16, 2009, at www.maine.gov/education/rf/newsletters/1106newsletter.rtf.

3. NAEYC Academy for Early Childhood Program Accreditation, "Standard 4: NAEYC Accreditation Criteria for Assessment of Child Progress"; accessed May 3, 2009, at http://www.grandmashouse.org/docs/assessment.pdf.

4. L. Shepard, S. L. Kagan, and E. Wurtz, *Principles and Recommendations for Early Childhood Assessments* (Washington, DC: National Education Goals Panel, December 14, 1998), 5–6.

5. J. Mueller, "What Is Authentic Assessment?" Authentic Assessment Toolbox, 2008; accessed March 30, 2009, at http://jonathan.mueller.faculty.noctrl.edu/toolbox/whatisit.htm.

6. Centers for Disease Control and Prevention, "Child Development: Using Developmental Screening to Improve Children's Health,"Department of Health and Human Services, September 20, 2005, http://www.cdc.gov/ncbddd/child/improve.htm.

7. Council of Chief State School Officers, The Words We Use: A Glossary of Terms for Early Childhood Education Standards and Assessment, "Informal Assessment"; retrieved April 1, 2009, from http://www.ccsso.org/projects/scass/projects/early_childhood_education_assessment_consortium/publications_and_products/2873.cfm.

8. Council of Chief State School Officers, "Informal Assessment," 2009; accessed September 16, 2009, at http://www.ccsso.org/projects/scass/projects/early_childhood_education_assessment_consortium/publications_and_products/2873.cfm.

Chapter 7

1. National Association for the Education of Young Children, Draft Core NAEYC Standards for Early Childhood Professional Preparation, August 7, 2008, 1–3.

2. Ibid.

3. Ibid.

4. U.S. Department of Health and Human Services, Administration for Children and Families, National Infant and Toddler Child Care Initiative, Zero to Three, "At-A-Glance Planning"; accessed February 27, 2007, at http://www.nccic.org/itcc/publications/planning.htm.

5. W. J. Cromie, "Looking for the Nature of Human Nature," Harvard University Gazette, May 27, 2004; accessed June 22, 2009, from http://www.news.harvard.edu/gazette/2004/05.27/01-pinker.html.

6. American Federation of Teachers, "Nurturing Language Development—Infants and Toddlers," accessed June 18, 2009, from http://www.aft.org/earlychildhood/language-dev.htm.

7. "Child Development, Toddlers Engage in 'Emotional Eavesdropping' to Guide Their Behavior," PhysOrg.com, March 26, 2007; accessed March 2, 2009, at http://www.physorg.com/news94143600.html.

8. S. Gable, "Nature, Nurture, and Early Brain Development," ClassBrain.com, May 3, 2008; accessed June 22, 2009, at http://classbrain.com/artread/publish/article_30.shtml.

9. P. Kuhl, Early Language Acquisition: The Brain Comes Prepared (St. Louis, MO: Parents as Teachers National Center, 1996).

10. S. Gable, "Nature, Nurture, and Early Brain Development," ClassBrain.com, May 3, 2008; accessed June 22, 2009, at http://classbrain.com/artread/publish/article_30.shtml.

11. E. Wilcox, "Straight Talk About Music and Brain Research," Teaching Music, 7(3), December 1999, 29, 31–35.

12. "Active Education: Physical Education, Physical Activity, and Academic Performance," Active Living Research, Fall 2007; accessed June 22, 2009, at http://www.activelivingresearch.org/alr/alr/files/Active_Ed.pdf.

13. Sharon Rosenkoetter and Lauren R Barton, "Bridges to Literacy, Early Routines that Promote Later School Success," Zero to Three, February/March 2002; accessed September 21, 2009, at http://www.zerotothree.org/site/DocServer/Vol_22-4f.pdf?docID=1182&AddInterest=1145.

14. "The Human Brain: Renew—Stress on the Brain," The Franklin Institute Online, 2004; accessed February 5, 2009, at http://www.fi.edu/learn/brain/stress.html.

15. E. Erikson, Childhood and Society, 2nd ed. (New York: Norton, 1963; first pub. 1950), 249.

16. Ibid.

17. A. N. Meltzoff, "'Like Me': A Foundation for Social Cognition," Developmental Science, (10)1, January 2007, 126–134.

18. Random House Dictionary, "bonding," Dictionary.com, 2009; accessed March 9, 2009, from http://dictionary.reference.com/browse/bonding.

19. J. Oats and A. Grayson, Cognitive and Language Development in Children, 2nd ed., (Oxford, England: Blackwell, 2004).

20. "Attachment Part One: The Dance of Relationship," AboutKidsHealth, June 16, 2004; accessed June 18, 2009, from http://www.aboutkidshealth.ca/News/Attachment-Part-One-The-dance-of-relationship.aspx?articleID=7933&categoryID=news-type.

21. A. Thomas, S. Chess, and H. Birch, "The Origin of Personality," Scientific American, 223(2), August 1970, 102–109.

22. G. Josse and N. Tzourio-Mazoyer, "Review: Hemispheric Specialization for Language," Brain Research Reviews, 44(1), January 2004, 1–12.

23. Society for Research in Child Development, "Children's Earliest Words Stem from What Interests Them," ScienceDaily, March 22, 2006; accessed March 9, 2009, at http://www.sciencedaily.com/releases/2006/03/060322141842.htm.

24. E. L. Newport, "Mother, I'd Rather Do It Myself: Some Effects and Non-Effects on Maternal Speech Style," in C. E. Snow and C. A. Ferguson, eds., Talking to Children (Cambridge, England: Cambridge University Press, 1979), 112–129.

25. L. Acredelo and S. Goodwyn, Baby Signs: How to Talk with Your Baby Before Your Baby Can Talk (Chicago: Contemporary Books, 1996).

26. JAMA and Archives Journals, "Babies Who Don't Respond to Their Names May Be at Risk for Autism or Other Disorders," ScienceDaily, April 4, 2007; accessed March 9, 2009, at http://www.sciencedaily.com/releases/2007/04/070402162106.htm.

27. National Institute for Literacy, Vocabulary Instruction, Eunice Kennedy Shriver National Institute of Child Health and Human Development; accessed April 9, 2009, at http://www.nifl.gov/partnershipforreading/explore/vocabulary.html.

28. S. Bredekamp and C. Copple, eds., Developmentally Appropriate Practice in Early Childhood Programs, 3rd ed. (Washington, DC: NAEYC, 2009), 9.

29. American Academy of Pediatrics, "Campaign Launched to Avoid Sudden Death in Child Care Settings," News release, January 29, 2003.

30. N. Engineer, C. Percaccio, and M. Kilgard, "Environment Shapes Auditory Processing," New Horizons for Learning, June 2004; accessed February 27, 2007, at http://www.newhorizons.org/neuro/engineer%20percaccio%20kilgard.htm.

31. U.S. Department of Health and Human Services, Administration for Children and Families, FY 2007 PRISM Protocol: Safe Environments, 2007.

32. L. Lloyd-Jones, "Relationship as Curriculum," Head Start Bulletin No. 73, 2002; available online at http://eclkc.ohs.acf.hhs.gov/hslc/ecdh/eecd/Curriculum/Definition%20and%20Requirements/edudev_art_00101_072305.html.

33. Tulane Institute of Infant and Early Childhood Mental Health, "10 Things You Should Know About Infant Mental Health," accessed April 7, 2009, at http://www.infantinstitute.org/tenth.htm.

34. U.S. Department of Health and Human Services, Administration for Children and Families, "A Commitment to Supporting the Mental Health of Our Youngest Children," October 23–24, 2000; accessed February 27, 2007, at http://www.acf.hhs.gov/programs/opre/ehs/mental_health/reports/imh_report/imh_rpt.pdf#search=%22A%20Commitment%20to%20Supporting%20the%20Mental%20Health%20of%20Our%20Youngest%20Children%22.

Chapter 8

1. National Association for the Education of Young Children, Draft Core *NAEYC Standards for Early Childhood Professional Preparation*, August 7, 2008, 1–3.

2. Ibid.

3. National Institute for Early Education Research, "The State of Preschool 2008"; accessed April 7, 2009, at http://nieer.org/yearbook.

4. Ibid.

5. Ibid.

6. U.S. Department of Labor, *Occupational Outlook Handbook, 2008–09 Edition,* "Teachers—Preschool, Kindergarten, Elementary, Middle, and Secondary," April 14, 2007; accessed June 22, 2009, from http://www.bls.gov/oco/ocos069.htm.

7. Culver City Unified School District, News and Announcements, "Christine Lyall Named Los Angles County Preschool Teacher of the Year," April 20, 2009; accessed June 22, 2009, from http://ccusd.org/apps/news/show_news.jsp?REC_ID=93423&id=0.

8. Healy Communications Inc., "First-Ever National Preschool Teacher of the Year Award Winners Announced by Story Reader™," September 18, 2006; accessed June 22, 2009, from http://www.pubint.com/about/dsp_pr_PTOTYWinnersReleaseFINAL.cfm.

9. Ibid.

10. Ibid.

11. Ibid.

12. National Association of Child Care Resource and Referral Agencies, "What Do Parents Think About Child Care?" 2006; accessed May 11, 2009, at http://www.naccrra.org/docs/policy/FocusGrpReport.pdf.

13. American Federation of Teachers, "Welcome Early Childhood Educators and Child Care Providers!"; accessed June 22, 2009, from http://aft.org/earlychildhood/index.htm.

14. W. T. Dickens, I. Sawhill, and J. Tebbs, The Brookings Institution, "Policy Brief #153, The Effects of Investing in Early Childhood Education on Economic Growth," April 2006, http://www.brookings.edu/comm/policybriefs/pb153.pdf.

15. Ibid.

16. California Department of Education, "Preschool for All: A First-Class Learning Initiative," State of Education Address, January 24, 2005; available online at http://www.cde.ca.gov/eo/in/se/yr05preschoolwp.asp.

17. L. J. Calman and L. Tarr-Whelan, *Early Childhood Education for All: A Wise Investment* (New York: Legal Momentum, April 2005); available online at http://web.mit.edu/workplacecenter/docs/Full%20Report.pdf.

18. Ibid.

19. The U.S. Department of Justice, "The High/Scope Perry Preschool Project," *Juvenile Justice Bulletin,* October 2000; accessed June 17, 2009, from http://www.ncjrs.gov/pdffiles1/ojjdp/181725.pdf.

20. S. Hoff, "Commentary: Investing in Early Childhood Education," KERA Public Broadcasting, Dallas, TX, September 3, 2008; available online at http://www.publicbroadcasting.net/kera/news.newsmain?action=article&ARTICLE_ID=1356160&sectionID=1.

21. National Governors Association, *A Governor's Guide to School Readiness: Building the Foundation for Bright Futures* (Washington, DC: National Governors Association Center for Best Practices, 2005).

22. C. Bruner, S. Floyd, and A. Copeman, "Seven Things Policy Makers Need to Know About School Readiness, Revised and Expanded Toolkit," *State Early Childhood Policy Technical Assistance Network* (Des Moines, IA: Child and Family Policy Center, January 2005), 7.

23. D. S. Strickland and S. Riley-Ayers, *Early Literacy: Policy and Practice in the Preschool Years* (New Brunswick, NJ: NIEER, April 2006).

24. J. P. Shonkoff and D. A. Phillips, eds., *From Neurons to Neighborhoods* (Washington, DC: National Academy Press, 2000), 338.

25. Charlottesville City Schools, "Preschool Program"; accessed June 17, 2009, from http://www.ccs.k12.va.us/programs/preschool.html.

26. Ibid.

27. U.S. Department of Health and Human Services, Administration for Children and Families, "Head Start Child Outcomes Framework Domain 6: Social and Emotional Development," March 4, 2005; accessed May 13, 2009, at http://www.headstartinfo.org/leaders_guideeng/domain6.htm.

28. Santa Clara County Partnership for School Readiness and Applied Research Survey, "Does Readiness Matter? How Kindergarten Readiness Translates into Success," April 2008; accessed February 11, 2009, at http://www.appliedsurveyresearch.org/www/products/DoesReadinessMatter_ALongitudinalAnalysisFINAL3.pdf.

29. M. Conn-Powers, "All Children Ready for School: Approaches to Learning,"*Early Childhood Briefing Paper Series,* Indiana University, 2006; available online at http://www.iidc.indiana.edu/styles/iidc/defiles/ECC/SRUD-ApproachestoLearning.pdf.

30. Ibid.

31. S. Hawley, "Kindergarten Prep: New Guidelines Outline What All Pre-Kindergartners Should Know," *ACF Newsource,* December 31, 2006; retrieved May 10, 2009, from http://www.acfnewsource.org/education/k_prep.html.

32. National Early Literacy Panel, *Developing Early Literacy: Report of the National Early Literacy Panel* (Washington, DC: National Institute for Literacy, 2008).

33. Kids Count Data Center, "Children That Speak a Language Other Than English at Home (percent)—2007"; accessed June 17, 2009, from http://datacenter.kidscount.org/data/acrossstates/Rankings.aspx?ind=81.

34. "Indicator FAM5: Language Spoken at Home and Difficulty Speaking English"; accessed February 9, 2009, at http://www.childstats.gov/americaschildren07/famsoc5.asp.

35. Ibid.

36. U.S. Census Bureau, "Detailed List of Languages Spoken at Home for the Population 5 Years and Over by State: 2000"; available at http://www.census.gov/population/cen2000/phc-t20/tab05.pdf.

37. Ibid.

38. E. Jones and S. Cronin, "Play and Culture," *ExchangeEveryDay,* April 16, 2009; retrieved May 10, 2009, from http://www .childcareexchange.com/eed/news_print.php?news_id=2234.

39. D. Phillips and N. A. Crowell, eds., *Cultural Diversity and Early Education: Report of a Workshop National Research Council* (Washington, DC: National Academy Press, 1994).

40. M. Parten, "Social Participation Among Preschool Children," *Journal of Abnormal and Social Psychology,* 27, 1932, 243–269.

Chapter 9

1. National Association for the Education of Young Children, Draft Core *NAEYC Standards for Early Childhood Professional Preparation,* August 7, 2008, 1–3.

2. Ibid.

3. Ibid.

4. International Reading Association and National Association for the Education of Young Children, "Learning to Read and Write: Developmentally Appropriate Practices for Young Children," *Young Children,* 53(4), July 1998, 39; available online at http://208.118.177 .216/about/positions/pdf/PSREAD98.pdf.

5. D. J. Ackerman, W. S. Barnett, and K. B Robin, NIEER Policy Report: *Making the Most of Kindergarten,* March 2005, http://nieer.org/ resources/policyreports/report4.pdf.

6. U.S. Census Bureau, "School Enrollment: Social and Economic Characteristics of Students," October 2006; accessed at http://www .census.gov/population/www/socdemo/school.html.

7. Education Commission of the States, "How States Fund Full-Day Kindergarten," *State Notes Kindergarten,* updated August 2005; accessed at http://www.ecs.org/clearinghouse/63/10/6310.htm.

8. S. Martinez and T. Akey, *Full-Day Kindergarten 1997–98 Evaluation Report,* unpublished evaluation from Park Hill Public Schools, Kansas City, MO, March 1998, with follow-up study summary, May 1999.

9. A. Matturro Gault, "Off to the Write Start," *Scholastic,* June 1, 2005; available at http://www2.scholastic.com/browse/article.jsp?id= 3745857.

10. This digest was adapted from a position paper of the Association for Childhood Education International by Vito Perrone, "On Standardized Testing," which appeared in *Childhood Education,* Spring 1991, 132–142.

11. Eye Care America, American Academy of Ophthalmology, "Learning Disabilities," May 2007; accessed May 12, 2009, from http://www .aao.org/eyecare/conditions/Learning-Disabilities/index.cfm.

12. U.S. Department of Education, Building the Legacy: IDEA 2004, "Statute: Title I/A/602/30"; accessed May 12, 2009, from http://idea .ed.gov/explore/view/p/%2Croot%2Cstatute%2CI%2CA%2C602% 2C30%2C.

13. E. Gootman, "Preschoolers Grow Older as Parents Seek an Edge," *New York Times,* October 19, 2006; accessed at http://www.nytimes .com/2006/10/19/nyregion/19kindergarten.html.

14. National Association for the Education of Young Children, "Still Unacceptable Trends in Kindergarten Entry and Placement," *NAEYC Position Statement,* revision and updated, 2000; available at http:// www.naeyc.org/files/naeyc/file/policy/state/Psunacc.pdf.

15. L. Starr, "Kindergarten Is for Kids," *Education World,* June 4, 2002, http://www.educationworld.com/a_issues/issues325.shtml.

16. J. DeFao, "Kindergarten 'Redshirting' Is a Hot Topic," (Salt Lake City) *Deseret News,* November 14, 2006; available at http:// findarticles.com/p/articles/mi_qn4188/is_20061114/ai_n16845725.

17. D. Stipek, "At What Age Should Children Enter Kindergarten? A Question for Policy Makers and Parents," *Social Policy Report,* 16(2), 2002, 11.

18. M. M. Martini, *Research Brief of Full-Day Kindergarten,* December 2007; available at http://www.leg.state.nv.us/lcb/research/ researchbriefs/FullDayKindergarten.pdf.

19. Ibid.

20. Education Commission of the States, "Access to Kindergarten: Age Issues in State Statutes," *State Notes Kindergarten,* 2005, http://mb2.ecs.org/reports/Report.aspx?id=32.

21. K. Kauerz, "Straddling Early Learning and Early Elementary School," *Young Children: Beyond the Journal,*)3, March 2005, http://www .journal.naeyc.org/btj/200503/01Kauerz.pdf

22. K. Kauerz, *Full-Day Kindergarten: A Study of State Policies in the United States,* Education Commission of the States, June 2005; available at http://www.fcd-us.org/usr_doc/FullDayKindergarten.pdf.

23. J. T. Downer, K. M. La Paro, R. C. Pianta, and S. E. Rimm-Kaufman, "The Contribution of Classroom Setting and Quality of Instruction to Children's Behavior in Kindergarten Classrooms," *Elementary School Journal,* 105(4), March 2005, 377–394.

24. M. Brendgen, B. Wanner, and F. Vitaro, "Verbal Abuse by the Teacher and Child Adjustment from Kindergarten Through Grade 6," *Pediatrics,* 117(5), May 2006, 1585–1598.

25. E. Y. Jung and M. M. Ostrosky, "Brief #12: Building Positive Teacher–Child Relationships," Center on the Social and Emotional Foundations for Early Learning; accessed March 2, 2007, at http:// www.vanderbilt.edu/csefel/briefs/wwb12.html.

26. Kansas Parent Information Resource Center, *How to Help Your Child Become a Better Reader: A Parent Guide,* 2008, http://www.kpirc .org/uploads/BetterReaderArranged2color.pdf.

27. Ibid.

28. J. Reyhner, "The Reading Wars; Phonics Versus Whole Language," December 13, 2008, http://jan.ucc.nau.edu/~jar/Reading_Wars.html.

29. Entire section on shared reading adapted by permission from J. D. Cooper, *Literacy: Helping Children Construct Meaning,* 5th ed. (Boston: Houghton Mifflin, 2003), 155–157.

30. M. Hubbard, "Shared Reading," accessed April 13, 2009, at http:// www.hubbardscupboard.org/shared_reading.html.

31. L. M. Morrow, *Literacy Development in the Early Years: Helping Children Read and Write,* 5th ed. (Needham, MA: Allyn & Bacon, 2005). Copyright 2005. Reprinted/adapted by permission of Allyn & Bacon.

32. Texas Education Agency, Texas Essential Knowledge and Skills for Mathematics, "Mathematics, Kindergarten," amended August 1, 2006, http://ritter.tea.state.tx.us/rules/tac/chapter111/ch111a.html.

33. Mathematics Standards, accessed September 21, 2009, at http:// www.sbec.state.tx.us/SBEConline/standtest/standards/8-12math.pdf.

34. *EnvisionMath,* Scott Foresman/Addison Wesley. Pearson, Kindergarten. 2009.

35. National Council for Social Studies, "About NCSS," http://www .socialstudies.org/about.

36. K. L. Maxwell and S. K. Elder, "Children's Transition to Kindergarten," *Young Children,* 49(6), 56–63.

Chapter 10

1. National Association for the Education of Young Children, Draft Core *NAEYC Standards for Early Childhood Professional Preparation*, August 7, 2008, 1–3.

2. Ibid.

3. Ibid.

4. T. W. Briggs, "All-USA Teachers Strive to Give Confidence, Changes," *USA Today,* November 6, 2007; accessed June 29, 2009, at http://www.usatoday.com/news/education/2007-10-17-teacher-team_N.htm?csp=34.

5. Arkansas Department of Education, "Milken Family Foundation, National Educator Awards", October 10, 2008; accessed June 28, 2009, at http://arkansased.org/teachers/recognition_milken.html.

6. Milken Family Foundation "Milken Educator—Elizabeth Parker". Accessed June 28, 2009, at http://www.mff.org/mea/mea.taf?page=recipient&meaID=22570.

7. T. W. Briggs, "All-USA Teachers Strive to Give Confidence, Changes," *USA Today,* November 6, 2007; accessed June 29, 2009, at http://www.usatoday.com/news/education/2007-10-17-teacher-team_N.htm?csp=34.

8. U.S. Department of Education, Institute of Education Sciences, National Center for Educational Statistics, *The Condition of Education 2009,* "Commissioner's Statement," June 2009; available at http://nces.ed.gov/pubs2009/2009081.pdf.

9. Ibid.

10. Ibid.

11. Ibid.

12. P. L. Ritchie, "Pine Grove Elementary Students Write Cookbook," *St. Petersburg Times,* June 4, 2009; accessed June 5, 2009, from http://www.tampabay.com/news/education/k12/article1006748.ece.

13. "Children and Computer Technology: Analysis and Recommendations," *The Future of Children,* 10(2), Fall 2000, 4–30; accessed March 5, 2007, at http://futureofchildren.org/futureofchildren/publications/docs/10_02_Analysis.pdf.

14. Pew Internet and American Life Project, "Home Broadband Adoption Increases Sharply in 2009 with Big Jumps Among Seniors, Low-Income Households, and Rural Residents Even Though Prices Have Risen Since Last Year," June 17, 2009; accessed June 24, 2009, at http://www.pewinternet.org/Press-Releases/2009/Home-broadband-adoption-increases-sharply-in-2009.aspx.

15. American Academy of Child and Adolescent Psychiatry, "Facts for Families: Obesity in Children and Teens," May 2008; accessed July 1, 2009, at http://aacap.org/cs/root/facts_for_families/obesity_in_children_and_teens.

16. Institute of Medicine, "Schools Can Play a Role in Preventing Childhood Obesity," September 2004; accessed November 15, 2007, at http://www.iom.edu/Object.File/Master/22/615/Fact%20Sheet%20-%20Schools%20FINALBitticks.pdf.

17. D. Satcher, "Healthy and Ready to Learn," *The Whole Child,* 63(1), September 2005, 26–30; available online at http://pdonline.ascd.org/pd_online/significance/el200509_satcher.html.

18. U.S. Department of Education. Institute of Education Sciences, National Center for Educational Statistics, "Calories In, Calories Out: Food and Exercise in Public Elementary Schools, 2005"; accessed March 5, 2007, at http://nces.ed.gov/pubs2006/nutrition.

19. "Lawmakers Call for Increased Activity to Combat Child Obesity," *Dallas Morning News,* February 8, 2007.

20. "Parents Launch 'Rescuing Recess' Drive," *CBS News,* May 16, 2006.

21. Mental Health America, "Factsheet: Childhood Depression: Tips for Parents," 2007; accessed March 5, 2007, at http://www.mentalhealthamerica.net/index.cfm?objectid=C7DF9240-1372-4D20-C81D80B5B7C5957B.

22. Mental Health America, "Factsheet: Depression in Children," 2007, accessed March 5, 2007, at http://www.mentalhealthamerica.net/index.cfm?objectid=CA866E0D-1372-4D20-C8872863D2EE2E90.

23. Mental Health in Illinois, "Ideas on Promoting Good Mental Health for Children," 2009; accessed June 24, 2009, at http://www.mentalhealthillinois.org/childrens-health/promoting-childrens-mental-health.

24. National Association of School Psychologists, NASP Resources, "Supporting Children's Mental Health: Tips for Parents and Educators," 2009; accessed June 24, 2009, at http://www.nasponline.org/resources/mentalhealth/mhtips.aspx.

25. Michigan Department of Education, "Okemos Elementary School Teacher Named Michigan Teacher of the Year," May 14, 2009; accessed June 4, 2009, from http://www.michigan.gov/mde/0,1607,7-140-6530_6526_6551-214772—,00.html.

26. Saskatoon Public Schools, "Instructional Strategies Online: Guided Reading," 2008; accessed May 15, 2009, at http://olc.spsd.sk.ca/DE/PD/instr/strats/guided/guided.html.

27. National Council of Teachers of Mathematics, "Algebra Standards for Grades Pre-K–2," © 2000–2004; accessed June 4, 2009, at http://standards.nctm.org/document/chapter4/alg.htm.

28. S. Feeney and N. K. Freeman, *Ethics and the Early Childhood Educator: Using the NAEYC Code* (Washington, DC: NAEYC, 2005).

29. Public Schools of North Carolina, Standard Course of Study, "Social Studies: 2006: First Grade Neighborhoods and Communities Around the World"; accessed December 20, 2007, at http://www.dpi.state.nc.us/curriculum/socialstudies/scos/2003–04/021firstgrade.

30. "Dancing to Music," CanTeach; accessed March 5, 2007, at http://www.canteach.ca/elementary/pedance1.html.

Chapter 11

1. National Association for the Education of Young Children, *NAEYC Standards for Early Childhood Professional Preparation: Initial Licensure Programs,* NAEYC Initial Licensure Standards (Washington, DC: NAEYC, August 2008), 2.

2. Ibid.

3. Ibid.

4. Council for Exceptional Children, CEC News, "National Special Education Teacher of the Year to Be Honored at Convention," March 11, 2009; accessed May 4, 2009, from http://www.cec.sped.org/Content/NavigationMenu/ProfessionalDevelopment/ConventionExpo/Press/National_Special_Edu.htm.

5. Individuals with Disabilities Education Act (IDEA), Public Law 105–17, 1997.

6. Ibid.

7. U.S. Census Bureau, Newsroom: Facts for Features, "Americans with Disabilities Act," May 27, 2008; accessed May 12, 2009, from http://www.census.gov/Press-Release/www/releases/archives/facts_for_features_special_editions/011953.html.

8. U.S. Department of Education, National Center for Education Statistics, *The Condition of Education 2005,* NCES 2005-094 (Washington, DC: U.S. Government Printing Office), 172.

9. A. Turnbull, H. Turnbull III, M. Shank, and D. Leal, *Exceptional Lives: Special Education in Today's Schools,* 2nd ed. (Upper Saddle River, NJ: Merrill/Prentice Hall, 1995), 64–71.

10. D. P. Hallahan and J. M. Kauffman, *Exceptional Learners: An Introduction to Special Education,* 10th ed. (Boston: Pearson/Allyn & Bacon, 2006), 31.

11. U.S. Department of Education, Building the Legacy: IDEA 2004, "Sec. 300.321 IEP Team," 2004; accessed May 5, 2009, from http://idea.ed.gov/explore/view/p/%2Croot%2Cregs%2C300%2CD%2C300%252E321%2C.

12. U.S. Department of Education, Office of Educational Research and Improvement, *Reaching All Families—Creating Family Friendly Schools,* 1996.

13. Autism Society of America, "What Is Autism?"; accessed May 18, 2009, at http://www.autism-society.org/site/PageServer?pagename=about_whatis.

14. Ibid.

15. Ibid.

16. Ibid.

17. Autism Speaks, *Building a Community of Hope: 2007 Annual Report,* "About Autism"; retrieved June 25, 2009, from http://www.autismspeaks.org/docs/Autism_Speaks_Annual_Report_2007.pdf.

18. Ibid.

19. J. J. Woods and A. M. Wetherby, "Early Identification of and Intervention for Infants and Toddlers Who Are at Risk for Autism Spectrum Disorder," *Language, Speech, and Hearing Services in Schools,* 34(3), July 2003, 180–293.

20. S. Mastrangelo, "Play and the Child with Autism Spectrum Disorder: From Possibilities to Practice," *International Journal of Play Therapy,* 18(1), January 2009, 13–30.

21. J. J. Woods and A. M. Wetherby, "Early Identification of and Intervention for Infants and Toddlers Who Are at Risk for Autism Spectrum Disorder," *Language, Speech, and Hearing Services in Schools,* 34(3), July 2003, 180–293.

22. K. Painter, "Science Getting to Roots of Autism," *USA Today,* January 12, 2004; accessed March 5, 2007, at http://www.usatoday.com/news/health/2004-01-12-autism-main_x.htm.

23. Autism Society of America, "What Is Autism?"; accessed May 18, 2009, at http://www.autism-society.org/site/PageServer?pagename=about_whatis.

24. L. Neergaard, Associated Press, *International Herald Tribune,* "Gene Clues from Mideast Suggest Autism Occurs When Brain Cannot Learn Properly from Early Life," July 11, 2008; accessed July 13, 2008 from http://www.encyclopedia.com/doc/1A1-D91R8GI84.html.

25. K. L. Spittler, "New Evidence Supports Theory of an Environmental Trigger for Autism," *NeuroPsychiatry Reviews,* 10(1), January 2009, 6.

26. J. J. Woods and A. M. Wetherby, "Early Identification of and Intervention for Infants and Toddlers Who Are at Risk for Autism Spectrum Disorder," *Language, Speech, and Hearing Services in Schools,* 34(3), July 2003, 180–293.

27. S. Mastrangelo, "Play and the Child with Autism Spectrum Disorder: From Possibilities to Practice," *International Journal of Play Therapy,* 18(1), January 2009, 13–30.

28. T. Wigram and C. Gold, "Music Therapy in the Assessment and Treatment of Autistic Spectrum Disorder: Clinical Application and Research Evidence," *Child Care, Health and Development,* 32(5), September 2006, 535–542.

29. Mental Health America, "Fact Sheet: Adult AD/HD in the Work Place"; accessed June 24, 2009, from http://www.mentalhealthamerica.net/go/information/get-info/ad/hd/adult-ad/hd-in-the-workplace.

30. American Psychiatric Association, *Diagnostic and Statistical Manual of Mental Disorders: DSM-IV-TR* (Washington, DC: Author, 2000).

31. Ibid.

32. Ibid.

33. Ibid.

34. Centers for Disease Control and Prevention, "Attention Deficit/Hyperactivity Disorder (ADHD): Facts About ADHD," February 20, 2009; accessed May 6, 2009, from http://www.cdc.gov/ncbddd/adhd/facts.html.

35. Centers for Disease Control and Prevention, "FastStats: Attention Deficit Hyperactivity Disorder (ADHD)," April 2, 2009; accessed May 18, 2009, from http://www.cdc.gov/nchs/fastats/adhd.htm.

36. C. Adams, "Girls and ADHD: Are You Missing the Signs?" *Instructor,* 116(6), March/April 2007, 31–35.

37. Ibid.

38. Ibid.

39. Ibid.

40. Ibid.

41. Ibid.

42. Mental Health America, "Fact Sheet: Adult AD/HD in the Work Place"; accessed June 24, 2009, from http://www.mentalhealthamerica.net/go/information/get-info/ad/hd/adult-ad/hd-in-the-workplace.

43. Ibid.

44. Centers for Disease Control and Prevention, "Attention Deficit/Hyperactivity Disorder (ADHD): Facts About ADHD," February 20, 2009; accessed May 6, 2009, from http://www.cdc.gov/ncbddd/adhd/facts.html.

45. C. Tomlinson, *How to Differentiate Instruction in Mixed-Ability Classrooms,* 2nd ed. (Alexandria, VA: Association for Supervision and Curriculum Development, 2001).

46. Embedded Instruction for Early Learning, "What Is Embedded Instruction for Early Learning?" 2008; accessed June 24, 2009, from http://embeddedinstruction.net/node/16.

47. Indiana's Academic Standards—Mathematics, Core Standards, Grade 1, Standard Indicators 1.1.1 and 1.1.4, updated August 21, 2006; available at http://dc.doe.in.gov/Standards/AcademicStandards/PrintLibrary/index.shtml.

48. A. Morse, "A Look at Immigrant Youth: Prospects and Promising Practices," National Conference of State Legislatures, Children's Policy Initiative, March 2005; available at http://www.ncsl.org/documents/immig/CPIimmigrantyouth.pdf.

49. Kids Count Data Center, "Children in Immigrant Families (percent)," 2007; accessed May 6, 2009, from http://datacenter.kidscount.org/data/acrossstates/Rankings.aspx?ind=115.

50. Children's Action Alliance, "Going Beyond the Immigration Hype: Children and Our Shared Destiny: Facts and Recommendations"; accessed May 13, 2009, from http://www.azchildren.org/MyFiles/PDF/Immigrant_Children.pdf.

51. Kids Count, Data Snap Shot, "One Out of Five U.S. Children Is Living in an Immigrant Family," March 2007; accessed May 12, 2009, from http://www.aecf.org/upload/publicationfiles/da3622h1267.pdf.

52. Kids Count Data Center, "Children Living in Linguistically Isolated Households by Children in Immigrant Families (percent)," 2007; accessed May 6, 2009, from http://datacenter.kidscount.org/data/acrossstates/Rankings.aspx?ind=129.

53. Children's Action Alliance, "Going Beyond the Immigration Hype: Children and Our Shared Destiny: Facts and Recommendations"; accessed May 13, 2009, from http://www.azchildren.org/MyFiles/PDF/Immigrant_Children.pdf.

54. Ibid.

55. Kids Count, Data Snap Shot, "One Out of Five U.S. Children Is Living in an Immigrant Family," March 2007; accessed May 12, 2009 from http://www.aecf.org/upload/publicationfiles/da3622h1267.pdf.

56. Children's Action Alliance, "Going Beyond the Immigration Hype: Children and Our Shared Destiny: Facts and Recommendations"; accessed May 13, 2009, from http://www.azchildren.org/MyFiles/PDF/Immigrant_Children.pdf.

57. Kids Count Data Center, "Children Living in Linguistically Isolated Households by Children in Immigrant Families (percent)," 2007; accessed May 6, 2009, from http://datacenter.kidscount.org/data/acrossstates/Rankings.aspx?ind=129.

58. Children's Action Alliance, "Going Beyond the Immigration Hype: Children and Our Shared Destiny: Facts and Recommendations"; accessed May 13, 2009, from http://www.azchildren.org/MyFiles/PDF/Immigrant_Children.pdf.

59. U.S. Census Bureau, Newsroom: Facts for Features, "Asian/Pacific American Heritage Month: Languages," May 2008; accessed May 12, 2009, from http://www.census.gov/Press-Release/www/releases/archives/facts_for_features_special_editions/011602.html.

60. Kids Count, Data Snap Shot, "One Out of Five U.S. Children Is Living in an Immigrant Family," March 2007; accessed May 12, 2009, from http://www.aecf.org/upload/publicationfiles/da3622h1267.pdf.

61. U.S. Department of Commerce, Minority Business Development Agency, *Minority Population Growth: 1995 to 2050,* September 1999; accessed March 5, 2007, at http://www.mbda.gov/documents/mbdacolor.pdf.

62. Miami–Dade County Public Schools, *Statistical Abstract 2002–2003,* July 2003; accessed March 5, 2007, at http://drs.dadeschools.net/StatisticalAbstract/sa0203.pdf.

63. I. Ryabov, and J. Van Hook, "School Segregation and Academic Achievement Among Hispanic Children," *Social Science Research,* (36)2, June 2007, 767–788; accessed September 30, 2009, from http://www.sciencedirect.com/science?_ob=ArticleURL&_udi=B6WX8-4K42DHF-2&_user=452995&_rdoc=1&_fmt=&_orig=search&_sort=d&_docanchor=&view=c&_searchStrId=1029881865&_rerunOrigin=google&_acct=C000007818&_version=1&_urlVersion=0&_userid=452995&md5=7d10f5f842fd471b753185a81fd128f2.

64. M. Cabo, R. Dunn, and K. Dunn, *Teaching Students to Read Through Their Individual Learning Styles* (Boston: Allyn & Bacon, 1991), 2.

65. D. L. Voltz, M. J. Sims, B. Nelson, and C. Bivens, "A Framework for Inclusion in the Context of Standards-Based Reform," *Teaching Exceptional Children,* 37(5), May/June 2005, 14–19.

66. V. Hildebrand, L. A. Phenice, M. M. Grey, and R. P. Hines, *Knowing and Serving Diverse Families* (Upper Saddle River, NJ: Merrill/Prentice Hall, 2000), 107.

Chapter 12

1. National Association for the Education of Young Children, Draft Core *NAEYC Standards for Early Childhood Professional Preparation,* August 7, 2008, 1–3.

2. Ibid.

3. W. M. Reinke, J. D. Splett, E. N. Robeson, and C. A. Offutt, "Combining School and Family Interventions for the Prevention and Early Intervention of Disruptive Behavior Problems in Children: A Public Health Perspective," *Psychology in the Schools,* 46(1), January 2009, 33–43; available online at http://www3.interscience.wiley.com/cgi-bin/fulltext/121549478/PDFSTART.

4. L. S. Vygotsky, *Mind in Society* (Cambridge, MA: Harvard University Press, 1978), 86.

5. S. Gupta, "Child Rearing in Self Regulation Through Private Speech," February 19, 2008; available at http://www.articles-r-free.com/articledetail.php?artid=17986&catid=162.

6. L. E. Berk and A. Winsler, *Scaffolding Children's Learning: Vygotsky and Early Childhood Education* (Washington, DC: NAEYC, 1995), 45–46.

Chapter 13

1. National Association for the Education of Young Children, Draft Core *NAEYC Standards for Early Childhood Professional Preparation,* August 7, 2008, 1–3.

2. Ibid.

3. A. T. Henderson, V. Johnson, K. L. Mapp, and D. Davies, *Beyond the Bake Sale: The Essential Guide to Family/School Partnerships* (New York: New Press, 2007).

4. A. T. Henderson and K. L. Mapp, National Center for Family and Community Connections with Schools, Southwest Educational Development Laboratory, *A New Wave of Evidence: The Impact of School, Family, and Community Connections on Student Achievement,* 2002; retrieved June 5, 2009, from http://www.edmonds.wednet.edu/diversity/documents/A%20New%20Wave%20of%20Evidence.pdf.

5. Data from L. C. Rose and A. M. Gallup, "The Thirty-seventh Annual Phi Delta Kappa/Gallup Poll of the Public's Attitudes Toward the Public Schools," *Phi Delta Kappan,* 87(1), September 2005.

6. A. T. Henderson, V. Johnson, K. L. Mapp, and D. Davies. *Beyond the Bake Sale: The Essential Guide to Family/School Partnerships* (New York: New Press, 2007).

7. H. T. Knopf and K. J. Swick, "Using Our Understanding of Families to Strengthen Family Involvement," *Early Childhood Education Journal,* 35(5), April 2008, 419–427.

8. J. S. Solochek, "Program Empowers Parents to Get More Involved with Children's Lives," *St. Petersburg Times,* April 5, 2009; accessed May 21, 2009, from http://www.tampabay.com/news/education/k12/article989668.ece.

9. S. Kolomer, "Chapter 13: Grandparent Caregivers," *Journal of Gerontological Social Work,* 50(4), May 2008, 321–344.

10. U.S. Census Bureau, Facts for Features, "Grandparents Day 2008: Sept. 7," July 7, 2008; accessed May 19, 2009, from http://www.census.gov/Press-Release/www/releases/archives/cb08ff-14.pdf.

11. S. Kolomer, "Chapter 13: Grandparent Caregivers," *Journal of Gerontological Social Work,* 50(4), May 2008, 321–344.

12. U.S. Department of Education, No Child Left Behind, Part A: Improving Basic Programs Operated by Local Educational Agencies, Subpart 1: Basic Program Requirements, "Sec. 1118: Parental Involvement," 2005; accessed May 19, 2009, from http://www.ed.gov/policy/elsec/leg/esea02/pg2.html#sec1118.

13. Ibid.

14. "Teacher Visits Hit Home," *Education World,* October 9, 2001 (updated May 25, 2009); retrieved June 4, 2009, from http://www.educationworld.com/a_admin/admin/admin241.shtml.

15. Milken Family Foundation, "Milken Educator Awards 2002: Susan Drinker"; retrieved June 5, 2009, from http://www.mff.org/mea/mea.taf?page=recipient&meaID=12427.

16. O. C. Moles, ed., "Personal Contacts," *Reaching All Families: Creating Family-Friendly Schools,* U.S. Department of Education, Office of Educational Research and Improvement, August 1996 (updated January 8, 2002); available online at http://www.ed.gov/pubs/ReachFam/index.html.

17. The Teachers' Podcast, "Twitter Used to Develop Second Graders' Writing Skills"; accessed April 23, 2009, from http://teacherspodcast.org/2009/03/31/ep-36-digital-catchup-and-21st-century-learning-debate.

18. INFOlathe, Unified School District 233, "Students Partner with Parents, Teachers in High-Tech Conferences," April 6, 2009; accessed May 21, 2009, from https://online.olatheschools.com/departments/infoolathe/2009/04/06/students-partner-with-parents-teachers-in-high-tech-conferences.

19. M. Sacchetti, "Teachers Take Bulletin Boards Online: Blogs Reaching Out to Students, Parents," *Boston Globe,* September 7, 2006; accessed May 21, 2009 from http://www.mackenty.org/images/uploads/boston_globe_blogging.pdf.

20. Centers for Disease Control and Prevention, National Center for Health Statistics, NCHS Data Brief, "Changing Patterns of Nonmarital Childbearing in the United States," May 2009; accessed May 20, 2009, from http://www.cdc.gov/nchs/data/databriefs/db18.htm.

21. U.S. Department of Education, National Center for Educational Statistics, *The Condition of Education 2009,* June 2009; accessed June 3, 2009, from http://nces.ed.gov/pubs2009/2009081.pdf.

22. Ibid.

23. The National Center on Family Homelessness, "America's Youngest Outcasts: State Report Card on Child Homelessness," March 2009; accessed April 29, 2009, from http://www.homelesschildrenamerica.org/index.php.

24. Ibid.

25. K. Kingsbury, "Keeping Homeless Kids in School," *Time,* March 23, 2009, 42–43.

26. The National Center on Family Homelessness, "America's Youngest Outcasts: State Report Card on Child Homelessness," March 2009; accessed April 29, 2009, from http://www.homelesschildrenamerica.org/index.php.

27. Ibid.

28. K. Kingsbury, "Keeping Homeless Kids in School," *Time,* March 23, 2009, 42–43.

29. The National Center on Family Homelessness, "America's Youngest Outcasts: On the Ground: How McKinney-Vento Liaisons Help Children Who Are Homeless," March 2009; accessed April 29, 2009, from http://www.homelesschildrenamerica.org/pdf/stories/on_the_ground/pg_mckvento.pdf.

30. Ibid.

31. K. Kingsbury, "Keeping Homeless Kids in School," *Time,* March 23, 2009, 42–43.

32. E. Burmaster, State of Wisconsin Department of Public Instruction, *Homeless Bulletin Series 01,* August 18, 2003; accessed April 29, 2009, from http://www.caction.org/research_reports/reports/hmls_identification.pdf.

33. Ibid.

34. Durham Public Schools, "Business Leaders Get Involved in Durham," January 30, 2009; accessed June 4, 2009, from http://www.dpsnc.net/news/community-news/business-leaders-getinvolved-in-durham.

35. Oregon School District 24J, Salem-Keizer Public Schools, "Business Partnerships," January 8, 2008; accessed May 21, 2009, from http://www.salkeiz.k12.or.us/content/business-partnerships?page=1.

36. S. Covel, "Businesses Emerge to Help School Fund-Raisers Go Green," *Wall Street Journal,* July 15, 2008, B6; accessed June 5, 2009, from http://online.wsj.com/article/SB121607802464352547.html?mod=us_business_biz_focus_hs.

GLOSSARY

Accommodation The process of changing old methods and adjusting to new situations.

Active involvement The feature of Piaget's theory of cognitive development stating that children's active hands-on experiences with the physical world provide the foundations for a "minds-on" ability to think and learn.

Adult–child discourse A conversation between an adult/parent and a child.

Advocacy The act of engaging in strategies designed to improve the circumstances of children and families. Advocates move beyond their day-to-day professional responsibilities and work collaboratively to help others.

Alphabetic knowledge (AK) Knowledge of the names and sounds associated with printed letters.

Anecdotal record An informal assessment tool that gives a brief written description of a student's behavior during a single incident.

Antibias curriculum An approach that seeks to provide children with an understanding of social and behavioral problems related to prejudice and seeks to provide them with the knowledge, attitude, and skills needed to combat prejudice.

Applied behavior analysis (ABA) The theory that behavior rewarded is more likely to be repeated than behavior ignored.

Approaches to learning Inclinations, dispositions, and learning styles necessary to interact effectively with the learning environment.

Assessment The process of collecting and recording information about children's development, learning, health, behavior, academic process, need for special services, and attainment in order to make a variety of educational decisions about children and programs.

Assimilation The taking in of sensory data through experiences and impressions and incorporating them into existing knowledge.

Asthma A chronic inflammatory disorder of the airways.

Atelier A special area or studio in a Reggio Emilia school for creating projects.

Atelierista A Reggio Emilia teacher trained in visual arts who works with teachers and children.

Attachment An enduring emotional tie between a parent/caregiver and an infant that endures over time.

Attention deficit hyperactivity disorder (ADHD) The inability to maintain attention and constrain impulsivity, accompanied by the presence of hyperactivity.

Authentic assessment Assessment conducted through activities that require children to demonstrate what they know and are able to do; also referred to as *performance-based assessment*.

Autism spectrum disorder A neurological developmental disorder characterized by a deficit in communication and social interactions as well as by the presence of restricted and repetitive behaviors. It is considered a "spectrum" of disorders because different people can have very different symptoms, ranging from mild to severe.

Autonomy An Erikson concept that says as toddlers mature physically and mentally, they want to do things by themselves with no outside help.

Balanced approach An approach to literacy in which there is a balance between whole-language methods and phonics instruction.

Basic trust An Erikson concept that involves trust, security, and basic optimism that an infant develops when nurtured and loved.

Behavior guidance A process by which teachers help all children learn to control and direct their behavior and become independent and self-reliant.

Benchmarks Statements that provide a description of student performance expected at specific grade levels, ages, or developmental levels. Benchmarks often are used in conjunction with standards.

Bias-free An environment, classroom setting, or program that is free of prejudicial behaviors.

Bilingual education Education in two languages (for example, the student's native language and English).

Bipolar disorder A mood disorder involving cycles of depression and mania that are severe and often lead to impaired functioning.

Bonding A relationship between a parent and offspring that usually begins at the time of birth and that establishes the basis for an ongoing mutual attachment.

Bullying To treat abusively or affect by means of force or coercion.

Challenging environment A learning environment that provides achievable and "stretching" experiences for all children.

Checklist A list of behaviors or other traits, used in informal assessment to identify children's skills and knowledge.

Child care Comprehensive care and education of young children outside their homes.

Child development The study of how children change over time from birth to age eight.

Child Development Associate (CDA) An individual who has successfully completed the CDA assessment process and has been awarded the CDA credential. CDAs are able to meet the specific needs of children and work with parents and other adults to nurture children's physical, social, emotional, and intellectual growth in a child development framework.

Childhood depression A disorder affecting as many as one in thirty-three children that can negatively impact feelings, thoughts, and behavior and can manifest itself with physical symptoms of illness.

Children with disabilities As defined by IDEA, children who need special education and related services because of mental retardation, hearing impairments, speech or language impairments, serious emotional disturbances, orthopedic impairments, autism, traumatic brain injury, other health impairments, or specific learning disabilities.

Chronosystem The environmental influences and events that influence children over their lifetimes, such as living in a technological age.

Circular response Behavior that typically begins to develop in early infancy, in which an infant's own actions cause the infant to react or when another person prompts the infant to try to repeat the original action; similar to a stimulus–response relationship.

Civil behavior In interactions with others, treating them well and in turn being treated well.

Classification The ability, developed during the concrete operations stage of cognitive development, to group things together according to their similar characteristics.

Cognitive sensory stimulation The process of providing appropriate sensory stimulation, which in turn supports cognitive development.

Cognitive theory Jean Piaget's proposition that children develop intelligence through direct experiences with the physical world. In this sense, learning is an internal (mental) process involving children's adapting new knowledge to what they already know.

Concrete operations Piaget's third stage of operational or logical thought, often referred to as the "hands-on" period of cognitive development because the ability to reason is based on tangible objects and real experiences.

Constructivism Theory that emphasizes the active role of children in developing their understanding and learning.

Constructivist process The continuous mental organizing, structuring, and restructuring of experiences, in relation to schemes of thought, or mental images, that result in cognitive growth.

Content knowledge Knowledge about the subjects (math, science, social studies, art, music, etc.) that teachers plan to teach.

Content standards Standards that are specified by content area and grade.

Critical periods Periods that represent a narrow window of time during which a specific part of the body is most vulnerable to the absence of stimulation or to environmental influences.

Culture A group's way of life, including basic values, beliefs, religion, language, clothing, food, and various practices.

Curriculum The subject matter taught; all of the experiences children have while in school.

Curriculum alignment The process of matching curriculum to the standards and tests that measure student achievement.

Data-driven instruction An approach to teaching in which analysis of assessment data drives the decisions about how to meet the instructional needs of each child.

Developmentally and culturally responsive practice (DCRP) Teaching methods that are sensitive and responsive to children's and families' developmental, cultural, and ethnic backgrounds and needs.

Developmentally appropriate practice (DAP) Teaching methods based on how children grow and develop and on individual and cultural differences.

Differentiated instruction (DI) Instruction that involves planning and teaching in response to the diverse needs of students, so that all students within a classroom can learn effectively, regardless of differences in ability.

Dyslexia A learning disability characterized by difficulties in reading, spelling, writing, speaking, or listening, despite at least average intelligence.

Early childhood professional An educator who successfully teaches all children, promotes high personal standards, and continually expands his or her skills and knowledge.

Egocentric Centered on the self; an inability to see events from other people's perspectives.

Embedded instruction An approach to teaching that embeds lessons into naturally occurring classroom activities.

Entitlement programs Programs and services that children and families are entitled to because they meet the eligibility criteria.

Environmental theory A theory of language development stating that while the ability to acquire language might have a biological basis, the content of language is acquired from the child's environment.

Epilepsy A neurological disorder in which electrical discharges in the brain cause a seizure.

Equilibrium A state of balance between the cognitive processes of assimilation and accommodation, allowing children to successfully understand new data.

Ethical conduct Responsible behavior toward students and parents that allows you to be considered a professional.

Event sampling An informal assessment tool that focuses on a particular behavior during a particular event.

Exosystem The environments or settings in which children do not play an active role but which nonetheless influence their development.

Expanding horizons approach *or* expanding environments approach An approach to teaching social studies in which the student's world is the center of the initial units, with children at each grade level being exposed to a slowly widening environment.

Expressive language A readiness skill that includes the ability to articulate fluently, to communicate needs and ideas with teacher and peers, and to express oneself.

Formal assessment Assessment utilizing standardized tests that have set procedures and instruction for administration and have been normed, thus making it possible to compare a child's score with the scores of children who have already taken the same exam.

Free appropriate public education (FAPE) The requirement under IDEA that children must receive a free education suited to their age, maturity level, condition of disability, achievements, and parental expectations.

Healthy environment A learning environment that provides for children's physical and psychological health, safety, and sense of security.

High-stakes testing Using assessment tests to make important and often life-influencing decisions about children, such as whether to admit children into programs or promote them from one grade to the next.

High/Scope educational model A constructivist educational model based on Piaget's cognitive development theory, providing realistic experiences geared to children's current stages of development.

Holophrases One-word sentences that toddlers use to communicate.

Home visitor program A program that involves visitation of children, parents, and other family members in their homes by trained personnel who provide information, training, and support.

Individualized education program (IEP) As required by IDEA, a written instruction plan for a child with a disability, assessing the child's needs and setting clear goals and objectives so that progress can be evaluated.

Individualized family service plan (IFSP) As required by IDEA, a plan created for infants and toddlers with disabilities and their families, specifying what services they will receive to help them reach their specific goals.

Infancy A child's first year of life.

Infant mental health The overall health and well-being of infants and young children in the context of family, school, and community relationships.

Informal assessment Assessment of students' learning, behavior, and development using means other than standardized tests.

Inquiry learning Involvement of children in activities and processes that lead to learning.

Integrated curriculum A curriculum in which one subject area is used to teach another.

Interpretation A three-step process that includes examining the information that has been gathered, organizing and drawing conclusions from that information, and making decisions about teaching based on the conclusions.

Interviewing An informal assessment tool by which observers and researchers obtain information about children by asking questions and engaging them in conversation.

Language experience approach (LEA) A reading instruction method that links oral and written language.

Learned helplessness A condition that can develop when children lose confidence in their abilities and, in effect, learn to feel that they are helpless.

Learning The acquisition of knowledge, behaviors, skills, and attitudes.

Learning centers Areas of the classroom specifically set up to promote student-centered, hands-on, active learning.

Learning disability A disorder in one or more of the basic psychological processes involved in understanding or using spoken or written language, which may manifest itself in an imperfect ability to listen, think, speak, read, write, and spell or to do mathematical calculations.

Learning style The way a child learns—specifically, how the child's environment, emotions, sociological needs, physical characteristics, and psychological inclinations come into play as he or she works to master new or difficult information or skills.

Least restrictive environment (LRE) As part of IDEA, the notion that a child with a disability should have the opportunity to be educated with children who are not disabled, to the greatest extent possible.

Linguistically diverse parents Parents whose English proficiency is minimal and who lack a comprehensive knowledge of the norms and social systems in the United States.

Literacy The ability to read, write, speak, and listen.

Locus of control The source of control over an individual's behavior; the locus may be external (controlled by others) or internal (within oneself). The goal of behavioral guidance is to help children learn that their locus of control is internal, that they are responsible for their own behavior.

Macrosystem The broader culture in which children live (absence or presence of democracy, societal violence, religious freedom, etc.), which influences their development.

Mastery-oriented attributions Personal characteristics that include trying hard, paying attention, determination, and stick-to-itiveness.

Mathematics disorder A learning disability characterized by decided lack of ability to calculate or comprehend mathematical problems.

Maturationist theory A theory of language development stating that language acquisition is innate in all children regardless of culture, and that speech production and other aspects of language will develop as children mature, according to built-in biological schedules.

Mesosystem The links or interactions between microsystems that influence children's development.

Microsystem The various environmental settings in which children spend their time (e.g., children in child care spend about thirty-three hours a week in the microsystem of child care).

Montessori method A system of early childhood education founded on the philosophy, procedures, and materials developed by Maria Montessori. Respect for the child is the cornerstone on which all other Montessori principles rest.

Moral development The process of developing culturally acceptable attitudes and behaviors, based on what society endorses and supports as right and wrong.

Motherese The distinctive way of adapting everyday speech to young children. *See also* parentese.

Multicultural awareness Appreciation for and understanding of people's culture, socioeconomic status, and gender.

Multicultural infusion A situation in which multicultural education permeates the curriculum to influence the way young children and teachers think about diversity issues.

Multiculturalism An approach to education based on the premise that all peoples in the United States should receive proportional attention in the curriculum.

Multiple intelligences Howard Gardner's concept that people can be "smart" in many different ways; those intelligences include verbal/linguistic, musical/rhythmic, mathematical/logical, visual/spatial, bodily/kinesthetic, interpersonal, intrapersonal, and naturalist.

Neural shearing The process of brain connections withering away when they are not used. *See also* pruning.

No Child Left Behind Act A landmark act in education reform designed to improve student achievement and change the culture of America's schools.

Obesity A condition characterized by excessive accumulation and storage of fat in the body.

Object permanence The concept that things out of sight continue to exist; this intellectual milestone typically begins to develop at four to eight months of age.

Observation The intentional, systematic act of looking at the behavior of a child or children in a particular setting, program, or situation; sometimes referred to as *kid-watching*.

Operation A reversible mental action.

Parent/family involvement A process of helping parents and family members use their abilities to benefit themselves, their children, and the early childhood program.

Parentese The distinctive way of adapting everyday speech to young children. *See also* motherese.

Pedagogical knowledge Knowledge about how to apply instructional practices in order to develop meaningful learning experiences for children.

Performance standards Specific examples of what students should know and do to demonstrate that they have mastered the knowledge and skills stated in content standards.

Pervasive developmental disorders (PDDs) A category of neurological disorders characterized by severe and pervasive impairment in several areas of development.

Philosophy of education A set of beliefs about how children develop and learn and what and how they should be taught.

Phonics instruction A teaching method that emphasizes letter–sound correspondence so children can learn to combine sounds into words.

Phonological awareness (PA) The ability to detect, manipulate, or analyze the auditory aspects of spoken language (including the ability to distinguish or segment words, syllables, or phonemes), independent of meaning.

Phonological memory (PM) The ability to remember spoken information for a short period of time.

Plastic Capable of adapting to conditions, such as the neurons in a child's brain, which are constantly arranging and rearranging connections to form neural pathways.

Play therapy A method that incorporates social experiences and enjoyable interactions into a therapeutic approach to working with children with developmental delays in order to enhance communication skills and other appropriate behavior.

Portfolio A compilation of children's work samples, other artifacts, and teacher observations collected over time.

Poverty The state of a person who lacks a usual or socially acceptable amount of money or material possessions.

Pre-kindergarten A class or program preceding kindergarten for children usually from three to four years old.

Preoperational stage The stage of cognitive development in which young children are not capable of mental representations.

Primary grades Grades one to three.

Private speech An internal conversation between a person and himself or herself. Also called *self-discourse*.

Professional dispositions The values, commitments, and professional ethics that influence behavior toward students, families, colleagues, and members of the community and affect student learning, motivation, and development as well as the educator's own professional growth.

Program standards Expectations that define the characteristics for quality in early childhood settings, centers, and schools.

Project approach An educational approach that encourages in-depth investigation by an individual student or small group of students, or even by the whole class, of a topic the students want to learn more about.

Pruning The process of brain connections withering away when they are not used. *See also* neural shearing.

Psychosocial development Erik Erikson's theory that cognitive and social development occur simultaneously and cannot be separated.

Rapid automatic naming (RAN) The ability to rapidly name a random sequence, such as a random sequence of letters, digits, colors, or pictures of objects.

Rating scale An informal assessment tool, usually a numeric scale, that contains a list of descriptors for a set of behaviors.

Readiness Being ready to learn; possessing the knowledge, skills, and abilities necessary for learning and for success in school.

Receptive language Language that a person "receives" or understands through spoken, written, or visual communication.

Reflective practice The active process of thinking before teaching, during teaching, and after teaching in order to make decisions about how to plan, assess, and teach.

Reggio Emilia approach An early childhood educational program named for the town in Italy where it originated. The method emphasizes a child's relationships with family, peers, teachers, and the wider community; small-group interaction; schedules set by the child's personal rhythms; and visual arts programs coordinated by a specially trained atelierista.

Research-based programs Programs based on scientific research that demonstrates they can increase student achievement. *See also* scientifically based programs.

Respectful environment A learning environment that shows respect for each individual child and his or her culture, home language, individual abilities or disabilities, family context, and community.

Response to Intervention/Response to Instruction (RTI) A multi-tier approach to the early identification and support of students with learning and behavior needs; it evaluates assessment data and employs differentiated instruction, so that students who are struggling can receive more intense intervention.

Responsive relationship The relationship that exists between yourself, children, and their families where you are responsive to their needs and interests.

Reversibility The notion that actions can be reversed. Awareness of reversibility develops during the concrete operations stage of development.

Running record An informal assessment tool that provides a more detailed narrative of a child's behavior, focusing on a sequence of events that occur over a period of time.

Scaffolding Assistance or support of some kind from a teacher, parent, caregiver, or peer to help children complete tasks they cannot complete independently.

Scheme A unit of knowledge that a child develops through experience that defines how things should be.

Scientifically based programs Programs based on scientific research that demonstrates they can increase student achievement. *See also* research-based programs.

Screening The process of identifying the particular physical, social, linguistic, and cognitive needs of children in order to provide appropriate programs and services.

Screening procedures Procedures that give a broad picture of what children know and are able to do, as well as their physical and emotional status.

Self-actualization Abraham Maslow's theory of motivation based on the satisfaction of needs; Maslow maintained that children cannot achieve self-actualization until certain basic needs—including food, shelter, safety, and love—are met.

Self-discourse An internal conversation between a person and himself or herself. Also called *private speech*.

Self-regulation The ability of preschool children to control their emotions and behaviors, to delay gratification, and to build positive social relations with each other.

Sensitive periods Periods of development during which it is easier to learn something than it is at other times.

Sensorimotor stage The first of Piaget's stages of cognitive development, when children primarily use their senses and motor reflexes to develop intellectually.

Shared reading A teaching method in which the teacher and children read together from a book that is visible to all.

Sight word approach Also called *whole-word* or *look-say*, an approach to reading that involves presenting children with whole words so they develop a "sight vocabulary" as opposed to "sounding out" words using phonics.

Social constructivist approach A theory that says children construct or build their behavior as a result of learning from experience and from making decisions that lead to responsible behavior.

Social story A personalized, detailed, and simple script that breaks down behavior and provides rules and directions.

Standards Statements of what pre-K–12 students should know and be able to do.

Standards-based education (SBE) Curriculum, teaching, and testing based on local, state, and national standards.

Supportive environment A learning environment where professionals believe each child can learn and where they help children understand and make meaning of their experiences.

Symbolic language A readiness skill that involves knowing the names of people, places, and things; understanding that words represent concepts.

Symbolic representation The understanding, which develops at about age two, that something else can stand for a mental image; for example, a word can represent a real object or a concept.

Synaptogenesis The formation of connections, or synapses, among neurons; this process of brain development begins before birth and continues until age ten.

Technology The application of tools and information to make products and solve problems. With this definition, technology goes far beyond computers and video games, but the most common use of the term refers to electronic and digital applications.

Telegraphic speech Two-word sentences, such as "Go out" or "All gone," used by toddlers.

Temperament A child's general style of behavior.

Theory A statement of principles and ideas that attempts to explain events and how things happen.

Time sampling An informal assessment tool that records particular events or behaviors during specific, continuous time intervals, such as three or four five-minute periods during the course of a morning.

Title I A federal program designed to improve the basic skills (reading and mathematics) of low-ability children from low-income families.

Toddlerhood The period of a child's life between one and three years of age.

Tourette's syndrome A genetic neuropsychiatric disorder characterized by multiple physical and/or vocal tics.

Traditional assessment Assessment done with standardized tests or teacher-created tests, where students typically select an answer or recall facts, measuring how well children have learned specific information.

Transition A passage from one learning setting, grade, program, or experience to another.

Typically developing Reaching the majority of developmental milestones at the appropriate time and not presenting deficits in social areas.

Unfolding Rousseau's belief that the nature of children—who and what they will be—unfolds as a result of development according to their innate timetables.

Universal design The process of adapting teaching strategies and technology to make the learning environment, the curriculum, and the instruction methods accessible to each young child, regardless of physical limitations or learning disabilities.

Universal preschool The idea that all children and families should have access to preschool, in the same way that kindergarten is available now.

Universal public kindergarten The availability of kindergarten to all children.

Whole-language approach Philosophy of literacy development that advocates using all aspects of language—reading, writing, listening, and speaking—to help children become motivated to read and write.

Work sample An example of a child's work that demonstrates what the child knows and is able to do.

Zero reject principle A rule under IDEA that prohibits schools from excluding any student with a disability.

Zone of proximal development (ZPD) The range of tasks that children can perform with help from a more competent partner. Children can perform tasks below their ZPD on their own, but they are not yet able to learn tasks or concepts above their ZPD, even with help.

NAME/AUTHOR INDEX

SUBJECT INDEX